MAN, MYTH & MAGIC

VOLUME 10

Ship – Tibe

Library of Congress Cataloging in Publication Data

Main entry under title:

Man, myth, and magic

Bibliography: p.
1. Occult sciences. 2. Psychical research.
I. Cavendish, Richard. II. Deutch, Yvonne.
BF1411.M25 1983 133 82-13041
ISBN 0-86307-041-8 (set)
ISBN 0-86307-051-5 (v.10)

British Library Cataloguing in Publication Data

Man, myth and magic.
1. Mythology - Dictionaries
2. Religion - Dictionaries
I. Cavendish, Richard
291.1'3'0321 BL303

ISBN 0-86307-041-8 (set)
ISBN 0-86307-051-5 (v.10)

Reference Edition Published 1983

Printed and Bound in Italy by L.E.G.O. S.p.a. Vicenza.

Published by Marshall Cavendish Corporation,
147 West Merrick Road,
Freeport, Long Island
N.Y. 11520

Distributed in India by Standard Literature.

MAN, MYTH & MAGIC

The Illustrated Encyclopedia of Mythology, Religion and the Unknown

Editor-in-Chief
Richard Cavendish

New Edition edited and compiled by
Yvonne Deutch, B.A. University of Exeter;
M.A. University of Kansas, Lawrence, Kansas.

MARSHALL CAVENDISH
NEW YORK, LONDON, TORONTO

CONTENTS Volume 10

Österreichische Galerie Vienna

SHIP

The black-sailed 'ship of death' travels over the land and sucks into itself the souls of damned seamen; the belief that the dead are transported to their final destination by boat is common to many religions

THE FIRST SUCCESSFUL navigations of wide stretches of water by primitive man must have seemed as much of an achievement as the development of space travel in our own day. Apart from the physical hazards of venturing on the ocean, this unknown element was believed to be ruled by dangerous spirit forces and gods; and as with all other apparently superhuman achievements, navigation has always been closely associated with the supernatural.

The ship, like the sea itself, is rich both in symbolism and superstition. Because it crosses the unknown ocean where it may encounter unexpected dangers, it is a symbol of confidence, adventure and enterprise. A ship in full sail symbolizes safe conduct, while a similar motif displayed on a coin is a token of joy and happiness. The ship is the Christian symbol for both Church and State; the barque which bears the faithful over the stormy seas of life to the promised land on the distant shore. Medieval Christians wore badges in the form of a ship to show their faith in salvation, and these were also thought to provide protection against the temptations encountered by a traveller on life's voyage. In this sense the ship may be seen as a symbol of transience and spirituality, of faith and hope. The

Ship of Fools **by Oscar Laske; engrossed in worldly pursuits, the passengers 'sail' through life, heedless of the need for a spiritual goal and the futility of an existence based on material pleasures**

'ship of fools', a constantly recurring theme in Christian imagery, is a symbol of the belief that to 'sail' through this world, treating life merely as an end in itself, is futile; man's spiritual goal must be transition, evolution and finally, salvation.

In some ancient mythologies a ship was said to carry the sun and the moon in their journeys across the heavens. The Egyptian sun god travelled in a ship, and there was much ship symbolism in the worship of Isis (see ISIS). The Babylonian moon god, Sin,

Superstition surrounds the life of a ship, from the time of its building until it reaches the breaker's yard

was also known as the 'ship of life'. The ship with its mast is a fairly obvious fecundity symbol, representing the sexual union of the male with the female, and its motion as it is tossed on the ocean waves represents the action of coition.

As a heraldic symbol a ship represents swiftness and succour in extremity. Its rudder generally symbolizes guidance, truth and wisdom, while the anchor stands for hope, patience and steadfastness. Noah's Ark is the symbol of God's covenant with man, the human race's hope of survival; it appears in the crest and coat of arms of the Company of Shipwrights.

Superstition surrounds the life of a ship, from the time of its building until it reaches the breaker's yard; and even after its natural lifetime, there are many stories of the ghost ship which continues to haunt the site of its wreck. The landsman's custom of laying a foundation stone is paralleled by the laying of the ship's keel, which may be seen as the foundation of the boat, its backbone. At Boulogne-sur-Mer, no alteration to the design of a fishing boat was ever permitted once the keel had been laid down, as this brought bad luck. In Scotland it was customary to hide a gold coin in some hidden recess in the keel to bring good fortune, the hiding-place being known only to the builder and never to the ship's owner. The first nail knocked into the keel was sometimes tied with red ribbon, to protect the craft against storms and similar misadventures.

It was axiomatic among shipwrights that they were free to curse anything on board ship except the keel, which was sacrosanct. It was forbidden to lay down the keel on a Friday, and an old legend tells of a shipbuilder who flouted this prohibition, named the ship *Friday*, gave its command to a Captain Friday and despatched it on its maiden voyage on a Friday; the craft was never seen again.

In Pomerania, in Germany, it was

Figureheads used to mean a great deal to sailors, and were most carefully tended. At one time it was generally thought that it was impossible for a ship to sink without her figurehead, possibly because it was connected in seamen's minds with the life and soul of the craft; in fact, these figures were originally effigies of the female deities of the sea, and libations, sometimes in the form of human blood, were made to propitiate them. The custom of breaking a bottle of champagne across the bows of a ship at its launching ceremony is a modern version of this old tradition *Below, left to right* Figurehead on a tea clipper; effigy of William Wilberforce, the English politician who fought to abolish the slave trade; matronly figure known as 'Old Goody', possibly symbolizing a kindly spirit who cares for sailors *Facing page* Partly-draped figurehead on the *Cutty Sark*; sailors have always regarded the naked body of a woman as a luck-bringer, whether in reality or in the form of an effigy

Bardo Museum/Sonia Halliday

believed to be lucky to use stolen timbers for the construction of a boat. In the North of England, during the caulking of a wooden boat a shipwright could claim a 'caulking kiss' from any passing girl. If she refused him, she had to pay a shilling. The painted eye on the bow of a Mediterranean boat guides the craft to its destination and protects against the Evil Eye (see EYE).

Even today it is customary for shipbuilders to lay a silver coin beneath a ship's mast. An emblem of the moon, this coin, usually a silver sixpence, is supposed to preserve ship and crew from storms. There are also a number of 'topping-out' ceremonies, intended to provide magical protection against storms, during which the ship is decked with laurel leaves and woodland flowers.

The figurehead on sailing ships was often in the form of a naked woman, who was in reality an idol or divine figure to whom propitiation had to be made in the form of a libation. In the past this female figure meant a great deal to seamen, and was most carefully tended. The breaking of a bottle of champagne across the bows of a craft at its launching ceremony is a modern version of the pagan libation. Mediterranean fishermen sometimes pour an offering of wine into the sea to lull a storm, and it is not at all uncommon for European yachtsmen to drop a coin into the water when the weather is threatening. In primitive societies, the libation was often in the form of human blood.

Throughout the recorded history of seamanship, ships have been blessed, in one form or another, during their launching ceremonies. While the boat of an Indonesian fisherman is charmed by a sorcerer, that of his European counterpart is blessed by a priest. In both cases a boat is doomed either to disaster or to a run of misfortune if it does not receive this benediction.

Whatever the size or importance of a craft, the act of naming it is an event of profound psychic significance; the selection of an unlucky name can have dangerous consequences. Seamen object to any name ending in the letter a, and the sinking of the *Lusitania* in 1915 reinforced this superstition. Once christened, a ship's name must never be changed or disaster will fall upon craft and crew alike. The ill-fated *HMS Victoria,* which in 1893, while on

The act of naming a craft is an event of profound psychic significance; the selection of an unlucky name can have dangerous consequences

A symbol of confidence and enterprise, the ship is sometimes also a bearer of good fortune, carrying treasures from one part of the world to another *Left* Dionysus is said to have brought the vine across the seas to Greece; a legend tells that he was attacked by his crew on one occasion, and drove them mad so that they jumped overboard, and were changed into dolphins: mosaic, 3rd century AD, from Dougga in North Africa *Right* Netsuke, by Masshiro, depicts the Japanese gods of luck aboard a treasure-ship

manoeuvres, collided with another battleship in mysterious circumstances, leading to appalling loss of life, is an example of a ship which had been given a new name. The story is told of a skipper who decided to rename his boat after his new wife, with the result that it sank.

Many customs and superstitions that originated far back in the past have survived relatively unchanged, and are still part of shipboard life. When naval officers salute the quarter-deck they are in effect paying their respects to what was the site of the altar, with its image of the Virgin Mary, in pre-Reformation times. Among the Greeks and Romans, every ship had an altar upon which sacrifices were offered to the sea and sky gods as an insurance against storms and wrecks. The albatross, which is a 'soul bird', is sacrosanct today, largely as a result of Coleridge's *Ancient Mariner*; and its arrival is regarded as a sign of coming storms. If it leaves its mark on the deck in the form of excrement, this must never be removed but must be left to weather away.

It is said to be unlucky to step forward with the left foot first when boarding a ship and highly ominous to sneeze to the left while doing so. The prejudice against whistling aboard ship, which is still very much alive, is because this was supposed to invoke an adverse wind to the detriment of ship and crew; an example of a superstition which has outlasted the days of sail. One long-standing tradition, now almost forgotten, was to tie a broom to the masthead if a ship was for sale. In Holland this device was used to raise a favourable breeze. In some parts of the British Isles owners of small craft consider it unlucky to pull a boat out of the water stern first.

Portuguese cod fishermen who sail in Newfoundland waters believe that it is unlucky

Victoria & Albert Museum/Michael Holford

Universitets Oldsaksamling, Oslo

Axel Poignant

to fish close to the mother ship, and regard Greenland as a 'bad luck area', an island of the dead. Most seamen, however modern their outlook, believe that it is extremely unlucky to have a dead body aboard ship. A corpse should be buried at sea as soon after death as possible, but if it is necessary to bring it ashore, it must always be taken off the ship before anyone else disembarks. In the meantime, for the safety of all on board, the corpse should be laid athwart the ship, and never parallel to the line joining bow and stern. This point is specifically discussed in a 17th century work which inquired as to 'whether a dead body in a ship causes the ship to sail slower and if it does so, what is the reason thereof'.

Fishermen attempt to preserve the luck of a boat, or attract good fortune to it, in various ways. In Ireland a fisherman may refuse to give a light from his pipe on a Monday, in case he should inadvertently surrender his luck for the whole of the ensuing week; and a fisherman will sometimes try to steal someone else's luck by rubbing the bows of his own boat against those of a more fortunate craft. Irish fishermen object strongly to being in the third boat to leave harbour for the fishing grounds as this is said to bring in a poor catch.

In past centuries, boatmen attached stones with holes in them to the bows of their boats, to ward off psychic attack. Called 'holy flints', these were made of the same kind of stone as that used to protect houses against witchcraft. Until comparatively recently it was customary in British ports to throw shoes after a departing ship for luck, a tradition reminiscent of the custom of hurling shoes after the car of a newly-married couple to ensure fertility. Wearing a cap made of hazel catkins was said to protect a vessel from shipwreck.

Above The belief that the souls of the dead have to cross a stretch of water in some kind of craft before reaching the otherworld is widespread, and many communities practised ship-burial in ancient times _Left_ Ship in a grave in Norway; Vikings were seated in their boats before being buried _Right_ Viking grave in Denmark, with stones laid out in the shape of a ship _Below_ Illustration of a phantom ship; the concept that a ship is a living entity with a soul has resulted in many legends that tell of ghostly craft

Harry Price Library/University of London

Any ship cursed with a long run of bad luck is said to be a 'jinx'. In some communities in Britain a small craft with an ominous reputation will be set on fire 'to kill the death in her'. The most notorious of all jinx ships was Brunel's *Great Eastern*, launched in 1858. She was so vast that she had to be launched sideways, in itself an ominous portent. The ship's career was associated with disasters, and she was also uneconomic to run. She acquired a reputation as an ill-fated ship, not only because of her much publicized misfortunes, but also because the ghosts of a riveter and his assistant, who had been accidentally built into the ship's hull, were said to be on board.

There are distinct traces of pagan sacrifice in the 'crossing the line' ceremony, during which anyone who is crossing the Equator for the first time is ritually 'shaved' and ducked. In the days of sail, the ceremony was intimidating to say the least. Tar brushes and bilge water were used, and the razor was usually a rusty iron hoop.

It was at one time customary in various parts of Europe to throw young boys over the ship's side when passing by important headlands, or within sight of temples on the coast. This was apparently a nautical replica of the 'beating the bounds' ceremony on land. A curious tradition, long current in

It was at one time customary in various parts of Europe to throw young boys over the ship's side when passing by important headlands, or within sight of temples on the coast

Devon, associated Sir Francis Drake with throwing a ship's boy from the *Golden Hind* when 'on the other side of the world'. Drake was credited with having supernatural powers of a high order; in one legend, he is said to have cast into the English Channel pieces of wood, which were immediately transformed into the warships with which he overcame the Spanish Armada. In another story, Drake's drum was heard to beat from the flagship of the British Fleet at Scapa Flow in 1918.

A considerable amount of ship lore may be found in sea shanties and ballads belonging to the days of sail. The concept that a ship is a living entity, capable of responding in an intelligent manner to the demands made upon it, is implicit in the song of *Young Allan:*

'Spring up, spring up, my bonny ship
And gold sall be your fee'
Whan the bonny ship heard o' that
That gold sall be her fee
She sprang as fast frae the salt water
As the leaf does frae the tree

An extension of this animistic approach is the ancient concept that a ship has a soul. In Japan, ceremonies were held after a shipwreck and the custom of offering up prayers on behalf of ships that had been despatched to the breakers' yard continued into the present century.

The custom of preserving the bell of a ship after the vessel itself has been broken up is in effect a gesture of respect towards the ship's soul. Like the bell of a church ashore, the ship's bell once had the task of keeping at bay all hostile influences including storms and devils. Understandably enough, the bells of sunken ships are supposed to ring from beneath the seas, from the places where the craft itself lies wrecked. It is said that a ship's bell that rings without human aid is an omen of death; and similarly, a wine glass that emits a ringing sound of its own accord is a sign that a ship and its crew will soon die. The tradition that a captain goes down with his ship is based to some extent upon the old belief that the ship, customarily referred to as 'she', is a living entity.

Ghost ships which haunt the sites of wrecks are often omens of disaster:.

The spectre ship in vivid glympsing light,
Glares balefully on the shuddering watch
at night,
Unblest of God or Man.

A ghostly ship with supernatural associations is the 'ship of death'; this vessel has black sails and leaves the water to travel over the land where it sucks into its dreadful vaporous mass the souls of seamen who are doomed to rot in hell. The tradition of the 'ship of death' has a close affinity with that of the phantom coach, the sight of which is supposed to herald a death.

The belief that the souls of the dead have to cross water in some kind of craft in order to reach the otherworld is widespread and there are parallels in many religions: the River Styx of the ancient Greeks, the Vaitarani which borders one of the hells of Hinduism, and the River Jordan which separates the world from the Promised Land of the Christians. The Fijians believe that they can only reach their abode of bliss in a canoe, and the Samoan islanders say of a chief who has recently died that 'he has sailed'. According to Finnish belief, the dead had to travel over nine and a half seas in order to reach the otherworld, and in Arthurian tradition the King was conveyed to the Celtic underworld in a boat.

Apparently working on this assumption that the soul had to be ferried to the underworld, many communities practised ship burial in ancient times. Clay models of barges have been found in Egyptian graves dating back to the Stone Age. Vikings were seated in their boats before burial, as at Sutton Hoo in Suffolk where a king was interred with his longship and treasure, and according to Norse mythology the body of the Scandinavian god Balder was laid in a ship on a funeral pyre (see BALDER). In Denmark Viking graves may be seen on which stones have been laid out in the design of ships.

For the sailor, life after death was represented by 'Fiddler's Green', a happy land where a fiddle never stops playing, where there are wild dances, barbaric music and uninhibited women; in short a place of never-ending shore leave. However, if the seaman had suffered a violent death he would be condemned to haunt the site where he had died as a 'seabound' ghost.

(See also SEA.)

ERIC MAPLE

The Case of the 'Calpean Star'

On 6 July 1959 the *Calpean Star*, a British 14,232 ton cargo liner owned by the Calpe Shipping Company Ltd of Irishtown, Gibraltar, docked at the Huskisson Dock, Liverpool, with a cargo of seals, penguins and an albatross bound for a German zoo. The ship had sailed from Antarctica, picking up the albatross at Bird Island, South Georgia, and was due to sail on to Oslo, concluding a five and half month trip. When the ship docked, 50 of the crew staged a sitdown strike, demanding to be paid off.

The immediate cause of the strike was the crew's objection to having to continue to Oslo instead of being paid off at Liverpool, said the ship's master, Captain Philip Everett-Price, but they also complained of 'misfortunes' which had occurred during the return voyage – engine trouble amongst them.

A report in the *Liverpool Echo* for 7 July said: 'It had been suggested that superstition about the "bird of ill-omen" was a part cause of the trouble, but this the men denied.' In fact, the 'bird of ill-omen' was found dead in its cage after the ship had docked.

The following day, 8 July, a report appeared in the *Liverpool Echo*: 'Violent explosions of propane gas followed by sheets of flame engulfed the new Mersey Docks and Harbour Board shed under construction on the Huskisson Dock early today. Twelve fire engines from all over the Liverpool area fought the blaze.'

According to mariners' tradition, the *Calpean Star* was ill-fated even without having to carry an albatross as part of her cargo, because her name had been changed early the same year from *Highland Chieftain*, when she was taken over by the Calpe Shipping Company and converted from Royal Mail Vessel to whaling transport and cargo liner.

In June 1960 she grounded in Montevideo Harbour and became a total loss – whether the albatross or the name change was responsible is a moot point.

Victoria & Albert Museum/C. M. Dixon

SHIVA

IN MEDIEVAL and modern Hinduism Shiva (or Siva) has come to share with Vishnu the honour of being the supreme deity. 'Share', perhaps, is the wrong word, since for his own devotees Shiva *is* the Supreme Deity, the Absolute, universal Creator and Destroyer of all things, while for Vishnu's devotees the same holds true.

How Shiva came to achieve this supreme position is not clear since in the oldest Hindu scriptures, the *Vedas*, he is not mentioned at all by name. Later tradition, however, associated him with the Vedic god Rudra who himself plays a very minor part in the earliest texts. Of all the Vedic gods Rudra-Shiva is the most magnificent, and yet even there he has two sides to his character, a terrible one which is uppermost and a benign *(shiva)* one which is subsidiary.

In the earliest text, the *Rig-Veda*, Rudra-Shiva is rather a lone wolf. He is rarely associated with other gods except the Maruts (also called Rudras), the gods of the storm. As the divine archer he pursues a solitary course, shooting his arrows indiscriminately at whom he will. These arrows bring death and disease, 'fever, cough and poison'. His anger is unpredictable and all his devotees can hope for is to transfer it to their enemies. In the *Vedas* he is 'black, swarthy, murderous and fearful' and, stranger still, 'the lord of thieves and robbers'.

But there is another side to him: for he is not only the great destroyer, but also the divine physician, and his hand is 'soothing, healing and cool'. In him the opposites of unbridled erratic force and an almost maternal gentleness meet.

In the last of the *Vedas*, the *Atharva-Veda,* Rudra is called the 'Lord of Beasts'; and it is in this form that one of the sects devoted to him were to worship him in later times, for they saw themselves as Rudra's flock and Rudra (-Shiva) himself as the divine shepherd. And yet the full status of the later Shiva was only faintly indicated in the earliest Vedic texts. Scholars, therefore, assumed that his origins must have gone back to a more ancient period before the Aryans invaded India. This view has now been vindicated by the discovery of figurines of a deity whose head is adorned by the horns of a bull and who is surrounded by wild beasts. This has very plausibly been identified with the 'Lord of Beasts' of the *Atharva-Veda*. What is more, the god is squatting in a position later characteristic of the contemplative yogi and he has an erect phallus. This surprising bringing together of the posture of contemplation and the symbol of sexual power is in fact characteristic of the later Shiva.

Left **Universal Creator and Destroyer of all things, Shiva is often depicted as a slayer of demons; one of his victims was Andhaka who attempted to steal the Parijata tree of Indra which perfumed the whole of paradise: illustration to a 16th century Mogul manuscript**
Facing page **The male and female principles are united in Shiva; 18th century miniature showing Shiva as a fair man with five faces**

The mythology of Shiva is fully developed in the *Mahabharata*, India's great epic poem, and in the various *Puranas* dedicated to him or to his symbol, the phallus. His original (Vedic) name Rudra gradually gives way to Shiva, the 'auspicious' or 'benign'. And yet the fully-developed figure of Shiva is anything but 'benign'. He is wrathful, incalculable, jealous in the Old Testament sense of that word, devoid of comeliness, wild, sometimes raving mad. He haunts the cremation-ground, clad in elephant hide or tiger skin, his neck encircled with a necklace of skulls, with serpents in his hair. He wears the matted locks of an ascetic and his austerities are prodigious.

But this fierce asceticism is only one side to his character; he is also the 'Lord of the Dance'; and his dance is twofold. Either he dances in the sheer joy of overwhelming power – he dances creation into existence; or else, in the Tandava dance, he careers down the mountainside, like a madman or a drunkard, surrounded by a rout of half-human, half-animal creatures who urge him on in his mad career. This dance represents the destruction of the world. His constant companion is the white bull Nandin and his consort is variously called Parvati, Uma, Kali, and Durga, the last two represented as even more terrible than himself (see KALI).

The significance of Shiva is that he is the reconciliation of all opposites: therefore he is both creator and destroyer, terrible and mild, good and evil, eternal rest and ceaseless activity. His consort is really only a part of himself – his 'power' by which he creates, sustains, and destroys. In the so-called Shakta cults (cults of Shakti or 'power') this 'power' is worshipped to exclusion of Shiva himself as being the active and 'committed' side of his nature.

In the full figure of Shiva, however, the male and female principles are united, and he himself is sometimes represented as half male and half female. The emblem under which he delights to be worshipped is the *lingam*, or phallus, which is always erect. Lingam and *yoni* (the female organ) together represent the totality of Nature and of all created existence. Unlike the discus of Vishnu, Shiva's lingam is the *natural* symbol of supreme creative power, and even the gods bow down in worship of it.

In the *Shvetashvatara-Upanishad* Shiva is identified with the Absolute but he is also the Supreme Deity who created and sustains all things. The sexual mythology is still there but 'spiritualized': 'With the one unborn Female . . . who produces many creatures like herself lies the one unborn Male, taking his delight: another unborn Male leaves her when she has had her pleasure.' Both the one and the other are Shiva, for he is forever involved in the creative process and forever unaffected by it.

'Who over wisdom and unwisdom rules, he is Another': that 'other' is Shiva, 'the One God hidden in all beings, pervading all, of all beings the Inmost Self, of all works the overseer, . . . witness, observer, absolute, alone, devoid of attributes', the one *personal* God who transcends both time and eternity. (See also HINDUISM; INDIA.)

R. C. ZAEHNER

Sven Gahlin

Blasted to Death

The legend goes that after the tragic death of Sati, Siva returned to Mount Kailasa where he sat wrapt in meditation. In the interval Sati was reborn as Parvati and when she came of age she desired to marry Siva. Accordingly she made her abode not far from the scene of Siva's meditations, and worshipped him.

It was at this time that the demon Taraka began his tyranny over the fourteen worlds, and it became imperative that Siva be the father of a child, since only a son of Siva could be expected to cope with Taraka. The love-god Kama was entrusted with the task of distracting Siva, and he waited for a suitable opportunity and shot an arrow at the god just as Parvati was walking past. Opening his eyes and beholding the voluptuous form Siva emitted his seed, which fell into a fire and from this was born Karttikeya who eventually killed Taraka.

Another version has it that Siva merely blasted Kama to death with a flash of his third eye, scorned Parvati for her dark complexion, for she was an aboriginal deity, and resumed his meditations. Parvati thereupon took to asceticism to win the god's love.

Benjamin Walker *Hindu World*

The prophecies of the Sibyls were manifestations of a power to which they felt they were enslaved, and usually referred to disasters such as war and famine; wanderers without regular succession in most places, the Sibyls have been described as freelances in prophecy

SIBYLS

THE PROPHETESSES who bore the title of Sibyl in antiquity are celebrated in literature, and many are mentioned in allusions scattered through Greek and Latin texts, but their historical character is not easy to grasp. Some of their personal names are known, but even in ancient tradition these appear unimportant. The classical Sibyls originated in Greek Asia Minor and were probably of oriental origin. They are always connected with Apollo, the god of prophecy (see APOLLO), who also originated in Asia Minor. But they are not his ordinary priestesses, nor even his ordinary prophetesses, for by comparison with the Pythia of Delphi, who was protected and controlled by a skilful priesthood, they appear as freelances in prophecy without regular succession in most places. They would be little more than a minor curiosity of classical lore if Virgil had not assigned a crucial role in the *Aeneid* to the Sibyl of Cumae. Indeed, when the Sibylline books of Rome are added to this account, it is clear that the renown of Sibyls in later literature and art is Roman rather than Greek.

Sibyls do not appear in Homer and are not well established elsewhere in Greek epic. But one character who has the marks of a Sibyl and is occasionally called one, is the Trojan princess Cassandra, whom Apollo loved but could not win, so that he gave her the gift of prophecy, but always as a painful fit of inspiration, in which her utterances were never believed. In Lycophron's iambic poem *Alexandra,* written in the 3rd century BC, Cassandra is made to give a long and exceedingly obscure prophetic monologue on the future fates and wanderings of the Greek chiefs returning from Troy, and of Aeneas, their opponent, who reached Latium in western Italy. This tradition reappears in the *Aeneid,* where the Sibyl leads Aeneas eventually into the presence of the dead Anchises to hear him foretell the future greatness of Rome.

In Greece the best-known Sibyl, typical of all of them, belonged to Erythrae on the coast of Asia Minor facing Chios. She is probably the one mentioned by Heraclitus as quoted by Plutarch, who says of her, 'The Sibyl with raving mouth, uttering things without smiles, without graces and without myrrh, reaches over a thousand years because of the god.' Sibyls were in fact believed to live for 900 or 1000 years, and it was thought that sometimes even after death they could make their voices heard in the air. Other Sibyls, of whom little is known, were those of Marpessus of Alexandria in the Troad, of Phrygia, of Sardis, of Delphi, of Thessaly, of Egypt, and, in the west, of Cumae in Campania. Very little remains of their actual prophecies except for inscriptions such as one at Erythrae in the Sibyl's dwelling, and such late compilations as the book *On Long Lived Persons* by Phlegon of Tralles, who lived in the 2nd century AD. In one utterance there a Sibyl claims a status between the human and the divine, and in another expresses jealousy or dislike of Apollo's priests or even of Apollo himself. The prophecies generally refer, like many others in history, to expected disasters such as war, plague and famine. The Sibyls were very loosely attached to the pan-Hellenic Olympian religion and even to local cults, and are often said to have been wanderers. Their prophecies were compulsive manifestations of a power to which they felt enslaved.

In the *Aeneid* Virgil makes the Sibyl a figure already established at Cumae at a time corresponding to the Greek heroic age. Such traditions at least suggest the antiquity of the influence of Greek religion in

Metropolitan Museum of Art, New York, Purchase 1924, Joseph Pulitzer Bequest

'The Sibyl with raving mouth, uttering things without smiles, without graces and without myrrh, reaches over a thousand years because of the god'; Heraclitus was probably referring to the Sibyl of Erythrae, on the coast of Asia Minor, but in fact these prophetesses of antiquity were commonly thought to live for as long as 1000 years. It was sometimes said that, even after death, they were able to make their voices heard in the air: Michelangelo's studies for a Sibyl, one of the hundreds of figures in his series of paintings in the Sistine Chapel, Rome

Italy, even if it is here exaggerated. The Sibyl, in frenzied inspiration, prophesies the terrible wars which will follow Aeneas's landing in Italy. She then conducts him through the entire extent of the infernal regions before leading him to meet his father Anchises among the blessed, and from there into the upper world again, through the ivory gate of dreams. No Sibyl of old Greece had a role of such grandeur.

The Sibylline Books

The celebrated legend of the Sibylline books, recorded by Varro and Dionysius, is among the more historical of Roman traditions of Sibyls. These were offered for sale to King Tarquin of Rome (reports vary between Tarquinius Priscus and his son Tarquinius Superbus) by a mysterious woman who was perhaps the Sibyl of Cumae. Nine books were offered but rejected because the price was too high; then, when she had destroyed three, six were offered at the same price as the nine but were again refused. Finally on the insistent advice of the augurs, the last three were bought at the price of the original nine. They were kept by the Roman state for centuries under the special care of a board of magistrates, were concealed from public view, and were consulted, with the help of Greek slaves, at moments of crisis or when alarming prodigies such as monstrous births occurred. They were used during the Latin wars and much later when Rome was threatened by the Gauls and Hannibal. Exceptional sacrifices were ordered for the infernal powers after consultations and once in 226 BC the burial alive of a Gaulish and a Greek couple. Sibylline oracles had much earlier been mocked by the Greek Aristophanes as texts of nonsense, but the Romans, perhaps following Etruscan tradition in such matters, regarded them as sacred texts giving practical rules for dealing with abnormal, uncanny and perilous situations.

Apart from the classical Greek and Roman framework, a large collection of Jewish, Chaldean and Christian prophetic poetry, in Greek hexameters, was formed in the eastern Mediterranean region in Hellenistic and Roman times. This collection is now known as the *Oracula Sibyllina*.

E. D. PHILLIPS

Based on the teachings of Guru Nanak, Sikhism requires its followers to 'avoid all conduct that does not conform to the truth that is God'

SIKHS

THE ROOTS of the Sikh tradition lie in the Punjab, a region in north-western India where Hinduism and Islam have confronted one another ever since the 10th century AD. At various times religious movements arose which combined features of Hindu and Islamic thinking, and the 11th and 12th centuries saw the development of a mysticism based on the ecstatic experience of saintly men, the Sufis (see SUFIS). Though they were adherents of Islam, the Sufis accepted certain Hindu ideas and practices, and converted many Hindus to their own faith. The interaction of the two religions did not lead to a true synthesis, however, and repeated attacks by fanatical Moslem invaders destroyed such mutual tolerance as the Sufi movement had created.

In the 15th century there was another upsurge of syncretistic ideas, and it was in this atmosphere that Sikhism arose as a new and distinct religious movement. The Sikh community gradually assumed the character of an ethnic group of distinct cultural heritage and national sentiment. Today there are about eight million Sikhs in India, and expatriate Sikh communities which retain their sense of identity exist in Britain, Canada, the United States, Afghanistan, Iran, Thailand, Malaya, Indonesia and East Africa.

The undisputed founder of Sikhism was Nanak, believed to have been born in 1469 in a village not far from Lahore. The story of his life is embedded in a welter of legends, but there is no doubt that his family background was that of a high Hindu caste, and that he became familiar with Moslem concepts and practices at an early age. His father was a village accountant, but Nanak showed little interest in the family profession, although he entered the service of a Moslem prince and held this position for 13 years in order to support his wife and children. Though he was deeply religious, and often consorted with both Hindu and Moslem ascetics, Nanak did not envisage complete renunciation of secular life. He was middle-aged when he had a mystic experience while taking a ritual bath in a river. It is believed that in this vision he received the divine command to go into the world and teach mankind to pray to one supreme Creator god. Nanak then disappeared for three days, and was believed to have been drowned; but he returned to announce his newly-found faith which was epitomized in the declaration: 'There is no Hindu, there is no Moslem.'

Camera Press

Religious power is vested in the entire Sikh community, and their actions are guided by the scriptures set out in their holy book, a focal point of their ritual: gold tablet inscribed with the sacred tenets of the Sikh religion, in the 'golden temple' at Amritsar

This incident marked the end of the first phase in Nanak's life. The search for truth was over, and he was intent on proclaiming his faith to the people of the world. He left his wife and home, and travelled widely, visiting many places sacred to Hindus and Buddhists as well as to Moslems. He saw how religion was practised by the adherents of various faiths and he determined to do away with superficial ritual, and concentrate in his teaching on the essence and purity of faith in a supreme deity.

From then on he became known as *Guru* (teacher) Nanak, and it is believed that his mission took him to Baghdad, Mecca and Medina. He certainly mixed with both Hindus and Moslems, and dressed in a manner combining the styles of the ascetics of both faiths. Many incidents of his life as a wandering ascetic are reported in the biographies compiled by his disciples, and though historical facts are interspersed with legendary elements, the picture that emerges is of a preacher of great independence of mind, who discounted the value of many traditional ritual practices, and advocated a religion focused on the love of God and the love of man.

On his travels Nanak gathered as his disciples many men and women who dissented from both Hinduism and Islam. The earlier Sufis had prepared the ground for a religion which dispensed with elaborate ritual and sought mystical union with God. Nanak's teaching appealed especially to the underprivileged Hindus of the lower castes, and to the poorer Moslems.

In later life Nanak returned to his family and settled down at Kartapur, where he combined work on his farm with teaching the disciples who flocked to him from many parts of the Punjab. He made them observe

William MacQuitty

a strict routine of prayers and work, and set up a communal kitchen where people of all castes and social status ate together, a practice diametrically opposed to the traditional segregation of the various Hindu castes. Nanak is believed to have died in 1539 and, according to legend, his body disappeared from among the flowers which surrounded it, thus obviating the problem of whether it should be cremated in Hindu style or buried according to Moslem custom.

During his wanderings as a preacher Nanak had set up centres of worship in widely separated areas, but those in distant places did not last very long. He had spoken and written in the language of the Punjab and it was in the Punjab that his message took root. His concept of God was derived more from Islam than from Hinduism. He was a strict monotheist and his disapproval of the worship of images placed him in conscious opposition to Hindu ritual. He believed that God was truth as opposed to falsehood and illusion; to tell a lie is to be ungodly, and untruthful conduct not only hurts one's neighbour, but is also irreligious. A good Sikh therefore must believe that God is the one omnipotent reality, and he must avoid all conduct that does not conform to the truth that is God. Nanak believed that the power that was God could not be defined because God was formless.

This abstract definition of God did not prevent Nanak from referring to him by a variety of names, such as 'Father of all mankind', 'Lover and Master of the devotee', and 'Great Giver'. He insisted that in order

Camera Press London

Top The 'golden temple' at Amritsar, the central sanctuary of Sikhism; built by Ram Das, the fourth Sikh guru, it contains the *Granth Sahib* or 'master book' of sacred scriptures *Above* Pilgrim outside the 'golden temple'; because they are forbidden to shave or cut their hair, orthodox Sikhs have beards, and long hair which they tie up under turbans

to understand the nature of God, man needed a guru, a religious guide inspired by God. Hinduism was the source of Nanak's belief in rebirth and his doctrine that man's fortunes are shaped by his deeds in a previous existence. Fortune and misfortune and all social inequality are said to be the natural products of individual conduct. Linked with this idea is the belief in retribution and rewards after death. A bridge as narrow as a knife's edge leads to the world beyond, and sinners, unable to cross this bridge, fall into an abyss filled with blood, while the pure walk safely across. Redemption is achieved neither by rigid asceticism nor by pilgrimages and the endless repetition of prayers, but by faith in the truth of God, and by integrity of conduct.

As well as being a preacher of a new doctrine, Nanak also organized and advocated social and religious reforms. His message has been preserved in a book of hymns which he recited so frequently that they became firmly lodged in the minds of his followers. Today they are a central part of Sikh sacred scriptures. They were composed in metric form and in a peculiar language, known as Gurmukhi, the 'tongue of the Guru'. In the same way that Nanak's teaching embraced Hindu and Moslem ideas, so the literary Gurmukhi language was a conglomerate of Hindi, Arabic and Persian elements. His successors developed a special alphabet for the Sikh scriptures.

Although Nanak did not formulate a rigidly defined doctrine to be adhered to by all Sikhs, he made arrangements for his succession and by doing so laid the foundations for what became in practice a Sikh 'Church'. In preference to his own sons Nanak chose Guru Angad (1539–1552) to be his successor. Angad was a former devotee of the fierce Hindu goddess Durga. Like his master, he tried to avoid the formation of a separate sect, and sought to preserve Sikhism as a movement of reform and a medium of reconciliation. But he was conscious of the twin dangers of absorption in Hinduism and eradication by militant Moslems.

Angad's successor was Amar Das and under him Sikhism assumed an attitude of conscious opposition to Hinduism. He rebelled against the practice of burning widows, a Hindu custom that had continued among Sikhs, he castigated the avarice of many Brahmin priests in his poems, and he argued against the evils of worshipping images and a multitude of gods. He emphasized the sad state of the world and the virtue of humility and penitence, and spoke of a God dwelling in men's hearts. He made the communal kitchen an integral institution of the Sikh Church by insisting that anyone who wanted to see him had first to accept his hospitality by eating with his disciples. In the case of high-caste Hindus, doing so showed willingness to abandon narrow caste-prejudices. Among Amar Das's innumerable visitors was the Mogul Emperor Akbar, who was so impressed by the lofty ideals of the community that he assured the Guru of his patronage.

Amar Das was succeeded by his son-in-law Ram Das, who founded the town which later became known as Amritsar, 'pool of nectar'. When Ram Das died, his own son Arjun (1581–1606) became the fifth Guru and during his term of office the Sikhs turned more and more into a distinct religious and political community. By compiling the writings of his predecessors and adding hymns and poems of his own, he created a large body of sacred scriptures which subsequently came to be regarded as the religious heritage of Sikhism. Arjun also built the 'golden temple' at Amritsar, which became the central sanctuary of Sikhism.

Martial Tradition

After the death of the Emperor Akbar, the Sikhs suffered from the oppressive policies of less tolerant Moslem rulers. This forced them into a defensive position and accelerated the growth of a political organization. Under Arjun's successors, and particularly the tenth Guru, Gobind Singh (1675–1708), the Sikhs created a theocratic state, of which the Khalsa, an elite group, became the military arm. Gobind Singh did not appoint a successor but decreed that after him the power of the Guru should be vested in the entire Sikh community, whose actions should be guided by the sacred scriptures, to be referred to as Guru Granth Sahib, 'Master Book'. This book has been venerated ever since, and has been treated as if it were the Guru himself.

In the 17th and 18th centuries the Sikhs became involved in armed conflicts with the imperial Moslem power, as well as with the Hindu states that surrounded the Sikh region. Gradually they carved out several principalities which were integrated into a sovereign state by Ranjit Singh, the most prominent military Sikh leader of his time. In 1809 he concluded a treaty with the British, which defined the southern limit of his kingdom. Subsequently the Sikhs fought successfully against invading Afghans, but a clash with the British in 1849 ended with the subjugation of the Sikh state and the annexation of the Punjab by the British rulers of India. By that time, however, the Sikhs had developed as a separate ethnic and cultural group, distinct from all other communities of India.

After the establishment of the Khalsa as a military elite, the Sikhs developed a strong martial tradition. They entered the British Indian Army in great numbers and distinguished themselves in many wars as tough and dependable soldiers.

A tragic situation arose when, in 1947, the division of the Indian sub-continent into India and Pakistan resulted in the partition of the Punjab, the Sikh's traditional homeland. While the majority lived in the regions allotted to India, substantial minorities remained on the Pakistan side of the newly-drawn boundary. Though the founder of Sikhism had envisaged his doctrine as a means of reconciling Hindus and Moslems, it now appeared that in the Islamic state of Pakistan there was no place for Sikhs, and in bloody clashes between Moslems and Hindus, the Sikhs found themselves on the side of the Hindus.

In a mass emigration triggered off by persecution and massacres, the Sikhs of West Punjab flooded into India, leaving their ancestral homes and many of their temples. Their cohesion as a community with a fanatical faith in its identity enabled them to establish themselves among their co-religionists in East Punjab. In the course of a long political struggle they finally obtained their own state, carved out of East Punjab, while the districts where Hindus are in a majority were established as the new state of Haryana. The fulfilment of the Sikhs' agitation was reached in 1970 when Chandigarh, the town designed by Le Corbusier as the capital of the undivided East Punjab and till then shared with Haryana, was allotted to the Sikh state.

Wherever their communities dwell, both in India and in Western countries, Sikhs follow the same practices in worship and the same pattern of living. The focal point of their ritual is the holy book. It occupies a central position in all temples and is solemnly displayed at every service. One room in the home should be set aside for this holy book, and part of it read every day. Most Sikh services include the distribution of communion food, and new members are initiated in a rite during which they must vow to adhere to the Sikh faith and to observe certain rules of behaviour. Among these is a ban on shaving or cutting any part of the body hair; it is for this reason that orthodox Sikhs have beards, and long hair which they tie up under their turbans. Any mutilation of the body, such as circumcision or piercing the nose or ears is also forbidden.

Sikhs in foreign lands consider the observance of these rules to be an essential part of their religion and tend to resist adaptation to local customs of hair style. Nevertheless, there is a class of young men among the educated and wealthy Sikhs in India who have begun to give up the practice of wearing their hair and beards unshorn. Although they may retain other symbols of Sikhism, they are regarded as renegades by the orthodox, who maintain that there is no such thing as a clean-shaven Sikh; at best such a person is a Hindu believing in Sikhism. Today there is a tendency where Sikhs are dispersed among Hindus to adapt to the Hindu pattern, and to dilute Sikh ritual and tradition. However, with the creation of the Sikh-dominated state of East Punjab, where nationalistic sentiment underpins religious practice, the Sikhs have acquired a national home and with it a new lease of life for their religion and their traditions.

C. VON FÜRER-HAIMENDORF

FURTHER READING: Khushwant Singh, *A History of the Sikhs*, 2 vols. (Princeton Univ. Press, 1963); W. Owen Cole & P. S. Sambhi, *Sikhs* (Routledge & Kegan, 1978).

Marsell Collection

Silenus

In classical mythology, one of the Sileni, woodland spirits who became associated with Dionysus and the satyrs (see DIONYSUS; SATYRS); represented as an elderly, fat, hairy but bald-headed man with the ears of a horse, riding an ass or a wineskin; he is profoundly wise and constantly drunk; sometimes said to have been the teacher of the young Dionysus or the father of the satyrs; Socrates was compared with him for wisdom and ugliness.

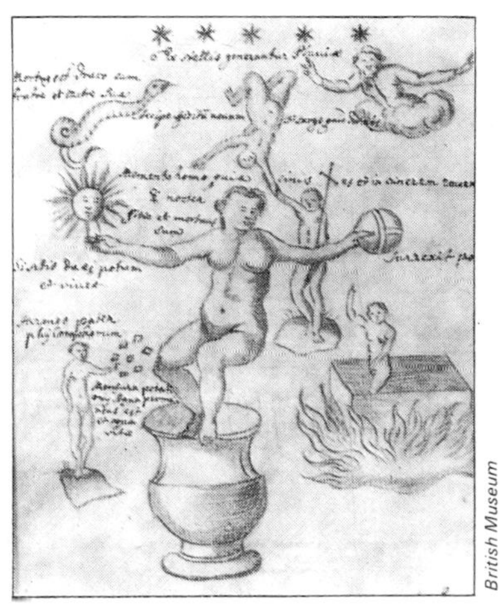

British Museum

Silver

Metal of the moon, because of its colour; according to some alchemists a stage in their work was the making of the White Stone, which turned all things to silver and which they connected with the white stone mentioned in Revelation 2.17: there is a widespread tradition that a silver bullet is needed to kill a sorcerer, a witch or an evil ghost.

See ALCHEMY; CORRESPONDENCES.

SIMEON STYLITES

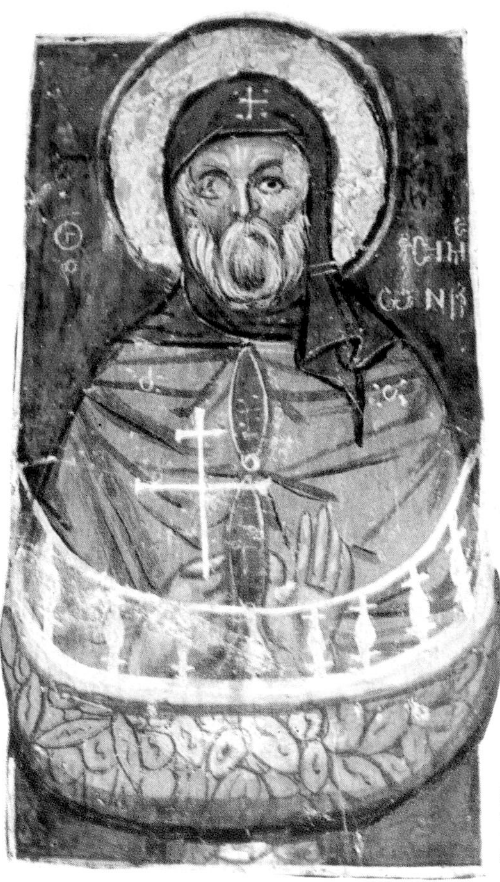
Sonia Halliday

Renowned for the fanatical austerity of his life, Simeon has nevertheless been described as modest, humble and sweet-tempered: wall painting from Asinou Church, Cyprus

A CHRISTIAN SAINT of the 5th century, Simeon passed 42 of his 70 years in the Syrian desert, perched on top of a pillar which he eventually built up to a height of 50 or 60 feet. Here he endured not only the scorching summer days and bitterly cold winter nights, clad only in a simple leather tunic, but also the rigours of frequent fasting, and the hideous discomfort of a platform too small to lie down on.

Simeon was born to Christian parents in 389 at Sisan, a village on the borders of Syria and Cilicia in Asia Minor. He never attended school, but from an early age helped to look after his father's sheep. When he was 13, he entered a local monastery as a servant, after hearing the Sermon on the Mount read in church. He had been deeply moved by the Beatitudes, and had a vision in which he was digging the foundations of a building, and heard a voice bidding him four times to dig deeper in order to build higher.

After two years as a novice, Simeon went to another monastery at Teleda, where he led a life of such fanatical austerity that he was finally ordered to leave, in case he exerted an undue influence on his brother monks. A typical incident was his attempt to mortify the flesh by tying a rope of twisted palm leaves round his waist so tightly that he caused ulcers, the stench of which, after a number of days, drew the attention of his superiors. Simeon fainted with the agony when the rope had to be cut out of his flesh with a knife, and lay on the floor for some time as if dead.

Leaving Teleda, Simeon went to Tell-neshin, near Antioch, where he persuaded a local abbot to wall him up in a cell during Lent, with ten loaves and a jug of water. At the end of Lent, Simeon was found stretched almost lifeless on the floor of his cell, with the bread and water untouched. He was revived with a moist sponge, and given a few lettuce leaves to eat. For the rest of his life Simeon fasted completely throughout Lent, standing and praising God to begin with, and gradually sinking to the ground as the strength ebbed from him. Later in life, on his pillar, he managed to remain standing throughout the fast, tied to a pole in the early years; gradually he was able to dispense with this aid.

When Simeon eventually took up the life of a solitary in the rolling stony hills to the west of Aleppo, he at first chained himself to a rock. But Bishop Meletios of Antioch advised him to scorn such a material bond, and to trust in his own will, sustained by divine grace, to keep him to his ascetic life. Simeon's first biographer, who knew him personally, reported that when the iron chain was removed from Simeon's leg, 40 large bugs were discovered on his skin underneath the shackle.

Simeon acquired a reputation as a healer of all sorts of sickness, and was an especial favourite of women who believed themselves to be barren. It was to get away from mobs of admirers and miracle-seekers that Simeon first resorted to the idea of building a column. He first built an enclosure, and then a column inside it. Accounts vary as to the exact size of this column, which he raised higher and higher as the years passed, but according to a Syriac biography written not long after his death, it rose finally to a height of 40 cubits (roughly 67 feet) and consisted of three huge drums, in honour of the Holy Trinity.

Simeon spent most of the time standing upright on a small platform at the top of the column, which could be reached by means of a rope ladder, though he varied his posture by leaning against a post, and inclining his head in prayer. An observer once counted 1244 obeisances during a day's prayer before coming to the end of his own, but not the saint's, powers of endurance. The constant standing gave Simeon an ulcer on his foot from which pus ran constantly. He is reported to have had spells of blindness, during which his eyes were open.

He regularly preached two sermons a day, and prayed all night with his hands raised. His sermons were greatly admired, and he is also described as a pleasing and ready conversationalist. He was at the disposal of the crowd who flocked to stare at him every afternoon, and to the end of his life listened to requests, healed the sick, and reconciled disputants. He was available to labourers, peasants and beggars, and also to the high and mighty of his time. He was in correspondence with potentates and Church dignitaries in many parts of Christendom, but also preached to pagans and prayed and spoke on their behalf. His extraordinary way of life had its detractors, but those who knew him well insist that he was humble, modest, easy and sweet-tempered. In spite of his solitary existence, he took part in many of the controversies of the day.

When he died thousands attended his funeral, which was celebrated with a torch-light procession through Antioch. A great church was built at Qalaat Semaan, which was unique in Christendom in being centred on the saint's pillar, instead of an altar. Simeon set an example for dozens of stylite (pillar) saints in the centuries that followed his death, and isolated examples have been reported down to modern times. The base of the original column is still standing at Qalaat Semaan to this day.

SIMON MAGUS

THIS SAMARITAN magician and, perhaps, Gnostic teacher of the first Christian century, is known from the New Testament book of Acts and from later Christian writers. According to Acts (chapter 8), Simon was a magician (hence called 'Magus'), baptized as a Christian after seeing miracles performed by Christian evangelists in Samaria. Two apostles, Peter and John, came from Jerusalem and laid hands on other converts, who then received the Holy Spirit. Simon offered money (hence the later term simony) for the power of transmission; Peter harshly rebuked him and predicted his doom. Conceivably, the author of Acts knew that Simon was also a Gnostic revealer and redeemer, for he is described as 'saying that he himself was somebody great' and as known in Samaria as 'that power of God which is called Great'. It may be that the author intentionally refrained from mentioning his dangerous Gnostic teaching, although it is possible that Simon had not yet developed it.

In any event, by the time of the theologian Justin Martyr (c 150) Simon was regarded as the founder of Christian heresy. Justin himself came from Samaria and knew that Simon was a native of the village of Gitthae. It was said that he claimed to be 'the first God' and that a prostitute named Helen embodied 'the first conception' of his mind. He was worshipped by 'practically all the Samaritans'. Justin had also been told that during the reign of Claudius (41–54) Simon had practised the art of magic at Rome; the Senate and the Roman People had erected a statue in his honour, with the inscription SIMONI DEO SANCTO ('to Simon, the holy God'). Unfortunately, in the 16th century this inscription, or one like it, was discovered. It read SEMONI SANCO DEO FIDIO, a dedication to the old Sabine deity Semo Sancus. Presumably the error was due not simply to Justin's poor eyesight but to the power of suggestion exercised over him by Simonians. It reflects Simonian propaganda of the mid-2nd century.

Other Church writers, perhaps relying on a lost work by Justin, tell more about Simon's system. He was the 'Father above all' and in the beginning emitted from himself the 'Mother of all', his first Thought. She descended from the height and generated angels and powers who, in turn, made the world. Because of their desire to be regarded as supreme creators, they imprisoned their Mother and made her pass from one female body into another – for example, into Helen of Troy, whose fatal beauty was the cause of the Trojan War. Finally she was a captive in the body of a prostitute from Tyre. Simon, who viewed her as his 'lost sheep' (compare Luke 15. 4–7), came down through the planetary spheres to look for her and save her. He appeared among the Jews as Son (that is, as Jesus), among the Samaritans as Father, and elsewhere as Holy Spirit; his followers also identified him with Zeus and Helen with Athene. His rescue of Helen was a model for his rescue of 'those who are his' everywhere. He freed her and them from the authority of the hostile angels, who not only had created the world but also had produced the Old Testament law and prophecies in order to enslave mankind under conventional morality. Simon's followers, saved by his 'grace' or favour, were free to do whatever they wished. What they wished, according to Christian critics, was to make use of incantations and magic.

With the passage of time, further details about Simon's life came into existence. Christians at Rome told of his flight over the city, terminated after prayer by the apostle Peter. Others claimed that he tried to emulate the burial and resurrection of Jesus but did not survive the experience. In the Jewish-Christian Clementine romances he was described as a follower of the Jewish or Samaritan heretic Dositheus, who recognized him as 'the Standing One', as God.

Regarded as the 'Father above all' by his followers, Simon Magus was credited with numerous magical feats; according to one legend he attempted to fly over Rome, but the evil spirits who had raised him were forced to cast him down to earth again by the prayers of Peter and Paul: Simon Magus with the Roman emperor and the apostles, from a 14th century Italian manuscript

Simon's magic was said to produce everything one could desire: invisibility, invulnerability, the animation of statues, tunnelling under mountains, transformation into a sheep or goat. Like Jesus, he was said to have been born of a virgin mother.

Since the 16th century the figure of Simon Magus has been merged, in Western culture, with that of the magician Faust, whose memory was combined with medieval tales about Simon and with the idea of a pact with the Devil (see FAUST). The first book about this Faust, by an anonymous author, was published at Frankfurt in 1587. In an English translation it inspired Christopher Marlowe's *Tragical History of Doctor Faustus*, published in 1604. Extremely popular during the 17th and 18th centuries, the story of Faust was given its greatest expression in the work of Goethe, who recast it and deepened its philosophical interpretation (see GOETHE). Composers were attracted by the story – for example, Berlioz, Liszt and Gounod in the Romantic era. The most successful treatment is to be found in the eighth (choral) symphony of Gustav Mahler (1907).

The modern Faust is not, of course, identical with the Simon Magus of the early Christian period, who was not described as making a pact with the Devil; and Faust's Helen is not Simon's. Goethe's emphasis on the goodness of human freedom and striving, however, is not unlike the Simonian stress on emancipation and magic.

Certain questions raised by the Simonians were faced more radically than was the case among their Christian opponents. Was man simply to accept (or, among ascetic groups, to reject) the world of Nature or was he to control it? To what extent were traditional and biblical ethical systems simply the products of convention? What was the place of woman or 'the female principle' in the created order and in the process of salvation? These questions were to be elaborated in the modern treatment of Faust, but in principle, at least, they were already raised among the followers of Simon Magus.

R. M. GRANT

FURTHER READING: R. M. Grant, *Gnosticism and Early Christianity* (Columbia Univ. Press, N.Y., 1966, 2nd edn).

The experience of sin is not the same as that of the difference between right and wrong, or good and bad; it is an essentially religious concept based on man's relationship with a transcendent reality or order

SIN

FEW CONCEPTS have been as significant and influential in the history of religions, and few have been so denigrated in modern times, as the concept of sin. Most religions have a variety of terms to render the idea of sin, and there is a wide range of nuances and emphases in the various religious cultures, and even within a single religion. One way of studying the concept of 'sin' would therefore be to analyse the meanings of the different terms used in the various religions, cultures and languages. For example, there is the Old Testament (*het, awon, pesha*, and so on), the New Testament (which mostly uses the Greek word *hamartia*), Hindu tradition (*papa*, which includes both ritual and moral sin), China (*tsui, o, kuo*), or Japanese Shinto (*tsumi, aku*). Practically all religions and cultures, even the most primitive ones, have terms more or less equivalent to 'sin', and very often the variety of terms in even a single culture reflects differentiations of various types of categories of sin (for example, *ama-tsu-tsumi* and *kuni-tsu-tsumi*, 'sins relating to heaven' and 'sins relating to earth' in Japanese Shinto).

Offending the Gods

Sin is an essentially religious concept since it implies an offence with regard to a religiously or supernaturally conceived reality: a personal god or gods, a divine order of things, or a set of taboos possessing supernatural sanctions. It is this added quality which distinguishes 'sinning' from 'wrongdoing', and renders the experience of sin different from the experience of the difference between right and wrong, or good and bad.

Sin is based on man's experience of, and his relation with, a transcendent reality or order. In the perspective of this relationship, all evil, wrong or unjust acts, and even the awareness of inescapable human inadequacy, acquire the additional quality and depth-dimension of 'sin'.

The elaboration of this concept, the interpretation and the consequences of the sense of sin, vary in different cultures, at different periods in the history of the same culture, and in the lives of individuals, even in any one period. So do the means devised for escaping the consequences of sin – rites of purification, atonement, remission of sins, penitential exercises and mortifications. Or means may be devised to escape the sense of sin itself, for instance by mobilizing psychological theories in defence of the assertion that there is no such thing as sin or sinfulness.

Rejection of God's Will

Because sin, as distinct from mere wrongdoing, is connected with man's relationship with the transcendent sphere, it is closely bound up with the ways in which the various religions represent this sphere and man's relation to it. There is a tendency in most religions to consider misfortunes of all kinds (sickness, famine, drought, defeat in war) as the result of sin (the anger of irate gods or spirits, punishment meted out by a just godhead, the automatic irruption of destructive forces resulting from a disturbance of the right order). Methods and rituals are therefore evolved for detecting sin, punishing the culprits or finding a scapegoat, or obliterating the sin by appropriate ritual acts or by obtaining forgiveness from the offended deity. By and large, most ancient religions do not distinguish between ritual and moral offences, and very often the former, the breaking of ritual taboos, for instance, appear to have been regarded as more serious.

The ancient Mesopotamian texts suggest a preoccupation with ritual offences. The ancient Egyptian texts (in which innocence from all sins is mentioned as a prerequisite for life after death) catalogue both ritual and moral transgressions, blasphemy and murder for instance, without distinction, whereas in ancient Greece and Rome the social character of religion also led to a greater emphasis on 'sins' relevant to the social order. The Hebrew prophets, who never tired of speaking of the sinfulness of the people and of God's wrath and imminent punishment, nevertheless shifted the emphasis from ritual to moral values as in the book of Micah (chapter 6).

"With what shall I come before the Lord,
and bow myself before God on high?
Shall I come before him with burnt offerings,
with calves a year old?
Will the Lord be pleased with thousands of
rams, with ten thousands of rivers of oil?
Shall I give my first-born for my transgression,
the fruit of my body for the sin of my soul?"
He has showed you, O man, what is good;
and what does the Lord require of you
but to do justice, and to love kindness,
and to walk humbly with your God?

A deepening of experience and of reflection on the character of human nature and its inherent failings and inadequacies led to a more systematic and fundamental consideration of sin and sinfulness. Whereas Islam takes it for granted that man is weak and always liable to sin, it holds Allah to be not only a stern judge but also compassionate and forgiving. Sins are essentially the result of human weakness which fails to obey the commands of Allah.

In Christianity, too, sin is conceived essentially as disobedience to, or a conscious rejection of, God's will; but the experience of sinfulness and the elaboration of the doctrine of sin have been carried further than in any other religion. In fact, sin can be regarded as one of the pivotal concepts of Christianity. Though essentially a religion of salvation, the salvation which it brings is primarily from sin. Christ on the cross took upon himself the sins of mankind, and by his suffering and death procured atonement and expiation. He was the 'Lamb of God who takes away the sin of the world', and in the account of the Last Supper, on which the rite of the Eucharist is based, Jesus says to his disciples as he gives them the cup of wine 'Drink of it, all of you; for this is my blood of the covenant, which is poured out for many for the forgiveness of sins' (Matthew 26.27–8).

Whilst bringing the good news of liberation from the power of sin, Christianity also did much to foster awareness of this power, sometimes to a pathological degree. Man is a poor and miserable sinner, and only contrition, continuous penance and resort to the sacramental means of grace provided by the Church will save him from the dire consequences of both his essential sinfulness and his specific sins. The source of sin and the nature of sinfulness were described in various idioms, ranging from mythology to a theological psychology. In mythological symbolism the Devil played a major role: it is he who tempts man away from God, hence the tendency to associate everything 'tempting', including the pleasures of this world and especially sex, with the Devil and lord of demons. Hence also the tendency of medieval Christianity to associate sin, heresy and magic.

The analysis of sinfulness as an inherent human trait and as a basic feature of the human mode of being in its actual ('fallen') state was first made by St Paul and subsequently developed by the Church Fathers, especially St Augustine, and by later theologians. Man's nature is so corrupted and vitiated that he cannot turn towards the better out of his own resources. Even his repentance, faith and conversion are the result of a divine grace moving him. In Christian doctrine this inherently sinful state of human nature was connected with the biblical account of Adam's Fall in Paradise (Genesis, chapter 3), giving this story of 'original sin' an importance it never had in biblical and rabbinic Judaism (see EVIL; FIRST MAN).

Whilst medieval Catholic belief held that it was possible for individuals to overcome sin and to rise to the level of sainthood, Martin Luther and the reformers reaffirmed the sinfulness of even the good Christian. To be saved is not to be free from sin but to acquire, through faith, the grace and pardon given in Christ. The role of sin in the experience and consciousness of Christianity in all its major historic forms is attested by its liturgy, traditional beliefs and practices, and literature.

The prevalence and omnipresence of a sense of sin were intensified by the teaching that sin was a matter of intention and desire no less than of overt action. 'You have heard that it was said, "You shall not commit adultery." But I say to you that everyone who looks at a woman lustfully has already commited adultery with her in his heart' (Matthew 5.27–8). 'For out of the heart come evil thoughts, murder, adultery, fornication, theft, false witness, slander' (Matthew, 15.19).

In due course Christianity developed very elaborate doctrines and catalogues of sins, as well as practices for dealing with them. There was original sin to which every human being is heir (according to St Augustine it was transmitted through the act of procreation), and the individual sins man committed during his life. There are the sins committed after baptism (which posed a serious problem to the early Church since it was believed that baptism had washed away not only all past sins but also the inclination to sin). These were divided into 'mortal' sins, which entail everlasting punishment, and venial or pardonable sins. The 'Seven Deadly Sins' became a favourite theme of medieval art. Around the basic idea of sin were built many other doctrines and practices; the sacrament of penance, confession and absolution, hell and purgatory,

Courtauld Institute Galleries/Colorific!

The Christian concept of original sin, the belief that sinfulness is an inherent human trait, was introduced by St Paul and developed by the Church Fathers and later theologians; it is traditionally said to stem from Adam's disobedience in the garden of Eden: *Adam and Eve* by Cranach the Elder

and the belief in the possibility of escaping the sufferings of purgatory. The abuses, such as the sale of indulgences, to which the latter belief led were important factors in precipitating the Reformation in the 16th century. But whilst the reformers did away with many Roman Catholic beliefs and practices, the doctrine of sin and sinfulness still remained central in their theology.

The significance attributed to the notion of sin can be gauged by, among other things, the practice of confession of sins. This flourishes wherever the reality of sin is taken so much for granted that the attempt to deny it would merely be compounding it, and wherever remission, expiation and atonement are considered to be real possibilities. Where these pre-conditions are lacking, 'declarations of innocence' may take the place of confession, as in the ancient mortuary ritual of Egypt, where the tomb inscriptions contain such declarations, evidently for the purpose of enabling the person buried to pass the Judgement of the Dead (see BOOK OF THE DEAD; JUDGEMENT OF THE DEAD). Confessions of sin are essential parts of the Jewish and Christian liturgies, and quite naturally precede every

The Christian Church taught that sin was a matter of intention and desire as well as of overt action. Elaborate doctrines were developed and sins were divided into various categories; as well as original sin there were individual sins committed during a man's life. Mortal sins entail everlasting punishment, and there are also venial or pardonable sins. The Seven Deadly Sins are those which are held to endanger the life of the soul if they are committed with full consent; a variety of sins were in fact depicted under this heading in art before the list was finally formulated *Above, left to right* Hypocrisy; pride; wrath; sloth *Below, left to right* Hatred; avarice; gluttony. All these illustrations are taken from a 13th century French manuscript which is now in the British Museum

prayer for forgiveness. In Psalms (51.1–4) the psalmist prays:

> Have mercy on me, O God, according to
> thy steadfast love;
> according to thy abundant mercy blot
> out my transgressions.
> Wash me thoroughly from my iniquity,
> and cleanse me from my sin!
> For I know my transgressions,
> and my sin is ever before me.
> Against thee, thee only, have I sinned,
> and done that which is evil in thy sight . . .

The General Confession in the Anglican Book of Common Prayer reads:

> Almighty and most merciful Father: We have erred and strayed from thy ways like lost sheep. We have followed too much the devices and desires of our own hearts. We have offended against thy holy laws. We have left undone those things which we ought to have done; and we have done those things which we ought not to have done; and there is no health in us. But thou, O Lord, have mercy upon us, miserable offenders. Spare thou them, O God, which confess their faults. Restore thou them that are penitent: According to thy promises declared unto mankind in Christ Jesus our Lord.

This type of confession, as well as the underlying doctrine of sin, presupposes a personal god who is a law-giver, judge and forgiving father. But the notion of sin is also found in religious cultures that do not recognize a personal godhead and where the problem of expiation is not conceived in terms of humble prayer and personal forgiveness. The Indian notion of sin is related to the general theory of karma (see KARMA); liberation from evil karma leads to the great and ultimate liberation. To assist man on his way to liberation, Hinduism has an elaborate system of penances to counterbalance and efface the effects of sin with corresponding merits.

In Buddhism, too, sin is essentially an act that produces evil karma. But although the commission of such acts is itself the outcome of earlier bad karma, man is thought to be sufficiently the master of his fate to break through the chain of karma and to advance on the path of right knowledge, insight and conduct to the great liberation.

Wrong acts have to be neutralized or balanced, and much Buddhist ritual is concerned with accumulating merit and applying it for the benefit of the departed. Rites of confession of sin were practised in early Buddhism, but these were chiefly the Buddhist monk's confession and enumeration of breaches of the rules of the order. In fact, early Theravada Buddhism thought of sin mainly in terms of individual offences against the rule. Mahayana Buddhism, on the other hand, developed a concept of man's fate and karma-bound existence which put the emphasis on his sinfulness in its totality, rather than on specific offences. This is clearly brought out by the form of confession of sins which is still in use in many Mahayanist circles. The text originally occurs in the *Avatamsaka Sutra*; it is still used among Zen Buddhists:

> All the evil karma ever committed by me
> since of old
> On account of my beginningless greed,
> anger and folly
> Born of my body, mouth and thought (that
> is, committed in action, speech and
> thought)
> I now make full open confession of it.

The notions of both 'original' and 'karmic' sinfulness go beyond the purely moralizing, and give to sin an almost ontological status. Modern psychology and existential philosophy, whilst doing away with many primitive, perverted and obsessive ideas of sin, illuminate the nature and character of human existence so as to place the problem and reality of sin in a new light.

R. J. ZWI WERBLOWSKY

Sinai, Mt

Holy mountain where God delivered the law and commandments to Moses (Exodus, chapter 19); which mountain it was is uncertain, but it was first identified as Gebel Serbal and later as Gebel Musa, in the Sinai peninsula; the episode of the burning bush (Exodus, chapter 3) was also placed there; the monastery of St Catherine on Gebel Musa became a centre of pilgrimage.

Mansell Collection

Sinbad

Or Sindbad, legendary Arab traveller who sailed on seven voyages in the Indian Ocean and the seas further east; he encountered all sorts of wonders and marvels, including a roc (see ROC) and the Old Man of the Sea, a monster which climbed on his back and would not leave him, until he killed it.

Mansell Collection

As long as the doctrine of hellfire was preached the sin eater, who took upon himself the sins of someone who had just died, could always find work; the unsaved dead were said to be doomed to the everlasting torments of hell: illustration from a 16th century Flemish manuscript showing the sinfulness of man

Bodleian Library Colour Filmstrip

SIN EATER

THE FUNCTION of the person known as a 'sin eater' was to act as a human scapegoat for the sins of someone who had just died. By eating bread and drinking either milk, beer or wine that had been placed on the body of the corpse, the sin eater took upon himself the sins of the departed, absorbing them into his own body. He was paid a small amount of money for saving a soul from hell in this way.

Sin eaters were first recorded by the antiquary John Aubrey in the 17th century, in his book *Remaines of Gentilisme and Judaisme*: 'In the County of Hereford was an old custome at funeralls to hire poor people who have to take upon them all the sinnes of the parting deceased . . . The manner was that when the corpse was brought out of the house and layd in the biere, a loaf of bread was brought out and delivered to the sinne-eater over the corpse as also a mazar bowl of maple full of beer (which he was to drinke up) and sixpence in money in consideration whereof he took upon him (*ipso facto*) all the sinnes of the defunct and freed him or her from walking after they were dead.' In North Wales, according to Aubrey, milk was used instead of beer.

A later writer, Bagford, referring to information obtained from Aubrey, described the sin eaters of Shropshire: 'Within the memory of our fathers . . . when a person dyed there was a notice given to an old sire (for so they called him) who presently repaired to the place where the deceased lay and stood before the door of the house when some of the family came out and furnished him with a cricket (stool) . . . Then they gave him a groat which he put in his pocket; a crust of bread which he ate, and a full bowl of ale which he drank off at a draught . . . (after which) he pronounced the ease and rest of the soul departed for which he would pawn his own soul.'

In the late 17th century sixpence or a groat (fourpence) were worth very much more than they are today but even allowing for this, it seems a ridiculously small fee for the redemption of a human soul.

The concept of a scapegoat, who takes upon himself other peoples' sins, is based upon the primitive idea that the qualities of a human being or animal, whether good or evil, can be transmitted to another by some supernatural agency (see SCAPEGOAT). Some primitive peoples ate the flesh of the newly-dead in order to acquire their strength. In ancient Europe human blood (which was identified with the soul) was frequently drunk in order that the living might share in the strength or valour of the dead. The Greek geographer Strabo writes that in the British Isles it was the custom for sons to eat the flesh of their dead parents in order to prevent their ghosts from returning to haunt them. It is probable that the bread consumed by the sin eater represented the body of the deceased and that the wine, beer or milk symbolized the blood.

Rites developed by human beings for the purpose of keeping the soul at rest seem to have been based originally on the principle that unless obligations to the dead were fulfilled, the soul was bound to suffer. For this reason it was imperative to remove the burden of sin from the person who had died.

As long as the doctrine of hellfire was preached, the sin eater could always find work. In *Sighs From Hell, or the Groans of a Damned Soul,* published in 1658, John Bunyan compared the agonies of the dying with those of the unsaved dead who were transferred from the discomforts of 'a long sickness to a longer hell – from the gripings of death to the everlasting torments of hell'.

Although later references to sin eaters are scarce, they probably survived in remote places in the British Isles until well into the 18th century. They were occasionally seen in the Lowlands of Scotland at this time; in this area it was essential that the sin eater was a stranger to the dead person, and that he did not consume the food and drink 'with a grudge in his heart'. There is reason to believe that vestiges of the custom continued to influence funeral rites in Welsh border districts for a considerable period; for instance, a poor man might be given a present of money at the graveside. In Derbyshire in the 19th century a glass of wine from a box resting at the foot of the coffin would be offered to mourners, the intention behind the ceremony being the sacramental 'killing' of the sins of the deceased.

It seems that in East Anglia an unsuspecting tramp or beggar who happened to apply for charity at the door of a household where an unburied body awaited interment, would sometimes be tricked into taking the sins of the dead person upon himself. A piece of bread which had previously been passed over the corpse would be given to the vagrant who would eat it in good faith, unaware of the meaning of this innocent act. The last relic of this ancient superstition is possibly the reluctance of tramps to beg where there is a dead body in the house.

In the Theravada school of Buddhism the highest ranking layman has always been considered of lower status than the youngest religious novice; the scriptures on which Ceylon's predominant religion is based were brought to the island in the 3rd century BC

SINHALESE BUDDHISM

THE MAIN INTEREST which Buddhism in Ceylon holds for the outsider is its long and continuous tradition. Introduced into Ceylon from India soon after 250 BC, less than 250 years after the Buddha's death, Buddhism has been the religion of most Sinhalese, who are the principal inhabitants of Ceylon.

The school of Buddhism preserved in Ceylon is the Theravada, which has since become dominant in Burma, Thailand, Laos, Cambodia, and the southern part of South Vietnam. The scriptures of Theravada Buddhism, the *Tipitaka,* are preserved in an ancient language called Pali, a word which originally means 'text'. The Pali language and the Pali Canon (see GAUTAMA BUDDHA) were first introduced to Europeans in the middle and late 19th century from Ceylon; and the size and importance of these scriptures persuaded many scholars that Theravada represented the 'original' form of Buddhism.

This is now considered to be an exaggeration. When Buddhism was brought to Ceylon, traditionally by Mahinda, a son of the Indian Emperor Asoka, Theravada was but one of many schools with equal claims to authenticity. That it has so well preserved its scriptures, and the doctrines and practices which they embody, is mainly due to the historical accident that Mahinda converted the King of Ceylon, Devanampiya Tissa, who established Buddhism as the official religion of the Sinhalese.

Since then the fortunes of Buddhism have usually been identified with the fortunes of the Sinhalese nation; and Sinhalese literature, art and education have predominantly used Buddhist materials. The Sinhalese view of themselves as a kind of Buddhist 'chosen people' is exemplified in the *Mahavamsa,* a chronicle written in Pali by Buddhist monks through the centuries. The first part, written in the 5th century, is especially interesting. In the first chapter are alleged accounts of three visits to Ceylon made by the Buddha in his lifetime. Vijaya, the reputed founder of the Sinhalese nation, is said to have landed in Ceylon on the day of the Buddha's death, while the Buddha was prophesying to the king of the gods that his doctrine would be established in Ceylon.

After describing Mahinda's mission the chronicle is devoted mainly to the exploits of King Dutugamunu (101–77 BC), the greatest Sinhalese folk hero. When Dutugamunu ascended the throne, the Sinhalese capital, Anuradhapura, was held by Tamil invaders. In his successful campaign against them he fought with a relic of the Buddha in his spear and monks (who left their order for the purpose) in his army.

William MacQuitty

One of the best-known Buddhist celebrations is the annual festival in Kandy, during which the Buddha's tooth, which is said to have reached Ceylon in the 4th century, is paraded through the streets of the town every night for a week; at one time possession of the tooth was thought to confer the right to rule: worshippers outside the Temple of the Tooth, a celebrated Buddhist shrine

Mahinda is traditionally held to have brought the complete Pali Canon to Ceylon. This is substantially correct in spirit, as most of the texts must antedate his arrival. However, all teachings at the time were preserved orally, and it is very doubtful whether one man could memorize the whole Canon. The Pali Canon was written down in Ceylon in the 1st century BC, probably the first time that the Buddhist scriptures had been committed to writing. Again, although it cannot be literally true that Mahinda brought with him the commentaries on the whole Canon, those composed in Ceylon certainly preserve Indian traditions. They were in Sinhalese, and were probably all completed by about 100 AD. These old commentaries have been lost.

In the early 5th century Buddhaghosa came to Anuradhapura from northern India, and wrote commentaries in Pali on most of the canonical texts, basing his work on the Sinhalese commentaries. His edition was regarded as definitive, and the Sinhalese originals were superseded. Buddhaghosa also composed a summary of Buddhist

William MacQuitty

The doctrine that an individual is responsible for his own salvation is explicit in Theravadin Buddhism; there are no millenarian movements, and the coming of Maitri, the only figure who could be regarded as a future Messiah, is thought to be immensely distant. Although Sinhalese Buddhists accept the concept of a Bodhisattva, one who is on his way to becoming a Buddha, this belief is not based on fact or demonstration: wall painting of a Bodhisattva in the Temple of the Tooth

Buddha's Footprint

Fa-hsien, a Chinese traveller, visits Ceylon in the 5th century AD

After fourteen days and nights he reached the Land of the Lion (Ceylon), said by the inhabitants to lie at a distance of seven yôjanas from India . . . This country was not originally inhabited by human beings, but only by devils and dragons, with whom the merchants of the neighbouring countries traded by barter . . .

When Buddha came to this country, he wished to convert the wicked dragons; and by his divine power he placed one foot to the north of the royal city and the other on top of Adam's Peak, the two points being fifteen yôjanas apart. Over the footprint to the north of the city a great pagoda has been built, four hundred feet in height and decorated with gold and silver and with all kinds of precious substances combined. By the side of the pagoda a monastery has also been built, called No-Fear Mountain, where there are now five thousand priests. There is a Hall of Buddha of gold and silver carved work with all kinds of precious substances, in which stands his image in green jade, over twenty feet in height . . .

The Travels of Fa-hsien (399–414 AD)
trans by H. A. Giles

doctrine, the *Visuddhi-magga*, 'the Path to Purity', which is still considered authoritative. His interpretation of the Canon is unquestioned in Ceylon and constitutes the touchstone of orthodoxy.

Buddhists traditionally believe that their religion is embodied in the *Sangha*, the community of monks and nuns, and for them their religious history is properly the history of the community, which depends for its continuation on the preservation of a valid ordination tradition: a monk must receive the full ordination, *upasampada*, from no fewer than five fully-ordained monks, and nuns must similarly be ordained by nuns. The community of nuns *bhikkhuni sangha*, died out in Ceylon in the 11th century, while the order of monks also died out during several periods of political turmoil, and was then re-established by contact with monks from abroad. However the discontinuity is of little importance, because succession has always been renewed by monks from Burma or Thailand, countries which themselves originally received their succession from Ceylon. The largest body of monks in Ceylon today, the Siam Nikaya, traces its ordination line back to the last such renewal, when monks came from Thailand to hold an ordination ceremony in 1753. It therefore has a strong claim to stand in the direct tradition of the *Mahavihara*, 'Great Monastery', of Anuradhapura, which was founded by Mahinda.

The Mahavihara was always the bastion of Theravadin orthodoxy in Anuradhapura, but the main currents of Mahayana thought seem to have reached Ceylon from India. The first Ceylonese schism occurred shortly before the beginning of the Christian era and throughout the first millennium AD, until Anuradhapura finally fell to the Tamils, the monks were split into three *nikayas*, or fraternities. For more than a hundred years there have again been three nikayas in Ceylon. Monks from different nikayas will not co-operate in religious acts, generally live apart, and do not recognize each other's ecclesiastical seniority or authority. In ancient times the lines of division, whatever their origin, were generally given a doctrinal basis; but in modern times this is not so, and Sinhalese Buddhists stress that they all follow Theravadin orthodoxy.

The reason for the modern split is caste. The Siam Nikaya in the late 18th century would ordain only members of the *goyigama*, (farmer) caste, the top caste and by far the largest. Early in the 19th century members of other castes went to Burma for ordination and started independent lines, which are known jointly as the Amarapura Nikaya. A similar renewal from Burma in the mid-19th century is the Ramanna Nikaya; it has a fundamentalist tendency, mainly in its monastic regulations, which insist, for instance, that monks handle no money. There are in fact many different nikayas, and the fact that they are usually grouped together and spoken of as three must be mainly due to the ancient model.

The appearance of caste criteria in the Sangha is only one aspect of the intrusion of secular institutions into the Sinhalese monastery. Though monasteries in ancient Ceylon, as elsewhere, continually received valuable gifts, and even held slaves, monastic landlordism in its present form is probably only about 700 years old. Individual monasteries own land, which the incumbent has the right to use, and some own the estates of entire villages and command the services of the cultivators, as did the kings of Kandy and members of the lay nobility. These service tenures are now diminishing greatly.

In other respects, however, monastic organization in Ceylon is still archaic. Nikayas are autonomous, and though each has an acknowledged head, who is usually elected by a small council of elders, there is little centralization, even within the nikaya, except in holding ordination ceremonies. For most purposes the unit that counts is still the individual monastery. Though king and government have at times had, and even exercised, the power to intervene in monastic affairs, this has never been formally acknowledged; the highest layman has always been considered of lower status than the youngest novice, and until recently lay participation in controlling monks has been unthinkable.

In Ceylon alone among the Theravadin countries has been preserved the ancient custom by which it is normally assumed that someone entering the Sangha does so for life. It is always possible to leave without formal stigma, although there may be social disapproval. Novices usually enter young, at any age from seven onwards, and receive the higher ordination at the minimum age of 20, or soon after.

There are now about $7\frac{1}{2}$ million Sinhalese Buddhists, about 17,000 monks and about 5500 monasteries. About two thirds of the monks and over half the monasteries belong to the Siam Nikaya.

Beliefs and Rituals

Buddhists have always believed in gods and lesser spirits, all of whom they regard as subject to the law of karma (see KARMA) and therefore to finite knowledge, power and longevity. Gods and demons exist for the vast majority of Buddhists just as other humans do; they accept their existence much as we accept that of nuclear particles, and consider them equally irrelevant to genuinely religious concerns, by which they mean the Buddha's *Dharma*, 'doctrine'. The Sinhalese believe that when the Buddha on his deathbed prophesied that Ceylon would be a stronghold of his religion, the king of the gods put the country under the particular protection of the god Vishnu. Gods and other spirits all hold authority under *varam*, 'warrants', which go back to this and similar events, so that ultimately they derive legitimacy from the Buddha. In granting material rewards and sending diseases and misfortunes, the gods and demons can only realize a man's karma: if by this moral law he is due for some good fortune, it may come to him from a god, but the god is only acting as a powerful man might act, and is likewise morally responsible in his turn. A demon who hurts a man will not go further than the man's bad karma will justify, for he is liable to have his warrant withdrawn by a higher, and therefore more just and more powerful spirit. Moreover, his malevolence creates more bad karma for himself. Relations with gods and demons are not considered religious matters.

Religion and mundane affairs do, however, meet occasionally. A ritual of very varied function and extent consists of monks chanting a collection of Pali texts called *pirit*, 'protection'. This occurs especially at set intervals after a death, when monks are also fed. Monks also officiate at funerals, but have nothing to do with any other life crises; birth and marriage are purely secular events. Monks serve the laity principally by enabling them to earn merit by listening to sermons and by giving food; the alms round is exceptional in Ceylon, as laymen usually take food to a temple.

Laymen also earn merit by observing the precepts. The Five Precepts (*pan sil*) must always be observed; the Eight Precepts (*ata sil*), which involve some abstention from normal indulgence, are taken on quarter days of the lunar calendar, especially full moon days, but traditionally only by elderly people. Those taking the Eight Precepts spend all, or most, of the day at the temple and wear white. More positive ways of earning merit include going on pilgrimages, especially to one of the 16 spots in Ceylon that were supposedly visited by the Buddha. However, the religious festival that is most widely known abroad concerns none of these. Once a year the Buddha's tooth, which reached Ceylon in the 4th century, is paraded through the streets of Kandy on the back of an elephant with huge tusks, preceded by dancers, drummers and many other elephants. This is repeated every night for a week.

Even a summary of ways of earning merit would be incomplete without mention of meditation, which is necessary to attain Nirvana, or even the highest (formless) heavens. It is conceived to be the supreme purpose of monasticism, but in neither theory nor practice is it confined to monks. However it seems likely that meditation has never been practised by more than a small minority of people. The recent propaganda for meditation, and its increased practice, is a result of modern developments, including rivalry with Christianity and lay Buddhist control over the state school system. This contrasts with the traditional belief that the last person to attain Nirvana in Ceylon lived 2000 years ago, and that no one on earth will do so again until the coming, aeons hence, of the next Buddha, Maitri. Most Buddhists are willing, even content, to postpone the attainment of Nirvana to a future life, and make rebirth in one of the lower heavens, or even in a good station on earth, their immediate goal.

In theory Theravada Buddhism has no place for devotional religion; in practice this rigour is mitigated. The doctrine that each individual is wholly responsible for his own salvation is universally explicit. Sinhalese Buddhism completely lacks millenarian movements, and the coming of Maitri, the only figure who might be considered a future Messiah, is conceived of as being immensely distant. Bodhisattvas play a purely notional part in the religion. On the other hand Gautama, the historical Buddha, is venerated as supreme. Whether one can describe him as deified depends on the level of analysis. No Sinhalese Buddhist would accept the term, for they say that the Buddha was human, and is dead and gone, but they certainly derive emotional satisfaction from his veneration. Every house has an image of the Buddha, even if only a picture, and the image house, the most essential feature of a temple after the residence of a monk or monks, contains at least one Buddha statue. Images are venerated as 'reminders' of him.

The other main features of a temple, the bo-tree and the stupa, are also venerated for their association with him: the one because under such a tree did he attain enlightenment, the other because it contains relics. Offerings (*puja*), most commonly of flowers, incense sticks or lights, are made before images, bo-trees and stupas, and people often recite Pali verses, some of them definitely devotional in tone, before representations of the Buddha.

(See also BUDDHISM.)

RICHARD GOMBRICH

FURTHER READING: Nanamoli Evans, *The Path of Purification (Visuddhi-magga)* distributed by Luzac, London; W. Rahula, *History of Buddhism in Ceylon: the Anuradhapura Period* (Intl. Pubns. Serv., 1966).

Gautama, the historical Buddha, is venerated as supreme by Sinhalese Buddhists; every house has an image of him, even if it is only a picture, and the image house of every temple contains at least one Buddha statue: feet of the giant reclining Buddha at the site of the ruined city of Polonnaruwa

Picturepoint London

IMMAMOU

SIRENS

Originally characters in Greek mythology, the Sirens have also become part of Voodoo belief; the consort of Agoué, the *loa* or spirit of the oceans, is the Lady of the Sirens: *The Mangé-Loa of Agoué*, a feast in honour of Agoué and his wife

Sheldon Williams

Left **The Sirens appear in the *Odyssey* as beautiful maidens who enchant passing sailors with their song so that they swim ashore and perish; Odysseus escaped this fate by commanding his men to bind him to the mast: *Odysseus and the Sirens,* 3rd century mosaic from Dougga *Below left* Formed partly like birds and partly like women, the Sirens are said to have attended Persephone before she was carried off to Hades: tripod, c 600–570 BC**

SIRENS

FEMALE BEINGS connected with the underworld, the Sirens were particularly dangerous to men; it is hard to find any story in which women suffered at their hands. They first appear in the *Odyssey* (book 12) as beautiful females who sit in a meadow by the sea, enchanting passing sailors with their song so that they swim ashore, or land, and perish miserably. Round them is a great heap of bones which come from the rotting corpses of men.

Odysseus was advised by the enchantress Circe (see CIRCE), when she warned him of the Sirens, to stop the ears of his rowers with wax as the ship passed them; and she told him that, if he wished to hear their song himself, he should make his men bind him to the mast and not release him however much he might implore them. A mysterious calm fell as the ship passed their island, so that it depended entirely on rowing to make headway. The Sirens sang to Odysseus that they knew of all his deeds and sufferings at Troy. In Homer they are mentioned in the dual number, so that he recognized no more than two. Their names are not given, and their physical form is not described. Like other such beings in the *Odyssey* they are not located in known or normal geography.

For the historical period corresponding to the heroic age, it is of some interest that tablets inscribed in the script known as Linear B from Mycenean Pylos seem to refer to decorations on furniture as *seremokaraoi* and *seremokaraapi* which has been interpreted as 'siren-headed'. If this is so, the word *serem,* in that form with M not yet changed to N, already existed in Mycenean Greek, and the Sirens were known in myth in some form. What form the Mycenean 'siren-headed' decorations had is not known.

In later periods poets and mythographers continued to write of Sirens, revealing more of their nature. Hesiod in a fragment of his *Eoiai* called their island Anthemoessa and named them Thelxiope, Molpe and Aglaophonus, daughters of Phorcys the sea god, saying also that they calmed the winds. In the 7th century BC the lyric poet Alcman spoke of the Muse 'the clear-voiced Siren' as if Siren and Muse were the same, and elsewhere mentions the Sirenides, but only for their music. A fragment of Sophocles makes them daughters of Phorcys and 'singers of songs of Hades'. The comic poet Epicharmus makes the Sirens try to attract Odysseus by descriptions of the food and drink that they enjoyed and which he might share; plump anchovies, sucking pigs, cuttlefish and sweet wine. When they begin to speak of their evening meal Odysseus cries 'Alas for my miseries'. Other comic poets, Theopompus and Nicophon, mention the abundant feasting of the Sirens and their taunting of the hungry wanderer Odysseus. This association with fabulous plenty is difficult to explain, even given the food-loving conventions of comedy.

'Barren Nightingales'

In Apollonius the island of the Sirens is Anthemoessa and they are the daughters of the river Achelous and Terpsichore, the Muse of choral dance and song. They once attended Persephone before she was carried off to Hades and they were then formed partly like birds and partly like maidens. The Argonauts would have been drawn into their power as they passed, but Orpheus with his lyre drowned the sound of their voices. Only Butes swam toward the shore, but Aphrodite snatched him up and set him on the height of Lilybaeum. In Apollonius the Sirens are placed on the coast of the Tyrrhenian Sea, as is usual in post-Homeric poetry. But the river Achelous belongs in Aetolia in north-west Greece, which may have been their original home in Greek legend. The tradition of this location is preserved later by Lucian and others, particularly by another Alexandrian poet, Lycophron, author of the poem *Alexandra,* in which Cassandra prophesies the future wanderings of the Greek chiefs, including Odysseus, on their return from Troy.

Lycophron calls the Sirens 'barren nightingales and slayers of the centaurs', because the centaurs were so charmed with their song that they forgot to eat. Later he says that Odysseus will be the death of the Sirens, who will hurl themselves from the cliff-top into the Tyrrhenian Sea. One will be washed ashore by the towering Phalerus (Naples) and the river Glanis (Clanius) where the inhabitants will build a tomb for her as the bird goddess Parthenope, and honour her with yearly sacrifices. Leucosia will be cast ashore by the strand of Enipeus (Posidon), that is, at Posidonia or Paestum. Ligeia will come ashore at Tereina and will be buried with honour in the stony beach. The tone of this passage shows that in Italianate Greek belief, on the coast of Campania and further south, the Sirens were regarded as beneficent beings, at least after their death. Their cult here and its centres, particularly on the Sorrentine peninsula south of Naples and its neighbouring islands, are also described by Strabo. This region became their regular location in myth, and this is where they had a temple. This lore, like most of the legends about Odysseus in Italy, was spread by the Greek colonists from Euboea who reached Italy by passing north-west Greece.

In later tradition Parthenope is presented by the medieval *Cronaca di Partenope* as a princess of Sicily who sailed into Naples Bay and died of the plague. She was buried there and became a sort of local saint who was consulted as an oracle. At some time in the Middle Ages the Sirens lost their bird form and acquired fishes' tails so that they became a form of mermaid. Earlier Greek art shows them always in the form of birds or birdlike women. One reason for locating the Sirens on or near the Sorrentine peninsula, while their character was still conceived as in the *Odyssey,* is the appearance of a cave on the coast. In this is a great mass of prehistoric bones preserved under transparent breccia (composite rock consisting of fragments of stone cemented together). The bones are in fact the remains of game that was killed and eaten by Paleolithic hunters. They must have been seen by generations of Mycenean and later Greek voyagers who thought they were human bones.

E. D. PHILLIPS

SIVANANDA

Kenneth Grant

Founder of the Divine Life Society, Sivananda believed that selfless service, and work without thought of personal gain, were vital factors in development; he maintained that just one sincere student could move the world by the power of his devotion

BORN ON 8 September 1887, in the small village of Pattamadai in south India, Sri Swami Sivananda was a descendant of the 16th century holy man Appaya Dikshitar, who wrote 104 works on *Vedanta* and the Sanskrit language. Named Kuppuswamy by his parents, he matriculated from the Rajah's High School at Etiapuram in 1903, and shortly afterwards took a course in medicine at the Tanjore Medical Institute.

In 1913 he was appointed doctor-in-charge of a hospital on a rubber estate near Seramban in Malaya, where he worked for nearly seven years. He then joined the Johore Medical Office, where he served for three years, until he experienced, in 1923, what Western mystics have referred to as the 'dark night of the soul'. He suddenly realized that however many people he might help by remaining a doctor, he could alleviate only the sufferings of a few.

Kuppuswamy withdrew from medical practice and sunk himself in deep meditation, striving to solve the problem of how he might bring relief, not to the few, but to all: not temporary bodily relief, but permanent spiritual peace. The solution came as a revelation which fully enlightened him; he would become a doctor of the Spirit. He would heal the entire universe of its worries and woes or, failing this, he would give people the means of healing themselves. Kuppuswamy had become Sivananda, the name by which he was soon to be known. He renounced the world and became a mendicant; he visited many sacred places in south India and stayed at the *ashram* (spiritual colony) of the celebrated sage Bhagavan Ramana Maharshi (see RAMANA MAHARSHI). Shortly afterwards, Sivananda met his own personal *guru.*

He travelled to north India and came to Rishikesh on the banks of the Ganges, in the Himalayas, where, on 1 June 1924, he was initiated into the Order of *Sannyasis* (celibate monks) by Paramahamsa Visvananda Saraswati. Finding Rishikesh alive with spiritual power, Sivananda engaged in intensive *sadhana* (spiritual culture). He made his home at various places in the region for the next 35 years.

He settled at Swargashram and lived in a small hut where he meditated deeply, gradually piercing the layers of illusion until he realized the *Atman,* or impersonal Self of the universe (see BRAHMAN). It was here that people first flocked to him.

On 12 June 1931 he began an arduous pilgrimage to Mount Kailasa in western Tibet, considered by millions to be the physical form of the god Shiva himself. He was accompanied by several saintly men and walked barefoot every inch of the 475-mile journey, despite chronic lumbago.

Swargashram swarmed with devotees and the regional authorities were soon unable to cope with them. Sivananda therefore decided to leave. He moved to a small and dilapidated hut nearby, where he stayed for eight years. It was here that he founded the Divine Life Society in 1936. Subsequently 300 branches were established in large cities, and by 1960, shortly before his death, the Society was in a position to maintain about 400 persons.

One of Sivananda's most important contributions to the science of the Spirit was *Namapathy,* healing by name; that is, by any name of God, or by a *mantra* (see MANTRA), a form of words or sounds which are believed to have a magical effect when uttered with intent. To perform Namapathy he composed a special ritual so that new life could pour into sick persons all over the world. Several Western centres of spiritual healing were modelled on the ashram in Rishikesh.

Sivananda's personal experience of all forms of yoga and religions enabled him to combine them for the rapid development of widely differing types of students. He reduced to their essentials all systems of spiritual attainment and called the result 'Synthetic Sadhana'.

The Divine Life Society, the Yoga-Vedanta Forest Academy and the Sivananda Ashram, all of which he founded and imbued with powerful spiritual impetus, attracted aspirants from all parts of the world. He stressed that work without thought of personal gain, and selfless service, were vital factors in development; and maintained that even a single sincere student could move the world by the power of his devotion.

He advised his helpers against refusing money from sympathizers on the grounds of non-attachment to worldly things. Money was needed for the work of printing and publishing great spiritual truths; for buying medicines for the sick; for clothing the poor and housing the homeless.

He treated women with the same courtesy, affection and generosity that he extended to men. Although he warned his male disciples against the wiles of women, and described them in some of his books as epitomizing uncleanness, he did so to obviate disaster to immature aspirants. He knew that it was not easy to acquire the perfect *samadrishti,* equal vision with regard to all, that enabled him and those of his stature to neutralize the glamour of women or, alternatively, to recognize them as channels of spiritual power. His own attitude was characterized by that supreme reverence to the feminine aspect of divinity that is one of the redeeming features of Hinduism.

Sivananda converted the villainous, lazy, and ill-tempered into ardent and cheerful workers who performed useful work in the ashram. Other, less successful, gurus who claimed astonishing occult powers, referred to him as 'a guru for thieves and rogues'. In fact he welcomed thieves and rogues as cheerfully as anyone else, knowing they would eventually become dynamic yogis after being transformed in a place charged with spiritual vibrations, and regarded the quip as a sublime compliment. However, he deprecated the use of the term guru in connection with himself, and asked his devotees never to describe him as a master or world teacher, but always as an ordinary *sadhu* (seeker). He never attempted to monopolize anyone who sought his help; on the contrary he recommended their visiting other ashrams and other gurus, if he thought it was necessary.

The mass of people he imbued with the spirit of devotion. He advocated *kirtan* (devotional singing and dancing), but likened its effects to the intoxication produced by drugs: 'Just as the intoxication from hashish, opium, or alcohol, lasts for some hours, so also this Divine intoxication that you get from kirtan will last for many hours during the following day, and at night also during dream.'

By this analogy he implied that there is a path, the effects of which are everlasting. This is the *Jnana Marga*, or path of Pure Wisdom, which he embodied and exemplified. But, although he had realized the Ultimate Truth of One-Self-in-All, he taught this interior science only to those who had pierced the last veils of illusion.

KENNETH GRANT

FURTHER READING: *Autobiography of Swami Sivananda* (The Yoga-Vedanta Forest Academy, Ananda Kutir, Rishikesh, 1958); Major-General A. N. Sharma, *Swami Sivananda, The Sage of Practical Wisdom* (The Yoga-Vedanta Forest Academy, 1959).

SIX

THE MAJOR characteristics allotted to the numbers in Western numerology fit neatly into a table of opposites (see NUMEROLOGY) and the qualities of 6 are in direct contrast to those of 5. Where 5 is jumpy, nervous, many-sided, erotic (see FIVE), 6 is settled, calm, simple and straightforward, and is the number of mother-love rather than sexual love. It is an even number, which means it is female and passive, but it is the least unlucky and disagreeable of the female numbers, because it is the only 'perfect' number in the first ten. A perfect number is one which equals the sum of its divisors other than itself, and $6 = 1 + 2 + 3$. The next perfect number is 28, followed by 496, 8128 and 33550336. Because its component parts produce the same total whether added or multiplied, 6 is considered a balanced and harmonious number and those whose names add to 6 (see ALPHABET) are described as well-adjusted, peaceable people who are not racked by inner conflicts.

Since 6 is mathematically perfect, it is appropriate that the book of Genesis describes God's work of creation as complete in six days, the seventh being the day on which God rested. St Augustine observed that 6 must be a perfect number, because God could have taken more or less time if he had so chosen, but generally in numerological theory 7 is a number of completeness (see SEVEN) and 6 is not. On the sixth day God created man and woman (Genesis, chapter 1), and the Tarot trump numbered 6 is The Lovers, frequently depicted in modern packs as Adam and Eve. In addition, 6 is the number of marriage from the female point of view because it is made of 2×3, the female (2) 'multiplied' or fertilized by the male (3).

As a result, 6 is essentially the number of the wife and mother, and people whose number it is find their greatest responsibilities and happiness in love and marriage, home and family. Decent, tranquil, unselfish, companionable, perhaps rather humdrum, they are warm, affectionate and kindly, thoroughly domesticated and staunchly respectable, at their best in the family circle. They tend to be conservative and conventional, plain and honest, wholesome and admirable, but they have the defects traditionally associated with the housewife, of being fussy, gossipy, limited in outlook, sometimes obstinate and unreasonable and a trifle dull.

The only 'perfect' number in the first ten, 6 is the number of love; God is said to have created man and woman on the sixth day, and the Tarot trump numbered 6 is The Lovers: sixth card of the Tarot pack

Someone whose number is 6 ought to make an excellent marriage partner and parent, loyal and sympathetic, faithful, dependable, and probably inclined to spoil his children a little, though it is said that a 6 gone wrong can be the worst sort of domestic tyrant. He is a conscientious worker, a good breadwinner, a good manager, much more thorough and reliable than 5, but without his versatility. Though he does not have the brilliance and sparkle associated with the number 3 (see THREE), he may be more successful in the long run. His failings in business tend to be a lack of firmness and self-assertion and, more crucially, a lack of ambition, since he really prefers his fireside and his slippers to the heights of business or artistic achievement. On the other hand, he is an able negotiator and peace-maker.

A 6 likes peace and quiet, and shuns quarrels, jealousy and all sources of discord. He is usually good with his hands and may be a capable cook or gardener (like Adam, created on the sixth day). He values comfort and ease, enjoys beautiful things and likes to surround himself with them, and is distinctly uneasy in any situation which is unsettled and uncertain.

A year which adds to 6 is supposed to have the same basic characteristics, as a time of peaceful harmony and quiet adjustment. It is naturally a good year for marriages, and an American numerologist says that, 'Marriage licence bureaux usually have to increase their staffs in a 6-year, or work overtime to take care of the applications.' It is a good year in which to set up a business partnership, acquire a pet or establish a permanent home.

Another set of ideas which contribute to the picture of 6 as the number of balance, equilibrium, symmetry, and the harmony of opposites, comes from the two interlaced triangles of the six-pointed star, or hexagram. One triangle points up and the other down, and they stand respectively for 'above' and 'below', God and man, male and female, fire and water, spirit and matter (see HEXAGRAM). On the sixth day of creation God made man 'in his image' and where 5 is the number of man as microcosm, 6 is the number of the Universal Man, man as macrocosm (see MACROCOSM; MAN). The number indicates, according to A. E. Abbot's *Encyclopaedia of Numbers*, 'that man's spiritual path lies in the balance of the spiritual and the physical, the external and the transitory. It represents harmony, proportion, co-operation, and implies order and harmony brought to manifestation.' In the Cabala, the sixth sefirah, Tifereth, is the central, balancing and harmonizing sphere of the Tree of Life (see CABALA). All this has bolstered the concept of 6 as signifying balance, harmony, settledness, peaceful married love. Someone whose name adds to 6 is 'good at making ends meet', not only because six is the number of the good housewife, but because of the joining of opposites in the hexagram.

SKOPTSY

ONLY ONE SMALL pocket of Skoptsy, a sect which originated in Russia in the 18th century, is known to exist today, and that is outside the confines of the Soviet Union. The descendants of those who fled to the islands of the Danube delta, one of the remotest and least-known areas of Europe, still survive. This wilderness of reeds harbours one of the strangest assortments of human flotsam in the world: Ottoman Turks, Nogai Tartars (relics of the Golden Horde), members of the Lippovan sect and Skoptsy. The total population of these islands is reputed to be no more than about 3000, so there cannot be many Skoptsy among them. However, they have managed to continue to populate several villages, consisting of houses built on stilts above the waters, and have even achieved economic stability as a self-supporting community. The Rumanian Government seems to have left them alone so far, but it is hard to believe that this can continue much longer. Before long, the Skoptsy will have receded into history as one of religion's more curious aberrations.

The name Skoptsy means 'eunuchs'. Castration as an adjunct of excessive religious zeal is a very old phenomenon indeed, dating back to the cult of Cybele (see CYBELE; MUTILATION) in the ancient world and further. In Christian times, Origen castrated himself in the 3rd century, basing his action on a literal interpretation of Matthew 19.12: 'And there are eunuchs, who have made themselves eunuchs for the sake of the kingdom of heaven.' The Christian Church has long since condemned as heretical the attitude which stigmatizes all appetites of the flesh as being essentially sinful. From time to time sub-Christian groups have gone against this teaching, but their malpractices have derived more from social factors than from adherence to misinterpreted doctrine.

This was certainly the case in Russia, one of the most fertile breeding grounds for religious fanaticism. Although Russia had no Reformation as such, there was a massive splintering of the population into centrifugal religious groupings, once the authority of the Russian Orthodox Church was broken in the 17th century (see OLD BELIEVERS).

Marxist historians are probably right when they interpret the more violent extremism in old Russian sectarianism as a form of social protest against a rigid system. Further, one of the surest ways for an individual who had nothing to achieve power within that system was to claim some special religious inspiration, and to use his personality to presume upon the naïveté of his followers. The force of much Russian sectarianism sprang from mesmerism of an individual rather from adherence to new doctrines.

'Self-mutilation is certainly a Russian trait in conditions of desperation': after the Second World War there was an outbreak among women whose husbands had been killed and who cut off their breasts

Centre for the Study of Religion and Communism

The immediate ancestors of the Skoptsy were the Khlysty ('Flagellants'), themselves one of the dozens of offshoots from the Old Believers at the end of the 17th century. Danila Filippov, the peasant founder of the Khlysty, was himself an ascetic, whom his followers considered to be of equal status with Christ. He sought the 'gifts of the Spirit' for his followers by denying them the right to have sexual relations with their wives, to drink alcohol and to eat meat. All sought the charisma or grace of the Spirit, but those who believed they had attained it considered themselves above human laws. Denied the right to cohabit with their wives, they considered extra-marital relations to be especially sacred. Filippov, however good his original intentions may have been, found himself quite incapable of controlling the excesses of his followers, or of preventing other rival petty would-be charismatic leaders from pressing their own claims to participation in the divine revelation.

So it was that the Skoptsy arose as a reaction against the Khlysty. Ironically, considering the original ascetic intention of the Khlysty, it was against their sexual excesses that the Skoptsy inveighed. The man who founded the new sect, Kondrati Selivanov, was himself a Khlyst. He, too, gave it out that sexual union was the fount of all sin; the only possibility of salvation for mankind, he said, was to renounce sex totally.

Baptism By Fire

It was in 1757 that Selivanov, then in his 26th year, first attracted a following. He said that to attain total purity and finally remove any possibility of sin, he must make himself a perfect example to his followers. He would undergo a second baptism – 'by fire' – and shed his own blood for Christ. As a public proof that he meant what he said, he had himself castrated.

The Skoptsy came to believe that as soon as 144,000 converts had been found to follow this path, the Last Judgement would descend upon all mankind. Selivanov himself was apparently in no hurry to meet his maker, for he lived to be 100 years old. As time went on, his followers imbued him with more and more attributes of the godhead, although he slightly confused the issue by making himself out to be the Tsar Peter III, who was murdered in 1762.

Portrait of Kondrati Selivanov, founder of the Skoptsy, who claimed that the only possibility of salvation for mankind was to renounce sex totally. As an example to his followers he had himself castrated

The Skoptsy never became numerous enough to be as important as many other religious sects in Russia, but for years they remained the most notorious. Groups sprang up in many areas of central Russia. Surprisingly, in view of the usual hostility of the authorities to any kind of sectarian deviation, they seem to have been treated with some awe by both the Tsarist regime and by the Russian Orthodox Church. The aura of super-monastic sanctity which seemed to surround the Skoptsy leaders was reinforced by a visit which Alexander I paid to Selivanov in St Petersburg. After this, Selivanov's own safety was guaranteed.

Some groups, however, were forced to flee and they established communes in remote areas of Siberia, which soon gained the reputation of being extremely clean and hard-working. Some also fled south-west to the Danube delta. In the main, however, they flocked in comparative safety to the towns, where they established themselves as economic, quasi-monastic communities, living in dormitories, but going out daily to work in factories.

Spiritual Castration

It became the practice for a male follower to father a small family before becoming a 'full member' of the sect. Before long, too, the Skoptsy doctrine became modified, so that some leaders preached 'spiritual castration' as the ideal. Physical mutilations had already become far less frequent by the time of the Revolution, but there was a tendency for them to increase in number as an act of violent protest when conditions became exceedingly hard. Soviet sources have admitted that in 1929 there were as many as 2000 adherents of the sect, that their number was increasing during collectivization and the mutilations becoming more prevalent. Self-mutilation is certainly a Russian trait in conditions of desperation, witness Anatoli Marchenko's prison experiences, recounted in *My Testimony*. In the terrible conditions prevailing after the Second World War, there was another outbreak, especially among women who had lost their husbands in the war (they mutilated themselves by cutting off their breasts). The last recorded instance of a castration in the Soviet Union was in 1951, by a certain Lomonosov, living near Rostov-on-Don, who was then the leader of the sect. He persuaded his brother to undergo this after the latter's demobilization. Such is the claim of F. I. Fedorenko, author of *The Sects, Their Faith and Practice* (1965), the most recent Soviet book to devote any considerable space to the Skoptsy.

With the rising Soviet standard of living and great improvements in universal education, there is certainly now much less of a tendency to be drawn into such extremism. The mainstream religions now are able to provide the antidote to Communist materialism which many in the Soviet Union, including the young, feel that they need.

MICHAEL BOURDEAUX

FURTHER READING: Walter Kolarz, *Religion in the Soviet Union* (Macmillan, 1961).

'The eyeless sockets peer back sightlessly into our own', a reminder that in the midst of life we are in death; the psychic qualities attributed to the skull, both human and animal, led to its use in religious practices, magical ritual and medicine

SKULL

THE HUMAN SKULL is a pre-eminent symbol of mortality and the vanity of this earthly life, representing at the same time a warning sign and a threat. Two beliefs which are found the world over, and which are shared by humanity past and present, are that all bones are centres of psychic energy, and that the head is the dwelling place of the soul; until well into the 17th century it seems to have been generally accepted as a scientific fact that the soul flowed in the fluids of the ventricles of the brain, while even in our own times there exists a strong tendency to regard mind as an aspect of spirit. These basic themes have had a profound influence upon social and religious attitudes down the ages.

A number of significant ideas emanating from the prehistoric cult of the dead continue even now to infiltrate religious thought, as they have done for many thousands of years. At the cave of Ofnet, between Augsburg and Nuremberg, nests of skulls were discovered in post-Magdalenian deposits, relics of a primitive European culture; one cache alone contained as many as 27 skulls, and each of the skulls was turned in a westerly direction, no doubt towards some mythical land of the dead. Modern graves too, lie in an east-west orientation. (See also CULT OF THE DEAD.)

From the discovery of large numbers of skulls buried separately from the other parts of the skeletons it is evident that some form of second burial must have taken place in former times. It is widely held by historians and archeologists that from the beginning of the Pleistocene period such burials took place following the extraction of the brains, perhaps for use as food. Rare artistry was often displayed in the decoration of human skulls, many being painted red, or decorated with sea-shells.

The skull motif dominated the ideology of northern Europe, and we find for example that the ancient Norse imagined the heavens to be constructed from the sky dome or skull of the giant Ymir. In the Swedish text of an old ballad – 'The Twa Sisters' – the frame of a fiddle is said to have been created out of a magic skull. The alchemists regarded the skull as the receptacle of transmutation or psychic change. The Irish swore solemn oaths upon skulls.

Skulls were frequently used to decorate the facades of buildings, only later being superseded by stone balls. They also had a vital, if gruesome, function in builders' rites for they have been found embedded in the foundations of very old churches. It was discovered in 1895, for example, that the west wall of Darrington Church near Pontefract rested upon the skull of an unfortunate individual who had apparently been buried alive some 600 years earlier (see BUILDERS' RITES).

That there was supposed to exist some supernatural quality in the human skull is evident from the custom in Easter Island in which sacred caverns were placed under the protection of skull guardians. In some places the heads of warriors have actually been found buried facing the direction from which danger has been anticipated. A comparable case occurring in the British Isles relates to Bettiscombe Manor in Dorset where a skull is preserved; it is said to be that of a Negro and is supposed to keep ghosts and other evil spirits from entering the house. Should it be removed from the house, however, the skull is reputed to scream at the top of its voice. Skulls are associated with other ancient homes including Burton Agnes Hall in the East Riding of Yorkshire, Higher Chilton Farm at Chilton Cantelo, Somerset, and at one time Tunstead Farm near Chapel-en-le-Frith in Derbyshire (see HAUNTED HOUSES).

Trophy and Symbol

The skulls of enemies were once extremely popular as drinking cups. The 17th century writer Sir Thomas Browne refers to this practice in *Urn Burial*: 'To be gnawed out of our graves, for our skulls to be made into drinking bowls and our bones turned into pipes to delight and sport our enemies are tragical abominations'. The barbaric Scandinavians and Germans imbibed human blood from the skulls of valorous foes in order to acquire the dead warriors' strength. Among certain peoples of the Far East, however, only a skull that had been picked clean by vultures made an acceptable libation bowl. As late as the last century, pious pilgrims would travel to the holy well at Llandeilo, south Wales, where they drank water from the brain pan of the pre-Reformation saint Teilo. Saintly skulls were once a common sight in churches all over Europe, but in Protestant countries few seem to have survived the Reformation in the 16th century. In Roman Catholic areas of Europe, however, thousands of skulls of martyrs and saints are displayed in the churches, bearing silent testimony to the continuing influence of the skull as a religious motif. The skulls of the 11,000 holy virgins of Cologne must have presented a truly imposing sight to the credulous. A relic preserved as the holy skull of St Thorlac at Skalholt in Iceland was later discovered to be a coconut shell washed up by the sea.

Regarded as the seat of soul power, the skull has played an immense part in primitive ritual. In New Caledonia pilgrimages were made by the natives to pay homage to the skulls of chieftains and others considered worthy of high honour. Skulls were also offered as gifts to the primal ancestors by the Wa people of Indo-China.

There is some reason for the belief that the original inspiration behind the preservation of the skull as a trophy was the ancient sport of headhunting which is still practised by a few isolated tribes today (see HEAD). To the headhunter, the skull of a slain enemy could represent not only considerable prowess in the field but a decided advantage over the victim. In the long-houses of New Guinea enemy skulls were displayed on racks, before each of which stood a shield representing the spirit of the warrior responsible for the murders. It was taken for granted that the ghost of the conqueror was in a position to command the services of the ghosts of those he had killed and in this way slavery could be perpetuated into the afterlife. The headhunters of Borneo used the skulls of enemies as pillows. Trobriand Island widows converted the skulls of their late husbands into lime pots. Widows of other peoples such as the Andaman Islanders sometimes suspended such skulls from their necks as ornaments after cleaning them thoroughly in sea water. Indians of the Amazon frequently adorned the ancestral skulls with feather head-dresses.

As a symbol, the skull appears frequently in art. The medieval painter Albrecht Dürer was fascinated not only by the visual aspect of the skull, but also by its symbolism. A grinning skull is frequently depicted in representations of the medieval Dance of Death and also of Ankou, the skeletal death-summoner of Brittany (see DANCE OF DEATH; BRITTANY). In Mexico the skull can be said to dominate certain forms of artistic expression. This can be seen, for instance, in the stone skulls carved on the temple of Tepoztlan and in Aztec models constructed out of wood, black stone or rock crystal. The Mexican death god Mictlantecuhtli, the skeleton with the conical hat, is probably responsible for the shapes of the toys and sweets of modern Mexican children, which often take the form of skulls.

The ancient Etruscans are said to have employed a skull impaled on a pole as a device 'to scare away death by his own likeness'. In New Guinea the same device is employed somewhat pointedly as a 'Keep Out' sign.

The skull and crossbones symbol is not only the hallmark of the pirate. This device was carved on gravestones in the 17th century, as a reminder of mortality. A British regiment, the 17th-21st Lancers,

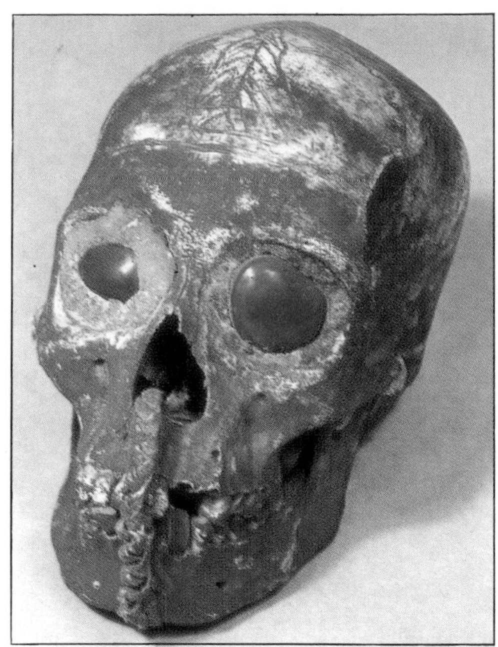

Horniman Museum

Axel Poignant

Below Nazi Death's Head badge in the shape of a skull and crossbones. Besides its associations with death, the skull is valued in many societies as the seat of a person's soul ***Top*** Skull from New Guinea, probably a headhunter's trophy ***Above*** Maori *tiki* amulet made from a human skull and thought to bring the owner good luck

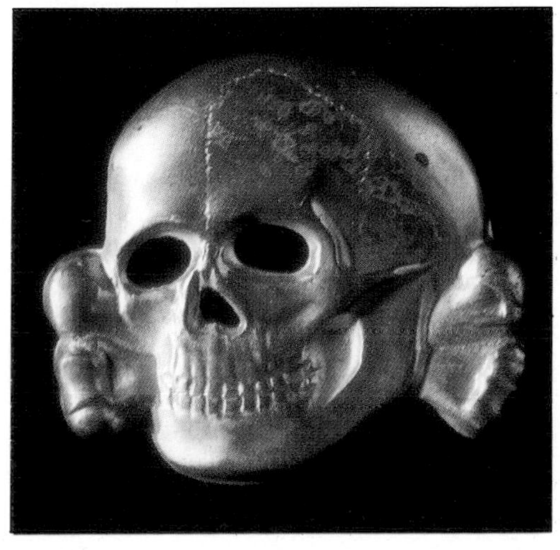
Andrew Mollo

Sonia Halliday

As the framework of the body and the part which lasts longest, bones and skulls are often regarded as the basis or root of life *Left* Skulls of former abbots are carefully preserved and named at Stavrouni monastery in Cyprus *Right* Detail from Signorelli's *Resurrection of the Body,* in Orvieto Cathedral, showing skeletons being clothed with flesh

known as the 'Death or Glory Boys', used the skull and crossbones as a regimental badge, and the helmet of the German Death's Head Dragoons bore this emblem as their insignia. In modern times it has become an international warning sign which is used, for example, on the labels of poison bottles in some countries and on Spanish electricity sub-stations.

Medicine and Magic

One curious feature of skull lore which has attracted the attention of archeologists and anthropologists is artificial cranial deformation as practised by the ancient Egyptians, among others; this was achieved by bandaging tightly the soft and malleable skulls of young children. Yet another type of deformation was trepanning, a surgical operation carried out by Stone Age savages apparently to relieve pressures on the brain caused by skull injuries. It was supposed that this operation permitted the evil spirit responsible for the headache or similar pains to make its escape, thereby freeing the sick person from discomfort. This primitive surgery must have been highly skilled in view of the fact that some of those operated upon are known to have lived for years afterwards.

The skull played a considerable part in medicine and magic. Epilepsy, a disease regarded with supernatural awe in the Middle Ages and later, was sometimes treated with a special elixir known as Spirit of Human Skull, which was prepared from the unburied skull of a criminal. Self-medication was readily available to those prepared to drink water from the skull of a suicide. Death by violence was an essential requirement when selecting a skull for medicinal purposes, and a flourishing trade in skulls developed between English apothecaries and Irish executioners. A distillation particularly favoured by King Charles II consisted mainly of filings of skull bone, spirits of wine and sage. A draught was administered to Charles on his deathbed with apparently little effect upon the outcome.

Irish skulls were particularly valuable by virtue of the greenish lichen which grew on them, known as usnea; they could realize as much as ten shillings each on the open market, a considerably larger sum in the 17th century than today. Severe headaches were said to be cured by an inhalation of snuff made from skull-scrapings, and in order to relieve toothache the sufferer had only to bite a molar out of a freshly disinterred churchyard skull.

Most medieval magicians, following the ancient theory that the skull was a centre of psychic power, included it in their ceremonies. At her trial in 1324, the notorious witch Dame Alice Kyteler (see KYTELER), was said to have brewed a potion consisting of the brains of an unbaptized child, scorpions, chickens' entrails and other horrors, using the skull of an executed thief as a cauldron. Some 50 years or so later, when a Surrey wizard was arrested he was discovered to have in his possession what was described in the indictment as the 'head and face of a dead man'. Both the skull and the wizard's book of spells were afterwards consigned to the flames. Skulls play an important part in the rites of modern black magicians; a skull impaled on a post was a prominent feature of the rituals carried out in Clophill churchyard, Bedfordshire, in 1963 (see CLOPHILL).

At about the time when magic was at long last giving way to scientific knowledge and most of the older medical superstitions were disappearing from the scene, skull mysticism reappeared in the form of the 'science' of phrenology. Dr Franz Joseph Gall, an 18th century Viennese physician, put forward the intriguing theory that a man's physical constitution determined his character and that the faculties of the brain could be assessed from the shape of the cranium. In the 19th century phrenology gained widespread popularity, both in Europe and in America. Although this latter-day cult of the skull has now been relegated to the fairground quack and the seaside pier entertainer, in the present century there has nevertheless been a revival of scientific interest in the possible effects of physique on character (see PHRENOLOGY).

Animal Skulls

In the 1st century AD the Roman writer Tacitus noted the curious custom of the ancient Germanic tribes of suspending the heads of animals from trees in sacred groves as offerings to the god Odin (see ODIN), while other early peoples offered the skulls of animals to their gods in return for success in battle. This idea is far from extinct, for modern huntsmen continue to exhibit the skulls of slain animals as trophies. It would appear that among some peoples the skulls of animals may have had a totemic significance similar to that of human skulls. In the Indian Archipelago turtle skulls were hung up to receive the prayers of turtle fishermen, and the Ainu of Japan offered libations of millet beer to the skulls of bears impaled on sacred posts (see BEAR). Nearer home, the 16th century historian John Stow in *A Survey of London*, recorded the discovery in 1316 of a huge cache of animal skulls, 'more than a hundred scalps of oxen and kine', in the vicinity of St Paul's Cathedral; this seems to indicate the existence of some kind of animal cult in England in prehistoric times. A further discovery of 1000 ox skulls buried on Harrow Hill, a pagan site at Angmering, Sussex, supports this theory. In 1895 a number of bullock and horse skulls were found under a building in south Devon.

Similar discoveries of horses' skulls buried beneath barn floors or concealed in church buildings remain as yet something of a mystery. In Ireland horse skulls were often deposited under the corners of threshing floors, so as to make the sound of the threshing reverberate and echo; this not only announced to passers-by that threshing was in progress, but was thought to be lucky. The skulls also magnified the music which accompanied dancing at the conclusion of threshing time. Towards the close of the last century, when the Presbyterian meeting house in Bristol Street, Edinburgh, was being demolished, the skulls of eight horses were found concealed behind a sounding-board. In some churches sounding-jars, usually of earthenware, were used to produce sonorous echoes; a number of these jars were discovered at Leeds Church, near Maidstone, in 1878. The practice of using jars for this purpose seems to have displaced the earlier use of horses' skulls. The horse skull motif also occurred in a number of folk ceremonies, well-known examples being the Welsh Mari Lwyd in which the skull was carried on a pole by a cloaked performer, and the related Hodening ceremony of Kent in which a skull which had been 'long buried in the soil' was occasionally used (see HOBBY-HORSE).

The skull is the emblem of finality, the perpetual reminder of death and the transitory nature of human existence. In the form of the libation cup, it is a hint to all to drink deeply of life while we yet have it. Its eyeless sockets peer back sightlessly into our own, and within them we may read Fate's immutable decree.

ERIC MAPLE

FURTHER READING: Barbara Jones, *Design for Death* (Andre Deutsch, 1967).

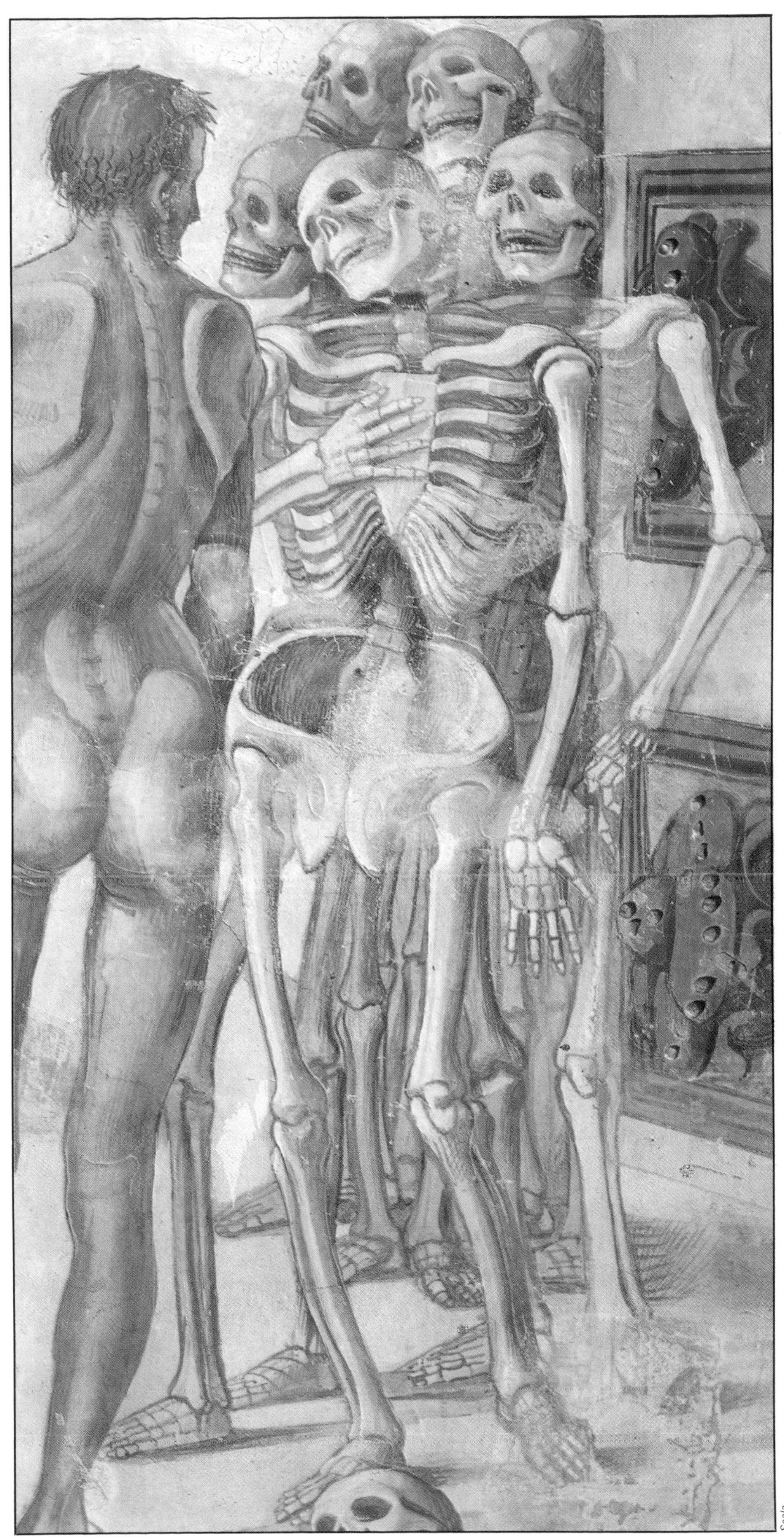

Scala

Giraudon

SKY

The Home of the Highest

'If many of us, still, are afraid of thunderstorms but welcome the rain falling on our gardens in due season, without associating meteorological phenomena with the divine, we can perhaps understand something of the emotions of people who did'

'OUR FATHER who art in heaven' is a familiar prayer to a Supreme Being in the sky, and the Old Testament is full of passages which associate God with phenomena of the sky, with light and darkness, clouds and winds, thunder, lightning and rain. When God was angry with the world he sent a deluge of rain which lasted for 40 days, and when he made an agreement with the survivors he set the rainbow in the sky as a sign (see FLOOD; RAINBOW). When he descended on Mount Sinai in the sight of all the people, 'there were thunders and lightnings, and a thick cloud upon the mountain', and when Moses spoke, 'God answered him in thunder' (Exodus, chapter 19). Psalm 18 describes the Lord coming down from the heavens in wrath, flying swiftly on the wings of the wind, with thick darkness under his feet and rainclouds as his canopy, thundering and flashing forth his arrows of lightning.

These passages are expressions of God's raging and overwhelming power. Elsewhere, he is not himself the tempest and the thunder, for when Elijah experienced his presence on Mount Horeb, the Lord was not in the wind which tore the mountain or in the earthquake that followed the wind or in the fire that followed the earthquake, but in the 'still small voice' which came after the fire (1 Kings, chapter 19). God wields the weapons of the sky because the sky is his eternal home, the place from which he watches and dominates the earth. It was there that Ezekiel and the author of Revelation saw visions of God, and still today, if you asked a broad sample of people what

Height is associated with power and moral superiority, and so the great gods often live in the sky *Above* Psyche is received by the Greek gods on Olympus, set among the clouds: painting by Caldara da Caravaggio *Right* Lucifer and his fellows are cast down from the heights of heaven into the pit, to the accompaniment of lightning and whirlwinds: *The Fall of the Rebel Angels* by Charles le Brun

Giraudon

British Museum

The sky god might control the weather himself or he might delegate these various functions to other deities: a lecturer in a 14th century manuscript expounds on the winds that blow from each quarter of the compass

area of the universe they particularly associated with the Almighty, the majority would probably point to the sky.

The sky is naturally the home of the Supreme Being, or may actually be the Supreme Being, because it is above the earth. We constantly associate height with power and often with moral superiority as well. The connotations of the words lofty, exalted, uplift and sublime (from Latin *sublimis*, 'high') indicate this double significance of height. High aims are ambitious or noble or both, to rise in life is to better your status, and Highness is a title of kings.

Access to the Divine

God is the highest of all things, the Most High, and in many traditions the righteous go after death to join him in a paradise high in the sky (see PARADISE). The pharaohs of Egypt were buried with rites to enable them to join the sun god in the heavens. Romulus, the founder of Rome, was taken up into the sky by Jupiter. After Jesus had 'risen' from the tomb, he ascended into the sky: 'he was lifted up, and a cloud took him out of their sight' (Acts 1.9). In Christian art, saints, kings and heroes are shown being carried up into heaven. The rebel Lucifer, on the other hand, was expelled from the sky and hurled down to the earth.

Because they can fly, birds were long believed to have access to the gods in the sky and to be in touch with power and knowledge denied to earthbound creatures (see BIRDS). Mountains are linked with the divine because they reach up to the sky (see LANDSCAPE; MOUNTAIN). Superhuman beings of all sorts have been observed careering through the sky, including phantom armies, dragons, visitors from distant planets, and the Wild Hunt (see ARMIES; DRAGON; FLYING SAUCERS; WILD HUNT). The astral body in which, according to occult lore, a man can rise into a higher plane has its origin in speculation about the souls of stars (see ASTRAL BODY).

There is no evidence of sky worship among the earliest of prehistoric men, but as supreme sky gods are known from most societies and as they are often more important in myth than in cult, it may be that one of the oldest and deepest of religious emotions is the sense of the immensity of the sky dominating and dwarfing the little figure of man walking on the earth. The sky contains the sun and moon, which provide heat and light, the rain which fertilizes the earth falls from the sky, the storm in which all the violence of Nature terrifyingly explodes brings the life-giving rain, and all this has affected the human view of the heavens. If many of us, still, are afraid of thunderstorms but welcome the rain falling on our gardens in due season, without associating meteorological phenomena with the divine, we can perhaps understand something of the emotions of people who did. And the fact that in changeable climates the appearance of the sky tends to affect people's feelings – bright and cheerful on a sunny day under blue skies, depressed on cloudy, overcast days – has probably contributed to the belief in dominant sky deities, as well as

The supreme sky god is the master and sovereign of all things... he is all-seeing and all-knowing, because the sky looks down upon every part of the earth

accounting for the passionate addiction to talking about the weather.

There are different sorts of sky deities and the god of storm is not always the same as the supreme power of the sky itself. The supreme sky god is the master and sovereign of all things, which he himself generally created. Usually, he is all-seeing and all-knowing, because the sky looks down upon every part of the earth, and even at night in the darkness he sees everything through his myriads of eyes, the stars. Though he lives in, or actually is, the sky, he may also be everywhere because the air is everywhere, and the air or the wind is his breath, which is also life (see BREATH).

The Father in Heaven

Because he is the supreme ruler and made everything and knows everything, the sky god is likely to be supremely responsible for law and order, both on a cosmic scale and in human terms, and he may be thought of as the Father, the heavenly parallel to the patriarchal father on earth, the author of life, the originator and upholder of rules and standards, the benevolent tyrant who loves and punishes and inspires and provides for his children. The sky's connection with law and order is strengthened when an orderly calendar is worked out by reference to events in the sky, when the stars are used as aids to navigation on sea or land, when the regular and predictable motions of the planets suggest that here in the heavens is the principle of order in an apparently chaotic universe, so much so that their movements can be used to calculate the future course of events on earth (see ASTROLOGY).

And yet the supreme sky being himself is frequently (though not always) unimportant in day to day matters. He made the world and man, he put the wheel of the seasons in motion and set the stars in their courses, but he is distant from the everyday world of humanity and does not much concern himself with it. Presumably this is a consequence of the fact that the sky really is far away and unreachable (at least until recently) and so the sky god is too.

The Andaman Islanders in the Indian Ocean, for instance, have a Supreme Being called Puluga, who lives in the sky. The wind is his breath, the thunder his voice and hurricanes his rages. He made the world and the first man, sent a flood to drown most of humanity when they disobeyed the laws he had made for them, and when later generations were still disobedient he went away and has never been seen since. People are frightened of him and respect his laws but they do not worship him or offer him sacrifices.

Similarly, in Africa there are traces of a great sky god who has practically no cult. The Ashanti people in Ghana, for example, say that he used to live close to the earth but moved far away into the heavens. He is everywhere and sees everything, you can speak to him by talking to the wind and place offerings to him in a pot which contains his thunder axe, but he has no organized cult, no set rituals or occasions for his worship, and rituals are mainly concerned with lesser and closer gods (see ASHANTI).

In many parts of the world Sky Father appears in myths as the great male principle who fertilizes Earth Mother with his rain (see EARTH), but little attention may be paid to him in cult and ritual. The gods who are more actively worshipped may be gods of the sun or the moon, or gods who have little to do with the sky at all. The general prevalence of Supreme Beings in the sky suggested the theory that the earliest religion was monotheism, which degenerated into polytheism, but this theory has not found general acceptance. Where a High God in the sky is believed in, there are also lesser gods who rank below him but may be regarded as more accessible to men. Sun, moon, storm, weather, may be the preserve of separate deities who are the High God's children, or they may be fully the preserve of the High God himself (see HIGH GODS; RELIGION).

Lord of Lightning

One High God who thundered for himself was Zeus. He is related to Dyaus, meaning basically 'bright, shining', the name of an early Aryan sky god, which lies behind Latin *deus*, 'god' and *dies*, 'day', French *dieu* and our 'divine'. The titles of Zeus demonstrate his connection with the sky and the weather – 'cloud gatherer', 'lord of lightning', 'rainy', 'thunderer', 'he who sends favourable winds'. Altars were sometimes dedicated to him in Greek houses as Zeus Kataibates, 'who descends', a reference to lightning, and sacrifices would be offered on the altar to prevent the house being struck by lightning. But he was, of course, much more than a weather god. He was supreme ruler, the father of gods and men, the giver of fertility and master of fate. He could be spoken of as being the sky itself: sometimes he shines brightly and sometimes he rains, and this is probably a statement of his oldest role, as the living sky whose overwhelming power dominates all things (see ZEUS).

One common function of a High God Zeus did not perform, according to Greek mythology. He was not the Creator. He wrested supreme power from his father Cronus, who had himself castrated his father, Uranus, in a myth based on the widespread idea that the sky and the earth were originally joined together and had to be separated (see CRONUS). Uranus was the Greek word for 'sky' and rain was sometimes represented as his seed, which fertilized the earth. But according to Hesiod's *Theogony* there was a sinister aspect to his virility, for the children he begot on the Earth included dangerous monsters, and Uranus hated his children and imprisoned them in the earth. He had no place in Greek worship: 'Zeus was the original Father Sky and consort of Mother Earth, and he remained the real Greek sky god' (see URANUS).

Bull of the World

Zeus's Roman equivalent, Jupiter (see JUPITER), was again a personification of the sky, father of gods and men, inspirer of Rome's greatness and guardian of law, armed with thunder and lightning, and sender of rain. 'Lo, through the clouds the father of the gods scatters red lightnings,' says Ovid's *Fasti*, 'then clears the sky after the torrent rain.' His temple on the Capitoline Hill in Rome was open to the sky, and thunder, lightning and the flight of birds could be interpreted as signs of his will (see AUGURY).

Dyaus Pitar, Zeus Pater, Jupiter, all mean Sky Father. Dyaus was a remote sky god by the time the Aryans reached India and was the father of nearer and more active deities, several of whom were connected with the sky (see INDIA). Indra was lord of the atmosphere between the earth and the far heavens, of weather and war. In early myths he wages successful campaigns against demons, who presumably represent the

C. M. Dixon

Michael Holford

Left **Roman statuette of the 2nd to 4th century AD, showing the god Zeus or Jupiter holding a thunderbolt: the supreme god of Greek and Roman religion was the power of the living sky *Above* In Canaan the most active deity was Baal, 'the cloud-mounter, god of storm and rain': stele from Ras Shamra dated 1900–1750 BC *Right* In this beautifully colourful Persian illustration, the sky is depicted thronged with angels**

native inhabitants who were defeated by the Aryan invaders. He was golden or red in colour and rode in a golden chariot drawn by tawny horses. The thunderbolt was his weapon, the rainbow his bow, and he wielded a great hook to trip and slaughter his enemies and a net of illusions to snare them in.

The heroic god of warrior chieftains (the poetic analogy between war and storm is obvious), Indra had superb and terrifying vitality. He lashed the world with tempests, he burst the clouds open to pour down the rain, he made the blood circulate and the sap. He had a thousand testicles, he was 'master of the fields', 'master of the plough', 'bull of the world', the god who made land and beasts and women fruitful, not himself the Creator but the virile promoter of life.

Another Aryan god, Varuna (the name means 'sky' and seems to be basically the same as Uranus), also had storm and weather attributes. The wind was his breath, he growled in the thunder, darkened the clouds and made the sky rain. But he was more important as the all-seeing, all-knowing sky. He had a thousand eyes, which were the stars, and he knew all acts and motives and secrets. He was responsible for the law and order of the universe, for the passage of the seasons and the moral code of men. Mircea Eliade comments that Varuna 'does not take to himself any rights, conquers nothing, does not struggle to win anything (as does Indra for instance); he *is* powerful, he *is* sovereign, while remaining a contemplative . . . power is his by right because of his very nature . . . the tendency to passivity is shown by all the supreme sky gods who live in the higher spheres, far from man and more or less indifferent to his daily needs.'

The Storming of Ur

In Egypt the sky itself was female, an exception to the general rule, but the principal sky deity was Horus, 'he who is on high' or 'the distant one', who was a falcon, 'the most fierce and terrifying of all the birds of prey which scoured the Egyptian sky'. Each of the pharaohs was identified with him as supreme ruler, and he was assimilated to another dominating power in the

William MacQuitty

sky, the god of the sun (see CREATION MYTHS; EGYPT; HORUS).

In Mesopotamia the god An or Anum ('sky') was the oldest of gods, the supreme father and king, the ultimate source of all existence, but in practice the divine power of the sky was more often exercised by the god of the atmosphere, Enlil, 'Lord Wind'. When the city of Ur was taken and sacked by invaders from Elam, to the east, the attack was described as an appalling storm, mounted by Enlil. The god summoned evil winds, he called the hurricane of heaven howling across the skies, the shattering storm, the relentless tempest which covered Ur like a cloth and wrecked the city. The attackers 'stormed' the walls, as we would say, but here not just as a vivid metaphor but in the sense that they embodied the terrible violence of the god.

There were also other powerful gods of the sky – the sun god, the moon god, the lady of heaven (Ishtar), and the weather god, Adad. Several of these deities were connected with the bull, an animal frequently linked with gods of sky and storm because of its dominance, its virility and fierceness, and its bellowing voice, like the thunder or the roaring of the wind (see ANIMALS; BULL; MESOPOTAMIA).

Powerful sky gods are also found among many other ancient peoples, including the Germans and Scandinavians, and the Hittites (see GERMANIC MYTHOLOGY; HITTITES). In Canaan the supreme god El remained in the background and the most active deity was Baal, the cloud-mounter, god of storm and rain. The bull was his cult animal and he wore the horns of a bull on his helmet. His weapons were thunder and lightning. Unlike most gods of sky and storm, he died and rose again, being both the fall of rain and the growth of vegetation (see BAAL).

St Swithin and Umbrellas

In religion the sky gods range from supreme but passive deities through supreme and highly active ones to gods with more specialized sky functions. In folklore and superstition it is naturally not so much the all-powerful and all-knowing sky that occupies attention as the more immediate phenomena of thunder, lightning and rain.

Church bells are still sometimes rung in parts of Europe during thunderstorms and hailstorms to shield crops from damage (see BELLS). Red coral, houseleek, St John's wort, hawthorn, mistletoe, sprigs of holly, and small branches of hazel gathered on Palm Sunday are all supposed to protect houses against lightning. When out of doors, you can protect yourself by wearing rosemary or mugwort (which will also ward off sunstroke and the malevolence of witches), or by carrying a nettle. Some people still cover mirrors and hide away all metal objects during a thunderstorm, and some say that the doors and windows should all be opened, so that if the thunder does get into the house, it can swiftly get out again.

The oak is generally considered the most protective tree against lightning (see OAK), which is probably a paradoxical result of the fact that oaks are peculiarly prone to being struck and so became sacred to Zeus, Jupiter and other gods of thunder and lightning, since anything struck by a bolt of lightning becomes a container of something of the god's force. All ferns are associated with thunderstorms and bracken is sometimes called Oak-fern. The marks on a stem of bracken that is cut across close to its root were thought to represent an oak tree, or alternatively an eagle, which is also sacred to sky gods (see EAGLE). There is an old belief that cutting or burning ferns will bring rain, and in 1636 when Charles I was going on a visit to Staffordshire, a letter was sent ahead of him asking the High Sheriff of the county to see that no fern was burnt during the royal visit, to make sure of fine weather.

If it rains during a funeral, this is a good omen for the dead person's soul. 'Happy is the bride that the sun shines on, happy is the corpse that the rain rains on', presumably because the sky is in harmony with the spirit of the proceedings.

Above Zeus, Sky Father and supreme god, was the lover of many mortal women; to approach Danae, who had been imprisoned by her father, he took the form of a shower of gold – a possible reference to the sky as the source of fertilizing rain: _Danae and the Shower of Gold_ by Titian _Below right_ A cartoon by George Cruikshank, 'St Swithin's Chapel', pokes fun at the fashion for carrying umbrellas: this modern defence against the rain soon attracted a variety of superstitions

'Happy is the bride that the sun shines on, happy is the corpse that the rain rains on', presumably because the sky is in harmony with the spirit of the proceedings

On the other hand, if a ray of sunshine lights up the face of somebody attending a funeral, he will be the next to die.

There is an old tradition that if it rains on St Swithin's day, 15 July, it will go on raining for 40 days afterwards, but if the weather is fine that day, there will be no rain for 40 days. St Swithin (or Swithun) was Bishop of Winchester in the 9th century and according to legend humbly asked to be buried in some vile and unworthy place. Years afterwards the monks of Winchester decided to dig him up and give him a more honourable resting place but they were prevented from beginning work, on 15 July, by torrential rain which fell for 40 days and 40 nights (as in the Flood story in the Bible).

'Rain, rain, go away, come again another day' and 'Rain, rain, go to Spain' are rain-repellent charms, still chanted by children. Even the modern adult's practical defence against rain, the umbrella, has attracted superstitions to itself. Through an obvious association of ideas, to open an umbrella in fine weather will cause rain, and to open one indoors at any time will bring bad luck. It is also unlucky to give anyone an umbrella, and if you drop one, you should never pick it up yourself but let somebody else pick it up for you. In the *Encyclopaedia of Superstitions* Christina Hole remarks that 'although these beliefs are themselves trifling, it is interesting that they should exist at all in Britain, in view of the late appearance of the umbrella there.' Long known in the East as an emblem of majesty held over the heads of kings on ceremonial occasions, presumably as a symbol of the sky, the umbrella was apparently used by a few women in England in the 17th century but was not adopted by men till the late 18th. A man named James Hanway appeared with one in London in 1778 and was jeered and hooted at in the streets.

(See also AURORA; AUSTRALIA; HAMMER; LIGHT; METEORS; MOON; STARS; STEPS AND LADDERS; SUN; WEATHER MAGIC.)

RICHARD CAVENDISH

FURTHER READING: M. Eliade, *Patterns in Comparative Religion* (New American Library); C. Hole ed., *Encyclopaedia of Superstitions* (Merrimack Book Services, 1979).

Chris Barker

Medieval Slav peasants at the confessional were asked: 'Have you worshipped animals, the sun, moon and stars, giving them the name of god?' Long after conversion to Christianity, the Slavs continued to worship the old gods of sun, fire, water, woods and fields

SLAVS

THE EVIDENCE relating to the existence of Slavonic tribes, who at this time were probably part of the Scythian and Sarmatian political units, does not go much beyond the 1st and 2nd centuries AD, though there is a tendency among the Russian chroniclers of later centuries to push their ancestry back as far as possible. References to the Slavs in the 6th and 7th centuries speak of them mainly as living near the estuary and central part of the River Danube. The period of their expansion covers the time of the decline of the Byzantine Empire between the advance of Attila in the 5th century and that of Genghiz Khan in the 13th century. The rapid spreading out of the Slavs over a large territory was facilitated by the fact that nowhere did they meet with a strong enough resistance to halt their progress. Slav tribes raided Macedonia and the Balkan peninsula; some of these scattered tribes remained on the Peloponnese until the first centuries of Turkish rule. By joining up with the Turkish tribe of the Avars the Slavs moved into the Hungarian Plain, settling as far as Dalmatia. In the north they pushed back the Finns who had settled in what is northern Russia today. Later too, the Slavs spread into what was then the Frankish Empire. They crossed the Rhine in the south and they even reached Spain. Lasting settlements in the west were to be near the river Elbe and the Baltic shore, including the island of Rügen, which became a centre of pagan Slav worship.

Mauritius in his *Strategicum* describes the ancient Slavs as follows: 'Physically they are strong, well able and accustomed to endure cold and lack of clothing and food. They have great reverence for the laws of hospitality and are very kind to strangers and prisoners. They are armed with two javelins, wooden bows, and small poisoned arrows, some use shields; they are supreme in the art of defence. When pursued by enemies or suddenly attacked, they dive under the water and, lying on their backs at the bottom, breathe through a long reed. They live in a continuous state of defence, having several exits to their houses and burying all their superfluous food.'

Geographically, the Slavonic tribes came to be divided into southern, eastern and western Slavs. All three groups are now distinguished by their different dialects and their own folklore but, as far as is known, the mythology was, in the main, similar among all Slavs. Information about the customs, religion and myths of the ancient Slavs has come down to us almost exclusively through their neighbours. Apart

from written sources, of which there are few that are reliable, there is some rather imaginative information to be found in Arabian travellers' accounts. The western sources are by far the most precise, but allowance must be made for their obvious Christian bias. These accounts tend to contain sweeping parallels to the Greek and Roman pantheon of gods. Russian chroniclers, who wrote their accounts when the Slavonic gods had long been dethroned, stress the inferiority of the old religion in comparison with the Christian faith.

More valuable is the archeological evidence and that of the existing folklore, such as the customs connected with the seasons, as well as Church records that deal with those pagan practices that have passed into Christian ritual. Folklore, songs, sayings, epics, sculpture, dances and games provide material that yields much reliable information. Slavonic folklore is abundantly rich and has survived well into the 20th century: in Russia major changes in the social structure and the way of life occurred only with the Revolution.

All-Pervading Life Force

The pagan Slav felt himself to be part of Nature and his feelings for it were of a religious kind – he worshipped all its manifestations. From these very close ties his gods were created and can be seen to be personifications of the life he experienced around him. He worshipped individual aspects of Nature, from an oak tree to a large stone, a swamp or a ravine. In an equal measure everything was endowed with an all-pervading life force with which he felt an affinity. From this intimate connection with Nature arose the knowledge of how to make use of its gifts and powers, such as were latent in springs and herbs, for example. The pagan Slav personified those powerful manifestations of Nature on which he felt most dependent, and these personifications entered the upper ranks of his mythology as gods. He also believed that each domain of Nature was inhabited by all kinds of spirits and demons. Whereas the ancient gods came to be forgotten soon after Russia became converted to Christianity, this lower order of beings survived in popular belief and magical practices and in folk customs, many of which merged with the Christian folk tradition.

Although many names of Slavonic gods and spirits have come down to us, in many cases their individual functions are not clear. Often it is not even known whether, perhaps, they originated in another people's mythology, or where exactly they were worshipped. The attempt has been made to establish their geographical distribution through an etymological analysis of place

***Kupala's Fire,* a drawing by a 20th century Polish artist. The worship of fire for its cleansing and healing properties was an important element of early Slav religion. Although condemned by the Church in the Middle Ages, some aspects of fire worship are still to be found in local belief**

names. As there is no written evidence of the gods of the Poles, Czechs, Serbians or Bulgarians, the information available covers mainly the areas of the eastern Slavs and the Baltic or western Slavs.

Opinions are divided as to whether a basic dualism underlies the Slavs' mythological concepts. According to the 12th century chronicler Helmold, whose evidence is confirmed by recent Soviet research, the Elbe Slavs used to offer prayers to the divinity of good and evil; these were personified in Chernobog and Byelbog, gods of darkness and light. Chernobog was regarded as very powerful, being the cause of all calamities, and prayers were offered to him at banquets to avert misfortune. 'The Slavs have a remarkable superstition, for on the occasion of banquets and festivities they carry about a round vessel, over which they speak words which are not a blessing but rather a curse, which they utter in the name of the gods of good and evil, for from the good god they expect good fortune, but from the evil god misfortune.' No other specific evidence concerning these two divinities has been preserved. Helmold testifies further that in spite of a fundamental dualism, the Slavs worshipped one god, ruler of all the other divine powers to whom they used to attribute parts of Nature, as fields or forests, as well as the human emotions of sorrow and joy. This god, he says, cared only for things celestial, whereas the rest, who sprang from his blood, obeyed the duties assigned to them, enjoying distinction in proportion to their nearness to the chief god. The name of this Supreme Being is not known.

The names of a number of gods and spirits that were worshipped at one time have been established with some degree of certainty. The sites of some of the statues of the principal east Slavonic gods were the hill before the palace in Kiev and by the River Volkhov in Novgorod. According to manuscripts dating from the 12th to the 16th century, these statues represented the gods Perun, Khors, Volos and Dazhbog. Perun's statue was erected by Vladimir, who later became the first Russian prince to accept Christianity. The idol is described as having been made of wood, with a silver head and a golden beard. Vladimir's uncle Dobrynya, a celebrated semi-legendary hero of many historical songs, was responsible for setting up a similar image of Perun in Novgorod. As no remains of temples dedicated to their gods have been found among the eastern Slavs, it is assumed that they used to erect their statues in the open. We are told that they were commonly placed on hills, facing east and the direction of water, a nearby river or lake.

When Prince Vladimir received baptism in 988 AD, he ordered all idols in Kiev to be destroyed. The statues of Perun in Kiev and Novgorod were dragged down to the river. The Novgorod idol was tied with ropes, pulled through the mire down to the river, where it was beaten with rods so as to cast out the demons that were thought to inhabit it. Perun appears to have been perhaps the most important east Slavonic god, being a solar deity, a god of lightning and of fire. His worship was widespread among the Slavs, judging by the many place-names in Slovenia, Bohemia, Bulgaria and Poland which are connected with his name. Worship of this god disappeared in about the 11th century. In the Christian era his worship was transferred to St Ilya. Nestor, the medieval Russian chronicler, tells that when Prince Igor was about to conclude a treaty with the Byzantines, the Christian Russians took oath in the church of St Ilya, while the pagans swore to Perun.

Gods of Sun and Fire

Dazhbog's statue also stood on the hill in the courtyard of the castle at Kiev. In old manuscripts this god is referred to as 'Tsar Sun'. According to the 12th century Russian prose epic *Slovo o polku Igoreve,* Vladimir and the Russians call themselves the grandchildren of Dazhbog; however, it is a common tendency of all people to explain their origins as having links with divine beings. Dazhbog also seems to have been known among the southern Slavs. A Serbian fairy tale relates that 'Dabog, the Tsar, was on earth and the Lord God was in heaven.' Dazhbog is here contrasted with God and is regarded as an evil being, for in early Christian times the memory of the previous pagan gods was linked with the Christian concept of evil and its personification, the Devil or Satanael. Dazhbog, who probably took over the role of sun god from Perun, played a significant part till long after Christianization because of his connection with fire and the Slavs' worship of the hearth as a sacred place in the house. The Christian clergy fought a long and difficult battle against this worship of fire. In a sermon we read that even 'priests do not scorn the company of the idol-worshippers, they eat and drink with them . . . they pray to the fire which they call Svarozhich' (another name of Dazhbog). As Christianity was introduced to the Slavs by their rulers, the common folk clung to their pagan beliefs for a long time, but gradually the old gods of the sun and the fire were replaced by Christian angels and saints.

The worship of fire and the hearth dates back to the days of nomads and hunters of Paleolithic times, to whom the fireplace and the spirit of the ancestors which lived in it was the central point of their religious worship (see FIRE; HEARTH). The names Ovinnik, Yarilo and Kupala, which were later used in folk ritual in connection with the worship of fire, stand for basically the same idea, since all are part of the customs of the sacred fire and its purifying power. Fire worship was frequently condemned by the Church, as in a sermon of the 12th century by the Bishop of Turov,

Left A Domovoy or Slav domestic spirit; usually conceived of as a hairy creature in human form, he protected the family and warned them of impending disaster in the home _Right_ Slav mythology abounds with stories of heroes and their legendary feats; Ilya-Muromyets tries to release Svyatogor from the coffin in which he has shut himself. Drawings by I. Bilibine

Hamlyn Group

Giraudon

И. Б.
1928

Giraudon

Left Volkh, a mythical being of Slav mythology, depicted as a hawk. He had the ability to assume a number of forms, such as a grey wolf or a tiny ant, and was renowned for his sorcery *Below right* Baltic Slavs pay homage to an image of the god Svetovit; he was famous for his prophecies, especially those to do with the success or failure of the harvest. Drawings by I. Bilibine

Cyril, who wrote: 'We do not worship fire. Now neither the forces of Nature, nor the sun, nor the fire . . . are called by the name of God . . . for idol-worship has come to an end and the devilish violence has been overcome by the sacrament of the cross.'

Many magical rites stemmed from belief in the capacity of fire to cleanse and heal. Until the 20th century, for example, Russian peasants believed that the most effective means of healing and protecting was the so-called 'new fire', which was obtained by rubbing together two pieces of dry wood. In the event of an epidemic, frightened superstitious villagers would put out all fires in their houses and then, after having said special prayers, would go out together to fetch this 'new fire' for their homes. The holy fire became part of Christian belief. It would be brought home from church on particular feast days, especially at Easter, and was regarded as a protection against unclean powers. On the whole, Christianity succeeded in banishing the old gods from the consciousness of the Slavonic tribes, but it did not succeed in suppressing the religious customs connected with them; these customs remained closely connected with Nature and the seasons.

Another major Slavonic deity was Volos or Veles, the god who protected cattle. What appear to be remnants of the worship of this god were still to be found until recently as part of the harvest festival customs in southern Russia. The peasants would tie the last handful of ears into a knot, which used to be called 'plaiting the beard of Veles'; in some districts a piece of bread was put among the ears. Veles was also known among the ancient Bohemians. Later his worship came to be transferred to St Blaise, a shepherd and martyr of Caesarea in Cappadocia whom the Byzantines called the guardian of flocks.

The Human Sun

Some Church records give an interesting indication of the Slavs' worship of the heavenly bodies. A sermon of John Chrysostom admonishes those who worship the sun, the moon and the stars to repent of their sins. Similarly, in a sermon, Cyril of Turov regrets that even now, in the 12th century, the Devil tempts people to believe in God's creatures, in the sun, the moon and the stars. In his 'Hymn of the Mother of God' he says: 'They have forgotten God and believe in the creatures that God has given us for work, and so they have called everything gods.' The questions asked by the priest during confession are also revealing: 'Have you perhaps worshipped animals, the sun, the stars, the moon, dawn and dusk? Or have you worshipped God's creatures . . . the sun, moon and stars, giving them the name of God, and the sun, the moon and the stars and the planets of the zodiac, looking at them, did you believe in them?'

In proverbs, songs and legends the sun has a human body, rises like a human in the morning and shows human emotions like happiness and sorrow. The setting sun is visualized as an old man with a golden head and a silver beard. The sun's sister is the *deva-zorya* or *solntseva sestritsa* which is dawn and dusk. The conviction was widespread that stars and humans are closely related, that there are as many stars as there are people, and that the luminaries of the night are the abode of the souls of the departed.

Various chroniclers give colourful accounts of the temples and idols of the western Slavs, who appear to have reached a considerably high cultural level, with a well-organized priestly caste and a definite ritual. The best known centre of worship was Arkona, on the island of Rügen in the Baltic Sea. The 12th century Danish historian Saxo Grammaticus reports of the image of the god Svantovit (or Svetovit) that it had four heads and necks, two facing the front and two behind. The faces of this image were clean-shaven and the hair cut short, as was the custom of the people of Rügen. In his right hand the idol held a horn, made of various metals and in his left he had a bow. He wore a tunic of wood reaching to the knees.

Svetovit was famous for his victories and

prophecies. Divining the success or failure of the crop of the following year was also connected with this god. After each harvest a great festival was held in his honour and people assembled from all parts of the island to sacrifice cattle and join in the rites. The king was held in very moderate esteem compared with Svetovit's priest. His temple was of wood and extravagantly adorned, for neighbouring tribes and nations sent abundant tribute to his sanctuary. The god had a magnificent sword and horse which were sacred to him; this horse could be ridden and tended only by the priest. Svetovit had 300 men-at-arms and horses attached to him and always received one third of their spoil. The priest of the image, so we are told, on the day before the celebration of the god's power, carefully cleaned out the sanctuary with a broom; this sanctuary no one was allowed to enter. He was careful not to breathe in the building and, as often as he was forced to inhale or exhale, he would run to the door, lest he should contaminate the presence of the god with the pollution of his mortal breath. In 1169 the Danish king Valdemar seized the treasures of the temple in Arkona, ordered the destruction of the sanctuary and then had the idol smashed to pieces and burnt. The name of this god suggests that he was probably a personification of the power of light.

Among the Elbe or western Slavs Svarozhich is said to have been a war god. His temple stood in Radegast, near Leipzig. The idol wore a helmet resembling a bird with outstretched wings and on its breast was the head of a black bison. The idol's right hand rested on this symbol, while the left grasped a double-edged axe. The temple was much visited by all Slavonic tribes to make use of the prophetic powers of this god, to whom human sacrifice was made. According to the records, in honour of a victory won in 1066, the head of John, Bishop of Mecklenburg, who had been captured in battle was offered to this divinity.

Tribute of a Bishop's Head

Apart from the sanctuary of Svarozhich there were other places of worship both in Radegast and in Stettin, near the mouth of the River Oder. Thietmar, Bishop of Merseburg, describes the town of Radegast with its three gates as being surrounded on all sides by sacred woods. The temple of Svarozhich, however, also contained the images of other gods and goddesses in armour. In time of war incantations and spells were used to induce a propitious sign from the gods. A sacred horse was used for divination, as in the ritual connected with Svetovit. Thietmar speaks of many temples and single images in these parts. Apparently, human sacrifice was common to appease the wrath of the gods.

Helmold mentions four temples in Stettin, all of which were devoted to the god Triglav. His three heads denote the three kingdoms: the heavens, the earth and the underworld. The image was made of gold and his eyes and lips were covered with a veil, that he might not see the sins of men. A black horse, used for divination, was sacred to him. The god's statue stood in a temple whose outer and inner walls are described as having such beautifully embossed figures of men, animals and birds that they seemed to live and breathe. All the temples in Stettin were full of valuables. Triglav's statue was broken by Otto, Bishop of Bamberg, and its head was sent to the pope. All pagan temples in the town were burnt to the ground, and churches in honour of St Peter and St Ethelbert were built on the hill that once had been sacred to Triglav.

Worship was also given by the Pomeranians of northern Poland to Gerovit (Herovit), another war god, in whose sanctuary hung an enormous shield, skilfully wrought and adorned with gold. It was carried before the army and was believed to ensure victory. Other colossal many-headed idols were those of Rugievit, with seven faces and seven swords hanging from his belt, and of Porevit and Porenutius, whose idol had four faces and a fifth one in his breast. It is assumed that all these gods were different versions of Svetovit.

The Pregnant Earth

The southern Slavs or Bulgarians accepted Christianity in the middle of the 9th century from Byzantium. About a hundred years later began the conversion of the eastern Slavs, followed by that of the Czechs. Other west Slavonic tribes became Christian much later; the Elbe Slavs, who today are extinct except for the Upper and Lower Lusatians, who occupy an area in East Germany

between Dresden and the Polish and Czech frontiers, were converted in the 12th century. For some time the old and the new faiths existed side by side, as is evident from references in many sermons and chronicles. In a 12th century work, *Slovo o khristolubtsa*, the author complains that there are many Christians who still believe in the old gods, making sacrifices to them and practising the old rites. Yet the early Slavonic chroniclers seemed to know very little of the old gods, and often remembered even their names wrongly. This ignorance is also reflected in the sermons of many of those preachers of the Christian faith who were concerned with propagating the new religion, and from the 16th century onwards the pagan Slavonic gods are only very occasionally referred to in the chronicles.

Finnish tribes who used to inhabit the region which is eastern Russia today influenced the beliefs of the Slavs to a great extent. The Finns worshipped the forces and manifestations of Nature (see FINLAND) and it appears that until about the 13th century the folk beliefs of the eastern and southern Slavs were largely identical, and pagan customs were retained for a considerable time. Such survivals are particularly to be found in north Russia which was far less accessible to Christianity, partly for geographical and climatic reasons.

The Slavs worshipped the earth, calling it 'Holy Mother Earth'. This reverence for the earth is also apparent in many agricultural customs and popular beliefs. In Russian villages, if the children were seen to strike the ground with a stick in the course of a game, older people would often stop and tell them, 'It is a sin to beat the earth, for she is our mother.' In White Russia (Byelorussia) the peasants believed that to injure the earth in any way in spring until about 25 March was a sin, as she was considered pregnant at this time. Since the earth was thought to be a pure element, the belief arose that she would not receive back into her womb the bodies of sinners, black magicians or suicides.

Water was an element in whose cleansing powers the Slavs believed deeply. It was thought to be neutral and could therefore carry positive and negative qualities. Because of its capacity to reflect, to mirror, water was used for divination and for healing magic generally. A custom which survived until the turn of the 19th century was to wash one's face three times in the first spring rain for beauty and good fortune, and to preserve this water for the whole of the year. The Slavs had holy springs and sacred lakes. This ancient cult of water is also linked with the belief in water spirits such as the Vodyanoy and Rusalki among various others.

Cult of the Dead

The Slav felt himself to be surrounded by spirits and demons who were mainly ancestral spirits, either helping or harming their descendants. Often they had no distinct features but might be recognized by general characteristics, such as a particular type of behaviour, a certain smell, or by leaving traces of their appearance. The memory of the ancestral spirit was honoured in a cult which was widespread among all Slavs, and which was linked with that of the domestic spirits and with animal worship. Ideas that are linked to ancestor worship have been handed down in proverbs and funeral laments, and in many folktales. Archeological material suggests that the Slavs believed that the soul had the same needs in the otherworld as on earth. The dead were therefore buried with food, clothes and household utensils. When they felt death approaching, old men used to go out in the fields and take leave of the earth and the light. A coffin would be made from a single tree trunk, with a little window cut into it; this was known as *domovina* (house, or boat). The funeral meal with the various offerings and the laments formed a substantial and obligatory part of the cult of the dead. The soul was believed to enter other people, birds or other winged creatures, or to become a spirit whose presence would be experienced by his next of kin; in this way the domestic spirits were the ancestral spirits who protected the family and their home and property; they were called Ovinnik or Domovoy.

The animal cult, such as the worship of the bear and deer, for instance, was closely linked with ancestor worship. In folktales the bear often figures as the protector and guide of man in the form of *Tsar-medved* (Tsar bear). The cock, as a bird that was at one time sacred to the sun and to fire, enjoyed particular respect among the Slavs. It was thought to banish evil spirits; it indicated the time of day by crowing, and predicted the weather. In an anonymous episcopal sermon for clergy and laymen alike, Christians are threatened with excommunication for several years who believe in 'bird song and who predict the future with bird omens'. A 16th century Russian book of rules and admonitions for the successful regulation of a household prohibits the belief in *rodoslovie* (genealogy) and in the forces of destiny, the *rozhanitsy*, that were believed to protect their descendants. Genii of fate would appear, according to a popular belief, at various crucial periods in life; at birth, for instance, three female spirits were thought to appear. Each of them would speak in turn of the fate of the newborn child. Bread, salt and wine were put next to the mother-to-be as a welcome for the rozhanitsy. Annual festivals, commemorating the dead, took the form of solemn banquets in which the ancestors were invited to take part. These old sacrificial customs were maintained long after the coming of Christianity.

The woods, waters and fields were the domains of Nature which belonged to various different spirits. The waters were the realm of the Vodyanoy, who was thought to live in deep rivers, lakes and brooks. He could transform himself in many ways and had nymphs as his wives and daughters. At night he would come to the surface of the water; when he appeared he could often be troublesome, but could be appeased by offerings. The Rusalki were water creatures who were believed to be women who had died a violent death; the Slavs visualized them as beautiful girls with long hair. At night, during the new moon, they would dance in forest clearings, luring the lonely wanderer. He who came into their power was doomed unless he could solve the riddle which they put to him. The Navy, also spirits like the Rusalki, were thought to be the souls of children who were killed or who had died in infancy. Sometimes at night they would appear in the shape of birds and give a shrill cry. The Serbians and Croats thought of them as big birds with the heads of children.

Dwarfs and Vampires

It was the task of the Leshy to guard the woods and to take care of all the animals and birds in them. He was thought to have green eyes that burnt like coals, his hair and beard were white and long; he was portrayed as an old man in white robes and a greenish-white hat; sometimes he would wear a crown. There were also a great variety and number of dwarfs, wild women, field spirits, 'mid-day women', and nightmares and vampires, all of which had a particular time when they appeared, often harming those who met them, playing tricks on people working in the fields, luring away little children or giving people hallucinations. These spirits had to be rendered harmless; countless magical practices existed for controlling their influence.

The belief in the supernatural and its manifestations in good and evil spirits was closely linked with the multiform magical practices and their exponents the Kolduny, Znakhary and Ved'my. The Christian clergy preached incessantly against the old gods and spirits and made the magical rites out to be 'devilish games'. But the belief of the Slavs in their traditional rites and customs was not to be uprooted easily. Instead of seeking advice from their local priest, the common folk turned to their wise men, their magicians and witches, who all had a well-tried remedy for anything from nightmares to toothache. They specialized in predictions, and would cast spells and cure with herbs and potions which only they knew how to apply. These exponents of traditional wisdom were both feared and hated as well as deeply trusted and revered. Almost every village had its own wise man and black magician who had often more power over the lives of the people, largely based on fear and superstition, than the Church ever succeeded in obtaining. But in due course the Church too produced its holy men, the 'Men of God', 'Elders' and 'Fools in Christ' who were believed to be endowed with supernatural powers. In the course of time, what was left of the former pagan beliefs and customs become emptied of their original religious content and survived as traditional customs that often merged with the Christian ones; they became incorporated into folk beliefs, children's games and legends.

MARIA-GABRIELE WOSIEN

FURTHER READING: L. J. Gray ed, *Mythology of All Races*, Vol 3: Slavic Mythology (Cooper Square Publishers, N.Y., 1964).

Rip van Winkle, a Dutch colonist, meets a strange band in the Catskill Mountains, tastes their liquor and falls asleep for 20 years, in an American version of a widespread folktale: illustration by Arthur Rackham

The connection between 'Death, and his brother, Sleep', occurs both in magical practice and also in legends of bygone heroes, who are not truly dead but lying in a death-like trance, ready to rise up in time of national danger

SLEEPERS

A CURIOUS ACCOUNT of an attempted robbery in County Meath appeared in the *Observer* of 16 January 1831. A group of thieves, who had entered a house without any attempt at concealing themselves, were discovered by the household and fled. The men supposed, wrongly, that a magic charm they had brought with them would act as a protection by casting a spell over the occupants. The charm, well known in Europe centuries ago, was called the Hand of Glory: that is, a hand cut from the body of a man who had been hanged. Dried and pickled, it was used as a holder for a candle made from the fat of a hanged man, or sometimes the fingers themselves were set on fire. When this charm was carried into a house and set alight, everyone inside would fall into deep sleep from which they would only wake if milk was used to extinguish it (see HAND OF GLORY).

Sleep and death are obviously closely linked here and the logic behind the charm may have been that, just as the dead sleep in their graves, so portions of a dead body may be used to induce a similar condition. The Hand of Glory was specifically a European charm but related objects have been used both in Europe and in other parts of the world, again chiefly by burglars, to induce a similar condition. Among the southern Slavs the thief threw a human bone over the roof, saying: 'As this bone will waken, so may these people waken', the significance of the spell lying of course in the fact that a bone remains as it is, an immutable object. In Java the thief strewed earth from a grave right round the house. Hindus placed ashes from a funeral pyre in front of the door, and Peruvian Indians also used charred human remains. The left arm stolen from the corpse of a woman who had died in her first childbirth was used by Mexican Indians. With this they struck the ground in front of the house to be burgled. In Indonesia, when a young man wanted to visit his girl friend at night, he threw soil taken from a grave over her parents' room. This was to prevent them from waking and disturbing the young couple. All these charms served the same purpose: to throw the householder and his family into a trance.

Methods for inducing magic sleep make an interesting comparison, and in some cases they are perhaps suggestive of a rudimentary knowledge of hypnosis. Combing the hair is one method occurring in certain fairy tales. Another is the sung or chanted verse, sometimes so reminiscent of a lullaby or sleep charm that one might assume this to be its origin.

A tale from Bengal, 'The Story of the Rakshasas', describes how a beautiful girl is placed in a death-like trance by means of a silver stick, and revived with a gold one. Slumber is produced by a spindle in the well-known story of 'The Sleeping Beauty', the princess who lies in enchanted sleep for 100 years until a prince arrives and revives her with a kiss. Opera-goers are familiar with Richard Wagner's treatment of Germanic legend in *The Ring of the Nibelungs*: Wotan lays Brunhild down on the mountain and causes a magic fire to blaze around her. Only a hero brave enough to pass through the flames can rouse her from this charmed slumber. Eventually it is Siegfried who awakens her with a kiss.

The converse of this idea occurs in the widespread legend of sleeping heroes, such as Sir Francis Drake in Henry Newbolt's poem *Drake's Drum*:

> Drake he's in his hammock till the great
> Armadas come
> (Capten, art tha sleepin' there below?),
> Slung atween the round shot, listenin'
> for the drum,
> An' dreamin' arl the time o' Plymouth Hoe.
> Call him on the deep sea, call him up the
> sound,
> Call him when ye sail to meet the foe.
> Where the old trades plyin' an' the old flag
> flyin'
> They shall find him ware an' wakin', as they
> found him long ago!

Inevitably human psychology plays its part. Popular leaders are not readily forgotten by the people from whom they sprang. They live on in the memory of the folk, and in times of peril and national emergency it is good to feel that they are there, waiting to be called upon. This expresses partly that basic human unwillingness to face up to unpleasant facts, and partly that dependency upon another greater than oneself, represented in its simplest form by the child who wants his parents to live for ever, and never die. The hero fulfils such a need. Bridging the gap between deity and man, he represents an image of transition, the pre-Christian version of a saint.

According to many accounts, King Arthur (see ARTHUR) is not dead but living, sunk in magic sleep and waiting to be roused. One of the best known is from Yorkshire, where Arthur and his host are believed to sleep beneath the ruins of Richmond Castle. Once, so it is said, a man called Potter Thompson was taken to an underground vault where they all slumbered. He was told to unsheath a sword and blow a horn, but though he tried to do so, he grew timid before the task was completed; the sleeping figures had begun to stir. As he left, a voice cried:

> Potter Thompson, Potter Thompson,
> If thou hadst either drawn
> The sword or wound the horn
> Thou hadst been the luckiest man
> That ever yet was born.

Parallel stories of slumbering heroes appear all over Europe: King Wenzel and his knights below Blanik mountain in Bohemia; Frederick Barbarossa with his men beneath the Kyffhäuserberg, a peak in Thuringia; King Marko sleeping in the mountain Urvina with his horse Sharatz, according to Serbian legend; Dobocz, the Carpathian robber chief; the founders of the Swiss Federation; Olaf Tryggvasòn; Ogier the Dane, one of Charlemagne's paladins; Charlemagne himself, and Don Sebastian of Portugal (see CONSELHEIRO). There are many others.

Sometimes there are references to treasure: King Arthur dreams in the Vale of Neath beneath the Craig-y-Ddinas

Robert Skelton

(Castle Rock) with his warriors and a quantity of gold. Of course, important leaders often possessed great riches during their lives, so the idea of the hero and his treasure is easily understandable. But it has also been suggested that such wealth was originally linked to the Nature spirit of the site, an idea perhaps associated with the ancient custom of killing a man so that his shade could guard buried treasure.

Slumbering Heroes

Certainly in many of these legends the hero sleeps, not in a distant land of the imagination, but literally underneath the ground, which could represent some earlier stage of folk belief and an identification with local earth deities. Legendary heroes exhibit a tendency to sink from the fortresses in which they lived to the clefts and caverns below. Norse tradition holds that aged heroes, dissatisfied with the world, shut themselves up in a hill. The subterranean location of the sites is of interest since a characteristic theme in mythology is removal: disappearance or translation to another sphere. A usual method is enclosure within the earth, which opens for the purpose.

Popular belief sometimes places the world of souls underground, and there the hero is secluded with his company. This suggests a possible association of ideas between the sleeping army and the host of the dead. Or there may be a memory here of the custom of slaughtering a man's retinue to keep him company and maintain him in his customary state in the afterlife. Such sleeping warriors occur in two examples from the Isle of Man and Rathlin Island, County Antrim. The first describes a hole called Devil's Den at the base of a mountain: one man brave enough to go in found a group of sleeping giants and, on a stone table in the midst, a bugle. He blew a blast, which woke the giants, and he fled in terror. On Rathlin Island, one of the traditional sites of Robert the Bruce's escape in a cave, where he was inspired by the spider and its web, there is a ruin called Bruce's Castle. Below it, in a grotto, the Bruce and his men lie in enchanted sleep. A man who ventured in found a group of slumbering men dressed in armour, and a sabre, partially sheathed, in the ground. When he tried to draw the sabre, the warriors woke and he ran away.

A Christianized sleepers myth, well known in the early centuries of this era, is the story of the Seven Sleepers of Ephesus. It appears in many versions and Mohammed used it in the Koran. According to *The Golden Legend*, a medieval collection of lives of the saints, seven Christians – Maximian, Malchus, Marcian, Dionysus, John, Serapion and Constantine – were living in Ephesus during the persecution by Emperor Decius in 250 AD. This group of Christian heroes, refusing to abandon their faith, hid in a cave on Mount Celion and fell asleep. Hearing a rumour to this effect, Decius caused the entrance to be blocked with stones. Several centuries later during the reign of Theodosius II, a workman chanced to remove the obstruction and the sleepers awoke. They were hungry so

British Museum

Left Vishnu asleep upon the coils of the serpent Ananta: the god was said to sleep for the four months of the rainy season *Above* The disciples beg Christ, asleep during a storm on Lake Galilee, to awaken and save them from sinking: from a 15th century French psalter. Many stories tell of sleeping heroes who wake in time of trouble to save their people

Malchus was sent to buy bread. Shopkeepers in the city, amazed at the ancient money with which he tried to pay, took him before the authorities and accused him of stealing treasure. The bishop agreed to go to Mount Celion and see the cave where the others were waiting. At that time there was a heresy in Ephesus denying the resurrection of the dead. The seven martyrs who were shown to Emperor Theodosius declared: 'God has resuscitated us before the great resurrection day, in order that you may believe firmly in the resurrection of the dead.' This said, they bowed their heads and died. The day commemorating the event is still venerated by the Eastern Church, and people suffering from insomnia ask the seven martyrs for assistance.

The timely appearance of these religious heroes when the Church was threatened with heresy resembles the sleeping patriots waiting to come when their country is in peril. These ideas may seem remote from us today, but are they really so? Siegfried, hero of the *Nibelungenlied*, traditionally slumbers in the mountain of Geroldseck, ready to fight for the fatherland; and, because the imagination of Hitler was fired by these old legends, the motif of the slumbering hero played a prominent role in Nazi ideology – the sleeper is Germany itself.

Rage! Rage! Rage!
The alarm bells sound from tower to tower . . .
The sleepers call from their chambers . . .
The dead call from their graves
Germany awake! . . .
Woe to the people that today dreams on!
Germany awake!

The refrain of the first Nazi party anthem – 'Germany awake!' – was the Nazis' favourite slogan. It was inscribed on their banners, which were designed by the Fuehrer himself, and it was also the title of the volume which commemorated their seizure of power.

VENETIA NEWALL

FURTHER READING: E. S. Hartland, *The Science of Fairy Tales* (Gale, 1968); Sabine Baring-Gould, *Curious Myths of the Middle Ages* (Oxford University Press, 1978).

Indispensable to the community, the smith was nevertheless regarded with a mixture of respect and fear; working amid darkness and flame, the master of fire was associated with all manner of underground beings, enemies of the gods, and sometimes with the Devil himself

SMITH

IN GERMANY, when speaking of someone who is trying to be a match-maker, the expression *'Er ist der Schmied von Gretna Green'* (He's the smith from Gretna Green) is commonly used, so widely known is the story of our Border blacksmith and his part in uniting runaway couples. In England it is still popularly supposed that eloping couples who slipped into Scotland needed the services of a smith to officiate on these occasions, although in fact other tradesmen were called upon as well. Behind this belief lies a persistent folk memory of the magic-religious role within the community once occupied by the smith.

Undoubtedly the ritual importance and significance of the smith were closely associated with his role as a worker with iron, a substance which, because of its comparatively late appearance in the history of the world, made a tremendous impact on the minds of our early ancestors (see IRON). A novelty when first introduced, its magnetic properties and the spectacular processes of smelting and forging must have invested it with a sense of mystery, which gave rise in turn to taboos and magic practices of all kinds.

For primitive peoples iron, which is dug from the depths of the earth or falls inexplicably from the sky as a meteorite, is charged with mysterious power. In folklore iron objects are traditionally protectives against witchcraft, evil spirits and malign influences, such as the universally dreaded Evil Eye. The kings of Malaya used to venerate a block of iron, and the famous Black Stone kissed by Moslem pilgrims to Mecca is probably a meteorite. The Bedouins of Sinai believe that whoever makes a sword from a meteoric iron will be invincible; death will come to an enemy who attempts to stand against this weapon. But iron serves not only the warrior; it can be seen as benefiting the new-born child. For example, on the birth of a child in the Nguon Son valley of Vietnam, the parents would sell it to the village smith, who would make a small iron ring with an iron chain attached and place it around the child's ankle. This hindered evil spirits from snatching the infant away, mortality being particularly high among new babies in undeveloped societies. When the child is grown up and this particular danger is over, the parents thank the smith for his help and ask him to break the ring.

Among some primitive peoples, such as the Tiv of northern Nigeria, if a death occurs, iron can play a part in making contact with the deceased; the metal acts as a mode of communication between the worlds of the living and dead.

Camera Press, London

In days past, when most economic necessities were supplied by a family for itself, the blacksmith, as maker of edged tools, was a particularly important craftsman. Even the water in which he cooled the iron was thought to possess medicinal properties. In Ireland he was credited with magic powers and, under the old laws, certain foods were ceremonially presented to him, since he was not himself a grower of food. He was given a tribute of corn and some of the first fruits of the crop. The head of any slaughtered animal was always his: a 19th century antiquary recollected seeing as many as 100 heads of pigs and cows preserved in the kitchen of a smith.

The blacksmiths of England liked to say that theirs was the first of the trades, since other craftsmen depended on them for their equipment. Indeed the blacksmith's tools themselves have been venerated in many countries. The people of Angola revered the hammer because it forged their agricultural implements. The Ogowe, who do not work with iron themselves, esteemed the bellows used by smiths of neighbouring tribes. The Ewes swore oaths before the hammer and anvil, which they believed fell from heaven. A smith among the Wachaga had to be very careful about handling his tools. If he pointed his hammer or tongs at anyone, or even allowed the iron-slag to spill over them, that person would die.

Here it is not only the substance from which the tools are made, but the tools themselves, forged by the skill of the smith, which possess magic properties. In certain myths, a smith god forges weapons which enable another god to defeat his foe: the Egyptian Ptah forges arms with which the god Horus defeats Seth; Indra, using weapons made by the smith Tvashtri, overcomes the demon Vritra; Hephaestus makes the thunderbolt with which Zeus will overcome Typhon; and Thor vanquishes the serpent with his hammer Mjölnir, forged by dwarfs (see HAMMER). These mythical smiths prepared thunder and lightning as weapons for the gods, and their stories stress the tremendous importance attached, not only to the manufactured tool, but to the craftsman capable of forging it.

Trade of the Devil

Another reason for the exalted position of the smiths arose from their often being outsiders, itinerant workmen who spoke a different language, practised different customs, and kept the secrets of their profession to themselves. In many countries metal workers have been found in separate groups, apart from the community: among north-western American tribes, the smith is a privileged person who hands on trade secrets to members of his family.

In Africa smiths are both respected and despised. Professor Eliade believes that

The village blacksmith *(right)* was formerly revered as a 'master of fire' and possessor of secret knowledge, acting as healer, charmer and practitioner of the occult. In Africa such beliefs continue, and this smith from the Sudanese bush *(left)* is priest and physician as well as craftsman

this ambivalent attitude arises from the history of each region. In areas where there is a culture based on iron, smiths are esteemed; but in pastoral civilizations, and among the hunters of the steppe, they are despised. To the Masai the surroundings of a smith's dwelling are infected with death, disease and misfortune. If a man has sexual relations with a woman from a smith's family, he will either go insane or die, and any children of the liaison will be unhealthy. It is most insulting to address anyone as 'smith', and if the word is spoken after sunset, the person who used it will be attacked by wild animals.

The same ambivalent attitude appears in Christian and other folklore, where the craftsman who worked with fire was often identified with the Devil, portrayed in hell-fire, with flames coming out of his mouth. In India, where smiths were generally out-casts, the mythology associates metal workers with demons, giants and other enemies of the gods. Perhaps there is here a hint of the curse which traditionally attaches to wanderers, in this case identified with those who work underground where fires burn. Myths of the Yakut people describe how the smith was taught his trade by K'daai Maqsin, chief smith of the underworld, living in a house of iron surrounded by splinters of fire.

The prayer known in Ireland as St Patrick's Breastplate invokes the protection of God: 'Against incantations of false prophets, against the black laws of paganism, against spells of women, smiths and druids, against all knowledge that is forbidden the human soul.' For all that, blacksmiths in England claimed St Clement as their patron saint and on 23 November, St Clement's day, anvils were fired with gunpowder and a dinner or procession held. A blacksmith in a long grey beard was dubbed Old Clem and carried in a chair by torchlight; or a dummy was prepared and put up over the door of the inn where the blacksmiths had their celebration. The dinner, known as a Clem Feast, featured a reading of the blacksmith legend. A Sussex version describes how King Alfred called together the seven trades which then existed, and said he would make that tradesman king over the rest who could manage best without the help of the others. A member of each trade was invited to a banquet and told to bring an example of his work, and the tool he had used for making it. The blacksmith brought his hammer and a horseshoe, the tailor shears and a new coat, the baker his shovel and a loaf, the shoemaker an awl and a new pair of shoes, the carpenter his saw and a trunk, the butcher his chopper and a joint, the mason his chisels and a cornerstone. Now the tailor's coat was so beautiful that he was by general consent declared King of all trades. The blacksmith, being furious at this, decided to do no more work so long as the tailor was king. After a time the King's horse cast a shoe and one by one all the other craftsmen broke their tools. Since the blacksmith had shut up his forge and gone away, they broke in and tried to do the work themselves. But the only result was a dreadful mess. The anvil was knocked over and exploded, and at this point St Clement walked in with the blacksmith. King Alfred then said: 'I have made a great mistake in allowing my judgement in this important matter to be governed by the gaudy colour and stylish cut of the tailor's coat, and in justice to the blacksmith (without whom none of us can do) proclaim him King.' The blacksmith then mended everyone's tools, and presented the tailor with a new pair of shears. The king proposed the health of the blacksmith, King of all trades, and everyone sang 'The Jolly Blacksmith'. While this was going on, the tailor crawled under the table and slit the blacksmith's leather apron with his new shears, and since then blacksmiths have always worn fringed aprons.

British Museum

The martyrdom of St Clement, who was bound to an anchor and thrown into the sea: from a 13th century manuscript. English blacksmiths claimed him as their patron saint, and on St Clement's day anvils were fired with gunpowder and a dinner or procession held

Master of Fire

The ambivalent attitude towards the 'King of trades' appears most closely in his role as the master of fire. If the smith is often assimilated to the Devil, there is also a considerable cycle of European folktales containing the idea of rejuvenation through fire. They describe how various saints, such as St Peter, and even Christ himself, appear in the forge as the blacksmith possessed of miraculous powers, rejuvenating the old by placing them in a hot oven or forging them on the anvil. The smith himself, the owner of the forge, then tries to imitate Christ and throws an old woman into the fire where, instead of regaining her youth, she changes into a monkey. Here the true master of fire is divine and not a demon.

As Christ carries the cross on the road to Calvary, a smith forges the nails for the crucifixion: from a 14th century English bible. In Christian society, the craftsman who worked with fire was often associated with the Devil

British Museum

In old Russian belief the celestial blacksmith Kuznets, the Vulcan of the Slavs, was transformed under the influence of Christianity into the double saint Kuz'ma-Dem'yan (St Cosmas and St Damian). The old pagan gods appeared in the role of protectors of marriage; crowns are traditionally worn by both bride and groom for an Orthodox Church wedding service, and the god who made the tools and the first plough for man was also said to have fashioned the first nuptial crown. Ancient marriage songs exist in the form of a prayer to a mysterious smith who is asked to make a golden bridal crown, and out of the tiny pieces remaining, a wedding ring and a pin to fasten the veil.

A legend about Kuz'ma-Dem'yan describes how, when he had just made a plough, a great snake tried to attack him. It licked a hole through the iron door of the smithy but the saint grasped its tongue with the pincers, harnessed it to the plough, and made it plough the land 'from sea to sea'. The snake prayed for a drink of water from the River Dnieper. But the saint drove it all the way to the Black Sea, which it drank half dry, and then burst. This tale is strongly reminiscent of the well-known legend in which St Dunstan seized the Devil by the nose with his tongs. Dunstan, patron saint of goldsmiths, was himself a blacksmith and a jeweller noted for his work in gold. Having been expelled from court, so the legend goes, he built a cell near Glastonbury, where he worked at these handicrafts. One day the Devil came and talked to him. St Dunstan kept him in conversation until the tongs were really hot, then turned suddenly and caught Satan by the nose, refusing to let go until the Devil had promised not to tempt him again.

The Iron Doctor

In mythology there is frequently a connection between trades which make use of fire, and the magic arts. Hence in Africa smiths are often greatly dreaded as possible sorcerers: the Ethiopians say that they can, if they choose, change into hyenas. Among the Wa Tchaggas, Bantu agricultural workers, if the wife of a smith is divorced, it is believed that she will be exposed to great danger. Only the smith himself can mitigate this to some extent by rubbing her all over with butter, in the presence of a female relative, before pronouncing the divorce. The 'iron doctor' of the Ba-ila tribe is a very important person. Without his magical assistance, it would be impossible to obtain iron from ore. Before smelting starts, a boy and a girl are put into the kiln. The iron doctor gives each of them a bean, to be cracked in the mouth. When this is done, it makes a noise and everyone shouts. It is forbidden to call the fire by name; it must be addressed as 'the fierce one', and the compliment will result in it burning the better.

The Kenyan Kikuyu believe that a

Wayland Smith

Puck describes how Weland has come down in the world

'. . . There was no trace of Weland, but presently I saw a fat old farmer riding down from the Beacon under the greenwood tree. His horse had cast a shoe in the clay, and when he came to the Ford he dismounted, took a penny out of his purse, laid it on a stone, tied the old horse to an oak, and called out: "Smith, Smith, here is work for you!" Then he sat down and went to sleep. You can imagine how *I* felt when I saw a white-bearded, bent old blacksmith in a leather apron creep out from behind the oak and begin to shoe the horse. It was Weland himself. I was so astonished that I jumped out and said: "What on Human Earth are you doing here, Weland?"'. . .

'He pushed the long hair back from his forehead (he didn't recognise me at first). Then he said: "*You* ought to know. You foretold it, Old Thing. I'm shoeing horses for hire. I'm not even Weland now," he said. "They call me Wayland-Smith."'

'Poor chap!' said Dan. 'What did you say?'

'What could I say? He looked up, with the horse's foot on his lap, and he said, smiling, "I remember the time when I wouldn't have accepted this old bag of bones as a sacrifice, and now I'm glad enough to shoe him for a penny."

Rudyard Kipling *Puck of Pook's Hill*

member of the guild of smiths can, by placing a spell, prevent anyone damaging a piece of forest land. If thefts have taken place in a village, the victim takes a dead person's iron bracelet to the smith, who heats and cuts it, saying: 'May the thief be cut as I cut this iron.' Or: 'May the members of that family have their skulls crushed as I crush the iron with my hammer! May their bowels be seized by hyenas as I seize the iron with my tongs! May their blood spurt from their veins as the sparks fly from beneath my hammer! May their hearts freeze from cold as I cool this iron in the water.' Curses like this are used to cast a spell over people who may be at a great distance. Most people would not dare to steal anything from the smith himself. The Bakongo are convinced that if anyone ventured even to sit on the blacksmith's anvil, his legs would swell up.

Traces of such beliefs embodying the supernatural powers of the smith can be found in traditions where he is healer, charmer, and practitioner of the occult. As possessor of the Horseman's Word, a secret charm, he was supposed to have complete control over even the wildest horses. Until the time of the Renaissance, smiths practised medicine: an Italian story places one in the role of dentist. Later still smiths were known to cauterize wounds. They were thought to possess the power of healing and to be able to read the future.

In England blacksmiths were often blood-charmers. This was a kind of magical 'first aid', used to stop bleeding in days when doctors were few and unskilful. A spectacular cure for a sick child involved seven smiths, all of whom had to be the descendants of smiths in unbroken line for three generations. The ailing child was taken at night to the forge and laid on the anvil. The seven smiths stood round, flourishing their hammers, as though about to hit the child, at the same time shouting the stroke-cry 'Heigh' very loudly. If the child seemed alarmed it would recover; and the converse was also said to apply. The men were given sixpence each and bread, cheese and ale in return for performing this service.

If the smith was a healer, he was also a divine being. Sometimes he appears in the role of culture hero. In Africa for instance, among some tribes, he taught people how to use fire, the arts of husbandry, and such knowledge as circumcision, how to give birth, and the sexual behaviour necessary for procreation. In other cultures, India for example, he is the creator of the world, and the Japanese smith god is Ame No Ma-Hitotsu No Kami, the one-eyed god of the sky. Celtic tradition associates the supernatural smith with the divine warrior, and Goibniu, the Irish celestial smith, presides over the otherworld feast. The forge of Hephaestus, the Greek Vulcan in classical myth, was situated beneath Mt Etna (see HEPHAESTUS). He worked there with the Cyclops, and the fires from the volcano were his furnaces. Homer says the god's workshop was on Olympus. Another of his establishments was on Lemnos, a volcanic island, and when Mt Moschylus rumbled, the smith was said to be hammering in his underground forge, the dwarf Cedalion working alongside him.

Where are Wayland's Bones?

Certain traditions identify smith and dwarf. The legends of small people living deep in the earth, devoted to metallurgy, appear in northern myth as well as in Africa (see DWARFS). Familiar to us is the tale of Wayland the Smith, sometimes represented as a dwarf, sometimes as a giant. In England he was an invisible smith, haunting a stone tomb called Wayland's Smithy on the Ridgeway in Berkshire, near the White Horse. If a horse was left there, together with a coin for payment, the owner would find on return, so it was said, that the animal had been shod and the money taken.

Similar traditions are to be found elsewhere in northern Europe. The smith appears as troll, headless man, dwarf, and his forge may be located in a variety of places, including an underwater cave. Germanic legend contains various supernatural smiths. Alberich, who appears in the famous *Nibelungenlied,* keeping guard over the treasure of the Nibelung, is sometimes giant and sometimes dwarf. In Old Norse tradition the smith Regin appears as both: his brothers are an otter and a dragon. To reach Mimir, the smith in Scandinavian mythology, it was necessary to make an arduous journey through cold and darkness: presumably the realm of the dead (see SCANDINAVIA).

The belief in supernatural smiths who live in subterranean regions beneath the ground or under the water, and who appear to be connected with the Land of the Dead, is not peculiar to Germany and Scandinavia. The Finnish national epic, the *Kalevala* describes how the smith Ilmarinen undertook to forge the *sampo*, a mysterious talisman, and in Estonian tradition, which is closely related to that of the Finns, Ilmarine forges a great sword in a mountain in the middle of the earth, located in the Land of the Dead (see FINLAND).

King Alfred, translating Boethius's famous work *De Consolatione Philosophiae* from Latin into Anglo-Saxon, wrote: 'Where are now the bones of that famous and wise goldsmith Wayland? I say the wise, since from the skilful man his skill can never depart, and can no more be taken from him than the sun can be turned from its course. Where are the bones of Wayland now, and who knows now where they may be?' In Anglo-Saxon poetry a particularly fine weapon or piece of armour is known as 'the work of Wayland'. Beowulf's corselet is so described, and in several countries of north-west Europe throughout the Middle Ages fine weapons were said to be made by Wayland.

Another tradition concerning Wayland, which dates back to Anglo-Saxon times, describes a gifted smith who was taken prisoner by a king, deliberately lamed, and forced to work for his overlord. One day the king's sons come to his workshop. He murders them, cuts off their heads, sets the skulls in silver, fashions ornaments from the eyeballs, and sends them to the parents. Their teeth are made into brooches, and given to the king's daughter, Bothvild. When she herself comes with a ring to be mended – a ring which was stolen from the smith and belonged to his wife – he stupifies the girl with drink, and rapes her. When the king asks what has happened to his sons, the smith taunts him and tells him to 'go to the smithy built for Wayland', where he will 'find the bellows covered in blood', and the sons' bodies buried beneath them. The smith then flies away, mocking his tormentor as he goes.

VENETIA NEWALL

FURTHER READING: Mircea Eliade, *The Forge and the Crucible* (University of Chicago Press, 1979); Lee M. Hollander ed., *The Poetic Edda* (Univ. of Texas Press, 1964).

Snail

Used for magical healing in the past, especially in wart cures; one method was to rub the warts with a snail and then impale the snail on a thorn, so that as it slowly died the warts would fade away: snail slime was considered effective against consumption and other diseases: shut in a box or dish on Hallowe'en, a snail would trace the initials of your future lover in slime during the night.

Snake

Appears in the myths and religious beliefs of almost all societies, playing many different roles: associated with rejuvenation, immortality, longevity and wisdom, because it sloughs its skin, and with sexuality because of its phallic shape: snakes which live under rocks or in holes in the ground are connected with the underworld, the dead, fertility, the unconscious mind: in Christianity, linked with evil and sex, because of its role in tempting Eve.

See ANIMALS; FIRST MAN; SERPENT; SNAKE-HANDLING CULTS.

Natural Historical Photographic Agency/Douglas Dickens

The power of the Indian snake charmer, playing on his pipe to entice the cobra out of its basket can be paralleled in some rural areas of the United States by snake-handlers who pick up snakes and even caress them

In 1909 George Went Hensley decided that the scriptures commanded the faithful to handle snakes; and even today among the depressed rural communities of some American states snake-handling cults are carried on

SNAKE-HANDLING CULTS

THE SNAKE is a powerful symbol in many different religious traditions. In Judaism and Christianity it has generally represented the power of evil and, perhaps because the snake resembles the phallus, it is frequently identified with unbridled sexual desire (see also SERPENT).

In Judaism snake imagery is plentiful, and circumcision, as a symbolic act that implies the regulation and social control of sexuality, also suggests the transcendence of the people, through a covenant with God, above the sinfulness of sexual behaviour into which Eve was led by the snake. Christianity employed snake imagery much less. In the gospel of St Mark, however, it is promised that signs shall follow them that believe, one of which is that 'they shall pick up serpents'.

It is this promise that is invoked to justify the snake-handling cult that has arisen in parts of the United States, and which today is practised in probably 30 or so different congregations by fundamentalists who accept Holiness teachings; they often regard themselves as anointed saints who have experienced the second blessing of the Holy Ghost that confers upon them entire sanctification (see HOLINESS MOVEMENT). Their services commonly include a variety of dramatic practices: speaking in unknown tongues; shaking, jerking and ecstatic dancing; faith healing; and foot-washing. These independent congregations are locally controlled and served, by lay, or self-ordained evangelists. They do not constitute an organized, centrally administered movement, and they

John Hillelson Agency

John Hillelson Agency

Camera Press, London

Camera Press, London

Though frequently associated with evil, the snake can also be regarded as a fount of power, partly because it is phallic and because in sloughing its skin it seems to possess the secret of rejuvenation *Facing page* In southern Italy villagers at the San Domenico festival (*far left*) twine snakes around their saints and touch them; (*left*) the local 'medicine-man' marches in the procession, snakes garlanded around his neck. In another culture, guides at the Snake Temple, Singapore (*below*) handle vipers fearlessly *Left* In Tanganyika, a snake is coiled around the body of a dancer: snake dancers attempt to invoke the magical powers of the serpent *Below* At a Tennessee snake-handling service, frenzy and ecstasy culminate in snake-handling in obedience to the words of the Bible: 'they shall pick up serpents'

William Sargant

are linked, if at all, only by itinerant evangelists. Some of these evangelists have been responsible for introducing snake-handling to congregations which already worship in an ecstatic manner.

Snake-handling appears to have begun in 1909. In that year, George Went Hensley decided that the scriptures commanded that the faithful should handle serpents; and he introduced the practice in churches in Tennessee and Kentucky. The cult spread to neighbouring states, particularly to North Carolina, Virginia and West Virginia, and in more recent years has been encountered in Georgia, Florida and California. Despite legislation introduced in some states to prohibit the cult, it has not been eliminated by being made illegal.

The practice appears to have arisen spontaneously in Holiness churches. It is true that some North American Indian tribes practised a snake dance, and that snakes were strongly associated with rain-making by many primitive peoples, but this idea has no echo in modern Christian tradition. Indeed the populations among whom snake-handling has arisen in the 20th century have had little, if any, recent contact with Indians. Their interpretation of the practice conforms to their general literal belief in the Bible: it is done in obedience to scripture. Its ultimate rationale may be beyond man's comprehending: just as God chose to give men the gift of unknown tongues so that they might worship him in ways that transcended their understanding, so, in his wisdom, the Lord decided that the truly faithful should handle serpents.

A Rattler Round the Neck

Snake-handling at Dolley Pond Church, Tennessee

The climax comes when the power is strong within the congregation, heightened by the clichéd preaching of the minister. A rope is stretched out by a member to separate the audience from the snake-handling devout, and visitors are warned that the snakes are about to be produced. This precaution may be barely accomplished before an impatient believer snatches up a snake from the angry knot in the opened box. Removing a snake from the box is regarded as a supreme test of faith, for the constantly jolted reptiles are by then thoroughly aroused and it is believed that they are most likely to strike when they are first touched. The box has been kicked, in a kind of half-jocular sin-baiting, because the snake represents the Devil, whom the spirit of God allows the true believer to overcome . . .

The snake may be held in various ways . . . Sister Minnie Parker, a buxom elderly gap-toothed woman – who walked barefoot among seventeen buzzing rattlesnakes in a homecoming service in the summer of 1946 – held a beautiful large timber rattler around her neck like a necklace, with the free neck and head of the snake along the outside of her left forearm, while cooing with closed eyes and a delighted expression on her face.

Weston La Barre *They Shall Take Up Serpents*

The snakes used in services are obtained some time beforehand, and the usual types are rattlesnakes, water moccasins and copperheads – all poisonous snakes. They are kept in a box while hymns are sung, spontaneous preaching occurs, healings are attempted and ecstatic emotions expressed. They are then taken out and handed from one believer to another. Great prestige is attached to those who first handle the snakes. In some services handfuls of snakes are taken up, thrown about, caressed: believers readily wrap them around their heads or push them under their shirts, or even kiss them. They admit that they fear snakes, but they handle them when the Lord anoints them to do so; and they see their activity both as a proof of their own sanctified condition, and as a demonstration of faith and a glorification of God.

The snakes are actually handled for about 15 or 20 minutes, a period which forms the high point of the service, which may last altogether about four hours. There is no question of these poisonous snakes having had their fangs drawn beforehand. Usually snakes are kept for only a few services and are then released, and new ones captured. Votaries of the cult are frequently bitten, but most of those who are bitten recover. There have, however, been a considerable number of fatalities in the course of half a century and most of these have been given widespread and adverse publicity. In 1955, Hensley himself, then aged

Museum of the American Indian, New York

The practice of snake-handling among white Americans seems to have arisen spontaneously, as an outgrowth of the Holiness Movement, though some North American Indians practised snake dances: painted hide of the legend of the snake clan, Arizona

70, received a fatal bite while practising in Florida. Adepts regard recovery from a bite as a miracle wrought by God, but they also profess their willingness to die when the Lord decides, since they believe that the true saint is then brought to God's throne.

The cult has been prohibited in Kentucky, Tennessee and Virginia, and also by some municipal authorities in North Carolina, but adherents are prepared to travel long distances to services in states where the practice is not forbidden. Some of the leading evangelists have been arrested at services, and police raids have occurred periodically. The notoriety that such attention from the police engenders appears to be not unwelcome. Insurance companies some years ago decided to refuse to regard death from snake-bite at church meetings as accidental but this has apparently not affected the practice of the cult.

Excitement in a Grey World

The congregations which practise snake-handling are all located in relatively remote country areas, particularly in the Appalachian mountains. There, Holiness religion of the more extreme type flourishes, and many sects indulge in ecstatic manifestations of Holy Ghost power, with free expression of their emotions, and sometimes with tongues, jerks and rolling. This is a typical economically depressed area, and among the snake cultists even the younger members are usually unemployed. Although rural, these areas are not farming districts, and many of the population live on government relief. Snake-handlers tend to come from the poorest section of the population, and their members have little education.

Holiness religion appears to have an important function in these culturally retarded areas in asserting that, despite poverty, its adepts are more worthy than the affluent and socially respected. Their sense of superiority is powerfully reinforced by what they regard as the tangible spiritual power evident in the emotional vigour of their services, and in their ability and daring in handling snakes. The cult offers the intense excitement of real danger for people who have fewer inner resources and little creativity, and whose daily lives are marked by boredom and lack of cultural interests. Their normal social relations are emotionally impoverished, and they live in areas characterized by frustration, cynicism and repression. The element of fatalism in the cult may also serve to absolve its members from blame as social failures.

Psychoanalytic interpretation of the cult might suggest that since the snake generally symbolizes the phallus, the manipulation of snakes represents the ability to handle phallic power: the cult thus appears as a significant and ambivalent undercurrent in response to the rigorous sexual morality that is demanded in Holiness religion. In his book *They Shall Take Up Serpents*, Weston La Barre considers that 'to dominate the snake is to dominate the guilty and dangerous sexual desire': it may also be a curious sublimation of sexual desire, as indicated by episodes in which women have gained immense elation from repeatedly kissing the snake over its whole body despite being struck repeatedly by it. Psychological tests do not suggest much abnormality in snake-handlers; the older members show more cheerfulness and fortitude in the face of old age and death than do members of conventional Churches. Nor have the young proved to be particularly maladjusted. Relations of young and old in these churches appear to be more harmonious than among the general population of people in similar social circumstances. Older people are accorded respect by the young for the greater frequency with which they handle snakes and for their greater knowledge of the Bible. These results may, however, reflect the amount of authoritarianism in the belief system of Holiness Churches.

BRYAN WILSON

FURTHER READING: Weston La Barre, *They Shall Take Up Serpents* (Oxford Univ. Press, 1961); Harold Preece and Celia Kraft, *Dew on Jordan* (Dutton, N.Y., 1946); W. D. Weatherford and E. D. C. Brewer, *Life and Religion in Southern Appalachia* (Friendship Press, N.Y., 1962).

SNEEZING

BECAUSE IT IS an involuntary process, the sneeze, like the yawn and the shudder, was once believed to have a supernatural quality. The Siamese, for example, believed that the gods were continually turning over the pages of the Book of Judgement and that a man would be forced to sneeze, whenever his name came under scrutiny. The Greeks and Romans regarded the sneeze as a signal from the soul, giving warnings of danger, or indicating good or evil prospects for the future. To sneeze during the course of a conversation was a clear affirmation from the celestial regions that the truth was being spoken. In 480 BC, just before the battle of Salamis, the Athenian leader Themistocles was offering sacrifices to the gods when an onlooker happened to sneeze; this was construed as a sign of divine favour.

In the supernatural sense, sneezing has always had a twofold aspect: there are good sneezes and there are bad. The sneeze can represent the spirit of life, as in the case of the image of clay animated by Prometheus with fire stolen from the sun, which gave proof of its vitality with a sudden sneeze, or it can represent, as it did in Aristotle's time, the first sign of recovery in a patient who was thought to be dying. In later European folklore, a sick person who sneezed could look forward to a restoration of full health, and even today in Yorkshire regular sneezers are supposed to enjoy long life. A 17th century writer observed that 'sneezing . . . is profitable to parturient women in lethargies, apoplexies and catalepsies.'

In its more sinister aspects, however, the sneeze provided clear evidence of some forthcoming tragedy: it was in fact an omen of death since it symbolized the expulsion of the breath of life from the body. According to a current American superstition, sneezing during a meal is a sure sign of a death in the family.

A sneeze was commonly regarded in the past as evidence of psychic attack or of diabolic possession, for it was believed that demons liked nothing better than to enter the human body by way of the orifices, especially the nostrils, unless these openings were protected by amulets or sometimes nose rings. The natives of the Celebes Islands in Indonesia secured the dead against the intrusion of devils by inserting fish-hooks through their nostrils, while the Chinese plugged the nostrils with pieces of jade. A Brahmin touches his ears when he sneezes, as spirits are supposed to enter through the ears at such times. A belated relic of this old attitude may be seen in the Scottish superstition that a baby remained under the control of the fairies until its first sneeze.

The social response to the sneezer almost invariably takes the form of a blessing. The Hindu says 'live' and his friends say 'with you'. The Englishman says 'bless you' and the Zulu 'I am now blessed'. In 1542 a Spanish explorer, Hernando de Soto, was surprised to find a similar type of response among the Indians of Florida. In 17th century England it was customary to raise the hat at the first blast of a sneeze.

The connection between blessings or other precautionary formulas and the sneeze has given rise to much speculation. The Romans used to say *Absit omen* (banish the omen) after someone had sneezed, and Aristotle mentions a similar custom among the Greeks. The fact that sneezing is a symptom of some types of plague – noted by the Greek historian Thucydides in the 5th century BC – greatly strengthened the feeling that there was a need for supernatural protection in the course of this frequently mortal disease. The custom of saying 'God bless you' after sneezing has been attributed to Pope Gregory the Great in the 6th century; he is said to have recommended its use during an outbreak of plague in Rome, and called for prayers to secure protection against the dangers of infection, accompanied by the sign of the Cross. During the ravages of the plague in the Middle Ages in Ireland, it became customary for the stricken to cry out 'God help me'.

Most modern sneezing superstitions confirm that the sneeze continues to be regarded as supernatural. When starting out on a journey or any important enterprise, it is a good sign if you happen to sneeze to the right, but a bad one if to the left, or in the general direction of a grave. It is almost as ominous to sneeze on New Year's Eve, unless you hasten to visit three houses before midnight, which offsets the curse. In parts of Europe three sneezes clearly indicate the presence of four thieves, while in Estonia, if two pregnant women sneeze simultaneously they may look forward to twins. Many Japanese believe that to sneeze once means that you are blessed, twice that you are guilty, and thrice that you will be ill.

It has been suggested that the familiar nursery rhyme *Ring A Ring O Roses* is a reference to the Great Plague: 'Atishoo, atishoo, we all fall down' refers to the sneeze, the fatal symptom of the plague, preceding death

Mansell Collection

Sodom and Gomorrah

The most notorious of the 'cities of the plain' which, according to Genesis (chapter 19), were destroyed by God in a rain of fire and brimstone because of the sexual depravity of their inhabitants (hence the term 'sodomy'): thought to have been located at the southern end of the Dead Sea and perhaps to have been overwhelmed in some natural catastrophe: they became symbols of exceptional wickedness.

Solomon

King of Israel in the 10th century BC, the builder of the Temple, a younger son of David and Bathsheba; renowned for his wisdom and wealth, and his long and prosperous reign, he flourished in legend as a master magician who controlled all demons by the power of his magic ring; he was said to have employed them in building the Temple; the *Key of Solomon* and other magical textbooks were attributed to him.

See GRIMOIRE; QUEEN OF SHEBA.

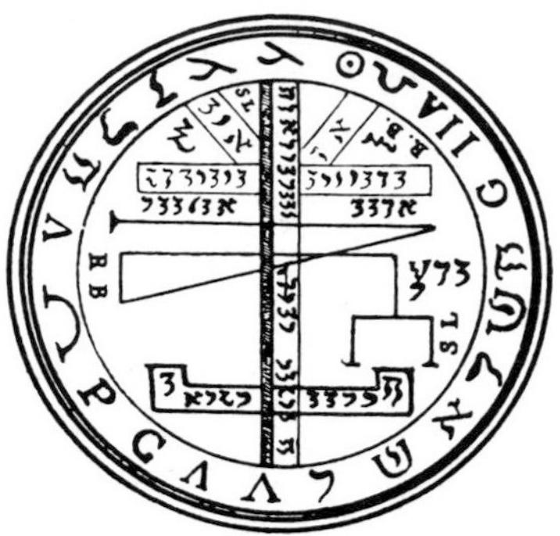

Soma

Sacred plant of ancient India, and the intoxicating drink obtained from it; it was the food of the gods and was also considered a god itself; the great warrior god Indra was particularly fond of it; the identity of the plant is uncertain but some authorities believe it to have been the mushroom *Amanita muscaria*.

See DRUGS; INDIA; MUSHROOM.

'A pox take it' was an all-purpose cursing formula used by the Somerset witches of the 1660s, who claimed to meet the Devil, 'the man in black', at their open-air meetings

SOMERSET WITCHES

'ON THURSDAY night before Whitsunday last, being met they called out *Robin*. Upon which instantly appeared a little man in black to whom all made obeisance, and the little man put his hand to his hat, saying, How do ye? speaking *low* but *big*. Then all made low obeisances to him again.' This description of a polite exchange between the Devil and his followers, and most of what is known of the Somerset witches in the 1660s, comes from Joseph Glanvill's *Sadducismus Triumphatus*, first published in 1681, a year after his death. Glanvill, who has been described as 'the father of modern psychical research', was a Fellow of the Royal Society and a former vicar of Frome in Somerset, who believed in the reality of witchcraft and had earlier published an account of the case of the Drummer of Tidworth in Wiltshire (see POLTERGEISTS).

The witches tried in 1665 seem to have belonged to two separate groups or covens. The Wincanton group numbered 14, six women and eight men, headed by Ann Bishop and including Elizabeth Style and Alice Duke. The other group, at Brewham, numbered 11, ten women and one man, and included four women named Green, who were perhaps related, and three named Warberton.

The Devil was described as 'the man in black' or 'a man in blackish clothes' and Elizabeth Style said he was handsome. He presided at the open-air meetings of the Wincanton group, sitting at the head of the white cloth spread on the ground, with his favourite, Ann Bishop, beside him, while they all feasted merrily on wine and beer, cakes and meat, which he had provided. He spoke a grace before the meal, but none after, and his voice was audible but very low. Sometimes he played a pipe or a cittern (an instrument like a guitar) and 'they danced and were merry', according to Elizabeth Style, 'and were bodily there and in their clothes.'

The other side to this peacefully rustic picture comes out in the description of the use of wax images, which the witches called 'pictures', to harm people. The doll was brought to the meeting and the man in black baptized it, with himself as godfather and two witches as godmothers, anointing its forehead and saying, 'I baptize thee with this oil', so as to create an additional link between the image and the victim whose name was given to it. Then they stuck pins into it and said, 'A pox on thee, I'll spite thee.' Margaret Agar, of the Brewham group, 'delivered to the little man in black a picture in wax, into which he and Agar stuck thorns, and Henry Walter thrust his thumb into the side of it; then they threw it down and said, *There is Dick Green's picture with a pox on it*' (and Dick Green died soon after). They were fond of the phrase 'A pox take it', which they used as an all-purpose cursing formula.

To go to the meetings, the witches smeared on their foreheads and wrists a greenish oil, which the Devil gave them, and were quickly carried to the meeting-place, saying as they went, 'Thout, tout, a tout, tout, throughout and about'. When it was time to leave again, they cried, 'A boy! merry meet, merry part', and then each said 'Rentum, tormentum' and another word which the witness could not remember, and was swiftly carried back to her home.

They said they were sometimes 'really' present at the meetings, 'in their bodies', but at other times they left their bodies at home and attended in spirit form, and it is interesting that the word trance occurs in Glanvill's account of their familiar imps. Alice Duke's familiar, in the form of a little cat, sucked her right breast, 'and when she is sucked, she is in a kind of trance'. Christian Green said that the Devil had what would seem the inconsiderate habit of sucking her left breast at about five o'clock in the morning in the likeness of a hedgehog: 'she says that it is painful to her, and that she is usually in a trance when she is sucked.' When Elizabeth Style wanted to do someone harm, she shouted for Robin, and when the familiar came as a black dog, she said, 'O Satan, give me my purpose', and told him what she wanted.

Alice Duke said that, 11 years before, Ann Bishop had taken her to the churchyard, where they walked backwards round the church three times. The first time round, they met a man in black clothes who went with them. On the second circuit a great black toad jumped up at them, and on the third round they saw something like a rat. Then the man in black spoke softly to Ann Bishop and they went home. It was after this that Alice joined the coven, and the Devil made his mark on her by pricking the fourth finger of her right hand, between the middle and upper joints.

The same mark in the same place was seen on the hands of Christian Green and Elizabeth Style. Elizabeth said that when the Devil first came to her, he promised her money and that 'she should live gallantly' and enjoy the pleasures of the world for 12 years, if she would sign in her blood a written pact giving him her soul. When she signed, with the blood he pricked from her finger, he gave her sixpence and vanished with the paper.

'Lead Us Into Temptation'

A little earlier, in 1663, a woman named Julian Cox, aged 70, had been tried at Taunton Assizes, accused of bewitching a servant girl who had refused to give her money. She had appeared to the girl in ghostly form, invisible to others, and had forced her to swallow several large pins. Evidence was given that she could transform herself into a hare, that she had a toad as a familiar, that she had driven a farmer's cows mad, and that she had been seen to fly in at her own window. She was found guilty and executed.

It was Julian Cox who gave the curious account of seeing two witches and a 'black man' flying towards her on broomsticks 'about a yard and a half from the ground' (see SABBATH). An interesting feature of her trial was that the judge attempted to test the belief that a witch could not say the Lord's Prayer. Julian Cox tried several times and repeated it correctly, except that she said 'And lead us into temptation' or 'And lead us not into no temptation' which, if she was really a member of the Devil's congregation, is the form of the prayer to which she might have been accustomed.

FURTHER READING: C. L'Estrange Ewen, *Witchcraft and Demonianism* (Muller, 1970 reprint); M. A. Murray, *The Witch-Cult in Western Europe* Oxford Univ. Press, 1967 reprint).

People the world over address their deities in song; in daily tasks, in the crises of life and in disaster, the human voice is used as a musical instrument to supplicate or thank the gods

SONG

SONG CAN BE a spontaneous expression of feeling or a sophisticated art form. At all times, in every part of the world, people have evolved modes of singing which originated in emotion. A mother softly lulls her child to sleep; a medicine-man tries to soothe a disturbed patient; so their songs are gentle and subdued. At the other extreme, war dancers of the American Plains scream at top volume and frenzied Negroes in the American Holiness Churches strain their lungs, as do other frenzy singers such as the rock and rollers. A lover may croon to his beloved or he may shout the agony of unrequited passion, with the glides and intense accents of flamenco singing. Between these two poles lie the *mezzo forte*, controlled renderings of folk singers and ballad singers, as well as many pleasurable song-dances. Sometimes the singers invent special effects, say, for comedy. Within the melody they may imitate a railroad engine's whistle, a pig's grunt, a duck's quack, or they may exaggerate the emotional wails.

Universally, these expressions depend on the functions of song. Singers may burst forth in spontaneous songs of joy or sorrow.

Songs have a flexible quality in that itinerant travellers may carry a song many miles when it will become an integral part of another culture: detail from *The Song* by Matisse

Usually they draw upon traditional repertoires or compose new songs for traditional functions. They may address supernaturals or fellow beings; they may tell about the glories of the deities or illustrious humans. They may celebrate crises of life, or accompany their daily tasks or hours of recreation. In different parts of the world and on different occasions, song has religious or secular intentions, although these purposes often overlap. All people sing to their deities, to avert sickness or disaster, to promote enterprises like hunting or harvest. Sometimes

they emphasize the supplication with dancing (see DANCE). Some people laud their deities in hymns of praise; or in dramas enacting their exploits, like the *Ramayana* and *Mahabharata* of India and its cultural satellites; or in great song cycles, like Manipur's Creation myths and the hero myths of America's Mohave tribe. Serbians, Finns and other Europeans sing long epics of demigods or heroes who liberated the people. The British sing of heroic outlaws such as Robin Hood. Faroe Islanders recall their history in song-dances which they mime. Roman Catholics invoke and praise the Virgin Mary on ritual occasions. In the past, youths of Spain, Portugal and Latin America would address worshipful serenades to their beloved, who might listen from a window or balcony.

Songs whose purpose is to mark the crises of life evoke manifold moods. Peasant weddings in some parts of Europe include a solemn ritual and chants for the exorcism of harmful demons; they conclude with gay songs for social dances. Negroes of the Bahamas sing mournful hymns in English for dying and dead relatives. However, Spanish singer guitarists sing gay tunes at the funeral wake of a child. Gabon pygmies in Central Africa lament a deceased chief with responsory songs and mimetic recreation of his exploits.

People who live close to Nature invoke or thank deities for every daily activity, especially in connection with hunting and agriculture. Even in the modern world, Iroquois and Pueblo Indians and Serbian peasants continue these song-dance rituals and social dances of celebrations for success. On a secular plane, many people, especially those who work in groups, such as the Negro field and chain-gang workers, have eased their labour by rhythmic group singing. With mechanization, the motivation for such songs is disappearing.

Gay gatherings with song and dance conclude many solemn occasions. But, increasingly, social gatherings lack any ritual connections, such as Serbian epic recitations, song contests of the Eskimos and Mexicans, the Latin American *romanceros* and calypsos with their manifold contents, concerts of protest or love songs, and the thriving meetings of folk dance and song clubs.

Technique, Range and Tone

Certain stylistic vocal tricks play a part in the singing styles of individuals, tribes, or geographical areas. For instance, when singers do not want to hit a note exactly, they use various devices to avoid an exact hit. One common device is a slide into a note upwards or downwards, as in many American Indian and hillbilly songs. Among the Great Plains Indians, barks or hiccoughs may announce a note; they also use *melismata* (melodic ornamentation) to adorn tones in their native songs. These strange techniques are most elaborate in Spanish flamenco songs, Yugoslav folk-tunes, Near Eastern chants, and art songs of India and Japan. More specialized techniques include bird-like trills by Ainu women in Hokkaido, Japan; and the *vibrato* (controlled undulation of pitch) of European opera sopranos. A technique that is apparently limited to North American Indians is pulsation, a repeated rhythmic impulse on one tone and one vowel. Pulsations are especially strong in the south-west region of North America, especially in male rain songs of the Pueblo tribes on the Rio Grande River.

Range can be extended by the yodel, a spasmodic breaking of the voice, and the falsetto, the forced high-pitch voice, usually used by male altos. The yodel of the Austrian Alps has tremendous carrying power, while the falsetto of Amerindian and Alpine ghost impersonators is eerie and unreal. There are other tricks for range extension although a trained singer can usually only reach a little over two octaves melodiously, women in the upper registers and men in the lower registers.

Tonality is determined by the limitations of vocal compass. Again, the tradition and purpose of particular songs have evolved scales of interest as art and local features. A scale is a series of tones that recur within a melody. It may consist of one or two adjacent tones as in some ancient medicine chants of the American Iroquois and the Ceylonese Vedda. It frequently contains four or five tones spread over an octave, termed tetratonic and pentatonic respectively. Pentatonic melodies are widespread in native North America, Scotland, China and Tibet. Some six-tone or complete diatonic scales occur in Pueblo corn dance songs; and they characterize many folk songs, hymns, and art songs of Europe and America. As the usual major and minor scales, they are focused respectively on scales beginning on C and A, as played on the white notes of the piano; scales starting on other notes – so-called modes – evidently evolved in ancient Greece and survive in chants of the Roman Catholic and Greek Orthodox Churches and also in many traditional songs of Europe and its colonies. In addition, there are microtonic scales with intervals less than a semitone. These scales coincide with the area of song which includes Spain, the Near East, India, Indonesia, and Japan.

Whatever the structure of the scale, melodies of all kinds of scales may descend, ascend, or waver. European songs tend to ascend and descend symmetrically, while Amerindian songs generally descend from a high to a low tone. However, many Pueblo rain songs have a pyramidal contour, like European songs. While a song may start on any tone, it usually (but not always) ends on the tonic, the first note of the scale. Significant exceptions are for emotional effects or in conformity with local practices, especially in the Far East.

To enrich the single melody, and to expand the range of a song, harmony is used. Harmony results from the parallel movement of voices in various intervals: often in seconds in the Balkans, in fourths or fifths in north-west Europe, Africa, and much liturgical music, in thirds in Central Europe, Iberia, and Latin America. The part singing of today involves complex counter-movements of voices in a variety of intervals, such as in the songs of Africa and Afro-America, and in modern hymns. The use of polyphony (two or more concurrent melodies) to produce harmony may be simple or complex and may produce startling effects from the transient relationships of voices. The round is the simplest device for polyphony. In *Three Blind Mice, Frère Jacques, O wie wohl ist mir am Abend,* singers or groups of singers start each of the three or four phrases successively.

A cappella (unaccompanied choral) singing or the combination of voice and instrument can produce harmony. A solo singer can produce harmony only in combination with another instrument. He may play his own accompaniment or depend on a collaborator. A solo singer or a chorus may combine with an instrument or an ensemble in stupendous chorales like the *Mass in B Minor* by Johann Sebastian Bach or the *Symphony of Psalms* by Igor Stravinsky.

Timing includes tempo, metrical divisions, rhythms, and total structure. Tempo defies categorization. Generally, laments and hymns are slower than dance songs, but there are slow dances and lively hymns. Though some prolonged art forms remain in slow tempo, like the Japanese *Noh* drama, many ceremonies like the Iroquois medicine rites start slowly and gradually get faster and faster; an entire dance ritual may alternate fast and slow episodes, according to mood. Metre ranges from the regular triple time of an Austrian or Spanish waltz or a duple-time polka or march to the 5/4 Basque folk dance *Zortziko* or the elusive, changeable metres of Serbian dances.

Rhythmic patterns rarely coincide with metrical divisions. In the triple-time *mazurka*, the melodic accent falls on the second metrical beat; and in the 'hot' rhythms of jazz, for example, syncopation occurs when the vocal rhythms conflict with the metre (marked by an instrument). Less extreme syncopations characterize Spanish dance songs. While European songs use relatively simple clusters of half-notes, quarter-notes, and so on, Scottish songs favour a form of syncopation called the Scotch snap, which also prevails in Hungary. North Africans and Orientals have devised infinitely complex rhythmic figures, accented and melodic.

The structure of song varies greatly. Rounds show a neat structure within their brief extent – a repeat of the first phrase on a higher level (termed a sequence). This form occurs in many ancient Iroquois songs. Many songs are 'through-composed', that is, developed ingeniously from one or several motifs, or freely moving through melodic inventions without any particular theme. The former has become a sophisticated art device; the latter characterizes improvisations in primitive songs of the pygmies and Australian aborigines.

The combination of a number of songs as part of a larger production is a sign of a highly-developed culture. A number of songs and their dances may constitute a ceremony

Singing is such an essentially spiritual activity that one of the principal occupations of angels and the blessed in heaven is said to be singing the praises of God: detail from a 15th century Italian fresco

Participation in singing depends partly on function and partly on social convention: religious services often use choirs to lead the singing and perform special anthems *Bottom* Boy choristers in a London church *Top* Singing in the rain at a funeral, marking the final crisis of life *Centre* Thomas Webster's *The Village Choir* evokes a sense of community in joining together for a religious occasion

such as the Iroquois food spirit rituals with a succession of songs in various tempi and qualities, each with its own rhythmic patterns. In great dance dramas, such as the *Ramayana* of India, songs and dances weave a complex pattern in obedience to the emotional intent of the successive scenes.

The Singer and the Song

Participation in singing depends partly on its function and partly on social conventions. For instance, in the home a woman may sing a lullaby, while a small group of friends may assemble for a 'sing-song' of an evening. During a church service several hundred worshippers unite in hymn-singing, listen to a specially-trained choir or soloist, or, if they are Roman Catholic, to the chanting of their priest. At festivities huge groups may assemble for choral singing, up to 700,000 pilgrims at the shrine of Our Lady of Fatima in Portugal, for example.

Sometimes particular social or racial groups assemble to sing together to the exclusion of other groups; for example the worshippers in a Negro church, or Germans living in America who meet to sing songs from their homeland.

While amateurs may be enthusiastic singers, professionals dominate some aspects of song, such as the epics, and in countries like Japan their specialization is highly regulated. The aristocratic male *Gakunin*, the royal choir of the emperor, specialized in religious *gagaku*, imperial court music. The *Genin*, of the merchant class, have a more secular repertoire, while blind musicians perform popular songs to their *koto* (zither) accompaniment. Female geishas, the tea-house entertainers, limit themselves to secular songs with *samisen* (three-stringed guitar) accompaniment.

In many societies sex determines the singers' roles. Women excel in lyric ballads and folk lamentations, while men predominate in strong epics, in dance accompaniments, and directing mixed choirs.

The nature of song texts seems largely a national or tribal characteristic, while the co-ordination of the three arts of melody, text and dance is a matter of skill, more highly developed among some peoples than others. A familiar type of text and melody co-ordination is the verse set to hymn or folk tunes. The text is paramount and may extend to many stanzas, with a recurrent melody. In European tradition there is a refrain, a response by a group to a soloist's narration of stanza after stanza.

Though Europeans may interpolate nonsense syllables, like 'Hey nonny no', this does not compare with the extensive use of vocables in Amerindian songs. Chorus syllables like *howajine* predominate in Iroquois and Cherokee songs, with an

Homer Sykes

Victoria and Albert Museum

Syndication International

occasional native word referring to, say, the bear. Indians of the Great Lakes tribes use more meaningful words; Oklahoma singers sometimes use English words of an amorous nature. Pueblo singers have some songs with chorus syllables, and others with elaborate, symbolic texts, which are mimed by a chorus of special singers.

When the chanters are also the dancers, as in the case of the Hawaiian *hula*, the liaison between the three arts is most intimate. The same is true for other singer dancers, like the Faroe Islanders; but this liaison is most skilled in India's art dance. According to Kapila Vatsyayan, author of *Classical Indian Dance in Literature and the Arts* (1968) each song has sections of pure melody, for abstract dancing; and of narration, for mime with the traditional *mudras* or gestures. Despite some improvisation, the interplay of singer and dancer is meticulous.

While the previous examples have indicated local qualities, such qualities, single songs, and large repertoires have travelled far from the homelands. A single man can carry a song over many miles, as did the medieval troubadours and the early French explorers in the New World. Groups of immigrants may establish their folk songs in the new settlements, like the Poles and Scots and Norwegians around the Great Lakes of America. They may preserve songs in variant versions that are lost in the homeland, such as those of the Appalachian mountaineers which developed from English ballads. Of course they also compose new songs, and develop new mannerisms. The following are a few examples of single itinerant songs and of large repertoires transferred with or without changes.

The national anthem of Great Britain, *God Save the King*, composed by Henry Carey in 1743, was fitted in 1781 to the Austrian words *Heil, Kaiser Josef*, in 1793 to the German *Heil Dir im Siegerkranz*. It is also the tune for *America* and for an Ottawa Indian hymn to the gracious Virgin, *Gwanatch Marie*. The hymn *Nearer my God to thee*, by Lowell Mason, is a favourite not only among white American Methodists but also among Christian Indians, in their native language: Cree on James Bay, Ottawa and Chippewa along Georgian Bay, Dogrib by the Great Slave Lake.

Repertoires of hymns spread far and wide, due to the efforts of missionaries. The hymns of Britain's Wesleyans have reappeared in America, in the original language or in versions prepared for Christianized Indian tribes. The converts have adopted the 18th or 19th century harmonies and followed the custom of interchanging texts and tunes.

In contrast, Spanish-Américans have formed ritual 'islands' in the mountains of New Mexico's Rio Grande area. They maintain a brotherhood, the Penitentes, and they continue their Easter Passion Plays, secret ceremonies in their *moradas* (sanctuaries), and self-flagellation. They mourn the agony of Jesus and they supplicate the Virgin Mary in their *Alabados* (paeans). In addition to medieval songs from Spain, Italy and Germany, they may present a new Alabado by a local minstrel. Some prototypes survive in Spain and also in other areas of Latin America.

While the Penitentes offer their blood and their songs as atonement for their transgressions, and as worship to their Saviour, the neighbouring Pueblo Indians offer traditional songs and dances to their rain gods. Indians and non-Penitente Spaniards sing Gregorian chants in the vernacular. In the Catholic churches they also render ecumenical hymns.

The fate of Protestant hymns among American Negroes illustrates another aspect of the diffusion of song. Though members of the Pentecostal Churches subscribe to Christianity and though they sing in English, they metamorphose the old hymns with words by Isaac Watts and the Wesleys, who went to America in the 18th century. Starting a tune in a recognizable fashion, they then transform it by a free, melodic rendering, or by elaborate, rhythmic syncopations in voice, hand clapping, piano, electric guitar, percussion instruments, and perhaps a trumpet. They also improvise responsory passages, which may be a fusion of African style and florid Puritan psalmody. Frequently they gesticulate or dance in the aisles.

The infectious rhythms and intense vocal style of Negro hymns reappear in the secular variants of jazz and blues, from the ragtime of the early 20th century, the later swing and boogie-woogie, to the rock and roll of the '50s and '60s. The musical and dance patterns have blended African, Spanish, French and British influences, and have diffused to many parts of the world. Rock and roll derived some of its modulations and vocal tricks from the Near East and, in 'raga rock', from India.

The ever-changing 'pop' music scene started as a teenage fad and it is still sometimes called 'the voice of the young people', in the expression of nostalgia, love, and frustration. It is now, however, demanding the attention of adults and even scholars. The difference between the British style, such as that of the Beatles, and American style is appreciated. Experts contrast black, white, psychedelic, and raga rock.

While most pop music has a secular, commercial motivation, it is showing an increasingly liturgical trend. Negroes say that except for the words it is like the singing in the Pentecostal Holiness Churches. The lyrics are becoming more sophisticated, using mystical, visionary ideas and words. New, anonymous rock hymns are springing up, for use in churches, predominantly in Roman Catholic, Lutheran and Episcopal services. In addition, serious composers are producing 'rock masses' and psalms in Africa and America. The texts range from English versions of the Nicene Creed to original verses on the theme of 'Praise the Lord with a New Song'. These creations appear in record albums, alongside Negro spirituals. They point the way to a new liturgical folk style, as hybrid as jazz.

While the dancing to pop is perhaps limited and monotonous, the secular and sacred music shows melodic and rhythmic resourcefulness, drawing on instruments old and modern, as well as on a vast range of vocal techniques.

GERTRUDE KURATH

FURTHER READING: **Bela Bartok and Albert B. Lord, *Serbo-Croatian Folksongs* (Columbia Univ. Press, 1951); Rose Brandel, *The Music of Central Africa* (Norton, 1971); Gilbert Chase, *America's Music* (McGraw-Hill, 1966); Francis James Child, *The English and Scottish Popular Ballads* (Peter Smith); Henry W. Foote, *Three Centuries of American Hymnody* (Shoe String Press, 1968 reprint); Gertrude P. Kurath, *Michigan Indian Festivals* (Ann Arbor Publishers, 1966); Bruno Nettl, *Music in Primitive Culture* (Harvard Univ. Press, 1956).**

Socio-economic factors are important in both the act and the accusation of sorcery; the Kikuyu, when deprived of their livelihood, resorted to black magic, and the African farmer who is more successful than his neighbours may have his prosperity put down to witchcraft

SORCERY

AN ACCUSATION of witchcraft can be regarded as a culminating stage in a special process by which an individual is psychically (and often, largely unconsciously) extruded from the group. Psychologically this is a process that resolves interpersonal tensions that might otherwise destroy the group itself. Any theory that hopes to delineate the motivation of the accuser has to recognize that much human behaviour stems from unconscious and sometimes atavistic impulses. Whatever the underlying motivation, socio-economic observations should apply not only to medieval European witchcraft but to contemporary case studies in Africa and elsewhere.

To a considerable extent the European witch persecution was developed by the Holy Office of Inquisition, formally created in the 13th century to expurgate heresy (see HERESY). So effective were the Inquisitors that by 1375 they had all but worked themselves out of a job. Certainly, those original medieval heretics, the Waldenses and Cathars, had been all but exterminated; and their confiscated lands and goods had provided princes and officials with considerable reason for zeal (see CATHARS; WALDENSES). It was Pope Innocent III (1160–1216) who provided that the goods and lands of those found guilty of heresy stood forfeit. But by the 14th century this lucrative process was drying up.

Attempts were made to persuade the Pope to allow the Inquisition to transfer its attention from heresy to sorcery; but for a while the Pope wisely resisted this ploy, insisting that unless the Holy Office could show that sorcery was in fact buttressed by heresy, it was not the concern of the Church.

It was only by reviving the notion of a pact between witches and the Devil, that earlier writers such as Augustine and Aquinas had touched on, that this particular theological problem could be solved, and the frequently lucrative benefits of the Inquisition restored (see EUROPEAN WITCH PERSECUTIONS).

The Dangers of Success

If both the act and the accusation of witchcraft (and sorcery) frequently involved socio-economic motives, it is interesting to observe that apart from expressions of jealousy of a more successful neighbour, English witch-hunting never really achieved the intensity that was found on the Continent during the 14th and 15th centuries. Even the consumptive Witch-Finder General, Matthew Hopkins, managed only a fair living during his self-imposed year of office in 1645. In Germany, however, in the same century, the direct connection between economic gain and a spate of accusations is seen clearly enough in the records of the Bamberg diocese. Between 1626 and 1629 there was an average of 100 executions a year for witchcraft. However, in 1630 an Imperial edict forbade the confiscation of the property of condemned witches. In that same year Bamberg's execution rate dropped to 24, and by 1631 it had fallen to nothing (see BAMBERG WITCHES).

In England, where the definition of sorcery and witchcraft was often so vague that the one frequently included the other, acts of so-called *maleficium* (supernatural evil-doing) were often transparent projections of village tensions in which the accusation was to a large extent a safety valve to protect a close-knit community. C. L'Estrange Ewen's survey of the indictments for the home counties in Elizabeth's reign contains many examples of envy of individuals who had achieved rural prosperity, resulting in acts of ill-will, for such successful people are felt to threaten the security of accepted norms.

Axel Poignant

Above Pressure to allow the Inquisition to try cases of witchcraft was partly motivated by greed for the property of those condemned: 18th century engraving *Left* In African societies economic and social success is frequently attributed to sorcery: Bakongo nail fetish, believed to contain or act as a conductor of magic power *Above right* Mau Mau was a reaction against economic pressures on the Kikuyu: members hand over their weapons *Below right* Poor and outcast gypsies are still widely feared as witches

Michael Gelfand, who has studied the Shona of Rhodesia, is not alone in pointing out that the modern African cultivator who is in any way successful lives in fear of the envy of his neighbour, who may point to his farming success as a clear demonstration of the use of sorcery. There is one story recounted by an anthropologist, M. G. Marwick, of an African migratory worker who returns to his village after months of absence loaded with purchases and savings; but he sneaks into his own dwelling after dark so as not to be seen. Members of his often large and extended family who felt he had

Camera Press, London

Spectrum Colour Library

been mean towards them might well accuse him of sorcery or might practise sorcery against him. In a way, sorcery acts as a levelling mechanism in the economic life of a community. And although this is only one aspect of the function of sorcery, it is a function that is often overlooked. In recent times an African cultivator who had most successfully adopted European agricultural practices was murdered. Parts of his body were distributed so that the magic that he had obtained could benefit the whole community. This act was probably a completely unconscious rationalization that restored the *status quo* in a manner wholly acceptable to everyone in the community, except the dead man.

The relationship of an outbreak of witch hysteria to socially unsettled times has been noted by a number of writers and may well explain in different terms much of the disquiet during the 1970s when there were extreme sub-groups opposed to society at large. Although the rituals of such groups are no longer centred on the Devil, they are supposed to have strong sexual undertones, and in their dance routines, their drug-taking and nakedness, they come close to paralleling the fantasies of the witches' sabbath. There cannot be much doubt that world society since the Second World War has been passing through a period of change, but whether it is more anxiety-provoking than the socio-economic turmoil that followed in the wake of the Black Death in the 14th century is another matter. Social and economic change was already in progress when the plague reached epidemic proportions, so that it merely enlarged a process that had been evident for some time. But it would be unwise to undervalue its importance. It has been estimated that some 25 million people died of plague in Europe alone; and that the population of England was reduced by a figure of between one third and one half.

Search for a Scapegoat

The already decaying manorial system crumbled after the Black Death, and its collapse smashed for ever the extended family system in England, with its group responsibility towards the individual, its comfortable social loyalties and ties. From this desolation was to emerge the modern nuclear family and eventually the tougher and much more individualistic mercantile practices that are the basis of modern capitalism.

It is significant that in Britain it was only in the trail of social desolation that followed the Black Death that there was an upsurge of witchcraft accusations. A close parallel has been established in the Eket district of Calabar, Nigeria, which had been decimated by the influenza outbreak in 1918–19. A spate of witchcraft accusations followed the epidemic, and 110 persons perished after ordeal by poison, while in one small village in the area, 18 persons were hanged. The great 19th century historian, William Lecky, noted collateral evidence of a similar nature in Switzerland and Germany, where plague deaths were subsequently attributed to the malice of Jews.

Epidemic and natural disasters concern us not only because our simpler rural forefathers required some sort of theological explanation, but because, in the resultant socio-economic dislocation, they produced states of acute anxiety in the afflicted communities. It is well known that as English manors disintegrated, because of acute labour shortages, landowners turned to less labour-intensive activities such as sheep-farming. The able-bodied were advantageously freed to sell their labour anywhere, but the old and infirm were rather like people whose pension rights had been suddenly removed. Often denied all privileges they had earned in the manor, and physically enfeebled, they had no welfare state to turn to. Robert Cowley thundered: 'They take our houses over our heads, they levy great fines, they enclose our commons. In the country we cannot tarry, but we must be their slaves and labour till our hearts burst and then they have all.' Despite their brutality, our forefathers could not consciously accept the extermination of unproductive or unwanted sectors of the population. But, with theological support, the witchcraft accusation provided a quasi-legal process to eliminate thousands of economically useless old women (see OLD AGE AND WITCHCRAFT).

Link with Mental Illness

The 16th century stereotype of the witch as a mumbling old crone was well expressed in the verbal cartoon of Reginald Scot, author of *A Discoverie of Witchcraft*, and perpetuated in our times by Walt Disney. Although J. C. Baroja has noted her appearance in Spain, she is central to the English tradition. German, French, and even Scottish witches are often young and pretty. In Africa the witch is more likely to be a jealous younger wife. But European society, and particularly English society, has experienced a good deal of stress in trying to accommodate the elderly. In fact, the unending spate of 'in-law' jokes indicates underlying tensions as little resolved today as they were centuries ago. If the *maleficium* continues to exist, the ducking-chair and the stake have gone. Of course, another factor has changed. Many elderly women in our present-day society have led economically active lives and their pensions render them relatively independent. Their final retirement is marred less by want than by loneliness. In Africa, the inchoate jealousies that so easily disrupt a psychically closely related group such as a family, take other forms. Marwick's brilliant depiction of Cewa society in Zambia shows that the polygamous family is often saved from collapse by the accusation of witchcraft brought against a disruptive wife. Behaviour that is disruptive of the social life of a group is also detrimental to its economic production.

There is a further interesting link between social disruption and economic well-being. Recent descriptions of the personalities of psychotics bear a close resemblance to contemporary verbal cartoons of medieval witches (see HYSTERICAL POSSESSION). In one study, a sample of the American psychotic population was examined by Hollingshead and Redlich, and divided into five classes. Class 5 was described as a group that was hostile, self-centred and suspicious. This group consisted almost entirely of factory hands and unskilled labourers, people with low educational standards, who had all the personality characteristics that lead to further isolation and discrimination. The authors of this study commented that these people had about them 'a spell of gloom and disaster which they exuded even when they were not depressed . . .' Centuries earlier the Swiss physician Thomas Erastus (1524–83) had described women accused of witchcraft as having a 'corrupt fantasy abounding with melancholic humour'. In the 1960s Michael Gelfand, speaking as an experienced physician, asserted that in Africa 'a sullen, sour, unfriendly personality is linked with the witch.'

If the psychotics in the American study resemble witches, both are frequently at the bottom of the economic ladder. The gradual extrusion of these difficult, uneconomic members of society has been examined in a recent study by Y. Talmon. Working among ageing women in Israeli collectives, she found that they tended slowly to retreat from communal affairs and to show increasing anxiety about their shrinking economic and, therefore, social status.

The importance of the economic factor in social cohesion (and hence an important element in the dynamics of witchcraft) is evident in the work of M. J. Field in Ghana. There, shrines manned by priests are open several times a week to ordinary men and women who want to discuss their problems and troubles. These therapeutic sessions are a source of significant socio-psychological information. In Dr Field's analysis of some 2500 cases at one shrine, it is interesting to note that the highest single class of consultation was 'Complaints of "not prospering".' 'Not prospering' includes the wrecking of one's lorry, failure to let property, bad marksmanship on the part of a hunter or personal sickness. But the African goes further with such human complaints. Why, he wants to know, is he not prospering whilst his neighbour is? Sometimes, Dr Field found, patients had their own solutions for their troubles. 'Witches have caused people to dislike me,' one reported.

The Cause of Failure

Failure is seldom seen as a personal responsibility. In African psychology there is always the outside power, apparently a projection of internal anxieties, that is responsible – the witch or the evil power that bears a personal animosity. Among the consultants at the shrine were two policemen asking for protection from their colleagues, a dismissed teacher and various schoolboys who had failed their examinations. Some applicants for help demand support because 'I want help in destroying my enemies' or 'I am not prospering because of my envious brother'. In Ghana the alcoholic is the victim of witchcraft. Economically disintegrating, the drunkard laments: 'You see how my house is spoilt. Witches have done that. My house is full of witches, and they have made me a drunkard.'

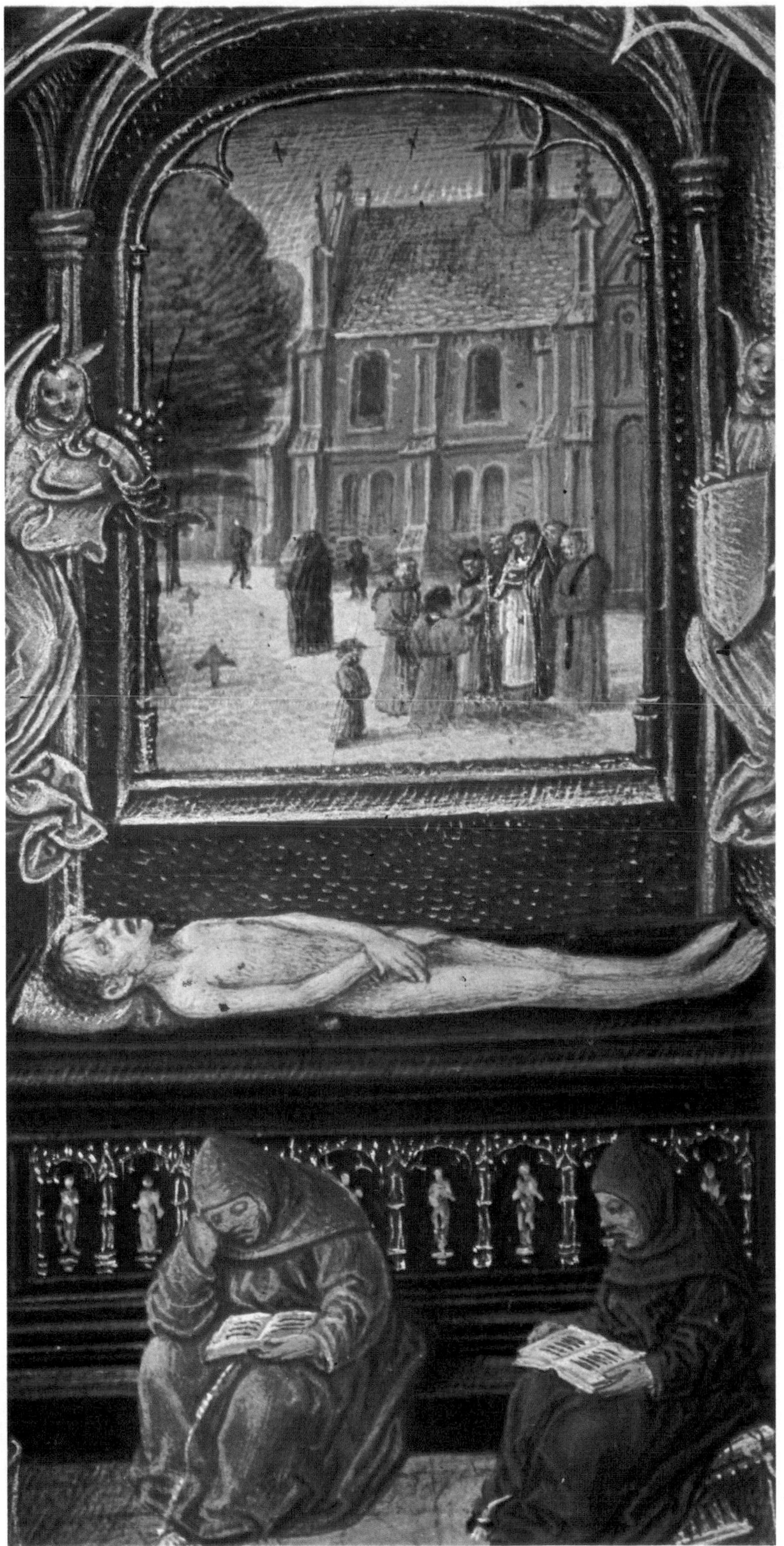
British Museum

In the trail of desolation that the Black Death left in its wake there was an upsurge of accusations of witchcraft, and a similar reaction to social and economic stress is known from other societies: illustration from a 15th century Book of Hours, reflecting the terror of plague

And just as English witch lore is full of complaints about envious neighbours who have caused crops to be bewitched and reduced, so the Ghanaian farmer attends a shrine to complain about pests and disasters of climate – but he generally regards these as instruments of witchcraft and bad medicine. As Dr Field comments, financially successful men are certain that envious kinsmen will do their best by means of bad medicines to 'bring them down'.

If we move from the stresses of inter-personal relations to the macroscopic tensions that erupt into inter-group conflict, we find a close association between economic forces and atavistic expression. The Mau Mau insurrection which marred the British withdrawal from East Africa is an example (see KIKUYU). Reports during the Mau Mau period suggested a return to the practices of black magic, and although much that was sensational was frankly hysterical, it is of interest to realize that the Kikuyu revolt only came about as a result of British administrative pressures which attempted to confine the Kikuyu to agriculturally depleted reserves that were incapable of supporting the population.

The Mau Mau leadership came from migrants who had flocked to the towns, had been deported to their own reserves by the authorities and, driven by hunger, had returned again to the towns. Their oath, like almost any ritual, was a device to create unity. The Mau Mau was a large fragment of society that had splintered from its matrix; and oaths, rituals, symbols were essential anthropologically to give positive stance to a negative commitment.

The Kikuyu were described as endemically secretive, a sour, inward-looking people – an obvious stereotype, of course, and not far removed from Hollingshead's Class 5. The rehabilitation of Mau Mau detainees closely resembled many of the medieval practices. T. G. Askwith, who led the psychological cleaning-up operations, postulated the necessity of attacking feelings and emotions. Consequently the first step in the process was a confession that 'would get rid of the poison of Mau Mau'.

Living in a different period of history, we have not completely interpreted the Mau Mau insurrection as a manifestation of witchcraft, although in its rituals and in the administrative treatment of rehabilitation, it had many elements in common. Almost always, sorcery and witchcraft are associated with pressures that are not resolved by normal social procedure. They offer a means of expression to the extruded: they express the anxiety of the economically unviable without, unfortunately, in any way resolving his deeper inadequacies.

(See also FINDING OF WITCHES; WITCHCRAFT.)

BRIAN ROSE

Sortilege

Divination by lots, from Latin *sors,* 'lot', and *legere,* 'to read': *sortes* is the type of divination which picks a passage at random from Homer, Virgil, the Bible or some other work as a guide to the future: more generally, a term for magic, sorcery and witchcraft.
See DIVINATION; LOTS.

Barnabys

Soteriology

Technical term, from Greek *soter,* 'deliverer' or 'saviour', for the branch of theology concerned with the doctrine of salvation, the redemption of fallen man by Jesus Christ.

The idea of the soul as an entity which can exist outside the body occurs among many primitive peoples, some of whom believe that each person has more than one soul

SOUL

THE BELIEF in a spiritual element of the human personality distinct from the visible and tangible body is widespread among primitive peoples. Ideas about the nature of this element vary greatly and its equation with the 'soul' as conceived by Christians is only of limited relevance. There is, however, the fairly general assumption that an invisible substance, separable from the material body, is responsible for the phenomena which distinguish the living from the dead. According to the views of some peoples, this element is the 'soul' or 'life-substance' of a person, and its temporary separation from the body leads to illness or loss of consciousness, while permanent separation causes death.

The enlivening element which may be described as 'soul' is not necessarily considered as totally immaterial, for it is sometimes associated with the breath or the shadow of a person (see BREATH; SHADOW), and under certain circumstances it can manifest itself and become perceivable as a phantom or ghost. Yet the idea that the soul is not merely a function of the living body, such as the breath, but an entity by itself capable of existing outside the body occurs among many primitive populations. Frequently this element is described in terms suggesting not complete insubstantiality but a finer type of materiality such as that of breath, shadow or double (see DOUBLE). It is in the nature of a soul to be capable of surviving after the body's decomposition following death. But there is a common belief that a disembodied soul is not necessarily freed from the exigencies of earthly life; it may be in need of the attention of the living and depend on their offerings of food.

The experience of dreams has certainly influenced the development of the belief in an immaterial part of the personality which can move about freely and encounter people in distant places while the body of the sleeper is known to remain static. In the 19th century, anthropologists such as E. B. Tylor, made a great deal of the role of dreams as the source not only of the concept of the soul but also of the belief in ghosts and spirits, beings conceived in the image of disembodied souls existing and acting independent of a tangible and visible body. This theory, generally known as animism (see ANIMISM), may well explain certain concepts of ancestor spirits and demons, but it cannot account entirely for the belief in spirits and gods belonging to a sphere outside the world of men and of a nature different from that of the human soul.

National Gallery

In major religions the fate of the soul is generally believed to be determined by the dead person's conduct in life, an idea which is frequently absent from primitive beliefs: *The Soul of St Bertin Carried up to God,* by the 15th century Dutch painter Simon Marmion

How Many Souls to a Body?

Christian doctrine assumes that man is endowed with a single soul, in which his personality survives after death, but which during his lifetime has no perceivable separate existence. The views of many primitive peoples on the composition of the human personality are far more complex. Beliefs in a plurality of invisible elements associated with one body are widespread, and the idea of multiple 'souls' is current in many primitive societies. Sometimes they are thought to be localized in different parts of the body during life, and almost invariably they have separate fortunes after death. The Menomini, an American Indian tribe, used to assign one soul to the head and another to the heart. After death the former was believed to roam about aimlessly, to linger about the grave and whistle in the dark, and this soul was given offerings by the kinsmen of the deceased. The other soul was believed to travel to the realm of the spirits and to dwell there without ever returning to earth. The Bagobo of the Philippines distinguish a right-hand and a left-hand soul. The former is manifested as the shadow on a person's right side, and is believed not to leave the body until death. When a person dies, this soul goes straight from the grave to the underworld, and by purification it becomes a naturalized spirit, who joins his predecessors in a mode of life closely patterned on that of

A dead Egyptian and her soul in the form of a bird receive water from Nut, protectress of the dead: illustration on a funerary casket, c 1000 BC. The Egyptians believed that at death a free-moving entity separated itself from the body but remained in close proximity to it

C. M. Dixon/British Museum

the living. The left-hand soul appears as the shadow on the left side and also as a man's reflection in water (see also MIRROR). It is this soul which leaves the body at night to go flying about the world. These adventures are fraught with danger, for were a demon to catch it, the owner of the soul would fall ill and ultimately die. At the moment of death the left-hand soul leaves the body and then becomes merged in the company of demons who cause disease. The left-hand soul is associated with sickness and pain, whereas the right-hand soul is a source of health, activity and joy.

Some American Indian tribes attributed four souls to every human body, and certain Melanesians believe that a man possesses seven souls of different type. The implications of a belief in several distinct elements in a person's spiritual make-up are exemplified by the Gonds, an aboriginal tribe of central India. The Gonds share with many Indian tribes the belief that a child in the mother's womb is lifeless until a *jiv*, or life-substance enters and animates the embryo. This life-substance is sent into the child by Bhagavan, the supreme deity, and failing the arrival of the life-substance the child will be still-born. During a Gond's life little attention is paid to the life-substance, which is unrelated to a man's consciousness or emotions. But when a Gond's span of life draws to its end, the supreme deity recalls the life-substance and thereby causes death. When a life-substance has returned to the deity, it is added to a pool of such life-substances available for reincarnation, and the link between the personality of the deceased and the life-substance comes to an end as soon as the latter returns to this pool. Thereafter it may be reincarnated in any living creature, be it animal or man, but there is a likelihood that a man's life-substance will be reincarnated in the son of one of his sons.

Despite this belief in the possibility of reincarnation within the same family, the personality of the deceased does not adhere to the life-substance but to another element, the *sanal*, which corresponds to the 'shade' or soul of the dead in the Homeric view of the underworld. Nearly all the rites and ceremonies of Gond funerals and memorial feasts, as well as the subsequent cult of the ancestors, relate to the shade in whom the personality of the departed is perpetuated. While in the moment of death the life-substance moves to the realm of the supreme deity, the shade is believed to linger near the corpse and throughout the funeral rites the presence of the shade is very much in the minds of the mourners. From the house of death the shade follows the bier bearers to the grave or the cremation-ground and hovers close by while the mourners dispose of the corpse. Immediately after the burial or cremation the mourners go to a stream and put down a miniature seat, a twig such as Gonds use for cleaning the teeth, and a cup of water. They then address the departed and admonish him to sit on the seat and to rinse his mouth, in the belief that the shade should purify himself from the pollution of death. Then a goat or fowl is sacrificed, and the cooked flesh is offered to the shade with the request to eat of it and to grant his favour to the living.

A soul in need of purification by means of a twig and water, and capable of partaking of food, is clearly not thought of as completely immaterial, but its substantiality is of a different and more subtle kind than that of living persons.

After the funeral the Gonds perform a rite whereby the shade of the deceased is joined with the company of the shades dwelling in fields and forest. This rite reflects the belief that for some time after death the shades roam the world of the living, but normally they live in the Land of the Dead, and an elaborate ritual is designed to introduce the shade of a recently departed to the company of the ancestors and the clan deities who reside with them in the underworld. There the shades lead a life very similar to life on earth, and every man and woman is believed to join ultimately his or her original spouse, even though several other marriages may have followed the first marital union. Although the souls of the departed live in a sphere of their own, they are not far removed from the living, and they come to the houses of their surviving kinsmen and partake of the food offered to them on the occasion of feasts. Far from dreading contact with the shades of the departed, the Gonds believe in their beneficial influence and the blessings they can bestow on the living. It is only when their cult is neglected that they may withdraw their favour.

Condemned to Roam the Earth

In so far as the afterlife is concerned, the shade approximates the Western concept of the 'soul' much more closely than does the life-substance to which adheres very little of a man's personality. Being the dead person minus the material body and the animating life-substance, the shade retains the personality of the deceased, and remains within the framework of the social system which places him in certain prescribed relationships to the living as well as to the dead members of Gond society. However, Gonds believe that in exceptional circumstances, a deceased may be unable to join the company of ancestors in the Land of the Dead, but turns into an evil spirit condemned to roam this earth and haunt the living. This may be the fate of a woman who died in pregnancy or childbirth. To encounter the ghost of such a woman is highly dangerous; the mere sight of her may cause a wasting disease or even death, and women who died in childbirth are buried in such a way as to make their emergence from the grave as difficult as possible.

Different from the concept of the soul or shade, which represents a man's personality surviving after death in a transformed state, is that of a soul which can leave a man's body even during his lifetime. Many primitive peoples, such as the tribes of central and northern Asia, believe that a man's soul has a separate existence, and they attribute disease to the soul's having strayed away or been stolen. Treatment is in principle reduced to finding it, capturing it, and obliging it to resume its place in the patient's body. Only a shaman or spirit-medium can undertake a cure of this kind, for only he recognizes that the soul has fled, and is able to overtake it. In a state of trance or ecstasy he 'sees' the spirits who may have abducted the soul and can follow them into their realm and bargain with them for the soul's release. While an ordinary person's soul may detach itself from the body involuntarily, the shaman is capable of sending his own soul into the world of the spirits and there searching for the truant soul of his patient (see SHAMAN).

Here the soul is clearly a separate entity and not merely the personality which after the death of the body appears as a shade, as believed by the Gonds. Certain Himalayan tribes, for instance, perform at every wedding an elaborate rite in order to induce the soul of the bride to reside happily in her new home. For it is believed that if her soul were to escape from her husband's house, the bride would pine and die.

As the soul of a dying man is breathed out of his body, angels and demons fight for control of it; for many peoples the soul is not merely a function of the living body but is capable of survival after death: drawing from De Plancy's *Dictionnaire Infernal,* 1835

The soul-concepts of north Asian peoples are complicated by the belief that man can have as many as three or even seven souls. At death one of them remains in the grave, another descends to the realm of shades, and a third ascends to the sky. Some north Asian tribes believe that at death one soul disappears or is eaten by demons, and during earthly life may cause illness by its flight.

The Vengeful Ghosts

Among primitive peoples we find two contrasting attitudes to the souls of the dead. Most Indian tribes, such as the Gonds, endeavour to maintain contact with the departed, believing that their support and favour will aid the prosperity of surviving kinsmen. In Africa, on the other hand, there is a widespread desire to turn the dead away from the living and to prevent them from meddling in their affairs. Thus the Nuer of the southern Sudan (see NUER) bury the dead with their backs to the homesteads and their eyes to the bush, in order to induce the ghost of the dead person to look outwards and leave the living alone. There is no cult of the dead and their graves are soon forgotten. The Nuer, like many other African tribes however, believe that ghosts may come to trouble the living. The dead are resentful of injustice and bear malice to those who have wronged them. Hence those who have recently become ghosts may take vengeance on anyone who harmed them in their earthly life.

We can conclude that most primitive people have a belief in an element in the human personality which survives in one form or other after death. Less general but still of considerable currency is the assumption that an intangible part of man can separate itself from the body and stray to other spheres, but that permanent separation inevitably results in the death of the body. The Christian idea of one single immortal soul, completely identified with a man's or woman's personality, is only one of numerous ideas regarding the spiritual side of human nature. The fate of the soul or other spiritual entity after death is rarely connected with a person's moral conduct in this life. More common is the belief that the circumstances of a person's death determine the future life of the surviving soul, and that those who died an accidental or violent death turn into malignant ghosts who cannot find rest and constitute a source of danger to the living.

Most of the assumptions of modern Spiritualism regarding the nature and fate of the souls of the dead are anticipated by the beliefs and practices of primitive peoples, and it would seem that a great variety of attitudes towards the spiritual elements in the human personality has persisted throughout the ages.

(For the soul in major religions, see MAN; and see also BRAHMAN; BURIAL; CULT OF THE DEAD; GHOSTS; HAUNTED HOUSES; IMMORTALITY; JUDGEMENT OF THE DEAD; PACT; PSYCHOLOGY; REINCARNATION; SPIRITUALISM.)

C. VON FÜRER-HAIMENDORF

SOUTH AMERICA

In the candomblés of Brazil, descendants of slaves beg favours equally from St Peter or the African Xango; while among their wealthier white countrymen a girl who wants her lover back will offer perfume and champagne to Iemanja, and a man who seeks Exu's help in a lawsuit will pour whisky over the roots of a certain tree

BRAZIL IS UNIQUE in South America for it has its own language – Portuguese – and its own religion – spiritism. The Vatican refers to Brazil as 'the largest Catholic nation in the world', but the majority of its 90 million people practise a form of spirit worship that has never received the approval of Rome.

Spiritism in Brazil (not quite the same thing as Spiritualism) goes back centuries to Africa, to the enlightened and progressive West Africa of the Yoruba culture and the nation of Benin, famous for its magnificent bronze sculptures and masks. The Yoruba developed in the region known today as southern Nigeria; they had their own cities, armies, priesthoods, elites and political systems. The people were guided by a host of deities and spirits that were all-seeing and all-powerful. They were everywhere: in the sky, in the trees, under rocks and inside animals. They could be called upon at any time and for any reason, but they demanded gifts and devotion.

The god Orolum was their Jehovah. He was so omnipotent that there was no direct way to approach him. An intermediary, or *orisha,* had to be used, and he would have to be convinced of a mortal's sincerity before he would take the request to his chief.

The two most important messengers were a black Adam and Eve who descended from heaven to the African jungles to intercede for Yoruba tribesmen. They had a son named Aganju and a daughter called Iemanja; brother and sister married and had a son named Orungan. When Orungan

Keystone Press

Blood is poured over the head of a young boy holding a sacrificed cockerel during a Brazilian spiritism ritual: many old African beliefs and practices, originally brought by Negro slaves, have survived and have coalesced with aspects of Christianity to create vigorous new religious movements

Keystone Press

The Umbanda cult of Brazil is a unique hybrid religion combining African paganism, spiritism, and Christianity; at a beach initiation ceremony drums and bottles of champagne play as vital a role as statues of Christian saints

grew to be a man he fell in love with his own mother. Iemanja repulsed his advances and tried to run away, but he caught her, knocked her to the ground and raped her. Iemanja was so ashamed of what had happened that she went into the jungle and hid. There her belly began to grow at an alarming rate. From her breasts spurted two fountains of water that became lakes. Then her womb burst open and out came the hierarchy of Yoruba spiritism: the god of thunder and the god of twins, the god of hunting, the goddess of disease, the god of wealth, the god of war, and five others. After 11 children had been born to her, she then gave birth to the sun and the moon. Thus Iemanja became the mother of all spirits and the most powerful and venerated of women in Yoruba mythology.

When the Portuguese initiated the slave trade at the beginning of the 16th century, Arab buyers attacked the villages and bound the tribesmen in chains. They were herded and branded like cattle, marched to the sea and stacked in layers inside slave ships. Many of them had never seen the sea, and when the ocean rolled, and the ships felt as if they were sinking, the slaves had only one hope of salvation; the goddess Iemanja. They begged her not to let them drown and prayed to her to calm the waters. When they arrived safely on Brazilian soil they were positive it had been Iemanja who had listened to them and who had delivered them from the terrors of a watery grave. She had guided them to safety. She and all her sons and daughters were immediately venerated in the New World.

Saints Merged with Spirits

The Portuguese were generally comparatively lenient masters, and they were also easy-going Catholics. Many of their religious beliefs were mixed with superstition and folklore, relics of centuries of Moorish influence. They believed in the Evil Eye, black magic and the power of amulets. Ideologically, Rome had always been at a

One by one the Christian saints became confused with the Yoruba spirits, and in less than a generation they were one and the same personality

distance from Lisbon, but it was almost on another planet from Brazil. The Portuguese masters were uninterested, therefore, in the gods their slaves worshipped as long as the work was done. When the Blacks set up altars to Iemanja and the other spirits they were allowed to keep them. The masters even allowed them to beat drums and light candles; and as long as the services did not end in physical injury, the masters were unconcerned.

But visiting Catholic priests were concerned, and admonished the Portuguese, insisting that their slaves should be converted to Christianity. The Church even threatened to take away slaves who remained pagan. So the masters held classes where the lives of the saints were read, and gave the slaves plaster statues of their various Christian heroes; and told them to worship them. The slaves were delighted because it gave them a new and very powerful collection of deities to pray to. If their masters worked through these white spirits, then they must be very strong indeed. They were pleased that the Virgin Mary was so important and looked so much like Iemanja. They put the image of Mary right up on the altar beside the goddess of the waters. Soon the two women were fused into one deity who would answer to either name. Other saints were also mingled with their jungle counterparts: Oxala was the god of purity and goodness, so he merged easily with Jesus. Xango was the spirit of the wilderness; he and St John the Baptist became one. Omulu was the spirit of disease and therefore a natural partner for St Lazarus, the poor man who was 'full of sores', mentioned in the parable in Luke, chapter 16. One by one the Christian saints became confused with the Yoruba spirits, and in less than a generation they were one and the same personality.

When the slaves of the northern states, Ceara and Amazonas, were freed in 1884

C. Waterson

C. Waterson

Iemanja, the mother of all spirits, and goddess of the sea, who saved the slaves from the perils of the journey from Africa to the New World, is still venerated; every New Year's Eve, crowds gather on the Copacabana Beach, Rio de Janeiro, to honour her *Above right* The faithful prostrate themselves before her picture *Right* The 'mother' and 'father' of the saints carry her picture to the sea

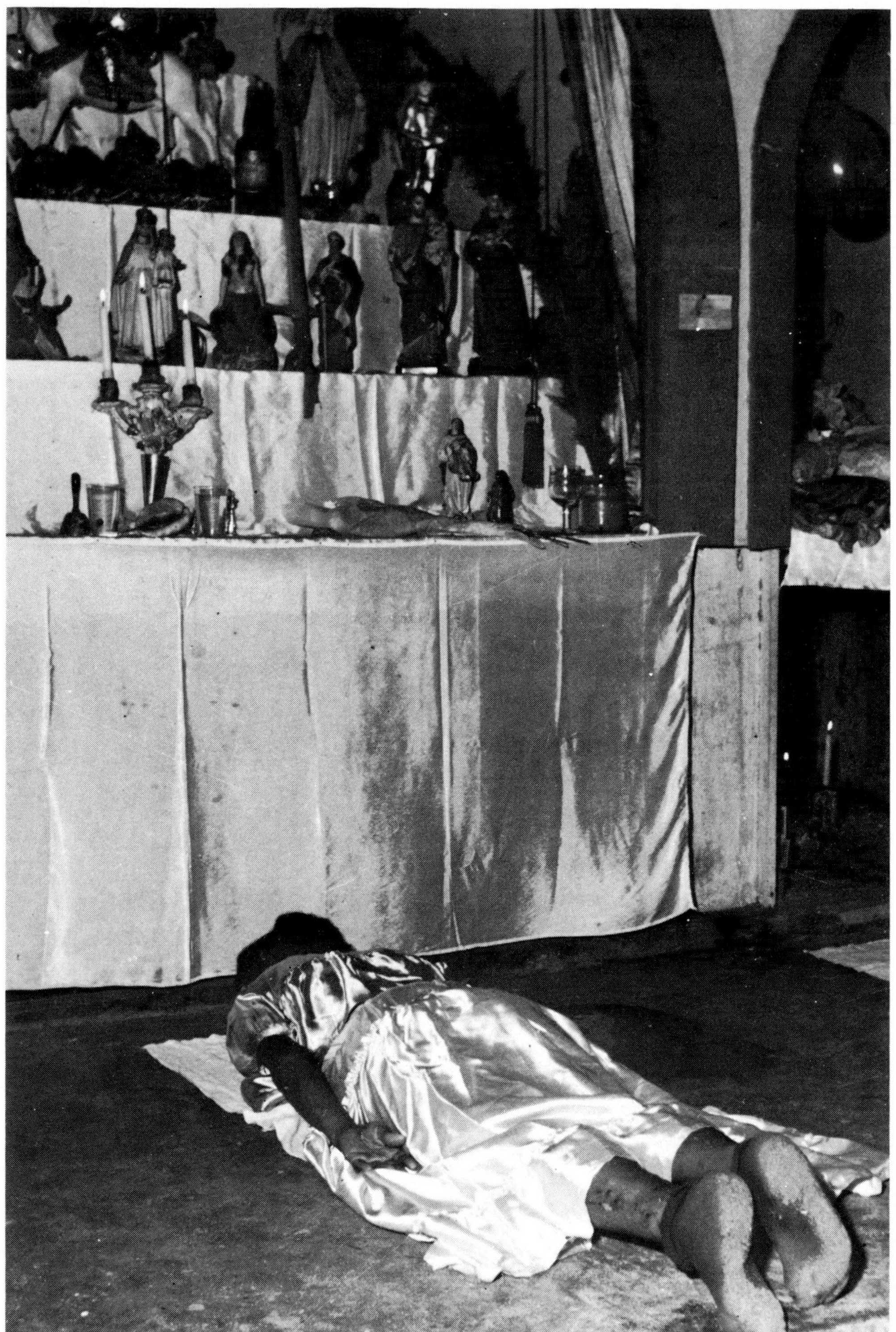

London Express News & Features

Left A woman prostrates herself before an Umbanda altar decorated with the images of Catholic saints: Umbanda is full of beliefs, rituals and recipes to smooth out life's daily problems, and appeasements are offered to the spirits for everything from success in business to good-fortune in love
Right Brazilian spirit doctors play a vital role in a society where there are too few medical facilities: a spirit doctor blesses a cripple whom he has just cured

they set up churches and called them *candomblés* (meeting places). Black women, who were the religious leaders during captivity, because they had more free time than the men for elaborate rituals, became the high priestesses. Their acolytes, also women, were chosen from the devout who wished someday to move up the hierarchy themselves. The men were limited to beating the drums.

There are some 700 Candomblé spirit temples in the city of Salvador, Brazil, today that are faithful to the rituals of the Afro-Christian slave churches of the past. The high priestess (called 'Mother of the Saints') trains her 'daughters' in the art of charms, spells, ritual, African dialects and cures. The congregation sits divided, men on one side of the room and the women on the other. Drums beat and candles are lit in the four corners while special food and alcoholic drinks are placed outside to keep Exu, the Devil, away from the ceremony. The dancers swirl to the rhythm of the drums and sing imploringly for the spirits to descend. One by one the dancers become possessed and take on the physical characteristics of their particular deity. Then they are dressed in the costume of that specific spirit and are led in a trance around the room blessing and embracing those who believe.

For true adepts, it is important to be present. They believe that the spirit saints are in that very room. The devout can touch the Virgin Mary. They can ask a blessing of St Peter. They can have their lives bettered by Xango. They claim they cannot become so intimate with the gods at the Catholic Church because the spirits there do not live and breathe: they just stare down from niches on the wall. At a candomblé the people are in the actual presence of the gods.

Faith for the Upper Class

Down the coast, in wealthy Rio de Janeiro, the upper-class Brazilians wanted something else in a religion. Catholicism failed to provide the answers to all their questions, as did the pagan African transplant of Candomblé. The wealthy and educated believed in spirits and spirit healing but could not reconcile themselves to worshipping beings such as Iemanja and Orolum. The whites needed a more 'civilized' way of believing in spirits, and found it through a Frenchman.

Alan Kardek (whose real name was Denizard Rivail) was a 55-year-old doctor of medicine in Paris. A scientist and sceptic, he trusted nothing he could not see. One evening, when he was present at an exclusive Parisian *salon*, the hostess, much to his astonishment, made her guests play 'table-rapping'. Kardek sat at a heavy round table and placed his hands on its surface along with everyone else. Shortly the table began to rap out messages. It told where Mme 'X' had misplaced her jewels and whom M 'Y' would marry. The spirit of the table identified itself as being that of a famous and long dead poet. The guests laughed at the table's messages but Kardek was not amused. He was incredulous, then appalled, and finally intrigued. He contended, as a doctor and scientist, that if these messages really came from the departed they should be taken seriously and should not be used for idle parlour games but should be seriously investigated. And if there really were spirits, then did not their very existence put an entirely new aspect on all the sciences?

He sent out teams of researchers armed with the same set of questions, to visit table-rapping parties across France. When they returned to Paris their answers were compared and found to be amazingly similar. Kardek became certain that spirits did exist and that they were trying to contact the living. He devoted the rest of his life to questioning them and compiling their answers.

In 1857 Kardek published his research,

Right As the dawn of the New Year breaks on Copacabana Beach, the crowds still cluster round their offerings to the goddess Iemanja _Facing page (left)_ flowers placed in the sand in honour of Iemanja and _(right)_ candles still burn after the long night celebrations

Foto Hetzel

calling it *The Spirits' Book*. It dealt with the spirit world, its origins, its various planes and its various classes. A small group formed around Kardek and supplied him with funds to continue his research, but on the whole he was ignored in France. In England there was a brief flurry of interest in his views, but this also died away. Then a nobleman of the Brazilian emperor's court returned to Rio de Janeiro from Europe with a copy of Kardek's book. It was just what upper-class Brazilians had been looking for. It was by a cultured Frenchman, he was a scientist and he was white. Also, he said what they had been waiting to hear: 'There is no death.'

His writings were quickly translated into Portuguese, and Kardekian centres sprang up all over Brazil. The better educated attended meetings, joined hands and received messages. They studied the rules that the spirits laid down to govern human behaviour, they learned to combine the spirits' ideas with those of Christ, and they learned how to heal by the laying on of hands.

Laying on of Hands

Kardek temples, numbering some 3000 in present-day Brazil, specialize in curing the body so that the mind can do its necessary work. Cures are performed by a medium stretching out his hands and letting jets of electricity speed from his fingers into the patient's aura, which is believed to be imbalanced. The aura, transmitter of physical health and mental balance, is regulated, thus stopping its damaging effect on the flesh of the patient.

Kardek doctors claim cures for thousands of believers after just one visit to an *Espiritista* service. Cripples have been reported to walk again, skin diseases have disappeared and the blind have regained their sight. A well-known psychic surgeon, Jose Arigo, has performed operations under strict surveillance, yet no sign of fraud or subterfuge has ever been noted. Kardek spiritists also work to orientate lost souls back to the spirit world, claiming that many confused 'souls', especially after an accident or an unexpected illness, are roaming the earth in search of their missing mortal bodies.

There is yet another form of Brazilian spiritism. It is called *Umbanda* and, at times, referred to erroneously as *Macumba*. Umbanda was created about 50 years ago by a Kardek medium who felt that African Candomblé was too 'low' for the average man and Kardek spiritism too 'high'. What was needed was a mixture of the best of both creeds. Umbanda was the result. The primitive gods (including Iemanja), the drum beats, the candles and the body-wracking possessions are present, taken from the African rituals. The Kardek rituals that were retained were veneration of Jesus Christ, communication with the dead and curing by the laying on of hands. It is a unique, hybrid religion with some 500 churches and meeting places across Brazil.

At last the majority of Brazilians had found a religion with which they could identify. At an Umbanda session the spirits spoke in Portuguese, not in African dialects. One could converse directly with the Old Slave, the Devil and even the Virgin Mary. The spirits advised, they cast spells and they cured. The spirits were with the people, on their level.

Umbanda is full of beliefs, rituals and recipes to smooth out life's daily problems. There are *despachos* (appeasements) to the spirits for everything. If a shopkeeper wants success in business he lights three candles to Ogun behind his closed shop door and hangs up a carved jacaranda fist called the *figa*. If a girl wants a missing lover to return home, she lights three candles on the beach at midnight and throws such gifts as flowers, combs, perfume or champagne into the sea for Iemanja. If a man wants to win a court case he makes a photostat copy of all

C. Waterson

Foto Hetzel

the important documents and buries them at the base of a tree standing at a deserted crossroads; then he lights seven candles to Exu and pours a bottle of cheap whisky over the tree's roots. He also leaves a fresh cigar and an unopened box of matches for the spirit. When he wins the case he brings a whole box of fine cigars and a better brand of whisky in gratitude for the spirit's services.

Meeting a Secular Need

Brazil is a gigantic, sprawling land and it is difficult for the bureaucratic federal government to supply the populace with their basic needs. Both the Kardek churches and the Umbanda temples have therefore set up schools, orphanages, homes for old people, free clinics and pharmacies for their members. These charitable institutions far outnumber anything established by the government or the local Roman Catholic Church. Spirit doctors perform an important service in a nation where the ratio is around one doctor for every 4400 citizens. In some areas of the interior there is no doctor for 15,000 square miles and the people depend on spirit doctors and priests for cures. Whether the treatment is completely effective or not is not the point; the important thing is that the people do not feel abandoned. 'To be an Umbandista,' a popular saying goes, 'is to practise good for others'.

The Roman Catholic Church has made some attempt to combat spiritism in Brazil but has completely failed. Some years ago a young Franciscan priest named Bonaventura Kloppenburg was appointed by the Vatican to denounce the various religions and reveal them, on television and in meeting halls, as fraudulent. He lectured and travelled around the nation; he made tables 'talk' and defied curses and hexes. Once he even healed a boy who was blind. He became a celebrity in his own right and was called to Rome where he tried to tell Pope Pius XII all about Brazilian spiritism. Later John XXIII asked the young priest to stop his work against the spirits and help him organize the Vatican II Congress. No one replaced him in his fight against the spirit religions.

It must be emphasized that the followers of spiritism in Brazil are not just the poorer, blacker and more ignorant classes. Such lines of wealth, race and education cannot be drawn. While it is true that the upper classes will deny their beliefs when asked about them by a foreigner, they will never do anything against a spirit organization nor belittle any deity or ritual. Almost everyone in Brazil has a friend or a relative who was cured, hexed or saved by a spirit. Wealthier homes may have a Picasso print in the living-room but they will almost always have an image of Iemanja or the Old Slave in a back bedroom. Appeasements to the gods can be seen glowing under neon lights on fashionable street corners. Steaks, bottles of alcohol and dishes of cornmeal are set out to the gods in central areas of Rio de Janeiro, yet starving dogs and hungry humans never touch them. Each New Year's Eve, Copacabana beach, Rio de Janeiro's wealthy coastal area, is filled with thousands of spirit believers who come to honour Iemanja. They wear full white skirts or white shirts and trousers. They light candles in the sand and beat on drums, and strew the beach with flowers and gifts. Some of them will sacrifice chickens or goats. Then at midnight, as fireworks are exploding and radios from the expensive beach-front apartments play *Auld Lang Syne*, they surge into the ocean tossing presents and praying to the goddess.

The rest of South America has accepted the teachings of the Vatican almost completely. The Spaniards, who conquered the whole of South America except Brazil and the Guianas, were devout and merciless Catholics. There are a few pockets in Ecuador, Peru, Bolivia and northern Argentina where Inca gods and beliefs are still venerated, but these ceremonies are heavily laced with Catholic ritual and ideas. The few Inca festivities that have remained take place under the tolerant eyes of local padres. Almost nothing is left of the rituals once observed by the Indians of Paraguay. Moslem mosques can be found in Guyana and Surinam because of the large immigrant population from India. Negroes from Colombia, Surinam, Guyana and French Guiana have a kind of 'voodoo' that is closer to the New Orleans and Haitian versions than the spiritism of Brazil.

(See also NEW RELIGIOUS MOVEMENTS.)

DAVID ST CLAIR

FURTHER READING: D. St Clair, *Drum and Candle* (Macdonald, 1971).

JOANNA SOUTHCOTT

'WAR, DISEASE, crime and banditry will increase until the Bishops open Joanna Southcott's box' – so say the advertisements which the Panacea Society of Bedford, England, still place in newspapers. The society is the descendant of the groups of people who surrounded a remarkable prophetess of the early years of the 19th century. A dairy-maid, turned domestic servant, born in Devonshire in 1750, Joanna Southcott had joined the Methodists in 1791, but only a year later had discovered that hers was no ordinary vocation but that she was indeed the 'woman clothed with the sun' of Revelation, chapter 12. This assurance was backed up by a prophetic gift which caused an enormous amount of stir in the Exeter area, so much so that by 1801 she had been carefully vetted by the Rev T. P. Foley, an Anglican rector, who pronounced himself convinced and was rewarded by Joanna by being named as one of the stars which adorned her crown.

In essence, her teaching was simple. She saw that as man had first been led astray by a woman, so by another woman would he be saved. In Christian thought this parallelism is, of course, already present in the comparison between Eve and the 'second Eve' – the Virgin Mary who, as the Mother of Christ, is the instrument of man's redemption from the original sin precipitated by the first woman.

Joanna Southcott, however, took this second Eve to be herself and set about establishing her followers as the 144,000 of the elect who were to be saved (Revelation, chapter 7). She 'sealed' them into the faith and about 14,000 people took part in such ceremonies – each paying between 12 shillings and 21 shillings for the privilege. Her followers were called upon to observe many of the Jewish laws and particular emphasis was laid upon keeping the Sabbath as well as attention to the dietary restrictions of the Old Testament. She presented each of those who were 'sealed' with a signed certificate, on which was written: 'The

Sealed of the Lord – the Elect-Precious Man's Redemption – To inherit the Tree of Life – To be made Heirs of God and Joint-Heirs with Jesus Christ.' Those who received the paper were said to be already saved.

Unfortunately, in 1809, one of the elect was hanged for murder and thus some doubt was cast on the infallibility of Joanna's selection procedures. She therefore ceased the practice but continued to bombard the bishops of the Church of England, the peers of the realm, and every member of the House of Commons with letters putting forward her views. In all, Joanna Southcott produced some 60 publications, and her correspondence books as well as some writing in her own shorthand are preserved. It is, however, not by her known writings that she is best remembered, but through the two remarkable claims she made. She left behind her a sealed box which was only to be opened by the bishops of the Church as foretold in the Apocalypse. It was this 'ark' which contained the revelations necessary to avoid the dire consequences mentioned by the Panacea Society in its advertisements, and it was the guardianship of this box and the continued pressure on the bishops to open it which has kept the Southcottians alive for nearly 200 years.

More remarkable at the time was Joanna Southcott's assertion that she was about to give birth to Shiloh, the Prince of Peace and the male child destined to rule the nations with a rod of iron (Revelation, chapter 18). She was by then, in 1814, 64 years old and was visited by large numbers of doctors as the phantom pregnancy proceeded. Her followers' hopes were unfounded and she died at the end of the year.

But they were undaunted by the non-appearance of Shiloh and set about arguing among themselves as to who was the true successor of the prophetess. Later the dissension hinged on the theological dispute as to whether Joanna actually gave birth to a spiritual child, or whether instead she would return and actually present the world with a baby.

From these arguments emerged several sects. In the north, the Christian Israelites were founded by John Wroe, while much later, their Chatham branch was taken over by James White and renamed the New and Latter House of Israel. He took the new title of James Jershom Jezreel, and with it the mystic letter J, which stood for Joanna (see JEZREEL). The 'orthodox' followers dwindled away until, by the end of the 19th century, there were only a handful left, mainly concentrated in Walworth, where they met under a railway arch.

An X-ray of Joanna Southcott's second sealed box reveals a pistol but no sealed writings

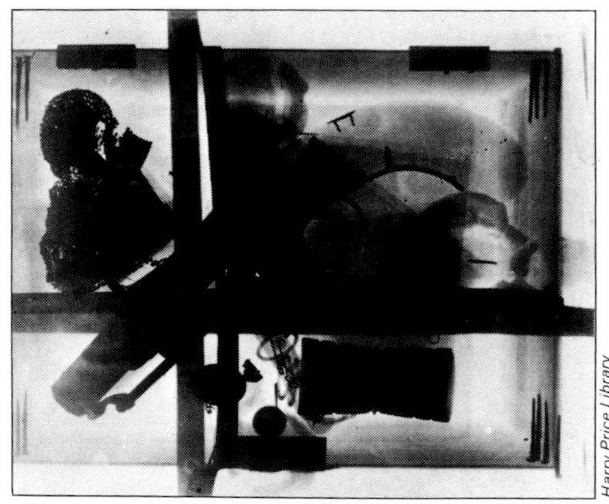

Harry Price Library

The Sealed Box

Yet their story was not over, for in 1902 Alice Seymour was attracted to the sect and began to read Joanna Southcott's writings. In 1909, she published 'The Express', which put forward the Southcottian doctrines again. This proved popular enough for her to set up the Panacea Society, whose activities were mainly concentrated upon getting the Archbishop of Canterbury, Randall Davidson, to open up Joanna Southcott's box. He refused to do this, but the publicity was enormous and finally the box was opened unofficially, in 1927, with no bishops present. It was found to contain a lottery ticket and a woman's nightcap.

Undeterred, the followers of Joanna Southcott claimed that this had been the wrong box and that they still retained the real one, which was full of sealed writings only waiting for the bishops to open it up. There is no likelihood of this happening, but it says much for the effect of Joanna's writing and for the appeal of the mystery of a locked chest, that even after the mammoth set-backs of the phantom pregnancy and the lottery ticket, there are still those who continue to look back to the prophetess.

JOHN SELWYN GUMMER

SOUTHEAST ASIA

THIS AREA has been the scene of a second flowering of several of the great religions of mankind, but unlike India and western Asia it has not been the birthplace of any religious movement powerful enough to shape the ideology of a civilization. Today Buddhism and, in a few regions, Islam dominate the cultural life of the countries of the Southeast Asian mainland, while Hinduism, though no longer practised to any great extent in its original form, has left its imprint on folk belief and ritual traditions.

Indian cultural influence spread into Southeast Asia as early as the beginning of the Christian era. It was characterized by the introduction of a way of life based on a specific philosophical and religious doctrine. Once accepted, the Hindu ideology provided a total pattern for the organization of the social and political system such as is exemplified by some of the ancient Hindu kingdoms of Southeast Asia, but Hinduism's tolerance of a variety of cultural forms facilitated the assimilation of numerous cultural and indigenous elements. Christianity reached Southeast Asia only during the colonial period, and has become established mainly among certain minority groups, such as some of the hill tribes of Burma and some communities in Vietnam.

Throughout Southeast Asia the historic religions introduced by colonists and missionaries from India and other countries have overlaid ancient indigenous religious traditions; but many of these traditions are still alive and are expressed in ritual practices, even among people who consider themselves Buddhists or Moslems. An analysis of the religious pattern peculiar to Southeast Asia must thus focus on the indigenous religious ideas and attitudes rather than on the doctrines imported from the homelands of such historic religions as Buddhism and Islam. These local religious phenomena are found among populations which have remained untouched by external influences, and in their comparative isolation preserve their traditional way of life. Typical of such populations are the hill tribes of Burma, Thailand and Laos as well as some of the simpler indigenous peoples of Malaya. The Lamets, a primitive hill tribe of Laos, for instance, exemplify by their beliefs in a great variety of supernatural beings, and their complex ritual practices, an ideological system unaffected by any of the higher religions. They share with other tribes the firm conviction that the human personality survives after death, and the ancestor cult occupies a central place in their religious thinking and acting. The Lamets believe that if they look after the spirits of their ancestors properly, they will enjoy good health and prosperity. These spirits are believed to live in the house, and if a new house is built they are formally invited to reside there. They are given sacrifices of buffalo and other animals when any change in the fortunes of a family occurs, such as at marriages, burials and adoptions. The greatest feast, combined with the largest economic expenditure, is directed towards the ancestor spirits, who in return for the sacrifices are expected to give happiness and success in all undertakings of the family. Thus the ancestor cult acts as an important factor in the life of a family, and contributes to a feeling of security.

Many of the religious practices of the Lamets and similar tribes are directed towards the increase of their food supply and specifically towards the prosperity of their crops. The Lamets attribute to the rice a 'soul' which is referred to by the same term as the soul of a human being. The soul of the rice is believed to exist not only in the grains but in the whole plant and indeed in a whole rice field. Numerous rites are concentrated on the rice, and many sacrifices are performed in order to protect the soul, which is the growing power of the rice. Such rites aim not only to increase the crop, but also to keep the harvested rice securely. To a certain degree the 'soul' of the rice is treated like a spirit and equated with the soul which enlivens man.

The coexistence and interpenetration of different religious ideas and practices in Burma may serve as an example of the religious scene in all those countries of Southeast Asia where old beliefs dovetail with the ideology of Buddhism. All tribal populations of Burma, as of other regions of Southeast Asia, share the belief in a multitude of spiritual beings. Among these are personal spirits attached to individuals, family or house spirits, communal spirits, Nature spirits inhabiting forests, hills, streams and lakes, and the disembodied spirits of the deceased. Buddhist Burmese believe in spirits of the same types, and the Buddhists retained and reinterpreted many of the beliefs in supernatural beings held by their pre-Buddhist forbears.

Most prominent among these spirits are the *nats*. They are the objects of an elaborate cult which forms part of an organized religious system. The cult of the nats rivals Buddhism in its elaboration and ideological systematization. The term nat is used to describe supernatural beings of a great variety of types, but in general they are considered more powerful than humans and able to affect men for good or evil. Most distinctive among the nats is a group referred to as the 'Thirty-Seven Nats', each of whom possesses a distinct, historically or mythologically determined identity. They are conceived as the spirits of outstanding men and women, who suffered a violent death, and on account of this became nats. They are potentially dangerous and easily offended, and some of them personify qualities abhorred by Buddhism, such as sexual profligacy, aggression and drunkenness. The festivals connected with their cult express a general saturnalian spirit, and function as an outlet for the human drives frustrated by the puritanical aspects of Buddhism. The cult of the nats received the support of the ancient Burmese kings, and in modern days political leaders have continued to allocate government resources to the maintenance of nat shrines and the lavish performance of festivals in the honour of these spirits.

Distinct from the nats with malevolent tendencies are benevolent spiritual beings who protect men and accede to their prayers for help. Among them are the gods of the Buddhist pantheon, whose images stand on the platforms of many pagodas, where they enjoy the worship of those visiting the Buddhist sanctuaries. The assistance of these deities is invoked by ritual offerings of food consisting of fruits and other vegetarian items.

In Burma and other countries of Southeast Asia, there is also a widespread belief in ghosts and demons. Among the ghosts are the souls of those dead who were denied proper mortuary rites and therefore remain near houses and settlements and haunt the inhabitants. Since any soul is potentially dangerous, certain rites are performed to prevent it from remaining attached to the scene of its previous existence. In the case of government officials, for instance, it was customary to prepare a special document, signed by the superior officer of the deceased,

Picturepoint, London

Popperfoto

Picturepoint, London

In Southeast Asia the worship of a multitude of spirits dovetails with Buddhism: spirits are propitiated to obtain earthly benefits, while Buddhism is the means of obtaining spiritual goals *Top* Buddhist priest at Angkor Wat, Cambodia *Centre* Buddhist priests in the gallery of the Reclining Buddha Temple, Bangkok *Bottom* A family shrine in a Balinese village; the appeasement of spirits is still an important feature of everyday life

discharging the soul from all connections with his past position. Such discharge statements were often buried in the grave with the deceased.

Cannibal Ghosts

Ghosts are thought to be usually invisible, but to become visible in certain circumstances. Those claiming to have seen ghosts describe them as monstrous in size and terrifying in appearance. They are believed to feed on corpses, but to enjoy also the flesh of living persons whom they attack when particularly hungry or malevolent. Children are believed to be specially vulnerable to an attack by ghosts. Epidemics are attributed to the action of ghosts or evil spirits, and if an epidemic breaks out, special rites are performed to drive away the supernatural being responsible.

Ghosts and evil spirits can be controlled by practitioners of witchcraft, and those who obtain power over a spirit can compel him to do their bidding. The belief in witches is widespread, but the Burmese distinguish between those witches whose powers are innate and those whose powers are self-acquired. The former, who have become witches on account of evil deeds in a previous existence, are more powerful than those who have learned the art of sorcery. Not only can they cause illness and death, but they can transform themselves into animals and fly through the air. Sexual jealousy is a frequent motive for the malice of witches, for witches are not immune from falling in love, and they attack those who frustrate their desires.

To ward off the attacks of witches the Burmese employ various types of protection. They place trays of food outside the house, in the hope that the witch will eat of the food and desist from harming the inhabitants, or alternatively obtain protection by wearing amulets. If these preventive measures are ineffective and a witch has caused a person to fall ill, the only remedy is exorcism. Should this fail too, so that the patient dies, attempts are made to take revenge on the witch by enlisting a more powerful witch or sorcerer.

Although in Burma and in other Southeast Asian countries some intellectuals educated in Western ways of thinking are sceptical about the power of spirits and witches, the great majority of the population believes implicitly in supernatural beings of various types. This belief is in accordance with Buddhist doctrine, which acknowledges the reality not only of gods but also of harmful supernaturals. Buddhist cosmology postulates six realms, inhabited by gods, humans, demons, ghosts, infernal beings and animals, and those believing in the existence of such beings in their appropriate realm find no difficulty in accepting the idea of their influence on human affairs.

The Buddhist Way of Life

Although the belief in gods, spirits and ghosts is firmly rooted in the thought of the people of Southeast Asia, there exists a clear division between these supernatural cults and the Buddhist religion. Gods and spirits, and in Burma specifically the great nats, are propitiated in order to obtain benefits in the mundane sphere, while Buddhism is the exclusive means for attaining otherworldly goals. To avoid rebirth in one of the subhuman realms, to achieve rebirth in the celestial abode of the gods, or to escape altogether from the cycle of rebirth and achieve the state of ultimate liberation known as Nirvana, are goals which can be achieved only by Buddhist means. Exertions in the worship of nats or other spirits have no influence on the attainment of these goals. Buddhist ritual and the cult of the nats of Burma, or equivalent supernaturals in other countries, appear thus as two distinct religious systems, though in popular practice there is some overlap, and Buddhist means are sometimes used to achieve worldly ends.

The values of Buddhism, however, clearly dominate the ethical outlook of the majority of the peoples of Southeast Asia. This is reflected in the veneration accorded to those whose conduct exemplifies the Buddhist way of life. The monk who has renounced the world and devotes his life to meditation and religious practices is highly respected by all sections of the population. To the people of the countries within its cultural influence Buddhism is the measure of all things and the criterion by which all ideas and all conduct are judged.

Not only the monks who have dedicated their lives to the pursuance of Buddhist ideals but also the ordinary laymen are conscious of the desirability of obtaining merit in the terms of Buddhist doctrine. Thus in Thailand, villagers regularly perform various acts with the specific intention of increasing their store of merit. Providing food for monks is the most common way to acquire merit, and as Thai monks are no longer wandering ascetics, but normally live in village monasteries, the monks do not go with their begging bowl from house to house, but are daily brought food by the village women. In the monastery the women serve the monks, watch them eat and receive the monks' blessings. The construction or the repair of a temple, the attendance of calendrical rites at a temple combined with the giving of gifts, and the strict observation of the principal Buddhist precepts, especially the avoidance of the taking of life and the excessive use of intoxicants, all rank highly as ways of acquiring merit.

Buddhism is the national religion not only of Burma and Thailand, but also of Cambodia, Laos and Vietnam. In all these countries, both of the main branches of Buddhism, known respectively as Mahayana and Theravada, flourished at various times over more than a millennium, but in recent centuries the Theravada ideology, which prevails also in Ceylon, has in most regions attained prominence at the expense of Mahayana sects. The function fulfilled by Buddhism in the countries of Southeast Asia resembles the role played by Christianity during a large part of the history of the West. As the state religion it is a symbol of national and social cohesion, and enjoys the protection of the king or the head of state. Religious and moral education is largely in the hands of the Buddhist clergy, and the monks have been the main agents in the spread of literacy. In these countries it is customary that at least once in their life all young men spend several months as novices in a monastery, and during that time they wear the saffron robe and lead the celibate life of monks. This practice tends to even out social differences, for all monks, from whatever social stratum, are regarded as equals and are subject to the same rules. Apart from the purely religious instruction given in the monasteries, much of the general education is imparted by members of the clergy, and the classical languages of the Buddhist scriptures, Pali and Sanskrit, occupy a position comparable to that which Latin used to occupy in the Christian world. In these countries the Buddhist 'Church' *(sangha)* also maintains such charitable institutions as hospitals and orphanages, for the emphasis on the importance of compassion and charity has always been a characteristic feature of Buddhist societies.

Even though Buddhism preaches detachment from worldly affairs, the members of the clergy as representatives of a state religion have sometimes been drawn into political controversies, and within the Buddhist Church there are two distinct trends. The more conservative elements advocate a certian aloofness from secular problems and seek to influence the faithful simply by their example of adhering strictly to the austere pattern of the traditional monastic life. Others wish to modernize the Buddhist community and to participate more actively in the secular life in order to make it into a more useful and positive force, and prevent its decline into insignificance. In all those Southeast Asian countries which have not fallen under the sway of Communism, Buddhism has so far retained a considerable vitality, and its ideological primacy is not seriously threatened. (See also BUDDHISM; SINHALESE BUDDHISM.)

There is only one country on the mainland of Southeast Asia where Buddhism has virtually disappeared from the scene. In Malaya, Buddhist sects were already active in the first centuries of our era, and in the 8th century the Mahayana doctrine was introduced from Sumatra. But with the coming of Islam in the 14th century, and its rapid acceptance by nearly the whole of the Malay population, Buddhism as an organized religion met its doom. Many of the indigenous folk beliefs and practices have survived, however, and the Malayan Moslem is no less inclined to believe in spirits, ghosts and the power of exorcists than the Buddhist of Burma or Thailand. Thus a common sub-stratum of archaic religious concepts and practices persists throughout Southeast Asia irrespective of the nature of the historic religion which their inhabitants officially profess.

C. VON FÜRER-HAIMENDORF

FURTHER READING: Melford E. Spiro, *Burmese Supernaturalism* (Inst. Study Human, 1978); C. Coedes, *The Making of South East Asia* (Univ. of California Press, 1969); Maung Htin Aung, *Burmese Buddhism* (Oxford Univ. Press, 1966).

Mansell Collection

When the apostles met on the day of Pentecost, 'they were all filled with the Holy Spirit and began to speak in other tongues': glossolalia has recurred on rare occasions ever since, and has greatly increased in recent years

SPEAKING IN TONGUES

SPEAKING IN TONGUES, or glossolalia, is best known as the practice of Pentecostalists (see PENTECOSTALIST MOVEMENT) but it is very much older than the Pentecostalist movement and, in recent years, the incidence of glossolalic experience within Christendom has extended far beyond the boundaries of the various Pentecostal denominations and sects. Although there is some evidence of glossolalia in the Old Testament and in ancient Egypt, and reports of it in China and among various tribes in Africa and Burma, it is in Christianity that speaking in tongues is best recorded and has been of most significance doctrinally.

Although the authenticity of the text is disputed by scholars, there is in the gospel of Mark (16.17) a promise concerning tongues. In Acts (chapter 2) the outbreak of speech in unknown tongues on the occasion of Pentecost is recorded. A case at Caesarea is reported in Acts 10.44–46, and the speaking in tongues at the baptism by the Holy Spirit in Acts 19.1–7. St Paul describes the gift of speaking in unknown tongues as a gift of the Holy Spirit in I Corinthians,

***The Descent of the Holy Spirit,* by Pinturicchio; Acts, chapter 2, describes the experience of Christ's disciples at Pentecost, when they 'began to speak in other tongues, as the Spirit gave them utterance'**

chapters 12 to 14, and specifies the circumstances of the use of this gift. Pentecostal writers usually also consider that the gifts of the Spirit are alluded to in I Thessalonians 5.19–20, Ephesians 5.18–20, and in the Old Testament in Joel (2.23 and 28–29) and Isaiah (28.9–11).

The nature and purpose of speaking in unknown tongues has been disputed, but Paul appears to have regarded the use of unknown tongues at Corinth as ecstatic utterance that was not to be understood

iiij. tenere dicitur passuum: paulatim altitudo angustior coartata erat. ut pondus imminens facilius sustentaret
Hanc turrem nembroth gigas construxerat. Qui post confusionem linguarum migravit inde ad persas. eosque ignem colere docuit.

except by divine inspiration. On the other hand, the scriptures make clear that when the apostles spoke with tongues at Pentecost, the Jews who had gathered, and who spoke many different languages, all heard them each in his own native language. However, some have regarded that incident as a miracle of hearing rather than of speech.

The Church Fathers had relatively little to say of the phenomenon of glossolalia, and it may be that after the early development of Christianity speaking in tongues became disregarded, except among those whose Christianity was doubtful or heretical, the Montanists being a case in point (see MONTANISTS). Subsequently theologians believed that the gift of tongues was not a permanent endowment, but was a sign confirming the divine authority of the teachings of Christ, especially adapted for the proclamation of the gospel in the beginning, but thereafter withdrawn. Nor did they continue to expect evidence of the baptism of the Holy Spirit such as occurred at Ephesus (Acts, chapter 19).

As the Church became fully institutionalized, control of its practices led to a severe circumscription of inspiration. The view that generally prevailed, instanced by the stories of St Pachomius, St Hildegard and later St Francis Xavier, was that God might grant men a gift of tongues, which was in fact a gift of languages, for scholarly purposes or, more usually, for promulgating his word among the heathen. Unknown tongues were clearly much more suspect and more readily simulated, and increasingly were looked upon as dubious if not heretical: most of those who gave utterance of this kind were already recognizable as heretics from their teachings.

Tarrying Meetings

A considerable number of Protestant sects have experienced glossolalia at different times. The most celebrated are the Camisards, among whom a number of children suddenly broke out into speeches in eloquent French that was considered far beyond their natural capacity (see CAMISARDS). In the 1780s, Mother Ann Lee, who had become the leader of a small religious group in Lancashire known as Shakers (see SHAKERS), whose origin is traced to the missionary activities of refugee Camisards, spoke in a number of apparently recognizable languages.

During the Welsh Revival of 1904–5 a number of converts who spoke little or no Welsh suddenly broke out into eloquent prayer in that language, which impressed observers. One of those who was deeply influenced by what he saw in Wales was an Anglican clergyman, the Rev Alexander A. Boddy who, in 1907, as Rector of All Saints, Monkwearmouth, was a leading figure in England in introducing 'tarrying meetings' at which believers prayed together for the descent of the Holy Ghost upon them and its manifestation by glossolalic utterance. The expectation of such experience had arisen principally in Holiness groups (see HOLINESS MOVEMENT) in the United States between 1901 and 1906, and had spread to Europe in that year, after T. B. Barratt, Methodist minister in Oslo, had been converted to the new movement, Pentecostalism.

The Pentecostal denominations, which trace their beginning to the American meetings at which Barratt experienced glossolalia, were not, however, the first Christian denominations to incorporate the gift of tongues in their regular worship. In 1830 a reputedly dying woman in Scotland was reported to have spoken in unknown tongues and to have instantly recovered her health. The news fired the interest of a group of devout Christians gathered round Edward Irving, a celebrated Presbyterian preacher, who soon after established his own Catholic and Apostolic Church, in which glossolalia became a dominant feature (see IRVING). For the Irvingites, tongues were a distinct sign of the nearness of the coming of Christ, and they devoted themselves to warning the established Churches of the need to accept Irvingite teaching and organization before it was too late. Tongues had also broken out spontaneously in a church in southern Germany, and this congregation joined the Catholic and Apostolic Church, which enjoyed rapid growth, in particular in the United States and Britain. Tongues continued as part of its devotional practice until, disappointed in the falsification of the prophecies on which the Church was based, the movement went into a decline in the 20th century.

Gift of the Spirit

Although the gift of tongues is officially accepted as part of Mormon belief, its practice was never of great importance in that movement. Only in contemporary Pentecostal churches is speaking in tongues a well-integrated, theologically justified and spiritually essential element of religious belief and practice. The need for the experience of the baptism of the Holy Spirit was accepted by many Holiness believers before speaking in tongues had actually occurred, but the full theological justification for glossolalia, and the distinction of the different occasions of its occurrence were only gradually worked out. Inevitably, some differences in doctrine arose between the various groups who came to accept tongues as an authentic experience prompted by the Holy Spirit but there is, despite differences of detail, broad agreement among Pentecostal bodies in respect of these phenomena, which are indeed the determining factors in the distinctiveness and separation of Pentecostal groups from other evangelical fundamentalist Protestant bodies.

Pentecostalists distinguish between two main occasions and one subsidiary occasion when glossolalia might occur. The first of the two principal circumstances in which a

William Sargant

British Museum

Left **The Tower of Babel, French, 15th century: the original 'confusion of tongues', the many languages of humanity, was said to have resulted from man's attempt to ascend to heaven, while the gift of speaking in tongues is said to come from the descent of the Holy Spirit from heaven**

Right **Worshipper believed to be possessed by the Spirit, in Barbados**

Giraudon

Illustration from a 15th century French Book of Hours, showing the Holy Spirit as a dove descending at Pentecost: St Peter described the event as a fulfilment of Old Testament prophecy

believer might speak in tongues is on receiving the baptism of the Holy Spirit. This baptism is an event that occurs after conversion, sometimes months or even years after, although there is a tendency for it to be expected sooner rather than later. Its purpose is to confer power for God's service, and it is said to prepare men for deeper communion with God and better understanding of his gospel. Not all Pentecostalists believe that the baptism must be marked by glossolalia, although all agree that it is a charismatic experience of transcendent and miraculous character, producing extraordinary effects that are visible to the onlooker. In practice, it is almost always assumed that the baptism will be evidenced by glossolalic utterance.

The baptism of the Holy Spirit is an event that occurs only once to a believer, but after the baptism he may receive one or more of the gifts of the Holy Spirit. These gifts are listed in I Corinthians, chapter 12, as: the word of wisdom; the word of knowledge; faith; the gifts of healing; the working of miracles; prophecy; discerning of spirits; various kinds of tongues; the interpretation of tongues. Without doubt the gift most frequently claimed by Pentecostalists is the gift of tongues, even though Paul regarded it as one of the lesser gifts. The gift is not at the disposal of the recipient, so contemporary Pentecostals insist: it is a gift to the Church rather than to the individual, and it should be used as the Holy Spirit directs.

Following St Paul, the large Pentecostal denominations expect there to be only two, or at most three, speakers in tongues at any one meeting. It is said that many who receive messages in tongues may never be anointed to speak forth, and it is also maintained that the Spirit is always 'subject' and need never cause a speaker to burst forth in tongues when someone else is speaking or, indeed, at an inopportune moment in the meeting. Insistence on this precept has, of course, improved the order and decorousness of Pentecostal meetings. The glossolalia occurring at the baptism of the Holy Spirit requires no interpretation, but at other times Pentecostalists maintain that when someone uses the gift of tongues there should be an interpretation from a person with this gift who is inspired by the Spirit to speak. The interpreter must be the same for all messages received in one meeting, and may be one of those who has spoken in tongues.

In the early days of Pentecostalism, before these precepts were well established, speaking in tongues was much more frequent in the meetings than (at least in the larger denominations) it is now, and often several spoke in tongues simultaneously. In the early days some used the claim to Holy Spirit inspiration to work off spites, to upbraid rivals, and to acquire influence in Church affairs. Pentecostals have increasingly come to stress that messages given in tongues must be in confirmation of the Bible, and today the interpretations often tend to be exhortatory messages, quoting or paraphrasing passages of scripture.

The third, and very much the least important, use of glossolalia is in the devotional exercise known as 'singing in the Spirit', which is merely a particular way in which God may be praised quietly in public, or in private, by a believer who has the gift of tongues. This use of tongues requires no interpretation. Pentecostalists acknowledge that the gift of tongues can be easily simulated, and it has become a general and informal assumption that the ministers of the Pentecostal churches possess the gift of the discernment of spirits, by which they are enabled to distinguish genuine from doubtful gifts, and on the authority of which they may counsel individuals to desist.

The Lost and the Last

In general, it is believed that the unknown tongues given to believers are all actual languages of some people who have lived on earth, even though they may be no longer spoken. Pentecostal writers claim many occasions when foreigners have recognized their own language spoken perfectly by someone speaking under the power of the Holy Spirit, but such demonstrations of the miraculous cannot, of course, be prearranged. The theoretical justification for glossolalia is not its possible practical use, but simply that God wishes to be praised in all languages, and that it is spiritually beneficial for man to have the experience.

There is no obvious or pre-ordained form for glossolalic utterance. Many speakers in unknown tongues do not appear to be speaking a language, but rather to be uttering a few repeated syllables, often in a rhythmic and lilting way. Many of those who speak in tongues are people whose powers of articulation in ordinary speech are rather limited, and such evidence as is available suggests that women are more frequent speakers in tongues than men.

Those who have been converted to the modern Pentecostal movement come very largely from the least educated sections of the population, and some Pentecostal writers have boasted that their fellow religionists are 'the lowest, the least, the lost and the last' among men. On the other hand, the Irvingite congregations of the last century were drawn much more extensively from the middle and upper classes. Glossolalia demands an atmosphere of considerable emotional freedom, and is itself a means by which inhibitions are reduced.

The incidence of glossolalia has probably very much increased during the last decade, with the development of a large number of informal prayer meetings by small groups of orthodox Christians who have become convinced of the authenticity and desirability of glossolalic experience. This 'charismatic movement' is now well organized, and its membership includes priests and prominent laymen from the Roman Catholic and Anglican churches and from the major Protestant denominations. Among its well established organizations is the Full Gospel Business Men's Fellowship International, but there are also many small groups in which speaking with tongues occurs.

BRYAN WILSON

FURTHER READING: N. Bloch-Hoell, *The Pentecostal Movement* (Humanities Press, 1965); C. Brumbach, *What Meaneth This?* (Gospel Publishing House); D. Gee, *Why Pentecost?* (Elim Publishing House, 1944); M. T. Kelsey, *Speaking with Tongues* (Epworth Press, London, 1965); *Catholic Pentecostals Now,* ed. by J. Kerkhofs (Alba Books, 1977).

Spectre

From Latin *spectrum,* 'vision', a ghost or apparition, especially one which is frightening: the Spectre of the Brocken is a huge shadow, often accompanied by rings of coloured light, cast by an observer on top of a hill on the upper surfaces of clouds which are below him.

See GHOSTS; HAUNTED HOUSES; SPONTANEOUS PSI EXPERIENCES.

Spell

A word, set of words or procedure, frequently of a relatively minor kind, believed to have magical effect: an enchantment, as in the case of a person or country which has been placed under a spell.

See INCANTATION; PSYCHIC ATTACK.

Layton-Sun

Sphere

One of the hollow, transparent, concentric globes formerly believed to revolve round the earth, carrying with them the sun, moon and planets; their motion was thought to produce a harmonious sound, the 'music of the spheres'; allotting one sphere to the Prime Mover, the fixed stars, and each of the seven planets, gave a total of nine, with the earth at the centre; or the earth itself could be allotted a sphere, making ten, as in the Cabala.

See CABALA; MAGIC.

Sphinx

Hybrid creature combining human and animal parts, typically a lion's body and the head of a man (or sometimes of a hawk or ram): pairs or avenues of sphinxes guarded the entrances to palaces, temples and tombs in Egypt; the Great Sphinx is a colossal image near the pyramids of Giza; in Greek mythology, the woman-headed Sphinx of Thebes strangled passers-by when they failed to solve the riddle she put to them.

See RIDDLES.

SPIDER

'WILL YOU come into my parlour, said the spider to the fly?'. The spider inevitably suggests an evil arch-intriguer, weaving a web of duplicity in which fragile innocence is entrapped, or a blood-sucking money-lender who entangles the unwary borrower in his toils. In fact, the spider is as much preyed on as predator, providing food for lizards, wasps and other foes, and it is ironic that the fly, a creature of dirt and disease, should be equated with the innocent victim who is ensnared.

Some people have a deep loathing of spiders and could not bear to touch one, but although the spider can be a type of evil and betrayal, and so of Satan, it has also been seen as a model of industry and wisdom, and a spider motif engraved on a precious stone makes a talisman which is supposed to confer foresight on the wearer.

Attitudes to spiders vary considerably, in fact. In West African and West Indian folklore, there is a great body of stories about Ananse, or Anansi, a spider who is a hero and trickster of infinite cunning and resource, and in some cases the Creator of the world. In European lore the spider spun a web to conceal the child Jesus from his enemies, and spiders also saved the lives of Mohammed and Frederick the Great. The famous story of Robert the Bruce and the spider points the moral that faith and persistence can bring victory out of defeat. Or the spider's web can be regarded as the home of the eternal weaver of illusions, and the spider which spins and kills, creates and destroys, can symbolize the perpetual alternation of forces on which life depends for its precarious balance.

The cross on the back of the common garden spider has helped to preserve it from the hostility of mankind, and the spider, like the toad, has played an important part in the folklore of medicine, since both creatures were believed to contain within their bodies a powerful health-giving stone. The 17th century antiquarian Elias Ashmole claimed to have cured himself of the ague by suspending three spiders around his neck. To relieve whooping cough it was once customary to wrap a spider in raisin

靱負尉碓井貞光

Victoria and Albert Museum

Left and above **'Earth Spider making magic in the palace of Raiko', a triptych by Kuniyoshi: the warrior Raiko is lying sick while his guards are playing *go* and the Earth Spider marshals its hordes of goblins above them; the picture was a satire on contemporary politicians**

or butter, or shut one in a walnut shell, the malady fading away as the spider died. Spider's web was used as a bandage for wounds and was supposed to cure warts.

On the other hand, in Suffolk in 1645, an accused witch named Mirabel Bedford admitted possessing a familiar imp in the form of a spider called Joan. In another trial, one of the accused defended himself with such eloquence as almost to sway the court in his favour, until the prosecutor noticed a spider crawling close to the prisoner's lips and cried out warningly, 'See who prompts him'. The prisoner was sentenced to death.

Spider's venom was once in demand as poison, and in Shakespeare's *Winter's Tale*, Leontes remarks, 'There may be in the cup a spider steeped'. The bite or sting of the tarantula spider was supposed to cause Tarantism, a hysterical disease characterized by an extreme impulse to dance, and the Italian Tarantella was a wild dance which was thought to be the only cure for it.

The golden money spider, the living symbol of a gold coin, confers riches on anyone upon whose body it runs, and if caught and put in the pocket ensures plenty of ready cash, or a new suit of clothes. The superstition is current in Norfolk that a money spider suspended over the head is a charm for winning the football pools.

'If you would live and thrive, let a spider run alive' is an old saying. In Britain to kill a spider brings unwanted rain, and in Scotland and the West Indies the spider-killer is sure to break his crockery or his wine glasses before the day is out. The appearance of numerous spiders is a sign of much rain. A long thread of spider's web hanging from a tree or a beam symbolizes the ladder or rope by which you can ascend to heaven, and if you should find a web inscribed with your initials near the door of your house, it will bring you luck as long as you live there.

ERIC MAPLE

Spinning

Activity symbolically connected with fate; in classical mythology the three Fates spin the thread of each man's life, weave it, and sever it; the fact that spiders spin webs to catch flies has contributed to their folklore and symbolism.

See FATE; SPIDER.

Spirit

Related to Latin *spirare*, 'to breathe', the animating principle in living things, contrasted with the body or matter: a being or intelligence which has no earthly body, or is separated from it, such as an angel, demon, fairy, ghost or poltergeist: sometimes equivalent to 'soul', or sometimes distinguished from it, when man is said to be made of body, soul (roughly, emotions and feelings) and spirit (mental faculties).

See ANIMISM; BREATH; GHOSTS; GUARDIAN SPIRITS; POLTERGEISTS; SHAMAN; SOUL; SPIRITUALISM.

SPIRITUALISM

Offering man a new view of the universe and proof of survival after death, Spiritualist beliefs derive from communications believed to emanate from the spirits of the dead

THE TERM Spiritualism has been used to refer to two distinct types of ideas. In the 18th and 19th centuries it referred to those philosophical theories which held that spirit was the ultimate reality. Today the term is used to denote a movement which is characterized by two major beliefs; that the human personality, in some form, survives the death of the body, and secondly that it is possible to communicate with the spirits of the dead. During the 19th century the critics and opponents of modern Spiritualism used the word Spiritism to describe the movement.

A belief in spirits is not restricted to modern Spiritualists, indeed as the anthropologist Sir Edward Tylor suggested in his study of *Primitive Culture* (1871), a belief in spirits is a universal feature of human societies (see ANIMISM). This is linked with a belief in life after death and that spirits may be contacted by the living. Amongst the earliest forms of religious specialists were the shamans and spirit mediums who in different ways were concerned with the contact between the 'spirit' world and the human world (see PRIESTS; SHAMAN).

It has been claimed that Christianity itself originated as a 'spiritualist' movement and that Jesus himself was a highly-developed medium. Spiritualists have argued that such an interpretation enables us to understand the 'miraculous' elements in the biblical accounts of the life of Jesus. There is also evidence which indicates that mediumship was practised in the early Christian Church, but it had certainly ceased to be a regular feature of Christian practice before the 3rd century AD, although the Church continued to recognize the possibility of occasional communications with saints and angels.

The Reformation led to what the sociologist Max Weber described as 'disenchantment', a growing disbelief in the supernatural associated with the rise of rationalism and modern science. By the 18th century rationalism was triumphant amongst the educated classes in Western Europe but while rationalism was still growing, a reaction against the extreme forms of materialism was already appearing. Within Christianity this reaction took the form of the development of mystical movements, such as the Quakers and the Quietists, and of 'enthusiastic' movements such as Methodism. But the sources of modern Spiritualism are to be found outside the Christian tradition, in the work of the alchemists, in the theories of Paracelsus, of Franz Mesmer and Emmanuel Swedenborg (see ALCHEMY; MAGNETISM; MESMER; PARACELSUS; SWEDENBORG), in ideas derived from eastern religions and from contact with the shamanistic practices of the North American Indians.

The modern Spiritualist movement arose in America in 1848 as a result of the publicity given to the events that occurred in the home of the Fox family in Hydesville, a small hamlet in New York state. The Fox family moved into the house in December 1847, and for the next three months they were disturbed by strange noises that frequently kept them awake at night. The family consisted of John Fox, his wife and two young daughters, Margaretta and Kate. On Friday 31 March 1848 the family retired to bed early. Mrs Fox described the events of that night in the following statement:

> It was very early when we went to bed on this night – hardly dark. I had been so broken of rest I was almost sick – I had just lain down when it commenced as usual – the children, who slept in the other bed in the room, heard the rapping, and tried to make similar sounds by snapping their fingers.
>
> My youngest child, Cathie, said: 'Mr Splitfoot, do as I do', clapping her hands. The sound instantly followed her with the same number of raps. When she stopped the sound ceased for a short time.
>
> Then Margaretta said, in sport: 'Now do just as I do. Count one, two, three, four, striking one hand against the other at the same time' – and the raps came as before. She was afraid to repeat them.
>
> I then thought I could put a test that no one in the place could answer. I asked the 'noise' to rap my different children's ages successively.
>
> Instantly, each one of my children's ages was given correctly, pausing between them sufficiently long enough to individualise them until the seventh – at which a longer pause was made, and then three more emphatic raps were given, corresponding to the age of the little one that died, which was my youngest child.
>
> I then asked: 'Is this a human being that answers my questions correctly?'
>
> There was no rap.
>
> I asked: 'Is it a spirit? If it is, make two raps.'
>
> Two sounds were given as soon as the request was made.

Left **The Fox sisters, who in 1848 claimed to have discovered a way of communicating with the spirit of a dead man: the intense interest this aroused was the starting point of the modern Spiritualist movement** ***Right*** **That the dead can communicate with the living is, of course, a very old belief: a ghost warns of approaching doom in this illustration from** ***The Astrologer of the 19th century***

British Museum

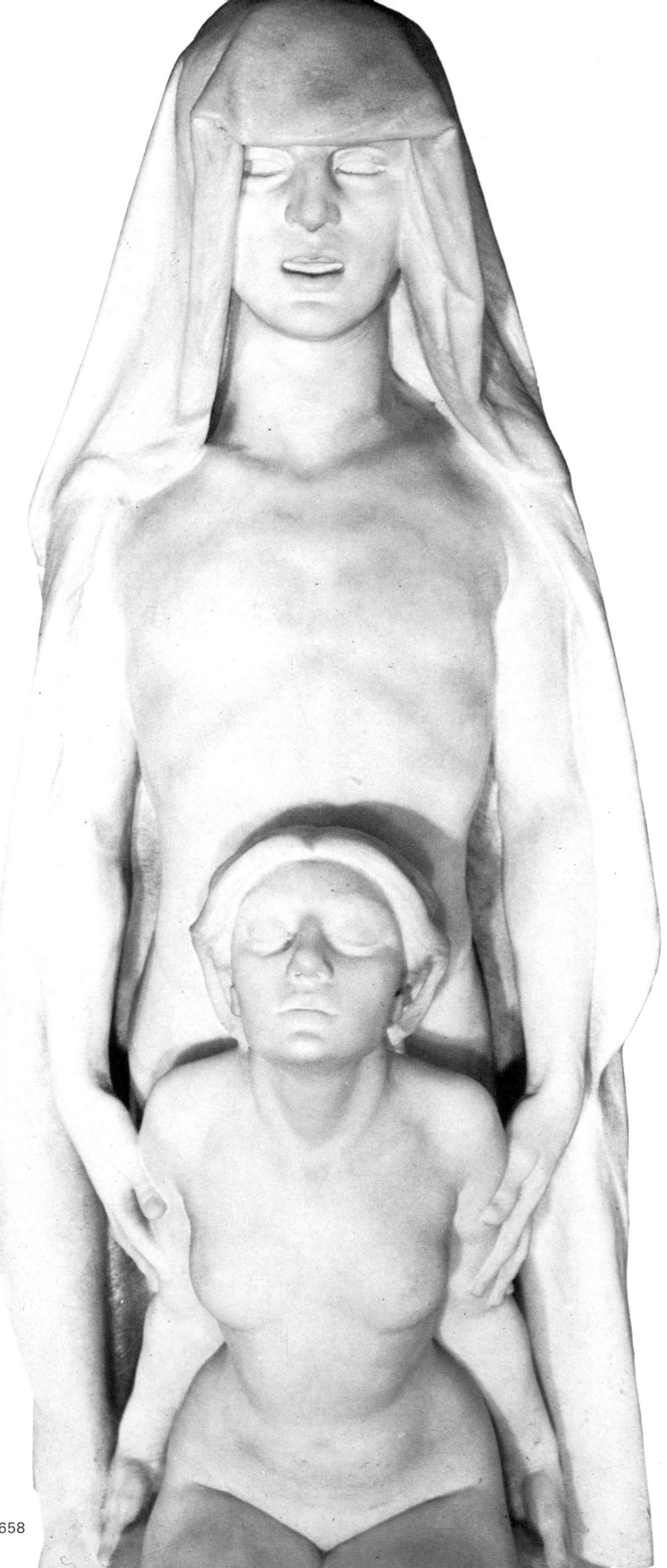

A medium and her spirit guide, a statue by G. H. Paulin. The key role in the Spiritualist movement is played by the medium, through whom the spirit world communicates with the material world: in some cases messages from the dead come through a spirit 'guide' or 'control' whose personality temporarily replaces the medium's normal personality, and whose function is to protect the medium and to regulate the attempts made by the departed to communicate through her

John Moses

In this way Mrs Fox and her daughters believed they had discovered a means of communication with a spirit who claimed to have been murdered in the house. Sir Arthur Conan Doyle in his *History of Spiritualism* (1926) says that subsequent excavations on the site disclosed human remains.

The Fox family were now plagued not only by spirit noises, but by sensation seekers, and Mrs Fox and the girls went to live with her married daughter in Rochester. Their psychic abilities continued and around them developed the first Spiritualist circle. In 1849 the girls gave a first public demonstration in Rochester and followed this up with demonstrations in many other towns in the eastern states. Their activities created a sensation in the popular Press, and their popularity was not affected by pronouncements made by three professors from Buffalo University, following an investigation in 1851, that the raps were produced by movements of the knee-joints, or by the subsequent alleged confession by Kate that they were produced by cracking her toes.

'Spirit rapping' rapidly became a craze in the United States, but in the early stages Spiritualism was as much a popular scientific movement as a religious movement. People who had attended a mediumistic demonstration, or had read about such events, held seances in their own homes attended by relations and friends. They were often motivated by curiosity and the spirit of scientific enquiry. They met in an attempt to test the claims of Spiritualists, they continued to meet if they felt that such claims were being confirmed by their experiences within the circle, and it was on the basis of such successful groups that permanent organizations, societies and churches began to develop.

The National Union

The Spiritualist movement was introduced to Britain in 1852 when Mrs Hayden, an American medium, gave demonstrations. She was followed by other mediums and, as in America, a short-lived craze swept the country. The early days in Britain were similar to those in America, the movement of that period consisting of 'home circles', either of friends who met to experiment or of followers who gathered round a successful medium.

The visits of D. D. Home to Britain in

Non-Christian Spiritualists frequently held that Spiritualism was a new religion which would ultimately replace Christianity, while others saw Spiritualism as the basis of all religion

the 1850s and '60s created considerable interest. Home was probably the most remarkable medium of the 19th century and unlike most well-known mediums was never detected committing a fraudulent act (see HOME). There were only two known professional mediums in London as late as 1867, though there were many private mediums in that period, including the infant prodigy of mediumship, Master Willie Turketine.

During the 1860s Spiritualist societies began to appear, as the more successful circles developed organizations. These first appeared in London and in the Keighley area of Yorkshire, which formed the two centres from which Spiritualism spread. Outside London the movement in the second half of the 19th century was most successful in the industrial towns of Yorkshire and Lancashire, and in the mining areas of the north-east. The first national organization, the British Association of Progressive Spiritualists, was formed in 1865 at a meeting held at Darlington. The Progressive Spiritualists were attacked by more conventional Spiritualists for being 'anti-Christian' and their organization collapsed in 1868.

At this time many Spiritualists feared the development of organizations which they held would destroy the freedom and spontaneity which were essential to the movement, and would lead to the growth of bureaucracy and oligarchy. A writer of the period expressed these feelings by pointing out that the movement would become 'controlled by the lower stratum of minds – minds that live and work almost solely for the interests of organizations.'

In spite of misgivings of this sort a further attempt to establish a national organization in 1873 led to the rise of the British National Association of Spiritualists. It consisted mainly of Spiritualists from the London area and was gradually forced to recognize its failure to acquire national status. In 1883 it was re-constituted as the London Spiritualist Alliance.

In the 1870s and '80s local Spiritualist societies in many areas began to associate with each other for mutual benefit and to form district organizations. The first of these, the Lancashire Association, was formed in 1875, and by 1912 there were fifteen of these associations. The first effective national organization was formed in 1890; the Spiritualists' National Federation was a federation of local churches which made rapid progress mainly in the north and by 1896 had 58 societies affiliated to it. In order to enable the movement to obtain legal status the Federation was re-constituted as the Spiritualists' National Union Ltd in 1902, and this remains the largest organization of Spiritualists in Britain.

In Britain the Spiritualist movement grew most rapidly in the period between the two World Wars, a period in which there was no lack of able mediums, including Rudi Schneider and Mrs Leonard (see LEONARD; SCHNEIDER BROTHERS), and the movement was also greatly assisted by the work of three able proponents, none of whom seem to have had any psychic gift themselves. Sir Oliver Lodge was an eminent scientist whose account of communications with his son, who had been killed in the First World War, was published under the title of *Raymond* in 1916. Sir Arthur Conan Doyle, then at the height of his fame as the creator of Sherlock Holmes, was converted in 1917 and until his death in 1930 worked ceaselessly to promote Spiritualism (see DOYLE). Hannen Swaffer set out to investigate Spiritualism for *The People*, of which he was the editor. In the course of his investigations, Swaffer believed that he had received evidence of the survival of his old 'chief' – Lord Northcliffe. He organized a public meeting at the Queens Hall in January 1925 to announce his conversion. Swaffer became an active protagonist and it was through the medium in Swaffer's private circle that the messages of the guide named Silver Birch were communicated.

Harry Price Library

Photograph by A. Martin, of Denver, Colorado, showing Houdini, the famous escape artist and fierce opponent of Spiritualist mediums, with spirit forms

Science or Religion

Although the Spiritualist movement seems to have arisen out of a semi-scientific curiosity about the nature of 'psychic phenomena', religious aspects began to appear at a very early date. The idea of communication with spirits is readily associated with religious concepts, and since many early Spiritualists were searching for a system of belief to replace Christianity they quickly seized on the 'messages' that were given by spirits through the mediums, for although these were often evidence intended to prove survival, many spirits could not resist the temptation to preach their philosophy. Spiritualist meetings also began to develop a ritual which included music, hymn singing, prayer and Bible reading. Such ritual is claimed to create an atmosphere conducive to the appearance of psychic phenomena and to the prevention of the disruption of the seance by evil spirits. By the 1870s many societies were adopting the title of churches.

Non-Christian Spiritualists frequently held that Spiritualism was a new religion which would ultimately replace Christianity, while others saw Spiritualism as the basis of all religion. The Christian Churches as a whole attacked Spiritualism, arguing that communication with the dead was forbidden by the authority of the Bible, and that the spirit communicators were evil entities dispatched by the Devil to mislead men. The Roman Catholic Church has maintained this

The Mediumship of W. S. Moses

Mr. Moses himself, in his published writings, was wont to attach considerable importance to the evidence for the doctrines of Spiritualism afforded by the communications, ostensibly from the spirits of deceased persons, received through his mediumship. Of communicators who thus claimed to furnish definite proof of their identity, Mr. Myers, who has collected the evidence under this head in a convenient form, reckons thirty-eight in all. Of these thirty-eight persons some had been known in life to Moses himself or to other members of the circle; some, such as Bishop Wilberforce, Swedenborg, or President Garfield, were historical personages; yet others were individuals of no special eminence, and without any point of contact with Mr. Moses or his circle.

In one important particular the evidence of identity in these cases is superior to that generally furnished through so-called clairvoyant mediums. In marked contrast to the vague generalities which commonly pass for tests, Mr. Moses' spirits were prodigal of names, dates, and other concrete facts which lend themselves to ready verification. Here is an example: "On February 28th, 1874, a spirit came by raps and gave the name 'Rosamira'. She said that she died at Torquay on January 10th, 1874, and that she had lived at Kilburn. She stated that her husband's name was 'Lancaster'"; and added later that his christian name was "Ben". As a matter of fact the whole of these particulars, given at the séance at the end of February, are to be found in the notice of the death in the *Daily Telegraph* of January 15th preceding.

The case is typical. Mr. Moses' spirits habitually furnished accurate obituaries, or gave such other particulars of their lives as could be gathered from the daily papers, from published biographies, or from the *Annual Register* and other works of reference.

F. Podmore *Modern Spiritualism*

attitude, as have such sects as Jehovah's Witnesses and the Pentecostal movement, but the 'Free Churches' and the Anglicans have moved towards a more tolerant position, reflected in the establishment of the Churches' Fellowship for Psychical Study in 1953. Christian Spiritualists have always argued that they were attempting to restore to the Church those practices which were commonly accepted by the early Christians.

Spiritualists were subjected not only to verbal attack by the Churches, the Press and rationalists, but to legal prosecution up to 1951, with the passing of the Fraudulent Mediums Act. As late as 1945 a Spiritualist church at Redhill had closed as a result of threats of prosecution. In the previous year the famous medium Helen Duncan had been sentenced to imprisonment for nine months. Under earlier acts the professional practice of mediumship (even if admitted to be genuine) could be construed as illegal, but the new act made it necessary for the prosecution to prove that fraud had been committed, thus implicitly accepting that genuine mediumship was a possibility.

One of the main sources of conflict within the movement has centred around the acceptance of Christian teachings. While accepting a broadly religious basis, the Spiritualists' National Union has consistently refused to adopt specifically Christian doctrine. After the failure in 1928 of Conan Doyle's attempt to convert the S.N.U. to Christianity and of a number of attempts to organize Christian Spiritualists, the medium Winifred Moyes established the Greater World Christian Spiritualist League in 1931. The League was an immediate success and by 1935 it had 580 affiliated churches.

Until the middle of the 20th century Britain and the U.S.A. were the main centres of Spiritualism. In recent years the movement has grown most rapidly in Latin America, particularly in Brazil, where there are said to be at least two million Spiritualists. The movement in Brazil is divided into two broad groups, the Western type based on the teaching of Kardec and largely supported by the middle-class, and native Spiritualism or Spiritism which is derived largely from African and American-Indian influences and is practised mainly by the poor (see SOUTH AMERICA).

The Seven Principles

Spiritualism is a movement and not an organization. It consists not only of international and national associations but of many independent local societies and of numerous 'home circles' and individuals who are unattached to any formal organization. You do not have to join any organization to be a Spiritualist. There is no agreement on a Spiritualist creed of beliefs, beyond the two broad beliefs already mentioned. Spiritualist beliefs are the result of messages received from the spirits through a medium, and the teachings of the spirits display wide differences. Spiritualists explain that spirits are human beings who have survived death; transition to the afterlife does not immediately make a man wise, he takes with him the ideas he had in life, and continues to hold to these beliefs at least during his stay in the lower planes of the afterlife. Spirits who have moved upwards after death, to increasingly high planes of existence, find it more difficult to communicate through mediums, so that communications usually come from the recently dead and those who have made little progress in the afterlife. It is not surprising therefore to find a wide diversity of belief held by Spiritualists. In Europe and Latin America, where the teachings of the French Spiritualist Alan Kardec predominate, most Spiritualists believe in reincarnation, in England and America few Spiritualists do. Some Spiritualists are agnostic, since there appears to be no greater proof of the existence of God in the lowest levels of the spirit world than on earth.

If there is no Spiritualist creed neither is there a Spiritualist bible. The most widely accepted book is *Spirit Teachings*, a series of communications from the spirit world transmitted through the automatic writing mediumship of Rev W. Stainton Moses (see AUTOMATIC ART).

A widely accepted credal statement is to be found in the Seven Principles subscribed to by all members of the Spiritualists' National Union, which were derived from a spirit communication received through the medium Emma Hardinge-Britten. The principles are: the fatherhood of God; the brotherhood of man; the communion of spirits and the ministry of angels; the continuous existence of the human soul; personal responsibility; compensation and retribution hereafter for all the good and evil deeds done on earth; eternal progress open to every human soul.

The S.N.U., which is the largest of the two national organizations in Britain, has about 460 affiliated churches with some 15,000 members and represents the non-Christian element in Spiritualism. The other organization, the Greater World Christian Spiritualist League, with over 200 churches represents the specifically Christian influence in the Spiritualist movement. There are also many churches not affiliated to either of these organizations offering a variety of beliefs and practices.

While it is difficult to generalize about Spiritualist beliefs, most Spiritualists in Britain and America would probably accept the following beliefs. Man is an immortal being composed of two elements, a body and a soul or spirit, and on death the spirit leaves the body and enters a phase of existence in a 'spiritual plane'. The universe consists of seven such planes of existence, of which the material (earth) is the lowest. After death most souls awake into the second plane, known to many as the Summerland, a level of existence in which life is not unlike that on earth except for the absence of pain and suffering. In this plane, as on earth, each soul has the opportunity for spiritual development which opens up the possibility of ascent to high planes.

Every individual has the opportunity of rising through the ascending order of spiritual levels until he reaches the seventh heaven, in which he will finally be united with God and all the great souls who have preceded him. Great souls such as Jesus are said to have risen directly to the seventh heaven, but just as goodness leads to spiritual advancement, so evil leads to decline; men are not punished, they punish themselves by opting for a course of action which prevents their spiritual development.

Spiritualism aroused violent antagonism and criticism, concentrating particularly on the physical phenomena occurring at seances, which opponents claimed were faked: the famous conjurer J. N. Maskelyne put on long-running shows (*above*) to demonstrate his ability to duplicate Spiritualist phenomena *Below* A 'rapping hand', used at fraudulent seances and probably controlled pneumatically through rubber tubing

Harry Price Library

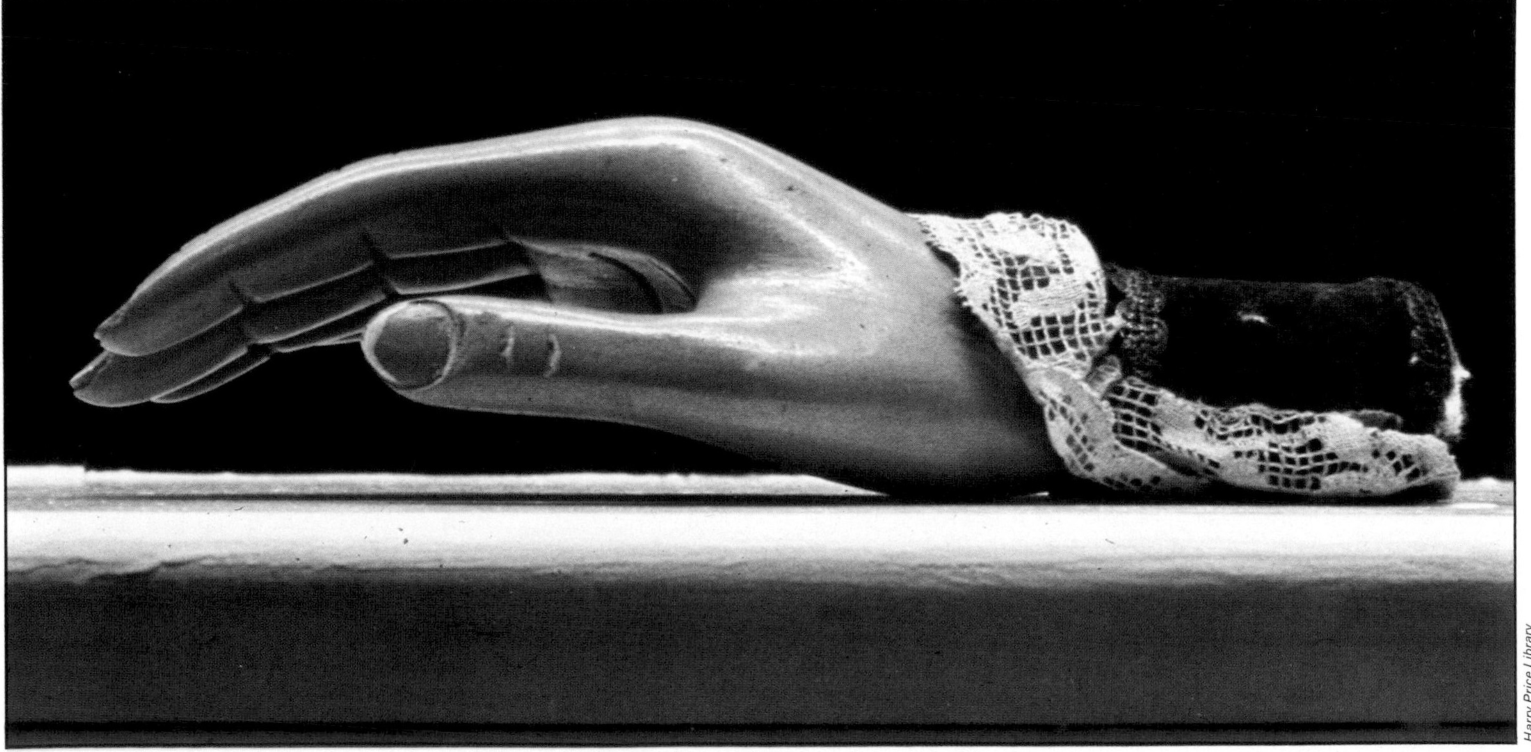

Harry Price Library

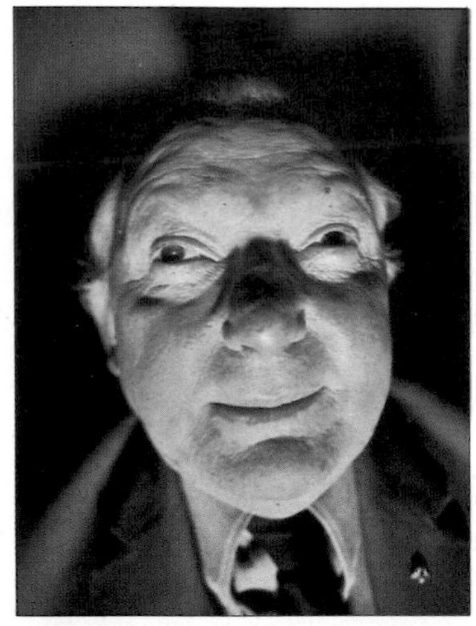

John Moss

John Moss

Evil men find themselves after death in a condition of limbo in which they perceive themselves as alone and lost in a fog, but this situation is not irretrievable. Through remorse and repentance they may find their way back to the light. Some Spiritualist societies organize 'rescue circles' with the aim of contacting and aiding such lost souls, and Lord Dowding's book *The Dark Star* (1951) contains graphic accounts of the work of these circles.

Those who are over-attached to earthly things may find themselves unable after death to leave the material world. Such 'earthbound' spirits may be perceived by those who have psychic abilities as ghosts, but these may also free themselves from their attachments and develop spiritually.

Many Spiritualists also believe that animals have souls and are active in anti-vivisection and other animal welfare movements. Some believe that the spiritual universe is not only inhabited by human spirits but by many spirits who have never been incarnated as humans, ranging from poltergeists and earth elementals, such as fairies, to cosmic powers of good and evil, angels and demons.

Spirit and Matter

Spiritualists' beliefs are derived from communication with the spirit world and such communication may take any one of a number of forms. The spirits may speak directly through the medium who is in trance, or the medium may use his own voice to convey the message. In the case of automatic writing the medium's hand is controlled by the 'spirit', and the ouija board is a device which facilitates this form of communication (see OUIJA BOARDS). Other methods (far less common today) are the raps (used by the Fox sisters) and slate writing, a popular Victorian technique, both of which methods were open to fraud. Clairvoyance and clairaudience in which the medium sees, hears, or senses information which he attempts to transmit to the sitter are the most common forms of mediumship.

From the early days Spiritualism has involved phenomena in which material objects have been moved by what many have claimed to be supernatural forces. As early as 1849 there is the record of a table

John Moss

Left and above **A medium in trance: though fraudulent mediums flourished in the earlier days of the Spiritualist movement, there have always been genuine mediums, and Spiritualists are convinced that communications coming through them constitute conclusive proof that human beings survive death**

being levitated six inches. The first instance of the levitation of a human being, a Mr Gordon, was reported in the journal *Spirit World* in February 1851. Materialization of a spirit and the 'apport' or mysterious appearance of a physical object were also early forms of manifestations. At some seances coloured lights appeared which floated round the room, and at others musical instruments were mysteriously played.

Spirit photography was first practised by William Mumler, a Boston photographer, in 1862, but his work was soon exposed as fraudulent. Frederick Hudson was the first spirit photographer in Britain, but he was exposed by the well-known Spiritualist writer W. H. Harrison in *The Spiritualist* in 1872. The most famous spirit photographer was William Hope (died 1933) who worked with the Crewe circle: his work was also exposed, but he found a faithful champion in Sir Arthur Conan Doyle.

There appears to have been a decline in physical mediumship since the Second World War, which cynics have attributed to the greater ease of detecting fraud by modern scientific methods. From the first, Spiritualists practised 'spirit healing' and this has become an increasingly important part of their work.

The key role in the Spiritualist movement is played by the medium, who is quite literally the medium through which the 'spirit world' communicates with the material world. In theory all men are potential mediums, but it is clear that while some people are endowed with psychic abilities which may appear spontaneously, others require years of training before they can make use of their abilities. Many of the most gifted mediums report that they had spontaneous psychic experiences when they were children. The claims of Spiritualists have frequently been investigated by critics and during the 19th century psychic phenomena were subjected to rigorous study by a series of eminent scientists. Some were convinced that not all Spiritualist manifestations could be explained by theories of fraud or illusion, but in spite of a considerable body of accumulated evidence most scientists have remained unconvinced by the Spiritualist interpretation.

If psychic phenomena are a universal feature of human life, why did the modern Spiritualist movement arise in the U.S.A. and Britain in the 19th century? Sociologists attempt to explain the rise (or decline) of social movements in terms of the conditions affecting the lives of the members of a society, in terms of the processes going on within the society and of the changes in the structure of that society.

The Sociology of Spiritualism

Modern Spiritualism is one of a particular type of religious movements known to sociologists as cults. Such movements are characterized by two general features; they are outside the major religious tradition of the society in which they originate (as already mentioned, Spiritualism owes more to non-Christian than to Christian sources), and they are attempts to solve the problems of individuals, particularly those problems that arise out of man's attempts to understand the world in which he lives, to give meaning to his life and to experiences of a psychic or mystical nature. Spiritualism certainly offers man a new view of the universe and man's place in it and is particularly concerned with the place of psychic experiences in human life.

Cults seem to arise in the greatest profusion, and to gain the most adherents, when a society is disorganized by rapid changes. In such circumstances the old religious traditions are challenged and men find the old views of life no longer satisfying. American society in the middle of the 19th century was going through a period of particularly rapid change as the result of the influx of emigrants, mainly from Europe, as well as the early effects of the industrial revolution. In Britain the industrial revolution was changing the traditional way of life; in particular this was the period of rapid urban expansion, and Spiritualism was from the first predominantly an urban religion.

The rationalism of the 18th century intellectual was beginning to spread more widely through society and following such publicists as Thomas Paine men began to demand proof of religious claims. While not claiming to offer proof of the existence of God, Spiritualism did claim to provide proof of the survival of the human soul beyond death.

Many of the early adherents to Spiritualism were agnostics or atheists, men who had ceased to find Christianity credible but who nevertheless sought a philosophy of life which went beyond scientific materialism while remaining consistent with science. Spiritualism was at first closely connected with psychical research though the two movements gradually drifted apart. In common with many modern cults, such as the Flying Saucer movement, Spiritualism started as an attempt to study phenomena which were not being seriously studied by orthodox science and indeed which did not 'fit' the established scientific theories of the time. In each case the movements developed into religions, because they offered solutions which were not only intellectually but emotionally satisfactory to certain key problems in the lives of individuals. The 19th century was obsessed with death but many people were losing faith in the Christian explanation, as a result of the growth of belief in science. Death was a major source of tension in the lives of such persons, who were not satisfied with faith but needed proof of the survival of the soul after death. Spiritualism was attractive because it offered evidence of survival.

It was during the First World War and in the following years that the movement experienced its greatest growth, thus reflecting the tension created by the high death rate. In the second half of the 20th century death has ceased to be such an obsession and many people are more concerned with a search for the meaning of life; this has meant on the one hand that the Spiritualist movement has ceased to grow, and on the other that within the movement there is less concern with proofs of survival and a greater interest in the philosophy of Spiritualism.

(See also MEDIUMS; PSYCHICAL RESEARCH.)

G. K. NELSON

FURTHER READING: M. Barbanell, *This is Spiritualism* (Smithers, 1959); William S. Moses, *Spirit Teachings* (Arno, 1976); G. K. Nelson, *Spiritualism and Society* (Schocken, 1969); Guy Lyon Playfair, *The Indefinite Boundary* (Souvenir Press, 1976).

SPITTLE

THE FLUIDS of the body, the blood and the saliva, have an importance in the history of magic in that they are both aspects of soul power. Among some communities in the past, expectoration was regarded as a deeply religious act since it involved the sacrifice of an essential element of the person to the gods. The close connection between the flow of saliva and the emotions probably contributed to this idea: one spits with disgust, or licks the lips in anticipation of some delight.

Since it is a holy fluid, spittle has had an important role in consecration and anointing, for it sanctifies and protects whatever it touches. In some primitive communities, property was protected against theft by being spat upon, and spittle was used for the ratification of agreements. Among the Masai in Africa the equivalent of the European handshake was mutual spitting, and in some societies it was customary for the respective parties to an agreement to spit into one another's mouths.

Saliva has also been credited with therapeutic properties, the most effective type being the first spittle of the day, known as fasting spittle. Pliny insisted that fasting spittle could cure snakebite and boils, and English country healers of the 19th century used it for the treatment of abrasions, skin irritations and eye disorders. A modern Japanese cure for headaches involves a matchstick steeped in spittle which is placed in the centre of the forehead. An old treatment for a crick in the neck was to convey spittle by means of the right hand to the right knee, and by the left hand to the left knee. To a minor extent the New Testament has been responsible for the continued respectability of saliva therapy among Christians, for Christ used spittle to restore sight and speech to the afflicted.

Then there is the importance of spittle as an aid to economic activity. Handsel money, the first coin of the day received by a trader, is frequently spat upon, ostensibly to attract further money, but basically to ensure that it does not vanish away like a fairy gift. Similar action is often taken in respect of money found in the street. Anglers, before casting their lines, spit on their hooks, and deep-sea fishermen are known to expectorate soulfully into their trawls.

Scala

In folklore, spittle has healing properties because it contains part of the body's life-energy: Christ touches a blind man's eyes with spittle, a fresco in Ravenna

At one time it was customary to spit on any member of the family before he or she embarked upon a long journey, as protection against the hazards of the road. A few years ago it was reported in the newspapers that a woman in Oxford always spat at her daughter on the day of an important school examination, and at her husband before he played in a bowls match. On the other hand, it is an old belief that your spittle can be used by an enemy to work magic against you.

Where the fear of the Evil Eye remains strong, spittle is sometimes used as an antidote. The stranger who unthinkingly praises the child of a Mediterranean fisherman may be astounded when the outraged mother spits into its face three times, three being a lucky number. In some cases a mixture of spittle and dirt is used to anoint the child's forehead and lips. The ill effects of boasting, a presumptuous act calculated to provoke the angry intervention of the gods, can be countered if you spit thrice into your own bosom. People who are conscious of having violated some taboo or feel vulnerable to psychic attack will often spit as a matter of course. Scottish fishermen who incur the wrath of higher powers by uttering tabooed words like 'dog', 'salmon', 'rabbit', 'pig', 'kirk' or 'minister', can restore their fortunes by 'spitting out the names'. The clergy are often in bad odour among the superstitious, and at one time the working men of Birmingham used to expectorate whenever they passed a parson in the street.

Dressmakers have been known to spit on their work to ensure the customer's satisfaction, boxers will spit on their hands before commencing a fight, and gardeners before they begin to dig. Although few people are still given to spitting into their right shoe or their urine for luck first thing in the morning, spitting superstitions have not quite died out. Some people invariably spit thrice on seeing the new moon for the first time, and others studiously spit three times whenever they see a dead dog, a magpie, or that rarity, the piebald horse.

ERIC MAPL.

Death or danger is somehow foreseen in dreams or hallucinations, people become aware of things which they have no normal means of knowing, messages are apparently received from the dead, a picture falls off the wall at the moment of a death: many curious experiences of this sort may be the result of an obscure mechanism of the human mind

SPONTANEOUS PSI EXPERIENCES

SPONTANEOUS PSYCHIC experiences include widely diversified kinds of unusual occurrences. They range over unaccountable 'awarenesses', true dreams, seemingly uncaused movements of physical objects, and unexplainable sights and sounds sometimes taken to be caused by the dead. The common element in all of them, however, is that by them the persons involved secure information not revealed by their senses, or produce effects not mediated by their muscles. This is the characteristic that divides these experiences from sensorimotor ones on the one hand, and instances of fantasy, imagination or delusion on the other.

Historically, psychic experiences had no rational explanation, since the phenomena were not caused by the senses or muscles, and therefore seemed mysterious, even supernatural. Research in parapsychology, however, has thrown light on their nature and origin. They turn out to be the result of normal but obscure mental processes, that do not operate like the sensorimotor ones but have their own laws and regularities. These processes constitute what is known as psi ability, the subject of parapsychological research.

Spontaneous experiences have played a part in parapsychological research and will continue to do so, even though the individual reports of them cannot produce conclusive reliability. Human testimony is fallible and the psi element is difficult to identify with finality. In large numbers of cases, however, the importance of individual or personal variations, even inaccuracies and mistakes, diminishes, while common aspects stand out and make the identification of psi more certain. In fact the relationship between this mental function as demonstrated in the laboratory and as evidenced in spontaneous experiences is, in a way, a reciprocal one. The experiences came under observation and study first, and because of their strangeness they were hard to take seriously as actual occurrences. The question of their validity led eventually to experimental tests, and the experiments eventually showed that there could well be something more to many of the manifestations that had been called psychic than a mixture of imagination, exaggeration and fraud. They showed, in short, that the human mind has two general types of psi ability, that of getting information without the senses through extrasensory perception, or ESP, and that of influencing physical objects without contact through psychokinesis, or PK (see EXTRASENSORY PERCEPTION; PSYCHOKINESIS.)

The experimental work, besides showing that psi ability exists, has also led to a degree of understanding of it, so that the experiences can now be taken as the probable spontaneous natural operation of a known human capacity. At the present stage their range offers a wider perspective on psi ability than the experimental researches have as yet verified. Therefore they can be the source of further suggestions about the still unknown aspects of it, suggestions that will be supported or discarded later according to the outcome of future experimental testing.

It is easy to see now why psychic manifestations have been baffling and mysterious, because it is now recognized that the psi process is an unconscious one. The person does not know when it operates or that he himself was involved in the operation. It was largely because of this unconscious origin that psi was long unsuspected and its effects generally misunderstood and often misinterpreted. For because the person is unaware of his own role in the production of a psi effect the tendency has been to assume it to be something imposed upon or communicated to him from the outside. This has been particularly true when a dying or deceased person seemed to play an active role in the phenomena or when it was possible to suppose that such an influence was involved.

Besides the mystery raised by the unconscious operation of psi, the manifestations themselves took many different forms and no unifying underlying principle was obvious. Only after decades of controlled research has it been established that the phenomena are the result of an underlying mental process (the psi process) that is expressed in various ways in different situations.

The concept of the psi process can be simplified by considering it as consisting of two stages. Stage 1 is that in which an item of information somehow becomes 'accessible', at an unconscious level. How this can occur is the true unknown of the psychic process.

The ghost of St Denis: if the dead do survive, 'psi would be the necessary form by which communications from the deceased to the living would take place' but methods of research which could establish the fact of survival have not yet been developed

Harry Price Library

Also unknown are the factors or influences that permit one specific item to be 'chosen', picked out from all others, as the topic of a given experience. Stage 2 is a psychological rather than a parapsychological one, for in it the selected item is transferred to consciousness in a psychological form or as a physical effect. Nearly all of the facts about the psi process that have now been established concern this psychological stage.

Even though psi effects occur in what superficially appear to be a great many different ways, the seeming confusion they represent is largely dispelled once the basic underlying processes are understood. First of all, although the two main types of psi are very different in their obvious effects, ESP being cognitive and PK physical, still they can now be recognized as two different aspects of the same basic psi process. Consequently, the phenomena produced by each are related. Then the phenomena of these two basic types, particularly those of ESP, can be even further classified into sub-types.

ESP experiences have been distinguished on the basis of the kind of subject matter involved. It may be an object or event, it may involve the thought of another person, or it may concern an event still in the future, and be clairvoyant, telepathic, or precognitive accordingly. And since ESP experiences are not limited by time, they are not limited by space, but may involve events at any distance. All three ESP types thus are in sharp contrast to sense perception, which is limited to events happening in the present and within a relatively short distance. Psi thus denotes an extraphysical aspect to human nature.

The following is an example of the clairvoyant type of experience, for in it the person's mind somehow 'made contact' directly with the object. A man in Ontario operated a sawmill in the woods, and occasionally stayed at the logging camp with the workmen. One day he found his wallet missing. After searching for it in vain, he gave up hope of finding it. About two weeks later he dreamed it was at the bottom of the well at the camp. The dream was so vivid that the next morning he drove the 13 miles to the camp. He baled out the water from the well and found the wallet, though he never knew how it got there.

Precognition cases can be illustrated by the experience of an Ohio woman. She reported that one Sunday morning in Cleveland while her mother was in church, her mother's new Oldsmobile was stolen from the parking lot. The police held out little hope of finding it. But two nights later the daughter dreamed that the car was at a certain location in downtown Cleveland. Telling her husband of her dream the next day, she drove to the place and found the car. However, the bystanders testified that it had only been parked there *minutes before she came.* The dream showed where it *would be*, not where it was. The case is typical, except that the time interval may cover years as well as minutes.

An instance of the telepathic type of case is the experience reported by a teacher in New Jersey. She was teaching spelling to her class by giving out a list of words for the children to spell. As she pronounced the words, slowly walking up and down the aisles, she saw that one little boy, Ralph, had misspelled the word 'grief'. But when she asked how many of the children had all the words correct, he raised his hand. She said, 'You missed one, Ralph.' He looked puzzled and she said, 'You misspelled grief.' They examined his paper and the word was not on it. Then a light broke over his face, 'Oh, now I remember. I wasn't sure how to spell it and as I was thinking you gave out the next word and I wrote it and forgot the other.' She asked him how he thought it should be spelled and he misspelled it just as she thought he had, though he had never written it, for he had written in ink and there were no erasures.

A Grim Case

In all three types of experience, it is as if the experiencing person's mind 'reaches out' and makes contact with the item of information. However, in some telepathy cases, because of the second person involved, the superficial impression is given that the action is initiated by him rather than by the experiencing person. An example was given by a woman in New Brunswick. She had gone downtown with a friend to do some shopping. Her husband was at home where he had a battery to recharge and replace in the car. Suddenly she knew she had to go home. She rushed off, regardless of her friend's remonstrances, and found her husband unconscious in his car in the garage. She was in time to get help and save him. She found that he had closed the garage door, thinking there would be ample air, but carbon monoxide fumes overcame him. The last thought he remembered was an urgent call to his wife to come home.

Apparently the wife was not thinking of her husband when she got the urge to go home, and presumably it was at the time that her husband in his extremity was calling to her. Thus the obvious suggestion would be that his mind, not hers 'reached out', and that her impulse to go home was a response to his message. Because of cases like this one, the experiencing person was called the receiver or percipient, and the second person the agent. These terms however are misnomers, for the sending is not the crucial part of the process, as was illustrated by the case of the teacher in New Jersey. The telepathic reception, just like that of the clairvoyant and precognitive types, can occur without it; although, possibly, it adds to the likelihood that the thought will be 'noticed' or picked up by the experiencing person.

Of course, to describe the psi process as one in which the experiencing person's mind 'reaches out' is only to employ a figure of speech based on sense experience, in which distance intervenes between the person and his environment. In ESP distance as such is not a factor. The language, however, lacks a word for mental contact without distance.

Cases cannot always be exactly classified as to type. For instance, experiences are often reported in which both a thought and an objective event are involved, so that it is not clear whether the situation was one involving telepathy or clairvoyance. The type of such a case cannot be determined exactly and consequently it can only be classified as general ESP (GESP). Today in the attempt to understand the psi process, it makes little difference just how an individual case is classified. The important point is simply that the types of ESP show its potentially great reach.

The PK type of psi is still in a comparatively early stage of investigation. The meaning or content of spontaneous PK experiences usually concerns the crisis of another person, and usually is one of strong emotional quality for the experiencing person. The situations thus tend to be similar to those of telepathy, and in any event their associated meaning falls within those of the types of ESP. Potentially the phenomena of PK fall into three sub-types, which are based on the state of the object affected. It may be moving, or at rest, or it may be a complex combination of the two in living tissue or organisms.

Research into PK on falling objects has now well demonstrated the PK effect, and very recently experiments have been reported on living organisms, in which positive results have been secured. If they are confirmed they should be significant for the treatment of disease, and have bearing on a wide range of psychosomatic functions. As yet no laboratory tests have been reported in which static objects have been caused to move, under adequately controlled conditions though, of course, many spontaneous cases that seem to involve PK deal with the movement of static objects.

Intuitions and Hallucinations

Psi experiences vary not only in the type of information they bring, but also in the way or form of manifestation. This is the product of the psychological process of Stage 2 by which the information secured by ESP in Stage 1 is manifested. Different forms are shown even in the three cases of ESP already given. The man who found his lost wallet did so by a dream. The woman who went home when her husband was in danger did so because of a strong intuitive compulsion. The teacher who knew her pupil misspelled a word 'saw' it written on his paper so realistically she was convinced that her eyes had actually seen it.

ESP experiences may take any of four different forms, but PK only one. They follow closely but not exactly the distinction between waking and dreaming mental states. Two of the ESP forms, the intuitive and the hallucinatory, occur when the person is awake, and two occur as dreams. The PK form is not known to be limited by the mental state of the person. Each form represents a different process and therefore they must be presented separately.

Certain psi experiences are just like the intuitions of ordinary life except that their subject matter was apparently received (in Stage 1) by ESP. The characteristic of intuitive experience, both when ESP is involved and when it is not, is the sudden 'awareness' of the given item of information without any recognizable reason for knowing it and without mental imagery, as in the case reported by a woman in Michigan. During the Second World War, when she was in hospital after the birth of her child, a letter came saying that her husband in France had died of a heart attack. But she said, 'It wasn't a heart attack. He was poisoned.'

'I honestly did not know I was going to say it,' she said. 'It was as if someone else had said it for me. I insisted that they check with Washington. They did and I was right. He had been poisoned. I never knew why they first said it was a heart attack.'

The experience brought a complete item of information without a reason and without imagery. The person 'just knew' it. The case given earlier of the woman who rushed home when her husband was in danger also was apparently based on an intuition. But the information in that instance was not complete. She knew she must go home, but she did not know why. Instances of incomplete information in the intuitive form are frequent. The degree of incompleteness varies, many of the cases consisting only of a strong emotion, or a compulsion to action. It is as if the information is entirely suppressed, unable to cross the threshold of consciousness. But the accompanying emotion or tendency to act breaks through.

Probably over half of the intuitive experiences reported are incomplete to some degree. This, along with the absence of detail even in complete cases, means that the transfer of an idea from unconscious levels to the conscious one of the waking state is accomplished with some difficulty. However, the majority of intuitions carry a strong feeling of conviction that the information is true. The case of the woman who knew that her husband had been poisoned illustrates this.

Hallucinations are pseudo-perceptual impressions; they occur when no external objective stimulus is present to cause them. Usually they do not involve ESP, but when they do the experience brings information about a real situation. In these any sense modality may be involved but the auditory is reported most frequently. The human voice is perhaps the sound most often 'heard'.

Probably better known, even if actually reported more rarely than the auditory, are visual hallucinations. Many of them coincide with the death of the individual 'seen', the experience thus seeming to serve as a communication to report it. A typical case comes from a woman in Kansas, who said: 'At an early hour one morning my father sat up suddenly in bed. My mother asked, "What is the matter, Bob?" he replied, "Mother is dead." She tried to convince him it was a nightmare, but he said, "No, I was never

Bouquet with Flying Lovers, **a 'dream' picture by Chagall: at least half of the spontaneous psi cases reported are dreams, in which an item of information that has somehow become accessible to the unconscious mind is transferred into the conscious mind, though often with deceptive alterations**

Tate Gallery/John Webb

'Because the person is unaware of his own role in the production of a psychic effect, the tendency has been to assume it to be something imposed upon or communicated to him from the outside': an automatic painting by Madge Gill, who attributed her work to the influence of a spirit

wider awake. Mother was standing by the bed just looking at me. She was pale, her hair was down, she was dressed in a white gown. There was a large red spot on the right side of her neck. I know she's dead." Word came that she died from an aneurism at about the same time on the same date.'

Since the message in such hallucinatory experiences is not expressed directly as an idea but by sensory imagery, its meaning must be inferred. The result is that only about a third of them transmit a reasonably complete item of information. In fact, when the information is reasonably complete, it usually means that more than one sense modality was involved, as for instance in the case reported by a woman in Illinois. During the Second World War her family received a telegram from the War Department saying that her brother, a Marine, had been killed in action. With the family distressed she had gone into a separate room, when she heard the front door open, and went to see who had come in. She writes, 'I "saw" my brother coming up the stairs in his Marine uniform. He said, "Shirley, don't cry. I'm all right", and then when he got to the head of the stairs, he vanished.'

The next evening the family got another telegram from the War Department, saying that a mistake had been made and her brother was alive and well. When he finally got home he did not know that he had been reported killed in action, but at the time he had been lost from his unit and knew his family would be so worried about him that in his mind he kept telling them he was all right. The experience thus may have been telepathic, although the vehicle of expression was hallucinatory, and used both the visual and auditory modalities.

In an occasional report of hallucinatory experience, a concomitant intuition brings added information and thereby gives a hint of the origin of the hallucinatory effect. An example was reported by a woman in

California. She had been divorced from her husband for some time, when as she says, one night 'I awakened around midnight in a cold sweat. I sensed I was not alone in the room. I felt a horrible suspense and I shivered as I stared straight ahead. Suddenly about six or eight feet directly in front of my bed I saw the darndest thing I'd ever seen and I was scared out of my wits. It was a greenish grey whitish foamy substance – and then I knew somehow it was the spirit of my husband. And yet how could it be, when he was alive and in New York?' The next morning she saw an account in the paper saying that her ex-husband had drowned in the East River the night before. It happened about the time of her experience.

The point in this case, of course, is that she knew 'somehow', or in other words she intuitively identified her husband in connection with what she saw, although it was not even in the shape of a human being. The intuition and the hallucinatory image together expressed the idea of her husband's death, or were the vehicles by which the fact, accessible by ESP, was brought to consciousness.

Cases like this suggest that the intuition and the hallucinatory effect develop together at the start of Stage 2. For instance, a message in Stage 1 about the crisis of a family member, might create, in Stage 2, an incipient intuitive idea, and along with it in those individuals for whom a sensory pathway is easily stimulated an auditory or visual impression of him. Then if the intuitive idea was repressed and did not cross the threshold of consciousness, the result would be a typical visual or auditory hallucination, and this would become the 'figment in consciousness', the only sign that an ESP impression was received in Stage 1. Thus the hallucinatory form may be an adjunct of the intuitive, and limited to those individuals for whom the internal activation of sensory centres is possible.

ESP Dreams

At least half of the spontaneous cases reported are dreams. They carry their meaning by imagery, and the development of this is the point of special interest. Of course, it is not the imagery of pseudo-sense experience as in hallucinations, but it is rather a dramatization of elements of *memories* of sense experience. The person usually recognizes this upon waking and does not believe, as in hallucinations, that his senses were involved.

On the basis of the kind of imagery used, two dream forms can be distinguished, the realistic and the unrealistic. The imagery of realistic psi dreams is detailed and true to the actuality on which presumably it is based. Details may be so profuse as to suggest that the imagery must have been made by a kind of photographic copying process. An example was given earlier in the case of the woman who dreamed of the location of the car. However, occasionally a dream of this kind is defective and does not completely disclose the item on which it is ostensibly centred. In such cases the nature of the defect shows that the mental process involved is not one of automatic copying after all, for it was possible to alter the meaning that presumably lay back of the imagery. The defects in different cases seem to have originated in different stages of the process. Some of them apparently came in the construction of the imagery, in others even before it, and in still others after the imagery had been made.

An instance in which the imagery was defective and did not reveal correctly the identity of the person involved was reported by a California woman. She dreamed that she was attending a funeral. In it she was impressed especially by the rays of the afternoon sun coming through the stained glass windows of the funeral parlour. She also noted many floral wreaths, not only banked around the casket but hung on the walls. (She had never actually seen this done before.) She went up to the casket and saw her mother in it. She was awakened then by a phone call telling her of a friend's accidental death. Later she attended his funeral which was held in the late afternoon. The sun and the wreaths were the same as in the dream. Only the corpse was different, and this fact shows that the copying was not automatic, but that changes could indeed be made in it.

Cases of the second kind, those in which the defect seems to have occurred even before the imagery was made, involve the scene 'selected' to convey the information. It may not be the proper one, as in the experience of a woman in Washington. She dreamed she answered the doorbell and a brother she had not seen for years was there. She saw the details of his clothing, a camel hair coat on his arm, the peculiar kind of suitcase he carried, and an especially serious look on his face as he walked in the door. Upon waking she wondered if it might have meant that her brother was intending to pay her a visit. Several days later her father passed away quite suddenly. Her brother came to her house and the dream scene was enacted, down to details of the suitcase and the camel hair coat. Now she knew the reason for the serious look on her brother's face, but the scene of the dream had given no hint of the real reason for the visit. It obviously had not been 'selected' to inform her of her father's death.

The third kind of defect, the one that occurs late in the process, involves the interpretation of the imagery. Even though the person himself has constructed it, in some deep unconscious level, that does not mean that he knows it on a higher (conscious) level. This is shown by instances in which this higher level interpretation is wrong. Such a dream was reported by a California woman. It was in the early stages of the First World War, when a man still needed his wife's consent to enlist in the army. This woman's husband wanted to enlist, but she had not consented because of their small children and the need for her husband's support. Very worried one night, she fell asleep, to dream that she saw her husband in a field crushed by a big heavy machine. She told him of it and said she thought it was a warning that if he went to war he would be killed. The next day a neighbour found her husband dead under his big tractor. He had gotten off it to take some trash from behind it. The gear slipped into reverse and the tractor ran over him. Although she had constructed the imagery of her dream, she did not interpret it correctly upon waking.

While incomplete realistic dreams do not occur very frequently (probably not more than one in ten of those reported is incomplete), the fact that they do occur shows that the person does not have to copy the reality, but can influence the message by changing the imagery, selecting the wrong scene, or misinterpreting the situation. In each instance the influence that leads to the defect seems to be personal. Even though the reasons vary from case to case, they appear in the main to be emotional. While they cannot be pinpointed exactly in material like this, they appear to include factors like hopes, fears, anxieties, memories and desires. In view of these possibilities, and since presumably all individuals who have dreams of this kind could so distort the pictured reality, it is rather surprising that a large percentage of these dreams present an essentially true and complete item of information, and so make this form a comparatively effective message-bearer.

Hail and Farewell

Unrealistic dreams, as well as realistic ones, carry their meaning by detailed imagery but in these the details are not true, as can be illustrated by the dream of a woman in New York. She lived away from her parents' home at the time. Though her father was 79, he was in good health and she was not worried about him. But in this dream she thought she was at home and with the family sitting around the dining table. She, but none of the others, looked at her father. He rose from the table, smiled at her, pointed to his heart, turned, left the table still smiling and waved his hand at her as if in farewell. He said nothing, but she thought he meant that he was going to die because of a heart ailment. The dream troubled her. A few weeks later her father had a heart attack, his first, and died.

In this form, obviously the imagery is not a copying process based on the item of information secured in Stage 1 by ESP. Instead, at the beginning of Stage 2 a process of suggestion goes on first, and the result of it becomes the basis of the dream scene, as when the woman dreamed that her father waved goodbye to her from the family dinner table. Even though the elements of this fantasy were realistic in that they were true to memory, the scene itself was a dramatization. If the reality was the father's approaching death, it suggested the fictitious scene which then was embodied in the dream imagery. However, the meaning in this instance was fairly clear.

But incomplete cases are frequent, and again the defect may occur in a number of different ways. One fairly common one is that personalities are substituted in the imagery. A frequent substitution is that of the dreamer himself for the one actually involved. Such was the case of a woman who dreamed she was driving along a lonely stretch of road when suddenly a heavy black car loomed up ahead in the early morning light. A woman and child were in the front seat. The woman lost control of the car, swerved into the other lane and a head-on collision resulted. All three persons were thrown against a lone tree, and she 'saw' all of them including herself, hanging as if dead from its limbs. The reality was that her brother Bill and his wife set out on an early morning trip. They were on a lonely highway with few trees when suddenly a heavy black car loomed up with a woman and child in the front seat. The woman lost control of her car and headed for Bill's. But just *before* he saw it his wife grabbed the wheel and jerked the car to one side where it came to a stop beside a lone tree. Although the woman's car swerved into Bill's lane, she got control of it in time and no one was hurt. The tendency toward fantasy introduced by the initial substitution of identity was plainly illustrated here by the striking embroidery that went on in the dream beyond the reality, although that had been reproduced fairly realistically.

In other cases the fantasy may be so remote from the actual situation that the latter may not be shown at all. The suggestion made by the actual situation takes off from it without embodying any recognizable detail of it. In 1948, when automobiles were scarce and expensive, a man in Los Angeles dreamed one night that a salesman was trying to sell him a two-toned grey Hudson. He tried to explain to the salesman that he could not buy it, but the latter was insistent and the contract was eventually signed. The next morning the man's sister called to say that the night before at a charity ball she had drawn the lucky ticket and won a two-toned grey Hudson. She said her first thought was to call her brother.

Sometimes a dream is repeated under circumstances that make it appear to be symbolic. For instance, if a dream fantasy is recognized as being connected with a given situation, then a similar dream may precede a comparable situation if one occurs. A man in Minnesota had been convicted as an accessory to a serious crime. As the result of much pressure he pleaded guilty and was held for years without a hearing. His family worked for his parole, but each time when their efforts seemed about to succeed he would dream he saw his dead parents sadly turning their heads from side to side as if saying no, and each time the parole effort was unsuccessful. But finally he did secure a hearing and was freed. A few days before it he again saw his parents in a dream and they were smiling and giving every evidence of joy. He felt the appeal would be successful, and it was.

In cases like this the repetition of the precognitive dream appears to stamp it in. The first time it is fashioned on the event, and then it is repeated so that with some reason it comes to be taken as an indication of the coming event.

One feature of dreams like the preceeding two is that the fantasy is obviously suggested by the person's own individual situation. It is not really symbolic, as it was in the case of a woman who dreamed for three nights of swirling muddy water. When ten days later her sister died of peritonitis after an appendectomy, the dreams were taken to have been 'signs' of it. This woman's grandmother, who died before she was born, was said also to have dreamed of muddy water as a sign of death, so that muddy water taken to mean a death had no doubt been mentioned in the family. It therefore could have been a natural association from which an apparently 'stylized' and impersonal symbol had developed.

However, when the fantasy has no personal connection the likelihood that it was based on ESP is questionable. Take for instance the kind of dream imagery reported by a man in Michigan, who said, 'When I dream of ice or snow I always have trouble on the job or am laid off. It has happened so many times that I can't ignore it.'

In such cases, if no time or other limit was set, the next 'trouble on the job' could be taken as a fulfilment of the dream without any necessary ESP impression at all. As a matter of fact, the unrealistic ESP dreams most frequently reported scarcely support the commonly held belief that dream imagery tends to be symbolic. In the first place the majority of unrealistic dreams that are reported do not show the impersonal imagery involved in symbolism, and many dreams that appear to be symbolic do not involve ESP.

Not quite all of the ESP experiences that feature imagery occur in sleep. Occasionally a person while awake may have an experience involving imagery (day-dream) which also brings information by ESP. Since the form is the same as that of a dream such experiences, whether realistic or unrealistic, can be classed as dreams even though the person was not sleeping.

All ESP experiences come in one or other of these forms – intuitive, hallucinatory, or realistic or unrealistic dreams, and bring items of information in varying degrees of completeness. The forms usually are fairly distinct from each other, although in occasional instances a tendency to change from one to another in the same dream may occur.

The Falling Picture

PK, the second main type of psi, is manifested by effects on objects without physical contact. They usually appear to bring messages, much as do the forms of ESP experience; as if the physical manifestation was a method of signalling a message without using the ESP channels. In them, instead of a hallucinated effect, a real objective one occurs. Such occurrences can thus be considered a fifth form of psi. While theoretically the information might concern a thing, a thought or a future event, just as in ESP experiences, it generally concerns another person, often one at a distance, and usually one who is undergoing a crisis at the time. The other person, the target person, almost invariably is one with whom the experiencing individual is emotionally involved. The physical effect then appears to the experiencing person to be a message or 'sign' of the crisis.

The crisis very frequently is that of dying, but sometimes the person is already dead, sometimes still living. There seems to be no connection between his state or condition and the specific kind of effect that marks his crisis. It may be different or the same from case to case, regardless of whether he is dying, dead, or still living.

One frequently noted effect is the falling of a picture at the time of the crisis of the target person. The following three cases, in which a picture fell and seemed to mark a target person's crisis, illustrate similar effects related to different conditions of the target person.

The first case involved a dying person. (The timing in cases when the target person dies, however, is seldom sufficiently exact to make it possible to tell if the person was still living or already dead when the physical effect occurred.) It was reported by a college girl whose father frequently flew his own plane. She was accustomed to the idea and not worried about him, but one Sunday morning in her dormitory room she was

Mansell Collection

Another way in which information known to the unconscious mind through ESP is sometimes transferred into the conscious mind is through a hallucination, seeing or hearing or otherwise sensing something which 'is not really there', as we say (though many hallucinations do not involve ESP)
Facing page **Banquo's ghost appears to Macbeth, though no one else can see it** ***Left*** **A night phantom, traditionally believed in Normandy to lure men to their deaths in marshes**

lying on her bed, her roommate sitting by the closed window, both reading, when her father's picture fell off the desk. Both girls looked up in surprise for there had been no motion in the room to cause it. Before long the message came that her father's plane had crashed that morning and he had been killed. The accident occurred about the time the picture fell, and its falling was taken as a sign to the girl of her father's crisis.

The next example is of an experience involving a person already dead. It was reported by a woman in Argentina. She tells of her father's death after a serious heart illness. She was sleeping in the room with him when she was wakened by his loud breathing followed by silence. Uneasy, she arose and found him no longer breathing. It was half past three in the morning. She decided she would not wake her mother since there was nothing to be done at that hour, and it would be better to 'prepare her for the mournful news when she had wakened'. She dressed, went into an adjoining room, took down a medical book and was reading and thinking about her father when a loud noise from his room caused her to go back into it. She found that her grandfather's picture had fallen from the wall where it had hung for years. The wire had broken and it seemed to her more than a simple coincidence that it broke just then. She reflected that her father had been her grandfather's favourite son-in-law and she felt that this had been his signal of awareness of the death.

The third is an instance of a picture that fell when the target person, though in a crisis, did not die at the time. It was reported by a woman who was then in Budapest. She and her mother were in their apartment when 'spontaneously a big heavy picture jumped from the wall and dropped with a loud crash to the floor'. Soon a message came that her sister in Vienna had had a stroke, that the case was hopeless and that they should come immediately. The sister died soon after, but was living when the picture fell.

Regardless of the actual kind of effect observed, such an occurrence until recently was usually taken as a message from the target person, particularly in cases in which the target person was dying or dead. Instances in which he was still living were seldom taken into consideration, and probably, if noticed at all, were put down to 'coincidence'. The natural though unspoken assumption when the dying or dead were involved was that an unusual ability to affect objects at a distance must have been activated, an ability that living persons were not known to have.

However, since PK has been demonstrated in the laboratory to be a capacity that does belong to the living, the interpretation now is different. It now hinges on the question whether the messages did come from the target person, or were instead spontaneous PK effects produced by the persons in whose presence or vicinity they occurred. The question is whether the effects were produced by the target persons or by the experiencing persons.

Harry Price Library

This question of who is responsible for a PK effect comes up in the laboratory as well as in life-situations. If an individual subject produces evidence of PK when alone, he himself of course can be assumed to have caused it. But the exercise of PK, like that of ESP, is an unconscious process and can only be recognized by its end product. Therefore if a subject and an experimenter are both present in a PK test, both aware of the target and both eager to succeed, and do then succeed, it is not possible to decide with certainty which one is responsible.

The experimental results thus may not show which of two individuals involved in PK is the effective one. But they do show that living persons can exercise the PK effect. Whether or not the deceased can do so, or even whether they 'survive' death at all, are still unsettled questions. Further, in occasional cases the likelihood that the target person created the effect is ruled out entirely by the fact that he did not know (or perhaps, even know of) the experiencing person. These are mostly instances in which the target person is a public figure. Such a case was reported by a man in Colorado, who said that a clock in his home stopped on 22 November 1963, at the very time that President Kennedy was assassinated. It had run perfectly for years and he did not feel that it stopped at that precise time just by coincidence. The effect, of course, could not be ascribed to an influence from the target person. Instead some of those in the home who were shocked, as was the nation, must

Harry Price Library

Collective hallucination, when several people experience the same apparently 'unreal' phenomena, has been suggested as a possible, if highly tentative, explanation of some strange cases reported in the past: from a broadsheet of 1681, describing a battle between two phantom armies in the sky

be supposed to have exercised PK, if indeed something other than coincidence was involved. But in all cases the experiencing person could have caused the effect. He could have done so regardless of the nature of the crisis of the target person or whether he was dying, dead, or still living.

The experiencing person thus appears to be the one who causes the physical effect. It would be, in a way, a sign to himself of the unconscious reception at Stage 1 of the item of information. There is reason to think that in Stage 2, the PK effect may occur in a way quite analogous to that of a hallucinatory effect; that is, in conjunction with an incipient intuition which is then usually blocked. The reason for thinking this is that here, too, in an occasional report, an intuitive component is recognizable. For instance the daughter of a coal miner, asleep in her home miles from that of her parents, was awakened by her bedroom light suddenly coming on. She says, 'I knew something was wrong down home', an intuitive idea, of course. It was correct, for at the time a motor down in the mine fell and crushed her father.

The physical effect in such cases thus appears to have originated with the intuition at the start of Stage 2. The origin of the PK form thus appears to be quite parallel with that of hallucinatory experiences.

The PK form never produces a complete item of information, and is also the form least frequently reported. This may mean that relatively few personalities can produce cases of spontaneous PK. It also may be partly because this is the most difficult form of all to identify with a degree of certainty. For not only must the effect be timed with the crisis but the absence of ordinary causes, too, must be established. These points often are difficult to make, for usually it is only some time afterwards that the details are noted. Consequently they are often unconvincing.

The general observation that follows from this catalogue of the forms of psychic experiences is that psi ability has no form that is exclusively its own, except that of PK. All of the other forms, and especially the intuitive and the dream forms, are common mental experiences that usually have nothing to do with psi. Hallucinations, while not so common, do occur in situations that have nothing to do with psi. They have been associated mostly with abnormal mental states rather than normal ones. Psi hallucinations, however, are not commonly associated with abnormality.

Since ESP does not have a characteristic form of its own, and the PK form occurs so obscurely that it is seldom recognized, psi is difficult to identify and can only be recognized tentatively in everyday life by considering the meaning of the information transmitted. It must be such that it could not have been supplied by sense experience. Also it must be beyond reasonable explanation as a case of chance coincidence. Reliable identification of psi has therefore depended on experiments, in which sensory cues were ruled out by the conditions and in which the unlikelihood of coincidence could be estimated.

The classification of cases as to form thus indicates that they are not really a heterogeneous manifestation of a mysterious, perhaps supernatural, order. Instead they appear to be the result of normal psychological processes, bringing parapsychologically received information to conscious attention.

Who Chooses the Message?

Even though psi experiences may bring information about a practically unlimited range of topics, the message in any particular case concerns only one specific topic. Obviously it is selected from all other thoughts, things or future events that might have concerned the person. But is it a topic that impresses itself upon the person from the outside, something like a telegram bringing an item of news? Or does he himself 'reach out' and pick this particular item from all the others, because of his interest in it? Indirectly, if not directly, it is possible now to get something of an answer to this question, both logically and by studying the range of topics involved in a large number of experiences.

Logically, the choice between the two

alternatives is different now than in the past. Before the occurrence of precognition had been recognized, it seemed more likely that the person was the receiver of a message impressed upon or communicated to him from the outside, for all experiences under consideration then were contemporaneous with the time of the event. But now no such necessary temporal connection exists. Presumably an experience involving a future event could occur at any time beforehand, and besides that it would be difficult to think of a future event as being 'sent' to a person.

Earlier, another impression was also current, which was that psychic experiences nearly always concern crises of great importance to the person, and that they frequently involve communications from the dead. Both ideas implied that the psi message was at least urgent, if not that it actually induced a sensitive person to have an experience about it.

The impression of the usually critical nature of the topics of spontaneous psi was based in part on 19th century studies in psychical research, in which special emphasis was put on crisis cases and those that involved the deceased. In the background of this work was interest in finding evidence that had a bearing on the survival question, and so there was naturally an emphasis on experiences involving crises.

But in addition to establishing the occurrence of precognition, research in parapsychology has shown that the psi process is essentially unitary; not only do ESP and PK seem to be aspects of the same process, but the types of ESP too are the result of a single process acting on different kinds of subject matter. Even telepathy, as shown above, is not dependent on outside initiative, but is a function of the experiencing person just as are the other types. This changes the likelihood that the event triggers the experience, rather than the experiencing person's interest in it.

A few years ago I made a special study of the subject matter of psi experiences. For this I turned to a collection of cases at the Parapsychology Laboratory of Duke University, and used the reports in it that came in the form of realistic dreams. About a third of them were contemporaneous (experience and event occurring at the same time) and the rest precognitive (experience occurring before the event). This particular form of experience was chosen because in it the detailed and accurate imagery makes the connection between the experience and the event it concerns more certain than in any other form. The distribution of topics in these dreams is fairly representative of reported psi experiences.

The study was made from the viewpoint of the experiencing person who in these cases, of course, was the one who had the dream. The objective was to see whether the topics of the cases as far as the dreamer himself was concerned, seemed to be distributed as if they had been forced on him from the outside, as an inordinate number of crisis cases might suggest, or whether he seemed to have selected the topics himself.

Since emotional relationships seem obviously to be involved in many psi experiences, the study began by dividing the cases into groups according to the emotional involvement of the dreamer with the individual who seemed to be the main character in the dream. Four such groups in descending order of involvement were formed. The first included all dreams in which the dreamer himself was the person most concerned, and also instances in which no other person was primarily involved, but which were situations the dreamer would later experience. For example, a girl in Texas dreamed she was at an outdoor theatre and, looking to one side, she saw a man in a cowboy hat lift a whisky bottle to his lips and take a drink. A few nights later she was at an outdoor theatre, looked to one side and saw a man in a cowboy hat lift a whisky bottle to his lips and take a drink.

The group next most important to the dreamer was that of his immediate family; his parents, his children, husband or wife. The third group included his remote relatives, grandparents, uncles, aunts, cousins, in-laws, neighbours, acquaintances and pets. The fourth was made up of strangers, people he had never met. In the case of public figures, he may have known of them.

Each of these four groups was then subdivided according to the importance of the subject matter, into crisis and non-crisis topics. Crisis cases involved death, serious accident, illness, operations, and weddings. The non-crisis cases were then further divided into two groups according to whether their topics were important or unimportant. The important topics included job incidents, honours, visits, journeys and contests. The unimportant were quite incidental experiences that seemed to have no particular purpose.

The percentage of the entire number of dreams which each subdivision represented was then found, as in the following table.

Harry Price Library

Broadsheet of 1833, giving an account of the death of Mrs Jane Pallister in Yorkshire in that year, with 'a faithful Relation of the wonderful Appearances which rested upon the Corpse, as represented in the Engraving, after the decease, with the Names of the Persons who witnessed the wonderful Phenomena'

The results showed no inordinate proportion of crisis cases, for only half of the total fell into that category, and many concerned trivial topics (15%). Besides, over a quarter of the dreams were either about distant relatives (15%) for whom the dreamer's emotional attachment was low, or strangers (13%) for whom it was practically non-existent. On none of these counts did it look as if the pressure or urgency of the event would have been the reason why it became the subject of the psi experience.

However, in the contrast between the distribution of cases involving the dreamer himself, and that of the other groups, especially that of his immediate family, a clue could be seen as to the basis of selection of the topics. The contrast begins in the difference in the percentage of crisis cases in these two groups, 7% in the first, 27% in the second. The 7% is very low, although it must be remembered that it is to some extent depressed because people can scarcely have experiences about their own crises in the present. These experiences are therefore practically all precognitive, while in contrast, half of the crisis experiences involving the immediate family were contemporary. But the percentage of crisis cases of the dreamer himself is low also in comparison to the rest of his experiences. His important but non-critical topics (17%) are more than twice as frequent as his crises. Even the unimportant cases (9%) are more frequent.

But the pattern is quite different in all of the groups except that in which the dreamer himself is concerned. In the immediate family

Distribution of Subject-Matter of 2878 Realistic Dreams

Relation to Dreamer	% of Crisis Cases	% of Non-Crisis Cases Important	Unimportant	Total %
Himself	7	17	9	33
His Family	27	10	2	39
Distant Relatives	10	4	1	15
Strangers	6	4	3	13
Total %	50	35	15	100

British Museum

Dreams carry their meanings by imagery, not the imagery of pseudo-sense experiences as in hallucinations but a dramatization of memories of sense experience. In the *Romance of the Rose* the hero dreams of his quest for love – the Rose: he finds the Rose in a beautiful garden but is driven away by Danger, Scandal and Shame; French, 15th century

group, not only is the percentage of crisis cases high (27%), but important non-critical topics are low in comparison (10%) and unimportant topics almost negligible (2%). Distributions in the last two groups, though less pronounced, are similar. In both, crisis cases are the most frequent, unimportant topics rare. In all three, the total frequencies reflect somewhat the degree of emotional attachment (39%, 15%, 13%), the percentages tapering off, although not disappearing entirely when it is non-existent.

A great difference is thus shown between distributions when the person is dreaming about his own affairs and when he is dreaming about those of others, and especially those of his immediate family. This, of course, is the group with which his emotional links are strongest, the group for which his concern and anxiety presumably is the greatest. However, in the low-emotion groups, too, crisis cases still are more frequent than others, although in these his concern or anxiety would certainly not be so strong, and he would have only a general interest. But it could well be strong enough to be aroused by a death or other critical event, while it would leave him fairly oblivious to less important happenings.

From these results, it looks as if the topics, in a general overall way, are oriented from the viewpoint of the dreamer himself. They do not appear to be random choices forced upon him. Instead they follow psychological rules recognizable in ordinary life, for the distribution of cases involving the dreamer himself seems similar to the interests of normal healthy-minded persons. They do not dwell overlong on their own crises or worry about those sure to come sometime in the future. They are of course interested in many of their own important but non-critical affairs, but they also have frequent occasions when, as it were, their reflections are merely 'idling', when a myriad of inconsequential thoughts and episodes occupy their minds. The distribution of their psi experiences appears to reflect this same pattern.

But in real life the pattern is different when the emotionally close circle is involved and here, too, it is different. With that circle, crises are highly important. The smaller the items of their lives, the less is the inducement to follow them, whether by sense perception or ESP. In both, each individual must first of all live his own life, and although in a sense he also lives the lives of his children and other close relatives, he cannot follow them in detail as he does his own.

However, in the situation in areas in which the link of emotion is weak, here, as in the sensory world, a change in motivation comes in. The person does not lose all interest where stronger emotions cease, but it becomes less personal. It becomes the general kind that makes each person want to know something of the outside world even if beyond his immediate contact, the kind of interest that makes him read the newspapers. And of course if anyone doubts the general interest there in crisis as against non-crisis topics, a glimpse of the headlines of almost any daily paper will remind him.

It seems, then, that the dreamers in the realistic dreams of this study were in general acting normally and in some way influencing or selecting the topics of their dream experiences. They selected them, not from some otherworldly idealized principle but according to inherent – one might almost say – primitive interests. The selecting, of course, was done on a deeply unconscious level, and consequently the principles that guided it were also unconscious ones, far removed from those that perhaps would be chosen if upper levels of mind were making the selections.

It looks as if the experiencing person himself is the measure of his ESP experiences, within the limits of his sensitivity to non-sensory targets. And with this picture of the topics that he selects for his psi experiences, his horizon, which in earlier days was supposed to be limited closely to his own calamities, is much expanded. In his psi contacts the person appears to be more broad-minded, more a citizen of his world, after the correction introduced by experimental parapsychology, than he would have considered, much less have known, himself to be before it.

Psi Experiences and the Dead

Psi experiences in which someone dead appears to play an active part are infrequent in comparison to those in which no such personality is involved. They occur, but since all types of spontaneous ESP, and especially the precognitive, are now recognized, those that involve the deceased make up a very small part of the total number.

Reported cases that seem to involve the deceased are of two general kinds which are different superficially, though not in the basic psi process. One of these is the simple isolated kind, like those mentioned above; the other is more complicated and the phenomena tend to recur in much the same way for an indefinite time. The second category includes haunting and poltergeist phenomena.

Unrepeated experiences in which deceased persons appear to be involved take some of the same forms discussed in earlier sections. One of these is the dream. Dreams involving the deceased are usually realistic in details, but the appearance of someone dead in an active role in a dream of course cannot be considered to be realistic. Such dreams are therefore classified as unrealistic in form. An example was reported by a woman in Detroit. She said that after her mother died, her father said she should have her mother's jewels; they lived in the same apartment and he kept them in his possession. Later he moved to another city and she supposed he took the jewels with him. After his death there, she did not find them among his belongings and she began to worry about them. One night in a dream her father appeared and told her she had worried enough, and she would find the jewels in the dresser in his old room. She should pull out a certain drawer and at the back she would find a small box built into the dresser, so that it could not be seen unless one knew where to look. She did as he said and found the jewels.

Even better known than dreams of the deceased are hallucinatory experiences involving them. (Hallucinatory, it should be recalled, is a term to denote that the person thought a sense, or senses, was involved when no objective reason was present.) A visual hallucinatory experience was reported by a woman in Connecticut. Her father had died some years before. She was awakened very early one morning. She heard nothing but saw her father standing at the foot of her bed. Somehow, though he did not speak, she got the command to go to her mother's home at once. She felt it was so urgent that she got up and within the hour had started on the trip home, a distance of over four hundred miles. She found her mother very ill and alone, and almost certainly she would have died without the help of her daughter.

Even more frequent than visual hallucinations are auditory ones involving someone deceased. An example comes from a woman in South Dakota. Her father, on whom she had depended a great deal, had recently died, and she felt very much alone and helpless in the midst of many troubles. Her husband had long been ill and the family was badly in debt. They were behind in their car payments, and a man came one day to repossess the car. As she reports, 'While I was talking to the man at the front door, just as clear as my own voice, I heard my father say, "Tell him to wait till Friday." Without hesitation I told him to wait till Friday and I would pay him. He agreed and went on. Then I began to wonder how I could raise the $280 due. Thursday afternoon my father's lawyer called me and told me to come to his office and pick up a check for $417. The court had collected an old account owed to my father.'

PK effects that seem to relate to the deceased also occur. Such an experience was reported by a woman in New York. The occasion was a dinner party that she gave for five couples, all of whom had known a man who had suddenly died of a heart attack two days before, while on a trip to South America. When the wine was passed, the closest friend of the deceased rose and proposed the toast. She was holding her glass by the bowl, the stem broke off and fell to the floor. Her glass had not touched anything – she was just holding it. They all felt that their deceased friend was present.

These are the main forms of spontaneous cases in which the dead seem to play an active part – dreams, hallucinatory experiences and instances of PK. Of course, the question in all of them is whether the communications do actually come from discarnate personalities. Before the establishment of ESP and PK as abilities of living persons, it was necessary in the interpretation of such cases as evidence of survival to suppose that the deceased somehow had powers beyond those of living persons. And it was by these unusual powers that they could return and communicate with the living as they purported to do. But it is now known that living persons could themselves secure the needed information in ESP cases like the three above, and that the person or persons present could be responsible for effects like the breaking of the wine glass at a moment of strong emotion.

The imagery of dreams carries information secured by psi to levels of consciousness where memory of the dream can take over, and it is clear that the imagery itself is unconsciously constructed to fit the case. The hallucinatory forms and PK are also

Clairvoyant Reading

In general, the senses (of certain people, at least) are sometimes capable of surprising feats of hyperacuity. In the 1880's, for instance, two Frenchmen, Bergson and Robinet, discovered a boy who, under hypnosis, appeared to be able to 'read' by clairvoyance book page numbers chosen at random by one of the experimenters. The conditions under which he could do this, however, were extremely specific: the experimenter had to stand with his back against the light, the book had to be held nearly vertical, about 4in. from the experimenter's eyes, but slightly below them so that he could look sometimes at the page and sometimes at the boy. It occurred to one of the experimenters that the boy might conceivably be reading the numbers from their reflection in the cornea of the reader. F. W. H. Myers, in reporting this case, calculated that the corneal image would have been about 1mm. in height, while two people who carried out some experiments on reading similar letters in this way found they could only succeed when the letters were about 10mm. high. This may seem to put the boy's performance beyond the bounds of (normal) possibility, but there is no knowing to what extent he was endowed with abnormal visual acuity, and, furthermore, it is possible that, whatever the boy's normal acuity may have been, it was enhanced under hypnosis.

Charles McCreery *Science, Philosophy and ESP*

National Gallery/Brompton Studio

Visual and other hallucinations sometimes carry a powerful and terrifying sense of impending danger, which may prove to have been justified: King Belshazzar sees a hand writing on the wall of his palace during a drunken feast; painting by Rembrandt

vehicles for the expression of information below the conscious level, and are forms in which information may be expressed when no deceased person is involved. Presumably, therefore, when a spirit agent appears as a character in the drama he could be another imaginary creation. The *forms* of the experiences in themselves can thus have no definitive significance for survival.

If spirit personalities exist after death and are in any way actually involved in these experiences, then detection of the fact would have to depend on evidence other than that the dead person *appeared* to play an active role in the drama of a psi experience. It would have to distinguish between influences ascribable to the deceased and those that might be exerted by the living person.

Possibly such evidence might be found in differences between the reasons or motives for communicating which the two persons, the living and the dead, might be presumed to have had. If the motive of the dead person in making the specific communication was much stronger than that of the living, then the bearing of the case would at least favour the idea that the deceased had influenced or caused the experience.

In the examples already given no great difference in motives exists, and it is only fairly rarely that a situation is such that the deceased person's interest in the communication can be presumed to have been much greater than that of the living person. One such, reported by a woman in Florida, happened some years ago, when she was a young girl in her 20s and travel was still mainly by train. In her Pullman one night she woke up, she said, 'to see the face of a nice man, probably in his late 50s, brown hair and eyes and a Van Dyke beard. He apologized, said his family was on the train and he was looking for them, and that I looked so much like his daughter that he thought he had found them. I went back to sleep resolved to waken early and try to get a look at the girl who looked like me. I did not find her until I was in the station. Then I saw her and with her were her mother and brother. The brother looked just like his father. Just then from the baggage car a coffin was taken off the train, and the girl, her mother and brother, in deep mourning and weeping followed with sad eyes the transfer of the coffin. I did not have the presence of mind to tell them of my experience, but I realized then that the buttons of my berth had not been opened and it was dark in it, yet that face and head had certainly been very visible.'

In this instance, as in many of the cases when the emotional situation is strongly weighted toward the deceased, he was a stranger to the experiencing one. The latter had no apparent reason for making the contact implied in the psi experience, while the deceased one seemed to have a motive. But still the evidence is not conclusive.

It can be observed, however, that experiences in which the dead seem to play an active role, if considered as unconscious dramatizations, do involve more complicated levels of it than other unrealistic psi dreams usually do. In these not only do the deceased appear as self-activated characters, but they also deliver the message. This may mean that these appearances of the deceased are not purely dramatizations, but actual influences; or on the other hand, it may mean that the unconscious dramatizing ability of very few dreamers is sufficient to produce this level of fantasy.

The situation regarding these experiences, therefore, is that they cannot be finally interpreted now that psi is known to be an ability that living persons possess. But at the same time that psi prevents an interpretation for or against the survival hypothesis, it does permit the question to be raised. If survival does occur, psi would be the necessary form by which communications from the deceased to the living would take place. But if it does occur, the methods of research by which the fact could be established have not yet been developed.

(See also DREAMS; GHOSTS; HAUNTED HOUSES; POLTERGEISTS.)

LOUISA E. RHINE

FURTHER READING: L. E. Rhine, *Hidden Channels of the Mind* (Sloane, Duell and Pearce, 1961), and *Mind Over Matter* (Macmillan, 1970); C. Greene & C. McCreery, *Apparitions* (State Mutual Books, 1977).

SPRING

John Moss

The renewal of life in spring has been celebrated since very early times and some pagan rites blended with the Christian festival of Easter: children dressed as angels, in an Easter procession in Brazil

The celebration of returning fertility, and its magical stimulation, is the basis of all spring rituals and festivals, from the Great Dionysia of the ancient Greeks to the Mardi Gras which is still an annual event in modern New Orleans

DRINKING, DANCING, FEASTING, noise-making and love-making have been the usual ways in which men have celebrated occasions of communal happiness; the winning of a war, for instance, or an election, the birth of a royal heir or the death of a tyrant. But ever since prehistoric times man has reserved special celebratory energies for the turning of the seasons, and has reacted with perhaps the strongest surge of emotion to spring, the time when the earth is freed from the shackles of winter.

This emotion was expressed in the form of religious rites, mainly because for ancient man no aspect of life could be kept apart from religion. Modern commentators have seen in the Paleolithic cave paintings of dancing figures in animal masks or disguises a form of hunting magic that itself was probably seasonal; but later ages brought agriculture to mankind, and the seasonal rites became of crucial importance. The celebration of returning fertility along with the magical stimulation of fertility form the basis for all ancient spring rituals and festivals, and so through them for most modern ones.

Something of their essence can be seen in the ancient spring customs of Mesopotamia in which the Babylonians performed ritual re-enactments of a Creation myth, reflecting the re-creation of spring. And they staged the sacred intercourse of the king and a priestess in a room set aside for the rite and decorated with leaves and flowers.

Sex and drama also occur in the rituals of the Greeks, a festive people who took every opportunity available for some sort of celebration. And the eastern cults that were introduced during later centuries offered many opportunities. Before that the early Greeks held a spring Festival of Flowers to

The sexual and dramatic aspects of springtime revelry sometimes overlap with another common motif in which the normal order of things is overturned

praise fertility and the god Dionysus (see DIONYSUS), with plenty of sacrificing, feasting and drinking. There was also some placation of the community's dead, the ancestral ghosts, a practice that found its way into many later traditions.

In March, the Great Dionysia was celebrated, which by the 6th century BC had come to be a time not only for general revels of a wildly unrestrained nature, but also for the presentation of drama in Athens. Evolved from older choric hymns and rites of Dionysus, the tragedies of Aeschylus, Sophocles and Euripides developed first, but comedy followed fast. And the latter retained explicit aspects of its fertility rite origins, as in the traditional flaunting of over-size phalluses.

Rome's spring festivals took up many of these older threads and entwined them with new ones. In early Republican days there were minor festivities such as the dancing and processions of the *Salii*, in March (see MARS), or the uninhibited merrymaking of the April *Parilia*, originally a shepherds' rite (see SHEEP). Also in April was a movable feast, the beautiful *Floralia*, which in the true primitive tradition combined vegetation magic and ritual sexuality.

The better known ceremonies of the *Lemuria* in May recall the Greek festival that paid homage to the dead: for the Romans it was also a time for laying restless ancestral spirits, and preventing them from wreaking harm. Something of the same intention functioned in another well-known late Roman festive occasion, the *Lupercalia*, which was held in February, at the very start of the Roman spring. It involved sacrifices, offerings of the first fruits of the previous harvest, and the other usual basic enjoyments. But it also required some ritual flagellation of people, most usually of barren women, to stimulate their fertility and perhaps to drive off whatever evil baulked that fertility. The priests also 'beat the bounds' of the communities, or of the fields, again to set up magical protection against evil for the year to come.

The declining Empire came to know many new cults and their festivals (apart from the novel worship of Christianity). One was the *Bacchanalia*, the frenzied Roman version of the Greek Dionysia, but another more austere festival developed with the cult worship of Attis (see CYBELE). This was the March celebration called *Hilaria*. It involved processions and sacrifices, followed by abstention from meat, and general restrictions, to accompany the ritual mourning of the god's death. The god's eventual resurrection was followed by ritual joy and festivity. Christians will find the pattern not unfamiliar.

First and Last Flings

From the earliest Christian times, the celebration of spring tended to begin on or shortly after Twelfth Night, but to come to a head especially in the few days before Ash Wednesday and the austerities of Lent. Many pre-Christian festivals were held at this time, and again this is an example of Christianity superimposing itself onto paganism. In fact, the folk festivals, as opposed to the liturgical ones, always tended towards the secular, not to say the profane. Nevertheless, the Church's terminology took over: the final day of the festivals is invariably Shrove Tuesday, presumably so called because it was a day for priests to shrive folk in preparation for Lent. Yet, although the festivals may appear to be in the nature of 'last flings' before Lenten asceticism, they were, and are, also 'first flings', expressing universal joy at the spring renewal. The pre-Lenten festivals were not the sole spring festivities, but for Christian Europe and the Americas, they were the first.

Some motifs are found in most of these early spring celebrations. Feasting is always important, especially for Christians who had to give up meat and any kind of rich delicacy in Lent; but sometimes the feasting is merely symbolized by the eating of some special Shrovetide food. Dancing invariably takes place, as always at times of communal joy; some special dances may be mimetic and dramatic, concerning some suitable springtime theme, while others might be processional, the ancestors of later parades. The modern idea of parades with great decorated 'floats' was foreshadowed in the Germanic rite praising the goddess Nerthus, which involved processions with sacred objects borne on a strange 'boat-on-wheels' called a ship-wagon or ship-cart.

Masks and costumes are always part of the festivities, perhaps recalling the prehistoric dancers in animal head-dresses, and the primitive belief that fearful masks provided a way of keeping evil spirits at bay. But in more modern times the costumes are worn largely for the sake of competitive splendour, and the masks have always helped the celebrants to shed their inhibitions in relative safety.

The motif of warding off or driving off evil crops up in many places in forms other than masking. Sometimes it is a magical ritual to protect the crops, at other times it appears as a magical destruction or exorcism of the demonic winter or some other appropriate symbol of evil. Noise plays a large part in the expulsion, as it does in many primitive rites; often an effigy figure is burned or suitably destroyed.

Mock battles of one kind or another occur frequently, and are probably linked with the motif of driving off evil. For while they may have taken on special colourations, such as re-enactments of historical combats, or riotous sport, their presence in a spring festival links them with more ancient ritual battles symbolizing the conflict of winter and summer.

Spring festivals all naturally incorporate some form of sexuality – not only private sex activity, which has always accompanied drinking, feasting and dancing, but also ritual sex that long antedates the Christian traditions. Some traditions incorporate variants of the sacred marriage; others merely bring in rude songs, the coarse antics of clowns, and earthy folk drama.

Drama, on any level, is a spring motif of its own. The incomparable Greek drama grew from much older, primitive rites; and the high traditions of English drama had their roots in choric liturgical rites of the Church at Easter which gave rise to later mystery and miracle plays, and the folk dances, mimes and mummery of the people, performed at Shrovetide, which developed the morality thread of the English tradition. Many lands still have special folk dramas and masques which are performed before Lent as they have been for centuries (see DANCE; DRAMA; MYSTERY PLAYS).

The sexual and dramatic aspects of the revelry sometimes overlap with another common motif, in which the normal order of things is overturned. Servants or fools become rulers, Lords of Misrule dominate the festivities of many countries, men dress as women.

It may seem odd that countries of the far

The celebration of fertility, and its magical stimulation, form the basis for spring rituals all over the world *Right* Fertility dance, in a village on the Ivory Coast *Below right* The maypole with its phallic symbolism is a traditional feature of springtime celebrations, and the custom of performing a dance around it is widespread: young men raising the maypole in Sweden

Uniphoto

Spectrum Colour Library

North start their festivities to celebrate spring and fertility at a time when the snow is usually no less deep than at Christmas. Similarly, it may seem strange that customs left over from Catholic observances of Lent still survive in primarily Protestant countries. The latter fact may be accounted for simply because the old ways die hard, especially when they are enjoyable, and the former may be because the combined pagan and Christian jollity, though perhaps imported to the northern lands, proved able to overcome even the frost and ice of February.

Indeed, a Finnish tradition makes use of the snow: outdoor games are part of the holiday, and old lore says that if the children's sleds can coast long distances on Shrove Tuesday, the year's crops will be bountiful. Elsewhere in Scandinavia, feasting, processions, games and dances are hallmarks of the pre-Lent time as is the custom of playful ritual flagellation with birch or willow switches, recalling the old purification theme, the driving off of winter and evil.

Driving off demons also seems all-important in Teutonic traditions, especially in the great *Fastnacht* celebrations of Germany, known as *Fasching* in Austria. The Austrian *Schemen,* a wild assortment of masked demonic dancers, which form the centrepiece of the Innsbruck festival the week before Ash Wednesday, are especially notable. Cologne's revelry features a Prince of Fastnacht with a court of fools, while Saxony was given to staging a mock battle between the forces of winter and summer. Munich's gorgeous pageantry is world-famous, but seems to dwell more on the city's medieval history than on folk custom or ancient rite; the German-speaking Swiss of Zurich have a tradition of killing an effigy of winter in their spring festivities.

British customs generally seem to have missed out the parades and pageantry so favoured in other lands, but some of the old spring motifs make their appearance. Shrove Tuesday is still Pancake Day in Britain, symbolic of the coming abstention from meat. But apart from this special food, Shrovetide for Britons once meant a time for rough games and hooliganism. In the past apprentices were given a holiday on the Tuesday, and showed their appreciation by all kinds of happy rowdiness. A special sort of Shrovetide football was played in many towns and rural villages (see GAMES).

The sexuality theme seems to be lacking in the British Shrovetide, though the traditional post-Easter fun, and especially the Maytime delights of the past, tended to make up for this lack (see MAY DAY).

In other countries pancakes are eaten as in Britain, and there are also splendid parades or dances. In Belgium where pancakes and door-to-door begging are both part of the tradition, glorious processions were staged. These were dominated by the Gilles, who wore beautiful costumes of silk embroidered with lace, and ostrich-plume head-dresses, and who used to pelt onlookers with oranges.

Old Russian and eastern European customs included eating special cakes: the Russians called them *blini,* and the time of celebration was known as *Maslenitza,* 'butter week'. Apparently the Soviet Union has retained some of these traditions – especially the blini – though stripped of any religious associations. However, it is unlikely that other Slavic customs have lasted; the eastern European dance where the women had to leap high, so that the crops would grow tall, for instance, or the Bulgarian processions with men, dressed as women, performing mimetic ploughing and sowing dances.

Farther south in Europe, terms meaning 'Shrovetide' are replaced by the word carnival, which has come to mean unrestrained festive gaiety. Italy sometimes begins its *carnevale* in mid-January or earlier, and keeps up the feasting and

Barnaby's Picture Library

Barnaby's Picture Library

In Christian Europe, and later in North and South America, the first celebrations of spring were also in the nature of a 'last fling' before the strict fasting of Lent; the Shrovetide celebrations of Britain were paralleled further south by carnivals, times of unrestrained festivity *Above* and *Left* Scenes from the Mardi Gras held annually in New Orleans; brought to Louisiana by French settlers when the state was a colony of France, it has developed into a major tourist attraction *Above right* Masks are always part of the festivities, possibly recalling the primitive belief that they keep evil spirits at bay: masks for sale in Rio de Janeiro which is the scene of the most famous carnival in South America *Far right* Effigy used in celebrations held in May in Portugal

John Moss

Robert Estall

The spring fiesta in Spain includes many folk dramas on sacred marriage or Resurrection themes, and dramatic dance battles between Moors and Christians

dancing and pageantry until Shrove Tuesday. Venice crowns an overweight effigy, the spirit of fleshly indulgence, as King of Carnival and ritually burns him to bring in Ash Wednesday. Florence, among other centres, is noted for the delightful rudeness of traditional carnival songs.

The Spanish carnival spirit produces most of the usual traditions, especially public dancing and masked processions. In northern Spain, a stuffed effigy again acts as the emblem of carnival licence; it rides in a cart decorated with greenery, reflecting the ancient belief in vegetation magic, and is duly burned. Elsewhere in Spain an effigy representing the King of Evil is ritually buried; and the spring *fiesta* also includes many folk dramas on sacred marriage or Resurrection themes, or on the symbolic battle theme, which is sometimes in the form of dramatic dance battles between Moors and Christians.

The Spanish concepts of pre-Lent fiesta were widely adopted in Latin and South America, and there too the motif of the mock battle seems to be strong. A Mexican drama ritually depicts the capture of a famous bandit by soldiers, while in south-east Mexico a mock battle dance concerns 'priests' and 'devils'. Throughout Latin America maskers represent devils and the dead, signifying the supernatural forces that are to be warded off.

But the Spanish ex-colonies take fiesta to its heights in their immense variety of special dances, such as the quadrille-type dance of central Mexico, for instance, in which participants wear medieval garb. Many of the dances incorporate elements of pre-Columbian Indian dances and rites. In Mexico, for instance, the time that is now carnival was once given to revelry in praise of the Aztec god of agriculture.

Portugal's carnival spirit rivals that of Spain. It was once especially famous for the extreme coarseness of the songs, dances and jokes of the masked Fools who dominated it, though this feature has diminished in recent times. The mock battle theme recurs abundantly: in the town of Loulé, for instance, the ritual conflict is fought out with flowers.

Portuguese carnival traditions were naturally exported to Brazil, where in 1840 the urban carnival of Rio de Janeiro began;

Victoria & Albert Museum

it is now regarded as the most lavish on the continent. All the expected features of carnival can be found in costly abundance, especially parades with vast resplendent floats and ornate costuming, in which various societies and clubs ruthlessly compete. Otherwise, besides the street dancing and music, noise and drinking and wild revelry, Rio finds some quiet corners to stage a major song contest, with rich prizes. And the whole festival culminates in a masquerade ball in the Municipal Theatre.

'Fat Tuesday'

The French have always enjoyed many different kinds of carnival, including a now extinct festival of butchers in Paris, which featured Le Boeuf Gras, a fattened ox decorated with ribbons, which was probably another emblem of the indulgence to be forsworn in Lent. But the chief festival is the carnival of Nice, with glorious parades and pageants, dominated by King Carnival and his court of clowns and harlequins, embodying the free wild spirit of the season. This spirit flourished especially in the French colony which is now the American state of Louisiana. There the significant French name for Shrove Tuesday took on new meaning as the general term for the whole festive time. The name is Mardi Gras, 'Fat Tuesday'.

Mardi Gras traditions date from the mid-18th century, in New Orleans, when private masquerade balls often exploded onto the streets to become public, sometimes violent, merrymaking. By the early 19th century the city's revellers had taken to parading through the streets on horseback or in carriages to display their finery; and tableaux, masques and similar light dramas had become a part of the occasion.

By the mid-19th century, the Creole domination of this essentially French tradition had begun to be eclipsed by the eager 'Saxons'. Then in 1857 a group of the latter formed a theoretically secret society called the 'Mystic Krewe of Comus', and staged a colourful street parade depicting the demons from Milton's *Paradise Lost*. So the modern Mardi Gras was born.

The Civil War interrupted the tradition but the Krewe of Comus formed itself again afterwards and continued its parades, always with a special theme that might be allegorical or sometimes satirical. There was always a torchlit night parade on the Tuesday. The Krewe also staged tableaux, and topped off the night with a grand ball that rapidly became a major social occasion.

The festivities were often marred by Creole-Saxon conflicts and general riotous behaviour, but the protests of some citizens could not stem the Mardi Gras tide. In 1872 the day was declared a legal holiday, though by then the festival had been getting under way much earlier. Indeed, in 1870 a Lord of Misrule figure had briefly appeared, with a parade of his own, on Twelfth Night. But in 1872 he faded out, for Rex, King of Carnival, and his court of Dukes, came into being partly to impress the Russian Tsar's younger son, who was visiting the city. The parades were enormous that year, the decorations lavish, the merriment frenzied. On the Tuesday more than a dozen bands played a song called *If Ever I Cease to Love,* supposedly a favourite of the royal Russian; and though he must have been heartily sick of it by the end of the day it remains a traditional tune of Mardi Gras. That year also there was a Boeuf Gras in the old French tradition. Rex, whose parade was at noon on the Tuesday, initiated the now fixed custom of acquiring a Queen, usually a pretty society debutante, and escorting her to the 'court' of Comus at midnight, to pay respects to the first lord of Mardi Gras.

Soon other krewes, as the clubs and societies are still generically known, began to take part. The Knights of Momus led the newcomers, and at first paraded on New Year's Eve, later switching to the Thursday before Fat Tuesday. In 1882 the Knights of Proteus began parading on the Monday; the Krewe of Hermes took over the Friday; and krewes of Orpheus, Osiris, Mithras, Elves of Oberon, the Harlequins, Pierettes, Marionettes and dozens of others found room where they could for their own parades and displays.

Some citizens thought it was all getting out of hand. Sometimes the festivities began before Christmas, as they still do: in 1965 the society balls began on 23 December and there had been 62 of them by Fat Tuesday. From the start, the inter-krewe rivalry had been lavishly expensive. But there was no stopping the flood. Neighbourhood parades began to spring up, smaller versions

Intended to promote fertility and reinvigorate the year, the *Holi* is celebrated in northern India when the crops of the spring harvest are almost ripe; festivities include ritual dramas in which women battle with the men, and generally culminate in a procession; on the second day dust and coloured water are flung over the spectators *Left* 18th century gouache, showing men of a village spraying red water over the women during the spring festival *Right* Dyes for use in the celebrations, for sale in an Indian market place

Brian Mondhe

of the great downtown processions, and on the Saturday schoolchildren organized their own parades. After the First World War the Negroes of New Orleans introduced a parade on the Tuesday itself, before Rex's parade began. The black contribution was headed by the Zulu King, with a ham-bone as sceptre, who was clearly in the Lord of Misrule tradition of overturning the usual order of things. He parades still, though black militants deplore his presence.

Others now tend to deplore the New Orleans' Mardi Gras as a whole, feeling that its French antecedents and the pre-Lent gaiety have been forced into a back seat by the more modern spirit of public relations. Mardi Gras remains still the high point of the social calendar, with an invitation to the Comus ball being a testimonial to social success; otherwise, the ruling theme is not snobbery but civic promotion and commercialism. The two may overlap, of course, for many of the krewes are somewhat identified with businessmen's lunch clubs.

Mardi Gras has been taken over by the promoters because it is a vastly successful tourist attraction. Though the carnival spirit of the citizens is supposed to be the mainspring of the festivities, the Chamber of Commerce is in fact a more likely one, and the city itself pours hundreds of thousands of dollars into the occasion. Nor are private promoters far behind: the trinkets traditionally thrown to the crowd from Rex's parade, once considered luck-bringing souvenirs, now carry advertising matter.

Once again, citizens are calling for the abandonment of the celebration because, they say, commercialism and violence have distorted the original 'folk-celebration' spirit of Mardi Gras. But it is doubtful if that folk spirit truly survived much past the 1850s. After all, the originators, with their self-conscious title of a Mystic Krewe, their high literary themes from Milton, and their expanding sense of their own social cachet, could hardly be said to have represented a spirit that had much to do with the simple, age-old human urge to celebrate the earth's renewal in spring.

DOUGLAS HILL

FURTHER READING: E. O. James, *Seasonal Feasts and Festivals* (Barnes and Noble, 1961); Errol Laborde, *Mardi Gras!* (Picayune Press, 1981).

Many holy wells were pagan sacred springs which were re-dedicated by Christian missionaries; some were prophetic, others therapeutic, and others again had power to work evil

SPRINGS AND WELLS

THE SACRED character of particular springs and wells, like that of many rivers, lakes and waterfalls (see WATER), is an exceedingly old tradition which has its roots in one of the most ancient and universal forms of worship. Water itself was considered to be essentially holy by primitive peoples because it was a basic necessity of life. It was also mysterious, as its movements were often unpredictable and beyond man's control, and it could destroy by drowning or by flood.

Where rivers flowed, or springs welled up out of the ground, or waterfalls thundered over rocks, there some divine force was felt to have its abode, and was worshipped in fear and hope by all who approached. To the unseen spirits who dwelt there, prayers and propitiatory sacrifices were offered, that their dangerous anger might be averted and the life-giving waters continue to flow. To them also, men came to be cured of their ills, or to seek answers to their problems, or to call down destruction upon their enemies. Such beliefs and practices were very deep-seated and, in one form or another, they managed to survive all the religious changes of many centuries, including the advent of Christianity. Even today, their traces are clearly visible in numerous legends of healing or wishing-wells, or life-demanding rivers, and in some wellside ceremonies.

Certain springs and streams were believed to have foreknowledge and, from time to time, to predict the future by sudden variations in level or colour, or the manner of their flow. The now-vanished Drumming Well at Oundle in Northamptonshire gave warning of coming changes in the state of the nation by sounds resembling the persistent beating of a drum. In his *Certainty of the World of Spirits* (1691), Richard Baxter, who heard it once during the Civil War, said that the noise continued for several days together, and was clearly audible some distance away. St Helen's Well at Rushton Spencer in Staffordshire dried up before any calamity, even in the wettest seasons. Tradition says it did so before the outbreak of the Civil War, before the execution of Charles I, and at the beginning of the Popish Plot terror in 1679. Other springs, normally dormant, foretold misfortune by suddenly breaking out and flowing very freely for a short time. One such is the intermittent Assenden Spring, in Oxfordshire, which traditionally runs before a war, and is said to have done so in 1914, and again in 1939. The uncertain land-springs found in chalk country, which appear only occasionally and are known as levants, or corn-springs, were believed to predict by their sudden uprising a dearth of corn, and consequently its high price.

Prophetic waters of this kind seem to have concerned themselves only with matters of national importance or, at least, with coming events likely to affect a fairly wide area. There were other springs which had knowledge of a different kind, and to which inquiries of a more personal character were often directed. The famous Holy Well of Gulval, in Cornwall, used to be visited by people anxious about the welfare of absent friends. Kneeling by the well, and looking into it so that they could see their faces reflected in its depths, they put their questions to an old woman who acted as guardian of the spring, and the water replied. If the friend was well, it bubbled up as if it were boiling, if he was ill, it became muddy and discoloured. If he was already dead, it remained unchanged.

Many ancient holy or healing wells now associated with particular saints started life as pagan sacred springs, and were re-dedicated and given a new spiritual significance by the Christian missionaries of the early conversion period. It was the wise policy of the Church at that time to transform and purify, rather than destroy, whatever was innocent and harmless in the older

Homer Sykes

Found in parts of Derbyshire, the Christian custom of well-dressing is a survival of the pagan belief that each well had its own guardian who had to be propitiated every year if the crops were to grow. Ceremonies usually take place on Ascension Day, immediately following the three days on which God's blessing is asked for the crops *Left* Ceremonial blessing of the Yew Tree Well at Tissingdon in Derbyshire *Facing page* Plaques depicting Cain and Abel, and illustrating a text from the book of Isaiah

faith and, by consecrating familiar sanctuaries anew to the service of Christ, to make the transition from paganism to Christianity easier. This is why the first small churches were often built inside or near stone circles, or close to heathen holy springs, and the water of the latter was used for the baptism of converts. The little wooden chapel that was the humble predecessor of York Minster was built over one such spring, which still exists in the crypt of the present cathedral. The healing virtues of medicinal wells were no longer attributed to the power of pagan indwelling spirits, but to the intercession of saints in whose honour the wells had been re-named; and as new legends replaced the old, their very existence was often thought to be due to the prayers of holy men or, occasionally, to the blood of martyrs shed at that place.

Tradition says that St Augustine's Well at Cerne, in Dorset, came into being when that great missionary, finding himself astray and thirsty in a dry countryside, struck the ground with his staff. Another version of the tale says that he performed this kindly miracle when certain shepherds complained that they lacked water for their flocks. At Binsey, near Oxford, a healing well, into which coins are still dropped by people seeking relief from eye ailments, was called up by the prayers of St Frideswide.

The famous medicinal well at Holywell, in Wales, had its legendary origin in the 7th century, when St Winifrid was murdered in what was then a waterless valley. Because she repulsed his advances, Caradoc of Hawarden killed her by cutting off her head with a single stroke of his sword. Where the head fell, a strong spring burst out of the stony soil, and has run unfailingly ever since. A further legend relates that St Beuno reunited the severed head to the body and restored her to life, and that she lived to meet a second death long afterwards.

Wells dedicated to St Anne exist in many parts of Europe. In England they are often known as granny-wells because, being the mother of the Virgin Mary, she was the grandmother of Christ. A Breton legend says that, in her old age, she made her home in Brittany, and there, just before she died, Christ came to visit her. At her request, in order to help the sick people of the province, he struck the ground three times with his staff, and so called into being the spring of St Anne-de-la-Palue. St Anne's Well at Buxton in Derbyshire has no such personal legend attached to it, but there is a tradition that it is dedicated to her because, in the Middle Ages, a statue representing her was found in its depths. A figure of the saint, enshrined in a wellside chapel, certainly existed in Henry VIII's reign, for it was removed then and subsequently destroyed, but whether this was the one so curiously discovered is now uncertain. Nor can we be sure that the original image was in fact one of St Anne, or any other Christian saint. The spring was venerated in Roman times, and perhaps earlier, and the statue may quite possibly have been that of some pagan water nymph or goddess. It need hardly be said that no such idea crossed the minds of the countless pilgrims who came to the spring to be cured of their ills, and deposited their offerings in the chapel of the saint by whose intercession they had been healed. In 1538 the well was arbitrarily closed by one of Thomas Cromwell's agents, 'for that,' as he said in his report, 'there should be no more idolatry and superstition there used'. Some 30 years later, by a curious turn of fortune, it was once again a centre of healing, though not for religious reasons. It became one of the main medicinal wells of the then newly-founded spa at Buxton, and as such it endures to this day.

A Source of Evil

In some holy wells that were once pagan springs, the ancient indwellers seem never to have been altogether forgotten, or perhaps they raised their hoary heads again as the saints who replaced them gradually lost their influence on everyday life. St Nun's (or Nonna's) spring at Pelynt in Cornwall is sometimes called the Piskies' Well, and pins used to be thrown into it to gain the goodwill of the pixies, rather than that of St Nun, the mother of St David. Its water was used for baptisms in the parish church, but according to a story collected in the late 19th century, it was the fairies who were blamed for the misfortunes that befell a farmer after he had rashly tried to steal its granite basin.

When St Aelian in the 6th century prayed for water and so called up the Denbighshire spring named after him, he can hardly have imagined that it would become notorious,

Spectrum Colour Library

Spectrum Colour Library

Because of their mysterious nature, wells are sometimes depicted in legends as being suitable refuges for malevolent beings; in the Persian *Romance of Amir Hamza,* the giant Zamurrad is lured into a well, and beaten by gardeners: 16th century Mogul miniature

Victoria & Albert Museum

and universally dreaded, as a cursing-well. It seems at one time to have been a simple healing spring, like many others, but during the 18th and 19th centuries, it had an extremely evil reputation. People came to it to curse their enemies. They gave money to its guardian, who wrote the victim's name in a book. His initials were then scratched on a slate, or inscribed upon parchment, and thrown into the well. A pin was also thrown in, and some passages from the Bible were read aloud. The seeker was then given water to drink, and some was thrown over his head, while he stated the nature of the evil he wished to inflict. It was widely believed that any person so cursed would become very ill, or would meet with constant misfortune, or that he would die. Exactly how these malevolent powers became attached to this spring is unknown; the well has now been filled up (see also CURSE).

Some venerable holy wells, to which pious Christians once came in true faith and devotion, have degenerated into simple wishing-wells, where secretly-formed wishes have taken the place of prayers, and pins or coins, or occasionally small pebbles, are dropped in. Those who visit such springs today are not actuated by religious motives, and probably they have only a very vague notion of who or what it is they expect to grant their wishes. Yet it can hardly be doubted that this is a curious reversion to heathen beliefs, unrecognized though they may be by those who offer their pins or coins. The wheel has come full cycle, and the pagan spirit, which some saint displaced for a time, has come into his own again.

CHRISTINA HOLE

FURTHER READING: Christina Hole, *English Shrines and Sanctuaries* (Batsford, 1954); Francis Jones, *The Holy Wells of Wales* (Univ. of Wales Press, 1964).

STAG

ANIMALS WITH HORNS or antlers are depicted in paintings and carvings executed by men of the Old Stone Age; and the 'Horned Sorcerer', a painting of a man wearing antlers, in the cave of Les Trois Frères in southern France, suggests that such beasts were of ritual importance (see ICONOGRAPHY). Among the Hittites a god whose sacred animal was the stag was worshipped. His cult, which dates back to the third millennium BC, was widespread, and models of stags have been recovered from tombs. A god of the countryside, he is represented standing on a stag, holding a falcon and a hare, and it is possible that, before the Hittite city states arose, he may have presided over the chase.

The Celtic divinity Cernunnos was depicted wearing antlers and, usually, in a squatting posture, as on the Gundestrup cauldron found in Jutland, where he is shown surrounded by animals and may have been regarded as a Lord of Beasts. A rock carving in Val Canonica in northern Italy shows a phallic figure apparently worshipping before a horned god who wears a torque (metal ornament). The god was probably regarded as a source of fertility and power. Evidence from the Near East indicates that horns represented supernatural power (see HORNS).

At Syracuse in Sicily women singers wore garlands, and antlers on their heads, and at a festival in honour of Artemis men were similarly adorned. In another such ritual men postured like women. There was yet another ceremony in which men wore phalluses, and one in which women wore imitations of the male organ. There were evidently ambivalent ideas concerning Artemis, the huntress goddess, who was represented in art with one or more stags. Animals, and even human beings, were sacrificed to her. Actaeon, the young hunter who inadvertently interrupted her bathing, was transformed into a stag and torn to pieces by his own hounds (see DIANA).

There is a curious connection between the stag and precious metals. The hinds captured by Artemis and harnessed to her golden chariot bore horns. Hercules's third labour involved capturing the Ceryneian hind which had brazen hooves and golden horns, and which was sacred to Artemis, and bringing it to Mycene (see HERCULES). The *Rama Yana*, an Indian epic, mentions a golden-antlered stag whose coat was flecked with silver, and in China deer are associated with places where precious metals are mined. Silver models of deer were placed in Christian sanctuaries because the stag was regarded as a symbol of Christ; when confronted with a serpent it represented the Christian overcoming evil.

A ritual stag-hunt took place on Mt Lycaeum at the beginning of the Christian era, and as late as the 5th century AD stag mummers danced in the south of France. In North America deer dances were performed by antlered dancers to increase fertility by causing rain to fall, and to encourage the growth of wild crops. Men wearing antlers still perform a dance in September every year at Abbots Bromley in Staffordshire.

Deer Women

The abundance of legendary lore concerning deer where Celtic culture and languages survive confirms that the stag was regarded as a supernatural animal. In the Scottish Highlands and islands the deer is associated with supernatural beings, always female, and there are many tales of deer-human transformations. These fabulous creatures are seldom malicious, but they are sometimes thought of as being gigantic. There was one, for instance, who was so colossal that when she waded across the Sound of Mull the water came only up to her knees.

A Gaelic tale relates that after a tragedy in which her baby was killed, a woman took to the hills where she lived with the deer and eluded her husband's attempts to capture her. After seven years he decided to marry again, but when the day for the wedding arrived his wife appeared at the church and took her place by his side; she was covered in fine fur like that of a red deer fawn. In other tales a hunter sees a deer turn into a woman and falls in love with her. He arranges to meet her at a church where they are to be married, but their plans are foiled by a witch.

Axel Poignant

The stag was widely regarded as a supernatural animal; in some areas it was thought to be connected with the underworld, but there are also signs that it was associated with the sun. Carving of a stag and a Viking, on a cross at Middleton in Yorkshire

British Museum

After many adventures they meet on a distant island and marry.

According to another Celtic legend Ossian hurled his spear at, but missed, a beautiful white deer, who turned out to be his mother. She led him to a rock in which a door mysteriously opened, and closed after them, and then revealed herself as a lovely woman. Yet another story describes how a hunter wounded a deer which managed to escape. Later she appeared to him in a dream, in human form, and returned the arrow with which he had shot her.

The ghosts of deer were thought to change into supernatural women. In some areas the lore concerning deer suggests that they were connected with the underworld but there are also signs that they were solar animals; a rock engraving in Scandinavia shows stags drawing the disc of the sun.

Fairies' Cattle

Folklore in Scotland and elsewhere refers so frequently to deer serving mankind in various ways that it has been suspected that red deer were domesticated at some time in the remote past. However, with the exception of the reindeer, there is little firm evidence of their having been tamed in ancient times. In Scotland they were said to be the fairies' cattle, and tales of benevolent deer go back to ancient times. Telephus, Hercules's son by the virgin priestess of Athens, was abandoned in a forest, and was said to have been suckled by a doe. Stories of Christian saints and hermits similarly describe their receiving sustenance from these creatures. Hermits gave sanctuary to hunted deer, who aided them in various ways, by carrying baggage, or providing an antler book rest or antler candlesticks.

The antlers of deer have often been regarded as having special powers, often magical. Picks made from deer-horn, and a chalk phallus, which were found at the end of a worked-out seam in a Neolithic flint mine at Grimes Graves in Norfolk may have been placed there in the hope that the mine could be made more productive. Practically every part of the deer has been believed to have medicinal qualities, in one part of Europe or another, while in China powdered antlers was thought to be an aphrodisiac. In some areas antlers are hung up on buildings to ward off evil influences.

E. A. ARMSTRONG

Homer Sykes

Victoria & Albert Museum/C. M. Dixon

Left The relationship between stags or deer and human beings is generally a benevolent one; the Roman general Sertorius gained the goodwill of the inhabitants of Spain because he had a pet fawn which they regarded as a sign of divine protection: Sertorius and his fawn, 15th century Italian manuscript _Above right_ Horned animals were of ritual importance to primitive man, who regarded them as sources of fertility and power: the Horn Dance, performed in Abbots Bromley every year, is a relic of pagan worship. There are many tales of people being transformed into deer; in Greek mythology Diana turned Actaeon into a stag because he saw her bathing: a 16th century Italian dish _(right)_ and a painting by Giuseppe Cesari _(following page)_ both depict Actaeon's transformation

Museum of Fine Arts, Budapest/Corvina Press, Budapest

STARS

Mansell Collection

18th century map of the northern hemisphere: the Mesopotamians regarded the movement of the planets in relation to the fixed stars as the 'writing of heaven'; although Christ was said to have disrupted the planets' courses, and to have broken their control over human destiny, belief in astrology has survived throughout the centuries

WHETHER STARS have ever been worshipped purely as stars is doubtful. For, mysterious though they surely were to ancient man, those remote points of light in the night sky had no obvious effect on his life as, for example, the sun had. However, they have been associated with divine beings from a very early period, often as their place of abode or form of manifestation. The ancient Sumerians identified the planet Venus with an important goddess called Inanna, the 'Lady of Heaven'; the Babylonians knew her as Ishtar (see ISHTAR). Since the planet appears as both the Morning and Evening Star, the two forms under which the goddess was conceived could be conveniently represented: as the goddess of the Morning Star, Ishtar presided over war and carnage; as the Evening Star, she was the fertility goddess, associated with love and luxury. Her symbol was a star of eight or 16 rays, inscribed in a circle. The awful god Nergal, the ruler of the Mesopotamian underworld, who was also associated with war and pestilence, was identified with the red planet Mars.

The locating of the gods in the stars and the origins of astrology are graphically recorded in the famous Babylonian Creation epic, known as the *Enuma elish* (see CREATION MYTHS). It is related of Marduk, the great god of Babylon: 'He constructed stations for the great gods, fixing their astral likenesses as constellations. He determined the year by designating the zones: he set up three constellations for the 12 months.' The movement of the planets in relation to the constellations of the fixed stars was, consequently, regarded by the ancient Mesopotamians as the 'writing of heaven', by which the will of the gods for the state or individual persons was signified. This resulted in the development of astrology as a science of divining what was portended by the stars, and the casting of horoscopes, which can be traced back to at least 410 BC (see MESOPOTAMIA). The belief that the gods revealed the fates of nations and men through the stars, in which they resided, inevitably led to the idea that human destiny was controlled by the stars or planets. This idea became very influential in the world of Graeco-Roman civilization.

In ancient Egypt, the stars were objects of great significance, although none achieved the status of a major god, apart from the sun (Re), which was worshipped as the chief state deity, and the moon god Chons, the 'lord of time' who counted the years of both kings and men. The Egyptians imagined the stars, which 'grow not weary', as manning the boat in which the sun god journeyed across the night sky. The circumpolar stars, that never set in the west, were seen as 'the imperishable ones', and in the Pyramid Texts the dead kings hope to fly up to heaven and join their company, to be for ever safe from change and decay. The association of the dead with the stars was a long-established tradition in Egypt, which finds expression in the depiction of stars on coffins, often in connection with the protecting image of Nut, the sky goddess.

The Egyptians, like the Mesopotamians, formed pictures in the stars, seeing in the various groups the figures of gods, animals and things. The Plough suggested to them both the implement used in the ceremony known as the 'Opening of the Mouth' in the Osirian mortuary ritual (see MUMMIFICATION), and the thigh of an animal. Because the latter symbolized a sacrificial offering, which in turn was connected with the evil god Seth (see SETH), the Plough was also called the 'thigh of Seth'. The constellation of Orion was held in particular veneration; like many other peoples, the Egyptians saw in it the form of a man, whom they identified with Osiris (see OSIRIS). The equation had a deep significance, in view of the ancient connection of the dead with the stars: for Orion, the 'king of the stars', was also Osiris, the ruler of the dead.

Another star of great significance was Sothis (Sirius, the 'dog star'). Because of its apparent proximity to the constellation of Orion, which represented Osiris, Sothis was identified with the goddess Isis (see ISIS) the wife of Osiris; and because Isis had succoured the dead Osiris and helped him to rise from the dead, Sothis was accordingly deemed to help those who had died. Further, the Egyptian calendar had originally been based upon the fact that Sothis's rising near the sun coincided with the commencement of the annual flooding of the river Nile. Consequently, since the prosperity of Egypt depended upon the fructifying flood waters of the Nile, the equation of Isis with Sothis was endowed with even greater meaning. According to the Greek writer Plutarch (1st century AD), Sirius (Sothis) was the soul of Isis. In iconography Isis is often depicted with a star between the two horns of her crown.

The ancient Egyptians did not come to believe that the stars controlled human destiny until the Hellenistic period (330–30 BC). Then, most probably under the influence of Mesopotamian astral beliefs, they adopted the idea with enthusiasm and developed a form of astral religion or mystical philosophy which became widely influential in the world of Graeco-Roman culture. Star charts were elaborated, comprising 59 deities who presided over the various time units of the year: months, decades, and supplementary days. Astrological writings were composed c 150 BC, doubtless in Alexandria, and were ascribed to a fictitious king Nechepso and a priest Petosiris, who were associated with the attribution of each day of the week to one of the planets, although the notion probably originated with Chaldean astrologers. The importance of horoscopes became so great in Egypt that they were inscribed on the roofs of tombs. How this astrological lore assumed that the fates of individual persons were decided by the planets is set forth, with pseudo-scientific detail, in the *Tetrabiblos* of Ptolemy, who wrote in Egypt in the 2nd century AD. For example, he attributes to each planet a particular form of death; Saturn controls death by pulmonary consumption and rheumatism; Jupiter by apoplexy and cardiac affections; Mars by strokes and kidney diseases. The planets similarly determined the temperament and length of life of each man and woman.

Slaves of the Universe

The idea that mankind was subject to demonic powers, resident in the planets, was elaborated into a complex doctrine of salvation in the *Corpus Hermeticum* (see HERMETICA). This remarkable collection of mystical scriptures purport to be revelations made by Hermes Trismegistus, who was in origin the Egyptian god Thoth. In one of the texts, known as the *Poimandres*, the subjection of mankind to the planets is explained in an esoteric imagery. In the beginning the Primal Being, who is described as Mind, *Nous*, Life, *Zoe*, and Light, *Phos*, generated a second demiurgic Nous, who created the universe. In the course of his creation the demiurge made the seven planets called governors, *dioiketai*, whose cycles envelop the material world, which they govern; their government being called *Heimarmene*, Destiny. Next, the Supreme Nous generated an archetypal man, *Anthropos*, in his own image. This Anthropos, seeing the creation of the demiurge, desired himself to create. Passing through the celestial spheres, he descended to the material world, where he cohabited with Nature, *Phusis*. From their union mankind was born, having a dual nature: their mortal bodies derived from Nature, and their immortal souls from divine Man. But owing to their situation in this material world, human beings are subject to the planetary powers, who control their destiny. It was the purpose of the *Poimandres* to show how the human soul could be saved from this fatal enslavement to the planets, and ascend through the spheres to the highest heaven from which its divine progenitor had come.

This explanation of the human situation, variously adapted, constituted the basic doctrine of the many forms of Gnosticism which flourished in the Graeco-Roman world (see GNOSTICISM). Its ideology appears in many writings of St Paul and it obviously influenced his doctrine of salvation (see PAUL). He uses a number of terms which relate to this astral doctrine: he reminds the Galatian Christians that before their conversion they 'were slaves to the elemental spirits of the universe' (Galatians 4.3); he explains that God misled the 'rulers of this age' into crucifying Christ, which enabled mankind to be delivered from their power (1 Corinthians 2.6–8); he tells how Christ, through his crucifixion, 'disarmed the principalities and powers' (Colossians 2.15); and he asks the Christians of Galatia whether they desire to return to their bondage to the planets, because they 'observe days, and months, and seasons, and years' (Galatians 4.10).

In Christian Gnosticism these ideas were further developed. It was maintained that Christ had broken the control of the planets over human destiny by disrupting their courses. The star which announced his birth to the Magi (Matthew, chapter 2) was explained as a new star that changed the old inevitable astral order to one that was providential. This subjection of the planetary powers is dramatically symbolized in the book of Revelation (1.16), where Christ as the Cosmocrator, ruler of the world, appears holding the seven stars in his right hand.

Although Christ was deemed to have delivered mankind from the dominion of the stars, Christians continued to regard them with awe. Astrology survived the downfall of paganism, and its practice continued on through the Middle Ages with even popes consulting the prognostications of the stars. The planets still remained associated with the pagan deities, and their depiction in medieval manuscripts reveals that they were still conceived of in personified forms.

(See also ASTROLOGY.)

S. G. F. BRANDON

FURTHER READING: S. G. F. Brandon, *History, Time and Deity* (Barnes and Noble, 1965); F. Cumont, *Astrology and Religion Among the Greeks and Romans* (Peter Smith); J. Doresse, *The Secret Books of the Egyptian Gnostics* (AMS Press reprint); J. Seznec, *The Survival of the Pagan Gods* (Harper and Row, 1961).

Axel Poignant

Stations of the Cross
A series of paintings or sculptures representing the 14 stages of Christ's Passion; usually ranged round the walls of a church, they depict scenes, from the condemnation of Jesus by Pilate and his reception of the cross, to the crucifixion, descent from the cross and burial; in the Roman Catholic Church a form of devotion is to pray before each station in turn

The extraordinary originality of Rudolf Steiner's mind led him to a philosophy which linked up the world of natural science with the world of Spirit; his revolutionary ideas took form in a number of enterprises, ranging from art and architecture to education and farming

RUDOLF STEINER

THE SON of a minor official on the Southern Austrian Railway, Rudolf Steiner was born on 27 February 1861 at Kraljevic, then on the borders of Austria and Hungary, now in Yugoslavia. The modest schooling available made little impression on him but he was intensely awake to Nature, and to the personalities with whom he came into contact. A conviction as to the reality of the inner life, 'a soul space in man' as he called it, which manifested itself in some clairvoyant experiences and was strengthened by a delighted discovery of the world of pure ideas in geometry, gave the first promise of his future activity. At his secondary school he studied science but taught himself the classics, and even tutored other pupils in the humanities. He continued this practice when he entered the Technical College of the University of Vienna, and laid the foundation of the extraordinarily wide-ranging knowledge for which he was so remarkable. Outside his official science course, philosophy was his principal interest, but he was keenly interested in literature and the arts.

The unusual combination of scientific and artistic interests led him to Goethe, and at the age of 23 he edited Goethe's scientific works for an edition of *Deutsche Nationalliteratur*. The connection with Goethe was later to take him to Weimar to work at the Goethe Archives on the scientific side of another edition of Goethe's works. One special activity he undertook in Vienna was the tutoring of a backward boy, an experience of great importance for his later work. Meanwhile, however, he was elaborating his own philosophy in *Truth and Science* (for which he received a Ph.D. from the University of Rostock) and *The Philosophy of Freedom*, in which he argued that thought can become an organ to perceive a spiritual world. He was attracted to the mystics but differed from them in wanting to experience the sources of human wisdom through ideas – 'a mystical experience of thoughts'.

The work in the Goethe Archives at Weimar, begun when he was 29 years old, was Steiner's first settled job. His elucidation of Goethe's *Theory of Colour* later deeply influenced Kandinsky, the Russian painter. Nor did Steiner confine himself to Goethe. He also edited the works of Schopenhauer, and concerned himself with the Nietzsche archives.

Weimar, however, gave him no opportunity for the expression of his own growing spiritual experience, and in 1897 he accepted an invitation to go to Berlin to edit the *Magazine for Literature* which was associated with a stage society which produced 'modern' plays that were not likely to reach the ordinary theatre. Here Steiner, always devoted to drama, had his first experience of stage management. In Berlin he also joined the staff of a working men's college, which gave him a deep insight into prevailing social conditions. In the magazine he could only express his ideas exoterically, in a form adapted to its readers.

Meditation, however, had become a necessity to him – that 'experience of the whole man through which he reaches the actual spiritual world far more than through ideas'. His first opportunity to speak to an audience esoterically was when a certain Count Brockdorff, having read an article of Steiner's on Goethe's esoteric fairy tale, *The Green Snake and the Beautiful Lily*, invited him to lecture to a theosophical circle.

This led to a ten-year connection with the Theosophical Society, to visits to London where he met Annie Besant, Colonel Olcott and other leaders of the movement (see BESANT; THEOSOPHY), and to his accepting the position of General Secretary to the German branch of the Society. He reserved the right, however, to speak only of his own spiritual investigation. He was already lecturing on 'An Anthroposophy' and in 1909, being totally opposed to the declaration of a further incarnation of Christ and other theosophical trends, he broke with that society and founded the Anthroposophical Society (from the Greek words *anthropos* and *sophia*, 'man' and 'wisdom'). Speaking of the Anthroposophical movement in a letter written the year before his death, Steiner said: 'Anthroposophy has its roots in the perceptions – already gained – into the spiritual world. Yet these are no more than its roots. The branches, leaves, blossoms and fruits of Anthroposophy grow into all the fields of human life and action.'

Earth-Memory

From the beginning of his theosophical connections, Steiner had given independent lectures in many places, helped by Marie von Sivers (whom he subsequently married), and had produced the monthly magazine *Lucifer* ('light-bearer'). In this he published his first two anthroposophical works, *Knowledge of the Higher Worlds* and *From the Akashic Chronicle*. The former contains his description of the path of initiation for modern Western man, with exercises leading to successive stages of development. Characteristic of the book is the recognition of the dangers as well as the difficulties of initiation, and the need to take three steps in morality for every one in higher knowledge. The second begins the teaching about Universe, Earth and Man which he was to elaborate during the next 20 years. For Steiner claimed that there is such a thing as an earth-memory, written in the earth aura, and that this memory, accessible to a trained and conscious clairvoyance, is valid for a new interpretation of human and geological history. This interpretation must, however, take fully into account all the discoveries (not necessarily the theories) of modern scientific investigators.

During this early period of his theosophical or anthroposophical activity, Steiner lectured widely on the gospels. He had never been able to accept Christianity as a religion 'revealed from without'. It was his own inner experience of the event of Golgotha that led him to see it as the fulfilment of what had been presented in the ancient Mysteries. He had expressed all this in his book *Christianity as Mystical Fact* (1902). He now expounded the gospels as esoteric documents, that is documents meant only for the initiated. The 'Mystery of Golgotha' became central to his teaching of the evolution of world and man.

To this period also belongs *Occult Science – An Outline*, a compendium of 'spiritual science' (as he often called Anthroposophy) dealing with the four 'bodies' of man, his soul members, and his spiritual principles; with life in the spiritual worlds between death and a new birth; with the evolution of the earth through the four embodiments as Saturn (warmth), Sun (air), Moon (water), and Earth (mineral). In Steiner's monism (the position opposed to dualism) even physical substance had its origin in living spirit, and man himself – the last to appear in evolution – was the first in conception, though indeed as macrocosmic man. The section on Earth evolution introduces the seven epochs and the seven historical civilizations, developed in great detail in later lectures, and the two opponents of human evolution, Ahriman and Lucifer, fundamental to Steiner's teaching on ethics, psychology, history, and all his 'science of man'. The book ends with a chapter on initiation, complementary to *Knowledge of the Higher Worlds*.

During the years of his association with the Theosophical Society, between 1902 and 1912, Steiner travelled on lecture tours with Marie von Sivers over almost the whole of Europe, also studying the art and architecture in all the places he visited. He wanted to express his spiritual vision in the form of art. With the help of Marie von Sivers, who was a trained actress, he first produced Eduard Schuré's *Drama of Eleusis* at a congress in Munich in 1907, after which he wrote, in successive years, four mystery plays dealing with the karmic connections of a group of people in successive incarnations, with scenes in the soul and spiritual worlds as well as on earth. He was also developing eurythmy, an art of movement to speech and music, based on the gestures latent in the sounds of speech and in the tones and intervals of music. This new art is used effectively in representing the soul and spiritual scenes in Steiner's mystery plays.

Rudolf Steiner: founder of the Anthroposophical Society, and a prolific teacher and author, in the last years before his death in 1925 he 'developed with special intensity the subject of karma and reincarnation (the latter in a new and Christian form), which he considered vital for the modern age'

All this artistic activity, together with Steiner's conviction that a new spiritual impulse demanded a new form of architecture, led to the building of the first Goetheanum, at Dornach near Basle in Switzerland, as the headquarters of the Anthroposophical Society, which had been founded in 1912. It was built largely of wood and consisted of two intersecting domes, the smaller over the stage, and the larger (bigger than the dome of St Paul's in London) over the auditorium. Notable features in it were the interior columns made from different woods, the change of form in their capitals and bases, the windows of sculptured glass (since copied in many places) and the painting of the dome. During the First World War men and women from all combatant nations worked on its construction. It was burnt down on the night of 31 December 1922, only the great sculpture of the 'Representative of Man between Lucifer and Ahriman' surviving: it had been carved by Steiner with the help of an English sculptress. Steiner immediately designed the second Goetheanum in a completely different and equally original style of moulded concrete.

At the end of the First World War Steiner won much support for his suggestion of a threefold commonwealth to solve the tangled problems of central Europe. This arose out of a view which he had developed in great detail, over many years, according to which the whole physiology (not the brain and nerves alone) is related to the psyche. Steiner maintained that thinking finds its physical basis in brain and nerves, feeling in the rhythmical processes of heart and lungs, and willing in the system of limbs and metabolism. He now extended this threefold conception into social life, which he saw as three spheres of human activity, each of which should have its own suitable organization: a cultural sphere with the ideal of liberty, a political or 'rights' sphere with the ideal of equality, and an economic or production sphere with the ideal of fraternity. Rightly conducted, these spheres would find a natural harmony (comparable to that of head, heart and hand), but these spheres of operation would by no means necessarily coincide.

The Waldorf Schools

An example of an institution free from political control within the cultural sphere was the Waldorf School in Stuttgart, originally founded in 1919 for the employees of a local factory. As its educational director, Steiner gathered teachers from all walks of life, and lectured to them on the three great psychological and physiological periods of childhood, on the temperaments, on the curriculum, and so on, as well as discussing with them the problems of individual children. This educational work roused particular interest in England, where he was invited to the 'New Ideals' educational conference in Stratford-on-Avon, and in the same year to a summer school in Oxford under the patronage of H. A. L. Fisher, Professor L. P. Jacks, and other well-known educators. At this time he also met Margaret McMillan, pioneer of the nursery school movement, who became his fervent admirer. The Waldorf School movement has now extended itself over most of Europe and the English-speaking world.

Among other groups who approached Steiner at this time for help and guidance in their special tasks were teachers of backward children, farmers, actors, doctors and a circle of ministers and others concerned with religion who wished to work for religious renewal. The lectures and practical advice which Steiner gave to these groups led to a widespread movement in curative education, to the biodynamic method of agriculture (in which soil, plant and animal live in a healthy and natural relationship), to stage productions at the Goetheanum and other

Steiner's conviction that a new spiritual impulse demands a new form of architecture led to the building of the first Goetheanum in Dornach, Switzerland *(right)* as the headquarters of the Anthroposophical Society; constructed largely of wood, it was burnt down on the night of 31 December 1922; the second Goetheanum which replaced it *(below right)* is made of moulded concrete. Both buildings were designed by Steiner, who believed that their form should correspond, to the smallest detail, with the activities that would take place within them

places, to a school of medicine centred on a clinic near Basle (founded in conjunction with a Dutch doctor, Dr I. Wegman) and to an independent religious body known as the Christian Community.

In the years before his death Steiner's lecturing activity was of immense range, embracing mathematics, astronomy, science, medicine, theology, philosophy, drama, education, economics and many other subjects. Many lectures were for specialists who were astounded at his knowledge in their special fields. But he continued to foster the esoteric character of the Anthroposophical Society, believing that esotericism should become an open secret for all who have eyes to read. In his last years he developed with special intensity the subject of karma and reincarnation (the latter in a new and Christian form), which he considered vital for the modern age. And in 1923 he founded the Anthroposophical Society anew, placing at its centre the 'School of Spiritual Science' for those who wished to follow a path of self-development. He died two years later, on 30 March 1925.

A. C. HARWOOD

FURTHER READING: Rudolf Steiner, *The Philosophy of Spiritual Activity* (1981), *Knowledge of the Higher Worlds and its Attainment* (1969), *The Threefold Commonwealth* (1966), *The Course of My Life* (1970), *Occult Science – An Outline* (1969), *Christianity as Mystical Fact* (1947), are all published by the Rudolf Steiner Press. Books on Steiner include: A. P. Shepherd, *A Scientist of the Invisible* (Musson, 1954); H. Poppelbaum, *Man and Animal* (Anthroposophical Publishing Co., London, 1960).

Amulets representing ladders, the means by which a king was thought to ascend to the sky after death, have been found in Egyptian tombs; and in the Mithraic Mysteries, the worshipper climbed the seven steps of initiation, symbolized by a ladder with seven rungs

STEPS AND LADDERS

IN THE GAME of Snakes and Ladders the snakes, being betraying and evil creatures, lead downwards. The ladders lead up, which is perhaps a reflection of the main role of ladders, steps and stairs in symbolism, as means of ascent. They lead up from the earth into the sky and to climb them is to rise above the human condition to a higher plane. St John Climacus (from *klimax*, the Greek for 'ladder'), a monk of Mount Sinai in the 7th century, wrote a book called *Ladder to Paradise*, which helped to bring into Christian iconography the picture of the souls of the dead climbing the rungs of a ladder towards heaven, with the unrighteous being snatched off it by demons (see JUDGEMENT OF THE DEAD). There is a tradition that Mohammed saw a ladder rising into the sky from Jerusalem, on which the souls of the just ascended to God.

We connect height with spiritual superiority and power, and when the source of ultimate power or the final home of the blessed is located in the sky, kings, heroes, shamans and the souls of the good are naturally thought of as rising into it (see SKY). Among the methods of ascent, besides ladders and stairs, are climbing a mountain, a tree, a rope, the rainbow or a spider's web, or being carried up by angels or in a chariot. The Tree of Life in the Cabala (see CABALA) and the idea of rising through its spheres to God is an example of the same underlying idea. A Maori hero reached the sky by climbing a vine and the folktale hero Jack by shinning up a beanstalk (see JACK). There is a widespread myth in the Pacific in which the hero fires an arrow into the air, then a second arrow which transfixes it, then a third, and so on until he can climb into the sky on a chain made of arrows.

The Pyramid Texts of ancient Egypt (see

British Museum

A means of ascent or descent, a ladder can symbolize the path from heaven to earth: *God's Covenant with Abraham*; in this 11th century Anglo-Saxon manuscript Abraham is shown lying on the ground while God, descending from heaven on a ladder, promises that he will make him 'the father of a multitude of nations'

BOOK OF THE DEAD), in spells meant to enable a dead king to ascend to the sky, speak of him climbing a ladder or staircase, as well as flying like a bird, leaping like a grasshopper or using other methods. He 'flies as a cloud to the sky' or 'kisses the sky like a falcon'. He 'goes to the sky on the wind' or 'stairs are laid for him' or he 'ascends upon the ladder' which the sun god made for him. Amulets representing ladders have been found in Egyptian tombs, and the Egyptians saw in the rays of the sun shining through a gap in the clouds a pathway to the sky, the radiant stair which the king ascends.

The Romans sometimes placed a miniature ladder, made of bronze, in a tomb, and in the Mithraic Mysteries of Roman Imperial times the worshipper rose to divine status by climbing the seven steps or grades of initiation, symbolized by a ladder of seven rungs, one for each of the planets (see MITHRAS). The staircase, with its steps corresponding to planets and metals and stages in the spiritual process, appears frequently in alchemical symbolism. The stairs lead to the summit of a mountain or to the gateway of the celestial city, and to climb them is again to transcend the ordinary human state and attain perfection and the divine.

The Ladder of Bethel

The golden ladder which Dante describes rising to the highest heaven (in *Paradiso*, cantos 21 and 22) he identifies with the most celebrated of all symbolic ladders, the one which Jacob saw in a dream at what is now the village of Beitin, some ten miles north of Jerusalem. He went to sleep with his head on a stone: 'And he dreamed that there was a ladder set up on the earth, and the top of it reached to heaven; and behold, the angels of God were ascending and descending on it!' When Jacob woke up, he said, 'How awesome is this place! This is none other than the house of God, and this is the gate of heaven' (Genesis, chapter 28). He named the place Bethel, 'house of God', and later the ark of the covenant was kept there and God was consulted there in time of stress (Judges, chapter 20). According to cabalistic commentators, the ladder had 72 rungs, corresponding to the 72 syllables of the great mystic name of God (see NAMES).

Christians interpreted the ladder of Jacob's dream as a sign that the righteous will attain salvation (and Bethel became a general term for a Nonconformist meeting-house). St Benedict in a vision saw his monks rising to heaven on a ladder, and in the 11th century St Romuald, founding a monastery at Camaldoli in Italy, dreamed of men in white robes ascending a ladder to the sky, and decided that he would dress his monks in white.

The ladder or stair leads down as well as up, of course, and the Pythagoreans saw the particles of dust which swirl and dance in a sunbeam as souls or life-sparks descending to the earth on wings of light. The Jewish author Philo in the 1st century AD and the Christian author Origen in the 3rd century both interpreted Jacob's ladder as the air through which souls descend and ascend before birth and after death.

Walking Under Ladders

Disinclination to walk under a ladder, even at the cost of stepping out into traffic on the street, is very common. The simplest explanation of it is that it is based on a sensible reluctance to risk something falling on your head. Another possible explanation is that to walk under a ladder is to break through the triangle formed by the ladder, the wall and the ground, and that this is dangerous because the triangle is a symbol of good luck in general and of the Trinity in particular.

In folk tradition, a dream of going up a ladder is a beneficent dream of good omen, and a dream of going down one is the reverse. A more modern interpretation, by Freud, is that dreams of going up or down ladders, stairs or slopes are symbolic representations of sexual intercourse.

(See also HOUSE; SUPERSTITIONS.)

Physical phenomena have appeared in holy men and women for which no 'natural' cause has so far been found; it may be, however, that 'profoundly religious temperaments may be correlated . . . with metabolic effects in which biochemical and psychosomatic factors participate'

STIGMATA

'WOUNDS', MARKS OR POINTS of bleeding which simulate the injuries of Christ are known as stigmata. Stigmatics (those who receive stigmata) can develop marks corresponding to any or all of the piercing of hands and feet, the *ferita* or lance-wound in the side, the bruise on the shoulder caused by the weight of the cross, chafing of wrists and ankles, weals of scourging and a coronet on the brow (Crown of Thorns). Allied to the stigmata is the mystic ring, a modification of the skin or flesh of the ring-finger of the right hand, appropriate to a nun's 'bethrothal'.

If healing miracles are omitted as essentially psychological (see MIRACLES), the curious physical phenomena reported variously of some mystics include: stigmatization, *incendium amoris* ('flames of love'), incombustibility, fragrance, bodily elongation, and *inedia*, the ability to survive without food. Physiological peculiarities alleged of the mystic's mortal remains comprise the ability to bleed, incorruptibility and absence of rigor mortis. Levitation, irradiance, telekinesis and 'miracles of abundance' may also be classified as physical phenomena.

It is difficult to reject all the alleged physiological and physical phenomena as frauds or fictions. Admittedly we can have little confidence in many of the reports, particularly concerning the elder saints, where hagiographers (writers of saints' lives) have been over-zealous. But the position has improved of late as a result of modern critical hagiography and the principles established by Pope Benedict XIV (1675–1758), who stressed that nothing should be ascribed to the supernatural if a natural explanation is possible. Extraordinary phenomena (other than posthumous miracles of healing) are not nowadays required in proof of holiness of life; and this diminishes the motive for ascribing wonders to the virtuous departed.

The tests of evidence in this field are the same as those in psychical research or in historical studies. Eyewitness depositions are preferred to hearsay evidence, and should be recorded soon after the event with circumstantial detail. The value of depositions made at processes for beatification or canonization is often, but not always, reduced by the lapse of time between the death of the candidate and the inquiry. Because of these or other uncertainties we cannot readily form a judgement concerning the status of fragrance, *incendium amoris*, bodily incorruption and so on, telekinesis or miracles of abundance. But with levitation, irradiance and stigmatization the evidential position is distinctly better.

A Kind of Trance

Little is known with any certainty of mystic phenomena in the orient, in Islam or in the Orthodox Churches; Protestants, it seems, incline neither to mysticism nor phenomena. Almost all the material worthy of study occurs in the Roman Catholic sphere. Non-Catholic students (including the present writer) have to overcome a lofty barrier of initial scepticism. But it is wrong to suppose that intelligent Catholics (to whom we are indebted for searching factual and critical studies) have all been gullible. Even in the 13th century, many ecclesiastical authorities would bear heavily on mystics suspected of fraud or love of notoriety.

In the present context 'mysticism' means 'mystical prayer' ('contemplation'). It is not given to all to graduate from ordinary prayer to any or all of the three stages of mystical prayer. At the first level the mystic concentrates his mind, by conscious effort, on divine themes. If the state of 'full union' supervenes, he enjoys a sense of divine presence but is still capable of voluntary withdrawal, unless the state of 'rapture' or 'ecstasy' has been attained. Ecstasy is, broadly speaking, a kind of trance in which the mind is cut off from the environment unless aroused by some drastic intervention such as a blow or an imperative command. Sometimes, when overtaken by ecstasy, the mystic continues in automatic fashion with his present occupation which may be preaching or saying Mass.

Attempts have been made to equate ecstasy with other forms of trance; hysterical catalepsy, somnambulism, hypnotism, the mediumistic trance or drug-induced states; but it is unsafe to suppose that these conditions are identical either to one another or to ecstasy, though as pointed out by St Teresa of Avila (see TERESA OF AVILA), distinguishing between 'natural' and mystic ecstasies, a hysterical trance can be confused with ecstasy. Religious mystics normally interpret ecstasy in terms of real contact with God. This is debatable in cases where they receive demonstrably false revelations concerning matters of fact. But in other cases the belief cannot be contradicted, though equally it cannot be logically proved true. Judgement has therefore to be suspended in the face of an important empirical fact; the majority of the alleged physical phenomena occur in persons who engage in mystical prayer and experience ecstasies. This goes some way to explain why, if the phenomena are not fraudulent or illusory, they belong only to religions where mystical prayer is practised. The link between ecstasies and phenomena does not, of course, prejudge the issue as to whether the latter are supernatural or due to obscure natural causes.

Few stigmatizations, if any, can be dated earlier than 1224 when, it is said, St Francis of Assisi (see FRANCIS OF ASSISI) received wounds in hands and feet after a vision of a seraph received during ecstasy. His stigmata were described as fleshy excrescences resembling the curved-over point of a nail on the palm, and a nail-head on the back of the hand. But examination of portraits of the saint and evidence from modern cases suggest that the excrescences were merely raised scar tissue, so that the problem is reduced to how the wounds originated. As many as 300 subsequent instances of stigmatization have been alleged but only a few provide data of value.

Bleeding Through the Skin

Elena Ajello (born in 1901 in Montalto Uffugo, Calabria, Italy) was especially devoted to St Rita of Cascia (1386–1457), who was said to have had an evil-smelling stigmatic wound which remained unhealed in her forehead. In 1923 Elena experienced a vision in which Christ injured her brow with his own Crown of Thorns. Some hours later, while she was still in an ecstatic state, a physician was called to her because blood was flowing copiously from her forehead. Dr Turano wiped away the blood and found that at intervals she would contract her brow in a painful spasm and blood would then exude from the pores. Similarly, when Dr Gerald Molloy wiped the blood from the backs and palms of the hands of the famous stigmatic Louise Lateau (1850–1883) of Bois D'Haine, Belgium, he found oval marks of a bright red hue about one inch long by half an inch wide. The blood forced its way through unbroken skin in sufficient quantity for visiting pilgrims to soak it up in their handkerchiefs several times in an hour. Dr Warloment of the Belgian Medical Academy enclosed Louise's arm in a special glass apparatus and showed that the bleeding was spontaneous and not due to prior irritation of the skin by Louise. Anne Catherine Emmerich (1774–1824) of Coesfeld, Rhineland, besides other stigmata, had the lance-wound on her right side and a Y-shaped cross on her chest, both of which were areas from which the blood exuded at certain times.

Bleeding through the skin is indeed an exceptional occurrence but would seem to lie within the limits of what is naturally possible. Various facts weaken the case for supernatural causation. On the supernatural hypothesis it is odd that 12 centuries elapsed without stigmatics. The historical facts of the Crucifixion are not made plain by the stigmata. Was Jesus pierced in the left side (Louise Lateau) or the right (Catherine Emmerich)? The shape of the stigmata vary between stigmatics and from time to time in the same person; the marks on the hands of Teresa Neumann (1898–1962; see NEUMANN) of Konnersreuth, Bavaria were sometimes square and sometimes round. Elena Ajello was devoted to St Rita. Catherine Emmerich's Y-shaped cross was unique to her, but resembled the unusual Y-shaped cross in the church of St Lambert at Coesfeld where Catherine had spent long hours in prayer. These oddities are suggestive of the influence not of the supernatural but of ideas that have become lodged in the mind of the stigmatic.

Indeed, if supernatural intervention be discounted, stigmatization cannot be explained naturalistically in purely organic terms such as haemophiliac bleeding because of the specific location of the stigmata. Analysis shows that in stigmatic bleeding actual blood is exuded, which further distinguishes the condition from haemathidrosis, which is characterized by red perspiration due to the presence of the bacterium *micrococcus prodigiosus*. The naturalistic explanation of stigmatization therefore sees the stigmata as the result of auto-suggestion on the part of the stigmatics who, almost without exception, have been given to brooding intensely on the sufferings of Christ.

This theory is well supported by the fact that many stigmatics show undoubted signs of having suffered from hysteria at some time in their lives. 'Hysteria' is employed in the technical sense to designate an illness that can take a bewildering variety of forms: temporary blindness, deafness, paralysis, losses of sensibility in the skin, or excessive sensibility; comas, fainting fits, spasms; miscellaneous aches and pains, and so on. Some stigmatics like Elena Ajello are described as manifesting hysterical symptoms. Others like Teresa Neumann and Berthe Mrazek (a friend of Nurse Edith Cavell who was shot by the Germans in 1915) suffer from mysterious paralyses of sudden onset, relieved by equally mysterious cures, which almost infallibly may be ascribed to hysteria.

A hysterical illness has no organic cause, and is psychological in origin (see FAITH HEALING). But the patient is not shamming; he is really ill and is the victim of a complex and mainly unconscious process of auto-suggestion. When hysteria is found in a stigmatic it is a good indication of a high degree of auto-suggestibility. The naturalistic theory of stigmatization ascribes it to auto-suggestion affecting blood flow and tissues, in persons endowed with unusual suggestibility and an obsession with the sufferings of Jesus. This is not quite the same as ascribing stigmatization directly to hysteria, which would go beyond the facts, as there are stigmatics like Father Pio Forgione (1887–1968), of the Capuchin monastery of San Rotundo near Foggia in Italy, who cannot at the present time be classified as hysterical. The link between hysteria and stigmatization is merely that each is a possible result, in appropriate conditions, of a temperament potentially auto-suggestible in certain ways.

Wounds that Open and Close

Advocates of the supernatural origin of stigmata have stressed the rather minor character of the effects such as blisters, rashes and eczemas, produced on the skin by suggestion under hypnotism. But this does not do full justice to Dr Adolph Lechler's results with 'Elizabeth', an Austrian peasant girl who was both very devout and under treatment for hysteria. On Good Friday 1932 she was deeply affected by seeing a film of the suffering and death of Christ, and (significantly) complained of pain in feet and hands. That evening Dr Lechler gave her the hypnotic suggestion that wounds would develop at the site of the pains. Moist wounds appeared during the night. Further suggestion deepened them, and resulted also in tears of blood, the Crown of Thorns and inflammation and sagging of the shoulder. Dr Lechler substantiated his claim with

'Drink of My Chalice!'

Day after day (Passitea) lay there upon her bed, motionless, and, as all believed, at death's door. Good Friday came, when suddenly between two and three o'clock she rose up on her knees with outstretched arms, a dazzling ray like lightning flashed through the room, a sharp loud clap as if of thunder was heard, and with a piercing cry, Passitea, her face radiant with some unearthly glow, fell swooning in utter collapse. Her two sisters who were in the room, alarmed, ran to lift her up when to their astonishment they saw that blood was pouring from her hands, her feet, and her head, whilst her white night-rail was crimsoned all down the left side with blood welling through as if from a deep wound. As quickly as they could they mopped up the stains with towels and ewers of fresh water; they changed the coverlets which were all spotted with blood, and even scoured the floor round the bed . . . a priest of much experience in mysticism was urgently sent for. Upon his arrival he at once recognized that Passitea had received the stigmata. In reply to his questions . . . Passitea under obedience described that she had seen as it were in a vision, Christ crucified, livid and bruised, and covered with wounds streaming with red blood. She heard the words "Daughter, drink of My Chalice", whereupon there darted out rays of transparent glory which struck her hands, her feet, and for a second's space encircled her head. The pain was so acute that she lost all consciousness.

Montague Summers *The Physical Phenomena of Mysticism*

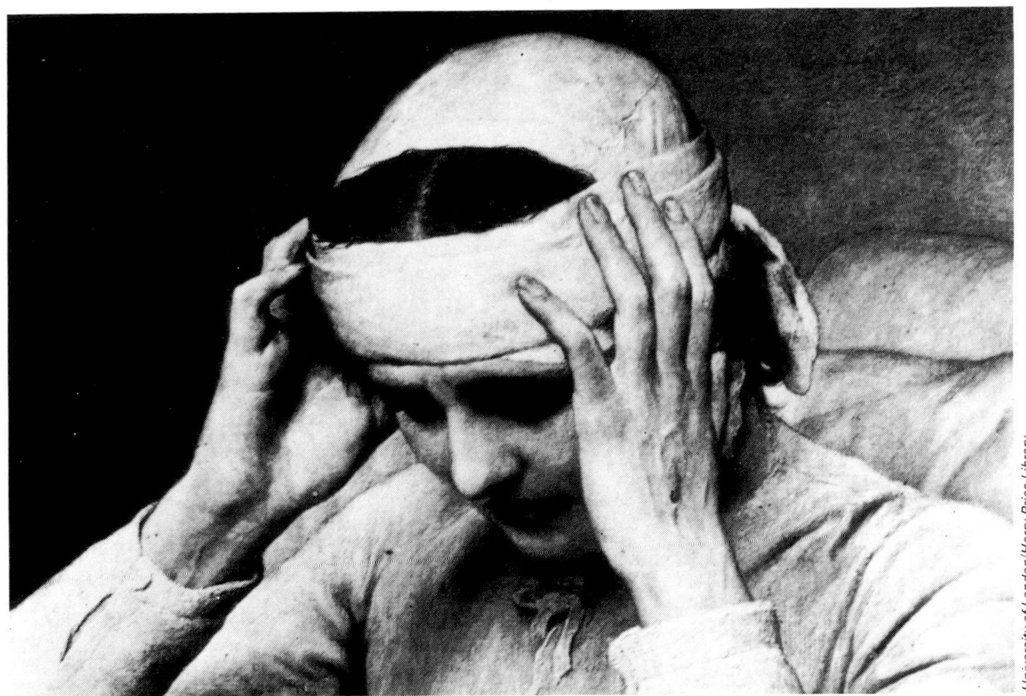

University of London/Harry Price Library

Scala

A naturalistic explanation of stigmatization is that the stigmata are the result of auto-suggestion on the part of the stigmatics who, almost without exception, have brooded intensely on Christ's sufferings *Left* Anne Catherine Emmerich: besides the stigmata shown in this picture, she also had the lance-wound on her right side, and a cross on her chest *Below left* St Catherine of Siena: she was said to have suffered the pain of the stigmata while undergoing a mystical experience at Pisa; painting by Sodoma

photographs taken before restoring normality by counter-suggestion.

In the light of Lechler's achievement it would be daring to say that stigmata are supernatural, and in modern canonization processes such as that of St Gemma Galgani (1878–1903) of Lucca the Church abstains from doing so. On the other hand, we cannot assert that stigmata have yet been proved entirely natural. Difficulty may rationally be felt concerning a naturalistic interpretation of St Gemma's stigmata. A beautiful Italian girl with a disposition of great sweetness, Gemma often had ecstasies each Thursday evening (a common pattern to which many stigmatics conform) when red marks showed on the backs and palms of the hands. A rent in the flesh opened by degrees, sometimes becoming very deep, the openings on each side almost reaching each other so far as could be ascertained without painful probing. The cavities were full of blood. On the Friday the flow would cease and the wounds close and heal with astonishing rapidity, usually leaving very little trace except sometimes a raised scar.

St Gemma's case lends credibility to the accounts of deep wounds in some of the older stigmatics such as St Mary Frances of the Five Wounds (1715–91). Extraordinary as these deep stigmata are, they do not decisively contradict the naturalistic hypothesis. 'Elizabeth's' wounds deepened under suggestion and we cannot say to what depth they might not have proceeded had Dr Lechler persisted with suggestion beyond the point that was medically ethical.

The genesis of the mystic ring is akin to that of stigmata. Marie-Julie Jahenny (1850–1941), a somewhat exhibitionistic stigmatic of La Faudrais in Brittany, was in the habit of announcing the particular stigmata she would receive some time before they appeared; a fact strongly in favour of the auto-suggestion hypothesis. In an ecstasy in January 1874 she predicted that she would plight her troth to her heavenly spouse on 20 February. On the predicted day in the presence of 14 witnesses the ring-finger of the right hand became swollen and red beneath the skin. Shortly afterwards it bled. Within 30 minutes a ring shaped formation appeared. There is evidence that Marie-Julie retained it for at least 20 years as a ring of fleshy tissue resembling a hoop which had sunk into the skin.

The tears of blood shed by St Gemma and others were observed by the French physician Dr Parrott in the last century in a patient (presumably hysterical) who shed them while affected by violent grief. She bled also from the breast, hands and knees.

Celtic lore the Little People are traditionally thought to have put up dolmens and cromlechs (megalithic tombs), they have been credited with Stonehenge too.

Present-day archeology has managed to sort out fairly clearly who the builders were. In doing so it has also managed to deduce a general dating of the construction, which apparently went on for some centuries. It was built in three stages, corresponding to stages in the cultural development of ancient Britain.

The first builders, it is thought, were a Neolithic people who moved into Britain before 3000 BC, bringing with them a penchant for circular earthworks. They also buried their dead in vast barrows, 100 feet or more in length, many of which are in the vicinity of Stonehenge. The tribes of this period left many enclosures surrounded by circular banks and ditches, and are usually thought to have made the ditch and inner embankment around Stonehenge, now mostly filled in by wind and time. They may also have set up the Heel Stone.

The next stage, from about 1800 BC, saw the arrival of the 'Beaker' people, who are known for their pottery and who buried their dead in individual tombs; they are also known for setting up many circular arrangements of standing stones along with 'henge' enclosures – like that at Avebury near Stonehenge. These were the people who brought the bluestones to Stonehenge from – it is now generally agreed – the Prescelly Hills in Wales.

The Beaker folk were a highly developed late Stone Age and early Bronze Age people. The ensuing stage introduced an even higher Bronze Age culture, the 'Wessex' people – workers in metal ruled by warrior chiefs, with direct trade links to Europe reaching perhaps as far as the Mediterranean. It was once thought that there might be Mycenean influence in the architecture of Stonehenge, but it is now known that Stonehenge was completed before Mycene. In their time, the mighty project became mightier. The older bluestones were uprooted and the huge inner 'trilithons' (structures formed of three stones), of sarsen sandstone from some 20 miles away, went up. Then followed the outer circle of uprights and lintels, also sarsen, and some crucial single stones including the Slaughter Stone.

So ended the construction of Stonehenge, somewhere about 1400 BC. Apart from the structures so far mentioned, there are various holes where no stones stand – like the 'Aubrey holes', named after the antiquary and surmised later to be pits dug for some sepulchral or chthonic rites.

A Prehistoric Computer

People have believed that Stonehenge was either a temple or a place of worship, or a vastly important meeting place for chiefs and kings, or a structure for observing and predicting the movement of heavenly bodies, mainly the sun and moon. This last idea is based on the belief that the sun rises, at the summer solstice, directly over the Heel Stone as seen from the centre of Stonehenge. And so, apparently, it does – depending on what spot you call the centre, what precise line you take to be the much sought-after axis of Stonehenge, what precise moment you take to be true sunrise, and how much margin of error you allow for erosion, cosmic adjustments over the millennia, and so on.

R. J. C. Atkinson, archeologist and leading authority on Stonehenge, insists that the midsummer sunrise alignment was only approximate, and that the reasons for it remain unknown. Nor does he accept the dating of the structure that is based on the alignment. But more recently G.S. Hawkins, an astronomer, turned to a computer and announced that he had 'decoded' the place. He found quantities of astronomical alignments, involving the Heel Stone, the outer 'Station' stones (from which diagonals give a putative centre), the Aubrey holes and much else. By his account Stonehenge is no less than a prehistoric computer, a device for making highly intricate astronomical calculations, including predictions of equinoctial sunrises and sunsets, moonrises and moonsets, and eclipses. But these findings are still very much in dispute.

FURTHER READING: E. Raymond, *Stonehenge & Druidism* (Artisan Sales, 1979); Gerald S. Hawkins, *Stonehenge Decoded* (Dell, 1966).

Stonehenge silhouetted against the sunset: its quality of awesomeness, and its antiquity, have made it the focus of romantic legends; modern Druids gather there to celebrate the midsummer solstice

Uniphoto

Even before man sculpted representations of his gods, he recognized in stones and pebbles a supernatural power to be venerated and, on occasions, tapped

STONES

THE PRESENCE of pebbles, ordinary stones and chunks of unhewn rock in so much mythical and magical lore reflects mankind's willingness to find the supernatural in anything and everything. Demons in wild animals, gods in trees, magical power in lightning or eclipses are readily comprehensible. But it must be an overwhelming, all-consuming myth-making urge that puts spirits in mossy old boulders, magical power in a handful of gravel.

In man's earliest myth-making days the stone would often be worshipped directly as a god in itself. Usually the object of such worship inspired awe because of its size, its odd shape or its colour. Pre-biblical Semitic peoples apparently possessed stone-worshipping cults, as did tribes in parts of pre-Hellenic Greece, Crete and Thessaly. Stones have also been worshipped as gods in parts of Africa, and widely in India.

But sophistication of a sort usually overtook these cults fairly soon, and the stone ceased to be a god, becoming instead the abode of a god. The god in the stone, the natural stone, not the sculpted, is a worldwide phenomenon. The ancient Greeks devoted much of their religious attention to such stones, including those that were vaguely phallic in shape and associated with Apollo. The Greeks also set up their famous *hermae*, cairns or heaps of stones ascribed to Hermes (see HERMES), which partook of some of his divinity as god of travellers. These were placed on roadsides, on boundaries, and in later days on street corners and outside houses. And though they eventually developed into carved representations of the god, erect phallus and all, many were originally plain, unwrought, columnar rocks.

The boundary stones of the Babylonians were often also plain, columnar rocks, though the boundary-makers carved inscriptions on them, mostly warning anyone who might dare to shift a particular stone that an awful curse would descend from the god to whom it was dedicated. In much the same way, the Celts scraped semi-abstract representations of gods onto tall, upright monumental stones known as menhirs. But the Celts, along with many other peoples, also made much use of unadorned, natural standing stones, sometimes in groups, as at Stonehenge, or as in the great dolmens of Celtic regions, flat, unhewn stones which rest horizontally across upright stones. Stones were also used singly, frequently as grave markers. The idea of erecting a tombstone over a grave may possibly have arisen from the belief that the spirit of the dead person would inhabit the stone. What is now a memorial may have once been a spiritual abode (see BRITTANY; CULT OF THE DEAD; STONEHENGE).

The Jungian psychologist Marie-Louise von Franz has written that ancient Germanic peoples believed in this role of the tombstone, adding that the belief may spring from 'the symbolic idea that something eternal of the dead person remains, which can be most fittingly represented by a stone'. This may explain much of the general mythological role of unwrought stone: its eternality symbolizes and magically confers spiritual eternality.

The most primitive form of boundary or marker stone, still widely in use, was the cairn, which was built up at holy places and to which each traveller added another stone. The practice is found throughout Celtic regions of Europe, including Britain, in the Middle East and Asia, and among Australian aborigines. The Celts dedicated many cairns to mountain gods on peaks and

Previous page **Deucalion and his wife Pyrrha, according to Greek legend the only survivors of a universal flood, created mankind anew by casting stones behind them: as they struck the ground, the stones thrown by Deucalion became men, while those thrown by Pyrrha turned into women: illustration from a 15th century Flemish edition of *The Romance of the Rose***

Below left **Stone dolmen in County Donegal: these constructions of flat, unhewn stones resting horizontally across stone uprights are numerous in Celtic regions**

Ianthe Ruthven

Below right **Formation in Cornwall dating from 1600–1000 BC; stones with natural holes were taken to represent the female principle, and sick persons or barren women might be passed through the hole in a symbolic rebirth**

John Moss

summits, believing that adding a stone magically swept away the traveller's weariness. Hikers and mountain-climbers still carry on the practice today, but as a pleasant tradition rather than a piece of magic or worship.

The 'god-in-the-stone' motif also occurs among North American Indians. Vast stones were worshipped by Plains tribes like the Sioux, Ojibwa and Canadian Cree, to whom, obviously, a solitary huge boulder on the empty face of the prairie would seem especially awesome. In the myths of these tribes, the great stones seem to be both dwelling places for special gods and almost ancestral spirit beings in their own right, as if they had not quite completed the transition from 'god-*as*-the-stone' to 'god-*in*-the-stone'.

The spirits in stones can often be lesser divinities, not much more than imps. Many old Irish and Welsh tales tell of stones that speak or move, usually on especially supernatural occasions, like Midsummer Eve; and there are moving stones in the folklore of France, Borneo, Central America and elsewhere. The Central American stones are on a mountain and are shaped rather like jaguars; they are believed to transform themselves into these animals at will. The Chukchansi Indians of California had a legend of a rock, about five feet high, that would grow, if anyone tried to jump it, just enough to scrape the jumper's backside. The belief that all stones increase in size is common to many peoples. According to an old American superstition, lightning aids this growing process.

Coronation Stones

In many parts of the world the concepts of the god-as-the-stone and the god-in-the-stone frequently develop into the belief that a particular stone is a sacred object merely because of some mythic association with supernatural powers. Perhaps the most famous example is the Black Stone of Islam, in the Kaaba at Mecca (see MECCA). It does not contain a god, but has traditional associations with God. Of course, as a meteorite it would be doubly venerable, as meteorites are considered to be extremely sacred in almost every mythology.

The Old Testament contains its share of sacred stones, like the one set up and anointed by Jacob at Bethel, after his dream of the ladder to heaven (Genesis, chapter 28). And Joshua set up a great stone to mark the covenant he made with the people of Israel that they would forsake 'foreign gods' and serve the Lord (Joshua, chapter 24).

According to a Greek legend, the centre of the world was found by Zeus to be at Delphi, and was marked by the conical 'navel stone' called *omphalos* (see NAVEL). Its shape and site undoubtedly made it sacred to Apollo; and a variant of the myth states that the omphalos marked the grave of the sacred snake of an older religion, supplanted by the worship of Apollo.

With the movement away from the concept of the god-in-the-stone to that of the less divine sacred stone, men developed the idea of the altar-stone: a sacred stone that still provided a way of access to the god, even if he no longer lived in it (see ALTAR). For instance, some tribes in Annam, now part of Vietnam, would wash natural, unwrought stones and place food and drink on them for the gods. The Aztecs and Maya used vast stones, partly hewn, and grooved to catch blood, as altars for human sacrifice; and Norse saga mentions Thor's stone, a sacred rock on which men being sacrificed to the god had their backs broken.

Another famous stone, which is not strictly an altar but which nevertheless is a feature of holy occasions, is the Stone of Scone, on which the kings of Scotland were once crowned. Edward I took it to Westminster Abbey in the 13th century, where it forms part of the throne occupied by British monarchs at their coronation. It was stolen by Scottish nationalists in 1950, but was recovered and returned to London the next year. A legend identifies the Stone of Scone with the coronation stone of the old kings of Ireland. Known as the Lia-fail, it was said to shriek aloud whenever the rightful heir to the throne stepped on it. The Anglo-Saxon tribes crowned their kings on a sacred stone at the present site of Kingston-on-Thames in England. The name Kingston is in fact derived from King's Stone.

Most sacred stones were believed to possess inherent magical powers and this is especially true of the chipped-flint tools of the Stone Age, when they were found in the fields of later peoples. Throughout Europe and much of the rest of the world these flint axes and arrowheads were thought to have dropped from the sky, or to have been hurled by the gods, and were called thunderbolts or thunderstones. Naturally they were associated with Zeus or Jupiter in the Graeco-Roman world, and with Thor in Scandinavia, although some ancient Scandinavians apparently worshipped them directly, almost as household gods in their own right.

Gravestones near Lake Awusa in Ethiopia, thought to belong to Arussi chiefs: 'the idea of erecting a tombstone over a grave may possibly have arisen from the belief that the spirit of the dead person would inhabit the stone'

Fire and Magic-Maker

In North and South America the Indians venerated flint. The Cherokee, for instance, regarded this kind of stone as a god, as did the Quiché of Guatemala, for whom it was the fire god, because of its ability to create fire. The Pueblo Indians had flint societies among their numerous clans and secret cults; predictably, these groups were concerned with weather control and magic-making.

Throughout Europe, the old popular superstitions give a protective role to the Stone Age implements, which were thought to protect against lightning, disease, witches or (in France) difficult childbirth. Many Asians considered the sacred flints to be lucky charms, and also aids in searching for buried gold. In Britain the prehistoric axes and arrowheads were sometimes called elf-bolts, or fairy-shot, for they were said to have been fired by the little people at humans, to bewitch them. By reverse magic, it was said that carrying such a flint ensured safety from fairy-shot, an idea once also current in Sweden.

Europeans took these ideas about flint to the United States, where rural superstition says that a clean white flint will keep witches from a house, or hawks from the chickens. And rubbing with a flint cures goitre, if the flint is returned to the exact spot where it was found.

Apart from flints, everything from vast granite blocks to plain pebbles can contain magical virtue. The Irish Blarney Stone confers eloquence on those who kiss it; a sacred stone in British Columbia needs only to be struck to cause rain for nearby Indian tribes; special stones in Scotland, Fiji,

John Moss

Making string figures (such as 'cat's cradles') is a popular game among children, and in primitive communities all over the world, and these pastimes often possess magical overtones. In the Far East, ghost traps made from string are sometimes set on the outskirts of villages to ensnare prowling spectres.

The Power to Bind

The bulk of the lore relating to string and thread is concerned with knots, which represent tightly closed links, and have many psychic implications that arise from the fact that, in magic, that which has the power to bind the body can also be used to confine the spirit. The knot is also the symbol of the sealed bargain. The continuous knot in the form of a horizontal figure eight represents infinity.

The Gordian knot which was wrought so intricately that no one could undo it – until Alexander cut it with his sword (see SWORD) and thus became conqueror of the East – also had an occult significance. It stood as a symbol of the labyrinth, and it was said that to untie the knot to its heart was equivalent to finding the centre which formed such an important part of mystic thought. In certain religious orders and secret societies, ceremonies involving knotting and binding take place during the initiation of a new member, as in the case of high-caste Brahmins and, in the past, the Knights Templar. Modern witches use cords and knots in many rituals: for example, cord of a given planetary colour may bind an image in a restraining spell, or a knot may be tied as a focus of concentrated will in a healing spell.

Closely associated with the knotting of cords or garments, are a number of religious taboos. The *flamen Dialis*, the Roman priest of Jupiter (see JUPITER), was forbidden to have a single knot in his clothing; and Moslem pilgrims to Mecca are prohibited from wearing knots and rings. It has been suggested that the origin of the phrase 'the bonds of matrimony' is the custom of draping the priest's stole over the clasped hands of the bride and groom to form a symbolic knot. In former times, knotted ribbons were often worn at weddings to symbolize the binding effect of the marriage ceremony as well as for their decorative value.

Love, Birth and Death

A girl who used illicit love magic in an attempt to lure a reluctant lover into her clutches would tie knots in lengths of thread or wool, at the same time chanting:

> This knot I knit,
> This knot I tie,
> To see my lover as he goes by,
> In his apparel and array,
> As he walks in every day.

The symbol of fidelity and love, the love-knot, is a double knot of ribbon with two bows, and two ends.

One of the arts of the Age of Chivalry was point-tying, a method of inhibiting the sexual prowess of a husband on his wedding night by artfully tying a knot in his points, the tagged lace or cord that attached his hose to his doublet. Similarly, tying a knot in a length of thread or string was popularly supposed to render a man sexually incapable. If the knot were not discovered, the condition of impotence could be permanent. This practice, which savoured of black magic, was greatly frowned upon by the Church.

Tying knots to avoid an unwanted pregnancy was at one time practised by both men and women. A Moroccan husband would knot and then swallow the oviduct of a hen, while in eastern Europe a woman would tie ten knots in a length of flax which she would wear for nine successive days and nights before burying it.

During the Renaissance churchmen were often horrified by the superstitious practices associated with childbirth; in 1584, for instance, in Shropshire, the prevailing custom of unlocking all the doors and loosening every knot in the house in order to ease the mother's labour was roundly condemned. This curious custom persisted in some rural districts of Britain until less than a century ago.

Because untying knots was supposed to facilitate childbirth it seemed perfectly logical to ascribe difficult births to the malicious tying of knots by an enemy of the mother concerned. As a result of this reasoning, a great number of so-called witches ended their lives on the gallows or at the stake, having 'freely' confessed under torture to the crime of inhibiting childbirth.

Clotho spins the thread of human life, Lachesis measures its length and Atropos waits to cut it at the last: the three Fates, in a detail from a painting by John Melhuish Strudwick, *The Golden Thread*

Knots have been used in the magical treatment of disease from ancient times to the middle years of the 19th century. A well-known country remedy for nose bleeding was to tie a skein of red silk, which had previously been knotted by nine maidens, around the neck of the sufferer. The mystical number nine occurs yet again in the once popular cure for whooping cough, in which a string with nine knots was worn as a neck-band. A well-known treatment for warts was to knot a piece of string and then bury it in the earth. It was said that the wart would disappear as the string rotted. In ancient Babylon, 4000 years ago, a three-fold cord with twice seven knots was said to cure headaches if it was tied round the brow.

Before the development of sedative drugs a protracted death could impose an intoler-able burden upon both the dying person and his family and, understandably, every legit-imate method of hastening the inevitable end was explored. Every door in the house was unlocked, all windows were opened and all knots loosened to clear a way of exit for the departing soul. The relief that members of a family felt when death had finally claimed its victim often resulted in agonies of guilt, and these led, perhaps inevitably, to a growing fear that the angry ghost would return. To insure against this happening, a piece of knotted thread or string would be carried in a pocket to serve as an antidote. A holed stone suspended from the ceiling by a thread with nine knots was said to give protection against nightmares.

In Scotland, fishermen use knotted thread and string, in various different colours, as charms. Red thread is said to be the most effective, particularly when used in con-junction with a piece of rowan or mountain ash (see RED; ROWAN). There was an old saying:

> Rowan tree and red thread
> Will put the witches to their speed.

This charm was believed to be effective only if the thread had been knotted by an

C. M. Dixon

Above 'The continuous knot in the form of a horizontal figure eight represents infinity': magical knot inscribed with the name of Pharaoh Tuthmosis III, dated c 1450 BC

Axel Poignant

Below Games with string are popular all over the world, sometimes carrying magical or religious overtones: a Maori woman teaches her grandsons how to make the two volcanoes of the central highlands of North Island

individual 'having the knowledge'.

Even the most innocent forms of magical knot-tying could involve great dangers in 17th century Scotland, where all supernatural practices were constantly scrutinized by the clergy. Margaret Barclay, one of the witches of the town of Irvine in Ayrshire, was put to torture solely on the evidence provided by a length of knotted red thread and a twig of rowan which she carried as a protective charm. Witches were said to be able to steal the milk of cows, from a distance, by plaiting, or tying magical knots, and Isabel Gowdie (see GOWDIE), the Scottish witch, confessed to this crime. She declared: 'We plait the rope the wrong way (widdershins) in the Devil's name and thereby take with us the cow's milk.'

As recently as the 1870s Scottish farmers attempted to protect their stock against bewitchment by threading red cord through one of the ears of each new cow when it first entered the byre.

At a Rate of Knots

One of the best-known arts of the sea witches of Finland, the Orkneys and the Isle of Man was that of controlling the wind by means of magical knots. Three knots were to be tied in a length of string, and as each was undone the power of the wind increased. It was said of the women of the Isle of Man, especially those on the coast, that they would 'selle to shipmen wynde so it were closed under three knotes of thread, so that the more wynde he would have the more knotes he must undo'.

The last surviving relic of the ritual tying of knots is possibly the ornamental intertwining of cords known as knotwork, an art which was popular in Britain towards the end of the last century, and which under the name of Macramé is currently enjoying a revival of popularity in the United States.

ERIC MAPLE

SUBTERRANEAN RACE

AN ANCIENT PERUVIAN legend relates that four brothers and four sisters emerged from the cavern of Pacari-Tambo, east of Cuzco, the ancient city that became the capital of the Inca Empire. The eldest brother climbed a mountain and, throwing stones to the four cardinal points, took possession of the land. The youngest brother, Ayar Uchu Topa, contrived to dispose of his elders, married the sisters, and subdued the surrounding peoples. He founded Cuzco and many other cities.

The great Mammoth Cave in Edmondson County, Kentucky, in the United States, was discovered only in 1809. Bodies of an unknown race reputed to antedate the Indians were found in its recesses with reed torches beside them, but all crumbled to powder when touched.

There is a belief that a low type of subterranean being sometimes appears in astral form on the earth's surface, and that it is somehow attracted by manifestations of human sex-force. For example, in *Real Ghost Stories*, W. T. Stead tells of an apparition seen by a woman in an English suburb: 'I saw this light develop into a head and face of yellowish-green light, with a mass of matted hair above it. The face was very wide and broad, larger than ours in all respects, very large eyes of green which, not being distinctly outlined, appeared to merge into the yellow of the cheeks; no hair whatever on the lower part of the face. The expression was diabolically malignant.'

One of the most interesting accounts of the subterranean people, which purports in one sense to be factual, is by the Theosophist C. W. Leadbeater. Although he claims elsewhere to have up-to-date confirmation of some of the facts, his story is alleged to be a report of an experience undergone by two Indian youths, which took place in 10,402 BC and was recovered from the 'memory of Nature' (the record of history supposed to exist on the astral plane).

Both young men had some psychic faculty, and one heard a voice, from time to time, which guided him and suggested interesting enterprises. On the instructions of this invisible guide, who demanded a pledge of secrecy, they set out on the pretext of a pilgrimage to a certain mountain area where they ultimately found a cave entrance. They prepared food packages to last several weeks and bundles of torches, and with some reluctance entered the depths of the cave.

After a long, fairly level, penetration into the mountain, they reached a sloping rugged downward fissure, which they descended perilously for some days. Finally they reached an immense cavity in the earth. Their torches were unnecessary there, because the air overhead and around them was charged with a strange luminosity.

They found underground rivers, several varieties of vegetation (which lacked the green of the upper earth), semi-reptilian animals and, to their astonishment, naked humans. These were of less than normal stature, but broad and stocky, and their skin had a repulsive leaden hue. The people had no culture and no shelters, and merely caught the reptiles and ate them raw. They also fed on an abundant huge toadstool-like fungus.

The youths declined the reptile flesh, but found the fungus quite good and invigorating. After a week or so their unseen guide directed them to walk in a straight line away from the wall where they had entered. Having done this for some hours, they came upon a different type of people, of higher intelligence. Although they were ignorant of fire, like the primitives already seen, they availed themselves of hot springs or geysers to cook the flesh of turtles and goat-like animals that they kept, and they drank the animals' milk. They lived in chambers hollowed out in the rock, and wove a kind of matting and string from reeds. Some of the women wore coloured stones, and both sexes smeared themselves with rose, green and yellow mud from the edges of the hot springs.

They were able to draw, and incised meaningful sets of marks on the rocks. These were mainly cup-markings, rounded hollows ground on the surface and arranged in patterns, each pattern having a meaning. In other words they were not letters but ideographs, symbols in picture-writing. A certain number of these in a straight line had one meaning, a set making an angle had another. The two young explorers eventually found their way back to the entrance of the cave, as they had carried their primitive fire-making equipment with them, and could relight their torches.

'Mysterious race in the earth's interior': illustration from *The Occult Gazette*

A Scientific Possibility?

The existence of an underground race, or races, presupposes that there are great cavities in the rocks deep inside the earth. Surprisingly enough, there seems to be a possibility that these races could exist. Although the core of the earth is a molten ball, the mantle or overlying mass of rock must have two distinct zones, one nearer the core where heat and pressure put the solid rock in a state of 'flowage', and an upper zone where 'fracture' can occur. The depth of this upper zone is the crucial point. Professor Frank D. Adams of Montreal has shown by actual experiment that empty cavities might exist in granite at a depth of at least 11 miles, and his conclusions were supported by the mathematician Louis V. King, who calculated that, at normal temperature, a cavity could exist at depths down to between 17.2 and 20.9 miles. The newly-discovered 16 Rouse Belts, which give planes of fracture completely penetrating the globe, give additional support to the possibility.

(See also LYTTON.)

C. NELSON STEWART

Succubus

Female counterpart of the incubus: a demon in female form which makes love to men while they sleep; the Devil himself was said to serve his worshippers as incubus or succubus and the children of such a union were expected to be deformed and demonic; belief in these demons is often attributed to exotic dreams and nightmares.

See INCUBUS AND SUCCUBUS.

'Sufism is a concentrated essence which for the majority needs diluting'; yet paradoxically, its most remarkable quality is a universality which bridges East and West

SUFIS

JUST AS the Cabalists are the mystics of Judaism, the Sufis are the mystics of Islam. The Sufi orders fulfil in Islam something of the same function as that of the monastic orders in Christianity. They differ from the Christian orders in not being celibate, in not being under the control of any outside authority, and in not being so highly organized. They nevertheless have a certain organization, and many of them have accumulated rich endowments with the passage of the centuries, nearly always including a mosque which has in it the tomb of the saint who founded the order.

As in other religions, the mystical orders of Islam appear to have originated in groups which gathered spontaneously round some person of outstanding spirituality. One of the earliest of these guides was the Prophet Mohammed's cousin and son-in-law, Ali (d. 661), the fourth caliph. All the orders trace their spiritual ancestry back to Mohammed himself, and in most of these 'chains' Ali is the ultimate link, though one or two orders are descended from the Prophet through Abu Bakr, the first caliph (d. 634). By the end of the 9th century some of these groups had become organized brotherhoods, and the term 'Sufi', which was not used at the beginning of Islam, had become current. Junayd of Baghdad (d. 910) is something of a landmark in this early period, and most of the Sufi masters are his spiritual descendants, whence his title 'the Sheikh of the Sheikhs'.

Sufi means literally 'wearer of wool', and long before the beginning of Islam woollen dress had been traditionally associated with the spiritual life. But the Sufis have not made a speciality of wearing wool. The term, which has profoundly venerable implications, was no doubt first applied to

a 'backward' part, no doubt, in the eyes of the majority for, like all mysticisms, Sufism would be untrue to itself if it subscribed to any of those aspirations and ideals which dominate the modern world.

The orders differ considerably from each other. The Tijani Order which is fairly widespread in north-west Africa and particularly so in West Africa (Senegal and Nigeria, for example), and throughout the Sudan is not well disposed to other orders, which it claims to have superseded. It is less aloof and more proselytizing than they are. Some of the other orders, the Isawi and the Rifai, for example, have degenerated in certain of their branches to the point of being dominated by snake-charming and fire-eating, practices which originated as subsidiary tests of faith and of reliance upon God. But the main body of Sufism can be said to be still true to its medieval heritage.

In India the Chishti Order is of considerable importance, and so throughout the East is the Naqshabandi Order; but the most widespread in both East and West are the great Qadiri and Shadhili Orders, founded respectively by Abd al-Qadir al-Jilani (d. 1166), and Abu 'l-Hasan ash-Shadhili (d. 1258), who imposed on his disciples an intellectual approach which still characterizes the Shadhili Order in its many branches. One of the most eminent of these is the Darqawi Order, with its Alawi sub-branch, founded respectively by Arabi ad-Darqawi (d. 1823) and Ahmad al-Alawi (d. 1934), both outstanding amongst the Sheikhs of more recent times.

MARTIN LINGS

Dancing dervishes of the Mevlevi Order, one of the numerous Sufi sects: illustration from a Persian *Lives of the Mystics*

FURTHER READING: Martin Lings, *A Sufi Saint of the Twentieth Century, Shaikh Ahmad al-Alawi* (Univ. of California Press, 1972); Shaikh ad-Darqawi, *Letters of a Sufi Master* (Weiser, 1970); Frithjof Schuon, *Understanding Islam* (Allen & Unwin, 1976); Titus Burckhardt, *Introduction to Sufi Doctrine* (Weiser); A. J. Arberry, *Sufism* (Allen & Unwin, 1979).

British Museum

Sulphur

According to early alchemists, the element in a substance which enables it to burn: regarded as one of the basic components of all matter, the others being mercury and salt; in man's constitution, identified with the emotions and passions, the 'fiery' part of the personality; associated with hell-fire and the Devil because of its fiery stench.

See ALCHEMY; MERCURY.

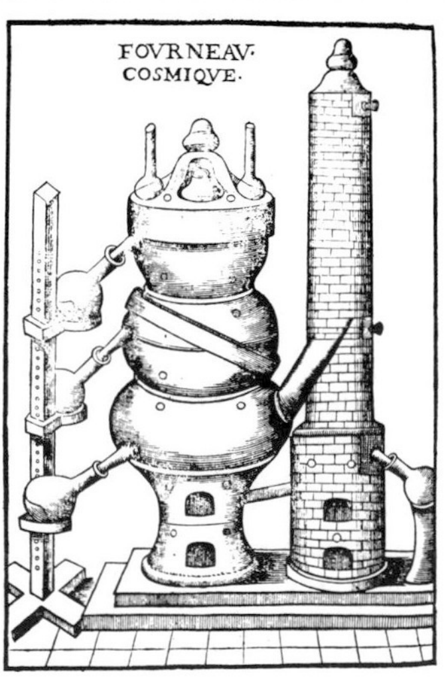

Sumerians

Early inhabitants of Mesopotamia: they had settled in Babylonia by 3500 BC and 'initiated a cultural revolution which gave the world writing, cities, and a corpus of religious practices and concepts'; each early settlement had its own local deity, so that there was a large pantheon of gods and goddesses, and a complex web of relationships between them.

See MESOPOTAMIA.

SUN

Orthodox Hindus begin the working day with an invocation of the sun: 'We meditate on the lovely light of the god, Savitri; may he inspire our thoughts'

ON THE FACE of it, there is no more obvious recipient of divine honours than the sun: visible and yet mysterious, beneficent and yet thoroughly dangerous, it is the giver of life and yet the most potent of destructive forces. In fact it can be regarded as summing up most of the characteristics which mankind has always attributed to its gods and goddesses, not least the characteristic of awesome remoteness. In the 6th century BC the Ionic philosopher Anaximander announced that the sun was not a deity, but merely a circle of fire. That he also said that it was only 28 times larger than the earth seems little more than curious; the denial of deity was the more important thing. To Anaximander's contemporaries, and the majority of his successors the world over, however, the sun was surely a deity, impinging upon the life of man at every point, measuring the rhythm of the days and the seasons, giving and withholding life, warming and burning by turns.

Nevertheless, the study of sun worship is by no means as straightforward as might at first sight appear. The simple adoration of the sun in its daily march, or ride, across the heavens can be observed and documented. But connected with this are a host of kindred notions. For instance, there is the matter of the daily and seasonal cycles which the sun establishes. Does the sun in fact establish the sacred rhythms, or is the sun itself subservient to a greater and more divine order, within which it acts essentially in the role, not of master, but of servant? Ancient Indian speculation spoke of a natural order, *rita,* of which the High Gods Varuna and Mitra (a sun god) were the guardians; but it certainly seems that they were not held to be the originators of this order. And from the other side of the world, Garcilaso de la Vega recorded the story of the Inca who was puzzled by the thought that if, as was supposed, the sun was the Supreme God, then why did he have to follow precisely the same path across the heavens every day? Was he not free to wander like the other planets? The Inca in

question is said to have concluded that there must be a god greater than the sun whom the sun was forced to obey, and to have set up an altar to that unknown deity.

The problem here is to know what is (or was) the relationship between the sun god and the High God of the sky. Other problems concern the relationship between the sun god and the world of men as reflected, for instance, in astrology; and the sun god's role in determining man's destiny after death.

When evaluating the mythology of sun worship, a great deal obviously depends on the geographical location of myth and cult. In tropical and sub-tropical areas, where the pattern of the seasons is not as clear-cut as it is in Europe, and where the omnipresence of the sun is taken for granted for the greater part of the year, particular importance is attached to the daily cycle of the sun's rising and setting; in temperate zones and in the Arctic, the seasonal cycle is by far the more important. It is significant that the nearest approach to a solar monotheism in the history of religion comes from ancient Egypt; such a belief would have been virtually impossible in northern Europe, where the sun emerged in the spring only after a bitter struggle with dark powers.

Explanatory Myths

The so-called primitive peoples of the world possess a vast store of myths concerning the sun, often coupled with moon myths, since sun and moon are frequently regarded as being related in some way.

Previous page **The rising sun brings light into darkness, a symbol of inward and spiritual illumination: from *Splendor Solis*, an alchemical work of the 15th century *Above* As Phoebus Apollo, 'bright Apollo', the Greeks identified the god of prophecy, healing and the arts with the sun: in a painting from the studio of Rosso Fiorentino, the sun god escorts the four seasons of the year**

The sun is sometimes male, sometimes female. Among certain Australian aboriginal tribes, for instance, it is personified as a woman who has a lover under the earth, among the dead. Every night she enters the underworld to be with him, and every morning ascends once more dressed in her lover's present, a red kangaroo skin. Another

Left Helios, a Greek solar deity sometimes confused with Apollo, rises from his palace in the east in readiness to drive his chariot across the heavens: chariots were also associated with the sun in Denmark and India _Below left_ 'It has been said that solar worship is the real religion of India': Surya holds in each hand a lotus, symbol of divine light, immortal life and fertility _Below right_ Pyramid to the sun at Teotihuacan, a centre of Mexican civilization of the 1st millennium AD: the similarities between sun worship in America and in ancient Egypt have led some scholars to believe that Egyptian culture must have crossed the Atlantic

tribe is said to have had a myth to the effect that every day the sun burns up her stock of fuel, and has to descend into the underworld each night for fresh supplies of firewood. Stories of the sun entering the underworld at night and emerging afresh every morning are legion, the sun having walked, ridden, or been carried from west to east.

Its daily course is similarly surrounded with stories and explanations. Ancient Indo-European myths usually picture the sun as driving across the sky in a golden chariot, drawn by horses, a belief which led to the horse being regarded as especially sacred. From Peru comes a variant, according to which the sun is tethered like a llama by an invisible cord to the pole of the sky, and driven round and round it by the power of the Universal Spirit. There are many such examples.

Another type of myth told of the sun concerns the need to 'tame' its power in some way. A Mexican legend tells that the sun was once a man who, to show his devotion, immolated himself in a sacrificial fire; in reward the Supreme Being conveyed him to heaven. He burned so fiercely, however, that the world was endangered by his very ardour, and arrows had to be shot at him to persuade him to temper his rays.

Myths concerning the relationship of the sun and moon explain why the two never meet in heaven. Usually it is held that sun and moon are brother and sister, but that for some reason they have become enemies, and the male partner, who can be either the sun or the moon, pursues the female for all eternity. There is a Masai legend to the effect that sun and moon were married, but fell out; in shame, the sun became bright in order that men might not look at him. From the Paiute Indians of California this is recorded: 'The sun is the father and ruler of the heavens. He is the big chief. The moon is his wife and the stars are their children. The sun eats his children whenever he can catch them. They flee before him, and are all the time afraid when he is passing through the heavens. When he appears in the morning, you see all the stars, his children, fly out of sight . . . and they do not wake to be seen again until he, their father, is about to go to his bed.'

These naïve explanatory myths take on a much more serious tone in Scandinavian mythology. There the daily rising and setting

Ancient Indo-European myths usually picture the sun as driving across the sky in a golden chariot, drawn by horses

of the sun was of less importance than the sun's battle with the powers that threatened to destroy her (once again, the sun is female). In Snorri Sturluson's *Edda* the question is posed: 'Swiftly rides the sun; it is almost as though she were afraid, and she would surely not fly faster, though she were pursued by death.' The questioner is told that the sun is indeed pursued, by two wolves, the offspring of giants. 'And it is said that one of that breed will be stronger than all others . . . He feeds on the blood of all those who die, and he pours blood over the air and the sky, so that the sun ceases to shine . . .' This is not only the vision of winter, but also the vision of the end of the world, heralded, among other things, by the howling of the Fenris wolf (see END OF THE WORLD; SCANDINAVIA).

To relate stories of the sun is not necessarily to worship it; but the power of the sun was in fact an object of active worship among many archaic peoples. Once more, though, elements other than 'pure' sun worship were frequently involved. The famous Sun Dance of the Great Plains Indians of North America, for example, was part of a major act of worship that lasted for eight days, and took place every summer after the buffalo hunt (see GREAT PLAINS INDIANS). On arrival at the place of meeting, the participating tribes formed a circle, leaving an opening to the east, the direction of the rising sun. A vast lodge, which might in some cases be open to the sky, was erected and an altar was placed to the west of the site. The dance itself lasted from two to four days, during which the dancers kept their gaze fixed on the sun or on the lodge's centre pole, which symbolized the cosmic tree. Self-torture was sometimes practised as an act of dedication and sacrifice, and as a means of obtaining that vision without which the Sun Dance was held to be incomplete.

It is perhaps justifiable to see in the Sun Dance an elaborate form of a type of sun ritual that was once found in many parts of the world, and which aimed at the annual renewal of the cosmic order by means of participation in the divine power of the sun, the greatest of the Great Spirit's manifestations.

William MacQuitty

Swedish National Museum

the remote past, adventurers, merchants or missionaries might have communicated something of Egypt's devotion to the sun god to other lands and races is an intriguing one. Unfortunately it is only a possibility, and one which archeology is very far indeed from having confirmed. There are two entirely independent lines along which a few scholars have believed this influence to have been transmitted. One leads from the eastern Mediterranean westward and northward into Spain, France, the west of Britain and Ireland, north Germany, Denmark and southern Sweden. Its evidence consists in the trail of vast stone structures, megaliths, in which the dead were buried, and in the stone circles and alignments, of which the best known are Stonehenge and Carnac in Brittany, at which the sun may have been worshipped. Unfortunately, speculation has tended to run riot as soon as this subject has been broached; but it seems to have been established that the megalith-builders were sun worshippers.

The second line leads directly westward, out across the Atlantic to the Americas. The most recent advocate of this theory is the Norwegian explorer Thor Heyerdahl, whose two voyages in the papyrus boats *Ra I* and *Ra II* aimed at demonstrating that such a culture-contact would have been possible. But the theory was expressed forcefully in the 1920s by a British scholar, W. J. Perry, who pointed out that the Peruvian royal family, like that of Egypt, mummified their dead, practised marriage of near relatives, built pyramids, and called themselves 'children of the sun'.

Writing about the megalith-builders in *The Growth of Civilization* (1924) he noted that: 'The presence of vast graves undoubtedly means the coming to Europe of members of a ruling family, for no one else could build them. The use of solar symbols suggests that the people responsible for these graves were sun-worshippers. Since, the world over, the sun-cult has been an ancestor cult in the family of the Children of the Sun, who ruled Egypt . . . for thousands of years, it would seem that these facts, when put together, mean that the Children of the Sun had begun to move out from Egypt, and had founded kingdoms in

The possibility of the withdrawal of the light was always present: it happened every winter in the North

Jeffrey Craig

Left The legendary inventor Daedalus made wings for himself and his son Icarus, but when the boy presumed to fly too near the sun the heat melted the wax, and he fell into the Aegean Sea and was drowned: *The Fall of Icarus* by Petrus Stevens and Joos de Momper *Above right* Embroidery representing the sun, from Isfahan, Iran

various parts of Europe, just as they had done when moving out to America.'

No doubt Perry's theories went too far; but the fact, not of sun worship, which needs no diffusionist excuse, but of certain forms of sun worship in various parts of the world, calls for explanation in terms of more than mere chance.

Warnings of Misrule

One other general feature of sun worship is the association of the sun with other heavenly bodies in patterns of astrological prediction. The sun was never isolated in the heavens. Subservient to the High God, linked in various mythical ways to the moon and the stars, maintaining the fabric of the universe by means of its regular rhythm, the sun served in many cultures as a pattern of natural order backed by divine favour. To be sure, sacrifices were always necessary, often, particularly in the Americas, blood sacrifices, in order to mark man's acknowledgement of his dependence; but the possibility of the withdrawal of the light was always present. It happened every winter in the North. And on rare occasions it would happen without warning, in which case it was taken as an omen of dire events to come (see ECLIPSE).

This extract is from an edict of the Chinese Emperor Ming Ti, consequent upon the solar eclipse of 233 AD: 'We have heard that if a sovereign is remiss in government, God terrifies him by calamities and portents. These are divine reprimands sent to recall him to a sense of duty. Thus, eclipses of the sun and moon are manifest warnings that the rod of empire is not wielded aright. Ever since we ascended the throne, our inability to continue the glorious traditions of our departed ancestors and carry on the great work of civilization has now culminated in a warning message from on high. It therefore behoves us to issue commands for personal reformation, in order to avert impending calamity.' There may be more spectacular, more bloody and evocative forms of sun worship in the history of religion; but there is none more moral. (See also ALCHEMY; AZTECS; INCAS.)

ERIC J. SHARPE

The Sun in Astrology

As the most important of the heavenly bodies, the Sun naturally plays a dominating role in the interpretation of a horoscope, and is said to be the most powerful single factor in the chart. In popular astrology columns in newspapers and magazines, you will find yourself classified under your Sun sign, the sign of the zodiac which the Sun was 'in' at the moment of your birth, with the implication that this is the major general key to analysis of your character and fortunes. More sophisticated interpretation tends to give great weight to the Ascendant, where the Sun rises, and the Mid-heaven, where it is at its peak of power, and both the sign and the house occupied by the Sun are taken as influential factors (see ASTROLOGY).

Since the Sun is the world's natural powerhouse of light and heat, it is believed to affect the creative abilities, vitality, ambition and will-power of human beings. Its position in the sky is generally said to indicate your basic temperament, the type of person you are, and sometimes your physical appearance. Some astrologers stress its role in influencing the conscious or 'lighted' part of your mind (with the unconscious mind being the domain of the Moon). If the Sun is favourably placed in the horoscope, especially if it is in its own sign, Leo, it is said to produce a commanding and kingly personality – powerful, proud, dignified, impressive, generous, faithful and affectionate. This symbolic link between the Sun and kingship is very old, and the good humour often associated with the Sun follows from the cheerfulness which its radiant appearance in the sky tends to promote in northern countries.

FURTHER READING: Glyn Daniel, *The Idea of Prehistory* (C. A. Watts, 1964); Jacquetta Hawkes, *Man and the Sun* (The Cresset Press, 1962); W. J. Perry, *The Children of the Sun* (Methuen, 1923); G. van der Leeuw, *Religion in Essence and Manifestation* (Allen & Unwin, 1938).

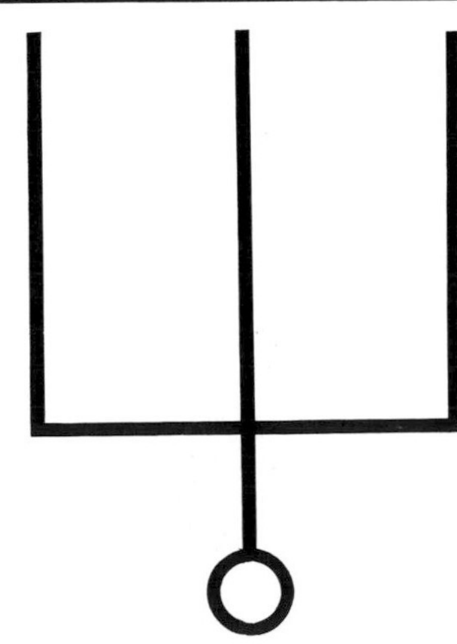

Sunday

The Christian sabbath, the day of rest, set aside for the worship of God in the tradition of the Jewish sabbath, and believed to be the day of the week on which Christ rose from the dead: named for the sun, with which the first day of the week was associated in the Roman Empire; a fortunate day to be born on, but unfortunate for any other secular activity.
See DAYS AND HOURS.

Sunnites

Members of the main branch of Islam, to which the majority of Moslems belong: they hold the Koran to be infallible, as the eternal word of God, and also place reliance on Tradition, originally transmitted orally and stemming from Mohammed or his Companions; the Shiites, the second principal branch, differ from them over the question of imams, over free will, and over other matters of doctrine, tradition and ritual.
See ISLAM.

SUNYAVADA

GAUTAMA, the Buddha, taught that the soul is a temporary combination of transient entities called *skandhas* (see BUDDHISM). Mahayana Buddhism, which arose about four centuries after the death of Buddha (c 483 BC), developed this doctrine more fully, and several of its early literary works, called Sutras, proclaimed the doctrine of emptiness, Sunyavada.

Whereas in early Buddhism wisdom is insight into impermanence, suffering and no-self, in Sunyavada the perfection of wisdom is the realization that all *dharmas* (doctrines or laws of life) are 'empty'. Transmigration and Nirvana (see NIRVANA) are both empty. The saviours are empty, and the beings whom they save are empty. From the absolute viewpoint, there is no difference whatsoever between the relative and the absolute, between *samsara*, the world of change and transmigration, and Nirvana, the perfect state beyond change. Emptiness, though, is not non-being, and Sunyavada is not nihilism, no matter how readily the charge springs to the lips of those bewildered and frightened by this doctrine. Emptiness is just that Middle Path between being and non-being that Gautama had declared. Things do not have being, because they are mutable and impermanent, and what is truly real does not change or perish. Things do not have non-being, because they arise and function, and whatever appears and acts is relatively real. That things are empty means that they lack own-being (*svabhava*), that is, they exist through the power of another rather than through their own power, they do not possess an inalienable set of marks, and they have no immutable essence.

The Hinayana Sutras say that all the skandhas, sense-spheres and elements are impermanent and devoid of self, which is tantamount to saying they are empty. However, the Abhidharma schools, especially the Sarvastivadins, drew up lists of 70 or so conditioned dharmas (force-factors), including all the skandhas, which they treated as realities. The Sarvastivadin doctrine that not only present but past and future dharmas are real comes perilously close to the theory that coming-to-be is just manifestation of what was already there in a latent state. Sunyavada was a reaction against this tendency in Abhidharma. Mahayana, charging that the Abhidharmists denied an *atman* (soul) in the person but admitted one in the dharmas, declared that both person and dharmas are empty of atman.

The Sunyavadin polemic against the Abhidharmists, and against Samkhya and Vaisesika (the two major Hindu philosophies at the time), was prosecuted most brilliantly by Nagarjuna (c 150–250 AD), founder of the Madhyamika school of Mahayana Buddhism. Born a South Indian Brahmin and well educated in Sanskrit and the Hindu philosophies, he became a Buddhist and proceeded to defend Mahayana principles using the logic and debating techniques of the Hindus. He reduces to absurdity all propositions that assume the existence of an own-being. This is not too hard, since the concept is self-contradictory as Nagarjuna defines it. Own-being exists and is immutable. But to exist means to change.

A sample of Nagarjuna's dialectic is his critique of causation. He says that a thing cannot arise from itself, since that would be the arising of the already arisen, an absurdity as great as the second cutting off of a head. A thing cannot arise from another thing, since that which is non-existent cannot be the agent of the action 'arising' or the object of the action 'production'; a real action requires that both agent and object be real, too. Nor can a thing arise from a combination of other things (the Abhidharma and Vaisesika position), since the effect does not exist in the separate causes before they are combined.

The Empty-ists introduced a whole new epistemology (theory of the grounds of knowledge) to the Buddhist tradition. Ordinary cognition is essentially deceptive, they held, because it involves thought-construction (*vikalpa*). What is changing is grasped as something persisting, class properties are superimposed on events that are really unique particulars, and consequently the imagination, like a magician, figments the ordinary world which is really an illusion or phantom. Ordinary language carries with it the acceptance of vikalpas and consequently the belief in the own-being of things. Nagarjuna's dialectic aims to purge thought and language by the use of thought and language, just as the physician uses poison to cure poison.

Man resorts to irrational beliefs whenever his faith wilts and he becomes afraid; superstition is a form of personal magic which is used for coming to terms with the unknown

SUPERSTITIONS

IT HAS been said that man is a religious animal, but it could equally be averred that he is a superstitious one. Throughout the whole of man's history an elaborate system of apparently irrational safeguards, often barbaric in character, has provided a foundation for much of his ritual life. The minor ceremonies which survive today in the form of superstitions, are a constant reminder of the fact that man's mind has probably changed but little from that of his primitive ancestors.

Many of these superstitions are apparently outward manifestations of deeply-seated anxieties, the precise character of which remains as yet relatively unexplored territory. Their very existence implies an unquestioning assumption that there is some power (or powers) external to man himself, which is capricious, tyrannical and highly dangerous, a force that must be cajoled and won over to one's side, or, if it is hostile, kept at bay.

The word superstition is related to the Latin *superstes*, a word which includes among its meanings that of outliving or surviving. Used in this sense, superstition became a useful term for the description of religious ideas which lived on when the religion from which they sprang had died. For this reason superstitions have usually been condemned as relics of outmoded ways of thinking, rather than as living expressions. More commonly the term has been used to denigrate forms of faith which disagree with one's own. In the 16th century 'Popish superstitions' were roundly condemned by Protestants, and in the 19th century pious missionaries risked their lives to rescue pagan savages from 'superstitious barbarism'.

Radio Times Hulton Picture Library

Most superstitions involve a simple, if unscientific, logic *Above* An eggshell stuffed with horsehair was rubbed on a patient's body and then thrown into the street, transferring the disease to whoever trod on it
***Right* Reversed symbols, the cat and the colour black belong to the Devil as the principle of rebellion, abnormality and darkness**

Yet however superficially absurd their character, unvarying features of behaviour deserve to be treated seriously. Any examination of contemporary superstitious beliefs indicates that these should not necessarily be written off as the result of errors of observation or reasoning, but should be considered as permanent traits of mind.

The thought-processes of pre-scientific man can be observed in the widespread and still current superstition that breaking a mirror (see MIRROR) brings seven years' bad luck. The reflected image was originally regarded as the *alter ego*, or other soul, and damaging it was supposed to cause an injury to the person who had broken the mirror. Fear of walking under a ladder (see STEPS) may be partly derived from the terror once felt at the sight of the gallows, which was often merely a ladder propped against a tree.

The Philosophy of Magic

All superstitions seem to have the dual purpose of attracting favourable influences and warding off unfavourable ones. The name we give to these influences may be good luck and bad luck but they correspond too closely to the good and evil spirits of our primitive ancestors to be dismissed as

Transworld

Unforeseen effects of observing popular superstitions: 'at the root of every type of superstition lies a belief in magic'

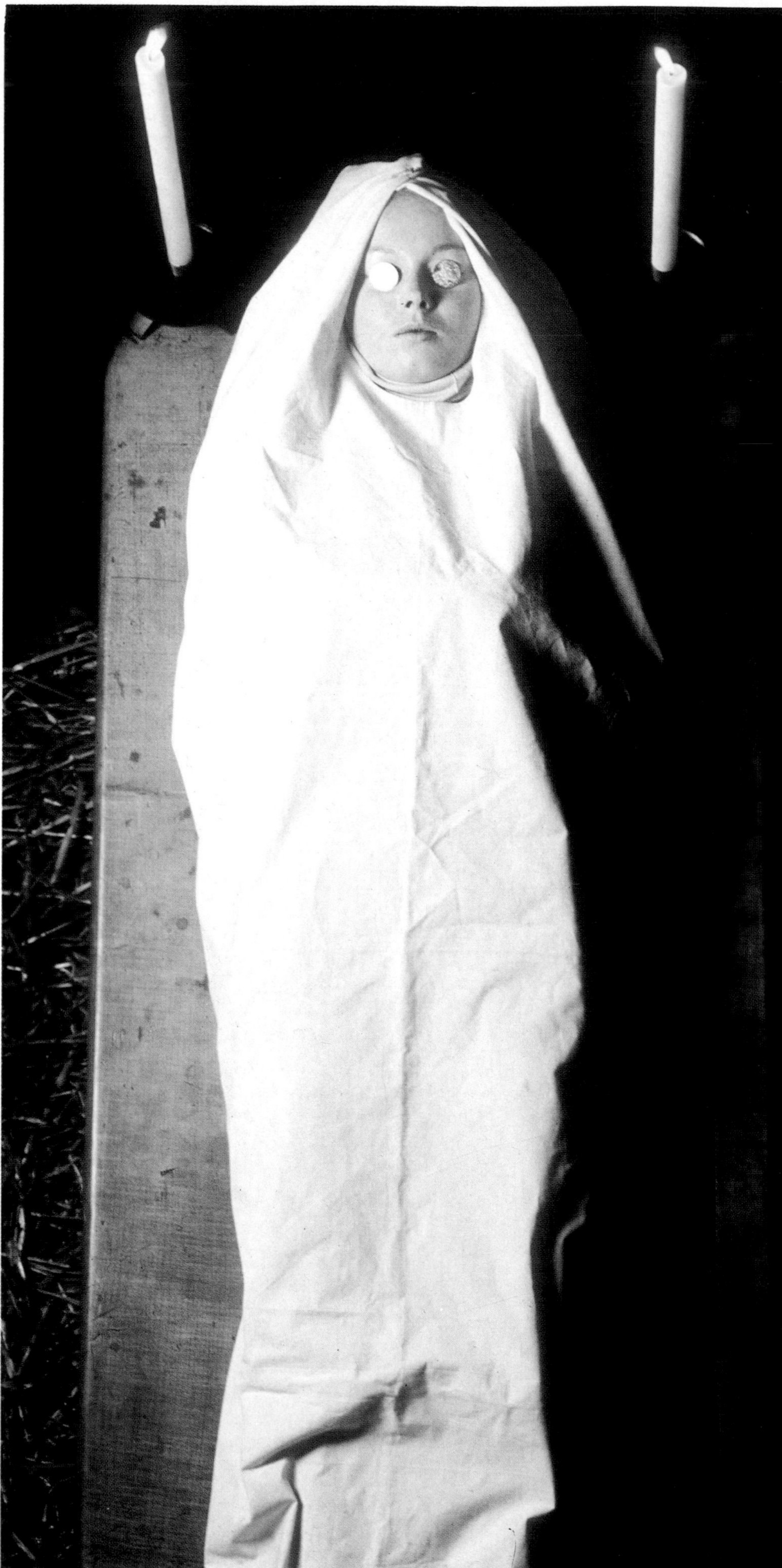

A corpse's eyes will be closed, sometimes by weighting them with coins: superstitious fears still govern our attitude to death

illogical fantasies. The curious predisposition of civilized man to revert in times of crisis to an archetypal mode of thought was noted by Paul Bauer in *Christianity and Superstition,* and he added that whereas the primitive man was perfectly at home in his superstitious environment, the civilized man most certainly is not.

It can therefore be argued that at the root of every type of superstition lies a belief in magic, which is a philosophy to which man resorts again and again whenever his modern gods fail him; in short, when his faith wilts and he becomes afraid. Superstition offers the comforting assurance that it is possible to influence one's fate for good and evil by will-power reinforced with ritual. There is obviously only a difference in degree between the act of worshipping a sacred tree and that of 'touching wood'. By physical contact with a piece of the magically charged wood one summons the power of the tree-spirit to one's aid. This magic is of the defensive type, however, for although the wood may hold bad luck at bay, it has no power to attract good luck.

More positive luck-bringing measures are the various uses of charms and talismans. Although to most people nowadays such objects have little real significance, the modern charm bracelet, first introduced about a century ago, has found ready acceptance as a luck-bringer. The symbolic meaning of the particular charms – the horseshoes, lucky pigs, and nowadays miniature golf clubs and cars – is quite lost upon the wearer, who is conscious only of the fact that they are supposed to exercise a collective power to attract good fortune. To an earlier generation, each particular charm would have had its clearly defined function; the pig, for instance, representing the Scandinavian Sun Boar, protected its domestic counterpart from evil; while the horseshoe, having the shape of a crescent moon, provided a safeguard against witches (see BOAR; HORSESHOE).

The most important characteristic of a luck-bringer is the source of the power with which it is endowed. How does a piece of wood or metal acquire its status as a charm, and what are the channels by which superstitions are transmitted? One of the ways in which an object may acquire supernatural power is through association; thus a toy animal given to a child by its grandmother is regarded as an embodiment of her love and is a powerful luck-bringer. In a series of experiments carried out among London children by the present writer, it became clear that superstitions are mainly communicated to the child by his mother or grandmother, and only occasionally by his father. In an almost literal as well as a figurative sense, they are 'taken in with the mother's milk'. The superstitious routines or lucky charms made their appearance at times of crisis, such as an examination. The particular type of charm employed included objects such as a lump of coal or a bent nail, the one originally representing the power of fire and the other that of iron (see FIRE; IRON). Charms that have failed to produce the desired results are rarely discarded but instead are hidden from sight in a desk or drawer. Luck-bringers are traditionally kept secret except in times of crisis, since discussing them is supposed to exhaust their powers. Protective charms, on the other hand, are more openly displayed since their function is to keep bad luck at bay, in other words to warn off evil spirits.

Stages in the Life Cycle

Two human fears may be found at the root of a vast number of widely differing superstitions: firstly, fear in the face of change at the various crises of life, and secondly, fear of presuming upon the future, thus inviting the anger of the gods.

Of the two, perhaps the most dominant is that aroused by the prospect of change. It was for this reason that new objects and occurrences were in the past greeted with elaborate ceremonies designed to ward off the hostility of the supernatural powers.

Among primitive peoples, the various stages of development in each individual from birth to death were always associated with protective devices, the vestiges of which survived until recently in the form of superstitions. With today's safer childbearing, many of the old birth taboos have disappeared, but some mothers-to-be continue to observe superstitious rites, such as those calculated to produce a child of the desired sex. A mother who wants a boy, for example, will wear a blue dress, and when hoping for a girl, she may still wear pink. A relic of the old uncertainty associated with birth survives in the belief that it is unlucky to take the pram into the house until after the baby has been born; an example of the superstitious fear of presuming upon the future (see BIRTH).

The onset of puberty was originally accompanied by magic rites designed to give protection against the hostility of evil spirits who were supposed to be particularly aggressive at this important period of one's life (see INITIATION; MENSTRUATION; RITES OF PASSAGE). The time has long since passed when menstrual blood was considered so threatening that a butcher would not permit his daughter to enter his shop during her periods, but it is still possible to find individuals who retain the belief that the sexual act carried out with a woman at such times can result in venereal disease.

With marriage comes a complete change of direction in the lives of both partners, and the marriage ceremony is a veritable museum of old superstitions (see MARRIAGE). Again out of fear of anticipating the future, the bride is careful not to see her image as a completely wedded woman in the mirror. If she has to take a last look before leaving for the church, she is careful to take off her glove. For the same reason, she will take care to avoid being seen by the groom before the actual ceremony. Every feature of this important magical occasion has its particular superstitions; even the dressmaker who inserts the first stitch into the wedding dress can expect to be a bride herself before the year is out. Should the wedding ring, which is in effect a magic circle, be removed or broken it becomes ominous for the marriage prospects.

Many primitive sexual superstitions have passed down the generations. Because the heat of the sun was once thought to be the source of life on earth, we continue to regard Mediterranean men as sexual athletes and Negroes as sexual dynamos (see RACE MYTHS). Because sexual activity was once regarded as a magical act, the seed or semen became sacrosanct; hence the long-standing myth that masturbation leads inevitably to a weakening of the physical powers, madness or even death. This may fairly rank as superstition.

Sickness and ill health, once the most feared of life's crises since they could lead to financial ruin, have lost some of their superstitious associations, thanks to modern medicine and welfare systems. Even so, to boast of excellent health is regarded as inviting psychic reprisals. The permanent fear of creating a situation by the mere act of referring to it by name is the real reason why certain diseases are mentioned only in hushed tones. For the same reason, the word death itself is often avoided.

The onset of death is even today associated with natural occurrences, prophetic visions and mystical utterances. Here, at the grand climacteric, superstition reaches its peak. The moment of death itself is signalled by stopping of clocks, and pious drawing of curtains and the covering of mirrors. The mourner, as Geoffrey Gorer has pointed out, has entered 'a special state of mind'. It is in the funeral ceremony that one observes an intensity of superstitious awe that no longer survives in the other departments of life. If the wreath has ceased to be regarded as a magic circle to contain the soul and prevent its return to haunt the living, it remains none the less obligatory even in cremations (see BURIAL).

War and Peace

A crisis in the life of a nation, as in the life-cycle of an individual, is the focus of superstition, and it is traditionally the onset of war which raises the tempo and intensity of irrational belief. During the First and Second World Wars a number of superstitions which were centuries old suddenly received a new lease of life. To paint the portrait of a battleship now became, to the seaman's mind, the equivalent of a sentence of death upon her. The jinx ship which is a commonplace of nautical life was discussed with even greater anxiety than previously. Sailors when about to embark upon a voyage considered it dangerous if a menstruating woman sewed a badge of rank onto a uniform. In 1914 German prisoners-of-war bore ancient amulets offering protection against death from bullets. In 1942 American servicemen carried iron-bound Bibles in their breast pockets for exactly the same reason.

Aircrews tended to resort under danger to a variety of death-defying fetishes, including amulets, mascots and lucky silk stockings, while their planes were invaded by those latter-day familiars, the gremlins. The belief in lucky and unlucky days was revived and one and all displayed a reluctance to presume upon the future.

In peacetime, the degree of superstition which a man is likely to display is usually related to the riskiness of his occupation. Stockbrokers, whose financial lives are so often balanced upon a knife's edge of chance, have a strong tendency to consult clairvoyants, and American bankers are reputed to derive a sense of security from furtively touching the backs of passing hunchbacks. Out-and-out gamblers, whether at the roulette or card table, wear their superstitions almost as badges, displaying a fervent belief in lucky seats and hunches. But the perfect example of a truly superstitious profession is the theatre. The life of an actor is extremely insecure, and every theatrical production is a hazardous venture. In these circumstances many actors have a complete philosophy of superstitious practices, some of which must be as old as the profession itself. To stumble is an omen of forgetting one's lines. The final line of the play is never spoken in rehearsal as any anticipation of completion is an invitation to disaster. If a long thread of cotton is found on an actor's back, it means that a contract is on the way. An actor will frequently treasure some little object associated with a successful first night's performance, regarding it as a form of magical insurance.

Another trade which was originally encrusted with superstitious usages is that of the seaman. In the hazardous days of sail, the men on the big ships surrounded their lives with a complicated system of rituals and taboos (see SEA; SHIP). Today the situation has changed radically as the direct result of a century-long revolution in shipping. Long sea voyages are now relatively safe and in consequence deep-sea superstitions of all kinds have dwindled. On the other hand, among fishermen, whose lives continue to be at risk and whose incomes are precarious, the majority of the older sea superstitions retain much of their original force. A skipper will frequently refuse to put to sea should he discover his hatch upside down on boarding his craft; a bucket lost overboard is still interpreted as a sign from the fates that the ship is doomed.

Sporting Chance

It would appear to be the rule that if the stock of superstitious beliefs remains undiminished, the point of emphasis is continually shifting from one situation to another in accordance with the amount of anxiety experienced at any particular time. Today at the factory bench, for example, a threat of unemployment at once brings all the old wives' tales to the fore. Placing a pair of new shoes on a bench is now seen as a threat to one's job, whereas in more settled times it was interpreted as an omen of death, the shoes being required for that long journey to the underworld.

All competitive situations, whether at work or at play, tend to create anxiety and therefore provide a solid foundation for the growth of superstition. In sport this principle is often paramount. The traditional belief that there is luck in odd numbers

Harry Price Library

Left A variety of superstitions illustrated: it is lucky to hear a goblin sneeze, unlucky to walk under a ladder or to be the third to share a lighted match _Below_ Members of the Eccentric Club defy the omens of bad luck at a luncheon held on Friday the 13th

Radio Times Hulton Picture Library

prompts punters to place their bets on threes, sevens and nines. Jockeys have their lucky caps, cricketers their lucky bats and boots, and some footballers not only touch the goal-posts at the commencement of a match but have been known to prevent their wives from looking at the game on television. In most cases a lucky object acquires its supernatural reputation because of its association in the player's mind with some important success in the field. The cricketer who makes his century while wearing a particular shirt will often go on wearing it until it is almost reduced to tatters. Luck by association is the rule in sport as in all other kinds of activity.

Any survey of the superstitious scene makes it clear that superstitions possess a powerful tendency to move with the times, changing in outward form although never in essence. Motorists advance down the motorways protected by lucky key-fobs, and automobile salesmen display a noticeable aversion to dealing in cars that have been involved in fatal accidents. Motor-cycle policemen and Hell's Angels alike believe it unlucky for their crash helmets to be touched by alien hands. Civil air pilots and even astronauts are reported to take amulets with them on their flights, while the computer operator is coming to believe that his machine has a life of its own.

Superstitious fears are likely to arise in anyone – irrespective of social class or nationality – who feels himself threatened by forces lying beyond the range of his power. The form of a particular superstition is determined by environmental and social factors, but the function of superstition itself seems to be unvarying.

Superstition may perhaps be defined as a form of personal magic which is used for the purpose of coming to terms with the unknown. By false analogy a particular course of action which has proved successful in the past is associated with some object worn or action carried out at the same time, which is then accorded a kind of talismanic quality. The object or action is then used again or repeated, in the expectation of achieving a similar result at another time. Negative superstition, which may be defined as the avoidance of certain acts with the object of preventing undesired contingencies, arises from a similar false association of ideas. In all this activity, however, can be detected an awareness of some law of cause and effect, but it is the cause and effect of the savage, not that of the scientific man, the rule of assumption rather than thought.

ERIC MAPLE

FURTHER READING: F. E. Planer, *Superstition* (Horizon, 1981); Gustav Jahoda, *The Psychology of Superstition* (Aronson, 1974); Eric Maple, *Superstition and the Superstitious* (W. H. Allen, London, 1971).

Mansell Collection

To perish in flames with her dead husband as an act of purification was the duty of the high-caste Hindu widow; a practice which survived here and there, in defiance of the law, until as recently as the 1940s

A Hindu widow leaps into the flames of her husband's funeral pyre; men with poles pinned the sati down if her courage failed her. Some believed that this sacrificial act expunged the sins of both husband and wife: 18th century engraving

SUTTEE

THE SELF-IMMOLATION of a Hindu widow on her husband's funeral pyre is described by the term *suttee*, more correctly spelt *sati*. The literal meaning of sati is 'a virtuous woman', but early European writers applied the term erroneously to the ritual burning of such a woman with her dead husband. The origin of the practice is not certain, but parallels are found in many ancient cultures. The kings of Ur, for example, were buried with their wives, attendants and possessions, so that in the next world they should have all the comforts they were used to on this earth. Similar customs prevailed among the ancient Chinese, among early Indo-European peoples and also among the nomads of Central Asia.

There is no direct reference to the burning of widows in the most ancient Indian scriptures, known as the *Rig-Veda*. A funeral hymn describes how the widow lies down on the pyre beside her dead husband, but she is then called back to the land of the living. A reference in the later *Atharva-Veda* suggests, however, that subsequently the burning of widows became common. The Greek accounts from the time of Alexander the Great's invasion of India (327–325 BC) contain references to the self-immolation of widows, and among the high Hindu castes the practice continued intermittently until the 19th century when the British authorities declared it illegal.

The earliest memorial to a sati is an inscription on a pillar dated 510 AD, and similar monuments from later days are found in many parts of India. Some medieval writers declared that the sati by burning herself on her husband's pyre expunges both her own and her husband's sins, and that the two would enjoy millions of years of bliss in heaven. There was also the idea that the self-immolation of a widow would purify her own as well as her husband's family. If her husband had died far from home she was advised to take some article of his dress, tie it to her breast, and then ascend the funeral pyre. In theory the cremation of a sati was always voluntary, but social and family pressures to follow the custom may often have been irresistible, particularly in the case of high caste widows of warrior class.

Criticisms of the custom were not unknown even in ancient times, and in the Middle Ages writers of tantric sects (see TANTRISM) even declared that a woman burning herself with her husband would go straight to hell. Yet, the fate of widows in orthodox Hindu families was unenviable, and women without young children may often have preferred a self-imposed death to a life of privation, scorn and domestic servitude in the house of unsympathetic kinsmen of a deceased husband.

The circumstances and methods of conducting the cremation varied. In northern India it was the custom for the sati on her way to the pyre to mark the chief gateway of a temple with the impression of her hand steeped in vermilion, or to impress her stained hand on a stone, forming marks which would afterwards be made permanent by chiselling. Stones bearing such marks were considered sacred, and a woman who chose self-immolation was revered as a divine figure. A blessing given by a sati on the way to her death was highly valued and her curses were feared. The actual cremation was accompanied by elaborate rites. In some parts of India it was customary for the widow to sit beside her husband's corpse in a straw hut erected on a pyre, which she finally set alight with a torch. Elsewhere she lay beside the corpse surrounded with inflammable materials, and if her courage failed her she was pinned down in the flames by men wielding long poles. In southern India a fire was kindled in a pit into which the widow had to leap.

The practice of self-immolation of women was particularly common among Rajputs, people from the present-day state of Rajasthan in north-west India. Not only did many Rajput widows burn themselves with their husband's corpse, but on the capture of a fortress many of the noble women burned themselves in the rite known as *Johar* in order to escape dishonour.

In many places in northern India, and particularly on the banks of rivers or tanks, small masonry shrines dedicated to satis may be seen. Such a shrine is often decorated with a carving in stone representing the husband and his faithful wife. Women come to such shrines to pray for male offspring or for the health of their husbands and children.

Detail from a 19th century engraving: a blessing given by a sati on her way to her death was highly valued and her curses were feared, for she was regarded as divine; the burning was accompanied by elaborate rites

Mary Evans Picture Library

With Snakes to the Flames

The self-immolation of widows is paralleled by other instances of ritual suicide once practised in India. In the Punjab mothers were known to burn themselves with their dead children, and in the past it was not unusual for men to kill themselves in order to accompany a beloved lord and master to the next world. There are many historical references to ministers, courtiers and servants voluntarily ending their life after the death of a ruler, and those who sacrificed themselves in such a manner were held in high esteem. The cult of such heroes as well as that of women who chose the role of sati is closely linked with the whole idea of worshipping the sainted dead. Representations of snakes rising out of the masonry of sati memorials to receive the adoration of the living suggests such a connection with the cult of ancestral spirits. A legend tells how once upon a time in the Narbada River valley of central India, when the three widows of a man were burnt on his funeral pyre, two great snakes appeared and entered the flames to be burnt with them. The bystanders were convinced that these were two wives of the dead man in a previous birth, and when the memorial rite was performed it was done for six souls instead of four.

The prohibition of the burning of widows, though enacted during the period of British rule, was the result of a campaign by progressive Indians. A Hindu sect known as the Brahmo Samaj, which combined ethical doctrines derived from Christianity with traditional Indian beliefs, agitated for the abolition of the custom, and though vigorously opposed by orthodox Hindu opinion gained the support of the British authorities. In 1829 the custom then officially described as 'suttee' was prohibited in Bengal, and similar legislation soon followed in the provinces of Bombay and Madras. But in the independent princely states not affected by British legislation the practice continued unchecked, and there were cases of people from adjoining British territories going there to perform the rite. Gradually, several of the rulers of the larger states, such as Baroda and Indore, were persuaded to prohibit the immolation of widows, but resistance to the reformist movement was strong in Rajputana. The opposition to abolition was weakened, however, by a ruling from the chief Brahmin priest of Jaipur to the effect that the immolation of widows was less meritorious than the 'living suttee' of chastity and devotion. In 1846 several Rajput states prohibited the practice but as late as 1861 the cremation of widows openly took place in Udaipur*(then a princely state). Secretly it continued very much longer, and in remote areas isolated cases of the immolation of widows occurred as late as the 1940s, though criminal proceedings were taken against those involved whenever a case came to the notice of the authorities.

C. VON FÜRER-HAIMENDORF

C. M. Dixon/British Museum

It was a common belief in many cultures that the human soul might leave its body in the form of a bird: Ani, a royal Egyptian scribe, is represented after death as a swallow, in the Theban Book of the Dead, c 1250 BC

SWALLOW

WHEN MAN BEGAN to erect solid buildings the swallows found that the eaves provided sheltered niches for their nests. An ancient Egyptian papyrus refers to a lovesick girl hearing the swallows early in the morning inviting her into the countryside. Greek writers often mentioned the bird which, in common with other European peoples, they looked upon as a harbinger of spring. And it was a Greek writer, Aristotle, who first wrote: 'One swallow does not make a summer.' A black-figured Greek vase now in the Vatican depicts an elderly man, a youth and a boy greeting the first swallow to appear in spring. The youth shouts 'Look, there's a swallow!,' the man cries 'By Heracles, so there is.' The boy exclaims 'There she goes,' and then, 'Spring has come.' In the 2nd century AD boys went from house to house on Rhodes singing:

> The swallow is here and a new year he brings,
> As he lengthens the days with the beats of his wings,
> White and black
> Are his belly and back.
>
> Pay his tribute once more
> With cheese in its basket,
> And pork from your store,
> And wine from its flasket,
> And eggs from your casket, and bread when we ask it.

A springtime swallow song is still sung in some areas of Greece. The Greeks had a low opinion of the swallow's song which they likened to a chattering in barbarous tongues. In spite of its joyous spring associations, the swallow became associated with wretchedness in the story of Philomela and Procne (see NIGHTINGALE). In this myth, Tereus cut out the tongue of his wife Procne lest she should divulge that he had violated her sister Philomela. Whereupon the gods transformed all three into birds: Tereus was turned into a hoopoe, Philomela into a nightingale and Procne into a swallow. Ever since, the swallow has only been able to utter incoherent twitterings.

Augurs claimed that they could interpret the bird's call, and inferences were drawn from its behaviour. The fluttering of a swallow around the head of Alexander the Great was regarded as a portent of tragedy, but returning swallows were considered to predict the safe return of Dionysus. Greek and Latin writers mention that weather was forecast from the swallow's flight; and throughout Europe low-flying swallows are still regarded, with some justification, as an indication of bad weather.

Observations of swallows flying low over lakes and rivers may have inspired the Chinese to throw swallows into water when they prayed for rain. The associations between swallows, rain and springtime growth were responsible for offerings being made to the genius of the house on the day when the swallows returned. According to one poem, heaven decreed that the swallow should give birth to the Shang Dynasty. Its egg was said to have caused the pregnancy of the ancestress of the Shang line.

The swallow has long been associated with gifts of healing. The white or red swallow-stones which were believed to be secreted in the bellies of the nestlings had medicinal value. During the Middle Ages, this belief became elaborated into the notion that the swallow fetches a pebble from the sea-shore to restore the sight of its fledglings. Confusion apparently arose between the swallow-stone legend and the ancient belief that the swallow brings to its nest a herb which cures the young swallows of their blindness. Parts of the bird were widely believed to cure various diseases: snake bite, epilepsy, rabies, and so on. Its droppings cured diphtheria and turned hair grey; and mud from its nest was a remedy for erysipelas (a fever accompanied by inflammation of the skin).

A Drop of Devil's Blood

In general the swallow has been viewed as a helpful, propitious bird, but as is often the case with other lucky birds, it has in some localities been regarded with suspicion. In regions of France and Hungary it was said that if a swallow flew under a cow's belly it would give bloody milk, and in Scotland it was reputed to have a drop of the Devil's blood in its veins. Yorkshire folk considered it a death omen when a swallow came down the chimney. If the first swallow seen by a girl in Czechoslovakia was alone she would be married within the year but if she caught sight of a pair she would remain unmarried.

It is widely believed that swallows should be kindly treated, and that ill luck befalls those who harm them. The Tyrolese say that if you destroy a swallow's nest your own house will be burnt down. In France it was believed that if a man robbed a swallow's nest his horse would go lame. The Chinese revere the bird, and although they use most organisms either as food or medicine, they do not molest the swallows nesting under the low eaves in city streets.

The helpful swallow plays a prominent part in Christian legends. The Swedes say that it hovered over the Cross crying '*Svala! Svala!*', 'Cheer up! Cheer up!'. The Norwegian version is that it twittered 'Console him!'. In France it is said that the swallow picked off the Crown of Thorns ignoring the wounds made in her breast by the spines. Ever since, the swallow has borne stains of blood on her breast. Similar stories are told of the robin and crossbill, both of which have red breasts. According to another French legend magpies pricked Christ's feet and head with thorns while he was resting in a wood, but swallows came and extracted them. Because of this the magpie has been hated and forced to build its nest in tall trees, but the swallow breeds in safety in man's dwellings.

In English folk rhymes the swallow is included among sacred birds:

> The robin and the wren,
> Are God Almighty's cock and hen;
> The martin and the swallow
> Are the two next birds that follow.

The disappearance of swallows in autumn and their reappearance in spring caused speculation and gave rise to one of the oldest ornithological fallacies, that they had hibernated in crevices or even under water. Aristotle mentions this belief which was substantiated by natural historians up to the 19th century.

E. A. ARMSTRONG

Swami

Or svami, a Hindu holy man and teacher: in certain religious and ascetic orders, title of initiates who have reached the highest stage of spiritual progress and have renounced the world: a popular term in the West for almost any Hindu adept, teacher or occultist.

Camera Press

The belief that the swan sings while dying has a long history endorsed by poets down the ages: Shakespeare wrote in Othello, *'I will play the swan and die in music'*

SWAN

SEVERAL CHARACTERISTICS account for the swan's importance in mythology and folklore: they are among the largest birds of the Northern Hemisphere and, except for the Australian black swan, all swans have conspicuous white plumage. Moreover, except for the mute swan which makes a remarkable musical sound with its wings as it flies, the other species – the whooper, trumpeter and bewick – utter loud vocal calls.

Engravings and designs from the Old Stone Age onwards of long-necked birds resembling the goose or swan indicate that such species had a magico-religious significance in various ancient cultures. The Middle Bronze Age Urnfield folk of Central Europe and other later cultures incorporated such long-necked birds in designs which included a sun disc, showing that these birds were associated with solar beliefs. As swans and geese fly high and also frequent water they became linked as well with ideas about growth and fertility (see GOOSE). Swans appeared over northern tundra areas when the days were lengthening, the sun's path in the heavens was getting higher, and the snows were melting and the flowers appearing. Thus swans are thought not only to accompany spring but to help usher it in. Even now, some of the inhabitants of the woodlands of northern Asia erect poles with wooden effigies of flying swans near sacrificial platforms; below they place carved wooden models of fish, symbolizing the powers of sky, earth and water.

Since myths in which people are transformed into swans are ancient and widespread, they evidently hark back to primitive modes of thought in which the distinctions between gods, men and animals were blurred. Aeschylus, the Greek playwright, mentions swan maidens; Aphrodite was represented in art riding on a swan or goose, and Ovid tells of Cycnus being turned into a swan by his father Apollo. Both Apollo and Venus rode in chariots drawn by swans. Zeus was said to have turned himself into a swan to couple with Leda. The sacred character of the swan is indicated by the belief held in areas as far apart as Siberia and Ireland that to kill a swan brings misfortune or death. In County Mayo the souls of virtuous maidens were said to dwell in swans.

For Love of a Swan Maiden

The most widespread swan transformation myth tells of a man who sees a flock of swans alight by the water, and watches them discard their feather garments, revealing themselves as beautiful maidens. He steals the robes of one of the swan maidens and lives happily with her until one day she finds the garments, puts them on and disappears. In an Irish account dating from the 8th century, Angus, the son of the Dagda, 'the good god', falls in love with the swan maiden Caer who appears to him in a dream. On visiting Loch Bel Dracon at the time of the great Celtic festival of *Samain* (1 November) he sees a flock of 150 swans, each pair linked with a silver chain, and among them his beloved Caer wearing a golden chain and coronet. When he calls to her she leaves the flock and he, too, takes swan form. Together they circle the loch three times and, chanting magical music which puts to sleep all who hear it for three days and nights, they fly to the royal palace. Among the Buriats of Siberia who regard the eagle as their paternal forbear and the swan as the mother of their race, a swan maiden tale is told which has close affinities with Irish stories. There are also Indian versions, and in Malaya and Siam the theme forms the basis of a dramatic performance. It appears to have inspired the Japanese Noh play, *The Robe of Feathers*.

Christian elements introduced into swan transformation stories are obviously later embellishments; this confirms that these stories date from pre-Christian times. In a Russian ballad, a swan maiden declares

The size of the swan and its flight high in the sky implies power, and its association with water implies fertility: Zeus turned himself into a swan to father children on Leda; *Leda and the Swan*, school of Leonardo

Myths in which gods or humans turn into swans are ancient and widespread, reflecting primitive concepts that blurred the distinction between gods, men and animals: Roman limestone relief of Leda and the swan, Crete

C. M. Dixon

that she will not marry the hero until he has been baptized, and a version of the beautiful Irish tale of the Children of Lir relates that after centuries had elapsed during which Fionnuala and her brothers, transformed into swans, swam the Irish sea, they were restored to human form in a very weak condition, and were baptized just before they died.

The belief that the swan sings while dying has a long history. Although Pliny contradicted this tradition it has been transmitted down the ages, and has been endorsed by poets almost up to our own times. This story may also have originated in the North. Although dying swans do not sing, a flock of bewick swans in full cry produces a resonant, mysterious, melodious tumult which seems to pervade the whole landscape. Chaucer refers in *The Parliament of Fowles* to 'swan-song'. Shakespeare wrote in *Othello* 'I will play the swan, and die in music', and in *The Merchant of Venice* 'He makes a swan-like end, fading in music'. Drayton in *Polyolbion* referred to 'swans who only sing in death' and Byron made the sad request:

> Place me on Sunium's marbled steep,
> Where nothing but the waves and I
> May hear our mutual murmurs sweep;
> There swan-like, let me sing and die.

Yet another poet to make use of this familiar theme was Alfred Lord Tennyson, in *The Dying Swan*.

The notion that swans are linked together or wear chains is also ancient. In *As You Like It* Celia says:

> And whereso'er we went, like Juno's swans,
> Still we went coupled and inseparable.

In Greek art, swans are depicted harnessed; a French medieval legend refers to six brothers and sisters whose transformation into swans depends on the possession of golden chains and in Grimm's tale of *The Six Swans* a golden chain is placed around the neck of the swan maiden. After Edward I had knighted his son at Westminster two swans with trappings of gold were brought into the palace. The stories of the Knight of the Swan both in France and in Germany also embody such traditions.

E. A. ARMSTRONG

SWASTIKA

THE WORD SWASTIKA is derived from the Sanskrit, *svastika,* which means well-being, good fortune, luck. Although the figure bearing this name has been extensively used as a decoration or mystical symbol in many parts of the world from prehistoric times onwards, the history of its origin and world-wide dispersion is obscure. Known as the *Hakenkreuz* (hooked cross) in German, its association with Hitler's Germany is universally familiar and the symbol is therefore generally equated with all the negative features of the Third Reich: antisemitism (including genocide), aggression, persecution and terror (see also CROSS).

Both before and after Hitler's rise to power in 1933, German archeologists and cultural historians studied every conceivable aspect of swastika symbolism, although without reaching definite conclusions. The subject inevitably attracted the attention of 'lunatic fringe' researchers, who went to irrational lengths to establish that it represented an ancient Germanic and therefore acceptably Nordic symbol.

Guido von List (see LIST), for example, confidently proclaimed that the runic equivalent of the letter G was a disguised swastika and quoted the *Edda* to prove that this rune had a secret and mystical significance for ancient Scandinavian bards.

For many, including List, the swastika also had a cosmic meaning, for example as a 'sun wheel', symbolizing eternal rebirth and eternal movement. One Germanic enthusiast asserted that it was an essentially Christian symbol until the Church adopted the crucifix in the 6th century. Friedrich Döllinger proposed in his book *Baldur und Bibel*: 'The hooked cross, also known as "Sun wheel", can be found as a common holy symbol with all Germanic peoples, in the Near East as in Crete, alluding to the religion of Odin (Wotan).' Ludwig Fahrenkrog (see NEO-PAGAN GERMAN CULTS), the founder of one of the many Germanic religious sects – non-Christian but not always specifically pagan – that flourished in Germany after the early 1900s, supposed that the form 卐 suggested 'cessation' or 'away from God', while its counterpart 卍 meant 'genesis' or 'to God'. Here he followed contemporary Theosophical concepts which were based upon Buddhist traditions.

The date when the swastika first became associated with the ideology of the German *völkisch* movement, emotionally inward-looking and intensely nationalist, is uncertain. The few available clues point in the direction of the Austrian Pan-Germans, that is, followers of Schönerer, in the 1870s. Guido von List, for instance, who was close to Schönerer, was probably speculating about the swastika as a Germanic symbol long before it became identified with völkisch groups in the Third Reich.

In Germany, Wilhelm Schwaner (b. 1863), the publisher of one of the earliest völkisch periodicals (*Der Volkserzieher*, 1897) displayed a swastika on the title-page of his publication, which was intended to inculcate truly Germanic (that is, völkisch) sentiments among its readers.

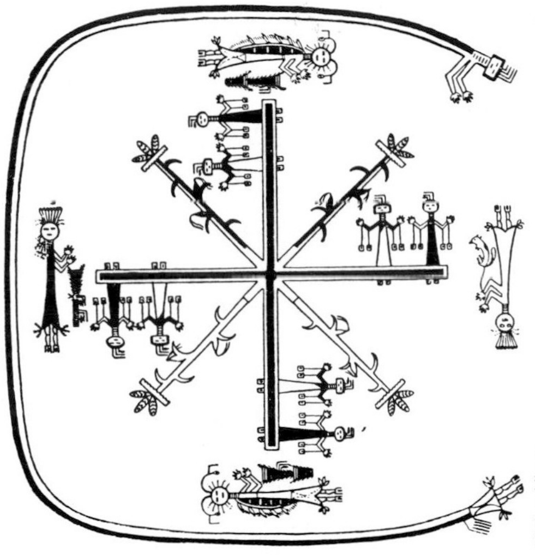

Weiner Library

The swastika has been used as a decoration or mystical symbol in many parts of the world *Top* Swastika pattern of the Navaho Indians *Above* Adopted by the Nazis as their party badge, the swastika came to stand for Hitler's Germany in general, and for Nazi racial policies in particular, since it was chosen on the mistaken ground that it was a 'Nordic' emblem: 'few other symbols have become so widely associated with evil' *Below* Swastika on a pot found at Argos in Greece, c 8th century BC

C. M. Dixon

By 1912 half a dozen or more völkisch groups, some of them quite large, were using the emblem on the titlepages of their periodicals and on their stationery. It had also begun to appear on private letter-headings, either printed, rubber-stamped or drawn with a pen. This insistent exhibition of the swastika was intended to advertise an emotional and complete identification with truly völkisch sentiments, and these invariably included rigorously antisemitic attitudes. The swastika had by this time become a symbol of recognition for like-minded people. A number of firms, such as Ecklöh at Ludenscheid in Westphalia, began to manufacture swastika badges, tie pins, amulets and belts or buckles incorporating the device.

The famous pre-1914 youth movement, the *Wandervögel,* inevitably encountered the swastika by way of various völkisch writers and periodicals and the symbol was therefore completely familiar to the generation that fought in the First World War. Soon after Germany's defeat in 1918 it was adopted by various paramilitary Freikorps units, which included many ex-students and members of the *Wandervögel.* The famous Erhardt Brigade, which participated in the liberation of Munich from the Communists in April 1919, arrived at the Bavarian capital singing their marching song which began with the words: 'Hooked cross on steel helmets . . .' The swastika was soon no longer an exclusively romantic völkisch symbol but became associated with the 'national revolutionary' right-wing opposition to the Weimar Republic.

Hitler's National Socialist German Workers' Party had its roots in Anton Drexler's German Workers' Party, a minute völkisch group founded in Munich in January 1919. Hitler joined the latter in September 1919 and was largely responsible for re-naming it as the National Socialist German Workers' Party in February 1920. When Hitler and the Nazis adopted the swastika as their party emblem they therefore chose a symbol that already reflected all or most of the tenets of National Socialist ideology, and antisemitism in particular.

The form in which the Nazis used the swastika was designed by Dr Friedrich Krohn, a dentist who had belonged to various völkisch groups, including the Germanen Order (see GERMANEN ORDER), before 1914. He was aware of the Buddhist theory that the 'anti-clockwise' swastika signified 'fortune and well-being' and made his first design accordingly. It was shown to Hitler and others. The majority readily accepted Krohn's arguments but Hitler insisted that the clockwise alternative be adopted – some would say with disastrous consequences. The Party flag, badge and armband, all based upon Krohn's design, were in official use by the summer of 1920. Almost exactly 25 years later the swastika became a symbol of shame and defeat in Germany. It is probably true to suggest that few other symbols have become so widely associated with evil.

SWEDENBORG

A scientist turned visionary, Swedenborg claimed that the real meaning of the scriptures was revealed to him through his conversations with God and the angels

EMANUEL SWEDENBORG was born in Stockholm on 29 January 1688, the second son of the Lutheran Bishop of Skara, who had himself once been a professor at the University of Uppsala. Emanuel's father had changed his name from Swedberg when his family was ennobled in 1719. He was a remarkably learned and saintly man who was to have a longlasting influence on his son Emanuel.

From the first, Emanuel showed great promise in his scientific studies and, after graduating from Uppsala, travelled in Britain, Holland and Germany, pursuing his investigations. In England he met and was befriended by the astronomers Sir Edmund Halley and John Flamsteed, and on his return to Sweden had already established such a reputation that, in 1716, King Charles XII made him a special assessor to the Royal College of Mines. This work so absorbed him that he turned down the chance to follow in his father's footsteps as a professor at Uppsala, in order to continue with the practical work associated with the mines.

In 1718, he invented a means of transporting boats overland for 14 miles. While still a student, he had been concerned in 'a plan for a certain ship which, with its men, was to go under the surface of the sea and do great damage to the fleet of the enemy'. He had designed an air-gun with a magazine which could fire 60 or 70 shots without reloading and he had even busied himself with an attempt to design a flying machine.

Yet it was not as an inventor that he gained his first international triumph. In 1734, Swedenborg produced a three-volume work *Opera Philosophica et Mineralia,* in which he developed his theory of 'nebular hypothesis' to account for the formation of planets, which predates the work of Kant and the French astronomer, the Marquis de Laplace, and is often erroneously attributed to them. Publication proceeded apace. In 1740 *Oeconomia Regni Animalis,* an anatomical work, was produced in Amsterdam; in 1743 *Miscellaneous Observations on Geology and Mineralogy* was published in Leipzig, and in 1744 he wrote, *On the infinite and final cause of Creation,* in which he attempted to discuss the relationship between the soul and the body. All these were major works of importance to the several branches of science to which they were addressed, yet all had the germs of his later religious preoccupation. Nevertheless, it was not until 1745, with the publication of *Worship and the Love of God,* that religion became his one and only concern.

No Flight of Fancy

His life became totally taken up with his religious work so that in 1747, at the age of 59, he resigned his assessorship and took a pension of half-pay so that he could devote himself to the new revelations. But he was in no sense a spiritist, for he believed that he had held conversations with these heavenly beings while still being very much aware of his surroundings and in much the same way that he might talk with another human being. His mysticism was not the mysticism of the trance or of the seance – it was a full-blooded avowal of his regular direct communication with beings from heaven. His religious writings are the record of these communications and he makes no concessions.

He was aware of the scepticism that such extraordinary claims would arouse, and in his first theological work he admitted: 'I am well aware that many persons will insist that it is impossible for anyone to converse with spirits and with angels during his lifetime in the body; many will say that such intercourse must be mere fancy; some, that I have invented such relations in order to gain credit; whilst others will make other objections. For all these, however, I care not, since I have seen, heard and felt.'

For statements of this kind to have any credence, it is important to remember that Swedenborg was neither a dreamer, nor an ascetic with little experience of the world, but a practical applied scientist who had preferred the real business of mining to becoming the Professor of Astronomy in the University of Uppsala.

Swedenborg's theological works are not easily read and they are certainly not the products of a slapdash mystical enthusiast. Just as in his earlier days he had learned about watch-making by apprenticing himself to a watch-maker, so he set about studying theology, becoming well-skilled in Greek and Hebrew and in the standard commentaries. Although his work was all based upon his own direct mystical experience of God, he did not neglect scholarship, and the large volumes, written in Latin, were intended for the serious student and were in no sense considered as the means of popularizing a new religion.

Despite the enormous claims made in his writings, Swedenborg remained throughout his life a modest and simple person, working enormously hard, never marrying, and without any intention of founding a new sect, believing that his followers could be of any denomination.

'God is a Man'

What then were the special doctrines which he taught, and how did he make his influence felt? The key to it all is in his belief that he was a divinely-appointed instrument of God's revelation to man. He put no special gloss on Christianity, except incidentally, for it was his view that his writings fulfilled the New Testament story, just as the gospels had fulfilled that of the Old Testament. He thus approached the gospels as one with superior knowledge. Swedenborg believed that his scholarship was informed by his own direct contact with God. His spiritual world was not seen through an inspired individual approach to scripture which Mary Baker Eddy, the founder of Christian Science, claimed as her contribution; nor was it seen as the result of the miraculous discovery of a new book of revelations, like the Book of Mormon; but it was revealed to him personally by God himself, who had led him along the paths of heaven, enabling him to talk directly to the angels. Indeed, Swedenborg spoke as if heaven and its inhabitants were his 'second home'. He knows them as he knows human beings and his knowledge enables him to maintain that man's real self is in form exactly as is his physical body, and if it had not been for the Fall, the body would have been sloughed off like a snake-skin. Instead, men need to die before they move on to a higher place. So important is this concept of humanness that Swedenborg continually emphasizes that it is only through man's own eyes that he can see God, that God exists only in the terms that man can see him, and that those terms are human terms.

This position undoubtedly comes from Swedenborg's reliance on his visions, and in these, God certainly does appear as a man. Of course, he would admit that God in his essence is unknowable, but insists that it is part of the essential God to be known in human form. It would be misleading, says Swedenborg, for us to think about God in human symbols if those symbols were not more than mere forms, but instead they must be an essential part of the reality of God himself. This explains the otherwise baffling comment: 'God is a man'. It cannot to taken totally literally and yet it is not merely symbolic. There is a real sense in which God shares the human form.

Swedenborg retained the doctrine of the Trinity, but twisted it slightly to fit in with the experience of his vision. The Father is absolute – God in his essence, unconditionally, worthy to be called Jehovah. When Jehovah determined to save mankind, he assumed the humanity of the Son. That humanity was complete, with all its defects and all its blemishes. Thus God took on the ignorance of the child, was tempted with real temptations, which played upon real human desires and weaknesses. Like all humanity, the humanity of the Son could reach towards perfection – he was not, as in orthodox Christianity, perfect God and perfect Man.

The redemption of the world was the mystical redemption of this humanity becoming perfect and thus reaching to the Divine Father and reuniting the now perfect humanity with him who is perfect Divinity. This example makes it possible for all men to come to the Father.

Staircase to Heaven and Hell

All this is based upon a very special doctrine of creation which acknowledges man as the highest form of life on earth, but does not see him as created. Man is a form which is capable of receiving the life which constantly flows into him from God. Life is, in fact, Love-Wisdom, and this was received gladly before the Fall, when man accepted the harmony with God. Once he began to ignore the fact that his life came from God, then he had to stand alone. God did not leave him without a help to perfection, but instead provided him with the old dispensation, which led him towards a stage at which he was able to receive the revelation of God's human form. God did not become man, but merely clothed his divinity in man's form. This revelation is to be found in the New Testament, and it in turn has been elucidated by the direct communication of God with Emanuel Swedenborg.

Once again, returning to this direct revelation, Swedenborg *saw* heaven and hell. He also saw the intermediate place to which we go at death and from which we move, as our spirit leads us towards perfection or destruction. For those on the upward 'escalator', the approach towards God is inevitable. For those on the downward, the Devil is reached by easy stages. Swedenborg describes the spiritual world, with its spiritual patterns of all that there is in the material world, and he calls this vision the Second Coming of Christ. For him, the Advent is not a physical return, but the spiritual vision of Christ in his true surroundings. This vision comes to us all as we near perfection and pass to that state of spiritual vision which Swedenborg reached and upon which all his religious writings are based.

The revelation which God makes to man is, in fact, a kind of distillation of the Word which is found in God himself. There is a great danger in revealing to unready minds the full force of this truth and therefore the Bible contains a 'sifted-down' version of the Word which has descended until it has reached the level at which man can understand it. Of course on other planets, says Swedenborg, there are beings far brighter than man, for whom revelation has been presented in more direct a form. Yet in the sifted state in which the scriptures reach us, they make a direct appeal to the spirit of man, who has the capacity to understand and search out the real meanings contained within them.

This enables us to see that there is among the books in the Bible, a true canon of books which are really the Word, and which can be read for their spiritual meaning, and some others which are merely devotional aids. This view allowed Swedenborg to concentrate his work on the Pentateuch (the first five books of the Old Testament); Joshua, Judges, I and II Samuel; I and II Kings; the Psalms, and most of the prophets. He also accepted the four gospels and the Apocalypse as of this specially divine nature. Their real meaning was revealed to him in his understanding which came from contact with the other world, and from his direct conversations with spirits and with God.

From this understanding, Swedenborg was able to see that the Atonement did not reconcile God with man, but made it possible for man to relearn the way to union with God – a way he had lost through choosing to love other than God at the Fall. When Christ had shown this way, he put off all the weaknesses of humanity and put on the divine humanity, given him by Jehovah. This was the glorification which is so much a part of Swedenborgian philosophy.

A Challenge to the Intellect

Now a knowledge of the truth is to be found in the Church. It is this knowledge that shows the way back to God. The Church is the true Church in so far as it has the truth. Therefore the founding of the Swedenborgian Church – or the New Church, as its adherents prefer – does not imply that other Churches are wrong; it is merely to help to point the way and to complete the revelation which may already be seen by people in other Churches. Nor is it the final revelation, for no doubt God may wish to show more of himself when the time is ripe. Swedenborgians claim, therefore, to be one of God's instruments, guided by the direct revelations made to Emanuel Swedenborg by God and his angels. These revelations they believe to be true, but in no way unique or exhaustive. They are not easy to assimilate, for the truths are theologically complicated and unarresting to the ordinary person, yet they have seized upon the minds of some great intellects. Much of William Blake's work, for instance, is imbued with the Swedenborgianism he embraced and then left behind. Despite his satire on Swedenborg's *Heaven and Hell* – which Blake called *The Marriage of Heaven and Hell* – he continued to be inspired by the directness of the revelations of a real other world which is the hallmark of Swedenborg's message (see BLAKE).

In our own day, Helen Keller, who was born blind and deaf, wrote of her love for the writings of Emanuel Swedenborg, 'If people would only begin to read Swedenborg's books with at first a little patience, they would soon be reading them with pure joy.' Miss Keller recognized that her hero was at first not easy to understand, and it is certainly true that for most people he does not get any easier even upon closer acquaintance, yet for some, he does appear to 'bring men by a wondrous way to God's city of light'.

His appeal is not universal. The New Church has never been very large, and its adherents have been few. Swedenborg presupposes a dedication to heavy reading. It would be surprising if the God who appeals to all men should have chosen so esoteric a character to continue his revelations made manifest in the carpenter's son. Nevertheless, here is obviously a mighty mind at work – a mind which was convinced of its personal and direct contact with God and which set out to describe that contact for the enlightenment of an inevitably dedicated readership.

JOHN SELWYN GUMMER

The founding of the Swedenborgian Church, or New Church, 'does not imply that other Churches are wrong: it is merely to help to point the way and to complete the revelation which may already be seen by people in other Churches'; etching of the New Church, Bath

SWEDISH WITCHCRAFT

BY CONTRAST with Germany, France, England and Scotland, the Scandinavian countries were comparatively free of organized witch hunts. But that fear of witches existed and could arouse hysteria and panic is shown by the case of the witches of Mora in Sweden, who were accused of taking children to a mysterious place called the Blocula and there enrolling them in the service of the Devil.

In July 1668 the Lutheran pastor of Elfdale in central Sweden, an area with a suitably evocative name in view of what was to happen, reported to his bishop that a girl named Gertrude Svensen had learned the art of magical incantation from a servant, Marit Jonsdotter, and had stolen several children of the district for 'the evil genius', the Devil. Her activities had been detected by a boy of 15, Eric Ericson, who also accused several others of stealing children for the Devil. One of them, a woman of 70, admitted that the accusation was true, but the others denied it. Officials of the royal government had investigated and discovered that the accused had stolen consecrated wine from the church, the implication being that they could only have a diabolical use for it.

The accusations caused great uproar locally. Rumours spread that hundreds of children had been delivered into the Devil's hand and that the evil genius himself had been seen going about the countryside. In May 1669 the royal government (King Charles XI was then aged 13) instructed the bishop to appoint worthy ministers to join members of the royal council in a commission to restore peace and order, without the use of imprisonment or torture. In June the bishop was told to order public prayers throughout his diocese to ward off the Devil's wrath, and this may perhaps have made the panic worse, for when the commission met, on 13 August, 3000 people came flocking to hear its deliberations.

After an investigation lasting till 25 August, the commission found that 300 children had been involved, and identified 70 witches. Far from being treated mildly, 23 who freely admitted their guilt were promptly beheaded and their bodies then burned to ashes. The other 47 were sent to the town of Falun, where they were later executed in the same way. In addition, 15 of the children were executed, 36 aged between nine and 15 were made to run the gauntlet and condemned to be publicly beaten on the hands with rods every Sunday for a year, and 20 more, aged under nine, were to be beaten on the hands on three successive Sundays.

Man in Gray

The atmosphere of dream or fantasy so often found in the confessions of accused witches hangs thickly round the Mora case. According to the evidence given to the commission, the children were dressed in red or blue clothes and carried by the witches to the Blocula, riding on goats or sticks or cooking spits or on the bodies of men who were fast asleep. The Blocula itself sounds like a place from a dream. It was 'situated in a delicate large meadow, whereof you can see no end'. There was a gate, painted in various colours, and behind it a smaller meadow and a house. The beasts the witches rode were left in the smaller meadow and the bodies of the sleeping men were propped up against the wall of the house. Inside, in one huge room there was a very long table at which the witches sat down to feast, and near it was another room, 'in which there were very lovely and delicate beds'.

Every witch had to take a child with her, such was the Devil's dubious fondness for young souls, and he bullied them and whipped them if they did not. Some of them took as many as 15 or 16 children with them. The children were made to deny God. They were baptized anew by the Devil's priests and their names were written in blood in the Devil's book.

The Devil appeared as a man. He had a red beard and he usually dressed in a gray coat, a high-crowned hat with linen of various colours wrapped round it, and stockings of red and blue with long garters. When they sat down to eat, those who stood highest in the Devil's favour were placed nearest him. The children stood by the door and the Devil himself gave them their food and drink.

Afterwards the witches danced, careering round and round astraddle on halberds (weapons which were a combination of a

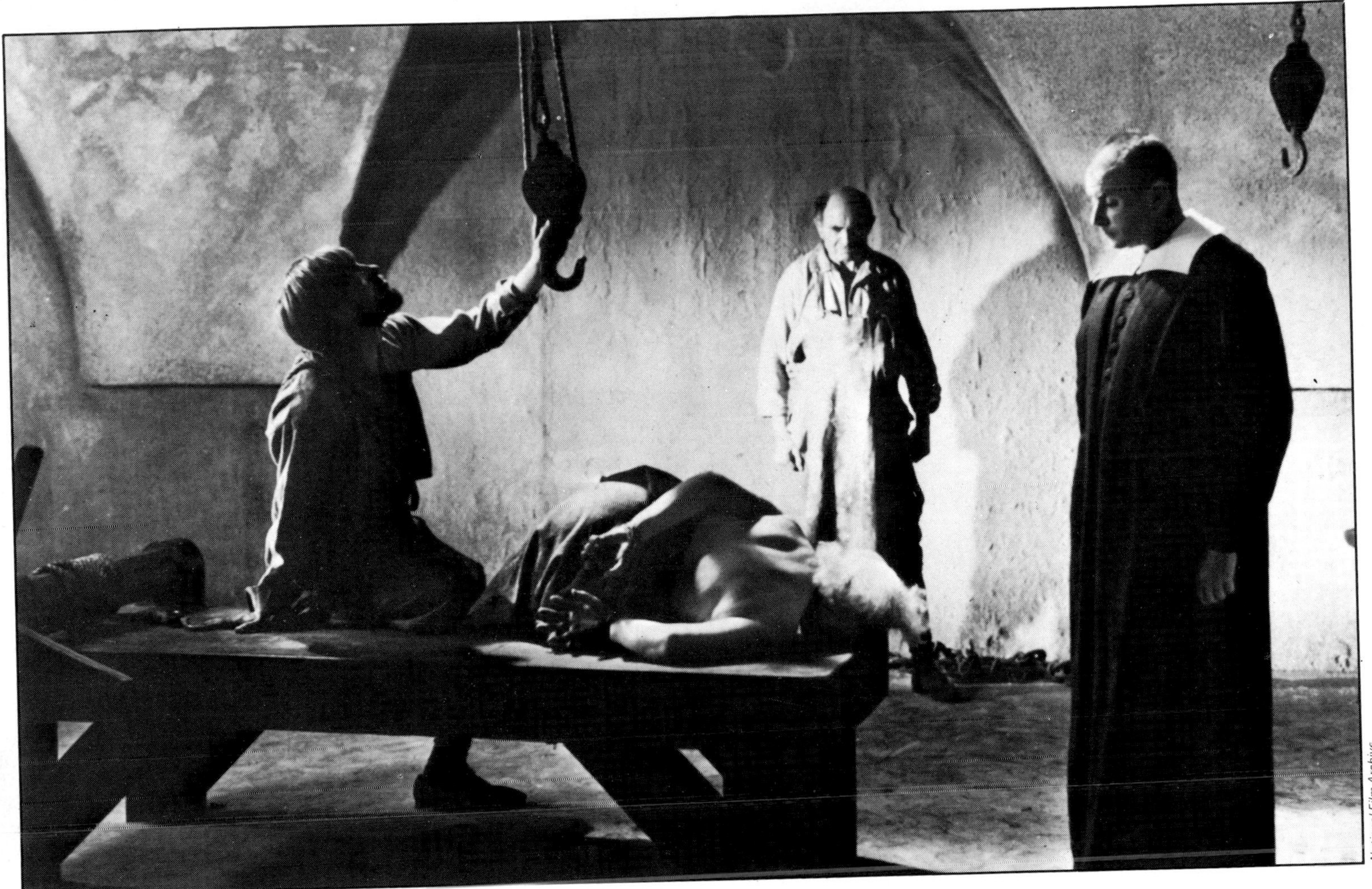

The Scandinavian countries were relatively free of organized witch-hunting, but fear of witches existed and could arouse panic and hysteria *Left* Detail from a contemporary illustration of witches in Sweden in 1669: they were accused of stealing children for the Devil *Above* A suspect about to be tortured, a still from the Danish film *Day of Wrath*

spear and a battle axe), while the Devil roared with laughter and played the harp with fingers which were like claws. The dancing culminated in a mixture of fighting and copulation. The Devil had children as a result of sexual intercourse with the witches, but they bore toads and snakes through their intercourse with each other.

The witches also said that they used to meet at a gravel pit which was near a crossroads, and there they would cover their heads with garments and dance. On the beasts or instruments which the Devil provided they would be carried over churches and high walls. He gave them ointment which they smeared on themselves, and a saddle to ride on. He would give a witch a purse in which were shavings filed off a clock. It had a stone tied to it, and the witch would drop it into water, saying, 'As these shavings of the clock do never return to the clock from which they are taken, so may my soul never return to heaven.'

The panic spread beyond Elfdale. In 1670 commissions of investigation were appointed in the Uppsala area and in Helsinki, in the Swedish province of Finland. In 1674 and 1675 a royal commission inquired into allegations of witchcraft in the parishes of Thorsaker, Ytterlannas and Dahl, and there was another holocaust.

In 1676 there were investigations in Stockholm and six women were executed. Many more were imprisoned, and many of them insisted that they were guilty. A Finnish woman named Magdalen Mattsdotter was accused by several children and servant girls, and her own two daughters said they had seen the Devil standing beside her. She denied the accusations and was burned alive, her younger daughter walking all the way to the stake with her trying to persuade her to confess. Later it became clear that the servants had accused her out of envy and malice, and they were condemned to death in their turn. The case contributed to a revulsion of feeling, Charles XI banned all further accusations, and the hysteria died away.

Christian Thomasius, a German lawyer and author of *De Crimine Magiae* (1701), who was head of Halle University (which his opponents nicknamed Hell University), said that he met one of the Swedish officials appointed to investigate accusations. The official told him that he and the other lay judges easily saw through the evidence, which was based on the lies and fantasies of children. But the Lutheran ministers, who dominated the proceedings, were convinced that the Holy Spirit spoke through the children and would never allow them to tell lies in such a case, citing the text 'out of the mouths of babes and sucklings' (Psalm 8, Matthew 21.16). After many innocent people had been put to death, one boy accused a man everyone respected. One of the commissioners offered the boy money to admit that he had made a mistake and had really meant to accuse somebody else. This the boy readily did, and the ministers on the commission decided that the Holy Spirit did not speak through the children after all. They gave the boy a beating and abandoned the inquiry.

Fighting in Germany during the Thirty Years War, Swedish generals had put a stop to witch trials in areas under their control, on the orders of Queen Christina, who believed that persecuting supposed witches simply entangled increasing numbers of people in 'an inextricable labyrinth', a conclusion which all the European evidence bears out. H. R. Trevor-Roper has commented (in *The European Witch-Craze in the 16th and 17th Centuries*) that the subsequent persecutions in Sweden itself followed on the new intolerance of the Swedish Lutheran Church in the 1660s. 'Like the established Calvinist Church in Scotland, it had shaken itself free from other, more liberal Protestant parties, and its Puritan leaders prepared to advertise their purity by a great witch-hunt.'

FURTHER READING: H. C. Lea, *Materials Towards a History of Witchcraft* (Yoseloff, 1957 reprint, 3 vols); M. A. Murray, *The Witch-Cult in Western Europe* (Clarendon Press, 1967 reprint); R. H. Robbins, *Encyclopedia of Witchcraft and Demonology* (Spring Books, 1959).

Although many sword dances are now show-pieces, it is thought that they originated as rituals honouring and promoting virility, victory and fertility. The swords may be used more as props than as weapons, but dances in which a combat is danced out are believed to be descended from mock battles between individual groups representing summer and winter, fertility and sterility *Below* Sword dancing at the Braemar Games *Bottom* The North Skelton Long Sword Dance, from the English Midlands *Right* Turkish dancers in mimic combat *Far Right* A Javanese fighting dancer

Picturepoint, London

Spectrum Colour Library

ornament, which accord with many literary indications that a sword was more than a utilitarian object. It was a living being with a name and a character. If not buried with its lord, it might be handed on in his family.

When Beowulf prepares for his combat with Grendel's mother, the royal herald Unferth lends him a weapon:

> Not the least or the worst of his war equipment
> Was the sword the herald of Hrothgar loaned
> In his hour of need, Hrunting its name,
> An ancient heirloom, trusty and tried;
> Its blade was of iron, with etched design
> Tempered in blood of many a battle.
> Never in fight had it failed the hand
> That drew it, daring the perils of war.

Many of the swords in other folklore and legend have outright supernatural properties. They shine, and discharge lightning-bolts. They grow and shrink at need, they make the owner invisible, they give him the power to travel fast over long distances, and they run with blood when he dies. Heroes pierce rocks with them, splinter arrows in flight, and create hills and springs by striking the earth.

Numerous tales of magic further reveal the personality of the weapon, and its independent wisdom and virtue. There are swords that can cause death whenever drawn, or throw enemies into an enchanted sleep. Some, on the other hand, can release the spellbound, keep the dying alive, and even resuscitate the dead. Swords act by themselves, striking out of the air in forests, or falling on an enemy. They speak to save their masters from danger, and understand when spoken to themselves.

Reserved for a Special Task

A number of stories tell of a sword's gift of discrimination. Some are unwilling to deal a wrongful blow. When the owner of one tries to attack a friend, it becomes too heavy for him to lift. Others turn to wood when somebody raises them against an innocent victim.

The use of these marvellous weapons is governed by many rules and hazards. Some can only be moved at all by the right person. Some are reserved for a single appointed task (as when a son must take up his father's sword to kill his father's murderer).

Sonia Halliday

Some must be handled in a special manner, for example, they must be drawn, and sheathed, and drawn again a fixed number of times before the battle.

A hero's vulnerability may be bound up with the magical qualities of his weapon. He may wear an impenetrable garment which his own sword alone can pierce, and eventually does. His sword may be bewitched so that it will break in one particular peril, or fail in one crucial crisis. However potent the sword's virtue, a hostile magic can be stronger. It can be dulled or otherwise neutralized, perhaps by an incantation, or by scratching a counter-charm on the blade. A magic wand may break it, or an evil spirit get into it. Grendel's mother is a case in point. She is a troll woman living in a cave under a

Picturepoint, London

C. M. Dixon/British Museum

emblematic of chastity, because of its brightness and also its power to separate. Many characters in legend, for example, Siegfried, sleep beside a woman who must not be touched, with a sword between them.

For alchemists the sword is a symbol of purifying fire. In the magician's hands, it is a protection against malevolent ghosts and hostile enchantments. Its polished surface can be used like a crystal ball for 'scrying'. It figures in Arthurian legend as one of the four Hallows or sacred objects seen by Grail seekers: the sword, the cup, the dish and the lance. Occultists assert a connection between these Hallows and the four suits of the Tarot pack, in which swords correspond to the spades in the ordinary pack.

GEOFFREY ASHE

Sword Dances

In sword dancing the swords are used as props and not necessarily as weapons; dancers wield swords to build up elaborate group figures or for use in dance tricks. There are many variations and types of sword dances, but they share some characteristics: for instance, they are exclusively performed by men, they are highly stylized even when they portray combat, and they derive from cultic and perhaps mythological sources.

Although many sword dances are now showpieces, they probably all originated in pre-Christian rituals in honour of virility, victory and fertility. For instance, the *Moriscas* ('Moorish dances', in which a ritualistic form of battle is mimed) and the various types of sword-or-stick dances have intrigued scholars over a long period. These dances have now been traced, not to Moorish origin, but to very ancient springtime seasonal rites for the return of the sun and of vegetation, culminating in a human or animal sacrifice. The combat signified the battle between summer and winter, night and day; and the leaps and high kicks promoted growth. In the Iron Age, the sticks and clubs were replaced by metal swords, especially in mining areas, and the symbolic developments became increasingly complex.

Whatever the aboriginal motivation, the overt meaning of the Morisca type of sword dance changed during the Crusades and the Moorish invasion of Spain. In the

The Sword of Arthur

'And there I saw mage Merlin, whose vast wit
And hundred winters are but as the hands
Of loyal vassals toiling for their liege.

And near him stood the Lady of the Lake,
Who knows a subtler magic than his own –
Clothed in white samite, mystic, wonderful.
She gave the king his huge cross-hilted sword,
Whereby to drive the heathen out: a mist
Of incense curl'd about her, and her face
Wellnigh was hidden in the minster gloom;
But there was heard among the holy hymns
A voice as of the waters, for she dwells
Down in a deep; calm, whatsoever storms
May shake the world, and when the surface rolls,
Hath power to walk the waters like our Lord.

There likewise I beheld Excalibur
Before him at his crowning borne, the sword
That rose from out the bosom of the lake,
And Arthur row'd across and took it – rich
With jewels, elfin Urim, on the hilt,
Bewildering heart and eye – the blade so bright
That men are blinded by it – on one side,
Graven in the oldest tongue of all this world,
'Take me,' but turn the blade and ye shall see,
And written in the speech ye speak yourself,
'Cast me away!' And sad was Arthur's face
Taking it, but old Merlin counsell'd him,
'Take thou and strike! The time to cast away
Is yet far off.' So this great brand the king
Took, and by this will beat his foemen down.

Tennyson *Idylls of the King*

view of the anthropologist George Foster, the trail of Iberian Moriscas spread from north to south along with the gradual expulsion of the Moors, from Lérida in 1150 to Andalusia in the 14th century. A further two centuries later, the Moriscas were taken by the Spanish to the New World.

Meanwhile, in the Middle Ages the sword dances of central Europe became attached to guilds as well as to male fraternities, and in Austria this is still the case. In Austria and in Spain and Portugal, the sword dances are traditional, while in England they were revived after 1900, thanks to the efforts of Cecil Sharp, the famous collector of folk song and dance; today they are losing their ceremonial meanings, even in the villages. In America they are kept alive by the enthusiasm of folk dance societies.

Despite the widespread diffusion of sword dances within the Old World and to the New, the celebrations have retained some of the original costuming and music, and a great deal of the aboriginal and medieval seasonal timing. They are held during the season of new life, from Epiphany to Corpus Christi. Moriscas abound during carnival time at Corpus Christi, sword dances on Plough Monday (first Monday after Twelfth Night) and during Whitsuntide or at May Day. Some dances are performed at unusual times, such as the September guild observance of the Hallein dancers from Austria, who also observe Whit Sunday.

Crossed and Wielded Weapons

Scholars have divided sword dances into various groupings. Solo dances which feature the brandishing of a sword or sabre predominate in the Near East. The Arab *Aissoua* is performed in a semi-trance culminating in self-mutilation. The Ukrainian *Zaporotchez* and the *Lezginka* of the Lezgis, Georgians, and Tartars in the Caucasus Mountains appear as a display of virtuosity, but probably originated in an old fertility rite, or at least a courtship rite for the display of masculine prowess. Before his female partner, the vigorous male leaps and whirls while he flourishes a sabre.

Stepping between two crossed swords or a sword and scabbard, or perhaps two crossed sticks, or pipes, originated as a victory dance. The best-known examples, all from Europe, are the Scottish *Gillie Callum*, the English *Bacca Pipes*, the Finnish *Skin Kompasse*, the Catalan *L'Hereu Riera*, and the Hungarian *Kanász Tánc*. Gillie Callum is now as popular among Scots in America as it is in Scotland, and women and children have been admitted as performers. The soloist follows a set routine to the traditional bagpipe music. With an elegant, erect carriage, and with extended arms and hands held to form a semi-circle, he lightly steps among the four spaces between the crossed sword and scabbard, excecuting a series of *jétes, pas de basques*, and other steps familiar to ballet dancers.

Left The Greek hero Theseus raises a stone to take his father's sword: Roman terracotta relief, 2nd century AD. In the Arthurian legends, Arthur becomes king by drawing a magic sword from a stone, which in some versions is identified with his great sword Excalibur _Below_ In alchemy the sword was a symbol of purifying fire; and when God drove Adam from the garden of Eden he placed an angel at the gate with 'a flaming sword which turned every way, to guard the way to the tree of life': detail from the Bedford Book of Hours

British Museum

Combat mime by a pair of opponents or two opposing factions involves the use of metal or wooden weapons. Among primitive tribes the weapon is usually a spear, a long staff or a war club, as in the Bontoc and Igorot war dances of the Philippines. More advanced civilizations have used metal in the construction of swords. In China and Japan swords feature in stylized, theatrical presentations of warrior dances. In Europe (except for Scandinavia), Latin America and the Caribbean, swords of metal or wood serve as weapons in the Moriscas. Closely connected to these are the Dalmatian *Moreshka*, a battle mime between two factions involving elaborate formations, and the Portuguese *Mouriscada* featuring the combat between beautifully-dressed men and demonic masked dancers. In Spain and Mexico *Los Moros y Cristianos*, the Moors and the Christians, is a drama of combat, ending with the victory of the Christians. The obvious reference to the Crusades has been reinterpreted by scholars such as Cecil Sharp and Curt Sachs as a medieval version of an ancient, pagan vegetation rite, a battle between the seasons, with the inevitable victory of the good, warm season. The drama usually includes dialogue, always elaborate costuming and masking, sometimes even realistic additions such as horses. If the Christian group has a leader called Santiago (St James, patron saint of Christendom), it is termed *Santiagos*. The English Morris Dance, despite the similarity of its name, differs from the south European Moriscas in the extreme stylization, the absence of actual conflict or the clash between sticks in set patterns, and the presence of side actors portraying a death and resurrection theme (see MORRIS DANCES).

When Spanish missionaries taught

Moriscas to their converts in Latin America, they apparently received a warm welcome. And they were able to substitute these vegetation combat dramas for the indigenous Indian dramas. Today, in Mexico, most religious fiestas include Los Moros y Cristianos under various names. The male dance-actors have substituted medieval costumes and masks for their aboriginal outfits; they clash with swords, usually of wood, instead of the aboriginal war clubs; the words spoken in Spanish or their native tongue are about the victory of Christianity. But they dance in a way that is earthly, relaxed, and retentive of ancient native styles.

Such importations have taken root in other areas colonized by the Spanish: the Philippines, Trinidad, Peru, Bolivia. In Brazil they have mingled with Negroid styles, as in the Mocambique of Sao Paolo, for the agrarian saint, San Benito. Here, the swords have become sticks and the battle features complex, syncopated rhythms and African steps. In the course of the fray, the swords are not only weapons, they are also used as percussion instruments. In time with the musical accompaniment usually of flute and drum, metal swords clang rhythmically and wooden swords clash with a duller sound. In some areas, such as Papantla in eastern Mexico, excitement is intensified by the dancers' high-pitched, monotone yells, and by the stamping of feet. These martial sounds synchronize with the visual effects of encounter, retreat, and advance.

Geometric Patterns

Sword dances of western Europe lack the element of combat; they create excitement by the steady evolutions of geometric patterns and metric beat of drum and stepping. In this dance, swords are not weapons. They connect the male dancers, usually six, sometimes ten or more. In her book *Sword Dance and Drama* (1962) Violet Alford describes the link:

> It begins by each man grasping his hilt in his right hand and in his left taking the point of his neighbour's sword. A closed chain or ring is thus formed, a sword between each man and the next, and except for the weaving of broadswords at fixed moments into a pentagon, hexagon, or octagon according to the number of swords and dancers, it never comes undone until each figure is finished.

In this book Miss Alford points to the frequency of sword dances in mining regions, perhaps as magical cults of sword forgers. She supports this discovery by giving lists of mining sites, in which she includes, however, some sites that are salt mines, such as the one near Hallein, Austria. Some scholars, like the folklorist Douglas Kennedy, regard sword dances as vestiges of seasonal rites. Kennedy supports this theory by describing two aspects of death and resurrection, the symbolic killing of a captain or the Fool in an associated acting group, and the revival by a doctor (see FOLKPLAYS).

In Kennedy's book *England's Dances* he also suggests a further theory, of influence from invading Norsemen. British sword dances are indeed concentrated in northern England, with long-sword dances in Danish Mercia (covering the present-day Midlands) and Rapper Sword Dances in Northumbria (much of northern England). They are further north than the Morris dances, and in distinct areas.

Elsewhere in Europe, hilt-and-point sword dances abound in the mountainous regions of northern Spain and the Basque provinces, and in the mountainous areas of Austria. Everywhere the dances share basic formations and types of costume and music, although regional differences are often evident.

The dances usually progress in a sunwise circle or weave within a circle, but the Flamborough Sword Dance straightens out into longways formations. The character of the figures depends on the length of the swords. A ring-and-step usually starts the dance, that is, a circling with a steady run, shifting the sword from shoulder to shoulder; this section concludes with foot-tapping, 'stepping' in place, and sometimes with a clash, that is, a meeting of the swords in a central pyramid. Afterwards follow evolutions such as the 'single-under' and 'double-under', in which the dancers in succession twist under the upraised swords; the 'single-over' and 'double-over', in which they successively step over the lowered swords; the 'roll' or 'waves', in which the parallel swords are successively raised and lowered and the dancers pass under and

The basis of the sword's mystique is its efficiency as a killer combined with its use by a warrior elite in advanced societies, skilled in metallurgy and comparatively sophisticated techniques of war *Left* Effigy of a crusader: the sword looked like a cross, it was wielded by Christian knights against the infidel, and its two edges could stand for truth and loyalty *Right* The triumphant Ottoman leader Mehmed II at the death of Uzun Hasan, ruler of northern Mesopotamia

over; the 'reel' or circular hey with raised swords; and 'threedling' with double overhead arches. In the final, triumphant 'lock' the swords are linked into a star shape. Then the leader displays the star during stepping, or the group wraps the lock around the neck of an attendant character and circles clockwise in the 'rose'. This leads to the decapitation and to the resurrection that follows.

Among the many variations, the dance figures at Dürrnberg near Hallein are particularly ingenious. In addition to the basic formations, they include symbolic presentations of mining activities, along with rhymed speeches by the sergeant. In the 'bridge' sequence the dancers stand in two parallel lines, with lowered swords. The sergeants step across and the files follow. For the shaft the dancers form a vault with their raised swords; they conclude with a rapid winding movement for the joyous return homeward.

Richard Wolfram, who has published many books and articles in German on the topic, considers these semi-realistic formations recent inventions, superimposed on older, basic patterns of sun-circling and interweaving. He agrees with Kennedy that the probable origin was an ancient vegetation cult, long preceding the first historical reference of 1398. He associates the custom with pre-Christian brotherhood initiations, since he has observed that these dances are always performed by members from within a closed fraternity group.

In every setting, from village green to gymnasium, the well-performed versions of these dances continue to enchant the performers and to captivate the audiences, not only due to the skill and beauty of the execution, but also thanks to a primordial magic of intent and geometry.

(See also DANCE; FOOL).

GERTRUDE KURATH

FURTHER READING: For sword: H. R. Ellis Davidson, *The Sword in Anglo-Saxon England* (Oxford Univ. Press, 1962); R. E. Oakeshott, *The Archaeology of Weapons* (Lutterworth Press, 1960). For sword dances: Violet Alford, *Sword Dance and Drama* (Merlin Press, 1962); Violet Alford and Rodney Gallop, *The Traditional Dance* (Methuen, 1935); Douglas Kennedy, *England's Dances* (Bell, 1949).

British Museum/C.M. Dixon

'It is the role of religious symbols,' said C. G. Jung, 'to give a meaning to the life of man': it is increasingly suggested in the West that the lack of adequate symbols is part of the Western malaise

SYMBOLISM

'THE GREAT function of symbols,' wrote the distinguished German Protestant theologian Paul Tillich, 'is to point beyond themselves, in the power of that to which they point, to open up levels of reality which otherwise are closed, and to open up levels of the human mind of which we otherwise are not aware.' There is no doubt that man's tendency to see in everything around him intimations of a veiled reality, and to perform actions which are themselves symbolic, has played an immensely important role in the history of religion and magic, but the elucidation of symbols is a highly precarious business. This is because a symbol is essentially an attempt to express what is otherwise inexpressible, which means that it cannot be expounded satisfactorily in words. The more powerful the symbol, the more this is so. Having caught it in your butterfly net, you can only display it with its wings spread out and a neat classificatory label underneath if you pop it in the killing bottle first. It is now unfortunately dead – it has lost the elusive quality which made you want to capture it in the first place.

Major religious symbols have about them a tantalizing vagueness or, put the other way round, a haunting richness, with an air of holding the key to a secret beyond the grasp of rational intelligence. It is because they are felt 'to open up levels of reality which otherwise are closed' that some Christian writers have suggested that if God has chosen to disclose himself to man, symbols would be the natural vehicles of his revelation. Whether this is accepted or not, it is at least impressive evidence of one of the cardinal facts about symbols (as distinct from minor conventional signs, like trademarks or traffic lights), that the impact they make on the mind is one of recognition, not of invention. They are felt to be discovered, not devised.

What is discovered, however, may vary considerably from one mind to another. Even within the same broad tradition, a symbol will have different connotations for different people (and even for the same person at different times). A telling example is provided by Mary Douglas in her book *Natural Symbols,* in connection with the Roman Catholic rule of abstaining from meat on Fridays. This was originally a symbol of 'personal mortification, a small weekly celebration of the annual celebration of Good Friday. Thus it pointed directly to Calvary and Redemption.' Among sophisticated Catholics the rule is increasingly ignored and its symbolism regarded as empty. But the rule is strictly maintained by many Irish immigrants to England, in a country where they have no roots and often no relatives or friends. To them, abstaining from meat on Fridays is a vital symbol of 'allegiance to a humble home in Ireland and to a glorious tradition in Rome.'

Another factor which makes the interpretation of symbols difficult is the confusing variety of ways in which the symbolic is related to the real. A symbol, by definition, is not what it represents. It stands for, suggests, reveals to the mind a reality other than itself. But in practice the symbol is frequently treated as if it *is* what it represents. When someone insults the American flag in the United States, for example, the violence of the reaction provoked among some patriots suggests that what has been maltreated is not merely a piece of cloth but America itself. Both the culprit and the patriot know perfectly well that the flag is not the same as America, but represents it, but they also feel that in a more profound sense it is America that has been damaged, not just the piece of cloth.

This principle applies to much religious

National Gallery/John Freeman

Left **Greek figure of the god Dionysus as a youth, holding a cock and an egg, symbols of creator and created, youth and age, death and rebirth** ***Right*** **At the simplest level, the cross merely represents the instrument of Christ's death, but it has a great wealth of symbolic references, leading the mind on to the idea of sacrifice and suffering, resurrection, a burden to be borne, trust in God's will, reconciliation between God and man, reconciliation of opposites, the essential unity of all things:** ***Crucifixion,*** **by Antonello da Messina**

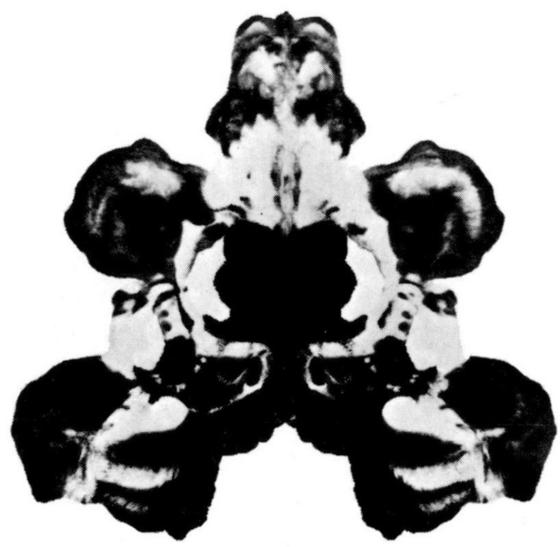

Practically everything of which human beings have become aware has been used as a symbol, but the same symbol will have different connotations for different people: the Rorschach test, devised by a Swiss psychiatrist, follows the principle of the child's inkblot game and takes the shapes, scenes and characters which you see in the blots as clues to your personality

and magical symbolism. When a sorcerer inflicts injuries on a puppet which represents his victim, he believes that he is inflicting the same injuries on the real body of the victim, and all imitative magic depends on the belief that the symbol of a thing *is* the thing (see IMITATIVE MAGIC).

Christ and the Host

The host, or communion wafer, is a symbol of Christ but when it has been properly consecrated in the Mass, it also *is* Christ. The Pope's Encyclical letter *Mysterium Fidei*, issued in 1965, observes that it is wrong 'to be so preoccupied with considering the nature of the sacramental sign that the impression is created that the symbolism – and no one denies its existence in the most holy Eucharist – expresses and exhausts the whole meaning of Christ's presence in this sacrament. Nor is it right to treat of the mystery of transubstantiation without mentioning the marvellous change of the whole of the bread's substance into Christ's body . . . Nor, finally, is it right to put forward and to give expression in practice to the view which maintains that Christ the Lord is no longer present in the consecrated hosts which are left over when the sacrifice of the Mass is over.'

On the other hand, there are many contexts in which the symbol is sharply distinguished from the reality, which it merely stands for. And between the two extremes is a large 'in between' area, in which the symbol is felt to be intimately connected with the reality without fully being it. Magical systems of correspondences, for instance, create links of this sort between symbols and realities (see CORRESPONDENCES). The Hungarian students who, in the uprising of 1956, hanged a bust of the Stalinist politician Matyas Rakosi from a lamp post, probably felt that they were doing something more effective than making a mere gesture of defiance. Going back to the Eucharist for a moment, there is a whole range of responses from Christians of different denominations to the nature of Christ's presence in the sacrament, as being 'real' or 'spiritual' or 'merely symbolic' (see MASS; SACRAMENTS).

Practically everything of which human beings have become aware has been recognized somewhere by somebody as a symbol of something. Unusual events are treated as omens, signs of an underlying maladjustment of the order of Nature which will bring death or disaster. The rustling of trees, the fall of lots, the speech of a person in trance, the lines on a hand or the stars in the sky, are interpreted as symbols of the will of the gods or the pattern of fate (see DIVINATION; OMENS; ORACLES). Animals, plants, features of landscape, thunder and lightning, parts of the body, clothes, numbers, buildings and innumerable other objects are felt to have greater significance than appears on the surface. A rolling wheel may be a symbol of the sun or the course of the year, and the sun and the year themselves may be symbols of the divine. An early Christian writer, Hippolytus of Rome, said of Christ: 'He the Sun, once he had risen from the womb of the earth, showed the 12 Apostles to be as it were 12 hours . . . Once they were gathered together, the 12 Apostles like 12 months proclaimed the perfect year, Christ.'

In Green Pastures

People and their occupations may be symbols. Among the symbols associated with the pharaohs in Egypt were the herdsman and the shepherd. 'The functions of the state,' said Henri Frankfort (in *Before Philosophy*), 'were to own, control, drive, discipline, and defend; they were also to cherish, nurture, shelter, and enlarge the population. The god-sent controller of the Egyptian people was the herdsman who kept them in green pastures, fought to secure fresh pastures for them, drove off the voracious beasts who attacked them, belaboured the cattle who strayed out of line, and helped the weaklings.' He went on to point out that, 'The concept of the herdsman has its negative pole in the implication that men are simply cattle, property on a lower stage of existence.'

Similarly, the king could be thought of as a shepherd. The sun god had appointed him, 'to be shepherd of this land, to keep alive the people', watching by night and by day. One of the earliest emblems of Egyptian kings was the shepherd's crook. The imagery of the shepherd has also played an inspiring role in Judaism and Christianity. In the Old Testament God is a shepherd ('The Lord is my shepherd, I shall not want' – Psalm 23) and, in the New, Jesus says: 'I am the good shepherd . . . and I lay down my life for the sheep' (John, chapter 10). Christ or the Church or the priest cares for the 'flock' of humanity, including its 'black sheep', and the crosier, or pastoral staff, of a bishop, may be descended from a shepherd's crook and is an emblem of firmness and mercy, and of the authority that combines both these qualities (see also GOOD SHEPHERD; SHEEP).

Evocative and long-lived myths are powerful symbols, stories which are felt to reveal otherwise inexpressible truths. Religious and magical rites and actions are symbols, ranging from an initiation ceremony in which the candidate symbolically dies and is reborn (see INITIATION) to such simple gestures as the kiss of peace, the finger held to the lips as a sign of silence, kneeling as a mark of humility, standing as a mark of respect, sitting as a mark of authority, in the case of a king or a judge (see also GESTURE). But even an apparently simple gesture may have unsuspected depths. In Islam, prostration is an expression of humility before God, but to the Sufi mystics it is something much more, meaning 'no less than extinction, a ritual affirmation that there is no room in the Divine Presence for more than the One' (see SUFIS).

The Key and the Net

Some symbols have a basic meaning which is obvious enough and depends on some evident resemblance or analogy, though many will see deeper significance below the surface. Inverted symbols, for example, things which are upside down, backwards, the wrong way round, are generally connected with evil, black magic and witchcraft because they reverse accepted standards of what is good. To turn a crucifix upside down, with deliberate intent, is to state allegiance to God's adversary, the Devil. A key opens a lock and so it stands for access to some spiritual truth or condition. In Christian art St Peter is shown with the keys of heaven as a sign of the authority and function which Jesus conferred on him (Matthew 16.19). More broadly, a key may be a symbol of the longing for God which opens the door of Christian hope. More broadly still, it may be a key of wisdom or eternal life, of initiation, of entrance into mysteries (see HOUSE). A net is an obvious image of entanglement, of difficulties and snares. It appears in the book of Ezekiel as a weapon in the hand of God, who will throw a net over an offender and entrap him. But also in Ezekiel, and in the New Testament, the net is connected with fishing, and in Christian symbolism it is linked with the apostles and their successors as fishers of men, the Pope is called the Fisherman.

Other symbols are not approached so simply (or deceptively simply). Receptacles are, in general, symbols of woman, for obvious reasons, but they are readily spiritualized: one of the emblems of the Virgin Mary, for instance, is a golden vase filled with white lilies (for purity). The cup is a female sex symbol but it also carries connotations of nourishment and abundance. When it becomes the cup of the Eucharist, and still more when it becomes

A dream-like painting by Chagall, *Time is a River without Banks*: both the Freudian and Jungian schools of psychoanalysis treat the scenes and images which appear in dreams as symbols which reveal unconscious mental processes, and Jungian methods of interpretation relate them to symbols in alchemy, myths, legends and folktales

the Grail, it has clearly far transcended its simple anatomical reference (see GRAIL).

One of the functions of a symbol is to act as what has been called 'a rallying point for meaning'. Through it the mind connects together several meanings which are not outwardly or immediately connected. Mircea Eliade cites as an example the symbolism of the moon, which links together the moon's changing cycle in the sky, the rhythms and cycles of life on earth, woman, the waters, death and rebirth, and human destiny (see MOON). 'The symbol is capable of revealing a perspective in which diverse realities can be fitted together or even integrated into a system.' This is why symbols are used in meditation, in many traditions, to lead the mind on to the realization of unsuspected truths or aspects of truth.

The Christian cross, at the simplest level, merely represents the cross on which Jesus died, but it has a great wealth and variety of symbolic references. The mind which dwells on it may be led on to ideas, among others, of death, suffering, sacrifice, resurrection, of a crisis to be endured or a burden to be borne, of God's love, of trust in God's will, of the reconciliation of God and man, the reconciliation of opposites, the unity of all things (see CROSS).

The cross can lead on towards the symbolism of the centre. The directions of east, west, north and south have their own symbolism, as do left and right (see DIRECTIONS), and up and down are naturally connected with ideas of progress and decline, superiority and inferiority, good and evil, heaven in the sky and hell underground (see SKY; STEPS). The cross on which Christ died can be thought of as an emblem which connects the directions and the centre, and in Christian tradition it was erected at the centre of the world. The cross was also thought of as a tree, and in various myths a great tree is the *axis mundi,* 'axis of the world', its trunk connecting the underworld, the earth and the sky, and affording a means of communication between the different levels. The tree reconciles the opposites of sky and earth, 'above' and 'below', as Christ's death on the glory tree made it possible for men below to be reconciled with God above. (Or the tree may be an *imago mundi,* a diagram of the world, as it is in the Cabala – see CABALA; TREES.)

Ronan Picture Library

A sacred mountain is sometimes thought to stand at the centre of the world, its 'roots', so to speak, beneath the surface and its summit in the sky. The Hindu heavens are located in a 'divine enclosure', said to lie somewhere north of the Himalayas, at the centre of which, marking the centre of the universe, is Mt Meru, a towering peak of pure gold, round which the heavenly bodies revolve. Alternatively, a shrine or city may be said to stand at the navel or centre of the earth, and sites where the divine is believed to have revealed itself become sacred 'centres', places where communication is possible between different levels of existence, between men and the gods, or the living and the dead (see MOUNTAIN; NAVEL; PILGRIMAGE).

In myths, legends and folktales a temple, a palace, a castle, may be a centre in which is concealed a secret goal of overwhelming importance, a holy of holies, the Grail, the enchanted princess, the treasure hoard. A maze contains a hidden centre, the way to which is hard to find, but in reaching the heart of the labyrinth a man penetrates perhaps to the Heavenly Jerusalem, perhaps to the underworld, perhaps to the innermost recesses of his own being (see MAZE). It is interesting that a map of Christian's journey in *Pilgrim's Progress,* reproduced earlier (page 2147), shows his path as a spiral, circling in from the periphery to the Celestial City at the centre, suggesting a journey inwards.

The Hero Within

That symbols illuminate the world within us, whether or not they reveal the world without, is one of the answers to the view which regards a symbol as at best unimportant and at worst undesirable, because it stands in place of a reality instead of being the reality itself. In practice, as suggested above, important symbols are not treated as reality substitutes but as things closely connected with a reality which could not be approached without them. In many societies outside the West symbols and symbolic actions are essential ingredients of human understanding of, and relationships with, reality, including relationships with the human as well as the sacred (see, for instance, MENSTRUATION; RITES OF PASSAGE; RITUAL). In the West, it is increasingly suggested that a lack of adequate symbols is part of the modern malaise.

For example, in his last book, *Man and His Symbols,* C. G. Jung said: 'It is the role of religious symbols to give a meaning to the life of man. The Pueblo Indians believe that they are the sons of Father Sun, and this belief endows their life with a perspective (and a goal) that goes far beyond their limited existence. It gives them ample space for the unfolding of personality and permits them a full life as complete persons. Their plight is infinitely more satisfactory than that of a man in our own civilization who knows that he is (and will remain) nothing more than an underdog with no inner meaning to his life . . .

'Today, for instance, we talk of "matter". We describe its physical properties. We conduct laboratory experiments to demonstrate some of its aspects. But the word "matter" remains a dry, inhuman, and purely intellectual concept, without any psychic significance for us. How different was the former image of matter – the Great Mother – that could encompass and express the profound emotional meaning of Mother Earth. In the same way, what was the spirit is now identified with intellect and thus ceases to be the Father of All. It has degenerated to the limited ego-thoughts of man; the immense emotional energy expressed in the image of "our Father" vanishes into the sand of an intellectual desert.'

Louvre/Hamlyn Group Library

Both the Freudian and Jungian schools of psychoanalysis maintain that the scenes and images which the mind throws up into consciousness, especially in dreams, may begin to make sense if treated, not at their face value, but as symbols which reveal unconscious mental processes. Jungian methods of interpretation relate these scenes and images to symbols in alchemy and in myths, legend and folktales from all over the world. Common features in numerous hero legends, for instance, suggest that the myth of the hero is really about the process of psychologically growing up. 'In the developing consciousness of the individual the hero figure is the symbol by which the emerging ego overcomes the inertia of the unconscious mind, and liberates the mature man from a regressive longing to return to the blissful state of infancy in a world dominated by his mother' (this and following quotes are from Joseph L. Henderson's essay in *Man and His Symbols*).

The 'tutelary' figure often found presiding over the upbringing and education of the hero (the centaur Chiron who taught Achilles, for example, or Merlin in the case of Arthur) becomes on this view a symbolic representation of the 'whole psyche, the larger and more comprehensive identity that supplies the strength that the personal ego lacks', and his role in the story suggests that 'the essential function of the heroic myth is the development of the individual's ego-consciousness – in a manner that will equip him for the arduous tasks with which life confronts him.'

When the hero does battle with dragons, monsters and evil beings, he is really in combat with his own 'regressive' trends, with the dark and negative side of his personality, with the shadow in himself. When he rescues a beautiful girl from danger – the damsel in distress theme – he is really liberating his own 'anima', the female component in his being (a woman's male component is the 'animus'). The hero eventually falls, betrayed or sacrificed, because 'the human ego can be exalted to experience godlike attributes, but only at the cost of over-reaching itself and falling to disaster' (a theme which many who are not Jungians have seen in the story of Adam and Eve, or in the Faust legend, and which flourishes in science fiction).

The hero myth, on this interpretation, is concerned with individuation, the process of becoming a 'whole person', which has parallels in the processes of alchemy and magic, where the attempt is made to find the true inner self and expand it, as it were, into the whole man, who is the divine man (see ALCHEMY; MAGIC).

The Jungian approach has been criticised on various grounds, among them that it involves talking about 'the' hero myth, when in fact there are many hero myths, which have to be stretched or lopped on a bed of Procrustes to fit them into the desired pattern, and similarly with other types of myth; and that it equally blurs the different meanings which people recognize in the same myth or symbol. The archetypes, or symbolic figures and patterns which the Jungians identify, do not appear as regularly as Jungians maintain; and when they do, they may be more easily explained as images drawn from the ordinary conscious experience of humanity than as images from the unconscious.

The Collective Unconscious

Jung explained the appearance of the same themes over and over again by locating them in the 'collective unconscious', but it was difficult to explain how this reservoir of images, if it exists, is transmitted from one generation to the next. In *Man and His Symbols* Jung suggested that the human mind has a tendency to form symbolic representations of a motif, 'representations that can vary a great deal in detail without losing their basic pattern', and that this tendency is 'an instinctive *trend,* as marked as the impulse of birds to build nests . . .'

Common themes and symbols in different societies can no doubt often be explained as the result of common human tendencies and common human experience, but

Left **Jung believed that alchemical symbolism expressed ageless realities of the human mind and that the alchemists were exploring their own innermost depths: symbols of alchemy and science mingled on the title page of Athanasius Kircher's *Ars Magna Lucis et Umbrae,* 1671**
Above right **Rembrandt's *Philosopher with an Open Book* suggests the light of illumination penetrating the darkness of ignorance, and the spiral stairs recall the alchemical motif of a return to the womb as a penetration of the recesses of the self**

The dignity of work, strength in unity, rejection of war and desire for peace – these concepts are symbolized in a Victorian trade union membership certificate

Chris Barker

symbols can also be seen migrating from one culture and religion to another. Obvious examples are Old Testament symbols which were adopted and adapted by the early Christians. In the Old Testament God is the Father, as he remained in Christianity, and he is king, judge and shepherd, which all became symbolic roles of Christ. He is also the cultivator of vines, which are his people ('My beloved had a vineyard on a very fertile hill' – Isaiah, chapter 5). Ignatius of Antioch, expanding on the theme in the 2nd century, said: 'Christ the tree of life . . . has the Apostles for branches, the redeemed for fruit, words for leaves; baptism is the root, and the Father, the gardener.' In St John's gospel again, Jesus is 'the bread of life' (chapter 6), referring back to the manna on which the Israelites fed in the wilderness, and this symbolism became linked with the host in the Mass.

The Christians saw figures and events in the Old Testament as 'types', or symbolic foreshadowings, of Christian figures and events. Jonah emerging from the belly of the whale, for example, was a type of Christ's resurrection from the dead (see JONAH). And, in one of the supreme examples, Christ was identified with the 'suffering servant' of Isaiah (chapter 53): 'He was despised and rejected by men; a man of sorrows, and acquainted with grief . . . upon him was the chastisement that made us whole and with his stripes we are healed.'

(See also numerous other articles, including ALPHABET; BODY; BURIAL; CIRCLE; COLOURS; DREAMS; ICONOGRAPHY; LANDSCAPE SYMBOLISM; MANDALA; PHALLIC SYMBOLISM).

RICHARD CAVENDISH

FURTHER READING: J. E. Cirlot, *A Dictionary of Symbols* (Philosophical Library, 1962); Mary Douglas, *Natural Symbols* (Pantheon Books, 1970); Mircea Eliade, *Patterns in Comparative Religion* (New American Library); G. Ferguson, *Signs and Symbols in Christian Art* (Oxford Univ. Press, 1966 reprint); C. G. Jung ed., *Man and His Symbols* (State Mutual Books, 1981).

Sympathetic Magic

Term coined by Sir James Frazer, in *The Golden Bough* for the principle that 'things act on each other at a distance through a secret sympathy'; combining two basic assumptions of magical thinking, the principle of mimicry, 'that like produces like, or that an effect resembles its cause', and the law of contact, 'that things which have once been in contact with each other contrive to act on each other at a distance after the physical contact has been severed.'

See IMITATIVE MAGIC.

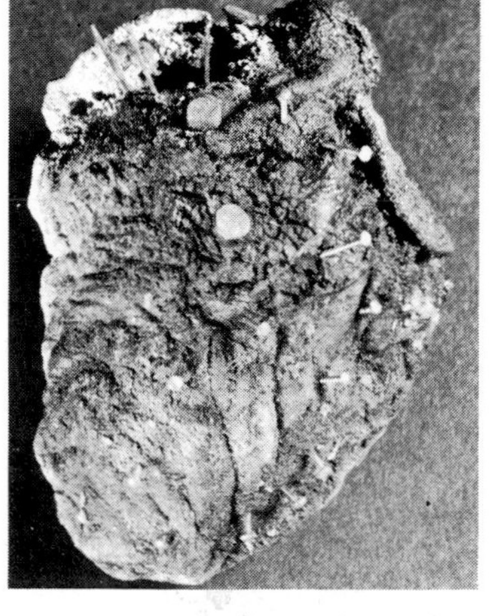

Syncretism

The mingling in one religious system of elements drawn from different systems: for example, the blending of cults in the Roman Empire as Eastern religions spread to the West and gods of different regions were identified with each other; or the blending of Egyptian, Greek, Christian and other elements in Gnosticism; or the mingling of eastern and western ideas in some modern occult systems.

The great bull god El and the dying and rising god Baal, with his consort Anat, were worshipped in rites which were ceaselessly denounced by the Old Testament prophets; yet nevertheless, their pagan temples wit[illegible] Syria's official adoption of Christianity

SYRIA AND PALESTINE

THE FULLEST contemporary record of religion in Syria is the texts in alphabetic cuneiform from ancient Ugarit, Ras Shamra, about 12 miles north of Latakkia and two miles from the coast. Theophoric names (personal name including in its form a divine name) as in the Egyptian Execration texts, lists of offerings to various gods, ritual texts, incidental references in legends and above all myths of the fertility cult illustrate the religion of Syria in the 14th century B[illegible]he many god[illegible]th Semitic and non-Se[illegible]itic, reflect t[illegible]xed population of this city in north Sy[illegible]ut only the cult of the fertility god Baal (see BAAL) and the goddess Anat and their associates is documented sufficiently to permit a reconstruction of the cult.

From these texts we learn that the senior god was El ('god'), the King Paramount, Father of the Exalted Ones and Father of Men and Creator, depicted as enthroned at the remote 'source of the streams'. His strength and procreative influence is expressed in his title 'the Bull', but he was the principal god in social relationships, and this aspect of his character is expressed by his title, 'the Kindly, the Compassionate'.

El's executive king is Baal, whose proper name was Hadad ('the T[illegible]erer') or Baal Ramman ('the T[illegible]erer'), which Jewish scribes parodied as Rimmon ('pomegranate'). He establishes his kingly power and order in Nature in a primeval conflict with Sea-and-Ocean Currents and associated monsters like Letan (Leviathan of the Old Testament) and Tannin, also

Goats figure frequently in the religious art of western Asia: he-goat in a thicket, in gold and lapis lazuli, from Ur in Mesopotamia, the city which Abraham, the Jewish patriarch, left to settle in Canaan

Michael Holford

known in this connection in the Old Testament, and has his 'house' built as a visible token that he is the reigning king. He is obliged, however, to reassert his kingship in a seasonal conflict against Sterility, or Death (Mot) in a myth which is believed to be related to the chief seasonal crisis in Syria, at the autumn equinox.

The Fertility Cult

In this myth Baal is the god of thunder, lightning and winter rains, 'He who Mounts the Clouds', and is, like the Mesopotamian Tammuz, a dying and rising god, whose fortunes fluctuate with the vegetation he promotes (see DYING GOD). In his eclipse in the summer season his sister and consort Anat (the north Syrian counterpart of Astarte; see ASTARTE) is particularly active. Baal, as the vegetation he promotes, succumbs to Mot. His dead body is sought over hill and dale by Anat, called in the Ras Shamra texts 'the Virgin Anat', a rite which had its counterpart in the fertility cult throughout the Near East (see APHRODITE; DEMETER; OSIRIS; TAMMUZ). There is definite reflection of the mourning of Anat on the recovery and burial of the body of Baal in the Old Testament (Zechariah 12.11) in 'the mourning for Hadad-Rimmon in the plain of Megiddo'. Anat proceeds to avenge Baal. She cuts down Mot, winnows him, parches him with fire, grinds him with a millstone and scatters his remains in the fields for the birds to eat. This obviously relates to the desacralization of the new crop, setting it free for common use, as in the offering of the first sheaf of 'new grain from fresh ears, parched with fire,' in Leviticus 2.14.

In myth related to ritual strict logical consistency is not expected, and Baal revives. His revival is anticipated in a dream by El, who is the final authority in these texts and intervenes at significant junctures to confirm a decision or to foreshadow the future. El's vision is of the skies raining olive oil and the wadis running with honey, which recurs in the liturgies of Israel reflected in Amos 9.13 and Joel 3.18. With similar lack of consistency Mot is introduced in a final 'showdown' with Baal, out of which Baal emerges victor and again vindicates his kingship. This conflict is set 'in the seventh year' and may be related to the seven-year cycle marked in Israel by an artificial famine, when the land lay fallow on the principle that drought must be given full play in order that its force might be exhausted. Thus in the seasonal tension after the long dry summer, pending the coming of the 'early rains', the Syrian peasant relieved his anxiety and predisposed providence by homoeopathic magic, which was the genesis of drama in Greece in the cult of the wine god Dionysus at Athens. In Syria no such dramas are attested, but all the elements of drama are in the Baal myth.

The Canaanite mother goddess Athirat or Ashera, was probably a form of the Mesopotamian goddess Ishtar, shown with a palm tree on this Assyrian seal: the fertility rites of Canaan were fiercely denounced by the Old Testament prophets

Michael Holford

It will be seen that Israel inherited this liturgic theme of the great autumn festival, which she developed in the light of her own historical tradition of the great deliverance from Egypt and the Covenant, but the essential features of the seasonal festival survive, conflict with the forces of destruction and disorder, the demonstration of the effective kingship of God and the establishment of his government, often by judgement. This is expressed notably in the Enthronement psalms in the Old Testament, in passages in the Prophets which reflect this liturgical theme and in passages on the Day of the Lord in Jewish and Christian apocalyptic, for example, Revelation. There the sea and certain sea monsters are arch-enemies of God's ordered government, as in the Baal myth of Ras Shamra in the New Year festival in Canaan.

The role of the king in his sacral function as executive of Baal as the Divine King in his 'passion' and triumph in the great autumn festival cannot be established on the evidence of the Ras Shamra texts, but on the analogy of the corresponding occasion in Mesopotamian religion it is likely. With the necessary changes, it may certainly be demonstrated that in Jerusalem the Davidic king was the temporal guarantee of the effective Kingship of God, which was expressed in the liturgy of the great autumn festival. For Canaan Ezekiel's denunciation of the King of Tyre (chapter 28) expresses the conception of the king as the representative of God, the channel of divine blessings, and, as representative of the community, the royal man in the garden of God. The Legend of King Krt at Ras Shamra speaks of the king as 'the son of El', and the crown prince is 'suckled by the fertility goddesses Anat and Athirat'. The conception of the king as the upholder of the social justice which is the concern of God is expressed in the royal texts from Ras Shamra and, as in Psalm 72 and Isaiah 11.1–9, he is the medium of blessings in Nature. It is not difficult to see here an ideology from which the conception of the Messiah in Israel developed.

The protagonists of this cult are well known through texts, sculpture and figurines. Baal is the active young warrior god, El is an elderly god on his throne and footstool, both being associated with the bull in virtue of procreative interests. Anat, like Astarte in the Old Testament, is the goddess of love, and appears naked in moulded reliefs and pendants, either devoted to shrines or given in return for the payment of a vow and used as amulets to promote childbirth. Sexual rites of imitative magic associated with the Canaanite fertility cult survived in Israel and are constantly denounced by the Prophets. Anat was also the goddess of war, like Ishtar in Mesopotamia, and is involved in what is evidently a bloody massacre in her temple in an episode in the Baal myth at Ras Shamra, which may really describe a blood-letting rite, like the self-laceration of the devotees of Baal at Carmel (1 Kings 18.28), or perhaps circumcision. The mother goddess Athirat (Ashera of the Old Testament) appears as the consort of El, and is probably the goddess represented as the nourisher of life who offers ears of corn to

C. M. Dixon

Bronze figures of Canaanite gods, thought to be El (*left*) and Baal (*right*): El was the paramount deity, father of gods and men, the kindly and compassionate; Baal, god of storm and the winter rains, was a dying and rising god, linked with the seasonal death and rebirth of vegetation; both El and Baal were associated with the bull

C. M. Dixon

two rampant caprids (goats) on an ivory relief from the seaward quarter of Ugarit. The motif is a development of the rampant caprids reaching up to the fruit of the Tree of Life, which is familiar throughout the Near East. In the references in the Old Testament to the *ashera* as a feature of sanctuaries this is a tree, either natural or stylized, representing the mother goddess Ashera as the receptive element in Nature and as the universal nourisher. The Tree of Life is closely associated in the ancient Near East with the king in his sacral function as mediator of the divine blessing, as in Assyrian sculpture and on the royal couch from the palace of Ras Shamra.

The Will of the Gods

Significant as the fertility cult of Canaan undoubtedly was, it is possible that the dramatic nature of the Baal myth gives an incomplete picture of the actual situation. In royal legends for instance, in dynastic succession and other historical and social situations the predominant deity is not Baal but El, to whom chiefly sacrifice is made in a fast-liturgy on the occasion of a national emergency. This and a certain text from Ras Shamra containing oaths by certain attributes of El indicate a more spiritual conception of El, which is nearer to the Hebrew conception of God.

Among many other deities in Canaanite religion Dagan, the god of corn (*dagon*), is known at Ras Shamra from offering lists, from Baal's stock epithet 'the Son of Dagan', and from dedication inscriptions on stelae from a temple adjoining that of Baal at Ras Shamra, which dates from c 2000 BC. Reshef was the god who slew men by war and plague. He is known from Egyptian sculpture and may be recognized in bronze figurines of a striding warrior with offensive weapon and shield, well known from archeological sites in Syria and Palestine. In one of the Ras Shamra texts he is called Reshef of the Arrow, and in the Graeco-Roman period he was assimilated to Apollo with his pestilential arrows. From later inscriptions from Sidon, Eshmun is known as the god of healing, assimilated to Asclepius in the Graeco-Roman period, as Baal was to Hercules, by whose labours also order was sustained against the constant menace of chaos. The sun, regarded as a goddess, is a minor figure in the Baal myth of Ras Shamra, and the moon god and his consort Nikkal were also worshipped, particularly at Harran in north-west Mesopotamia, and in north Syria (see HARRANIAN RELIGION). Ritual texts from Ras Shamra indicate that special rites and sacrifices, in which the king was involved, were observed at certain days of the month, probably at lunar phases.

The will of the various gods was consulted and communicated in various ways. In the 2nd century AD, Lucian of Samosata mentions oracles according to the movement of statues of the gods, doubtless at the manipulation of priests in response to specific questions, conveying a simple 'Yes' or 'No', like the sacred lots Urim and Thummim in early Israel. Divination by the entrails of sacrificed animals was also practised, the liver being especially significant, as is indicated by clay models from archeological sites, charted and annotated for consultation or instruction. The medieval Arab writer Ibn an-Nadim mentions divination at Harran by the direction of the gaze or the expression in the eyes of the dying victim. Texts from the Amorite city of Mari on the mid-Euphrates mention diviners who consulted the auspices in this way and communicated their findings to the king in matters of ritual or state. There were also communications by ecstatic devotees, who suggest 'the sons of the prophets' in the Old Testament and dervishes of later Islam.

At Byblos c1100 BC there is an instance of the will of the god communicated to the king in an affair of state by an ecstatic of his household and considered authentic by the king. The account of the distress of King Saul before his last battle (1 Samuel 28) mentions prophets and dreams as the media of the communication of the will of God in a crisis, and the patriarchal narratives in the Old Testament and the passage in the Baal myth where El sees the revival of Baal in a dream indicate the significance attached to dreams as communications of the will of God in future events or on the significance of the present situation. People would often resort to shrines in ritual incubation when dreams were taken as sure communications of the purpose of the god.

The temple in Syria varied in form, but the general conception was a large area within the sacred precinct in which the temple proper was the focal feature. This conception is best illustrated in the sanctuary of Bel, or Baal, in the early Roman period at Palmyra in the Syrian desert and the Moslem sacred precinct at Jerusalem. At Ras Shamra and Hazor in the 14th–13th centuries BC, the tripartite temple is known, comprising an outer court with a great altar, shallow vestibule, main nave and inmost shrine, or 'Holy of Holies'. This is the plan of Solomon's Temple at Jerusalem, which was constructed by Phoenician craftsmen. Administrative texts from Ras Shamra attest hereditary office in a large number of professions among temple personnel, priests, votaries both male and female, temple prostitutes, singers, makers of sacred vestments, sculptors, potters, launderers, slaughterers, augurers, or possibly Temple herdsmen, and merchants who traded on account of the Temple. The king of course was the supreme priest, though except on special occasions he would delegate his duties.

Sacrifice of the Infants

The myths and legends of Ras Shamra in their fuller context amplify the simple listing of various types of sacrifice in the offering lists. Thus from the description

Left **Statue of Baal Hammon, the principal god of Carthage, the Phoenician colony in North Africa: the name Hammon may derive from Ammon, god of the Siwa oasis in Libya; 1st century AD, from Tunisia** ***Below right*** **Ruins of a temple of Baal in Tunisia** ***Above right*** **Roman ruins at Palmyra in Syria, where the moon god was venerated by the caravan merchants**

of the duties of the son and heir of the king in the royal legend of Prince Aqhat at Ras Shamra it is known that communion meals were eaten in the sanctuary. The blood and vitals were offered to the god, and the rest was cooked and eaten by the community, thus effecting solidarity of the participants with the god and with one another. The shrine might also house memorials of the ancestors of the community, represented by standing stones, as in the Canaanite sanctuary of Hazor, and probably also at Gezer. By offerings at this tangible token of a favoured ancestor the community hoped to continue to share in the blessing which had been his.

Besides communion sacrifices there were those that were offered wholly to the gods either as food or as an act of total renunciation on the part of the worshipper, being wholly burnt on the altar; and other such offerings were made for purification, as doves were sacrificed in Israel after childbirth, and as firstlings of crop and flock and of game in hunting. In Israel and among the Carthaginians in North Africa animals were sacrificed in redemption of first-born sons, and this was almost certainly done also in Syria.

Archeological evidence has been claimed from Gezer and Tell al-Fara by Nablus for foundation sacrifice of children, but this is disputed. Multiple infant sacrifice, however, is attested by jars full of calcined bones of infants and young animals from the sanctuary of the fertility goddess Tanit at the Tyrian colony of Carthage (see PHOENICIANS), in Punic inscriptions and in the writings of the African Church father, Tertullian (3rd century AD). Those may have been first-born children dedicated thus as firstlings, but in King Mesha's sacrifice of his eldest son (2 Kings 3), like those in Judah in the latter period of the kingdom, they may have been sacrifices in extremity, to which Philo of Byblos (64–161 AD) alludes. Other cases, such as that which Diodorus Siculus attributes to the Carthaginians in Sicily after a victory over the Greeks in 307 BC, may be a case of 'death-devotion' (*herem*), a great act of renunciation of the spoils of war, to which King Mesha also refers in his inscription recording his war of liberation from Israel (c 835 BC). The sacrifices would thus correspond to Samuel's 'hewing Agag in pieces before the Lord' (1 Samuel 15.33).

The Dead and the Afterlife

Besides the commemoration of the dead as recipients of the divine favour ritual texts from Ras Shamra refer to the family god (*'il 'ib*), certain of these alluding to 'offerings at the aperture of the divine ancestor'. This is amplified by the discovery of grave-installations of such apertures as pipes of bottomless jars to communicate offerings, especially libations, to the defunct, probably to promote fertility of the earth, over which the dead were believed to have some influence. Such offerings to the dead may be the substance of the ban on offerings of a portion of the harvest to the dead in Deuteronomy 26.14. The dead were termed *repa'im* by the Phoenicians as in Israel, the name for the 'weak' shades in the Old Testament, and were possibly referred to in funerary inscriptions of King Tabnith of Sidon (5th century BC) as 'divine', or at least supernatural, as in the passage on King Saul and the Witch of Endor (1 Samuel 28.13), where the shade of Samuel is described as 'a god'. In this case the king sought revelation of the future.

As recipients of offerings, givers of fertility and revealers of the future, the departed in ancient Syria were regarded as not quite defunct. The Aramaean king Panammu in his inscription (c 750 BC) expects his descendants to invoke him when they make an offering to Baal, so that 'his soul may eat and drink with Baal'. The existence of the shade in the gloomy underworld is familiar in the Old Testament, particularly in Job chapter 3. Though quite undesirable this was apparently still an existence, however insubstantial, and this attenuated life was sustained by offerings, particularly libations, though one of the more recently discovered texts from Ras Shamra refers to animal sacrifice 'for the life of the family god', or the divine ancestor. The belief in

Alan Irvine

Sonia Halliday

this insubstantial life of the dead who require to be revived by libation survives among Arab peasants in Syria and Palestine, who believe that the dead come at dusk to wells, springs and rivers to drink; however, this was but a tenuous existence. In the Legend of Prince Aqhat in the Ras Shamra texts occurs the passage:

> As for mortal man, what does he get as his latter end?
> What does mortal man get as his inheritance?
> Glaze will be poured out on my head,
> Even plaster on my pate,
> And the death of all men will I die,
> Yea I shall surely die.

These lines express the typical view of the afterlife in ancient Canaan.

Incantations and Amulets

Apart from the regular cults, men in Syria, as elsewhere and at all times, sought to enlist the powers of the supernatural or to ward off their evil influences by charms and amulets. Prophylactic charms in Aramaic are known, and at least one excerpt from the Baal myth of Ras Shamra was probably used as an aphrodisiac charm. The figurines of the nude fertility goddess were probably also used to promote procreation and childbirth. Besides, a great number of amulets have been found in excavations. Those are chiefly Egyptian, the cat and the intelligent ape, the hippopotamus, which was both a sinister force to be placated as the representative of chaos or, in the form of an upright female, a beneficent patroness of mothers. The grotesque dwarf Bes, the protector of children and pregnant women was also popular. From the Egyptian cult of the fertility god Osiris, the goddess Isis and their son Horus, who survived a hazardous infancy to avenge Osiris' death (see HORUS), small images of the infant Horus were favourite amulets, and also the 'Eye of Horus' with its fertilizing tear-drops. Small gold flies and other insects resembling lice, which were found by Sir Flinders Petrie at a site at the mouth of the Wadi Ghazzeh in Palestine, may have had a prophylactic purpose to ward off disease, like the gold mice referred to in 1 Samuel 6.4, which were sent back with the ark by the Philistines.

In describing the religion of Syria the documents of Ras Shamra have been taken as the basis of this account, firstly because they are a contemporary statement, the fullest and most reliable that is available, and secondly because they document the fertility cult, which was the most conspicuous aspect of local religion that impressed Israel as she settled in Palestine. Ugarit, however, was but one city state in Syria, and in the history of the land it is notable that, despite a general community of religion in any given period, there were local variations and different emphases. So too over the long period of paganism, until Christianity was established as the faith of the majority (c 500 AD), different variations of the old religion developed through time and in different localities.

In the Graeco-Roman period the Canaanite gods were identified with classical deities: coins of the 2nd century AD show Baal (*top left*) who was assimilated to Hercules; Eshmun (*top right*) the god of healing, with twin serpents, assimilated to Asclepius; the sea (*bottom left*) assimilated to Poseidon, the city god of Beirut; the sanctuary of Byblos (*bottom right*)

British Museum

The Blood of Adonis

In the settled land the old gods were assimilated to the gods of Greece and Rome, as Baal to Zeus the sky god with his thunderbolt, the fertility goddesses Astarte, Anat, and Ashera to Aphrodite and Juno. Baal in his role as a dying and rising vegetation god was assimilated to Adonis, the lover of Aphrodite, or Venus, but retained his Syrian title Adonis ('lord'); their cult was practised at the source of the River Adonis just south of Beirut. When it ran red, as it did at a certain time in summer, it was considered to be discoloured by the blood of Adonis, who was lamented at that time by the Syrian women. Baal, the divine king who must always struggle to vindicate his kinship and order against the forces of chaos, was assimilated to the labouring Hercules, particularly at Tyre and her colonies in the coastal plain of Palestine south of Jaffa. The god Reshef, with his power of life and death, was assimilated to Apollo with his bow and arrows as plague-shafts, and Anat, the goddess of love and war was assimilated to Athene and Minerva. The sea was assimilated to Poseidon, who appears as the city god of Beirut on coins from the Graeco-Roman period, and the healing god Eshmun to Asclepius with his serpents. The latter was particularly venerated at Sidon, judging from the name Eshmunazzar, which was borne by two kings of Sidon.

In the caravan city of Palmyra, between Damascus and the Euphrates, the needs of the caravan merchants in the first three centuries of the Christian era are indicated by the cult of the moon, which was also venerated at Harran, another great caravan city in north Mesopotamia. The moon had evidently a peculiar significance for those merchants and their distant and protracted enterprises. The Venus star Athtar, the brightest star in those latitudes, the first to rise at evening and the last to disappear in the morning, was also greatly venerated at Palmyra, where as two gods Arsu and Azizu ('the Gracious and the Fierce') they are represented as mounted respectively on a camel and a horse.

Christianity did not easily oust the Nature religion of Syria, even after it became the official religion of the Roman Empire. Indeed when Porphyry the Bishop Elect of Gaza went to his see at the end of the 4th century AD the lusty heathen impeded his journey; and according to his deacon and biographer, there were eight pagan temples and many private shrines in Gaza and only 280 Christians out of between 50,000 and 60,000 inhabitants, and that after an Imperial edict against paganism.

JOHN GRAY

FURTHER READING: John Gray, *The Canaanites* (Thames & Hudson, 1965); *Near Eastern Mythology* (Hamlyn, 1970).

Table Turning
Or table tilting, a popular method of communicating with 'spirits'; the table tilts up and raps on the floor with its foot in response to questions, without being consciously pushed by the experimenters, who rest their fingers on it.
See OUIJA BOARDS.

Rules of behaviour which govern the human uses of things and people, taboos are not isolated restrictions; they are always part of a whole system and cannot be understood outside their social context

TABOO

A TABOO (sometimes spelt tabu) is a ban or prohibition; the word comes from the Polynesian languages where it means a religious restriction, to break which would entail some automatic punishment. As it is used in English, taboo has little to do with religion. In essence it generally implies a rule which has no meaning, or one which cannot be explained. Captain Cook noted in his log-book that in Tahiti the women were never allowed to eat with the men, and as the men nevertheless enjoyed female company he asked the reason for this taboo. They always replied that they observed it because it was right. To the outsider the taboo is irrational, to the believer its rightness needs no explaining. Though supernatural punishments may not be expected to follow, the rules of any religion rate as taboos to outsiders. For example, the strict Jewish observance forbids the faithful to make and refuel the fire, or light lamps or put them out during the Sabbath, and it also forbids them to ask a Gentile to perform any of these acts. In his book *A Soho Address*, Chaim Lewis, the son of poor Russian Jewish immigrants in London's Soho at the beginning of this century, describes his father's quandary every winter Sabbath: he did not want to let the fire go out and he could not ask any favour outright. Somehow he had to call in a passer-by and drop oblique hints until the stranger understood what service was required. Taboos always tend to land their observers in just such a ridiculous situation, whether it is a Catholic peasant of the Landes who abstains from meat on Friday but eats teal (a bird whose fishy diet entitles it in their custom to be counted as fish), or a Maori hairdresser who after he had cut the chief's hair was not allowed to use his own hands even for feeding himself and had to be fed for a time like a baby.

In the last century, when the word gained currency in European languages, taboo was understood to arise from an inferior mentality. It was argued that primitive tribes observed countless taboos as part of their general ignorance about the physical world. These rules, which seemed so peculiar to Europeans, were the result of false science, leading to mistaken hygiene, and faulty medicine. Essentially the taboo is a ban on touching or eating or speaking or seeing. Its breach will unleash dangers, while keeping the rules would amount to avoiding dangers and sickness. Since the native theory of taboo was concerned to keep certain classes of people and things apart lest misfortune befall, it was a theory about contagion. Our scholars of the last century contrasted this false, primitive fear of contagion with our modern knowledge of disease. Our hygiene protects from a real danger of contagion, their taboos from imaginary danger. This was a comfortably complacent distinction to draw, but hygiene does not correspond to all the rules which are called taboo. Some are as obviously part of primitive religion in the same sense as Friday abstinence and Sabbath rest. European scholars therefore took care to distinguish on the one hand between primitive taboo with a mainly secular reference, and on the other hand rules of magic which infused the practice of primitive religion. They made it even more difficult to understand the meaning of foreign taboos by importing a classification between true religion and primitive magic, and modern medicine and primitive hygiene; and a very complicated web of definitions was based on this misconception.

In the Eye of the Beholder

The difficulty in understanding primitive taboo arose from the difficulty of understanding our own taboos of hygiene and religion. The first mistake was to suppose that our idea of dirt connotes an objectively real class from which real dangers to health may issue, and whose control depends on valid rules of hygiene. It is better to start by realizing that dirt, like beauty, resides in the eye of the beholder. We must be prepared to put our own behaviour under the same microscope we apply to primitive tribes. If we find that they are busy hedging off this area from that, stopping 'X' from touching 'Y', preventing women from eating with men, and creating elaborate scales

Axel Poignant

Methods of purification in Arnhem Land, Australia: water is poured over a girl *(below)* and a man is purified by sweat from another's armpits *(above)*. Many of the rules of primitive societies, breach of which might cause a pollution that needed to be cleansed away, used to be termed taboos, with the implication that they stemmed from inadequate knowledge and inferior mentality: in fact, all societies have rules which may appear irrational in isolation but are part of a larger and necessary system of classification

Axel Poignant

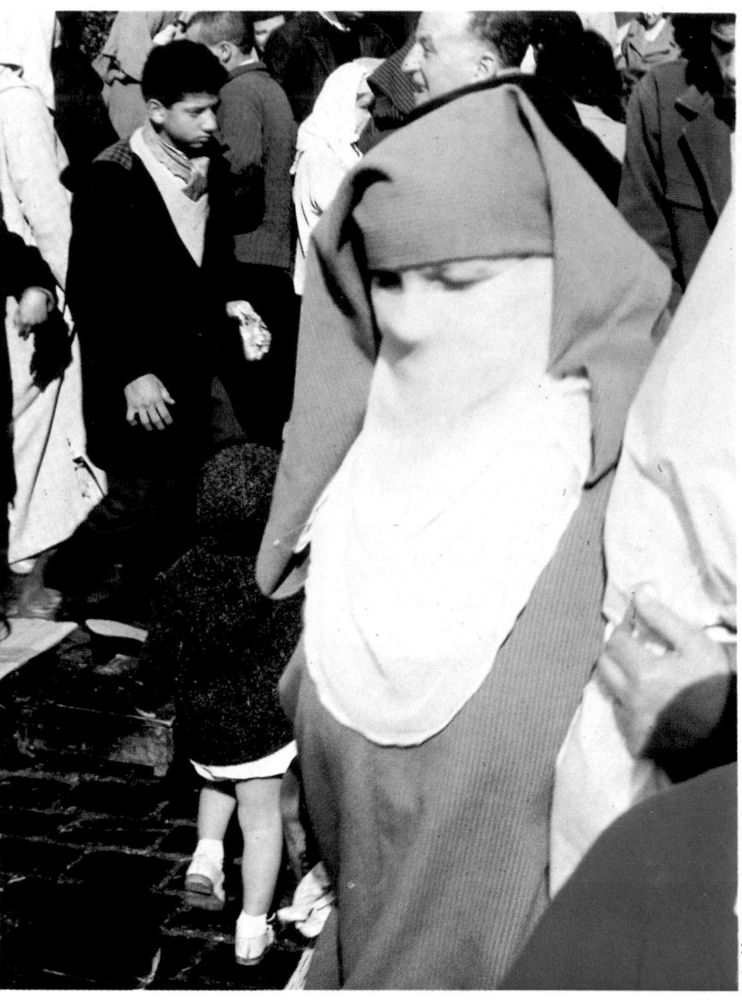

of edibility and inedibility among the vegetable and animal worlds, we should realize that we too are given to this ordering and classifying activity. No taboo can ever make sense by itself. A taboo is always part of a whole system of rules. It makes sense as part of a classification whose meaning is so basic to those who live by it that no piecemeal explanation can be given. A native cannot explain the meaning of a taboo because it forms part of his own machinery of learning. The separate compartments which a taboo system constructs are the framework or instrument of understanding. To turn round and inspect that instrument may seem to be an advanced philosophic exercise, but it is necessary if we are to understand the subject.

Above left **A seller of dye for caste-marks, in India: the Hindu caste system involves elaborate rules regulating behaviour between the castes** ***Above right*** **Street scene in Morocco: for centuries it has been taboo in Arab countries for women to appear unveiled out of doors** ***Below*** **A ban on wearing shoes on holy ground is a common religious rule: special slippers provided for worshippers at a mosque**

The 19th century scholars could not understand taboo because they worked within the separate compartments of their own taboo system. For them religion, magic, hygiene and medicine were as distinct as civilized and primitive; the problem of taboo for them was only a problem about native thought. But put in that form it was insoluble. We approach it nowadays as a problem in human learning.

First, discard the idea that we have anything like a true, complete view of the world. Between what the scientists know and what we make of their knowledge there is a synthesis which is our own rough and ready approximation of rules about how we need to behave in the physical world. Second, discard the idea that there can ever be a final and correct world view. A gain in knowledge in one direction does not guarantee there will be no loss or distortion in another; the fullness of reality will always evade our comprehension. The reasons for this will become clear. Learning is a filtering and organizing process. Faced with the same events, two people will not

necessarily register two identical patterns, and faced with a similar environment, two cultures will construe two different sets of natural constraints and regular sequences. Understanding is largely a classifying job in which the classifying human mind is much freer than it supposes itself to be. The events to be understood are unconsciously trimmed and filtered to fit the classifications being used. In this sense every culture constructs its own universe. It attributes to its own world a set of powers to be harnessed and dangers to be avoided. Each primitive culture, because of its isolation, has a unique world view. Modern industrial nations, because and insofar as they share a common experience, share the same rules about the powers and dangers aroused. This is a valid difference between 'Us' and 'Them', their primitive taboos and ours.

For all humans, primitive or not, the universe is a system of imputed rules. Using our own distinctions, we can distinguish firstly, physical Nature, inorganic (including rocks, stars, rivers) and organic (vegetable and animal bodies, with rules governing their growth, lifespan and death); secondly, human behaviour; thirdly, the interaction between these two groups; fourthly, other intelligent beings whether incorporeal like gods, devils and ghosts or mixtures of human and divine or human and animal; and lastly, the interaction between this fourth group and the rest.

The use of the word supernatural has been avoided. Even a small amount of reading in anthropology shows how very local and peculiar to our own civilization is the distinction between natural and supernatural. The same applies even to such a classification as the one just given. The fact that it is our own local classification is not important for this argument as the present object is to make clear how taboos should be understood. Taboos are rules about our behaviour which restrict the human uses of things and people. Some of the taboos are said to avoid punishment or vengeance from gods, ghosts and other spirits. Some of them are supposed to produce automatically their dreaded effects. Crop failures, sickness, hunting accidents, famine, drought, epidemic (events in the physical realm), they may all result from breach of taboos.

The Seat of Mana

Taboos can have the effect of expressing political ideas. For example, the idea of the state as a hierarchy of which the chief is the undisputed head and his officials higher than the ordinary populace easily lends itself to taboo behaviour. Gradings of power in the political body tend to be expressed as gradings of freedom to approach the physical body of the person at the top of the system. As Franz Steiner says, in *Taboo* (1956): '. . . in Polynesian belief the parts of the body formed a fixed hierarchy which had some analogy with the rank system of society . . . now the backbone was the most important part of the body, and the limbs that could be regarded as continuations of the backbone derived importance from it. Above the body was, of course, the head, and it was the seat of mana. When we say this, we must realize that by "mana" are meant both the soul aspect, the life force, and a man's ritual status. This grading of the limbs concerned people of all ranks and both sexes. It could, for example, be so important to avoid stepping over people's heads that the very architecture was involved: the arrangements of the sleeping rooms show such an adaptation in the Marquesas. The commoner's back or head is thus not without its importance in certain contexts. But the real significance of this grading seems to have been in the possibilities it provided for cumulative effects in association with the rank system. The head of a chief was the most concentrated mana object of Polynesian society, and was hedged around with the most terrifying taboos which operated when things were to enter the head or when the head was being diminished; in other words when the chief ate or had his hair cut . . . the hands of some great chiefs were so dangerous that they could not be put close to the head.' Since the Polynesian political system was very competitive and chiefs had their ups and downs, great triumphs or total failures, the system of taboo was a kind of public vote of confidence and register of current distributions of power. This is important to correct our tendency to think of taboo as a rigidly fixed system of respect.

We will never understand a taboo system unless we understand the kind of interaction between the different spheres of existence which is assumed in it. Any child growing up learns the different spheres and interactions between them simultaneously. When the anthropologist arrives on the scene, he finds the system of knowledge a going concern. It is difficult for him to observe the changes being made, so he gets the wrong impression that a given set of taboos is something hard-and-fast handed down the generations.

In fact, the classifying process is always active and changing. New classifications are being pushed by some and rejected by others. No political innovation takes place without some basic reclassification. To take a currently live issue, in a stratified society, if it is taboo for lower classes or Negroes to sit down at table or to join sporting events with upper classes or whites, those who assert the rule can make it stronger if they find a basis in Nature to support the behaviour they regard as right. If women in Tahiti are forbidden to eat with men, or in Europe to enter certain male occupations, some ultimate justification for the rule needs to be found. Usually it is traced back to their physical nature. Women are said to be constitutionally feeble, nervous or flighty; Negroes to smell, lower classes to be hereditarily less intelligent.

Rules of the Game

Perhaps the easiest approach is to try to imagine what social life would be like without any classification. It would be like playing a game without any rules; no one would know which way to run, who is on his side or against him. There would be no game. It is no exaggeration to describe social life as the process of building classification systems. Everyone is trying to make sense of what is happening. He is trying to make sense of his own behaviour, past and present, so as to capture and hold some sense of identity. He is trying to hold other people to their promises and ensure some kind of regular future. He is explaining continually, to himself and to everyone else. In the process of explaining, classifications are developed and more and more meanings successfully added to them, as other people are persuaded to interpret events in the same way. Gradually even the points of the compass get loaded with social meanings. For example, the west room in an Irish farmer's house used to be the room where the old couple retired to, when the eldest son married and brought his wife to the farm. West meant retirement as well as sundown. In the Buddhist religion, east is the high status point; Buddha's statue is on a shelf on the east wall of the east room; the husband always sleeps to the east of his wife. So east means male and social superior. Up and down, right and left, sun and moon, hot and cold, all the physical antitheses are able to carry meanings from social life, and in a rich and steady culture there is a steady core of such agreed classifications. Anyone who is prepared to support the social system finds himself impelled to uphold the classification system which gets meaning from it. Anyone who wants to challenge the social system finds himself up against a set of manifold classifications which will have to be rethought. This is why breach of taboo arouses such strong feeling. It is not because the minor classification is threatened, but because the whole social system (in which a great investment has been made) looks like tottering, if someone can get away with challenging a taboo.

Classification involves definition; definition involves reducing ambiguity; ambiguity arises in several ways and it is wrong to think that it can ever be excluded. To take the classification of animal species, they can be classified according to their obvious features, and according to the habitat they live in, and according to how they behave. This gives three ways of classifying animals which could each place the same beasts in different classes. Classed by behaviour, using walking, swimming or flying as basic types, penguins would be nearer to fish; classed by bone structure and egg laying, penguins would count more clearly as birds than would flying fish, which would be birds in the other classification. Animal life is much more untidy and difficult to fit into a regular system of classification than at first appears. Human social life is even more untidy. Girls behave like boys, there are adults who refuse to grow up, every year a few are born whose physical make-up is not clearly male or female. The rules of marriage and inheritance require clear-cut categories but always there will be some cases which do not fit the regularities of the system. For human classifications are always too crude for reality. A system of taboos covers up this weakness of the classification system. It points in advance to defects and insists that no one shall give recognition to the inconvenient facts or behave in such a way as to undermine the acceptability and clarity of the system as a whole. It stops awkward questions and prevents awkward developments.

Sometimes the taboo ban appears in ways that seem a long way from their point of origin. For example, among the Lele tribe, in the Kasai district of the Congo, it was taboo to bring fishing equipment direct into the village from the streams or lakes where it had been in use. All round the village fishing traps and baskets would be hung in trees overnight. Ask the Lele why they did this and they replied that coughs and disease would enter the village if the fishing things were not left out one night. No other answer could be got from them except elaboration of the danger and how sorcerers could enter the village if this barrier were not kept up. But another kind of answer lay in the mass of other rules and regulations which separated the village and its human social life from the forest and streams and animal life. This was the basic classification at stake; one which never needed to be explained because it was too fundamental to mention.

Injecting Order into Life

The novelist William Burroughs describes the final experiences of disgust and depression of some forms of drug addiction. What he calls the 'Naked Lunch' is the point where all illusions are stripped away and every thing is seen as it really is. When everyone can see what is on everyone's fork, nothing is classed as edible. Meat can be animal or human flesh, caterpillars, worms or bugs; soup is equally urine, lentils, scotch broth or excreta; other people are neither friends nor enemies, nor is oneself different from other people since neither has any very clear definition. Identities and classifications are merged into a seething, shapeless experience. This is the potential disorder of the mind which taboo breaks up into classes and rules and so judges some activities as right and proper and others as horrifying.

Keystone

In the West women and 'dirt' have long been the subjects of powerful taboos *Above* Suffragettes campaigning for votes for women *Below* The London Stock Exchange used to be barred to women *Right* Marcel Duchamp's *The Fountain* (1917): sent to a New York art exhibition, this urinal was greeted with a mixture of outrage and delighted shock

This kind of rationality is the justification for the taboos which we ourselves observe when we separate the lavatory from the living room and the bed from the kitchen, injecting order into the house. But the order is not arbitrary; it derives from social categories. When a set of social distinctions weakens, the taboos that expressed it weaken too. For this reason sex taboos used to be sacred in England but are no longer so strong. It seems ridiculous that women should not be allowed in some clubs or professions, whereas not so long ago it seemed obviously right. The same for the sense of privacy, the same for hierarchy. The less we ourselves are forced to adopt unthinking taboo attitudes to breaches of these boundaries, the easier it becomes to look dispassionately at the taboos of other societies and find plenty of meaning in them.

In some tribal societies it is thought that the shedding of blood will cause droughts and other environmental disasters. Elsewhere any contact with death is dangerously polluting, and burials are followed by elaborate washing and fumigation. In other places they fear neither homicide nor death

Keystone

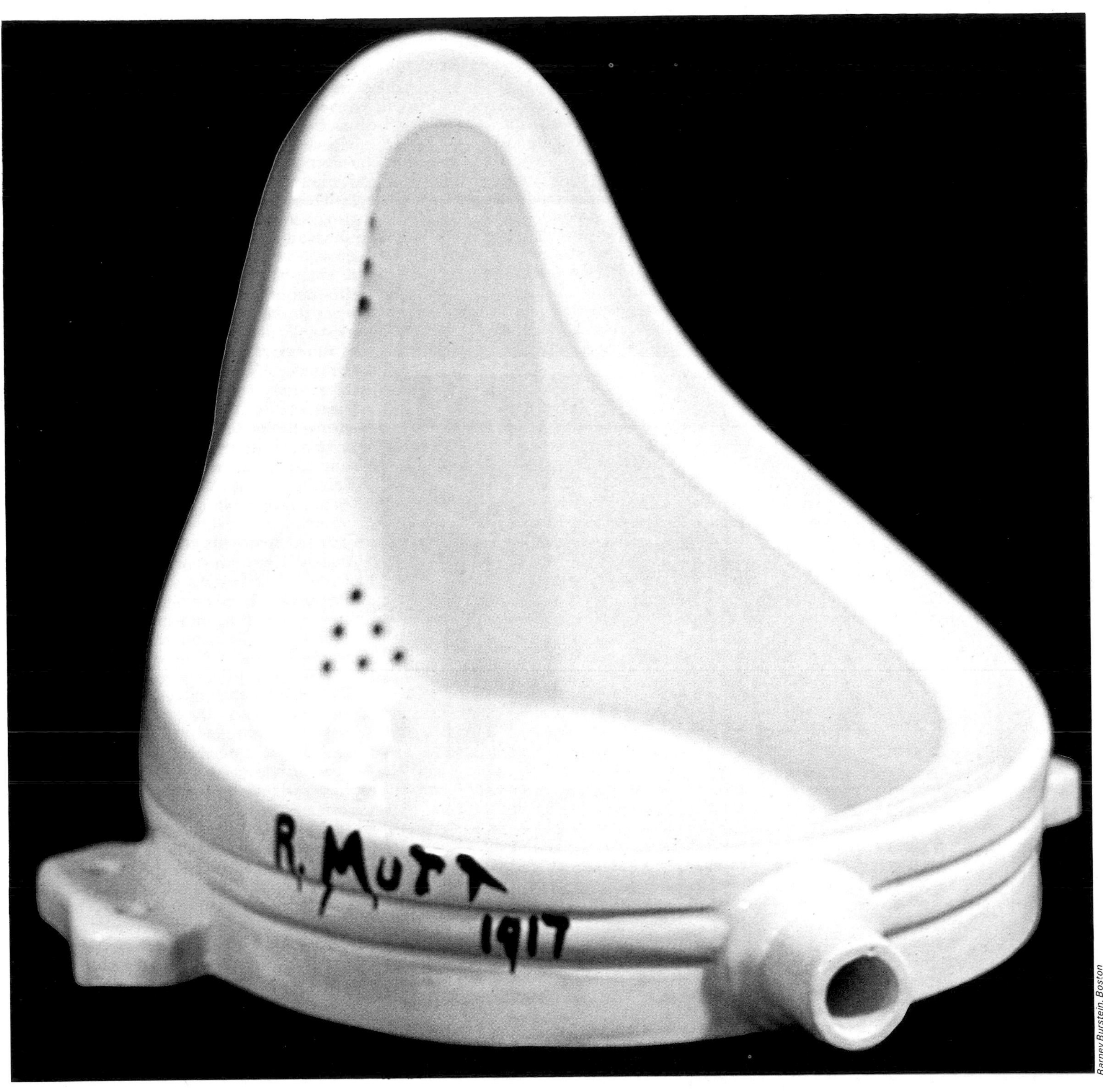

Barney Burstein, Boston

pollution but menstrual blood is thought to be very dangerous to touch (see MENSTRUATION). And in other places again, adultery is liable to cause illness. Some people are thickly beset with taboos so that everything they do is charged with social symbolism. Others observe only one or two rules. Those who are most taboo-minded have the most complex set of social boundaries to preserve. Hence their investment of so much energy into the control of behaviour.

A taboo system upholds a cultural system and a culture is a pattern of values and norms; social life is impossible without such a pattern. This is the dilemma of individual freedom. Ideally we would like to feel free to make every choice from scratch and judge each case on its merits. Such a freedom would slow us down, for every choice would have to be consciously deliberated. On the one hand, education tries to equip a person with means for exercising private judgement, and on the other hand, the techniques of education provide a kind of mechanical decision-making, along well-oiled grooves. They teach strong reactions of anxiety about anything which threatens to go off the track. As education transmits culture, taboos and all, it is a kind of brain-washing. It only allows a certain way of seeing reality and so limits the scope for private judgement. Without the taboos, which turn basic classifications into automatic psychological reflexes, no thinking could be effective, because if every system of classification was up for revision at every moment, there would be no stability of thought. Hence there would be no scope for experience to accumulate into knowledge. Taboos bar the way for the mind to visualize reality differently. But the barriers they set up are not arbitrary, for taboos flow from social boundaries and support the social structure. This accounts for their seeming irrational to the outsider and beyond challenge to the person living in the society.

(See also FOOD AND DRINK; MANA; MAORI; POLYNESIA.)

MARY DOUGLAS

FURTHER READING: Mary Douglas, *Purity and Danger* (Routledge & Kegan Paul, 1966); Franz Steiner, *Taboo* (Penguin, 1967 reprint).

translated the words to the woman, who was thunderstruck, but nevertheless cured.

This anecdote illustrates one aspect of the use and effect of talismans. The wearer's thoughts are constantly turning towards the talismanic object and picturing its purpose or quality. If it has been impregnated by the act of a powerful will, when one who has faith concentrates his thought upon the talisman, he draws from it a strong suggestion which his own will-power reinforces. Even where there is no 'magnetic charge', as apparently in the case of the roll of parchment, the wearer's belief quickly builds up a charge which is effective at subconscious levels.

A talisman kept by a Scottish family, the Lee Penny of the Lockharts which is said to have originated with the Moors in Spain in the 14th century, has a long record of healings by water in which it was dipped. Sir Simon Locard of Lee obtained the talisman as part of the ransom of an emir whom he took prisoner in Spain. The emir's mother explained the powers and method of using the penny, which was a silver groat with a dark red triangular stone set in the middle. It could stop bleeding, cure fever, and especially cure animal diseases by means of the water in which it was dipped three times and then swirled round. The last record of its successful use was before the First World War when one of Sir Simon Lockhart's guests accidentally sustained a deep cut in his hand which bled obstinately. Sir Simon 'magnetized' a basin of water with the penny, and the guest soaked his bandaged hand in it. The bleeding stopped, and the cut healed rapidly.

As J. G. Lockhart, who has written a full record of this famous healing stone, says: 'It might be observed that the Lee Penny appears to have been at least as successful in dealing with the complaints of its time as in a later day the Ministry of Agriculture has been in dealing with Foot and Mouth Disease. The Penny was at any rate reputed to cure where the Ministry can only kill.' It was the Lee Penny, incidentally, which inspired one title of Sir Walter Scott's novel, *The Talisman*.

How to Make a Talisman

An old work, Sepharial's *Book of Charms and Talismans* is still widely read for its delightful blend of Hebrew-inscribed medieval cabalistic diagrams and Victorian descriptions of their usefulness. Consider, for example, what the 'Talisman for Travelling on Land or Sea,' engraved on a Monday in silver, can do: 'Train drivers and guards should certainly wear it, and signalmen too. All those who hold any position on board ship from Commodores and Captains down to waiters and stokers should wear it as it will assist from the safety standpoint, will help to prevent seasickness and will cause the ordinary work to seem less arduous.'

Ancient Egyptian amulet, c 1250 BC, showing the head of the popular god Bes, a squat, dwarfish, cheerfully grinning deity, who presided over fun and music, and helped women in childbirth: numerous amulets depicting him have been found

C. M. Dixon

In making a talisman, your will, and to a secondary degree your personal emanation, can impregnate a suitable chosen piece of material with lasting power. You can set up in it a 'field' or charge of a particular type of force. But the material to receive this should be new or virgin, although used material can be cleaned and purified.

The type of material will affect the permanency of the result. Parchment is more enduring than paper and has other advantages; the nobler metals such as platinum, gold, silver, and even nickel, are less absorptive of gross vibrations; while gem stones, containing the most highly developed mineral life, can sing the same vibrational song over thousands of years. Sensitives will tell that this is so in the case of many of the Egyptian symbolic jewels and the inscribed gnostic gems used in initiation ceremonies in the past. The serpent-entwined rod of the caduceus was charged with power and when laid along the spine of the candidate in the Mysteries, produced a stirring of power and intuition in him.

On the other hand, for a temporary purpose, you can make an effective talisman for a friend from a short length of new cord. Holding it, you make a loose knot, and then concentrate with all the intensity you possess on the quality you are to give. When you feel supremely charged, picture that charge pouring down your arms and concentrating in the knot as you pull it tight with a fierce jerk. Make seven knots like this and you have your talisman.

Supposing you wish to give a ring or jewel for a talismanic purpose, the technique is to visualize a sheet of tense etheric matter between the curved forefinger and thumb of your left hand and, holding the object in your right hand, pass it through the web several times with the intent that all past 'magnetism' be combed out. The object can then be made potent by a process of tension and discharge into it, somewhat similar to the knotting procedure just described. All authorities agree that many types of talisman are better enclosed in silk, and not exposed to the gaze of the inquisitive.

Although the human will is the most powerful element in its creation, it is usual to take into account the best possible astrological conditions in deciding the time. It is unwise, say the astrologers, to wear the birthstone traditional for your sign if in your nativity map the sun has serious adverse aspects; so you require to know your personal horoscope. Very few occultists nowadays would care, however, to go through the elaborate ceremonial with dress, colours, and invocations at exactly appropriate times, feeling that they mainly serve as psychological props and aids to concentration.

C. NELSON STEWART

FURTHER READING: E. Clodd, *Magic in Names* (Gale, 1968 reprint); W. B. Crow, *Precious Stones* (Weiser, 1980); J. G. Lockhart, *Curses, Lucks and Talismans* (Gale, 1971); A. E. Powell, *The Etheric Double* (Theosophical Publishing House, 1925); W. G. O. Sepharial, *Book of Charms and Talismans* (Wehman, 1965).

Sven Gahlin

In tantric philosophy the interplay of two basic forces, Shiva and Shakti, male and female, underlies the entire universe: the female principle is the dominant one and the male the subordinate, for 'Shiva without Shakti is a corpse'
Previous page **Copies of statues from the temple of Konarak, c 1000 AD, showing the male and female principles embraced**
Left **and** ***right*** **18th century pictures of Kali, a personification of the elements of terror and dread in Shakti, dancing on and dominating her male partner, Shiva**

Believing that the generative organs are instruments of a supreme magical operation, the tantrics seek salvation through sex, but in their highly disciplined rites sensual pleasure is incidental

UNTIL THE END of the last century comparatively little was known in Europe about Tantrism, although it is one of the most extraordinary cults of the East. Today in one form or another it plays an essential role in certain occult societies, both in Europe and America. It is in a sexual context that this philosophy is usually considered because its treatment of sex is so remarkable, but Tantrism touches on a great deal more than sexual matters.

The name comes from *Tantra*, a general term used for the texts in which this system is expounded, as a rule in the course of a dialogue between the Hindu god Shiva and his consort Shakti (see SHIVA). Tantrism is practised with local variations in India, Nepal, Bhutan and Sikkim, and before the Chinese occupation it formed part of certain lamaist sects of Tibet. Its philosophy is as complex as any that can be found in the orthodox religions of these countries, and some of it reaches heights of subtlety and finesse to match anything in the more traditional theologies. But there are critics who maintain that it bears the same relationship to orthodox Hinduism and Buddhism that the Black Mass bears to Christianity. Though an outgrowth of Hinduism it is opposed to the *Vedas*, the sacred writings that are the fountainhead of all Hindu orthodoxy; and the Buddhist frowns upon most of its teachings and practices, which to the puritan border on the scandalous.

Tantrics, the followers of Tantrism, claim that theirs is perhaps the oldest religion in India. Yoga (see YOGA), now regarded as one of the six orthodox systems of Aryan Hindu philosophy, is in their view basically tantric. A figure in a typical squatting posture, and a priest gazing at the tip of his nose, which both suggest yogic breathing and meditative techniques, have been found impressed in seals of the Indus Valley civilization (c 2000 BC), which preceded the arrival of the Aryans in India by more than 1000 years.

This priority can, of course, be disputed, but the tantrics' claim to uniqueness admits of little doubt. Theirs is a special cult; its teachings confer personal and social emancipation; it liberates the follower from the bondage of all moral restraints. The tantrics regard themselves as the elect, and all those outside the sect as *pashu*, or the animal herd.

Most tantric writings are traceable to a period after the 10th century AD. Many of the earlier manuscripts were destroyed by Hindu zealots, and the bulk of the remainder by a succession of invaders who conquered India, and to whom the doctrines appeared unworthy of perpetuation or remembrance. The monasteries where they were taught were razed to the ground, the libraries burned, and the monks slain. The nucleus of the teaching was thereafter preserved with great secrecy.

According to tantric philosophy the whole universe is built up of and pervaded by two basic forces which are in intimate and intricate union. These forces, named Shiva and Shakti, are personified as male and female deities. Of this divine pair, Shiva is the subordinate one, for it is the Female Principle that ultimately underlies all manifestation, and everything, including Shiva himself, is contained within the Female Principle. There is a tantric saying, 'Shiva without Shakti is a corpse.'

So important is the Shakti concept in this philosophy that Tantrism is often known by the alternative title of Shaktism, the Tantras spoken of as the Shakta writings, and tantric cults often called the Shakta cults. Among the various reasons advanced by tantrics as the basis for their claim to

Women are treated on terms of complete equality with men, and in many of the rites are assigned superior status

superiority over orthodox Hinduism is the high place assigned to women. The latter are treated on terms of complete equality with men, and in many of their rites are assigned an even superior status, as living embodiments of Shakti, the mother goddess.

The main subjects dealt with in the Tantras include the creation of the world, and its final dissolution; the various gods and goddesses and the worship appropriate to their status and powers; physical culture; mental and spiritual discipline; and the rites by which magical powers can be acquired to enable one to control oneself, control others, the forces of Nature, and, on the highest plane, even the gods themselves. This emphasis on magic has brought Tantrism into further disrepute, and the term 'tantric' retains its overtones of black magic in India to this day.

Indeed, there is hardly an occult procedure that is not dealt with in Tantrism. Some of its rituals are reminiscent of the forms of ceremonial magic described in the Western grimoires. Candles, incense, bells, magical wands, spells, magic circles, bodily postures, occult gestures, symbolical designs, words of power, are as much part of the tantric's paraphernalia as of the Western magician's. Much of the ritualism has in fact been embodied into their own traditions by Western magicians who have been largely influenced, especially in rites of sex mysticism and sex magic, by what they have found in tantric manuals or learned from tantric teachers.

Long periods of preparation and training in techniques of highly specialized physical culture are a pre-requisite to tantric progress. In particular, great emphasis is laid on *pranayama* or respiratory exercises (see BREATH); on heliotherapy or invigorating the body by adoration of the sun and exposure of the body to the sun; on the control of certain autonomic functions, that is, of those physiological processes not under the direction of the conscious mind, such as body temperature, pulse rates, and the reflexes that trigger ejaculation; on methods of superconcentration that bring all bodily functions under the control of the will; and on very subtle processes of internal alchemy. Certain exercises are motionless stances with the limbs fixed in prescribed symbolic attitudes during which the internal exercises are carried out. Running parallel with these

Sven Gahlin

Victoria and Albert Museum

The terrifying aspects of Shiva and Shakti are the subject of tantric meditation in graveyards during rites of contact with corpses
Left **Lamaist temple banner from Tibet, 18th century, showing the goddess of terror surrounded by deities and demons**
Right **Mandala of Shiva in his awe-inspiring aspect as Bhairava (from *bhairav*, 'terror'): Bhairava was said to have been born from a drop of Shiva's blood and became the personification of his rage and hatred**

on the floor, this symbol being taken to signify the presence of the goddess. Then all the members partake of a ceremonial meal consisting of wine, flesh, fish, and bread, followed by a rite of sexual intercourse. These five items have been the subject of much philosophical speculation; they are said to represent certain fundamental categories and are equated either with the elements or with the interior faculties of the body. The wine symbolizes fire and the subtle draught of immortality that the tantric must learn to distil and drink; the flesh symbolizes air and the bodily functions that must be brought under control; fish stands for water and the techniques of sexual occultism; the bread is the earth, or the natural environment which must be understood and controlled. *Maithuna* or sexual intercourse symbolizes ether, the quintessence of all the elements, and is the final goal of all tantric endeavour, for through it one apprehends the ultimate reality. In this context the esoteric meaning of maithuna must be clearly understood. The sex act in its normal, gross form may occasionally bring a fleeting revelation of eternal truth, but that would be rare, for the smoke of passion clouds the mind. Sex as a sacred ritual, unclouded by passion can, on the other hand, help one to apprehend the ultimate Unity. The genuine rite can reveal Being, expand consciousness, confer bliss. The way through *bhukti* (pleasure) can lead one to *mukti* (redemption). Sex, in other words, can be a way of salvation. And this profoundly mystical belief is the tantric secret.

The gods have ordained that the evolution and purification of man's soul can only be achieved by living in an earthly incarnation and experiencing life on the physical plane. So it is the destiny of the initiate to utilize the sex organs for the purpose of discovering the ultimate principles of the universe. Union of male and female brings about the union of man and God. In the religious art of many Indian sects the procreative organs are stylized in the form of the lingam (phallus) and yoni. The lingam being the symbol of transcendent life is regarded as worthy of adoration, and anointed, garlanded and given homage. The yoni, symbolizing regeneration, is drawn on the ground in the form of mandalas (see MANDALA), often in composite designs of

Sven Gahlin

three or nine yonis; sometimes little vessels representing the lingam and yoni in union are used as lamps to keep the symbol of the divine encounter ever before the eyes of the worshipper.

Woman, the Opposite

The human organs that perform the divine rite of maithuna receive veneration for special reasons. In tantric theory the seat of pleasure during the sex act resides not in the active members but in the heart, so the members do not need to be venerated for the pleasure they are erroneously thought to give. The apparent purpose of food is the satisfaction of one's appetite, whereas only after the food has passed from plate to palate and the taste buds have been satisfied, does the actual process of nourishment take place. Only the pashu, or animal, thinks of sex in terms of pleasure or procreation. The gross product of the sex apparatus results in children, but such procreation is not a human prerogative. All animals procreate; in tantric belief they derive greater pleasure from the act than men; they produce more abundantly, and procreation is therefore rightly for the pashu. The human sex organs are instruments of a supreme magical operation of which no animal can possibly be aware. They help the participant of the sex rite to transcend the physical, to transcend the mental, and rise to a psychic and spiritual state. Sex, like every other blessing can be debased and become a mere lustful interlude in which the worst elements of human animality are given full play, and the erotic components of smell, sight, touch, taste and hearing are directed towards a purely sensual gratification. But to the tantric pleasure plays only an incidental part in the process.

Woman provides an element that nothing else can give a man, for she represents the Opposite, the contrasting and vitalizing component that brings the vision of the goddess. Again, only the pashu thinks of the female in terms of intercourse with her. There is no room in Tantrism for the man who seeks out women for their beauty, youth, status, wealth, pleasure or progeny. The unique quality about a woman is her sex, and it is imperative that one's motivation should be moved from all considerations of personal desire to the pure fact of experiencing sexual union.

The further a woman is removed from all deceptive allures the better, for then the power of the female can be brought into operation in a pure unadulterated state, transcending all considerations at the physiological or social level. To the adept it makes no difference whether his sexual partner is a Draupadi (a voluptuous heroine of the *Mahabharata*) or a dombi (a low-caste untouchable woman). Beauty is a snare and an impediment, and in order to avoid its attraction it is necessary to overcome the obstacles of conventional revulsion. To avoid all possibility of desire entering into the rite, the true adept often insists that his partner be an old or ugly woman.

In the tantric circle worship it therefore becomes important that no claim should be made on any partner, and that no personal preferences should be allowed to decide the selection. Various means are used to ensure that the partners should pair not by choice but by chance. One method is for each woman on entering the sanctuary to deposit her bodice in a box, and at the end of the preparatory ceremonies for each man to pick one and take as his partner for the occasion the woman to whom it belongs, be that woman his wife, another's wife, his daughter, sister or even mother. This last requirement is explained away by some tantrics as symbolizing certain other mysteries.

Each stage of the tantric exercise demands some form of personal discipline. The asceticism of the unenlightened person involves resisting, conquering and killing physical desire. This latter does not dam the turbulent stream of sex, but only muddies it. The tantric practises *tapas*, which means both 'heat' and 'asceticism', and in tapas sexual desire is not obliterated but vitalized and used. It is a means whereby sexual energy is brought to a controlled intensity and then re-absorbed into the system. In one curious rite the tantric undertakes to serve the female like a domestic, for three months. He sleeps in the same room with her, but on the floor, while she sleeps on the bed. Later he sleeps in the same bed, but at her feet; then beside her, but clothed; then they lie together nude in each other's arms. But at no time during this cycle of 'closed intercourse' does he have sex with her. He builds up an inner tension, deliberately controlled by long self-discipline and complex yogic techniques so that his system becomes a reservoir of power and he is ready for the very difficult sex procedures that follow. One tantric text says, 'The man who knows the fiery form of Shiva procreates himself anew at every intercourse. His body glows, his mind is crystal clear, his spirit in harmony with heaven'.

(See also BUDDHISM; SEX.)

BENJAMIN WALKER

FURTHER READING: Agehananda Bharati, *The Tantric Tradition* (Greenwood, 1977); S. B. Dasgupta, *An Introduction to Tantrik Buddhism* (Calcutta Univ. Press, 1950); Benjamin Walker, *Hindu World,* 2 vols. (Praeger, 1968) and *Sex and the Supernatural* (Macdonald, London, 1970).

Typical of the many paradoxes contained in this ancient philosophy is the fact that 'Tao' means the 'Way', yet it does not prescribe a particular path; Tao is simply 'the uncomplicated essence of what is right'

TAOISM

ONE OF THE THREE great religions of China, Taoism, like the other two, Confucianism and Buddhism, has a traditional founder. He is Lao Tze, born in 604 BC in a hamlet in Honan province. During his long life he held a number of public offices and was for a time the curator of the royal library in Loyang. Confucius, more than half a century his junior, visited him and was overawed by his presence and his phenomenal learning. After the interview Confucius told his disciples, 'I understand how birds move through the skies, how fish swim in water, how animals run over the hills. Things that fly can be snared; things that swim can be caught in nets; things that run can be trapped. But what can one do with a dragon that soars into the heavens, trampling on the clouds and riding the storms!'

At an advanced age Lao Tze retired from government service and travelled westward on buffalo-back to the borders of the barbarian lands somewhere in the region of the Gobi Desert. At the boundary warden's earnest plea for a record of his teachings, the sage paused long enough to inscribe a mere 5000 characters on bamboo parchment. Leaving this with the official he resumed his journey to an unknown destination, and was seen no more.

This small book, the *Tao Te Ching*, is one of the world's great religious classics; zealous Taoists claim that it enshrines the wisdom of the universe. As a result of speculation and commentary on its verses a vast library of Taoist scriptures grew around it. By the 1st century AD it comprised about 60 volumes; by the 7th century the number had increased to 4500. By that time, too, Lao Tze was worshipped as a god; temples were raised in his honour, and his original slender masterpiece was engraved on stone at the capital of every Chinese state.

The teachings of the *Tao Te Ching* are amongst the strangest ever propounded. They are paradoxical, inverse, passive, irrational. Although the term Tao means course or way, Taoism does not point to any particular way and there is no fixed track to be followed. Tao has reality but no form. Like the deep and obscure highways of the sea the waters close behind the moving ship and leave no trace of its passing. Little can be taught: 'The Tao that can be put into words is not the eternal Tao.' It opposes complexity, sophistication, 'cleverness', for these corrupt both mind and spirit.

This idea is well expressed in a famous Chinese story about the clever young fellow who saw a peasant watering his fields by the tedious process of carrying one pitcher at a time from the well, and told him about a mechanical contrivance that would enable him to get his water straight from well to furrow in a fraction of the time. 'I know of the contrivance,' said the old one, 'but I also know that those who use cunning contrivances soon begin to practise cunning ways. Practising cunning ways their hearts become cunning. Those with cunning hearts are incapable of being pure in their thoughts. Those with corrupted thoughts have restless and disturbed spirits. And those who are troubled in spirit are not fit vehicles for the Tao.'

Yielding Is Life

Tao is the uncomplicated essence of what is right. It overflows into everything that is in harmony with it. It is easy, but people still prefer the difficult and intricate little paths, straining to get 'there', when the way 'there' is best found by not making 'there' your goal. Ambition, fretful desire, thirst for fame, striving to be first, are the real hindrances along the way. Take long strides and your progress is unsure. On tiptoe you are unsteady. Grab and it eludes you. Action and achievement are limitations. The Tao has no shape but like an uncarved block of wood it holds within itself an infinity of shapes. Give it shape and it

The three great religions of China are Taoism, Confucianism and Buddhism: the founder of Taoism was Lao Tze, and Confucius, who visited him, was overawed by his presence and his learning *Below* The meeting of Confucius and Lao Tze *Right* Lao Tze, Buddha and Confucius, shown tasting saké on a 19th century Japanese sword guard

Sotheby's/Michael Holford

becomes fulfilled, formalized and limited.

The simple is better than the sophisticated. In the words of the *Tao Te Ching*: 'Relish unflavoured things'. Staying at home is better than wandering: 'The Tao can be known without leaving the house. The further one travels the less one knows.' Silence is better than speech: 'He who knows does not speak; he who speaks does not know.' Beware the distraction of the senses: 'The eyes of a man blind him; his ears make him deaf.' Cultivate less rather than more: 'Power and learning is adding to oneself more and more. Tao is subtracting day by day.' Submission is better than resistance: 'Rigour is death; yielding is life.' Bureaucracy is remorselessly greedy: 'The more government, the still more government.' Legalism defeats its own purpose: 'As laws increase, crimes increase.'

The *Tao Te Ching* is extremely susceptible to interpretation. When Christian missionaries first discovered the book they were so astonished to find what they thought were resemblances to the teachings of the New Testament, and particularly the Sermon on the Mount, that they called Lao Tze an inspired forerunner of Christ. Some even discovered hints of the doctrine of the Trinity, and found evidence of the Tetragrammaton, the four letters YHVH that make up the name of Jehovah.

Chinese scholars for their part read into the enigmatic verses many strange doctrines, and built up schools of thought and practice on innocuous words and isolated phrases. The expression 'divine man' sparked a search for immortality; 'long life' resulted in the manufacture of elixirs that would enable one to live for centuries; 'taste' inspired a system of dietary observances; 'harmonious infant' laid the foundation for a method of concentration which would create within one's body an embryonic seed that formed the nucleus of another, imperishable body; 'breath retention' started techniques of respiratory mysticism; the 'unknown female' sought the universal life essence in women; 'sex organ' was the beginning of a widespread cult of sexual mysticism.

Taoism actually existed long before Lao Tze, and is sometimes regarded as the primary religion of the Chinese people. One

C. M. Dixon

of its mythical founders was the fabled Yellow Emperor, Huang Ti, who lived about 2600 BC, ten centuries before the Jewish law-giver Moses. In Chinese tradition the Yellow Emperor, like Lao Tze, was reputed to talk at birth. But unlike Lao Tze a great deal of magic was linked with the personal life of the Yellow Emperor, particularly of a sexual kind. Through a combination of the names of these two founders, Taoism is sometimes called the doctrine of Huang Lao, and Taoism in later centuries came to be associated not only with the refined principles of the *Tao Te Ching*, but increasingly with occultism and with the black arts as well.

In the course of time its pantheon came to include ancient deities of sky and mountain, Buddhist gods, deified emperors, legendary and historical personages, a number of 'immortals', spirits of the stars, constellations, moon and sun, and of all things under the sun. There are guardian spirits of wind and cloud, kitchen and sewer, stone and stove, teats and intestines, tongue and teeth, literary works and account books, doors and hinges.

Most Chinese thaumaturgists have claimed kinship with the cult to add distinction to their particular brand of magic, and Taoism evolved an elaborate hierarchy of priest-magicians, both male and female, who were specialists in various branches of Chinese occultism. They communed with the dead, spoke with the ancestors, flew to heaven or hell as the occasion demanded, and cast out demons and invoked celestial spirits. They combined the role of medium, oracle, sorcerer and physician.

The Bandits

Taoism has drawn into its orbit all the floating traditions of Chinese magic and sorcery, adding considerably to the bulk of Chinese superstitions and permeating all branches of Chinese occultism. It absorbed the doctrine of the two basic principles that underlie the universe, Yang the active, male and positive force, and Yin the passive, female and negative force (see CHINA). These contrasting but complementary principles lent themselves to further elaboration along sexual lines. Yang and Yin were said to be found in greater concentration in

The Taoist pantheon came to include a bewildering number and variety of gods and spirits, including deified emperors, real or legendary people, and guardian spirits 'of wind and cloud, kitchen and sewer, stone and stove, literary works and account books . . .' *Left* Hsi Wang Wu, a Taoist deity, walking on the sea: Chinese saucer, 18th century *Right* Bronze mirror of the 3rd century AD, with figures of Taoist gods

C. M. Dixon

the human male and female respectively, but a mutual interchange was beneficial, and this was effected through sexual intercourse in certain special ways, first in normal partnership and later in group orgies, so that the Yang and Yin might be absorbed in greater variety.

Similarly the various forms of Chinese divination, including the highly respected method of the I Ching or Book of Change (see I CHING), were subject to interpretation along Taoist lines. Indigenous schools of medicine and healing, including acupuncture or the curing of bodily ills by pricking the surface of the skin (see ACUPUNCTURE), similarly claimed a Taoist derivation. Astrology or the influence of the heavenly bodies on human affairs; geomancy or the selection of propitious sites for cities, temples, palaces, private dwellings and graves, all developed on lines indicated by Taoist masters on the subject. Alchemy too evolved along Taoist lines. External alchemy concerned itself with the manufacture of elixirs of immortality. Internal alchemy combined breathing with sex techniques in which subtle fluids were manufactured by the body, and were then potentialized and reabsorbed into the system.

Pervading Unity

At the beginning of the present century we find Taoist religious beliefs and practices still carried on by numerous and mostly secret sects. Among these was the society of the 'Pervading-Unity Tao' (*I-kuan Tao*). This sect believed that the One is the root of all things and, as a principle, penetrates through and pervades all existence . . . Followers of the *I-kuan Tao* were much addicted to the use of charms, planchette, the practice of the 'three secrets' of finger signs, and magic phrases and incantations. They also abstained from meat, tobacco and alcohol. They worshipped images of all religions . . .

Werner Eichhorn, in *The Concise Encyclopaedia of Living Faiths*

Finally the *Tao Te Ching* provided the theoretical basis for a number of secret societies, many of which combined banditry, sorcery and the precepts of the *Tao Te Ching* with a shrewd knowledge of military strategy and tactics, and these societies remained the bane of Chinese political and social life for more than 18 centuries. The chiefs of these societies virtually ruled large areas of China, and their priest-magicians boasted dominion over the forces of Nature, and claimed to be able to divert rivers and command the lightning.

In 1912 the newly established Chinese Republic tried to put an end to these outlaw organizations, but made little progress as many in their own ranks were themselves Taoists. But the time of the secret societies had run out. In 1930 the Red Army stormed the strongholds of the most enduring of the great societies, entered the sanctuary in their mountain stronghold in the province of Kiang-Si, and smashed all the jars in which their magicians were said to have imprisoned the winds.

BENJAMIN WALKER

FURTHER READING: L. Giles, *The Sayings of Lao Tzu* (Paragon Books); H. Maspero, *Taoism & Chinese Religion* (Univ. of Massachusetts Pr., 1981); Arthur Waley, *The Way and Its Power* (Grove Press, 1958); Holmes Welch, *The Parting of the Way* (Beacon Press, 1966 reprint).

TARA

'NOW UPON another time it chanced that Eochaid Airem, the king of Tara, arose upon a certain fair day in the time of summer and he ascended the high ground of Tara to behold the plain of Breg: beautiful was the colour of that plain.' As the king looks out over his domains he sees a splendid warrior approaching him, unusual both in his beauty and in the splendour of his weapons: 'And Eochaid held his peace, for he knew that none such had been in Tara on the night before, and the gate that led into the enclosure had not at that hour been thrown open' (Cross and Slover, *Ancient Irish Tales*). The majestic warrior is in fact the god Midir coming to claim his wife Etain who, in her state of rebirth countless years later, is now married to the king of Tara.

This is the Tara of the ancient Irish tales, the seat of the High Kings of Ireland, and the focus of much mythological tradition and ritual practice. Here the supernatural is constantly present, and the tales frequently make the visitation of some god or goddess the introduction to some amorous or adventurous situation associated with the otherworld. In the story of the *Adventures of Art son of Conn*, for example, we learn concerning Conn (who subsequently marries a goddess after the death of his wife) that 'Conn the Hundred-Fighter son of Fedlimid Rechtmar son of Tuathal Rechtmar . . . was once at Tara of the kings, the noble conspicuous dwelling of Ireland, for a period of nine years, and there was nothing lacking to the men of Ireland during the time of this king, for indeed, they used to reap the corn three times in the year.'

According to ancient Irish belief, a good king, one whose conduct was in complete accordance with the moral attitudes of his tribe and whose physical being was entirely unblemished, brought prosperity and peace to the land and to the livestock and to the people; the lord of Tara had to be perfect in these respects or he was deposed by his followers. All these things we learn from the rich literary tradition of medieval Ireland which casts so much light on the darkness of the Iron Age world.

The Screaming Stone

There is, moreover, another source of evidence for 'Tara of the Kings' as it was called, the 'noble conspicuous dwelling'. This is the archeological record. Excavations of the site have provided convincing proof of the veracity of the story-tellers in their descriptions of this powerful royal seat, and have given concrete reasons for the recurrent mythological episodes which characterize references to the place in the early tales.

Tara is situated on a low hill in County Meath, 23 miles from Dublin. The remains consist of various earthworks, and a Neolithic passage grave which was used again in the Bronze Age; this suggests that the Iron Age occupants of the site took over a place which was already hallowed, and applied their own religious traditions to it. The Celts venerated divine ancestors, deities who gave their names to the various tribes, and several of their sanctuary sites can be seen to have had religious associations antecedent to their own occupation. At Tara, then, Celtic traditions were clearly attached to an existing hilltop shrine, which contained a passage grave with later burials in the mound which covered it. Just as the Romans tended to construct their temples on ground already sanctified by the presence of native shrines, thereby winning over and at the same time propitiating the supernatural forces already there (as did the Christians in respect to pagan shrines), so we must expect the innovating Celts to have created their holy places at sites which had been made sacred by centuries of ritual and belief. They would thus both conquer the older forces which were believed to control the territory, and at the same time render them quiescent by continuing to observe religious rites there, but in honour of their own deities. The fact that the patron goddess of the great Assembly of Tara was Tea, who is represented in the tales as having been kept in captivity, and that two other powerful goddesses of the early tradition, Etain and Medb, were also closely associated with Tara, suggests that these may have had an ancestry much earlier than the Celtic Iron Age, and linking them with such deities as the tomb goddesses of the ancient Mediterranean world.

Little is known, comparatively speaking

Tara's Halls

The harp that once through Tara's halls
The soul of music shed,
Now hangs as mute on Tara's walls
As if that soul were fled.
So sleeps the pride of former days,
So glory's thrill is o'er;
And hearts, that once beat high for praise,
Now feel that pulse no more.

Thomas Moore

. . . the exaggerated pretensions of St Columcille had come almost at once into opposition with the established laws of the land, the law which enjoined death as the penalty for homicide at Tara . . . Of precisely such a nature – only with far worse and far more enduring consequences – was the cursing of Tara by St Ruadhan of Lothra. The great palace where, according to general belief, a hundred and thirty-six pagan and six Christian kings had ruled uninterruptedly, the most august spot in all Ireland, where a 'truce of God' had always reigned during the great triennial assemblies, was now to be given up and deserted at the curse of a tonsured monk. The great Assembly or Féis of Tara, which accustomed the people to the idea of a centre of government and a ruling power, could no more be convened, and a thousand associations and memories which hallowed the office of the High-king were snapped in a moment. It was a blow from which the monarchy of Ireland never recovered, a blow which, by putting an end to the great triennial or septennial conventions of the whole Irish race, weakened the prestige of the central ruler, increased the power of the provincial chieftains, segregated the clans of Ireland from one another, and opened a new road for faction and dissension throughout the entire island.

Douglas Hyde *A Literary History of Ireland*

C. M. Dixon

Tara of the Kings, in County Meath, the seat of the High Kings of the Irish and 'the noble conspicuous dwelling of Ireland': a magical stone pillar, the Lia-fail, used in the ceremonies accompanying the enthronement of the High King, was said to scream in the presence of the rightful ruler

of the archeology of this ancient royal seat as yet. There are various features which have been named by antiquarians. The Mound of the Hostages, for example, which has been excavated in recent years, contains the primary passage grave and some 40 Bronze Age burials dating to c 1400 BC. The so-called Royal Enclosure consists of a hilltop enclosure with features which are again suggestive of ritual. It has also been suggested that the Banquet Hall is in fact yet another sacred enclosure of a kind known on the Continent. Other structures associated with the site would also seem to have been of a ritual rather than a domestic character.

Archeology, in conjunction with the vernacular literature, demonstrates that the Celts in general venerated stones of various kinds and that stone pillars in particular were worshipped. At Tara a magical stone pillar, known as the Lia-fail, 'Stone of Fail', was used in the inauguration ceremonies which accompanied the enthronement of the High Kings (see STONES). According to tradition, the stone used to scream when a rightful king was about to be inaugurated. A stone pillar which originally stood near the Mound of the Hostages and today marks an 18th century grave, has been taken to be the Lia-fail; it consists of a pillar of granite some five feet in height. The inauguration and choice of the High Kings was attended by much ritual, and a great bull feast (*tarbfeis*) used to be prepared whereby a seer could envisage in a trance the rightful King of Tara.

ANNE ROSS

FURTHER READING: T. P. Cross and C. H. Slover, *Ancient Irish Tales* (Figgis, Dublin, 1969); E. Evans, *Prehistoric and Early Christian Ireland* (Batsford, 1966); A. Ross, *Pagan Celtic Britain* (Routledge & Kegan Paul, 1967), *Everyday Life of the Pagan Celts* (Batsford, 1970).

TAROT

The strange and beautiful Tarot cards form a system of communication through symbols, showing the relation between God, man and the universe; the symbols act as stimuli to the imagination and it is for each student to interpret them for himself

THE UNINITIATED usually regard the Tarot as a system of fortune telling using a special pack of fancy cards. But this is the lowest, if not a debased, aspect of a method of communication by symbol which has behind it not only antiquity but esoteric knowledge. It may be described as 'the cosmic method in universal creation or emanation, including its purpose and result'. As practised by the Western user, it is generally associated with the Tree of Life of the Cabala (see CABALA) but it has also affinities with the pyramids of Egypt and with Indian theosophical philosophy. 'Like all ancient cosmic symbols which are but the reduction of natural law to the simplicity necessary for human use, the Tarot is of the utmost practical value in all senses.'

The origins of the Tarot are not clearly defined. A. E. Waite concluded that it had no exoteric history before the 14th century and the oldest examples of Tarot cards probably date from about 1390, while occult tradition places their origin at about 1200 AD. It is said that the gypsies are believed to hold the first set of cards and that they alone hold the secret of its meaning.

According to occultists, the system comes first from the East, probably from Chaldea. After the destruction of the seat of learning in Alexandria, the adepts of all countries converged upon Fez in Morocco and made it the pivot of their esoteric science; since they spoke in many tongues, they decided to create a set of common symbols which all could understand and in which their truths could be pictured. 'As a skeleton for their invention the wise men chose the relatively simple system of numbers and letters afforded by the Qubalah' (S. Mayananda, *The Tarot Today*). The Hebrew alphabet consists of 22 letters and these placed upon the 22 Paths of the Tree of Life gave a combination of bases for correspondences (see PATHS). By this system of a pack of cards containing four suits of 14 cards each and 22 trumps unconnected with the suits and called the Major Arcana, ideas could be exchanged without the necessity of either the spoken or the written word.

The four suits are designated Wands, Cups, Swords and Pentacles, symbolizing amongst other things fire, water, air and earth: in each suit are four court cards: the King, the essential Self, 'Spirit', in man; the Queen, the 'Soul' or inner pattern part of a particular human personality; the Knight, representing the special focusing of energies and a personal sense of selfhood; the Page or Esquire, standing for the Body or personal vehicle. These four court cards correspond also to the four letters of the sacred Name of God in Hebrew theology – *Yod, He, Vau, He* (see NAMES). Yod is represented by the Kings of the four suits, and more especially by the suit of Sceptres or Wands, and it stands for the First Principle – the origin of all things. The first He symbolizes substance, in opposition to essence, and this is represented by the four Queens and by the suit of Cups, the form which contains the Life and the Feminine Principle. Vau which indicates Affinity completes the Trinity, and is pictured by the bond of love and the mystery of union exemplified by the four Knights and the suit of Swords. To stop there would indicate Finality. So the fourth court card, that of the Page or Esquire, represents the second He, marking the transition from the metaphysical to the

According to occult tradition, the Tarot pack was invented by adepts and forms a complete symbolic system. Different packs use varying designs and symbols, but there is a rough general similarity. The pack has four suits – Wands, Cups, Swords and Pentacles (*below*) – of 14 cards each, plus 22 extra cards called trumps or Major Arcana

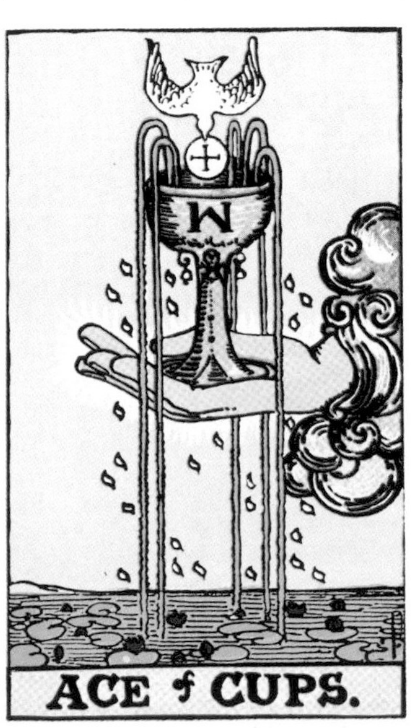

Tarot Production Inc.

O

THE FOOL.

The trumps of the 'Waite' pack, drawn by Pamela Coleman Smith under the direction of A. E. Waite: this is probably the best-known and most often used version of the Tarot pack though the cards, shown on this and the following pages, vary from the traditional designs of older packs in many respects

material world – God in man made manifest. This is the suit of Pentacles or Coins, the symbol of material gain but also the five-pointed star which leads man from the unreal to the real.

The Tarot in its cabalistic form sets out to show the relation between God, Man and the Universe, and amongst other things it is a symbol of incarnation. It is one of those immemorial systems which were destined to convey this abstruse fact to mankind in a form that could be appreciated even by almost submerged awareness. Oswald Wirth says that a symbol is designed precisely to awaken in our consciousness the memory of that which we have already known. In other words, the use of the Tarot evokes the associations which we have already formed in the past. In *Le Symbolisme Hermetique* he states that 'a symbol can always be studied from an infinite number of points of view and each thinker has the right to discover in the symbol a new meaning corresponding to the logic of his own conception. Symbols are intended to arouse a thought by means of suggestion and thus cause the truth which lies hidden in our consciousness to reveal itself.'

P. D. Ouspensky (see OUSPENSKY) postulates that only a symbol can deliver man from the slavery of words and formulas, and allow him to attain to the possibilities of thinking freely: '. . . occult knowledge cannot be transmitted either orally or in writing.

The Tarot in its cabalistic form sets out to show the relation between God, Man and the Universe; amongst other things it is a symbol of incarnation

It can only be acquired by deep meditation.'

Tarota or *Taro-Rota* means the Wheel of the Law and the Law of the Wheel, and is a widespread symbol of universal life; the same idea is found in Western symbology in the phrase 'spinning of the Web'.

Dance of Life

There are various methods of using the Tarot cards; reference has already been made to placing them upon the Tree of Life, they can be paired as opposites or complementaries, or they may be set out in a circle or wheel representing the universe.

There are no standard pictures on the packs of Tarot cards. While the pictures are basically the same the presentation may vary. There is one known as the Marseilles or French pack which is probably the oldest in design and can be found reproduced in many books; generally speaking, the designs are crude and not well drawn. Manly P. Hall produced a pack drawn by Augustus Knapp but this is no longer on the market. Paul Foster Case, founder of the Builders of the Adytum, had a pack drawn by Miss Jessie Burns Parke which was very similar to the one usually referred to as the 'Waite' pack, drawn by Miss Pamela Coleman Smith under the direction of A. E. Waite; this, in turn, is generally held to be based on the Oswald Wirth symbolism, though it has been considered that in certain details Dr Waite expressed his personal ideas of symbolism rather than the traditional esoteric ones. There is no reason why any interested student of the Tarot should not make his own pack, provided that he is prepared to undertake the necessary study to incorporate the correct symbols. Instructions for interpreting the meanings of the cards may be found either in booklets sold with the packs, or in the books on the Tarot written by authorities.

While there is an interpretation for each one of the 14 cards in each suit, either right way up or reversed, the ordinary person is chiefly concerned with the Major Arcana, the trumps, since these are the only cards used in dealing with the Tree of Life or with the system of the Wheel.

There are 21 numbers on the cards, and a zero. This is the attribute of the Fool and its position has been the subject of much discussion. Where does one place O and what is its significance? Taking the cards in numerical order it would seem clear that O should precede 1, yet Papus, one of the best known and most authoritative writers on the Tarot, places it between 20 and 21, and takes it to refer to the Animal Kingdom, that is the Kingdom of Instinct and not of Mind. If it precedes 1 the subsequent cards will fall sensibly upon their paths on the Tree, ending with the card called the Universe on the final path leading to Earth – the Plane of Matter. Israel Regardie says 'O must precede 1. This is the most logical place for it'.

If the method of the Wheel is worked O will be placed in the centre as the hub; the remaining 21 cards will fall naturally into three segments of seven apiece, and when studied their mutual correspondence, either complementary, fulfilling or opposing, will be clear. There is a legend that once upon a time a man made a magical table and placed on it statuettes of the major trumps modelled as small golden figures. By his own great knowledge of the mysteries he was able to set the figures in motion and they wove in and out of the figures of the Dance of Life, so that he could see the pattern of evolution. But it was not given either to that adept or to his disciples to be able to move the 22nd figure – that of O or the Fool; for if the Fool joins in the dance the world is completed and there is an end to all things as we know them.

In this case the Fool represents the mystery of the Divine Love; when that is understood and he takes his place among the dancers there will be no more sorrow and no more misunderstanding, for the former things will have passed away. It will be the Golden Age in reality; we shall see ourselves in proper relation to God and man; we shall

indeed be united with the Highest and therefore there will be nothing left for which to struggle.

The trumps of the Major Arcana, their sequence and their general meaning are:

0. ***The Fool.*** The picture is of a young man, a bundle over his shoulder, a dog at his heels, gaily treading a cliff edge with no regard for where his steps are leading him. To those who have begun to perceive the esoteric meaning of the cards, this carefree attitude is significant of the man who has followed the Divine Law and become as a little child. In German the title of the card is *Der Sille*, which means the Holy or Innocent one.

1. ***The Magician.*** In exoteric packs this card is sometimes labelled 'The Juggler'; in the Marseilles and other French packs it is called *Le Bateleur*, which means 'the holder of a small farm or estate' in Old French; no previous origin of the word is known, but it could be that the card is intended to represent a lesser Sun. The man in the picture has a figure eight shaped device over his head, a lemniscate, the sign of Universal Life. One of his hands points upwards and the other down, while before him lies a table on which are displayed the four suits of the Tarot pack.

2. ***The High Priestess.*** She sits between two pillars in the place of Equilibrium; partially veiled, a book upon her knees, she is typified in the Book of Wisdom and in the mystical poets; she is the feminine aspect, the reflection of God. In Egypt she represents the Isis of Nature whose veil must not be raised by the profane.

3. ***The Empress.*** This shows a fine woman with flowing hair; she wears a crown with 12 points, signifying the diffusion of the First Principle in the same way that the 12 signs of the zodiac are disseminated and yet form a perfect whole. The card signifies the basis of Reality.

4. ***The Emperor.*** He represents the positive or active form of the Empress; he wields a sceptre which has always been taken as an attribute of the progenitor.

5. ***The Pope or Hierophant.*** This is the complementary opposite of the High Priestess, who is the instructress of the initiates to whom she imparts occult knowledge. The Hierophant gives this knowledge to ordinary people in a practical and oral form that they can understand.

6. ***The Lovers.*** This card represents on one hand the dual nature of man: when the child is first conceived its sex is not determined; the potentials of both sexes are carried by every embryo and one sex is finally assumed in the material world. But the lovers also symbolize the most powerful of all the emotions; love properly expressed brings unity with the beloved, so that this dual card is both an analysis and a synthesis.

7. ***The Chariot.*** This portrays the man who has vanquished the elementary forces. It is the final card of the first seven into which the 21 numbered trumps are divided when they become a triad in the Wheel system; on the Tree of Life in the Hebrew version the card corresponds with the Hebrew letter *Zayin*, which signifies Victory in All Worlds.

8. ***Justice.*** This card stands for equilibrium in all worlds and in all forms. Occult science has been taught in word and in deed; the sword and the balance are the reward of a man's acts, whether they be black or white. As a man sows, so shall he

reap. (In the Waite pack, illustrated here, and in several later ones, cards 8 and 11 are transposed.)

9. ***The Hermit.*** This card sometimes pictures an old man and sometimes a young one. If he is old he is thought to be the man aged in years who yet has a young heart; if he is a young man, he is one who has already learned to walk in the right way. He wears the cloak of protection, carries the lamp of wisdom and is supported by the staff of righteousness. His quality is prudence, and some packs will give the card this name rather than that of the Hermit. His significance is silence regarding the Inner Knowledge.

10. ***The Wheel of Fortune or the Wheel of Life.*** This card does not denote anything in the way of chance but is the symbol of the eternal action of time, the continuous rotation of the aeons, the mutable laws each recurring in turn and then resting in Equilibrium.

11. ***Strength.*** This is the strength of the young girl closing the mouth of the lion; above her head is the lemniscate – the sign of spiritual life and virility. Here is the counterpart of the young child in the cockatrice's den; she is Sir Galahad in opposition: 'my strength is as the strength of ten, because my heart is pure'. Galahad the boy knight is as sexless as this maiden.

12. ***The Hanged Man.*** This most curious of all cards has been given different interpretations by different writers but it is generally accepted that it stands for Equilibrated Power. In the Hebrew alphabet the letter *Mem* accompanies this figure on the path of the Tree and is one of the three 'mother letters', standing for water. In all occult matters the element of water signifies a change of plane or of consciousness. This man has come far enough on the road to find absolute submission to the Will Divine.

13. ***Death.*** Death is the culmination of life in the exoteric sense; in the esoteric meaning it is the passing from one stage of progress to the next. Death has been termed the Negative of Realization, the universal link between material and spiritual. Nearly all versions of this card are based upon a skeleton, and include the very ancient phallic symbol of the sickle or curved blade.

14. ***Temperance.*** Here man is individualized. The water of life is being poured out and he has the power to accept or reject it for himself.

15. ***The Devil.*** This is a card which has puzzled many people but if it be looked at carefully it will be seen to represent No 1, the Magician, in reverse. The power is now misused. The right hand, the hand of power, points sometimes downwards and sometimes upwards, and those he has taken in bondage are in chains at his feet. The card is sometimes referred to as Pan, unbridled Nature, and his lighted torch is the symbol of destruction. He is to be feared and to be conquered. To allow him to gain the mastery is to allow Matter to overcome Spirit.

16. ***The Tower Struck by Lightning.*** This card is usually said to be symbolic of the Fall of man; here is the Tower of Babel; man is being hurled into materialism; as he proceeds down the Tree of Life he becomes more man and less God. But it must be noted that in two French versions this card is considered to be a divine happening; one refers to it as 'The Fire of Heaven' and the other as 'The House of God'.

Pat Keene/Mahlig

17. ***The Star.*** This picture represents the Word in action in Nature. The butterfly or ibis symbol is a sign that the spirit is not lost though man may have far to go; the spirit will survive and the Fall is not irreparable.

18. ***The Moon.*** Here again is comfort for the soul in involution. The material world is only a reflection; man can descend no lower, and the Spirit is now immersed in Matter from which it must eventually start to climb again. Yet other writers have other ideas. S. Mayananda says, 'The picture presented by this Trump is a terrible travesty of what should be shown, or rather it is but the negative half. It seems to have been dictated by sorcerers or the Church in whose teaching the "world" is merely an evil condition to escape from to "Heaven".' And an Indian writer, Govinda, says of this card 'the symbolism of the elements moves on many planes'.

19. ***The Sun.*** This picture represents the first of the elemental kingdoms beginning its slow progress by development back to God. Spirit is renewed in a different form; man is freshened for his evolutionary climb and the mineral kingdom is slowly individualizing.

20. ***Judgement.*** Life is progressing a little further up the stairway, for this trump governs the evolutionary development of the vegetable kingdom.

21. ***The Universe.*** Here in this last card the macrocosm and the microcosm have met. Here the Earth of matter is represented in the four quarters – the four Worlds – and here the four animals of the Apocalypse and of the vision of Ezekiel are depicted. It is the reconstruction of the synthesis of all and the figure of the androgyne is lightly veiled; as with the Lovers, sex is undefined. This represents in one form God in man at the foot of the middle pillar of the Tree of Life.

There are almost as many interpretations of the Tarot as there are interpreters, and the meanings attributed to each card vary with the understanding of the student *Above* The Tarot may be used for fortune telling, although occultists generally regard this as the lowest use to which the cards can be put; during a reading the client shuffles and cuts the cards of the Major Arcana (*left*); these are then returned to the reader, who spreads them into a fan (*right*) from which the client selects seven cards which are placed clockwise on the table *Below* The cards of the Major Arcana laid out according to the system of the Wheel; the Fool is placed in the centre as the hub, and the student of the Tarot then meditates upon the significance of the cards, either complementary, fulfilling or opposing

Pat Keene/Mahlig

These are the major trumps of the Tarot pack. Only one suggestion of meaning can be given by any one person in a limited space; and it must be remembered that there are meanings to each trump according to the understanding of each student, and that they are intended to act as stimuli to the imagination. Each and every writer on the Tarot will have something different to say, will develop another aspect; all anyone can do is to suggest an approach. This is a system of universal communication by symbol and therefore it must be sufficiently fluid to allow each man to use it as an expression of his ideas on the Absolute. The more that is read about the Tarot; the more the cards are meditated upon, the greater will be the flow of understanding and the wider the comprehension.

(See also CARDS; WALDENSES.)

CHRISTINE HARTLEY

FURTHER READING: P. F. Case, *The Tarot* (Macoy, 1977); Gareth Knight, *Practical Guide to Quabalistic Symbolism* (Weiser); R. Cavendish, *The Tarot* (Harper & Row, 1975); Papus, *Tarot of the Bohemians* (Weiser); A. E. Waite, *The Holy Kabbalah*; *The Pictorial Key to the Tarot* (Citadel).

John Moss

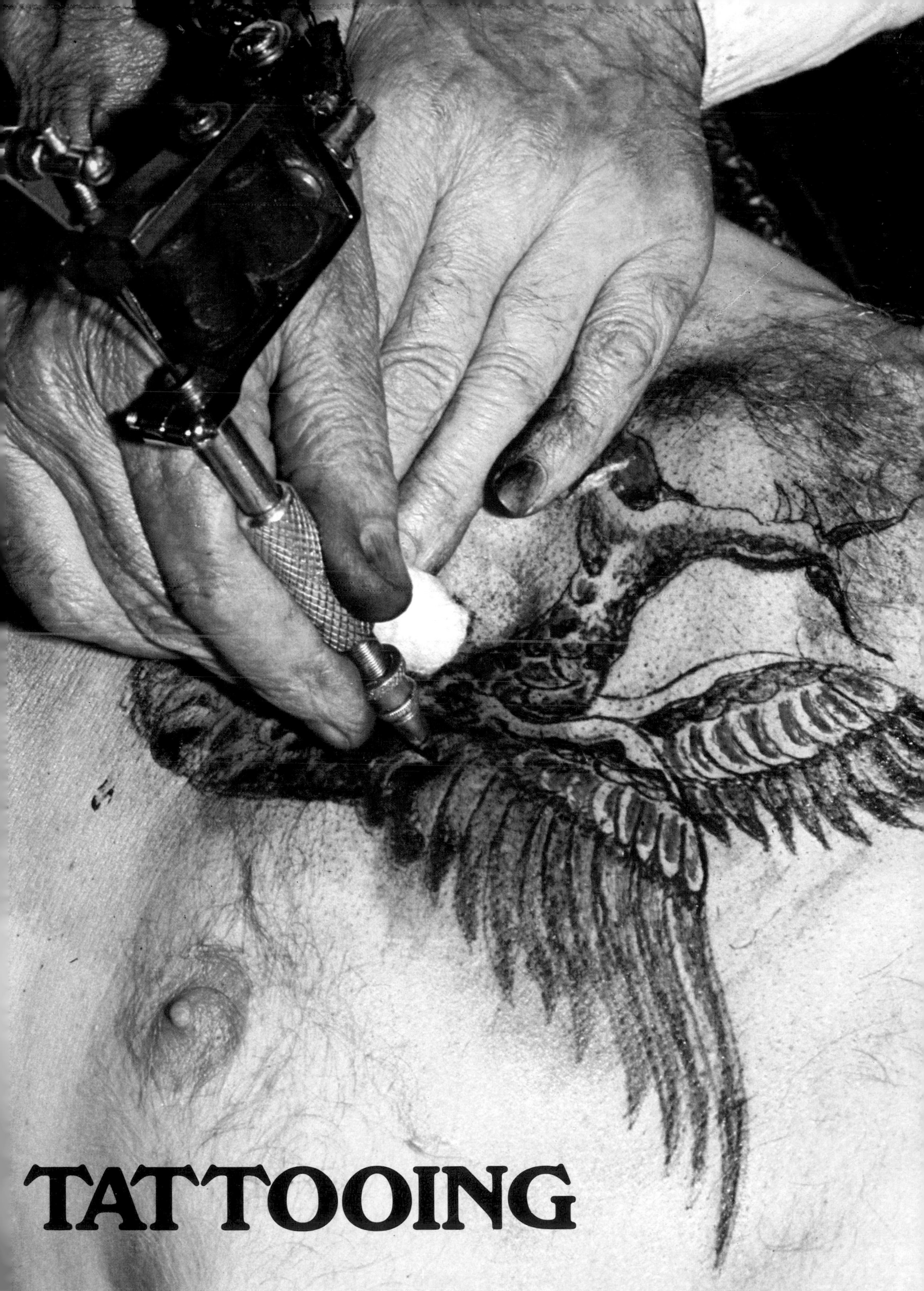

TATTOOING

John Bulmer/Uniphoto

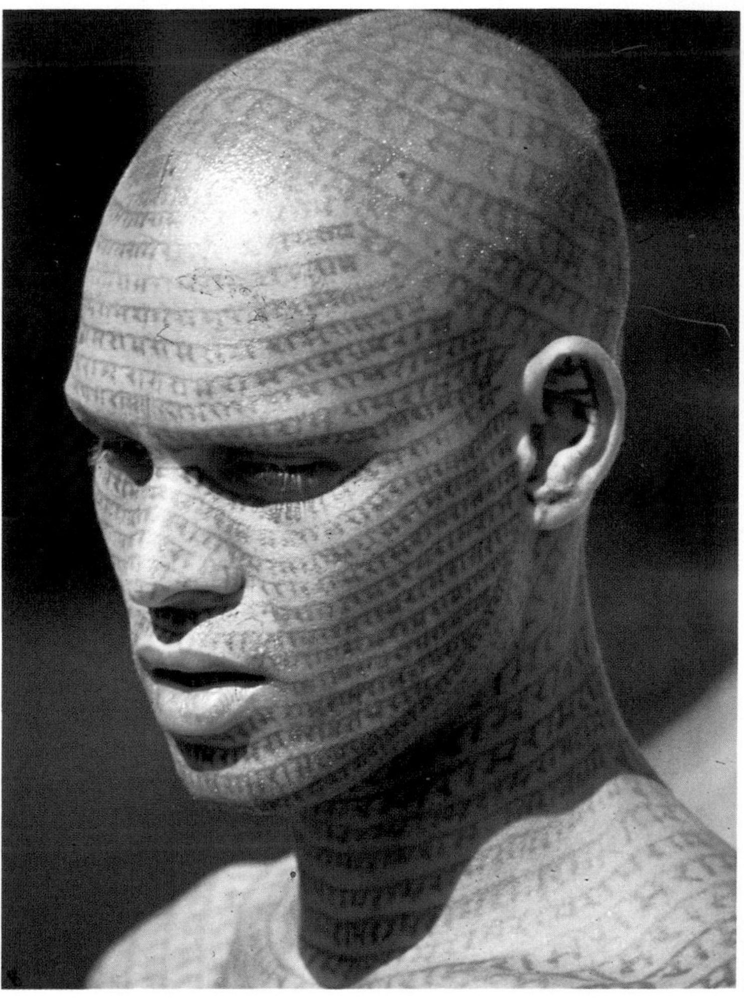

R. K. Singh

Among the Polynesians of the Marquesas every part of the body, face, trunk and limbs had to be tattooed; even lips, eyelids, gums and skull were not excluded

Elaborate decoration of the face and body satisfies an almost universal human drive; in many primitive societies tattooing and cicatrization have ritual importance as part of an initiation rite, and marks on the body often emphasize an individual's achievements or social status

THE URGE TO ENHANCE the beauty of the human body by artificial means is worldwide, but the techniques of doing so differ from culture to culture and age to age. Among peoples who do not wear clothes, or whose clothing is sparse, efforts at altering the body's natural appearance concentrate on the decoration of the actual surface of the skin. The most prevalent methods of achieving this may be classified as painting, tattooing and cicatrization.

Painting includes all types of decoration in which coloured substances are applied to the skin without causing permanent discoloration. Tattooing consists of pricking pigment into the skin in such a way as to produce, under a smooth surface, a permanent pattern, usually of black or blue. This may be done in two ways. A small chisel or adze-like implement can be used to produce grooves in the skin, into which pigment is rubbed; or a needle and thread covered with soot may be drawn under the skin. In some cases the desired design is painted or imprinted on the skin with a stamp before the tattooer sets to work.

Cicatrization, which involves the artificial creation of scars, is effected by scratching, cutting, piercing or burning the skin. The wounds may be allowed to heal naturally, forming plain scars which are usually slightly depressed, or they may be aggravated so that they form deep gashes. Raised scars may be produced by continued and extremely painful irritation which results in the proliferation of regenerative tissue.

All these methods of changing the appearance of the skin are widespread, but the most extreme forms of cicatrization are confined mainly to the dark-skinned peoples of Africa, Australia and Melanesia.

The word 'tattoo', sometimes spelt 'tatu', was introduced to the Western world by Captain Cook, and is derived from the Tahitian term *tatau,* which is used to describe the marking or puncturing of the

During tattooing pigment is pricked into the skin so that a permanent pattern is produced under a smooth surface *Previous page* A tattooist at work in London *Facing page* Patterns formed by tattooing vary in different parts of the world; plain stripes are imprinted on the face, neck and shoulders of a New Guinea woman (*far left*) while a formalized design (*left*) covers an Indian's shaven head *Right* Selection of implements used for tattooing and marking the flesh includes (*back row, left to right*) a skin-marker from Guyana, tattooing instruments from New Zealand, Borneo and Japan, and (*front*) implement used in making Hindu caste-marks and tattooing tools from Burma

Horniman Museum

skin for ornamental purposes. Although tattooing in its most elaborate form was found among the Polynesians of such islands as the Marquesas and New Zealand, the technique was well known to the ancient civilizations of the Near East and the Mediterranean countries.

The pre-dynastic tombs of Egypt (c 3500 BC) contained clay figurines which bear marks suggesting tattoos, and the Egyptians of the New Kingdom (1567–1085 BC) tattooed their breasts and arms with the names and symbols of deities. In more recent times the practice has been common in many parts of Egypt, reflecting a persistence of the custom throughout more than 5000 years. Today its purpose is mainly curative, and tattooing is used for such ailments as headache, toothache, weak eyesight and possession. There are suggestions that it is a sign of sexual maturity, and it is also used to enhance sex-appeal.

In Iraq tattooing is believed to increase a woman's fertility, and her chances of becoming pregnant. It is also used for protective purposes. A woman who has had several children who have died will try to save the next by having it tattooed, for the practice is held to confer a long and vigorous life.

In Europe tattooing was known to Greek and Latin writers of the classical period. Herodotus mentions that Thracian women were tattooed as a sign of noble status, while Pliny refers to Dracian and Sarmatian men being tattooed. The custom was also current among several tribes of ancient Gaul, but was not practised by the Greeks and Romans. It seems to have disappeared from all parts of medieval Europe. The revival of tattooing among certain classes, such as sailors, may be the result of contacts with Asian and African countries where it was widespread, and often practised by professionals whose services were available to European travellers. It was common among the pre-Columbian indigenous population of the West Indies, Mexico, Central America and South America. Other areas where there is a high frequency of tattooing are Polynesia, including New Zealand, Melanesia, Micronesia, Indonesia, Malaysia and Burma. It is practised to a lesser extent in India and Tibet. Although it was common in ancient China it soon ceased to be used as decoration and survived only as a distinctive mark. Today elaborate tattoos are found mainly among primitive peoples.

In traditional Maori society (see MAORI) men of aristocratic families had their entire faces tattooed, the patterns consisting of intricate designs of curved lines which formed spirals and arabesques and emphasized the nose and chin. Each chief was tattooed with the design peculiar to his family or tribe, while the figures marked on the faces of dependants and retainers were the same in form as those by which the chief was distinguished, although they were less elaborate. During the operation of tattooing a Maori chief had to be fed through a special funnel, for he was not allowed to touch his food, and a strict taboo prevented him from communicating with anyone not in the same condition. The pattern imprinted on the faces of Maori women was much simpler than that tattooed on the men, and covered mainly the upper lip and the chin. It was a disgrace for a woman not to have her mouth tattooed, for red lips were thought to be shameful. The operation was performed as soon as a girl had reached puberty. A girl's tattoo was also a sign of her maturity in Tahiti.

The most extensive tattooing found anywhere in the world was that common among the Polynesians of the Marquesas Islands. There every part of the body, face, trunk and limbs had to be tattooed, and even lips, eyelids, gums and skull were not excluded. The tattoo was applied in several stages, each taking three to six months. It was rare for a tattoo to be completed before a man reached the 30th year of his life. The women were not as extensively tattooed. The designs and motifs in Polynesian tattoo patterns are largely the same as those used in the decoration of implements and boats; it seems that they are chiefly ornamental.

In Polynesia it is commonly believed that tattooing originated among the gods, and a similar idea is current among the Ainus, in the northern part of the Japanese archipelago. Their women are tattooed on their lips and arms in order to keep away the demons of disease, who believe them to be the wives of gods, since the gods are tattooed in the same manner.

Tattooing is an essential part of an initiation rite among the inhabitants of the Indonesian island of Mentawei, and no man who has not undergone it is allowed to marry. The tattooing is done with the aid of two little sticks, on one of which is a vertical needle. This tool is used by tapping it with the other stick to make small punctures in the skin, into which the colouring matter, the darkened sap of sugarcane, is inserted. The design starts with a convex bow running from the chin to the shoulders, and lines are also made over the breast to the pit of the stomach. The hips, arms, legs and fingers are tattooed. A man's upper legs are always tattooed just before marriage. The calves of the legs, the backs of the hands, and the sides of the body are the last areas to be decorated. Formerly this was always done at the time of a special religious ceremony involving the

In some Naga tribes great ritual and social importance is attached to the tattooing of girls; the operation has the character of a 'rite of passage'

Left Fantastic animals tattooed on the mummified arm of a Siberian chief who lived in the 5th century BC *Below* Designs on a sailor's arms and chest; many seamen have themselves tattooed, as a mark of virility and heroic adventure *Below right* Intricate tattoo, typical of the elaborate designs that may still be seen in modern Japan

purification of the participants and the sacrifice of animals. This particular rite was performed to nullify the evil influence of blood shed when someone was stabbed inside the village or killed by a crocodile. A special porch was constructed to prevent the blood that flowed from the tattooing, and which was intended to 'cover the blood of the dead man', from falling on the ground. Every village has its own pattern of tattooing. After a headhunting expedition the victorious warriors were traditionally allowed to have the beheaded man's image tattooed on their bodies.

The custom of using tattoos to register martial deeds is widespread. Among the mountain tribes of the Philippines, such as the Kalingas, successful headhunters were entitled to cover their chests, and in some cases also their backs, with elaborate patterns. Even women who participated in headhunting expeditions as carriers were marked with a special sign. But not all tattooing has a symbolic character, and Kalinga women cover their necks and arms with intricate designs made from lines as a form of decoration.

The Naga tribes of the Assam-Burma borderland (see NAGAS) also tattoo the bodies, and in some cases the faces, of men who have been successful in headhunting raids. The Kanyak Nagas, in particular, cover the faces of warriors with an extensive pattern of curved broad lines, giving them a fierce expression. The tattoos on their chests consist of geometric patterns combined with small figures of men which represent enemies killed in war. However, tattooing is not confined to men and in some Naga tribes great ritual and social importance is attached to the tattooing of girls. For them the operation has the character of a 'rite of passage', symbolizing the transition from one stage of life to another.

The tattoo of an Ao Naga woman consists

Pat Keene

John Hillelson Agency

Strength from the Forest

With regard to preferences among the women as to where they give birth, it varies. But there is unanimity that if there is any difficulty at all, then the right thing to do is to go off away from the camp and into the forest, which will 'help'. The forest appears quite clearly as helper and protector in the vine and wooden medicines and charms, and in the scarification that will take place at the first sign of sickness. Even with adults this is done: the skin is cut in a number of small slits with an arrow, and some of the flesh is gouged out. The ashes prepared from forest woods and plants are made into a paste with spittle and rubbed into the wounds. When the skin grows back, the black ash is still visible beneath, and is regarded as a source of the strength and health and happiness that derive from the forest . . . Insofar as this strength is conveyed by washing the baby with the juice of forest vines, tattooing it with forest ashes and binding it with forest symbols, this may be regarded as sympathetic magic. But it is better regarded as the beginning of a lifetime of close intimacy between the Mbuti and the forest . . .

Colin M. Turnbull *Wayward Servants: The Two Worlds of the African Pygmies*

roughly of four vertical lines on the chin, a chain of lozenges from the throat to the bottom of the breast-bone, inverted V's on the front of the shoulders and the stomach, solid squares on the wrists, an arrow pattern on the knee and lozenges on the lower part of the leg. It usually takes five years to complete this elaborate ornamentation. When a girl is about ten or 11 years old her legs are tattooed up to the bottom of the calf; the next year her chin, chest and the front of her shoulders are completed; in the third year the pattern on the calf is done, and in the fourth year the knees are tattooed; in the final year her wrists and stomach are ornamented. All the girls of the same age are tattooed in the same year, although in small villages there may not be enough girls to make it worth while calling a tattooer every year. In this case some of them may have reached marriageable age before their tattoo has been completed. Once a girl is married the only addition that may be made is on the wrists, and there are numerous women whose tattoo pattern has never been completed.

The tattooing is carried out in the jungle near the village by old women, and no male may be present. The pattern is marked on the skin with a piece of wood dipped in colouring matter, and the girl is held firmly to the ground while the marked-out design is punctured all over with an adze-like instrument to which a little bunch of cane-thorns is attached. The black colouring matter is applied once again after the blood has been washed off. The process is exceedingly painful, and if a girl struggles and screams overmuch a fowl is sacrificed close by to appease any evil spirit that may be increasing her pain. The punctures sometimes become infected resulting in bad sores, and a girl may occasionally lose a leg. However, considering the lack of precautions against infection, the proportion of septic cases is small.

Passport to Heaven

The Baigas, a primitive tribe of middle India, also regard tattoos as greatly enhancing feminine beauty, and aesthetic considerations are foremost in their attitude to the practice. That they are inextricably linked with the function of tattoo marks as a powerful sexual stimulant is partly indicated by the fact that a girl's arms and breasts are not tattooed until she is adolescent, nor her legs until her marriage. Tattooing seems to play a role in the skin-eroticism that is a strong sexual agent in Baiga love-making. Women themselves take great pride in their marks, mainly no doubt, because they know it increases their attractiveness to their men. A woman's husband is forbidden to watch her being tattooed, and for two days afterwards she is treated as though she were menstruating. Her body is then covered with turmeric and oil, and she bathes. A triangular decoration on the forehead is generally made when a girl is about five years old, and on the breast is the figure of a peacock or of a basket, done when the girl reaches puberty. At the time of marriage, or later, a pattern is applied to the back of the hands and lines of dots are tattooed on the thighs.

Among the Muria Gonds of the middle Indian highlands, tattooing is used mainly for feminine adornment. The day when she is tattooed is an important moment in the life of a young Muria girl, a real step towards maturity. It is desirable that girls should be tattooed before marriage, and if possible before they are betrothed. The marks also appear to be a kind of passport to heaven. According to a Muria saying, 'the god of heaven will punish a girl who dies without being tattooed, but if she brings him beautiful drawings from the terrestrial regions, he will keep her with him and look after her'. The tattooing is done by women of a special caste, and a myth relates how a goddess performed the operation on a woman of that caste at the beginning of time, and then instructed her in the art of tattooing. The method followed today is still the same as that described in the myth. Lamp-black, charcoal and pounded incense are mixed with castor oil and then burnt in a potsherd over a fire. The resulting black deposit is used as colouring matter which is pricked into the girl's skin with needles.

Some Indian tribes ascribe protective qualities to tattoo marks, particularly if they represent symbols of family or guardian deities. But in other cases they are curative; tattooing over a tumour is supposed to relieve it, for instance, and applied to the belly it will cure colic. Some Gonds tattoo the figure of a horse on the front of their thighs, and of a saddle between the knee and thigh, to represent the horse god who can make their thighs as strong as those of a horse; or they mark each upper arm with the image of Hanuman, the monkey god who is a symbol of strength; this is believed to enable a man to carry unusually heavy weights. Cicatrization is not unknown among the tribal people of India, although it is not used as extensively as in Africa and Australia. The Oraons of Bihar brand young boys in five or six places on one arm with a piece of burning cloth before admitting them to the bachelors' hall, and Gonds brand their joints with burning wood in the belief that this will make them supple for dancing.

Tattooing is also widespread among the Indians of the tropical zone of South America. The usual tattoo of the Apiaca Indians consisted of three lines extending from each ear to the nose, mouth and chin. At the age of 14 a boy's face-tattoo was completed with a rectangle around the mouth, indicating that the wearer was allowed to eat human flesh. The designs on the body illustrated a man's deeds in war and hunting. They included crude representations of animals, fish, men and women applied to the arms and legs. Among the tribes of the Xingu region a person's social importance was indicated by the width of the vertical stripe running down the middle of the face. A chief's face was tattooed all over, and gave the impression of being totally black.

While in most societies tattooing is done mainly for aesthetic purposes, it may also fulfil a protective function. The women of certain Arab communities of Morocco, for instance, have small crosses or other designs tattooed on their cheeks or the tips of their noses to avert the Evil Eye.

Cicatrization is widespread among the dark-skinned races of Africa, and the scars,

Body painting may be practised for religious or ceremonial reasons, or it may be purely decorative *Above right* A tribesman, his face painted white in order to intimidate the enemy, and a child (*far right*), his face decorated with paint *Right* A woman in ceremonial costume. All these examples of body painting are from New Guinea *Far right* A young girl's sexuality is emphasized by the formal pattern painted on her body *Following page* New Guinea tribesmen; their bodies are covered in mud as a sign of mourning

Axel Poignant

Axel Poignant

Axel Poignant

Carl Perutz

Axel Poignant

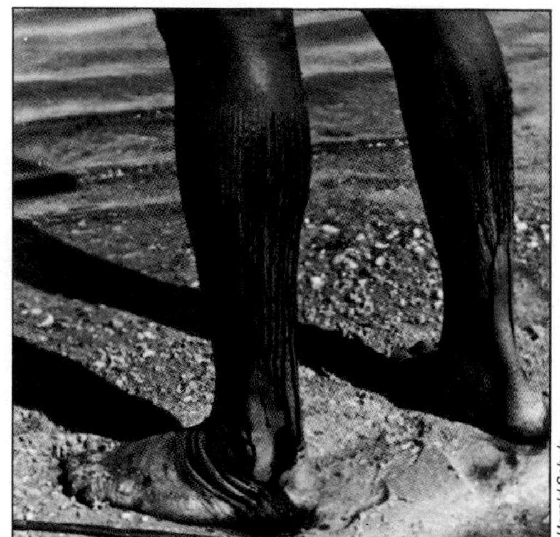

The artificial creation of scars, cicatrization is caused by cutting, scratching, burning or piercing the skin; the wounds may be allowed to heal naturally, or they may be aggravated so that a raised scar is produced *Above left* and *Above* A Brazilian Indian undergoes a form of cicatrization in which vertical lines are scratched into his leg *Above right* Aborigine woman: the cicatrix strengthens her breasts and is also decorative

which are produced artificially on the face as well as other parts of the body, often serve as distinctive marks by which members of a tribe or clan can be recognized (see MUTILATION). In many tribes the operation forms part of the initiation rites of boys and girls, and is therefore a sign that social maturity has been attained. Similar practices occurred among many of the aboriginal tribes of Australia, and also among the indigenous and now extinct inhabitants of Tasmania. The scars, which usually cover the chest and abdomen and sometimes also the shoulders and arms, were produced by cutting the skin with sharp shells or stone-blades and by rubbing clay or sand into the wounds to delay the healing process. The scars are partly decorative and partly indicative of social situations. For instance, bereaved persons may inflict scarification on themselves to express their sorrow over the death of a relative. As in Africa the operation is also performed during the initiation rites through which boys attain the status of fully privileged members of the tribe (see INITIATION).

Paint for Beauty and Status

In the course of these rites and other religious ceremonies, the Australian aborigines change their appearance by painting their faces and whole bodies in a variety of fantastic patterns. The only colours available are red, yellow, white and black, and these are applied in broad bands and stripes. The aborigines often use their own blood, which they draw from their veins, as a basis for the paint.

Body painting is also widespread among the tribesmen of New Guinea and other islands of Melanesia, where, in addition to wearing masks, it transforms the appearance of men who represent ghosts and ancestor spirits when performing the ritual dances which form part of initiation rites and agricultural ceremonies. But the face and body are also painted for cosmetic reasons, and Melanesians make a clear distinction between decorative painting, which enhances their beauty, and the custom of smothering themselves in soot to extinguish all their attractions as a sign of mourning.

The Indians of South America, many of whom wore no clothes before they came in contact with Europeans, make extensive use of paint to adorn body and face. The most common pigments are red and blueish-black, both of which are derived from locally available vegetable substances. Some of these pigments remain indelible for ten days or more, and travellers often confused these apparently permanent painted patterns with tattoos. Among the Indians of the Uapes-Caqueta region, body painting is widely practised by both sexes, elaborate designs being produced by a roller dye. Women paint the undersurface of the jaw and throat blue to achieve a curious sculptured effect for ceremonial occasions, and smear their faces with red pigment to ward off danger on working days. Their backs are crudely spattered with blue pigment, but care is taken with painted designs on the legs, thighs, breasts and face (see COSTUME).

Elaborate painted designs were also common among the Tupi Indians. The combination of arabesques, frets, undulating lines, and other motifs differed so greatly in the various groups that a person's tribal affiliation could be immediately discerned. The design was named after an animal, the markings of which were supposed to have served as a model.

The custom of decorating the body, either permanently or temporarily, appears to exist in primitive and more advanced societies throughout the world. Tattooing and cicatrization are the most common types of permanent decoration, and though similar methods are used in widely separated countries it can hardly be assumed that the wide distribution of such techniques is entirely due to diffusion. Specific styles, such as the elaborate tattoo patterns of Polynesia and the Philippines, which cover the whole body and represent an art form comparable to painting or sculpture, are certainly associated with a definable cultural tradition, but the actual technique of inserting pigment into the skin must have arisen independently in various parts of the world.

There can be little doubt that artificial modifications in the appearance of the body by tattooing, cicatrization and painting developed in early prehistoric times, but tangible evidence is limited by the impermanence of human flesh and the substances used. Tattooing has, however, been found on mummified corpses from tombs of the first millennium BC in the Altai region of central Asia, but such discoveries are rare; for the most part evidence is provided by stamps of baked clay which were used to apply paint to the skin, and earthen palettes used in the preparation of paint for cosmetic purposes. These palettes have been found on various Neolithic sites as well as among the ruins of higher civilizations. It seems that the modern practice of elaborate cosmetic make-up satisfies an almost universal human drive, and has its antecedents in the earliest civilizations accessible to archeological research.

Aesthetic considerations may be the most frequent, and are often the dominant, motives behind the practice of tattooing; but they are usually by no means the only reasons for the importance which many societies attach to body marks. Among peoples who lack a system of writing, tattoos and patterns painted on the body are a convenient means of recording and publicizing information about an individual's activities and achievements, and they may serve a similar purpose in societies where there are no distinctive clothes, uniforms or badges of rank to emphasize the status or social condition of persons and groups. However, their role as identifying labels becomes obsolete where more precise and sophisticated symbols are available to indicate the rank of individuals or the identity of groups.

C. VON FÜRER-HAIMENDORF

FURTHER READING: W. D. Hambly, *History of Tattooing* (Witherby, 1925).

Tau
Last letter of the Hebrew alphabet, and so connected with the end of the world and believed to be the sign with which the righteous would be marked, to protect them in the last days; as a result, a T-shaped cross, or St Anthony's cross, became a protective device against evil.
See CROSS; TALISMANS.

Taurobolium
Rite in the Mysteries of Cybele and Attis; the initiate descended into a pit and was drenched in the blood of a bull which was slaughtered above him; after this the initiate was regarded as 'reborn'.
See BAPTISM.

TAURUS

THE SECOND sign of the zodiac, Taurus the Bull was identified by the Greeks with Zeus's transformation into a bull when he abducted Europa; to the Babylonians he was the heavenly bull whose rising marked the beginning of spring.

Taurus is ruled by Venus, and people born under this sign are governed by their affections; they will go out of their way to avoid ill feeling. Modest, they do not seek popularity. Because he is associated with the earth, Taurus has been described as hefty, clodhopping, obstinate, lazy and the opposite of intellectual. However, these adjectives are no longer thought to apply to the constellation. The following description, by the 1st century AD Roman astrologer Manilius, has similarly been superseded:

> Dull honest Taurus to manure the field
> Strong Taurus bears, by him the Grounds are till'd:
> No gaudy things he breeds, no prize for worth,
> But blesseth Earth, and brings her Labour forth.

According to modern astrologers, although Taurus is not ambitious his rewards are the fruit of his toil, and not the result of getting others to work for him. Valens, a classical writer of the 2nd century AD, says: 'Those born will be good handicraftmen, hard-working, good at keeping things, fond of pleasure and music, and generous: but some of them will be labourers, planters, and builders. And if the benefics (that is, Jupiter and Venus) aspect the ascendant, or the ruler is well placed, they become high priests or athletic trainers, and are awarded wreaths and purple robes, statues and busts, and are given charge of sacred rites and become notable and famous.'

This is the origin of the association that Taurus is supposed to have with money. In fact, this sign actually symbolizes not money but real wealth, the result of the material forces of production. However, music is also a Taurean art, and people born under Taurus are competent musicians and singers. The influence of Venus means that the Taurean is fond of pleasure, generous and more than usually amorous. The bull is naturally highly sexed, but his attitude to sex is uncomplicated and he does not need to be stimulated by artificial glamour. Taurus's keynote is devotion, to a person, an ideal or simply to his work. His love is deep, lasting and undemanding. Humble by nature, he feels that he has no right to ask anything for himself.

The Babylonians associated Taurus with the heavenly bull whose rising marked the coming of spring. People born under this sign of the zodiac are said to be good-natured and reliable; fond of pleasure, they are nevertheless hard workers, often scholars or philosophers and often extremely creative: illustration from *Stars and Marvels of the East,* a 12th century English manuscript

Bodleian Library Colour Filmstrip

Faithful Friend

Because he is ruled by Venus there is nothing heavy or unimaginative about Taurus. Although sensitive and keen-witted, the Taurean is not afraid of hard work or dirt or the unpleasant aspects of life, but accepts them as part of living. He enjoys beauty, however, and tries to avoid ugliness.

Emotionally truthful, the person born under Taurus is good-natured, reliable and a faithful friend. But he is inclined to brood, and needs encouragement. If religious, he is not necessarily conventional in his beliefs even though he is strong in faith and devotion. The Taurean gift for profound study makes scholars, philosophers and artists, and people born under this sign excel at work that requires patience.

THOMAS TAYLOR

THE FIRST TRANSLATOR of Plato's work into English was Thomas Taylor the Platonist (1758–1835). His edition, published in 1804, includes nine dialogues by Floyer Sydenham (who had died in a debtors' prison). Taylor's edition includes long introductory essays, and extensive notes, with long extracts from the Commentaries of Proclus. He also translated much of Plotinus, founder of the Neoplatonist school of philosopy, and the principal works of his successors, Porphyry, Iamblichus, the Emperor Julian, Sallust and Proclus, besides the Chaldean Oracles, the Orphic Hymns and the works of Aristotle, and many minor works. To all these he added long introductory essays and notes; of his own writings, the most important is his *Dissertation on the Eleusinian and Bacchic Mysteries.*

His translations have been superseded; his English style has at all times been criticized; according to Coleridge he translated Proclus from 'difficult Greek into incomprehensible English'. S. Mackenna's translation of Plotinus is, as a work of literature, superior to Taylor's; in philosophic exactness of rendering this is not always so: he himself wrote that 'in perusing the works of these great men, the reader must not expect the sublimest truths to be explained in a familiar manner, and adapted, like many modern publications, *to the meanest capacities*'. G. R. S. Mead (whose own work on Orpheus is but an expansion of Taylor's preface to the Mystical Hymns of Orpheus) called him 'a wonderful genius and profound philosopher'; 'what was true of his critics then is true of his critics today: though they may know more Greek, he knew more Plato . . . Taylor was more than a scholar, he was a philosopher in the Platonic sense of the word.'

Taylor himself recorded that his interest in the Platonic philosophy came through mathematics; his first work (published when he was 23) was a mathematical essay; and in 1816 he published *Theoretic Arithmetic,* based upon the Pythagorean philosophy of number; a work which retains its value to the present time. But his first significant publication – one of the seminal works of the Romantic movement – was the anonymous translation of Plotinus *On the Beautiful* in 1787. This paraphrase translation of the epitome of the aesthetics of Plotinus lies at the root of that doctrine of the imagination as the formative principle of all art which Blake and Coleridge independently formulated. This little book may well be the common source of their similar ideas. Wordsworth too must have read it, for the theme of 'the inward eye' of the mind, as well as the phrase itself, comes from this tractate with its impassioned introduction and epilogue in which the young Taylor summoned his contemporaries to a revolutionary return to tradition: 'Let us then boldly enlist ourselves under the banners of Plotinus, and, by his assistance, vigorously repel the encroachments of error, plunge her dominions into the abyss of forgetfulness, and disperse the darkness of her baneful night. For, indeed, there never was a period which required so much philosophic exertion; or such vehement contention from the lovers of truth. On all sides nothing of philosophy remains but the name, and this has become the subject of the vilest prostitution: since it is not only engrossed by the Naturalist, Chemist, and Anatomist, but is usurped by the mechanic, in ever trifling invention and made subservient to the lucre of traffic and merchandise.'

For Taylor erudition was not an end but a means 'to diffuse the salutary light of genuine philosophy', which was for him '. . . that sublime theology which was first obscurely promulgated by Orpheus, Pythagoras and Plato, and was afterwards perspicuously unfolded by their legitimate disciples; a theology which, however it may be involved in oblivion in *barbarous*, and derided in *impious* ages, will again flourish for very extended periods, through all the infinite revolutions of time'. That Taylor took seriously the ideas of the Platonists and hoped to see these ideas carried into effect, was, to the 'pedants' and 'verbal critics' with whom he carried on a lifelong battle, intolerable. According to the *Encyclopaedia Britannica*, 'His efforts were unfavourably – almost contemptuously – received'. For this the chief reason was undoubtedly the extreme antipathy of the age of deism and pragmatism to the Platonic philosophy as such. Taylor's works nevertheless proved seminal for the three most significant intellectual revivals of the 19th century, in England, America and Ireland.

The texts Taylor placed in the hands of the Romantic poets were the same that Ficino, founder of the Platonic academy of Florence in the 15th century, had made accessible to the Florentine painters, and their transforming effect was the same. As a translator and exponent of the Platonic philosophy Taylor must be seen in the context of that renaissance at the end of the 18th century of which the Romantic movement in poetry is only the most discernible aspect. The Greek revival had its beginnings in the visual arts, with such works as Stuart and Revett's *Antiquities of Athens and Ionia*; in the publicity that was given to the Portland Vase by the Wedgwood replicas, made at the suggestion of Flaxman, the sculptor; and with work brought to England by collectors, notably Lord Elgin. Taylor must be seen in this context, as providing the Platonic texts and the exposition of Greek theology which accompanied this rediscovery of ancient Greece. He gave, in 1787 or 1788, a series of lectures on the Platonic philosophy at the house of Flaxman; and it is likely that among those present was Flaxman's friend William Blake. The substance of these lectures is probably to be found embedded in the several long essays included in Taylor's *The Philosophical and Mathematical Commentaries of Proclus* (1788–89). In the second volume of this work is included *A History of the Restoration of the Platonic Theology by the Latter Platonists*, an impassioned discourse upon the Neoplatonic philosophers.

This essay is a manifesto; and on the title page of the first volume (dedicated 'To the Sacred Majesty of Truth') is a quotation from Isaac D'Israeli's *Curiosities of Literature*: 'Mr. T. Taylor, the Platonic Philosopher and *The Modern Plethon*, consonant to that philosophy, professes polytheism.' Taylor's polytheism was of course of a philosophic kind; his profession was perhaps made in order to add greater force to his rejection of Christianity, and his challenge to the monopoly of 'the classics' by Anglican clerics who alone could hold Fellowships at the colleges of Oxford and Cambridge.

Taylor was educated at St Paul's School; his father was a Dissenter, and Oxford and Cambridge were therefore closed to him. His father intended him to go to Aberdeen University, but he made instead a rash (but apparently very happy) early marriage, and so never went to any university, working instead in a series of ill-paid posts. Nevertheless his reputation extended to France; and the Platonic Marquis de Valady stayed for a time in Taylor's house before returning to France, there to be guillotined under the Terror. Another lodger under Taylor's roof was Mary Wollstonecraft, one of the first champions of the rights of women, who described the philosopher's study as 'the abode of peace'.

Taylor's studies were pursued in such spare time as his employment allowed; he was for some years assistant secretary to the Royal Society for the Promotion of Arts, Industries and Commerce, whose President, the Duke of Norfolk, subscribed to the whole edition of his Plato. In later years

National Gallery of Canada, Ottawa

Left **Portrait of Thomas Taylor by Sir Thomas Lawrence; described as 'a wonderful genius and profound philosopher', Taylor exposed himself to satire because of his professions of polytheism. According to rumour he sacrificed a bull to Jupiter, and honoured other gods in equally appropriate rites** ***Right*** **Taylor's Neoplatonism influenced the poetry and paintings of William Blake, and his translation of Plotinus** ***On the Beautiful*** **may have been the source of Blake's belief that imagination is the formative principle of all art:** ***When the Morning Stars Sang Together,*** **one of a series of illustrations to the biblical book of Job by William Blake**

As a translator and exponent of the Platonic philosophy, Thomas Taylor must be seen in the context of his time, a period when there was a great revival of interest in ancient Greece and its works: part of the Parthenon frieze, one of the most famous of Greek antiquities, which was brought to England at the beginning of the 19th century

he found a patron, William Meredith, but it is his early works – those published before 1800 – which had the greatest impact upon his contemporaries. These were welcomed by the young Romantics for precisely those elements for which they were anathematized by the *Edinburgh Review*, Horace Walpole, and 'the black-coated gentlemen' of Oxford. The strong Neoplatonic element in Blake comes from Taylor; his works were among the 'darling studies' of Coleridge as a schoolboy; traces of Wordsworth's reading of his translations of Plotinus are to be discerned in many images and verbal echoes. Shelley possessed a copy of his Plato; and his friend Thomas Love Peacock was one of Taylor's circle of friends in later years.

By his open professions of polytheism Taylor willingly exposed himself to satire; according to rumour he sacrificed a bull to Jupiter in his house at Walworth, and honoured the other gods in no less appropriate rites. This was of course pure invention; but an episode in which the young Taylor started a fire at the Freemason's Hall while demonstrating the principle of the Perpetual Lamp of antiquity, is fact. That Taylor was a striking personality even in a generation of eccentrics is evident from his appearance in Isaac D'Israeli's novel *Vaurien*, as 'the modern Pletho'; and, many years later, as 'Mr Mystic' in Thomas Love Peacock's *Melincourt*. Coleridge refers to him as 'the English Pagan'; and he was in his lifetime always known, as he remains to the present time, as 'Taylor the Platonist'.

Taylor's 'polytheism' (or rather, his exposition of the symbolic language of Greek mythology) was for the Romantic poets the main source of the revival of mythological poetry which distinguishes their work. Blake's polytheism is contained within a Christian framework; both Blake and Coleridge gave modern guise to their gods and daemons; though Coleridge's *Ancient Mariner* evidently derives in part from Taylor's writings on Odysseus as symbolically understood by Porphyry and Plotinus.

Shelley and Keats revived the Greek pantheon, but in a living way made possible by Taylor's presentation of the gods as the ever-active divine energies of the cosmos. The most important of Taylor's works on the interpretation of Greek mythology are his

British Museum/Michael Holford

Dissertation on the Eleusinian and Bacchic Mysteries; *The Mystical Initiations, or Hymns of Orpheus*; Porphyry's *Cave of the Nymphs*; Apuleius' *Fable of Cupid and Psyche*, and his dissertation on daemons; Sallust's *On the Gods and the World*; and an Introduction to *The Republic*, books 2 and 3, *Containing an Apology for the Fables of Homer*. The great merit of Taylor's expositions is their fidelity to the tradition from which they derive. Bacon had set the fashion in euhemerist interpretation (referring myths to a historical basis), so congenial to the 18th century English mentality; Jacob Bryant (author of the *New System of Mythology*) and Bishop Warburton interpreted the Greeks in terms of a religion alien to them; whereas Taylor unfolded the Greek mythology in terms of the Orphic theology (see ORPHEUS) and Platonic metaphysics.

Through the enthusiasm of Ralph Waldo Emerson and Bronson Alcott the works of Thomas Taylor crossed the Atlantic to become one of the main sources of the inspiration of the Transcendentalist movement, that 'new declaration of independence made on behalf of literature and art and philosophy'.

When in 1842 Bronson Alcott visited England, he paid Taylor the compliment of collecting, with Charles Lane, a library which included as many of Taylor's books as they could find; of the 214 titles which were taken to America for the library of their 'new Eden' at 'Fruitlands' in Harvard, Massachusetts, 16 bore the name of Thomas Taylor as translator, editor or author.

In England there was little interest in Taylor from the time of his death until the beginning of the Theosophical movement (see THEOSOPHY). Through the movement Taylor became known to George Russell (the poet A.E.) and to W. B. Yeats. A.E. called Taylor 'the uncrowned king'; as Emerson had described him as 'a better man of imagination, a better poet, or perhaps I should say a better feeder to a poet, than any man between Milton and Wordsworth'. William E. A. Axon, who published in *The Library* (1890) a bibliography and memoir of Taylor wrote: 'He was an enthusiast, and only an enthusiast could have done his work. His translations represent a side of Greek thought that but for him would be unrepresented in English literature.'

KATHLEEN RAINE

FURTHER READING: *Selected Writings of Thomas Taylor the Platonist*, with an Introduction by Kathleen Raine, an essay on 'Taylor in America' by G. M. Harper, and a bibliography (Routledge & Kegan Paul, 1968).

TEA-LEAF READING

ALTHOUGH TELLING FORTUNES by consulting the patterns formed by tea-leaves on the base and sides of a cup is often regarded as drawing-room entertainment, it is not purely an amusement. The tea-leaves can act as a medium through which the clairvoyance of the reader is stimulated so that he or she is able to reveal truths that would otherwise remain hidden; or the figures formed by the leaves may be believed to reflect patterns that exist in the astral.

The method used in tea-leaf reading is time-honoured and simple. The client inverts her cup, turning it round three times; she places it on the saucer and then taps the bottom three times with her left index finger. The clairvoyant, who is in a light trance, picks the cup up and turns it round so that the leaves can be inspected.

All tea-leaf readers have their preferred methods of interpreting the patterns made by the leaves, and only some general indication of their meaning is given here:

Chain of small leaves: A journey, travel; if two larger leaves are in close proximity, the excursion is mental and not physical.

Serpentine chain of small leaves: a visit to the mountains; if two larger leaves are in close proximity, there will be ups and downs in daily life; inability to settle down.

Three small leaves close to one leaf: A man.

Two leaves close to a small leaf: A woman.

Group of small leaves in a triangular pattern: A child or children.

Heart: Love; a heart broken or crossed by a chain of leaves represents a broken love-affair or a divorce.

Triangle: Emotional involvement; jealousy; rivalry. If pointing downwards this shape indicates a *ménage à trois*, if upwards, ambition and success are suggested.

Square: Several different possibilities are suggested by this formation; it may mean that the person concerned is well-established, conservative and a solid character. But it can also imply a need for protection, or the client's failure to excel in his career.

Star: Great success; a sign of genius; spiritual enlightenment. However, if it falls on or near a heart formation, the passions may be crushed and replaced by a life of asceticism.

The appearance of more complicated symbols or geometric signs needs profound study; because of their rarity they are extremely significant.

Many leaves spread all over the cup: A rich or confused character; extravagance; negligence; generosity.

Very few leaves in the cup: Clarity; direct action in the future. However, this also indicates poverty in emotional life, and if the leaves seem to arrange themselves in a provocative way they must be read with great care so that they offset the poverty of the all-over pattern.

Cup-Tossing, a 19th century engraving: tea-leaf reading is a homely branch of the old art of geomancy, the reading of omens in the patterns formed by earth, sand, pebbles or shells scattered on the ground

Cross: This means that the client is at a crossroads in life, and that a personal sacrifice may be necessary. If this pattern is in conjunction with one large leaf, it can signify death. However, care and tact should be exercised in making such an interpretation, and it should be remembered that the possible death is not necessarily that of the client. Other leaves close by will ward off danger, and show a remedy for whatever ill is likely to befall him.

Circle: Marriage; a close partnership; fame. A good omen.

Circle with a cross on it: Enforced confinement, possibly in a hospital, prison, or other institution.

Two parallel lines of leaves: A propitious journey; dreams that will come true; a long and happy life. Reinforcement of all else seen in the cup.

Dots: Letters; messages; thoughts.

Stars: Good luck.

Dashes: Surprises.

Flowers: Joy; an engagement and marriage.

Fruit: Good fortune; children.

Daisy: Simple happiness.

Gun or dagger: Danger; strife.

Scythe: A good harvest; a death warning.

Musical instruments: Good company.

Scales: Justice; success at law.

Ladder: Increasing success.

Key: Secrets revealed; knowledge.

House: Stability.

Bottle: Excess; flirtation at a party.

Envelope: News.

Fan: An indiscreet love-affair.

Teapot or kettle: Good cheer; contentment.

Pair of scissors: Angry words.

Hammer: Hard work.

There are other general indications:

Time is represented by the different levels of the cup. The rim is the present, and below this lies the near future, while patterns formed on the base refer to events that are many years ahead.

Place is indicated by the parts of the cup in which the leaves settle. Those nearest the handle tell of events that affect the home; the leaves on the sides suggest distance according to their proximity to the handle, and the ones on the base show the place of birth, nationality and hidden nature of the client.

Letters of the alphabet represent the initials of people concerned in the reading; the nearer they are to the handle, the closer their relationship to the client.

Clear symbols are lucky, with the exception of those that represent illness or death. *Faint symbols* tend to be unlucky, suggesting a weak character or lack of purpose.

In occult lore the bowl of the cup corresponds to the dome of the sky, and the leaves to the stars, and there is therefore said to be a connection between tea-leaf reading and astrology. There are also correspondences between the cup, the sky and the palm of the hand, and tea-leaf reading is linked with palmistry as well as with the stars. Other correspondences, such as the link between the leaves and the moles on the body and the bumps on the head, have also been observed.

(See also DIVINATION; GEOMANCY.)

BASIL IVAN RAKOCZI

Marxist and 'hyper-Catholic', Teilhard de Chardin believed that the human race is still evolving; his vision was of humanity as a union of free persons propelled towards the God 'ahead', the point of convergence at which mankind is to find its consummation and meaning

TEILHARD DE CHARDIN

BORN ON 1 May 1881 at Sarcenat near Clermont-Ferrand in the Auvergne, France, Pierre Teilhard de Chardin died of a heart attack in New York on Easter Sunday, 10 April 1955. In 1901 he took his first vows as a Jesuit and remained within the order until his death. But Teilhard was not only a priest but also a scientist – a paleontologist – of some distinction. Before his death he enjoyed a considerable reputation in his chosen field and in 1948 was offered a chair in Prehistory at the Collège de France. This offer he had to decline because his Jesuit superiors in Rome would not allow him to publish his most famous book, *The Phenomenon of Man*. For Teilhard had ideas of his own, and these did not correspond to the official Roman orthodoxy of the day. Hence his superiors considered it more 'prudent' that he should spend most of his life working 'in the field', mostly in China, while the last four years of his life were spent in the United States where the impact of his ideas was less likely to be felt than in France where he was already well known. Right up to his death, however, he was not allowed to publish anything except papers of a purely scientific nature within his own speciality, but fortunately he had the prudence to entrust his manuscripts to a friend and not long after his death *The Phenomenon of Man* was published in the original French, the English translation appearing with a warmly sympathetic introduction by Sir Julian Huxley, in 1959.

The Soul of the World

The publication of *The Phenomenon of Man* created something of a sensation. The worlds of both science and theology were split down the middle in their attitude towards the 'phenomenon' of Teilhard. Some scientists denounced him as insufficiently grounded in biology, while others took up his ideas with enthusiasm. The theologians were also split, the orthodox remaining obdurately antagonistic while the liberals hailed his totally new approach to Christianity as a real breakthrough in that it seemed to make Christianity once again relevant to the modern world. Rome severely discouraged the reading of his works since they had been published without its permission under the auspices of a committee that was largely scientific and not by any means entirely Christian. Then came Pope John XXIII and the Second Vatican Council, and the rock of Peter, monolithic and unmoving since the Council of Trent in the 15th century, lurched forward with unforeseen and unforeseeable speed.

Teilhard was dead; but at last his ideas received a sympathetic hearing from the great majority of his fellow churchmen. Posthumously he had his reward, for the contradictions of his life reflected the integrity and completeness of his thought. Within the Church he was the apostle, prophet and mystic of a purposeful progress, and yet, despite constant setbacks, despite what often seemed petty and timorous persecution, he remained not only a loyal son of the Roman Catholic Church but also faithful to his vows of absolute obedience to the Society of Jesus and the pope. His non-Catholic friends could not understand why he did not break with such pusillanimous lack of understanding. But his own philosophy of life, and vision of the future, made it impossible for him to break away from what he saw as the one 'axis' of cohesion in a world in travail. He had been attacked as a theologian, as a scientist, and as a philosopher, but basically he was none of these things. True, he *was* a scientist but his science was the prehistoric past of this planet, whereas his real and absorbing interest was the goal towards which evolution was, in his opinion, guiding and pushing not only Earth, but the whole universe. As a theologian and philosopher he was never more than an amateur and he knew it. He was one of those awkward human beings who could not be pigeon-holed into any obvious category: he was a mystic, a visionary, and a prophet.

'One of those human beings who could not be pigeon-holed into any obvious category', Teilhard de Chardin was a mystic, visionary and prophet; because his ideas did not correspond to the official Roman orthodoxy of the day, it was considered 'prudent' that he should spend most of his life working in the field, mainly in China. Although he was only allowed to publish scientific papers, he entrusted his manuscripts to a friend and his most famous book *The Phenomenon of Man* appeared in French not long after his death

Basically he saw the salvation of the world in terms of a real reconciliation between science and religion, a situation in which religion would be able to re-interpret itself in terms of evolution, and in which science itself would be 'tinged with mysticism and charged with faith', in terms of a 'synthesis of the (Christian) God "above", with the (Marxist) God "ahead"'. In scientific terms he saw the world as evolving to ever-higher stages of 'complexity-consciousness', for, quite rightly, he saw that there was no reason to suppose that evolution had suddenly come to a halt with the emergence of self-conscious man. The very troubles of our times were a sign that the human race was undergoing a new 'mutation', a new qualitative change which would result in a new and higher form of consciousness in which the individual consciousness would be transcended in some form of collective consciousness. The precursors of this were the modern totalitarian movements. During the Second World War, most of which he spent in China where he was out of touch with the ghastly realities of the European situation, he refused to see the conflicting powers as black-and-white alternatives. Nazism, insofar as it was a cohesive and progressive force, he considered as an advance on what had gone before, although he was well aware that ultimately it could only lead to an 'ant-hill' civilization, which would be an evil parody of his own vision of the 'totalization' of humanity as a union of free persons animated and propelled forward by what he had once called the 'Soul of the World' towards a unique point of convergence. He was later to call this point 'Omega', that is, God or Christ as the ultimate term of human evolution and history.

The Cosmic Christ

At a time when the Vatican under Pius XII was fulminating against international Communism as the chief enemy, Teilhard saw in it the shape of things to come. In China where he had seen it at first-hand and had witnessed the vast human energies it had been able to unleash, he was convinced that here was a power working along the very 'axis' of evolution, which no earthly force could stop. Yet he saw that the new 'totalized' society could never be wholly valid unless it were underpinned by love. 'The world cannot endure, advance, or realize itself,' he wrote, 'without the action of a power that is a species of love. This is why, much as I sympathize with the "totalitarian" faith of popular fronts, I am forced to acknowledge that their *impersonal* forms of ideal "Humanity", "Society", (*a fortiori* the "Race" or "Empire of fascist doctrines") without soul or "face", are going to nip the Evolution that they want to promote and save in the bud.' What Teilhard had been anticipating actually came to pass for an all too brief period in Czechoslovakia, when

'Communism with a human face' became a living reality.

Despite the divisive tendencies that seemed to be tearing this world to pieces during two World Wars and their aftermath, he remained incurably optimistic; for he had an unshakable faith in Christ and the Catholic Church, which he liked to speak of in biological terms as the Christian 'phylum' (in biology a 'phylum' is a main division of the animal or vegetable kingdom).

But what kind of Christ did Teilhard worship? His was not Christ as preached by the 'orthodoxy' of the Roman bureaucrats but the cosmic Christ preached by St Paul in his letter to the Colossians in whom 'were created all things in heaven and earth' and who 'holds all things in unity'. As to the Roman Catholic Church (and Teilhard, far from denying his Catholic faith, described himself as 'hyper-Catholic'), according to this same letter of St Paul 'the Church is his body, and he its head'; and 'in this body lives the fulness of divinity, and in him you too find your own fulfilment, in the one who is the head of every Sovereignty and Power.' All this was vitally real to Teilhard, and this was the 'gospel' of which he felt himself to be the prophet.

'Spirit of the Earth'

In his vision the Church was not just a divinely appointed organization designated to save individual souls through a more or less mechanical administration of the sacraments. Rather, it was a living organism – a single phylum – which had to be saved in its totality, for he could not conceive of the salvation of the part except in the context of the salvation of the whole. Nor was his God simply 'our Father which art in Heaven,' but the God 'ahead', the point of convergence at which the human race, through the instrumentality of the Church, was to find its consummation and meaning. This vision presented itself to Teilhard with irresistible force when he was serving as a stretcher-bearer in the First World War; and it never left him till his dying day.

In his vision there were two ingredients always present. Christ as the point of convergence in the future and his own almost physical awareness of the 'Spirit of the earth' – an awareness of the 'holiness' of matter and the 'essence' of the world that had 'hit' him when he was still a child and from which his 'whole internal life had sprung and grown . . . a personal psychological experience: nothing more, but also nothing less.'

A Paroxysm of Love

Teilhard was a pantheist and he knew it; but according to him there were two types of pantheism. These were what he describes as Hindu pantheism – the pantheism of diffusion and dissolution of all individual personality into an indeterminate whole – and a pantheism of 'centration' in which personality, so far from being obliterated, is heightened and clarified through love and centred on to the cosmic Christ who is the point to which all creation (or at least all of it that can be saved) is destined by evolution itself to converge. The 'oriental' pantheism of diffusion, which he had himself experienced time and again, is a blissful experience all right, but it is nonetheless essentially retrograde, a step back into a state of 'co-consciousness' before *self*-consciousness was born. The new mysticism neither abolishes personality nor sinks back into the beatific peace of undifferentiated oneness, but throws itself in a paroxysm of love into him who is both the source and goal of all personality and the collective fulfilment of all personalities.

Teilhard was both a mystic and a Marxist. He looks forward to the Marxist 'association in which the free development of each will be the condition for the free development of all' and to a state of cosmic awareness which will be suffused by love, and concentrated on and towards that ultimate unity to which evolution is driving us and which is the true goal of Christianity and the Catholic Church – Christ Omega, the cosmic fulfilment of mankind. This is the gospel according to Pierre Teilhard de Chardin, humanist, Marxist, mystic, and 'hyper-Catholic.'

R. C. ZAEHNER

FURTHER READING: Pierre Teilhard de Chardin, *Hymn of the Universe* (1964), *Le Milieu Divin* (1960) and *The Phenomenon of Man* (1959) (Harper and Row); *Letters to Two Friends 1926–1952* (World Publishing, 1969); F. Neilson, *Teilhard de Chardin's Vision of the Future* (Revisionist Pr., 1979); R. Speaight, *Teilhard de Chardin* (Harper and Row, 1968).

Telekinesis

Paranormally caused movement of objects: examples include the fall of a picture at someone's death, the flight of the Communion wafer to the recipient's mouth, and the movement of furniture or flinging of stones or crockery in poltergeist cases; teleportation, or apportation, is the mysterious conveyance of objects into closed rooms.

See MEDIUMS; POLTERGEISTS; PSYCHOKINESIS; SPONTANEOUS PSI EXPERIENCES; STIGMATA.

Telepathy

Communication between one mind and another without the use of speech, gesture or any of the normal methods of communicating; thought transference; 'the direct experience of another person's mental state'; a type of extra-sensory perception.

See EXTRA-SENSORY PERCEPTION; SPONTANEOUS PSI EXPERIENCES.

A practical and down-to-earth mystic, Teresa of Avila at the same time attained lofty heights of spiritual experience; on the one hand, an able administrator and on the other, a saint who showed the way to the ultimate fusion of the soul's being with God

TERESA OF AVILA

RECOGNIZED AS ONE of the greatest Christian mystics, Teresa de Cepeda y Ahumada, in religion Teresa of Jesus, will always be known as Teresa of Avila, from the Castilian town in which she was born on 28 March 1515 and where she spent most of her 67 years until her death on 4 October 1582. She was one of ten children – mostly boys – and when her father's second wife died in 1528, Teresa became something of an anxiety to her father, who finally put her in a boarding school, which she had to leave after 18 months owing to ill-health. He opposed her wish to become a nun, but at the age of 20 she eventually entered the Carmelite convent of the Incarnation in Avila.

The Carmelite Order, which originated in Palestine at the foot of the mountain from which it takes its name, had been, in intention, a body of hermits dedicated to extreme austerity. The extension of the hold of the Moslems in the Levant in the 13th century made life increasingly difficult, and the members of the order left Carmel for Cyprus, France, England and Spain. Progressive mitigation of the primitive rule became the accepted thing, and the convent of the Incarnation was lax in its observance and worldly in its spirit. Teresa was to reproach herself in later years for her own unfaithfulness, yet we know that during the 18 years she spent in that first convent, she seems to have had authentic mystical experiences. As the result of one of these, a vision of Christ in his Passion, she experienced a 'conversion' and began to lead a stricter life. In the year 1560, together with a small group of like-minded nuns, she decided to found a convent of strict observance, and in August 1562 she left the Incarnation for the new house, dedicated to St Joseph, also in Avila. There she was to spend what she later described as the happiest years of her life, from 1562 to 1567. It was at this time that she wrote the first version of her *Life* and also her *Way of Perfection*.

In 1567 she was ordered by the general of the Carmelite Order, then on a visit to Spain, to make other foundations. The remaining 15 years of her life were largely spent in travelling, negotiating, working with her own hands – she was, a contemporary declares, the best cook in the order. For, whilst she enjoyed the most remarkable and lofty mystical experiences, she always kept her feet on the ground. 'The Lord walks amongst the saucepans', was a famous saying of hers. In all, she was personally responsible for setting up 19 establishments, including two for men. She was helped in her work by a Carmelite friar, Fr Jerome Gracian. But her chief support in the closing years of her life came from an even greater exponent of mystical theology, John of the Cross (see JOHN).

The seal was set on her life's work when, in 1581, the distinction between the 'calced' or shod, and 'discalced' or shoeless Carmelites, as the relaxed parent body and the stricter reformed order were respectively known, was officially recognized by their separation into two orders, with separate governing bodies. She died in the following year, at Alba, one of her many foundations.

'Suborned with a Sardine'

The first important work from her pen was the *Life*, written between 1562 and 1565. It falls into four main divisions: an account of her early years, down to her 'conversion' to a life of perfection; a treatise on prayer; an account of her spiritual experiences, graces and temptations after her conversion; and the story of the foundation of St Joseph and some account of further experiences. To be grouped with the *Life* are the *Relations* which, from time to time, she wrote for the benefit of her confessors and spiritual directors. We should bear in mind that there was in Spain at the time much suspicion of those who claimed to have had special revelations, and Teresa was always anxious lest she should be deluded. Equally, her spiritual directors needed reassurance about their remarkable penitent.

The Way of Perfection, probably written in the year 1565, and rewritten before 1571, was intended as a guidebook for her nuns at St Joseph. The first part is a treatise on the ascetical preparation necessary for the aspirant to the heights of mystical experience, together with some account of 'mental prayer', the preliminary to true mystical prayer. The latter is treated, in the second part of the work, in the shape of a commentary on the Lord's Prayer.

The Interior Castle, written in 1577 and revised three years later, is universally recognized as her greatest achievement. It treats of the progress of the soul from the earliest imperfect stage to the final achievement of the mystic marriage. The 'castle' is pictured as a fabulously rich building, consisting of seven 'mansions' or apartments, the seventh and central one being the dwelling place of the Blessed Trinity, residing in the depths of the soul. Thus the mystic way is a turning away from outward reality to enter 'into oneself', there to find oneself in the embrace of God.

The Foundations, written at intervals during the last nine years of her life, is basically an account of the travels, negotiations, adventures and difficulties that attended the work of setting up the different convents of the reformed order. But it also contains much practical and spiritual advice to her nuns and to their superiors.

Letters, written throughout her life, give us an invaluable picture of the woman of affairs, the negotiator, the mother, the friend, remaining a complete human being even in the times of her great mystical experiences. They bear the stamp of a remarkable personality the warmth of whose heart is equalled, it would seem, only by the range of her interests and the solidity of her common sense.

Like all mystics, who see the end of human existence as a union with God, Teresa used language which implied a disregard of, if not a positive contempt for, the ephemeral realities of this world. Since this seems to be a basic element in all types of mystical doctrine, it calls for a further study. It must be recognized that such an attitude of mind, even if it is often expressed in absolute terms, can be justified only as an appreciation of relative values. In any human situation, certain values, pleasures, satisfactions, have to be sacrificed for the sake of a more pressing, more important demand. We have seen that, in everyday affairs, Teresa was eminently practical; we know that she was immensely affectionate and sensitive; she had her natural preferences, as when she said: 'It must be my nature – I could be suborned with a sardine!'; she constantly exhorted her nuns to accept their daily, concrete responsibilities. If, then, she was fond of saying *'todo es nada'*, 'everything is nothing', she meant this in the sense that everything derives its value and its significance from its relationship to God, its creator. Apart from him – if such an expression has any meaning – 'everything' is worthless and meaningless.

The Carmelite convent of the Incarnation in which Teresa of Avila spent 18 years was worldly in spirit and lax in its observance, and she later reproached herself for her unfaithfulness during this period. However, she seems to have had authentic mystical experiences while at the convent, and as a result of one of these, in which she had a vision of Christ in his Passion, she was 'converted' and began to lead a stricter life: *The Ecstasy of St Teresa* by Cignaroli

Mansell Collection

In her description of the total process leading to final mystical union, she distinguishes two main stages – the stage in which the emphasis is primarily on human effort, and the stage where all the work is seen as done by the spirit of God. In a famous passage in her *Life*, she compares the soul to an orchard, in need of water. At first this water is laboriously drawn from a well by hand. Then, the labour is lightened by the use of a *noria* (windlass), and water pipes. Yet more effective is the irrigation of the soil by streams, but best of all is the beneficent rain of God.

The approach to God, the way of perfection, is to be achieved, then, first by the ascetical effort which 'detaches' the soul from created reality so that it may come to a clearer vision of the Creator. Such detachment, not merely from possessions but from the sort of 'natural' affection which is a kind of self-seeking, will pave the way for true charity, a total love of the other for the sake of the other. Humility, the recognition of our own insignificance before God, is seen as another kind of detachment – from comfort, health, even life, to say nothing of reputation.

Concurrently with this ascetical effort must go the cultivation of 'mental prayer', the use of imagination and intellect about the things of God. As distinct from 'contemplation' or what Teresa calls 'supernatural' prayer, this first stage is due primarily to our own striving. In general, she would lump together the asceticism and the kind of prayer that goes with it as forming our contribution, our active progress towards the stage when God 'takes over' and the soul becomes 'passive'. In the imagery of *The Interior Castle*, the first three 'mansions' represent the first stage of the soul's journey.

When the soul enters the fourth mansion, it is coming under the influence of those graces which become more and more powerful as the soul submits more and more to their influence. From a state of recollection, in which the aspirant finds less and less savour in the sort of human conversation which merely dissipates the mind, God brings the soul to the prayer of 'quiet', in which the faculties of imagination and intellect become almost completely suspended. It is, one may suggest, as though the specific qualities of the individual human personality are surrendering to the power of God. Yet, as Teresa insists, the personality does not thereby become weakened or impoverished. On the contrary, the effects of this kind of prayer are an increased liberty of spirit, a growing sense of the Infinite and 'a great mastery of earthly realities'.

The final stages of the mystic way are the steps leading to the ultimate fusion of the soul's being with the Godhead. In Teresa's analysis there are three successive experiences to be undergone. Using the analogy of marriage, she speaks first of the meeting, the introduction of the spouses. The soul is being prepared for betrothal and marriage by a minute conformity of its will with the will of God the Beloved. In the prayer of (infused) 'union', the understanding and the will become united with the Godhead, in such a way that the human being no longer understands or wills anything otherwise than as God sees and wills. During this phase, too, the soul undergoes the purification of the senses. Yet the pain of this purification, and the purification of the spirit which follows, are essential experiences in that fullness of union which, daringly described in language reminiscent of sexual ecstasy, is at once intolerably painful yet incomparably delightful. But, in the very heart and centre of the 'castle', where the mystical marriage is at last celebrated, the encounter is such that the soul, now totally forgetful of itself, lives only for God. Life is desired solely as an opportunity of serving him. A foretaste of eternal bliss, this full union represents the highest favour that God can bestow on a human soul. Perfection is achieved.

T. CORBISHLEY

FURTHER READING: A. Peers ed., *The Complete Works of St Teresa of Jesus,* 3 vols. (Sheed and Ward, 1946); C. Gasquet ed., *Letters of St Teresa* (Gordon Press, 1977). See also: Marcelle Auclair, *St Teresa of Avila* (Doubleday); R. Hoornaert, *Saint Teresa in Her Writings* (Sheed and Ward, 1931); G. Papasogli, *St Teresa of Avila* (Dghtrs. St. Paul, 1973).

Tetragrammaton

The four Hebrew letters of the name of God in the Old Testament, spoken as Jehovah or Yahweh; regarded with profound awe it was rarely pronounced, and in the ordinary services in the synagogue the names Adonai or Elohim were substituted for it; it passed into European magic as one of the major 'names of power'.
See NAMES.

Theogony

Birth of the gods, an account, myth or theory of the origin, generation and line of descent of the gods; specifically, Hesiod's poem on the genealogy of the Greek gods.
See CREATION MYTHS; CRONUS.

The Theosophical Society does not identify itself with any particular religion, but has been described as 'a philanthropic society in that it attempts to promote a love of mankind and it is religious in that it demonstrates a spiritual background to existence'

THEOSOPHY

THE GERMAN ORIENTALIST Friedrich Max Müller (1823–1900) defined theosophy as 'expressing the highest conception of God within the reach of the human mind, and the perception of the eternal oneness of human and divine nature.' The emphasis is on the intuitive, inner nature of the knowledge, something not experienced through facts open to ordinary intelligence.

It is an ancient conception, particularly in India, where the philosophical schools of Vedanta and Sankhya, and the Yoga *Upanishads* teach it. At Alexandria the philosopher Philo Judaeus (1st century AD) joined the ideas of Plato with Judaism in a theosophic system. It persisted in the Cabala and Neoplatonism, and adherents of the system appear down through the centuries. Paracelsus, Giordano Bruno, Jacob Boehme, Emmanuel Swedenborg, John Tauler and Meister Eckhardt – all taught the essential basis of theosophy (see BOEHME; BRUNO; CABALA; ECKHARDT; NEOPLATONISM; PARACELSUS; SWEDENBORG).

In modern times the name is associated with the system set out in the 19th century in her books by H. P. Blavatsky (see BLAVATSKY). She stated that she had received these doctrines from Indian teachers or masters who had reached a higher plane of being and of spiritual development. Her experiences and witness to occult feats made her salon a magnet for a wide variety of people, who usually found her in possession of out-of-the-way facts in their own special subjects. The Theosophical Society, which she founded in conjunction with Henry S. Olcott and W. Q. Judge, exercised an influence on many notable people, either by its books, or by recruiting them as members. A copy of Blavatsky's *The Voice of the Silence* was on Lord Tennyson's bedside table when he died. Sir William Crookes, chemist and psychic researcher (see CROOKES), was a member; so were Thomas Alva Edison, the inventor, and W. B. Yeats, the poet (see YEATS). Lord Crawford, the astronomer, was a frequent visitor in London, and the student Mahatma Gandhi made his first acquaintance with the *Gita* among the theosophists. Rudolf Steiner, editor of Goethe and founder of Anthroposophy, was for a time at the head of the German section of the Society (see STEINER).

Annie Besant (see BESANT) was criticized for her political activity in India, but she explained, in 1929: 'What I say of the Inner Government of the World I speak from personal knowledge, for I have studied and practised Raja Yoga steadily during 40 years. . . . the Freedom of India within the great Federation of Free Nations linked by the British Crown is a condition essential to the Great Plan which must ultimately succeed.'

On her death in 1933 the Vice-President, A. P. Warrington, took charge, and appointed in his own post C. Jinarajadasa, a well-loved and accomplished lecturer and author. There were two nominees for President, and some acrimony because a letter had been made public in which Mrs Besant had remarked to the recipient, Dr George S. Arundale, that he was to be her successor. The other nominee, Ernest Wood (Sanskrit scholar and former secretary to C. W. Leadbeater, who had been closely associated with Annie Besant) objected to this and himself circularized the membership. However, out of a 72 per cent vote he secured only 4825 votes against Dr Arundale's 15,604.

In 1934 Dr Arundale stated what he called the marks theosophy makes upon the chart of Life: '(1) Life is essentially one and universal; (2) Life is within a great evolutionary process whereby an infinitude of life-units move from lowliest unconsciousness through innumerable stages of unfolding to heights of self-consciousness; (3) This irresistible movement is under beneficent and immutable law, order and purpose; (4) That all good and ill fortune individual or collective are signs of this evolutionary principle at work; (5) Each life-unit can hasten or retard the pace of its own evolutionary process, through understanding or through ignorance.'

Dr Arundale married an Indian lady,

Shrimati Rukmini Devi, who did important work in the revival of the classical Indian dance, Indian art, and the education of women. As President he did not travel as widely and frequently as others, but that was partly owing to the Second World War. He did give a great deal of attention to the movement in Australia, with good results. His books on special subjects like *Nirvana*, *Kundalini*, *You* (some critics said it should be 'Me') and *Mount Everest, its Spiritual Significance*, were intended to stimulate the intuition of the reader. This applied still more strongly to his large book on symbolism, *The Lotus Fire*, which most people found too difficult.

Jiddu Krishnamurti

In the early 1900s some European male residents of the Theosophical Society's headquarters used to swim of a morning in the Adyar river. Two young Indian brothers used to watch them and then were given swimming lessons. C. W. Leadbeater had noticed the exceptional aura of the older boy, and it occurred to him that it would be interesting to look at the previous lives of an ordinary Indian boy like this and see what his history was. The boys were two of a rather large family who lived in the village on the estate, sons of a minor local official, G. Narayaniah. Ernest Wood claimed to have suggested to Leadbeater that he look up the past lives of Krishnamurti and Nityananda, and that this was done with the father's permission. Wood's idea was that most Indians he knew abhorred the suggestion that they might be reborn in the West, and he wondered if experience in different races was the general rule. Leadbeater found to his surprise that the boy had had previous lives of great significance, and he commented, 'surely he is not here by accident'.

An offer was made to the father that Mrs Besant would undertake the future education and development of Krishnamurti and Nityananda, and he signed a statement before witnesses that he had no objection to the boys being taken to England to continue their education. However, pressure from orthodox Hindu friends and relatives made the father change his mind, and he sued for the restoration of the boys; and the court ruled that they should be returned to the father by May, 1913. Mrs Besant appealed first to the High Court, Madras, where she lost, and then to the Privy Council in London. There the case was reviewed with the welfare of the boys as the first priority. The boys had stated that they wished the benefits of an English education and did not wish to return to India. The Council over-ruled the two previous decisions, allowing the father, if he so wished, to make application in England for restoration regarding the guardianship, custody and maintenance of his children.

In 1910 Dr G. S. Arundale had formed among the boys of the Central Hindu College a private association called 'The Order of the Rising Sun of India'. He meant it to include those of his pupils who believed that the coming of a great Teacher was near. This Order was opened to the public in 1911, at the instance of Mrs Besant, and shortly afterwards she altered its name to 'The Order of the Star in the East', and put Krishnamurti at its head. The Order brought out a magazine called *The Herald of the Star*, and through sympathetic members of the Theosophical Society it spread rapidly in many countries. Other members strongly opposed its intrusion upon the time and resources of its followers.

Much newspaper publicity was focused upon Krishnamurti, whom they concluded to be a 'Messiah'. This effectively prevented him being sent to an English university, as it seemed certain his life would be made intolerable. His first venture into print was while still a boy, a booklet in simple English titled *At the Feet of the Master*, in which he recorded the instructions said to have been given him in sleep by an adept. Later he tried to express his mystical feelings in collections of poems, and wrote editorials for the magazine of the Order.

In the middle and late 1920s large gatherings of Star members took place yearly, camping in the grounds of Castle Eerde, belonging to Baron van Pallandt, near Ommen, in Holland. At the time of the first Camp, an unusual and severe cyclone tore across that part of the Low Countries, and strangely seemed to bifurcate and pass on either side of the tented camp. The local villagers were much impressed in favour of the Star by this phenomenon. These gatherings with ritual camp-fires in the evening were like elderly versions of a Scout jamboree. According to Lady Emily Lutyens, on 10 August 1925 Dr Arundale brought through from his overnight experience the names of ten of the '12 apostles' of the new religious impulse that was to come through Krishnaji, as he was called.

However, Krishnamurti became increasingly impatient of being associated with theosophists. He had his own individual outlook and message. In 1929 he dissolved the Order of the Star in the East, and returned Castle Eerde and its grounds to Baron van Pallandt, who had wanted him, or a group on his behalf, to take it over. In the following years he made his base at Ojai in California, and there and elsewhere held seminars of talks and question and answer meetings. Many books, revised from these occasions, were published. He became a friend of Aldous Huxley and other original thinkers. From time to time he has visited Europe and India.

In 1927 he had a profound experience, and on 2 August he said: 'I could not have said last year, as I can say now, that I am the Teacher; for had I said it then it would have been insincere, it would have been untrue. But now I can say it. I have become one with the Beloved, I have been made simple. As I have changed, as I have found my end, which is the end for all . . . and because I have affection – and without affection you cannot attain the end . . . because I have suffered and seen and found all, naturally it is my duty . . . my pleasure, my dharma, to give it to those who have not . . . I am not going to be bound by anyone; I am going on my way, because that is the only way. I have found what I wanted. I have been united with my Beloved, and my Beloved and I will wander together the face of the earth.'

One cannot but agree with the English theosophist T. H. Redfern when he says: 'The strange and puzzling thing is that although his work has turned out much different from what was expected of him, yet Bishop Leadbeater, using his psychic faculties "picked a winner" in a lad of about

Founded by H. P. Blavatsky, in conjunction with Henry S. Olcott and W. Q. Judge, the Theosophical Society influenced many eminent figures including Mahatma Gandhi, the inventor Thomas Edison and W. B. Yeats *Below left* Mme Blavatsky, and (*left to right*) Dr G. S. Arundale, C. Jinarajadasa and N. Sri Ram, successive presidents of the Society

Psychic News

Theosophical Publishing House

12, described by Professor Wood as "a very frail little boy, extremely weak . . . He was bullied and beaten to such an extent that it seemed the boy might fade away from this life and die."'

On the death of Dr Arundale in 1945, C. Jinarajadasa, or 'Brother Raja' as he was affectionately called in theosophical circles, became President of the Society and so remained until 1953. He took his degree at St John's, Cambridge, and later studied languages so that he could lecture in French, Italian, Spanish and Portuguese. He continually pressed for the introduction of Beauty and Art into theosophical work. He branched out in original directions; interviewed Mussolini in 1923; inspired the formation of a Muslim League to study the relation between Islam and theosophy; and devised a Ritual of the Mystic Star. Apart from his many excellent books, students of theosophy hold him in high esteem for his care of the headquarters archives, and the editing and publication of many documents which would otherwise have slipped into oblivion.

The successor to C. Jinarajadasa was N. Sri Ram. He was assistant editor of Mrs Besant's paper *New India* from 1923 to 1933, and was also her private secretary. In 1937 he was made Treasurer of the Theosophical Society. His lectures and writings are logically structured and full of a limpid wisdom. In spite of his years he is an active and continual traveller, and inspires the national sections by his quiet emphasis on the truly spiritual and unselfish solutions to world problems. His tenure of office has seen the completion and opening at Adyar of a fine new library building, which in addition to printed books, houses a very valuable collection of palm-leaf manuscripts. Recently a new building has been erected for the printing and publishing department, with a bust of its founder, Annie Besant, in the forecourt. The North American membership has been generous in its support of these projects.

Blueprint of Evolution

The important divergence of viewpoint between modern theosophy and current scientific thought is that the former insists that the evolutionary plan, both in the material and the non-physical worlds, pre-exists in blueprint form in the Universal Creative Mind. It cannot be substantially interfered with by man or angel. The supposed chance emergence of an organizing force which we call life, owing to the juxtaposition of certain chemicals, water, and sunlight, is regarded by theosophists as confusing the predetermined suitable conditions for life manifesting, with the cause of life so manifesting.

Theosophy harks back to Pythagoras (see PYTHAGORAS), and indeed to ancient India, in underlining number as a guide to understanding the scheme of things. There is One Supreme, the Logos or Word, expressing itself in a triple mode or Trinity. Seven distinctive streams of energy from the One pour out into 12 areas of expression. Creation is a continuous, or rather cyclically recurring, process throughout the Universe.

The widespread variety of stages in cyclic development occurring among suns, planets, supermen, men, animals, and lower kingdoms, permits the maximum economy of energy by using the mutual aid and interaction between the older and younger lives. For example, man in his extraction and manufacture of metals for his own use is speeding the development of the minerals. The failures and backward units of one cycle become the wise and stable shining lights of another or later cycle.

Self-conscious man, in theosophical theory, is the product of an extraordinarily long evolution, not only as to his body, but as to his thinking and emotional consciousness. The innermost unit of consciousness is divine in origin – 'the One willed to become Many' – but the bridging sheaths, through which that unit or monad can contact the physical world, have been taken over by him from some animal which reached the peak of animal consciousness. Then a long pilgrimage of incarnations is required to develop the means to become self-conscious at the highest levels, and ultimately conscious of unity with the One. These lives or incarnations are linked and moulded by the operation of the law of adjustment, or Karma (see KARMA). This law continually tends to balance outgoing forces. Energy continuously expended towards an objective must bring success if it lies in the realm of the possible. But it can produce an imbalance in the individual, and a back-surge of unexpected results if it is selfishly motivated.

Shrimati Rukmini Devi; the wife of Dr G. S. Arundale, she played an important part in the revival of the classical Indian dance, Indian art, and the education of women

C. Nelson Stewart

The prehistory of mankind goes back, in the theosophical system, not tens of thousands, but millions of years. Seven great human types will develop during the earth's present cycle of activity, and we are already well through the fifth type. But there are natural phenomena which shut off the great races from each other – ice ages, subsidence into the ocean, earthquakes and volcanic storms. These catastrophic events are initiated and controlled by non-human intelligences under the command of the Planetary Logos. Hence the last word does not lie with man, who thinks he is now powerful enough to devastate his home in space.

Later theosophists have published what they claim to be life-stories and incidents recovered by clairvoyance from the 'memory of Nature'. Something similar is done by what are called object-readers or psychometrists in regard to more recent events. One extraordinary compilation by Annie Besant and C. W. Leadbeater purports to describe in detail the infra-structure of many of the chemical atoms and molecules. So far no bridge has been found between their diagrams and models and the mathematically-based arrangements of the physicists. They tell us that the ultimate physical atom is built in a spiralling vortex of about 14,000 million bubbles in *koilon*. Koilon, it seems, is what fills space. In this study of the building bricks of matter it is interesting to hear that the atoms themselves alter in their capacity to respond to vibrations as the cycles proceed. And it must be admitted that these seers stumbled upon isotopes before the scientists did.

An early Vice-President like A. P. Sinnett thought membership should be sought in the upper classes, and their acceptance of the ideas would filter down to the lower orders. When Annie Besant was at her peak as a travelling lecturer, the membership probably reached its highest level. When the post-Revolutionary spread of Russian power took place, the countries dominated were unable to maintain theosophical societies. To some extent counterbalancing the loss, many new centres opened in South American countries as a result of tours by C. Jinarajadasa, who was able to lecture in Spanish and Portuguese. In 1925, when the Order of the Star in the East was flourishing world-wide, its membership exceeded 100,000 or more than twice that of the Theosophical Society. The Theosophical membership figures (with some returns awaited) given in the General Report for 1966 were 26,487 in 49 countries. The three largest totals were India, 7664; United States of America, 4054; and England, 2252.

C. NELSON STEWART

FURTHER READING: H. P. Blavatsky, *The Secret Doctrine* (Theosophical Publishing House, 1980, abridged edn.); *Key to Theosophy* (T.P.H. reprint); W. Q. Judge, *The Ocean of Theosophy* (T.P.H. reprint); Mary Lutyens ed., *The Krishnamurti Reader* (Penguin, 1970); Victor A. Endersby, *The Hall of Magic Mirrors* (Carlton Press, 1969).

As legendary hero, Theseus is represented as the slayer of the monstrous Minotaur and an adventurer who went down alive to Hades; as statesman, he appears as magnanimous champion of the oppressed and author of the Athenian constitution

THESEUS

FOR THE ATHENIANS, as for us, Theseus was one of the more important heroes of Greek legend. But his full renown is of relatively late growth and peculiar to Attica. In fact Theseus has two aspects, which may be called the heroic and the political. In his heroic aspect he is an adventurer, subduer of monsters and chaser of women, after the fashion of Hercules, on whom he came to be modelled. In his political aspect he is a symbol of Athens and of Attic unity and power, indeed almost the only hero to become such an established symbol. He is treated for all purposes as a historical figure, even by sober writers of prose such as Aristotle. For this reason Plutarch brackets him with another legendary figure in his parallel *Lives* of Greeks and Romans, the founder of Rome, Romulus.

Though for ordinary Greeks legend was not separate from the history of earlier periods, in the case of Theseus this distinction must be made in some form. But it is not enough to argue simply that the heroic Theseus in his marvellous adventures is purely legendary, while the political Theseus is historical in the sense of being a man who really lived. For the political Theseus is a figure answering to other needs of the Attic imagination, but hardly less fictitious.

As a pan-Hellenic hero, Theseus is a relatively minor figure of the generation before the Trojan War, by no means of such stature as his contemporary Hercules or some other figures. He is connected in legend

***The Minotaur*, by G. F. Watts, suggests the pathos of the monster with a human body and a bull's head which in legend was kept in the labyrinth of Cnossus. With the help of Ariadne, daughter of the king of Crete, Theseus penetrated to the heart of the labyrinth, killed the Minotaur and made his way safely out again**

Tate Gallery/John Webb

Michael Holford/British Museum

Bulls occur frequently in the history of Theseus, adventurer, ravisher of women and subduer of robbers and monsters: he slew the bull-headed Minotaur and subdued the wild bull of Marathon, and his son Hippolytus was killed by a bull from the sea *Left* Black-figured Greek vase of the 6th century BC, showing Theseus killing the Minotaur *Right* Heroic statue of Theseus in Hyde Park, London

with Troezen in the eastern Peloponnese but otherwise only with Attica, apart from the regions visited in his adventures and wanderings. For the Athenians of classical times he was not only the slayer of the Minotaur but also the author of a great political change, the *synoikismos*, that is to say the incorporation of all Attic communities into a single state ruled from Athens. In Attic legend he is also the pattern of the humane ruler who receives refugees and unfortunates, since Attica is never in his time ravaged by war.

From Plutarch's *Life of Theseus* and from two other compilers, Diodorus and Apollodorus, the outline of Theseus's life can be told. This is fortunate because there is no continuous and complete narrative in extant poetry, and even vanished epic poems of Attica such as the *Theseis* and the *Minyas*, which are later than the *Iliad* and the *Odyssey*, do not seem from remaining fragments or from references in other writers to have told the whole story.

Sword beneath the Rock

Theseus was born in Troezen to Aethra, daughter of King Pittheus. In Athenian legend his father was King Aegeus of Athens, who returned to Athens before he was born, leaving under a hollow rock a sword and a pair of sandals, to be claimed by his son when he was big enough to raise the rock. In the Troezenian legend his father was the god Poseidon, who has an important part even in the Athenian legend. Having lifted the rock, Theseus then made his way to Athens.

However, he did not take the easy way by sea. He went by land, overcoming and killing dangerous robbers. Such were Periphetes, who attacked travellers with his club; Sinis who bent down pine trees, tied his victims to the tops and then let the trees spring up and apart to tear them limb from limb; Cercyon who forced men to wrestle with him until he killed them; Sciron who made travellers wash his feet on the top of a precipice so that he could kick them over; and Procrustes who forced them to fit one of his two beds, stretching out the shorter travellers to fit the longer bed and lopping the taller to fit the shorter. He also killed the ravaging sow of Crommyon. On being welcomed by Aegeus at Athens, he was very nearly poisoned by a drink offered by the witch Medea, then married to Aegeus; but Aegeus recognized him and cried out in time.

Aegeus then told Theseus of the affliction that the Athenians suffered at the hands of Minos of Crete. In vengeance for the killing of his son Androgeus in Attica, Minos every year carried off a band of Athenian youths and maidens to be given as victims to the Minotaur. This was a monster with a human body and a bull's head, usually said to have been kept in the labyrinth of Cnossus, a building designed in the form of an intricate maze, from which no one who entered could find his way out (see BULL; MAZE).

Food for the Minotaur

Theseus went voluntarily as one of the victims. When he arrived on Crete, he won the help of Ariadne, daughter of Minos. She gave him a ball of thread to unwind as he made his way into the labyrinth and follow so that he could find his way out again. He killed the Minotaur with his sword and then set off homeward in triumph with the captives, who were no longer needed as food for the Minotaur. He took Ariadne with him, but left her behind on the island of Dia off the coast near Cnossus or, as was more commonly said, on the island of Naxos, where the god Dionysus found her and took her as his wife.

As Theseus approached Athens, he forgot to change the black sail of the ship, a sign of mourning for the young Athenians, for a white one which would be a sign of deliverance. This he had promised to do if he came home safe. Aegeus, who was looking out for him, concluded that he had perished and hurled himself from a cliff.

Theseus thus became king of Athens. He had to fight rivals, the sons of Pallas, brother of Aegeus, but prevailed over them. He subdued the wild bull of Marathon, being sheltered on his way by an old peasant woman, Hecale. On an expedition with

Hercules and others to Themiscyra, where the Amazons lived on the south coast of the Black Sea (see AMAZONS) he carried off an Amazon, Antiope or, according to others, Hippolyta, and made her his wife; he later repudiated her and married Phaedra, daughter of Minos. The Amazons made war on him, invaded Attica and were with a great effort defeated. By his Amazon wife he had a son, Hippolytus. He also carried off Helen as a girl from Laconia, but she was brought home by force while he was away by her brothers Castor and Polydeuces.

Theseus was in Hades at the time with his friend Pirithous the Lapith, who was attempting to carry off Persephone, queen of the underworld. Pluto, however, cunningly persuaded Theseus and Pirithous to sit on seats, to which their flesh grew. Theseus was rescued by Hercules, who could not free Pirithous.

When Theseus eventually returned to Athens he found that the people were disaffected. He left for the island of Scyros, where the king Lycomedes, fearing that he meant to annex the island, treacherously thrust him over a cliff. A skeleton of great size, said to be his, was found on Scyros centuries later and carried to Athens by Cimon.

The adventures given in this framework appear here and there in surviving poetry, including some celebrated plays, which introduce something of his other aspect of statesman. Within extant poetry the earliest mention of Theseus is in a speech by Nestor in the *Iliad* (book 1). Nestor compares the warriors at Troy to their disadvantage with the earlier generation which included Pirithous and Theseus, son of Aegeus. 'They were like the immortals, the mightiest of men, who fought the mightiest of enemies, the beast-men of the hills.' The reference is to the centaurs whom Pirithous and his Lapithae subdued with the help of Theseus. In the *Odyssey* (book 11) there is mention of the ghost of Ariadne in Hades 'whom Theseus wished to bring from Crete to Athens but who was slain by Artemis on Dia by the witness of Dionysus': a puzzling passage. The *Odyssey* also relates that Odysseus, after seeing the phantom of Hercules, also hoped to see the ghosts of Theseus and Pirithous. The expedition of the two heroes to Hades must have been known to Homer.

According to Hesiod as reported in Athenaeus and Plutarch, Theseus abandoned Ariadne because he took a fancy to the maidens Hippe and Aegle. A damaged papyrus contains a fragment of a Hesiodic poem *The Descent of Pirithous*, in which the ghost of Theseus in Hades tells the ghost of Meleager how he and Pirithous came down to carry off Persephone. Meleager apparently hears the story with disgust.

In the remains of the Epic Cycle, poems of the same type as the *Iliad* and *Odyssey* but later and inferior, there is an occasional allusion to Theseus. In the *Nostoi* (Homeward Journeys of the Heroes from Troy) it is said that the love of Antiope for Theseus led her to betray Themiscyra to him and Hercules. In the *Cypria* Theseus is said to have carried off Helen and to have kept her

Jeffrey Craig

Spectrum Colour Library

The 'Horns of Minos' rise from the ruins of Cnossus, relics of the bull cult of ancient Crete: the legend of Theseus as national hero of Athens, who challenged the authority of Crete and founded Athenian greatness, seems to preserve memories of a time when Attica was dominated by Crete

until she was rescued by her brothers, the Dioscuri.

Among the lyric poets Alcman, as reported by Pausanias, tells how the Dioscuri, retrieving Helen, took Athens while Theseus was away and captured his mother Aethra. Stesichorus says that Helen was pregnant at the time of her rescue, and gave birth at Argos to an infant which she handed over to her sister Clytemnestra, before she herself married Menelaus. Pindar tells much the same story, explaining that Theseus kept Helen because he wished to become brother-in-law of the Dioscuri.

Palace under the Sea

But the most celebrated treatment of Theseus in lyric is found in two poems of Bacchylides. In *Dithyramb* 18, Aegeus is presented in conversation with a chorus about the approach of a remarkable stranger coming from Troezen. Aegeus has heard that he has killed Sinis and the other robbers and the sow of Crommyon. Two men are accompanying him; he wears a sword, a Laconian helmet, a red tunic and a woollen Thessalian cloak. His hair is flame-coloured and he darts from his eyes a red flame like the earth-fire of Lemnos. He is in the flower of his youth, his thoughts are of weapons and he is making for Athens. In *Dithyramb* 17, Theseus is shown sailing to Crete in the charge of Minos with the captive youths and maidens. He disputes with Minos, who is laying his hands on one of the maidens, claiming that if Minos is son of Zeus he himself is son of Poseidon. Zeus gives a clap of thunder as a sign for Minos, who throws his ring into the sea, challenging Theseus to dive for it. Theseus plunges in and reaches Poseidon's palace under the sea, where he is greeted by Amphitrite and presented with a bright garment. He comes up to the surface still dry, and the Nereids sing around him as he returns on board.

In Attic drama Theseus is prominent in Sophocles' *Oedipus at Colonus* and in Euripides' *Mad Hercules, Hippolytus* and *Suppliants*. In the *Oedipus at Colonus* the aged and blind Oedipus, exiled from Thebes, is received in Attica at Colonus as a refugee with his two daughters. Theseus gives him protection and will not allow Creon of Thebes to carry off him or his daughters. In reward Oedipus reveals to Theseus alone where he must die in Attica and how, when he has disappeared beneath Attic earth, his presence will be a blessing to Attica. Only Theseus sees the manner of his death, and on oath reveals it to no one except his heirs. For this service Oedipus will hold Athens unscathed from any attack that may come from the Thebans who cast him out. Sophocles also wrote a *Phaedra*, which has perished; it dealt with the adulterous passion of Phaedra, wife of Theseus, for her stepson Hippolytus, but details are not known. It is believed that at the time of the action Theseus is supposed to be away.

In *Mad Hercules* Euripides relates how Hercules, after recovering from the fit of madness in which he killed his children, is brought to Attica from Thebes by Theseus and cleansed from the defilement of his deed. He also receives the promise of a place to dwell in recognition of his services to the Greeks, including Theseus. So too in the *Suppliants* Theseus supports the claim of Adrastus, the survivor among the chiefs who led the great Argive expedition against Thebes, to receive back the dead from the Thebans. If the Thebans will not yield, Theseus will make war on them, after putting the proposal to the Athenian people for their approval. He receives back the bodies of the Argive troops which the Athenians bury on Cythaeron, while those of the leaders are brought to Eleusis in Attica for burning before the bones and ashes are taken to Argos.

Deceived Husband

In the *Hippolytus*, Theseus has a very different part. There were two versions, of which the older, now lost, presented Phaedra in the style of Potiphar's wife, as perhaps Sophocles did, attempting to seduce Hippolytus and, when she failed, denouncing him for an attempt on her virtue. In the later one, which survives, Phaedra at first takes no action and conceals her passion until she is ill with it. Her old nurse induces her to confess it and unwisely reveals it to Hippolytus, making overtures in Phaedra's name but without her permission. Hippolytus recoils in horror and upbraids Phaedra for advances which she did not make. Phaedra hangs herself, leaving a written message for Theseus, accusing Hippolytus of rape. On his return Theseus believes the message and curses Hippolytus, driving him into exile. As Hippolytus drives along the shore, Poseidon, carrying out Theseus's curse, sends a bull from the sea to terrify his horses. They smash his chariot and drag him until he is nearly dead. The goddess Artemis then appears to tell Theseus the truth, and he is reconciled to his dying son. Theseus appears here only as a deceived, outraged and hasty husband and father. But in the other plays he appears as a humane ruler with a certain leaning toward democracy.

Episodes of Theseus's career are treated in Alexandrian poetry. Bion remarks that all lovers are happy, even Theseus when he went down into implacable Hades, because Pirithous was at his side. The remains of Callimachus's *Hecale* tell how the old peasant woman, Hecale, entertained Theseus on his way to capture the bull of Marathon, but was dead when he returned.

It has been argued that Theseus was originally a hero of the Ionian Greeks, who lived in the northern Peloponnese as well as in Attica and Euboea before the Dorian and West Greek invasion, so that his connection with Troezen, a Dorian city in classical times, goes back to the Mycenean period. Within Attica he seems originally to have belonged to the north-eastern region about

Marathon. The power of Minos over Attica could represent the power of rulers in Cnossus, who were already, in the 15th century BC, Greeks rather than Minoans, though Cnossus fell later to other Greeks from the mainland. Theseus's defeat of the robbers between Troezen and Athens may be a fairly late development of his story, not much earlier than the 6th century BC.

Friend of Democracy

The political Theseus no doubt has ancient roots in Attic tradition. But he appears in definite form first in Thucydides, and in plays of Euripides which apply forms of thought belonging to the 5th century BC to heroic legend. According to Thucydides, Attica before Theseus's reign was divided between separate communities which had their own authorities and took little common counsel or action except in face of external peril. The shrewd and energetic Theseus abolished these local assemblies and directed their members to meet in Athens, though the rest of the local inhabitants still lived separately. By the death of Theseus, Athens had become a large and powerful state, and the Athenians date their political unity from that time. Euripides in his *Suppliants* even makes Theseus claim to have set the people free to exercise equal votes and to elect annual officers, an equal part of these to be chosen by the poor. Isocrates *(Panathenaicus)*, Aristotle *(Politics* and *Constitution of Athens)* and Plutarch *(Life of Theseus)* regard Theseus's constitution as a historical creation, a mixture of various elements which was intended to be just and stable and was later gradually improved, until finally it was transformed for the worse into extreme democracy. Some oligarchs regarded Theseus's concessions to the people as the remote beginning of decay.

The truth symbolized by this treatment of Theseus, alone among epic heroes, is that Attic society, and even the Attic state, had a continuous existence since heroic or, historically, since Mycenean times. In other regions of Greece overrun by the Dorians the heroic or Mycenean society had been swept away and no such continuity could be claimed.

E. D. PHILLIPS

'The similarities between ancient theurgy and modern Spiritualism appear too numerous to be dismissed as pure coincidence' and 'it is tempting to conclude that they have a common psychological basis in actual experience'

THEURGY

THEURGY WAS DEFINED by the Neoplatonist philosopher Proclus (5th century AD) as 'a power higher than all human wisdom and knowledge, embracing the blessings of divination, the purifying effects of the ritual art, and in a word all the operations of divine possession.' It can be described more simply as magic applied to a religious purpose and resting on a supposed revelation of a religious character. Its practitioners called themselves 'theurgists' because they claimed not merely to talk about the gods as 'theologians' did, but to *act* upon them in a direct manner. Whereas vulgar magic used names and formulae of religious origin to profane ends, theurgy employed the methods of vulgar magic primarily (though, as we shall see, not exclusively) to a religious end, the salvation of the soul through contact with the Divine.

The revelation on which the theurgists based their practice was contained in a long poem in Greek hexameters, known as the *Chaldean Oracles*. It was the last Sacred Book of classical antiquity, published and perhaps composed by one Julianus (called 'the Chaldean' to distinguish him from the Emperor Julian) who lived in the time of the Emperor Marcus Aurelius (161–180 AD). Of his life and personality we know virtually nothing, but later tradition represents him as a potent magician who could cause men's souls to leave and re-enter the body and could produce apparitions of divine beings; the timely thunderstorm which saved the Roman army from destruction during Marcus's campaign against the Quadi in 173 AD was attributed by some to the magic arts of Julianus. His book is unfortunately lost, but numerous fragments of it and descriptions of the rituals founded on it are preserved by the

Medieval Christian view of Julian the Apostate, the patron of theurgy

British Museum

C. M. Dixon

later Neoplatonists. It seems to have been a strange amalgam of oriental religious ideas, derived ultimately from Iranian, Babylonian, Syrian, Egyptian and Jewish sources, with Greek concepts most of which go back in origin to Plato.

Theurgy had a chequered history. For a century after Julianus's time it seems to have created little stir. Plotinus, the founder of Neoplatonism, never mentions it and is never described as a theurgist. Its heyday came later, when Plotinus's successors in the Greek-speaking Neoplatonic schools perceived in it a valuable ally in their long struggle against the rising power of Christianity. Iamblichus (*c* 250–325 AD) in particular exalted theurgy above philosophy, ritual above reason. 'It is not thought,' he says, 'that links the theurgists with the gods . . . Theurgic union is attained only by the efficacy of the unspeakable *acts* performed in the appropriate manner.' The last pagan Emperor, Julian 'the Apostate' (died 363), had complete faith in theurgy and elevated its practitioners to high office, but the subsequent Christian reaction drove it underground for a time. It re-emerged in the 5th century at Athens, where Proclus set the *Chaldean Oracles* beside the *Timaeus* of Plato as the two indispensable cornerstones of pagan orthodoxy and was himself an expert in theurgic magic (see NEOPLATONISM; PROCLUS). Under Justinian (527–565) it was finally prohibited along with other pagan practices, but the tradition of it lingered.

Animated Statues

From the many scattered sources the procedures of theurgy can be reconstructed in broad outline, though much remains uncertain. We can distinguish two main types – those which depended exclusively on the use of 'symbols' or 'tokens' and those which involved the employment of an entranced 'medium'. The former type seems to have been used mainly for the purpose of consecrating and 'animating' magical statues of deities in order to obtain oracles or other help from them. The 'symbols' were the animals, herbs, stones, scents and engraved characters appropriate to the particular god invoked; each god had his 'sympathetic' representative in the animal, the vegetable and the mineral kingdom which was

The theurgists' attempt to induce the temporary presence of a god in a human medium had a famous precedent at Delphi, where Apollo spoke through a priestess *Left* Apollo, on a bowl from Delphi, 5th century BC *Below right* Aegeus consults the priestess of Apollo: Attic vase of the 5th century BC

permanently *en rapport* with its divine cause. The symbols were hidden inside the statue, so that their identity was known only to the magician. The ceremony was completed by the recitation of certain secret 'life-giving names' which the gods had revealed to Julianus. If the consecration had been correctly performed, the statue would give omens to its worshippers by apparent movements or changes of expression, or would procure for them communications from the deity in sleep.

This practice, though foreign to classical Greek tradition, was by no means new. Its centre of diffusion appears to have been Egypt, where it was rooted in native religious ideas. The Hermetic dialogue *Asclepius* knows of it as an ancient Egyptian usage (see HERMETICA), and the magical papyri from Egypt offer recipes for the manufacture of such images. But from the 1st century AD onwards we begin to hear of the private fabrication and magical use of oracular statues outside Egypt. Its real vogue, however, came later with Iamblichus, who doubtless saw in it the most effective defence of the pagan cult of images against the sneers of Christian critics. From his teaching seems to derive the belief in consecrated statues as protective 'talismans' *(telesmata)* – enchanted images whose presence, concealed or visible, had power to avert natural disaster or military defeat. Such a 'talisman' was the statue of Achilles, dedicated in the Parthenon in 375 by the theurgist Nestorius, following instructions received in a dream, which is said to have saved Athens from an earthquake.

The Medium Possessed

Of greater interest to the anthropologist and the psychical researcher, since it invites comparison with 'possession'-cults elsewhere and in particular with modern Spiritualism, is the other branch of theurgy, which sought to induce the temporary presence of a god not in a statue but in a living human organism. This too was in principle no novelty. At Delphi the oracular god Apollo had for many centuries spoken in the first person through the lips of an entranced priestess, and in the Roman Imperial Age similar methods were in use at several other public oracles (see ORACLES). But this was institutionalized mediumship, confined to certain holy places and certain officially authorized persons. What seems to have been new in theurgy was the systematic exploitation of mediumship at private seances which had no official standing and might apparently be held anywhere.

The best mediums, says Iamblichus, are 'young and rather simple persons'. Ritual means, such as the putting on of a special dress, were employed to throw them into a state of dissociation and to secure the presence of the particular god desired. A distinction is drawn between trance automatism, in which the medium's personality is completely in abeyance, and automatism without trance, which the medium can both induce and terminate at will. The symptoms of trance are said to vary widely with different communicating gods and on different occasions: there may be anaesthesia, including insensibility to fire; there may be bodily movement or complete immobility; there may be changes in the quality of the voice. The gods, we are told, come at first reluctantly, but more easily when they have formed a habit (that is, no doubt, when a secondary 'trance personality' has been built up). Most of these observations can be paralleled from the annals of modern Spiritualism (see MEDIUMS; SPIRITUALISM).

The possessing gods, like 'communicators' today, claimed to establish their authenticity by exhibiting supernormal powers. In true possession, we are assured, the possessing spirit will 'utter things outside the medium's knowledge and sometimes predict future events'. Some gods even venture an answer to such questions as, 'Will it be a boy or a girl?' This may be thought risky, but in the event of failure there were explanations available: 'bad conditions', or the disturbed state of the medium's mind, or the inopportune intervention of his normal self; or again the intrusion of a lying spirit who 'jumps in and usurps the place prepared for a higher being'. All these excuses recur in the literature of Spiritualism.

The gods also granted to the theurgists visible signs of their presence. Sometimes these were seen by all present, though on other occasions only the operating magician claimed to see them. Iamblichus alleges that there may be dilatation or levitation of the medium's person; that lights may be seen, sometimes by all present, at the moment when the medium is falling into or emerging from trance; and that the operator may see spirit forms entering the medium's body (this last he calls 'the most important sign'). To the psychical researcher this is a familiar-sounding list. The apparition of lights, which seems to have been the most frequent phenomenon (and one of the easiest to fake, as the Christian writer Hippolytus showed) is frequent also in the modern seance-room. Levitation and dilatation have been ascribed to modern mediums. And the 'spirit forms' – which may appear either as shapeless masses or in recognizable shapes – are suggestive of the so-called ectoplasm which modern observers claim to have seen emerge from, and return to, the bodies of certain mediums. Iamblichus also seems to refer to what spiritualists call 'apports' (materializations of objects); and from other sources we hear of 'autophonic' oracles, corresponding to the so-called 'direct voice' which dispenses with the use of the medium's vocal organs.

The similarities between ancient theurgy and modern Spiritualism appear too numerous to be dismissed as pure coincidence. And it is not altogether easy to account for them by literary tradition or any diffusionist theory. It is tempting to conclude that they have a common psychological basis in actual

Staatliche Museum, Berlin

experience. It should, however, be remembered that with all these similarities there is associated one fundamental contrast: what the Spiritualists ascribe to the activity of a discarnate human mind the theurgists normally attribute to non-human spirits, 'gods' or 'daemons'. In this way they agree with the preponderant weight of ancient opinion. The *possibility* of communication with the dead was indeed seldom denied, save by Epicureans and sceptics, but religious feeling was strongly opposed to it. Under the Roman Empire necromancy was occasionally practised in secret, but it had no place in religious life and was subject to severe legal penalties. Nor is there any evidence that Graeco-Roman necromancers ever made use of mediums in their rites.

The pious theurgists, who did employ mediums, were not necromancers and had little interest in calling up the dead. They admitted, however, that cases of disputed identity – ghost or non-human spirit – might sometimes occur, since the lower orders of spirits were liable on occasion to simulate the higher. Thus for example Iamblichus was credited with having unmasked a self-styled Apollo, evoked by an Egyptian magician, who was in reality only the ghost of a gladiator. But such cases were thought to be exceptional, as were also the occasional intrusions of the evil spirits known as 'anti-gods' *(antitheoi)*: they happened, it was believed, chiefly where the operator was inexperienced or ritually impure. The motivation of the theurgist was religious. He was not interested in demonstrating survival, which he took for granted; his object was to achieve communion with the divine beings of a traditional faith and by their aid to transcend earthly experience and 'ascend to the intellectual fire'.

E. R. DODDS

FURTHER READING: Hans Lewy, *Chaldaean Oracles and Theurgy* (Cairo, Institut Français, 1956); E. R. Dodds, 'Supernormal Phenomena in Classical Antiquity', *Proceedings of the Society for Psychical Research* vol. 55 (1971).

The Tarot card numbered 13 is Death, the skeleton, and 13 is the traditional number of a coven of witches: the number's uncanny and ominous associations reach back to pagan times

Lady Westmorland and her 13 children pray to Christ, in a 16th century altar frontal: 13 is widely regarded as an unlucky number, possibly because it is one more than 12, a number of completeness, and so has the connotation of dangerously exceeding proper limits or starting on a new and uncertain course

THIRTEEN

THAT THE NUMBER 13 is unlucky is one of the most common and persistent of superstitions and one of the few that is openly catered to. Hotel managements still frequently take care to have no 13th floor and some builders and local authorities do not number a house 13, because if they do it will be difficult to dispose of. Gustav Jahoda records in his book *The Psychology of Superstition* that in 1965, when the Queen paid a visit to West Germany, the number of the platform at Duisburg railway station from which her train was to leave was changed from 13 to 12A.

A good many people dislike parties of 13 and it is thought to be extremely unlucky for this number of people to sit down to a table. One of them, sometimes said to be the first person to rise from the table, or sometimes the last, will die or suffer some damaging misfortune before a year is out. The belief has been recorded in Oxfordshire that it is ominous for 13 people to be together in one room, especially for the one who is nearest the door, and in London that if the number on a bus ticket adds to 13 it brings bad luck. The 13th day of the month is widely regarded as a most unpropitious day for beginning any new undertaking (though there is nothing unfortunate about being born on it) and even people who think of themselves as entirely unsuperstitious may show slight symptoms of unease when the 13th falls on a Friday, which is an unlucky day in its own right (see DAYS).

The reasons for this uneasiness about 13 are obscure. Though it has probably

The Last Supper by Damaskinos, a 16th century Cretan ikon painter: the fact that 13 people attended the Last Supper, which was followed by betrayal and death, has added to the number's evil reputation. It is still thought very unlucky for 13 people to sit down to a table

C. M. Dixon

been strengthened by the fact that 13 sat down to the Last Supper, the first person to rise from the table being Judas, who went out to betray Christ, the uneasiness is older than Christianity, for the Romans associated 13 with death and misfortune. The root reason may be that 13 is one more than 12, which is a number of completeness – the whole year consisting of 12 months, the whole day of 12 hours (see TWELVE) – and so it has the connotation of dangerously exceeding proper limits, of going beyond a natural cycle or starting on a new and uncertain course.

The Coven of 13

In early Christian numerology 13 was sometimes categorized as the number of sin, because it goes beyond the 12 apostles, though it could equally be a holy and admirable number which adds faith in the Trinity to the Ten Commandments. In the European magical tradition 13 is the number of necromancy, of bringing the dead back to temporary life, which again implies transgressing natural and proper limits.

One of the Graeco-Egyptian magical texts of the early centuries AD provides a method of animating a corpse which can then be forced to obsess a woman until she submits to the magician. It involves making a doll to represent the woman, piercing it with 13 needles and putting it on the grave of someone who died young or by violence, and then conjuring the corpse by incantation to rise up and stalk the streets to the woman's house, there to prey on her mind until she does the magician's will. The Tarot trump numbered 13 is Death, a skeleton who is mowing a field of human heads with a scythe while hands and feet grow in their place, a symbol of death and new life.

The fact that 13 is the traditional number of a coven of witches, with the 13th being the Devil or the local leader, may also have contributed to the number's evil reputation. Margaret Murray, in *The Witch Cult in Western Europe* and *The God of the Witches*, maintained that witches were in fact organized in groups of 13, each with a leader and 12 followers. Modern witches generally regard 13 as the proper number for a coven, though most real covens are smaller. The famous witch Isabel Gowdie (see GOWDIE) said that there were 13 in each coven, and in 1673 a woman named Anne Armstrong, of Morpeth in Northumberland, said that every 'covey' of witches had 13 members and 'every covey of 13 had a Devil, who danced first with those boasting the most evil'. But in general the evidence for real covens of 13 is slight and unconvincing.

It has been suggested that a 'baker's dozen' of 13 really means 'the Devil's dozen' and is derived from 'Boucca's dozen', Boucca being an old name for a god or spirit, surviving in the buccas of Cornish lore (see CORNWALL). Margaret Murray, who to the mingled scorn and amusement of more orthodox historians connected the founding of the Order of the Garter by King Edward III with the 'old religion' of witchcraft, noted that there were 26 knights, equivalent to two covens, and that Edward's mantle as head of the order was decorated with 168 garters which, adding the one he wore on his leg, makes 169, or 13 times 13, equalling 13 covens. However, it seems more likely that the number 13 here was drawn directly from the model of Christ and the 12 apostles.

A bluff, straightforward fellow who preferred strong-arm tactics to diplomacy, the red-bearded god of thunder, whose hammer laid low trolls and giants, was a god after the Vikings' heart

THOR

THE GOD OF THUNDER among the Germanic peoples, Donar, developed in the Scandinavian North into a vigorous, dynamic figure of mighty strength, with a red beard, a voracious appetite, and a great axe-hammer to protect gods and men from the evil forces of chaos and destruction. Thor remained a dominant influence until the end of the heathen period, and in the 10th century his silver hammer symbol was worn in opposition to the Christian cross, while his famous fishing exploit when he hauled up the World Serpent from the sea was carved on crosses and memorial stones in Scandinavia and the British Isles and celebrated in a number of Icelandic poems. He is presented in the literature as a god of considerable popular appeal, worshipped by the landowners of Norway in particular, and carried by them to Iceland.

Thor was a suitable god for a farming community, for he was closely linked with the earth. As the 11th century chronicler Adam of Bremen observed, he ruled not only thunder and lightning but winds and showers, fair weather and crops; while his wife Sif, famous for her bright hair, might be a variant of the ancient fertility goddess, typifying the golden corn. It was said that Thor's mother was Earth itself, so that the link between sky god and earth goddess is still reflected in the traditions concerning him.

Thus it is not surprising that Norwegians leaving for Iceland used sometimes to take with them earth from under the family shrine to the god, and also the two main pillars supporting the building, the 'high-seat pillars', which were sometimes said to have Thor's image carved on them. These could be thrown overboard as the ship drew near Iceland, so that Thor himself might lead his worshippers to the place where he desired them to dwell. The ancient Germanic thunder god was associated with oak forests (see GERMANIC MYTHOLOGY), and in Iceland, where forests were unknown, the wooden pillars sacred to the god served as an echo of the earlier tradition. Once a settler who had no wood for high-seat pillars prayed to Thor, and in answer a great tree was washed up on the shore, which provided pillars not only for him but for his neighbours also.

Whether indeed Thor had special temples built for him, as described in the sagas, is a matter for controversy. It may have been that he presided over the living quarters, and that the high-seat pillars were those of the hall itself, where the ritual feasts were probably held; certainly no convincing archeological remains of temple buildings have yet been found in Iceland.

His worshippers turned to Thor for blessing on hearth and home, and protection from wind and storms, as also from evil spirits haunting the waste places and bringing misfortune to the community. He presided also over law, which played an important part in Icelandic life. The Althing, the main Law Assembly held yearly at Thingvellir, opened on Thursday, Thor's day. When men made contracts with one another they swore oaths on Thor's ring, a heavy arm-ring of gold or silver which was said to lie on his altar.

An enthusiastic worshipper of the god would set up his home in Iceland only after careful consultation of Thor. He would organize feasts in Thor's honour along with the other gods at certain seasons of the year, and would turn to him at the important times in family life, at births, marriages and deaths. The hammer of Thor was raised over the new-born infant received into the community, and was laid in the lap of the bride and carved on memorial stones to the dead. Thor could help travellers, since he controlled the winds and the sea, and one Icelandic Christian from the Hebrides, Helgi the Lean, was said after his conversion to continue to pray to Thor for help whenever he had to make a sea voyage. The red beard of the god may be associated with the stormy sky, while his terrible blazing eyes and great voice remind us that he controlled the lightning and thunder.

The Sign of the Hammer

In the myths Thor is an active figure, frequently said to be off fighting trolls, and continually engaged in struggle and adventure. He does not ride on horseback like Odin, but is said to walk to the assembly of the gods, wading through rivers. In his passage across the sky, however, he is said to travel in a wagon drawn by goats, and the noise of its rattling wheels is heard as thunder in the world of men. When he hurled his hammer at giants, rocks split and boulders were shattered (see HAMMER). This was a magic weapon of great potency, held to be the greatest treasure of the gods; it was used as a throwing hammer and was said always to return to the hand. It is pictured on carvings with a long thong, as if the thrower whirled it round his head before letting it fly at his opponent. The hammer symbol long lived on in folklore, and was a protective amulet not only against lightning and fire, but against theft and flood and all kinds of calamities, while the sign of the hammer made with the hand, like that of the cross, conveyed a blessing and gave protection.

Sometimes in the myths Thor hurled glowing fragments of red-hot metal at his enemies, but his favourite technique was to smash their skulls with his hammer. The association with fire is suggested by the strange story of Thor's duel with the giant Hrungnir. Thor flung his hammer, and the giant, who was armed with a stone shield, threw a whetstone at Thor. Hammer and whetstone met in mid air; the hammer went on to shatter Hrungnir's head, but one piece of the stone lodged in Thor's forehead. A possible explanation of this myth might be sought in Lapp custom: the image of the thunder god of the Lapps had an iron nail in the head on which fire could be kindled with flint, in a ritual which re-enacted the lightning.

In accounts of Thor's temples in Norway, there are descriptions of large figures of the god seated in a chair or, in one case, in his wagon, with goats of bronze which could be pulled along by a cord. How common such impressive statues were in pagan times is uncertain, but we have one small amulet of the god in a chair, holding his hammer, which seems to grow out of his beard; this was found on a farm in Iceland. A number of runic stones in Norway and Sweden have invocations to Thor to hallow the memorial, and his protection evidently extended to the dead as well as the living. In one story Thor slew his own goats to provide a meal for himself and his companions, and then, raising his hammer aloft over bones and skin, called back the animals to life.

Thor plays a large part in the myths, and from these much of our knowledge of his powers and importance is drawn. Sometimes he appears as a figure of comedy, the bluff, simple fellow who trusts in his strong arm and has no time for the tortuous wiles of Loki and Odin. But the humorous tales do not indicate hostility towards the god, but rather testify to the affection felt for him by his worshippers. One of the most famous myths was that of his struggle with the World Serpent, of which several accounts survive. He went out in the boat of the sea giant Hymir, who did not recognize his divine passenger, and he had with him the head of Hymir's largest ox. The giant was alarmed by the speed with which the boat moved when Thor took the oars, and utterly terrified when the ox-head was thrown out as bait for the serpent which encircles the world, and the monster was hooked on Thor's line. As the struggle continued Thor took on his divine strength, pushing his feet through the boat and bracing himself against the sea bottom. The serpent's terrible head appeared and the two stared fiercely into each other's eyes; then according to one version Hymir cut the line, and the serpent fell back into the depths, there to await the world's end. Thor in wrath knocked the giant into the sea and waded back to shore. The struggle between the sky god and a monster of the deep is a pattern familiar in many mythologies. Originally Thor may have slain the serpent, although at the end of the pagan period the episode was set in the account of Ragnarok, the last battle between gods and monsters, and Thor, after slaying the serpent, himself perished from its poisonous breath (see SCANDINAVIA).

John Moss

Battles with Giants

The fishing story is linked with a visit to Hymir's hall and a battle with the giants. Hymir's wife assisted Thor, who had been challenged to break the giant's precious cup, by prompting him to hurl it at Hymir's head, against which it was shattered. Thor then marched away with the giant's cauldron, which was to be used to brew ale for a banquet of the gods. This is one of a series of tales in which Thor enters the realm of the giants and finally overcomes them, although the odds at first are against him. Once he visited the kingdom of Geirrod, who had forced the god Loki to bring Thor out without his hammer or his belt of might. Thor was again helped by a giantess, who lent him another belt, gloves of iron and her magic staff, so that he was able to survive the ordeals prepared for him. First he was beset by the swelling waters of the River Vimur, because one of Geirrod's daughters stood astride the river and was adding to the waters by her own efforts. He struck her with a well-directed rock and reached the shore with the help of a rowan tree. Next he sat down in the goatshed, and found his seat being forced up to the roof by two other daughters of the giant, but he pushed it down with his magic staff and broke their backs. Finally Geirrod himself flung a ball of hot iron at him, but Thor caught it in the gloves and sent it back to lay Geirrod low.

Another famous story reads like a satiric version of the myths, and is told with much wit by the antiquarian writer of the 12th century, the Icelander Snorri Sturluson. Thor set out with Loki and two servants to visit the realm of Utgard-Loki, a giant

Left **The hammer of Thor, the Scandinavian thunder god, as a talisman: in the North the sign of the hammer rivalled the cross as a sacred symbol and was a protective amulet against lightning, fire and calamities of all kinds *Right* 'The struggle between a sky god and a monster of the deep is a pattern familiar in many mythologies': Thor in the giant Hymir's boat, catching the World Serpent, an illustration from an *Edda* MS**

Royal Library, Copenhagen

Sm̄ XLI. Eddu Dæmisaga seig.

expert in magic. On the way, they encountered an enormous giant, who gave his name as Skrymir and offered to accompany them. Thor was continually frustrated, since he was unable to unfasten the giant's bag of provisions, and when he finally lost patience and struck Skrymir on the head, the giant only asked if a leaf had fallen, or a bird dropped something from the tree above. Finally he left them and they went on to Utgard, a stronghold of such size that they were able to creep through the bars of the gate. The king was rather contemptuous of such puny figures, but asked if they had any special skills.

Joke at Thor's Expense

In the trials of strength that followed Thor and his companions suffered further humiliation. Loki had an eating contest with a man called Logi, but although he devoured all the meat he was given his opponent ate the bones and the trough as well. Thialfi ran a race with a lad called Hugi, and was utterly outstripped. Thor himself undertook a drinking contest, but to his shame was unable to empty the horn offered him in three draughts: the liquid only fell a little below the rim. Next he tried to raise the king's grey cat from the floor, but could only get one paw off the ground. Finally he was asked to wrestle with the king's old foster-mother, but found himself unable to throw her. The king feasted them well after their defeat, and next morning they took their leave. Once outside the gates, the truth was revealed to them. The blows aimed at Skrymir, really Utgard-Loki in disguise, had been diverted by magic and had fallen on three mountains, leaving deep pits where the hammer had struck. The bag which Thor could not undo was fastened by iron bands; Loki's opponent in the contest was Fire, which can consume more than any god or man, while Thialfi had raced against Thought, swifter than any in its flight. The horn offered to Thor had its tip in the ocean, and his great gulps had lowered the sea, as if the tide had ebbed; while the cat was in reality the World Serpent, and all had trembled when Thor raised it so far by his strength, lest the universe should perish; his last opponent was Old Age, able to overcome the mightiest.

Thus the witty tale, by a clever series of reversals, reveals the mighty powers of the great sky god even as it makes merry at his expense. The indomitable Thor, trusting in his own strength and rejoicing in a good fight against heavy odds, is a fitting deity for the Viking Age; while in the conception of the mighty god of the sky, who supports justice among men and fights unceasingly against the forces of chaos, there is a deeper truth than at first might be apparent in the light-hearted myths of his exploits against the giants.

H. R. ELLIS DAVIDSON

Hamlyn Group

Small bronze statuette of Thor, of *c* 1000 AD, seated in a chair and holding the hammer; it was found in Iceland where Thor, who controlled rain and storms, was highly regarded by farmers and seafarers

FURTHER READING: H. R. Ellis Davidson, *Gods and Myths of Northern Europe* (Penguin, 1964); E. O. G. Turville Petre, *Myth and Religion of the North* (Weidenfeld, 1964).

The identity of the Thracian Rider, and what he meant to those who carved his figure, remains uncertain but clues to his character may be deduced from the way he is depicted on the numerous stone stelae on which he appears

THRACIAN RIDER GOD

OVER A WIDE AREA of the Balkans, especially in the territory known as Thrace in ancient times (now Bulgaria), great numbers of monuments have been found of what is called the 'Thracian Rider'. These monuments generally take the form of stone stelae, upon which the figure of a horseman is carved, together with other attendant figures or symbols. They date from the Roman Imperial period, mostly from the 2nd and 3rd centuries AD. Some specimens have been found further afield, in Anatolia and Western Europe. The identity of the 'Rider', and what he meant to those who carved his figure on these stones, remain uncertain, despite the research of many scholars. That he commanded the allegiance of many peoples is evident from the multitude of the monuments bearing his effigy, and the wide area of their diffusion.

There are a few deductions which can be made about the significance of this mysterious figure. First, it must be noted that the figures of a horse and rider frequently occur on classical Greek and Etruscan funerary monuments. Such representations had a mortuary significance — the deceased was departing from this world to the next. But the Thracian Rider does not appear on tombstones, and so cannot be reckoned as having a sepulchral character. Instead, his monuments were located in sanctuaries, indicating that he was a divinity of some kind.

Unknown Hero

Here the mystery of his identity becomes very puzzling. Although the monuments often bear inscriptions in Greek and Latin, and name the divine Rider to whom they are dedicated, the mystery is only deepened by what they record. The name most frequently given is 'Heros' or 'Heron'. This could be the designation of a dead man, for the dead were sometimes 'heroized' in Greek funerary inscriptions. But this is unlikely to have been the case here, since the monuments were not tombstones; some inscriptions, moreover, read *theo Heroti*, 'to the god Hero'.

In other inscriptions, the Rider is named Phoebus, that is, Apollo, or Asclepios, the Greek god of healing. Such names suggest that the mysterious Rider was being equated with well-known Greek gods, though himself remaining unnamed.

Clues to what the divine Rider meant to his devotees seem to be provided by various iconographic features of the monuments. The Rider was generally depicted with his cloak streaming out behind him, suggesting vigour and speed of movement. He frequently flourishes a club or double-axe, the latter being a symbol of many Near Eastern weather or sky gods. But more significant is the fact that a number of monuments show the deity with three heads. Such multiplication of physical features is usually a primitive way of suggesting superhuman ability. Three heads, so arranged that one looks forward, one backwards, and one full-face, would seem to indicate a deity who was all-seeing and all-knowing. Since these powers were usually attributes of a sun god, the Thracian Rider probably had solar associations, even if he was not actually a sun god. Then the fact that he is sometimes shown as hunting a great wild boar, often a symbol of evil, may mean that the deity was regarded as a divine saviour, who hunted and subdued the forces of evil and disorder.

These deductions are reasonable, but they cannot be proved. However, we may certainly conclude that, whatever his significance, the mysterious Rider god answered some deep need or aspiration felt by the various peoples inhabiting these rather savage regions in ancient times.

FURTHER READING: R. Pettazoni, *The All-Knowing God* (Arno Press, 1978).

Horse and rider, worked in silver on a helmet of the 4th century BC, found in the tomb of a Thracian chief and now in the Bucharest National Museum of Antiquities: the horseman motif appears in classical times over a wide area of the Balkans but its significance is still not fully understood

C. M. Dixon

THREE

THIS IS GENERALLY considered the luckiest of numbers and if your name adds to 3 (see ALPHABET), you will be described by numerologists as a fortunate being indeed. Creative, clever, charming, lively and entertaining, extremely successful, a 3 has a natural attraction for both money and the opposite sex. He is one of those people to whom everything seems to come easily, who succeeds without really trying. Rarely worried or depressed, he takes life as it comes and may have difficulty in taking anything seriously, though he will have a strong underlying sense of his own value and importance. One of the key ideas attached to 3 in numerology is 'expression', and those whose number it is express themselves wittily, effectively and with frequency. Imaginative and optimistic, cheerful, generous and agreeable, they get on well with everyone, but perhaps more because they are anxious to be liked than because of any deep concern for others.

A 3 enjoys the limelight and detests obscurity. Active, energetic and proud, he may have a commanding air about him and he will make a bad subordinate. He likes to show off and to be admired, but is probably more nervous and sensitive than his assured and brilliant exterior suggests. He has a tendency to expend his energies wastefully in too many directions and, since he loves pleasure and luxury, to scatter his money about. Though always the life and soul of the party, he can sometimes be exasperatingly vain, gossipy and superficial.

The Manifest Creator

Behind this picture of the creativity and self-expression of 3 are a number of converging numerological theories. To begin with, the number 1, though potentially all-creative, is regarded as barren by itself, for however many times it is multiplied (fertilized) by itself, it remains 1. The number 2 introduces a pair of opposites, but 2 multiplied by 1 remains 2. It is 3 which fruitfully reconciles these opposites and creates more numbers (3 + 2 = 6). As the French magician Eliphas Levi put it: 'Were God only one He would never be creator or father. Were He two there would be antagonism or division in the infinite, which would mean the division also or death of all possible things. He is therefore three for the creation by Himself and in His image of the infinite multitude of beings and numbers.'

Again, 1 is assigned to the point and 2 to the line, both of which are theoretical constructs. When 3 points are connected, in the triangle, the first plane figure is constructed, the first which has surface and is therefore observable. So 1 is regarded as the number of God as alone and complete in himself but hidden and unmanifested. In 2 something emanates from within God's wholeness to create the great opposite forces which run all through the universe. In 3

The Three Fates, in a 15th century tapestry; the number 3 occurs frequently in Greek mythology, as a mark of completeness

C. M. Dixon

the opposites are reconciled and God is for the first time manifest, for the first time comprehensible to human experience in having, as it were, a surface. This is followed by the creation of solidity in 4, when a fourth point is added above the triangle and a pyramid constructed (see FOUR). Then the 3 of spirit and the 4 of matter, added or multiplied, produce 7 and 12, the numbers which govern the rhythms and cycles of life in the universe – the 7 planets and days of the week, the 12 zodiac signs, months and hours of the day (see SEVEN; TWELVE).

Added to all this is the sexual symbolism of 3. It is the first of the masculine numbers (see NUMEROLOGY) and the number of the male genitals, which are threefold. The triangle is a natural symbol for the male genitals (though it can also be a symbol for the female). Where God as 1 is the hidden and unknowable Absolute, God as 3 is the manifest creator of 'the infinite multitude of beings and numbers', and this is the basic numerological interpretation of the Trinity, the three-fold godhead.

It follows that 3 is the number of creativity and self-expression on the human plane, as it is the number of God making himself known on the divine plane. The connection with 'surface' accounts for some of the other characteristics of 3 – sparkle and glitter, showing off, a tendency to superficiality. The triangle, facing 3 ways, accounts for the tendency to expend effort in many directions, but this and other traits allotted to 3 also have a genital reference – attractiveness, need for approval, pride, energy, love of pleasure. The idea of 3 reconciling the opposites in a third term which harmonizes and transcends them accounts for the harmonious progress through life attributed to 3, easy money and success, getting on well with everyone.

Three Blind Mice

As the number of the Trinity, in Christian numerology 3 is naturally linked with the most holy, the most perfect, the best. But the number's connection with the superlative is older, and is expressed in the Greek word *trismegistos* ('thrice-greatest', superlatively great) and the Latin *ter felix* ('thrice-happy', happiest). The notion of the superlative itself involves the third term in a series of 3 – good, better, best. And 3 is not only connected with 'best' but also with 'all', and is the most important of the numbers of completeness. Time is made of 3 ingredients (past, present and future) and so is space (length, breadth and thickness). All created things have a beginning, a middle and an end. The feeling that 3 is the basis of everything we experience may account for the belief that runs of luck, good or bad, tend to happen in threes. 'Third time lucky' is a common phrase and, on the other hand, if two unlucky things happen one after the other, some people will deliberately break a dish or do some other minor piece of damage in the hope of ending the run of ill luck.

Three of anything is somehow 'all' of it and 'enough' of it. 'I'll give you 3 guesses,' we say, with the feeling that 3 are enough. The hero of a folktale frequently has 3 wishes or 3 tries at a task, the heroine has

British Museum

Left **The godhead as both One and Three, from a 14th century manuscript**
Right **The 3 magi and their 3 gifts were regarded as foreshadowing the Christian Trinity: 6th century mosaic from the church of San Apollinare Nuovo, Ravenna**

3 suitors, and 3 frequently bobs up as a number of completeness in nursery rhymes. Goldilocks met 3 bears, there were 3 blind mice, 3 little kittens who lost their mittens.

In the distant past behind all this there may lie very early methods of counting which used special words for 1 and 2, but for 3 or more simply said 'many'. The Babylonian term for a constellation, for instance, regardless of how many stars it might contain, was 'three stars', meaning 'many stars'. In this way the connotations of 3 may have come to include 'many', 'all', 'abundance', 'best', and so 'lucky'.

Numbers of completeness are always important in magic, because they prescribe how many times an action must be repeated to be effective. To chant an incantation 3 times, for example, is magically to chant it 'enough' times or 'all possible' times. In European magic 3 is even more important than 7 or 9, and the instruction to repeat a process 3 times over occurs constantly.

The Threefold God

Medieval Christian numerologists remarked on various uses of 3 as a number of completeness in the New Testament, including the 3 gifts of the magi to the infant Jesus, the 3 temptations in the wilderness, the 3 denials of Christ by Peter, the 3 falls on the road to Golgotha, the 3 days between Christ's crucifixion and resurrection, the 3 appearances of the risen Christ to his disciples. These could all be taken as foreshadowings or reflections of the Trinity.

The period of 33 years is also regarded as significant by some modern occultists. A. E. Abbott observes in his *Encyclopaedia of Numbers* that 'important phenomena of history receive their special imprint through the fact that they unfold in a cycle of 33 years from their origin to maturity and fulfilment or to rebirth . . . The life of Christ, occupying 33 years on earth, has impressed its forces and rhythms into the earth-organism and into time, thus giving form to world history.'

The doctrine of the Trinity was officially recognized by the Council of Constantinople in 381. The earliest Christians were Jews who had been brought up to believe that God is One and to think of him as the heavenly Father. But in recognizing Christ as divine they introduced a second person into the godhead, the Son. And in their confidence that the spirit of God, which had descended on the apostles after Christ's death (Acts, chapter 2), was with them and working in them, they added a third divine personage, the Holy Spirit. The nature of God as Three-in-One, and of the relationship between the persons of the Trinity, caused an immense amount of philosophical speculation (see HERESY).

Occasional groupings of deities in threes can be observed in pagan pre-Christian religions: Osiris, Isis and Horus as father, mother and child in Egypt, or the triad of Serapis, Isis and Harpocrates (Horus) at Alexandria, or the three universal gods at the head of the pantheon in Mesopotamia (see MESOPOTAMIA). Numerous other examples come from the Celts, to whom 3 was a sacred number. They sometimes portrayed their deities in groups of 3, or with 3 heads or 3 faces (see BRIGIT; CELTS), apparently as a way of emphasizing their power and perhaps with the same basic idea of a single god making himself known in terms of 3 which underlies the numerological approach considered earlier.

Groups of 3 can also be found in Greek mythology, including the 3 Graces, the 3 Fates and the 3 Furies. Early in this century a German scholar counted more than 120 triads in Greek myth and ritual, but his conclusion was not that 3 was sacred to the Greeks but that it merely meant 'all' or 'many'. Greek triads attracted the interest of Renaissance humanists, who connected them with the Christian Trinity (even the 3 heads of Cerberus, the dog of the underworld, becoming an emblem of the Christian doctrine) and who saw them, again, in terms of a unity manifesting itself by displaying its 3 component parts, the opposites and the factor which reconciles them (see RENAISSANCE).

In Hinduism the concept of God as both 1 and 3 appears in Brahman, which in itself is One but which as it presents itself to the world is Three – Being, Consciousness and Joy, or the godhead which originates, sustains and destroys the universe, personified as the triad of Brahma, Vishnu and Shiva (see BRAHMAN). In his book *Mysticism Sacred and Profane* R. C. Zaehner comments on the remarkable closeness of the concept of the threefold Brahman as *Sat* (Being), *Cit* (Logos or Reason) and *Ananda* (Joy or Love) to that of the Christian Trinity of the Father (Being), the Son (Logos) and the Holy Spirit (Love).

That God must be both 1 and 3, One as he essentially is, Three as he is manifested and known, has been observed by mystics of Christian and other traditions on the analogy, to put it over-simply, that a complete sentence must have a subject, a verb and an object. If there is divine love, there must also be a lover and a beloved, if there is divine knowledge there must also be a knower and what is known. Professor Zaehner quotes the 13th century Jewish mystic Abraham Abulafia, who said that the Master 'is called . . . the knowledge, the knower and the known, all at the same time, since all three are one in Him'; and a Sufi mystic, who was asked about the divine Union, and replied, 'Union, He Who unites, and He Who is united – and that is three.'

FURTHER READING: A. E. Abbott, *Encyclopaedia of Numbers* (Emerson Press); E. Wind, *Pagan Mysteries in the Renaissance* (Penguin, 1967 reprint); R. C. Zaehner, *Mysticism Sacred and Profane* (Oxford Univ. Press, 1967 reprint).

C. M. Dixon

THRESHOLD

TO THIS DAY, a bridegroom will carry his bride across the threshold of their new home, even when the 'new home' is merely a hotel room in which they will spend their honeymoon. It is one of the pleasant minor customs attached to weddings but it has links with special ceremonies involving doorways and thresholds all over the world.

In Rome the god Janus (see JANUS) was present at the main doorway of every house and the threshold itself, a block of stone big enough to keep water and mud from spilling into the house from outside, was presided over by its own god and goddess, Limentius and Lima. When a bride came to her new home, she was lifted over the threshold by her husband. This was partly to prevent her from stumbling over it, which would have been a bad omen for the marriage, but there was evidently more to it than that, for she anointed the doorposts, preferably with wolf's fat, and fastened wool onto them before being carried in.

Similarly, the Chinese make sure that the bride's foot does not touch the threshold when she first goes into her husband's house, and in many other parts of the world the bride is either carried across the threshold or takes care to step over it without treading on it. Other rituals involving doorways include sprinkling blood or water or perfume on the threshold and doorposts to purify them, and hanging charms or sacred objects from the lintel or on the doorposts.

In his book *Folklore in the Old Testament* Sir James Frazer compared a number of threshold customs and beliefs, taking as his starting point the officials of the Temple in Jerusalem who were called 'keepers of the threshold'. They are mentioned several times in the Old Testament (2 Kings 25.18, for example). There is also the passage in 1 Samuel (chapter 5) which records that the worshippers of the Philistine god Dagon took care not to tread on the threshold of his temple, and the curious verse in Zephaniah (chapter 1) in which God vows to punish everyone who leaps on (or over) the threshold.

Frazer suggested that the function of the keepers of the threshold was to prevent people from treading on it. In the 19th century in Syria it was still considered unlucky to tread on the threshold of a mosque or a saint's shrine. The great 13th century traveller Marco Polo reported that each door of Kublai Khan's palace at Peking was guarded by men whose duty was to see that no one trod on the threshold in entering, and to punish anybody who did. Another traveller in the Far East at the same period said that anyone who touched the threshold of the hut or tent of a Tartar chieftain was liable to be put to death. It was equally considered a crime to tread on the threshold of the gate of the palace from which the caliphs of Baghdad held sway.

Frazer quoted several curious cases from 19th century England of farmers burying a premature calf under the threshold of a cowshed to prevent the other cows from giving birth prematurely. In Yorkshire, for instance, the traditional method was to remove the threshold, dig a deep hole there and bury the corpse of the calf on its back with its legs sticking up, then filling in the hole and replacing the threshold.

Arnold van Gennep pointed out, in *The Rites of Passage*, that the key to much magical and religious reverence, not merely for the threshold which must not be profaned by treading on it, but for the whole doorway, is the idea of passing through a door or gate or portal of any kind as a transition from one realm or condition to another. 'The door is the boundary between the foreign and domestic worlds in the case of an ordinary dwelling, between the profane and sacred worlds in the case of a temple. Therefore to cross the threshold is to unite oneself with a new world. It is an important act in marriage, adoption, ordination, and funeral ceremonies.'

Arch of Triumph

The Roman arch of triumph seems originally to have been a portal of this sort. A general returning to the city after a successful campaign passed through the arch as part of a rite of separating himself from the enemy world outside and returning to the world of Rome. The symbolism of transition is expressed nowadays at military weddings when the newly married couple pass through an arch of swords as they leave the church, as a sign of their entry into the community of the regiment.

Some doorways, as in Rome, are believed to be the domain of gods or spirits. In central

A. J. Huxley

The threshold, which marked the transition from one state of existence to another, might be emphasized by guardian statues: the Lion Gate, the main entrance to the fortified city of Mycene, dating from the 14th century BC, is surmounted by two great limestone lions

India the threshold was said to be the seat of the goddess Lakshmi. Others are guarded by statues, frequently of hybrid and monstrous creatures, such as sphinxes in Egypt, winged bulls in Mesopotamia, dragons in China. The main doorways of palaces, temples and churches are embellished with decorations or emphasized with porches or other architectural features to mark their importance as gateways to another world.

On a smaller scale, the same treatment is often applied to the main door of a house, and because it must not be polluted tradition says that a corpse must be removed through the back door or a window, or that women who are pregnant or menstruating must only be let in through the back door. In many farms and houses in the countryside, the front door is scarcely ever used, except on important and formal occasions. All everyday coming and going takes place through the back door, a faint reflection of the old reverence for the portal and its threshold. (See also HOUSE; RITES OF PASSSAGE.)

FURTHER READING: J. G. Frazer, *Folklore in the Old Testament* vol 3 (Macmillan, 1918); A. van Gennep, *The Rites of Passage* (Routledge, 1960).

Only chosen adepts were allowed to engage in the mystical disciplines known as 'the work of the chariot' and to encounter the dangers of the ascent to the heavenly throne

THRONE MYSTICISM

'IN THE YEAR that King Uzziah died I saw the Lord sitting upon a throne, high and lifted up; and his train filled the temple. Above him stood the seraphim; each had six wings: with two he covered his face, and with two he covered his feet, and with two he flew. And one called to another and said: "Holy, holy, holy is the Lord of hosts; the whole earth is full of his glory"' (Isaiah 6.1–3).

'In the thirtieth year, in the fourth month, on the fifth day of the month . . . the heavens were opened, and I saw visions of God . . . As I looked, behold, a stormy wind came out of the north, and a great cloud, with brightness round about it, and fire flashing forth continually, and in the midst of the fire, as it were gleaming bronze. And from the midst of it came the likeness of four living creatures . . . And each went straight forward; wherever the spirit would go, they went, without turning as they went. In the midst of the living creatures there was something that looked like burning coals of fire . . . and the fire was bright, and out of the fire went forth lightning . . . Now as I looked at the living creatures, I saw a wheel upon the earth beside the living creatures, one for each of the four of them . . . their appearance was like the gleaming of a chrysolite; and the four had the same likeness, their construction being as it were a wheel within a wheel . . . Over the heads of the living creatures there was the likeness of a firmament, shining like crystal . . . And when they went, I heard the sound of their wings like the sound of many waters . . . And above the firmament over their heads there was the likeness of a throne, in appearance like sapphire; and seated above the likeness of a throne was a likeness as it were of a human form' (Ezekiel 1.1–26).

These quotations from two of the major Old Testament prophets illustrate the visionary tradition of beholding the glory and majesty of the Lord upon a high and exalted throne. This tradition goes back to earlier prophets, like Micaiah who declared to King Ahab: 'I saw the Lord sitting on his throne, and all the host of heaven standing beside him on his right hand and on his left' (1 Kings 22.19). It was no doubt indebted to ancient Near Eastern forms and patterns of kingship. During the latter part of the Second Temple period and in the Rabbinic period (the period preceeding, and the centuries which followed, the destruction of the Temple in 70 AD), these records of prophetic visions provided the basis of the visionary and ecstatic forms of early Jewish mysticism.

But the more rationalist and non-mystical thinkers also concerned themselves with these biblical passages, since they raised a basic problem of theology and religious philosophy – that of anthropomorphism. Was there a throne in heaven? Could a purely spiritual God be 'seen'? Were these visions, if taken literally, not gross and crude heresies rather than expressions of mystical spirituality? Many of the great medieval Jewish thinkers discussed these questions and suggested various solutions: the biblical accounts were allegorical figures of speech; or perhaps God created visible forms of glory in order to enable mortal eyes to behold a reflection of the splendour of the invisible Godhead.

The Ascent to the Throne

But in the circles of visionary mystics these philosophical analyses played a minor role. The earlier Jewish mystics cultivated an ecstatic kind of mysticism which taught its initiates ways and techniques of achieving the visionary experience of the divine glory and splendour of light: the throne. In the literature of these mystics, the throne (Hebrew *kisse*) which is the object of the ecstatic vision is more often called 'chariot' (Hebrew *merkabah*), probably under the influence of Ezekiel's great vision with its description of wheels, and wheels within wheels. This is therefore known as Merkabah or throne mysticism, and is distinct from later forms of Jewish mysticism, which were largely speculative, and whose practice of meditation and contemplation culminated in the experience of communion, if not union, with God (see CABALA).

The Merkabah mystics seem to have experienced ascensions of the soul, which were not without danger. In rabbinic circles only chosen disciples were permitted to engage in these mystical disciplines, known as *ma'aseh merkabah* (the work of the chariot). The 'perils of the soul' which the adept encountered during his ascent through the various celestial spheres are described realistically and convincingly enough in the ancient texts. To overcome these dangers and pass the various celestial barriers the adept had to use mystical formulae and 'seals'. Hence Merkabah mysticism also had its magical side: an apparatus of incantations, spells and conjurations.

Within the Merkabah practice proper the magical part was subservient to the essentially mystical goal of the vision of the throne (and possibly of the splendour of the divine majesty on the throne). The outstanding feature of this kind of mysticism is its emphasis on the transcendent, majestic, tremendous and awesomely numinous character of the deity. The experience of loving communion, so common in later mysticism, is absent here. The initiate rises through worlds, spheres and heavens guarded by all kinds of terrifying celestial keepers until, at last, if all goes well and he be found worthy, he stands in awe and trembling before the supreme and blinding vision of the divine splendour. Merkabah mysticism is a mysticism of the *mysterium tremendum* (awesome divine mystery), and it left a permanent mark on the Jewish liturgy, inspiring some of the finest and most impressive religious poetry and hymns. The esoteric teachings and practices of the Merkabah mystics subsequently fell into disuse, but some of the Merkabah traditions and literary documents were absorbed by the Cabala.

R. J. ZWI WERBLOWSKY

FURTHER READING: G. Scholem, *Major Trends in Jewish Mysticism* (Thames & Hudson, 1955).

Merkabah mystics sought the visionary experience of the divine splendour of the throne of God, which was more usually referred to as a 'chariot', probably under the influence of the prophet Ezekiel's great vision: God appears seated in a fiery chariot in Blake's painting of the Lord passing judgement on Adam

Tate Gallery

THUGS

THESE ROBBERS and ritual murderers in India strangled their victims as sacrifices to the goddess Bhavani, a form of Kali, the Hindu goddess of terror and destruction. They believed that the goddess herself had founded their organization and had taught her worshippers the art of throttling, using a clay dummy for purposes of demonstration (see KALI). They are first mentioned in the 12th century but their history probably goes back much further, and some of them maintained that their rituals were portrayed in carvings of the 8th century in the caves at Ellora in Hyderabad.

The thugs had a secret language of their own and a system of secret signs. Their children were brought up to the craft and sometimes the children of murdered victims were adopted into the cult. Preying principally on travellers, a gang of thugs would join a party of traders or pilgrims and accompany them, perhaps for weeks, until they found a safe opportunity to kill them.

Apprentice thugs were taught the art of choosing suitable victims, gaining their confidence and luring them to a convenient place of execution, and strangling them in the prescribed manner. They would approach a victim from behind, pass a length of cloth round his neck, jerk it tight and relax it, whispering to the goddess to come and watch. Then the noose was tightened and relaxed again, and the summons to the goddess repeated, and finally the victim was slowly throttled to death – slowly so that Bhavani could enjoy his agonies.

The corpse was then mangled, the legs disjointed, the face cut and disfigured, the body slashed and gutted. Burial of the body was followed by a solemn feast, sometimes held on the grave. The stranglers sat on a sheet or blanket, near which were the sacred pickaxe of the goddess and an offering of silver. A little sugar was poured into a hole in the ground and a prayer spoken to the goddess, asking her to reward her faithful followers with plenty of loot. Holy water was sprinkled on the pickaxe and those who had

British Museum

A thug prepares to strangle a victim with a length of cloth, as a sacrifice to Bhavani, while his attention is distracted by others in the band: 19th century Indian painting

committed the murder ate a little of the sugar from their hands.

Before an expedition, a sheep was sacrificed before an image of the goddess, which was black and smeared with blood. Flowers, fruit and cakes were also offered to her, and near her effigy stood images of a snake and a lizard, and the tools of the thug's trade – noose, knife and pickaxe.

On initiation into the society each member was given a pickaxe, the tool with which graves were dug. Each band of thugs carried a sacred pickaxe, a symbol of the goddess in which something of her power resided. The pickaxe, which had been passed seven times through the fire to consecrate it, was treated with awed respect and solemn oaths were sworn over it. If it was dropped by its bearer, either his death or the break-up of the gang would certainly follow within a year.

Though the thugs worshipped a Hindu goddess, many of them were Moslems, especially in the Delhi area, where they held in reverence a famous Moslem holy man of the 14th century in Delhi, Nizam-ud-din Auliya, whom they believed to have been one of the founders of thuggee.

Instruments of the Goddess

Sir William Sleeman, a British army officer and administrator who took a leading part in suppressing thuggee, said that a thug thought of his human victims much as a priest of Jupiter must have thought of the sacrificial oxen. 'He meditates his murders without any misgivings, he perpetrates them without any emotions of pity, and he remembers them without any feelings of remorse. They trouble not his dreams, nor does their recollection ever cause him inquietude in darkness, in solitude, or in the hour of death.'

Though strangling was their preferred method of murder, the thugs sometimes poisoned or drowned their victims or burned them alive. Women were not acceptable offerings to the goddess and men following certain trades were also in theory exempt from the attentions of the thugs, but by the 19th century at least many of them had become indiscriminate killers, and some of them attributed their downfall to this disregard of their rules.

In the 1830s the British authorities waged what almost amounted to a war against the thugs. Many of them were killed in action and by 1837 more than 3000 had been captured, of whom over 400 were hanged. By about 1860 they had been almost entirely wiped out, and the last known thug was hanged in 1882.

FURTHER READING: N. Mackenzie ed., *Secret Societies* (Macmillan, 1971); B. Walker, *Hindu World* (Praeger, 1968).

THUNDERBIRD

Hamlyn Group

The widespread belief in the thunderbird, a gigantic winged creature responsible for storms, is connected with the fear that the fertility of the earth might fail for lack of rain: carved wooden thunderbird from Vancouver Island

IN THE PAST it was widely believed that birds were connected with the sun, wind, thunder and lightning. As aerial creatures seen ascending into the heavens, they were associated with the celestial powers and particularly with those controlling the weather. For this reason birds were often regarded as in various ways responsible for rain and the conditions which make life possible for man and the plants and animals on which he depends.

Since in many parts of the world outside the tropics migratory birds appear in spring, it was assumed that they were in some way responsible for the increasing warmth and fertility or, at least, in league with the powers responsible for favourable weather. The mysterious appearances and disappearances of migrating birds stirred the primitive imagination, and mythical birds were endowed with powers beyond those of any known species; commonly these birds were thought to be gigantic. Birds fan the air with their wings, and it was therefore supposed that storms and tempests were caused by huge winged creatures. And as some make drumming, booming and clattering noises with their wings, voices or bills, primitive folk supposed that thunder was caused in some such way by invisible, supernatural, monstrous birds.

Thus belief in a thunderbird, sometimes also conceived as a fire bird, lightning bird or storm bird, became widespread. Such birds could be regarded as beneficent because fire is useful to man and thunder showers foster fertility, but they could also be viewed with fear and awe because lightning can be destructive, killing men, shattering trees and setting forests on fire. Moreover, as giant birds were thought to act as the steeds of the gods, some of whom were not always friendly to man, their nature and activities might have an important bearing on human welfare.

The Flapping of Great Wings

In North America the thunderbird was pictured differently by various tribes. The Hareskin Indians spoke of a huge bird which spent the winter in the land of the dead with other migratory birds and beasts, returning with the warm weather. When it shook its tail thunder was heard, and lightning was the flashing of its eyes. At Eneti, in Washington state, a face said to represent the thunderbird was carved on a rock; the Indians believed that rain could be caused by shaking the rock and so arousing the anger of the thunderbird. According to the Dakotas, it was the parent thunderbird which made thunder; it was wise and did no harm, but the young were irresponsible and might cause destruction. These Indians claimed to have killed a thunderbird, and to have discovered that it had a man's face with a nose like an eagle's beak.

On the north-west coast the thunderbird was thought of as an eagle with an extra head on its abdomen; it was huge enough to be able to carry off whales. A story told how two hunters saw an enormous bird rise from a lake with the sound of thunder and then sink back with a terrific roar. An early traveller recorded that the Hurons regarded thunder as a large bird because a similar noise, on a smaller scale, was made by a bird like a swallow. In British Columbia the Indians likened the thunderbird to the ruby-throated hummingbird. The sound made by the hummingbird's wings probably suggested the connection with thunder, while its red throat feathers associated it with lightning.

In West Africa the spirit of lightning, So, is a flying being partaking of the nature of a god. Thunder is caused by the flapping of his wings and he casts lightning from the dark clouds. The image of the Nigerian thunder god is placed between two poles, on which are placed representations of birds. Among many Bantu tribes an image of a bird is placed on huts to ward off lightning; its form may vary from that of a flamingo to that of a bird of prey. Stone effigies of birds found at the ancient town of Zimbabwe have a crocodile or serpent carved at the base, suggesting that the powers of heaven and earth respectively were symbolized, as in some Asian cultures. In southern Africa the lightning is said to be a bird, brown or white-necked like the fish eagle. Persons struck by lightning are said to have been scratched by its claws. The Luyia in Kenya say that a huge red cock lives up in the clouds. He sends lightning when he shakes his wings and thunder is the sound of his crowing.

In Asia the thunderbird is widely associated with rain. The forest Tungus of north-east Asia say that thunder is caused by the rustling of a mighty bird's wings. Ancient Chinese literature reveals belief in thunderbirds: the pheasant is prominent in these traditions, probably because pheasants make a thudding noise when they flap their wings, and carry red markings on their heads. Young people in China used to perform springtime dances, in the course of which they imitated pheasants and flapped their arms to induce rain to fall. The connection between the bird and fertility also appears from the fact that in Chinese the word or character representing the sounds made by a pheasant also signified the noise of thunder and the 'agitation of a woman as she becomes pregnant'.

The Chinese thunder god, Lei Kung, is thought to have been originally a bird, possibly an owl. He is represented with a man's body, blue and hideous; he has a beak, wings and talons, and carries a wooden mallet, with which he beats a number of drums hung around him. He may carry a dagger or be shown shooting the arrows of lightning. The Japanese thunder god is also shown festooned with drums. In northern Asia tribal drums are painted with pictures of birds and frogs; as in other areas the drums are beaten, imitating thunder, to induce rain to fall.

The diver (see DIVER) is associated with rain in Europe, Asia and North America because of its close connection with water. Its cry is said to foretell rain and the Thompson Indians of British Columbia therefore imitate its call to make the rain fall. Belief in the efficacy of imitative magic extends to Mexico, where the Tarahumare Indians perform dances imitating the courtship antics of the turkey: they assume that as the gods grant the prayers of the bird, expressed in its dances, by sending rains, so they too must dance like the turkey to bring fertility to the countryside.

Imitative rain magic was also performed in Europe: near Dorpat in Estonia a man would climb a tree and rattle on a kettle, simulating the noise of a woodpecker drumming on a branch. The drumming noise which the bird makes with its bill as it hammers on a tree has been regarded from ancient times as rain magic, mimicry of thunder in order to create thunder and cause a downpour, a belief which still survives (see WOODPECKER).

A Potawatomi 'thunder war medicine bundle' from the Great Plains includes two stuffed birds. Birds were associated with thunder in America, Africa, Asia and Europe; these thunderbirds 'could be regarded as beneficent because fire is useful to man and thunder showers foster fertility, but they could also be viewed with fear and awe because lightning can be destructive'

Museum of the American Indian

Enemy of Snakes

In southern Asia the thunderbird belief appears to be superseded or obscured by the concept of a solar bird dominating a creature of the waters. The Hindu god Vishnu, who sometimes appears as a solar deity, rides the Garuda bird which is itself a solar divinity. In the art of Indo-China, Garuda is represented in immense stone sculptures as a winged and beaked human figure holding a snake in its taloned feet. This is interpreted as symbolizing the sun drying up the waters, represented by the Naga snakes, Garuda's traditional enemies. The Brahmanic god of the waters, celestial and terrestrial, Varuna, is depicted mounted on a monster, half-bird, half-reptile. Other gods also ride birds: Kama, the god of love, rides a parrot, Sarasvati, goddess of eloquence, a peacock (see PEACOCK). The immense birds of Near Eastern mythology such as the Simurgh and the Roc (see ROC), and even the huge birds of Irish legend, appear to have some affinity with the mythical birds further east.

The concept of opposing powers, celestial and terrestrial, is also found in Europe where the design of an eagle holding a snake or perched on an aquatic creature appears in ancient art. In Greece Zeus, the Thunderer, was symbolized by an eagle, and he disguised himself as an eagle in order to abduct Ganymede, the son of King Tros. The myth of celestial and terrestrial powers in conflict is very ancient. Among the Hittites there was a story describing the conflict between the weather god and the dragon (see HITTITES). In various forms this myth is represented in many cultures, including our own, for the legend of St George and the Dragon may be regarded as a variant.

(See also BIRDS; EAGLE.)

E. A. ARMSTRONG

Thyrsos

Ivy-twined staff tipped with a pine cone, or sometimes with a bunch of grapes and vine leaves, which was an attribute of the Greek god Dionysus and was carried by his worshippers: ivy was the plant of Dionysus and the phallic pine cone was an emblem of fertility and immortality; the grapes and vine leaves marked the god's link with wine and intoxication.

See DIONYSUS.

Tiamat

Monstrous personification of the sea in Babylonian mythology: from her mingling with the fresh waters the first generation of the gods was born; she threatened to destroy the gods but was killed by Marduk, the god of Babylon, who fashioned the universe from her body and created mankind from the blood of the leader of her army.

See CREATION MYTHS; MARDUK.

Marco Polo records that by their extraordinary powers, Tibetan lamas at the Mongol court could make the Khan's cup rise spontaneously from the ground to his mouth, thus convincing him that their religion was superior to Christianity

IN APRIL 1982 a British television programme in the series *The World About Us* described the impact of Chinese Communism on Tibetan life. By 1982, of the 3,500 original monasteries, only 13 were left. By 1979, the Cultural Revolution in China was over, and the Chinese asked the Dalai Lama to consider returning to Tibet from exile. He sent delegates to investigate conditions in the country, and the people turned out in their thousands to greet them. Clearly, despite the official ban on their religion, the Tibetans had kept faith in their personal lives, and evidence of this caused a distinct waning of support by the Chinese for the Dalai Lama's return. Tibetan religion and culture live freely only in the remoter Himalayan frontier lands, where people are Tibetan by race but for past historical reasons do not belong politically to Tibet. Also the Dalai Lama has founded a small, symbolic kingdom in Dharmasala, Northern India.

Mainly thanks to several scholarly officials, chiefly British, and to European scholars who have visited Tibet and studied its art, religion and literature during the course of this century, far more is now known about the life and religion of Tibet than is popularly imagined. The first European to write about the religious life of Tibet was Ippolito Desideri, a Jesuit missionary-priest, who lived happily in Lhasa from 1716 to 1721, saying mass regularly in his rooms at the great Tibetan Buddhist monastery of Sera. He learned classical as well as spoken Tibetan (they relate to one another rather as do Latin and Italian) and was thus able to engage in friendly written and oral disputation with his hosts. His description of Tibetan life and religion (*An Account of Tibet*) remains a classic to this day. While true to his own faith, he willingly recognized the merits of Tibetan religion. 'Not only do the Tibetans possess treatises and codes about contemplation, but they obey them. I have already said that during two months of the year the Lamas hold conferences, preach and give instruction to the monks in their monasteries. Others retire to some solitary place and pass the time in

Victoria and Albert Museum

A Jesuit who visited Lhasa in 1716 held the Tibetan faith to be 'wrong and pestiferous' - yet admitted that it led men towards heroic perfection

Victoria and Albert Museum

Tibetan religion is basically Buddhist, incorporating elements from the indigenous, more primitive religion of Bon; a main feature is belief in Bodhisattvas, who may be devotees on the road to Buddhahood or Great Beings who themselves chose to be reborn into the world to help suffering creation *Left* The Bodhisattva Avalokitesvara, national god of Tibet, was believed to become incarnate as each succeeding Dalai Lama: gilt copper figure of the 16th or 17th century *Above right* A lesser Bodhisattva was Vajrapani, wielder of the thunderbolt, gracious to the faithful and terrible to the impious: 5th or 6th century AD

peace and tranquil contemplation, while others withdraw from the world and devote themselves entirely to profound and subtle contemplation. If one considers what I have stated about Tibetan religion, although I believe the articles of faith to be absolutely wrong and pestiferous, yet the rules and directions imposed on the will are not alien to the principles of sound reason; they seem to me worthy of admiration as they not only prescribe hatred of vices and inculcate battling against passions, but what is more remarkable, lead man towards sublime and heroic perfection.'

Not until the end of the 19th century did another European attempt a serious evaluation of Tibetan religion. Even before going to Tibet, L. A. Waddell, a British member of the Indian Medical Services, made good use of local informants in Darjeeling on the Tibetan frontier, amassing much detailed information about popular Tibetan religion, especially charms, oracles, magical rites, prayer-flags and other religious symbols, as well as about more serious religious beliefs. His work, *The Buddhism of Tibet or Lamaism*, remains an important reference book. However, he had an excessive loathing for 'priestcraft' and Tibetan religion continually reminded him of Catholicism. He writes of Tibet as subject to its 'Dalai Lamaist Pope' and of its 'Lamaist priestly domination', for which he never has a good word. His general opinion of Tibetan religion is therefore far different from that of the saintly Desideri. 'The bulk of Lamaist cults,' writes Waddell, 'comprise much deep-rooted devil-worship and sorcery, which I describe with some fulness. For Lamaism is only thinly and imperfectly varnished over with Buddhist symbolism, beneath which the sinister growth of poly-demonist superstition darkly appears.' It was Waddell who popularized the unhappy term 'Lamaism', which had the same connotation for him as 'Papism' once had in England. His information, culled at a very popular level, is relatively accurate, but he simply never made contact with higher religious practice. The books of Sir Charles Bell, for many years British representative to Tibet, show a great progress, especially in the first-hand information they contain and in their serious attempt at a historical presentation of Tibetan religion.

However, the main incentive for modern Tibetan studies in the West derives from the travels and writings, the editions and translations of Tibetan works, which are the main fruits of the long life of Professor Giuseppe Tucci of Rome. He made eight expeditions in western and central Tibet between 1930 and 1948, and his discoveries brought to light whole past centuries of Tibetan art, literature and learning. From 1946 onwards other European scholars of Tibetan and Sanskrit, and of Tibetan and Chinese, although still a small select band, have done their share of research and writing, so that by now the history of Tibetan civilization, particularly relating to its religious and cultural connections with India on the one hand and its political connections with China on the other, is by no means unknown.

An Imported Faith

Buddhism became gradually established in Tibet from the 7th century AD onwards. The beginnings were slow, rather like the progress of Christianity in the British Isles about the same period, since those who practised the old indigenous religion, often supported by local chieftains, resisted the new faith. The Yarlung line of kings are represented with few exceptions as being its leading early patrons, but it is now historically certain that most of them continued to support the ancestral religion, while sometimes encouraging the founding of Buddhist temples and small monastic foundations.

Little is known with certainty of pre-Buddhist Tibetan religion, but it certainly comprised a cult of the king as a divine being, and special funeral rites involving the immolation of chosen companions together with the deceased king. There is mention of this rite being practised as late as 800 AD. The early religion also included the cult of local gods, especially mountain gods and warrior gods, and rites of sacrifice which were performed when special oaths were taken. This old Tibetan religion is often referred to by Western scholars as 'shamanism', and there were doubtless shamanistic elements, especially in the sense that some priests, through the practice of trance, might 'visit' or identify themselves with the divinities with which they were in special contact (see SHAMAN).

The assassination of the last of the Yarlung kings in 842 reduced the country to political chaos and so caused a further set-back to the introduction of Buddhism. However, new initiatives were taken in western Tibet by the descendants of the Yarlung dynasty, who established three small kingdoms there. From the 10th until the end of the 12th century trained Tibetan monks and scholars made continuous visits to India and Nepal, collecting and translating all the Indian Buddhist literature they could find. Central and eastern Tibet began to take an interest again, thanks to local aristocratic families who saw political advantage in supporting the new religion. Certainly Buddhism presented itself as a much higher culture than anything the Tibetans had possessed hitherto. Not only was a whole new written style developed in order to make possible the translation of obscure Sanskrit philosophical and religious terms, but this same Buddhist form of literature became the model for all Tibetan literature whatsoever. Thus when the representatives of the pre-Buddhist religion, known as *Bon* (perhaps simply meaning 'indigenous'), came to record their traditions, they inevitably made use of the new Buddhist vocabulary and introduced into their own teachings all kinds of Indian Buddhist doctrines.

High and Low Buddhism

During the last period of Buddhism in India (8th to 12th centuries) there were generally two kinds of religious practisers, the celibate monks who lived together in well-established monasteries, following a religious rule that went back to the earliest Buddhist period (5th century BC and onwards), and the yogis, who lived a much

Spectrum Colour Library

Since Tibet became part of the People's Republic of China, public practice of its religion survives only in surrounding regions and refugee communities *Left* Prayer flags stream from a stupa near Katmandu, Nepal, as trumpets are blown in a ceremony to welcome the Year of the Iron Pig *Right* A procession of monks symbolically carry the Dalai Lama's portrait back to Tibet in the hope of reconquest

freer life and might be either celibate or married. The yogis, with their greater religious freedom, were able to introduce the later theories and practices known as 'tantric' (see TANTRISM). They used as special means of invocation magical spells and formulas; they also employed symbolic cosmological designs called mandalas (see MANDALA), impressive initiation ceremonies, special forms of violent yoga (as still practised nowadays by some groups of non-Buddhist Indian yogis), and sometimes a particular kind of sexual yoga. Some of these yogis also practised everyday magic, for a fee placing curses on enemies, locating lost items or causing rainfall. All these higher and lower forms of Buddhism gradually entered Tibet, and some of them easily combined with Bon practices. From the first, Indian Buddhists seem to have adopted local gods as converted 'defenders' of their own, higher religion, and this process continued quite naturally in Tibet, where the pantheon was already quite large.

However, the main strength of the new religion lay in its scholarly and its higher religious aspects. Tibetan religious life was deliberately modelled on the Indian Buddhism of the 10th to 12th centuries AD. This included organized monastic life with its highly developed systems of philosophy and logic, complex forms of liturgy, disciplined behaviour and meditational practice, and the encouragement of literature, architecture and religious painting and iconography. When Buddhism disappeared from India about 1200 AD, the Tibetans were already its full inheritors. The Tibetan Buddhist canon, which reached its final state during the first half of the 13th century, comprises all the known Buddhist literature developed in India from the 1st century AD onwards, as well as part of the still older literature. It is arranged in two parts, known as the Kanjur, or translated (Buddha-) word, and the Tenjur, or translated treatises. The Kanjur, subsequently published in 108 large volumes, contains everything traditionally regarded as 'revealed' teachings (the word of Buddha). The Tenjur, subsequently published as 225 large volumes, contains translations of commentaries, exegetical literature and discourses by Indian Buddhist monk-scholars and yogis.

The pioneer discoverer of this wealth of Tibetan literature was a Hungarian traveller and scholar, Alexander Csoma de Körös. For years he lived like a monk in a small remote Tibetan monastery in the Himalayas, compiling a dictionary and cataloguing the contents of the Tibetan canon. His dictionary was published in 1834. His linguistic work was carried forward by another Hungarian, H. A. Jäschke, who likewise lived for years in the Himalayas, always under hardship, often in utter poverty. The chief fruit of his self-sacrificing labours was a Tibetan-English dictionary, first published in 1881, which remains an important standard work.

Reincarnating Lamas

The Tibetans have proved themselves great commentators and expositors of scripture, great compilers of manuals, great historians and biographers. Every religious order of Tibetan Buddhism has produced its own voluminous stock of writings, including the 'complete works' (*gsung-'bum*) of their leading scholars and prelates; these often run into many volumes. One order in particular, the Ka-gyu-pa, which goes back to the saintly yogi Mila Repa (1040–1123) and his religious master Mar-pa, developed a semi-popular religious literature in the form of delightfully written biographies combined with doctrinal teachings. Tibetan Buddhism is very much a religion of the written word, as well as of the mind and the heart.

There developed from Mila Repa's disciple,

Camera Press, London

sGam-po-pa, no less than six schools or sects, all based on his teachings. Some of these were connected with aristocratic families, whose members tended to be the leading lamas (lama simply means 'religious superior'). Others found their head lamas by making use of the traditional Buddhist belief in rebirth or reincarnation (see LAMAS). The process of rebirth is universal and inevitable; one is reincarnate as man or animal or tormented spirit, as a sufferer in hell or as a kind of petty god, depending upon one's good and evil acts. Release from this continual process is gained only by salvation in Buddhahood. Those who are especially aware of a religious vocation may take the vow to become eventually a perfect Buddha. Such a man becomes immediately a Bodhisattva (one who is intent on enlightenment) and, gradually overcoming his present imperfections, he advances through a series of lives towards final sanctity. This Buddhist path towards perfection remains perhaps the highest spiritual aspiration devised by man. The progress towards Buddhahood of Sakyamuni Buddha (6th to 5th centuries BC) was interpreted in this way, and at no time was it believed by his followers that he was the only Buddha. From the 1st century AD onward the 'career of the Bodhisattva path' was regarded by the followers of the 'Great Way' (*Mahayana*), which represents the 'great church tradition' of Indian Buddhism, as the ideal religious life, available to all, whether monk or layman, man or woman, who felt the workings of 'the thought of enlightenment' (see also BUDDHISM).

Having taken over all such doctrines and aspirations, the Tibetans would naturally assume that the head lamas of their monasteries were human Bodhisattvas on the gradual path to Buddhahood. Because of the merit they had already accumulated they were certain after death to be reborn in the human world as males, as this would present the best initial circumstances for religious progress. All one needed to do was to locate and identify the new child, and one would have rediscovered one's revered head lama returned to this world.

The system was already under way by the 12th century amongst the Ka-gyu-pas, and gradually other Tibetan religious

Eccentrics and holy madmen and mad women abound in Tibetan literature; even practical joking plays a part in the religious life

orders adopted it, usually where the interests of some great aristocratic family were not involved. As an example of a family monopoly, the succession in the important and powerful Sa-kya-pa order has continued through the centuries from uncle to nephew, down to the present day. By contrast the dGe-lug-pa or 'Yellow Hat' order, attached to no aristocratic family, soon adopted the system of reincarnation for the appointing of their chief lamas. These grand lamas (known in China and in the West as Dalai Lamas) have been the titular and sometimes the actual rulers of Tibet since the fifth Dalai Lama won political power in 1642.

Mongol Raiders Converted

As in medieval Europe, so in Tibet, religion and politics went close together. By offering political submission together with the services of their holy religion, the Tibetans managed to remain at peace with the murderous Mongol hords of Genghis Khan, who ravaged every other country in central Asia except Tibet. One lama in particular, abbot of Drikung, so overwhelmed a marauding Mongol chieftain by his magical powers, that he repented of his evil ways and paid for the restoration of the three monasteries he had raided. The Mongols were certainly impressed by Tibetan religion, and in 1249 Godan Khan, to whom Tibet came as part of his heritage, appointed the abbot of Sa-kya his vice-regent in Tibet. Religious rule in the country dates from this time. Seeing the material benefits of allying themselves with the Mongols, who also offered a rewarding mission field, other Tibetan religious orders began to seek Mongol patronage and to intrigue against Sa-kya.

Mutual jealousies amongst the various Tibetan groups at the Mongol court (from 1263 Kublai Khan was the effective Emperor of China) do not seem to have weakened the Tibetan religious hold on the Mongols. This spiritual conquest of a barbarian people is proof of the extraordinary ability of the great lamas of the day, who had to compete for Mongol favours against many other religious faiths, Christian (both Nestorian and Catholic), Moslem and Taoist, as well as the shamanism of the Mongols themselves. As for their magic, Marco Polo records that by their extraordinary powers they could cause the Khan's cup to rise spontaneously from the ground to his mouth, thus convincing him that their religion was superior to Christianity.

Even before the end of the Mongol dynasty in China in 1368, the hierarchs of Sa-kya were deprived of their rather feeble vice-royalty by a determined aristocratic layman named Chang-chub Gyal-tsen, who was closely connected with another religious order, the Phag-mo-gru branch of the Ka-gyu-pa. After his death in 1364 Tibet continued to remain independent of Mongol and Chinese encroachments for some 275 years, but it was internally divided by the mutual enmities of the main religious orders in league with leading aristocratic families.

But even this politically disturbed age produced scholars, contemplatives and poets, whose devout lives are portrayed in Tibetan historical works and indeed throughout Tibetan literature. For instance, in *The Blue Annals,* an English translation by G. N. Roerich of a religious history written by a famous Tibetan scholar named gZon-nu-dpal (1392–1481), there are numerous short biographies and anecdotes about Tibetan lamas, monks and yogis. One reads of the strict religious life of the Lama of Drikung and of that of the Karmapa Lama, who became spiritual adviser to the Emperor of China. Others studied religious texts and then withdrew to solitary meditation, acquiring spiritual and sometimes miraculous powers. Some described their experiences in poetry, and all of them were intent on transmitting their special knowledge to chosen disciples. There were others who were addicted to extreme asceticism, living naked in snow and ice, haunting graveyards, eating vile things and enduring all kinds of self-inflicted hardships; some of them gained great prestige and wealth from such a way of life.

Then there are the eccentrics and the holy madmen and mad women who abound in Tibetan literature. Even practical joking plays a part in the religious life: one story tells of a disciple who put on the dancing mask of the Lord of Death and chased his terrified teacher round the monastery by moonlight.

Tibetan religious life is hardly ever dull, and magical practices always played an important part. A certain lama of Drikung was famed in this way. Once a magician tried to transfer to him certain evils which were threatening the son of a local prince, but the lama's superior powers turned back upon the magician the whole complex of spells.

The Yellow Hats

In the midst of political strife and all the extraordinary variety of religious practice, a new religious order, founded by the saintly and scholarly Tsong-kha-pa (1357–1419), gradually grew in numbers and strength. During the first two centuries of its growth the dGe-lug-pa or 'Yellow Hats' remained largely uncontaminated by temporal power, and the simplicity, the religious devotion and the calm austerity of its life gradually won for its monks a

Killed by a Demon

A refugee worker describes the death of a young Tibetan woman

Suddenly the incense – or something else – took effect and Rinchin, who had been reclining against a bed-roll, sat bolt upright without assistance and began to talk in a low but very clear voice. At once the ayahs, who had by now reassembled, stopped their agitated chattering and seemed hardly to breathe . . .

I whispered an enquiry to the interpreter and he replied briefly that Rinchin had described her visions and concluded by affirming that a few months ago an Evil Spirit from Tibet had entered into her and she had known then that after the birth she would die.

Now the Lama anointed Rinchin's ears, eyes and nose with butter-fat, before going into a trance to attempt to exorcize the Evil Spirit. Within moments he had gone completely rigid as he sat cross-legged, his eyes open but blank and beads of sweat standing out on his face . . . Soon the Lama had gone so white and was sweating so hard and looking so odd that I feared he might die first. Two other Lamas now arrived, carrying the *Bardo Thödol* (a Tibetan Buddhist scripture recited for the benefit of the dying and the dead) rolled up in two silver cylinders. These manuscripts were immediately unfolded and the monks began to chant them *sotto voce* in that indescribable Tibetan manner which has to be heard to be believed . . .

An hour later the interpreter came to tell us that Rinchin was dead.

Dervla Murphy *Tibetan Foothold*

Travellers to Tibet often commented on the mingling of magic and mysticism in Tibetan Buddhism *Left* Tibetan magician: he works spells for his clients, besides dealing with unfriendly gods and demons – a survival of old shamanistic beliefs *Above* A feature of Tibetan worship is the use of prayer-wheels, cylinders containing mantras; both the mechanical repetition of the mantras and the turning movement itself conveyed a blessing, if turned from left to right, but 'demon-worshipping' Bon priests turned their wheels anti-clockwise

large measure of popular support. Then in 1578 the head lama of the dGe-lug-pa visited and befriended a Mongol chief, Altan Khan; he and his following proved ready converts. This head lama died in 1588, the third in the series of reincarnating lamas recognized by the Yellow Hats, and the first to use the title 'Dalai', meaning 'Ocean (of Wisdom)' given him by Altan. His successor was discovered in a grandson of Altan Khan, thus consolidating politically the relations between the Yellow Hats and an important Mongol tribe.

The now obvious political pretensions of the Yellow Hats provoked the older orders to violent opposition, and as a result the Mongols continually invaded Tibet in support of their favourite religious order. The next Dalai Lama, the 'Great Fifth', was supported by the Mongols with sufficient strength to win political control over the whole of Tibet from 1642 onwards, but his death in 1682 led to another period of political chaos. The Mongols and then the Manchu Emperor of China very soon interfered, and when the problems were finally resolved in 1721 Tibet emerged still subject to the rule of the Dalai Lama (or more often that of the high Tibetan ecclesiastical dignitaries who ruled in his name), but also as a religious protectorate of the Manchu emperors, who remained until their fall in 1911 Tibetan Buddhists by religion, and not Chinese Buddhists. For nearly two centuries they acted as patrons of many Tibetan monasteries. This unusual relationship, which ended in 1911, is the basis of the claim of Republican as well as Communist China that Tibet is politically part of China.

Desideri's appreciative comments on Tibetan higher religious life and Waddell's harsh words about devil-worship, sorcery and superstition represent the extremes of Tibetan religious practice. The higher religion of those who devote themselves single-mindedly to a purely religious and world-transcending goal (always a minority in any country and any culture) is fundamentally Buddhist. By strict control of all selfish tendencies and by the practice of concentrated meditation they seek to experience already in this life the joyful tranquillity which comes from such practice, and after death to pass into Nirvana (see NIRVANA).

Gods, Demons and Magicians

The majority of Tibetans, monks as well as laymen, scarcely hope for such an achievement in the course of one lifetime. But they hope that their continual practice of good works, particularly generosity to religious houses and to all in need, will build up a sufficient store of merit for them to be reborn as humans again. This concept too is entirely Buddhist. However, in the course of their everyday lives they meet with obstructions, especially illness or economic ill-fortune, and for these they want antidotes. Buddhism teaches patience in such circumstances, for is not all life a transient passing show, of no real substance whatsoever? But since for practical purposes most men who live in the world must treat it as real, the Tibetans (like ourselves) try to remedy the causes of their misfortune and ensure their continual good fortune.

Because of the Tibetans' ancestral belief in local gods and demons, these are readily recognized as the cause of troubles. A local god may be angry because a house has been built on his territory without suitable propitiation ceremonies. A house god may be upset by a dirty hearth, or a local water spirit infuriated by refuse thrown into his stream. Throughout the centuries the Tibetans have called upon local religious practisers, including Buddhist lamas of the older religious orders, to deal with these local gods and demons by either quelling or placating them, whichever proves more efficacious. The Tibetans believe that some local magicians are able to control natural phenomena and especially to keep off hail, which sometimes destroys whole crops in Tibet just before harvest. They also believe them capable of turning the same rites which quell troublesome local gods against the personal enemies of their clients.

In their extreme forms it is easy to distinguish between genuine Buddhism and local superstitious religion, but in practice the two were so closely combined in Tibet as to form in most people's minds a single religion. So long as a man was attached to worldly affairs, he simply had to take local gods, and therefore local magicians, into account. But in so far as he was detached from life, as in the case of the sincere monk intent on religious perfection, or of any man

Five of the 16 apostles of Sakyamuni, the Buddha, appear in a Tibetan temple-hanging of the 17th or 18th century: Tibet was until recently ruled by priests, and the monasteries were storehouses of art and learning

Victoria and Albert Museum

approaching death, his religion became ever more purely Buddhist. Yet even so, Tibetan religion sometimes introduces extraordinary non-Buddhist elements. There is the terrifying rite of deliberate sacrifice of oneself to local demons, as performed by some ascetic yogis. There is also the amazing *Tibetan Book of the Dead,* by means of which a competent lama might guide the consciousness of the deceased towards some satisfactory form of rebirth. The regions through which he guided the frightened human consciousness were peopled with terrifying divinities, which may only be called Buddhist in so far as most of them had already been accepted into the Indian Buddhist pantheon before the Tibetans imported such doctrines.

DAVID SNELLGROVE

FURTHER READING: Sir Charles Bell, *Tibet Past and Present* (Krishna Press reprint) and *The Religion of Tibet* (Oxford Univ. Press, 1969 reprint); Alexandra David-Neel, *Initiations and Initiates in Tibet* (Rider, London, 1958) and *With Mystics in Tibet* (University Books, 1958); V. Reynolds, *Tibet: A Lost World* (AM. Fed. Arts, 1978); W. Y. Evans-Wentz ed., *Tibetan Yoga and Secret Doctrine* (Oxford Univ. Press, 2nd edn., 1968) and *The Tibetan Book of the Dead* (Oxford Univ. Press, 3rd edn., 1960); D. L. Snellgrove, *Four Lamas of Dolpo* (Harvard Univ. Press, 1967); D. L. Snellgrove and H. E. Richardson, *A Cultural History of Tibet* (Great Eastern, 1980).

Tiger

Feared as a maneater and shape-shifter, and often regarded as a sensitive creature which must be treated with formal respect: in Sumatra apologies are offered to a maneating tiger, and its forgiveness asked, before it is killed; in Malaya tiger claws and whiskers are valued as charms and tigers are said to live in houses in their own village, where the roofs are thatched with human hair.

Tiki

Polynesian carving of a human figure, frequently worn round the neck as an amulet: the Maori said that the first hei-tiki was made for the goddess of childbirth by her father; also the name of the first man, created of red clay by the god Tane, or the phallus of Tane, or alternatively the name of the god who created the first man; tikis have become popular in the West as good luck charms.